REAL WORLD RESEARCH

"Robson and McCartan continue to highlight in a coherent manner the complexity and importance of social research. This is much more than a key textbook on research design and process. This is also a book on tactics and strategy that will increase both undergraduate and postgraduate understandings of real world research."

Richard Race,
Roehampton University, UK

"This has to be the most comprehensive book about doing applied social research on the market. Written in an accessible style, it is an important resource for new researchers, practitioners and old hands alike. It is full of practice examples and is a real 'how to do it' guide. This edition updates an already well-read best seller. The range of resources and tools presented is quite frankly, breath-taking."

Professor Hazel Kemshall,
De Montfort University, Leicester, UK

"This book is the best general resource that I know of for those wanting to conduct research in the 'real world'. The writing is clear and accessible, the coverage is remarkable for its comprehensiveness, and the focus is admirably practical."

Professor Joseph Maxwell,
George Mason University, USA

"This is a really useful book for anyone interested in conducting research that matters—that is, applied research, or as the authors here term it 'real world research'. This is a comprehensive text which manages to cover a broad range of research methods (how to do things), whilst also including all those other 'need to know' items, such as ethics and how to report findings to a variety of audiences. An excellent book, I can highly recommend it."

Dr Belinda Winder,
Reader in Forensic Psychology, Nottingham Trent University, UK

"*Real World Research* is an invaluable resource for academics wishing to engage in a rigorous manner with the world outside the University. For my own students of interdisciplinary design, this new edition will continue to provide a constant and essential reference guide, as well as a lucid introduction to the broader issues surrounding the creation of new technologies for human benefit."

Alan Blackwell,
Professor of Interdisciplinary Design, University of Cambridge, UK

REAL WORLD RESEARCH

A Resource for Users of Social Research Methods in Applied Settings

Fourth Edition

Colin Robson & Kieran McCartan

Registered office

John Wiley & Sons Ltd, The Atrium, Southern Gate, Chichester, West Sussex, PO19 8SQ, United Kingdom

For details of our global editorial offices, for customer services and for information about how to apply for permission to reuse the copyright material in this book please see our website at www.wiley.com.

Library of Congress Cataloging-in-Publication Data

Robson, Colin.
  Real world research / Colin Robson & Kieran McCartan. — Fourth Edition
     pages cm
  Revised edition of Real world research, 2011.
  Includes bibliographical references and indexes.
  ISBN 978-1-118-74523-6 (pbk.)
1. Social sciences—Research—Methodology. 2. Psychology—Research—Methodology. I. McCartan, Kieran, 1980- II. Title.
  H62.R627 2016
  300.72–dc23
                          2015033629

ISBN: 9781118745236 (pbk)

ISBN: 9781119144854 (ebk)

A catalogue record for this book is available from the British Library

Set in 10/12.5 Palatino LT Std by SPi Global, India

Printed in Great Britain by Bell & Bain Ltd, Glasgow.

Reprinted November 2018

Dedicated by Colin Robson to Mark and Catherine
Dedicated by Kieran McCartan to Sue and Isaac

CONTENTS

PREFACE

The central purpose of this book has remained essentially unchanged over the four editions: to give advice and support to those wishing to carry out a 'real world' research project. That is, one seeking answers to problems faced in areas such as healthcare, education, business and management and other people-related fields, rather than being concerned primarily with advancing an academic discipline. The focus is mainly on projects for which social research methods can be used. However, a change in this edition is the greater attention given to 'desk-based' projects based solely on existing research, which are common in some fields of research. This is partly because the real world, in the shape of the various agencies willing to provide funding for research, increasingly calls for this type of research – not least because it is quicker and cheaper than empirical projects collecting new data. It also recognizes that, in some disciplines and fields of study, the norm for students has always been for students to do desk-based research. And that, in others, students are now restricted to it for a variety of reasons, including financial ones when resources are limited, and ethical concerns where safeguarding those taking part in research and the students themselves is important.

As well as taking note of the real world for students, the book seeks to address the needs of researchers, both new and established. Their real world is ever more challenging. Pressures on those in universities intensify when their ability to obtain funding for research and complete projects with measurable impact is crucial not only for their personal careers but also for the future of their department, even for the institution itself.

Other changes in the context of carrying out research projects, highlighted in the third edition, are still with us. They include:

- an increased emphasis on ethical considerations when carrying out research involving people – and the need to come to terms with ethical committees;
- the mighty bandwagon of evidence-based everything; and
- the all-pervading Internet – particularly the rise of social media.

We try to provide an even-handed approach; recognizing their existence and importance, while pointing out problems that they pose.

The addition of a second author, discussions with colleagues and students directly involved with carrying out this kind of research, and feedback from users (and non-users) of earlier editions have all helped to provide an agenda for changes and development in this new edition. It has also proved very instructive to review the citations to 'Real World Research' in journal articles, these and other publications. Using the invaluable Google Scholar (see p. 53) in September 2014, citations of the third edition since 2013 covered work in 23 countries (Australia, Brazil, Canada, Chile, Egypt, England, Finland, Hong Kong, Iceland, Ireland, Japan, Nepal, Nigeria, Norway, Pakistan, Saudi Arabia, Scotland, South Africa, Spain, Sri Lanka, Sweden, Turkey, and the United States) and 14 fields of research (Business and Management, Computer Science, Criminology, Development Studies, Economics, Education, Engineering, Environmental Studies, Film Studies, Geography, Health, Psychology, Social Work, and Sociology.

This exercise, together with a search for other recently published real world-type articles, provided insights into the 'real world' of published journal articles which has informed the approach in this edition.

Another reality check has come from findings about how social researchers actually go about their research as distinct from how research methods texts say they should (e.g. Bryman, 2006b). This has reinforced the perception that jobbing researchers often seem to get on quite adequately without worrying about philosophical matters such as epistemology and ontology. We have tried to restrict such matters to a 'need to know' footing. On that basis, we continue to try to persuade readers of the value of a realist approach to applied social research. Further recent developments have gone a long way to rectifying the lack of material which shows the practical implications of going realist, and providing examples of doing this.

An increased interest in social research methods, and their teaching, in UK universities continues, fostered by the ESRC's (Economic and Social Research Council) highly successful 'Research Methods Initiative'. The various workshops, reviews and briefing papers produced under the aegis of the initiative, and their highlighting of methodological challenges for the 21st century, are invaluable, as will be seen in numerous references in the text.

This mention of a UK initiative is a prompt to make it clear that, while we are UK based and no doubt to some extent UK biased in the selection of materials, a conscious effort has been made to cast the net widely in both journal and text references. There appears to be a degree of unhelpful chauvinism in research methods texts (shown in extreme form in some from the US!). Appreciating the different approaches and traditions in other countries provides yet another example of the value of the anthropologists' advice to 'spend some time in the neighbouring village'.

The 'fixed design' and 'flexible design' distinction introduced in earlier editions is retained in preference to the more commonly used 'quantitative design' and 'qualitative design'. Also, the term 'multi-strategy designs' is preferred to the widely used one of 'mixed-methods designs'. There are good arguments for these deviations from accepted usages, which are presented in the text.

The references have been updated where appropriate. Several 'golden oldies' have been retained if older material makes a point better than more recent efforts. The text is heavily referenced so that readers can follow up topics and issues that interest them, or look likely to be relevant to their research efforts.

The preface to the previous edition of this text ended with the following credo:

I hold two diametrically opposed views about many aspects of life. On the one hand, I consider doing research, including real world research, as pretty straightforward and simple. Approached with integrity, and some forethought, anyone should be able to carry out a worthwhile project. On the other hand, it is enticingly complex, to the extent that some very bright people, who have devoted their working lives to the task, continue to dispute how it should be done. The book seeks to reflect both these views. I have tried to signpost a way through the minefield so that someone with little background feels empowered to produce a competent piece of work relevant to a problem or issue of concern.

I have also attempted to give an indication of what Baranov (2004, p. 8) refers to as the 'issues and debates below the surface of social research methods', and sufficient leads for the interested reader to follow these up (with some discussions of interesting but more peripheral matters placed on the website). As may be evident there are aspects of current practices and conventions in social research which I view as misguided, including the heavy reliance on significance testing in statistical analysis, and I have tried to give a voice to dissidents who articulate such discontents.

I remain convinced of the centrality of research questions to the process of carrying out real world research. Working out a good set of related research questions helps to get your ideas sorted out. Working out how you get answers to these questions shapes the design of the research. The answers are the key part of your findings.

As you will have noted, this text is now under joint ownership. I am very pleased that Kieran has agreed to share the task of keeping *Real World Research* up to date. And also that he is very much in tune with the approach taken in the book (having used it himself throughout his academic life, from BSc to PhD to academic researcher, and as a course text with his students for several years) – including this credo.

WAYS OF USING THE BOOK

Recommendations

- If you are following a course of some kind, then the needs and structure of the course will shape your use. It is likely that the course will be to prepare you to carry out your own project. To get a full appreciation of the range of issues involved it is best to start at the beginning of the book and work through to the end. Our own preference is to go through initially at some speed so that your momentum keeps you going through any bits that you don't take in fully. From this you get a feeling for the general lie of the land, and can then return at more leisure to sections which are important for your needs or which you found difficult.
- If you want to use the book to help carry out a research project – either by yourself, possibly for a research degree, or as part of a group – you have two main choices. Do the same as is suggested above and effectively use the book as a self-study course guide – then home into the bits you need.
- Alternatively, you could jump straight in and use it more as a 'how to' cookbook. (It is difficult to understand the denigration of 'methods' cookbooks by some commentators. Obviously some are mere recipe books but others are much more.) To do this, use the shaded pages which are intended to provide an overview of the main stages of the research process and appear at intervals throughout the book. They can be picked out from the Contents list where their headings are shaded in the same way as those in the text.
- If you are using this book as a course tutor or to help others to carry out research projects, you are likely to be familiar with much of the material in the text and a quick glance should locate aspects to recommend to your students. Some of the material differs from the traditional, however (particularly in the first two parts), and you are recommended to review these sections to key you in to the line taken.

Associated website

The website associated with the book (www.wiley.com/college/robson) has several different types of material which support and complement the text. These include:

- illustrative examples of recent journal and other articles in a range of different disciplines or areas of study for a wide range of topics;
- additional discussion on methodological and other topics which some readers may wish to explore; and
- annotated lists of further reading for each chapter.

A set of PowerPoint slides keyed into the different sections and chapters of the book, which may be useful for teaching purposes, is provided in a separate Instructors' website (www.wiley. com/college/robson). The material in the website will be updated on a regular basis.

Links to some of the many websites covering issues relevant to carrying out a real world research project are given in the text itself.

The Internet provides such amazingly extensive and valuable resources for anyone carrying out research that we would urge any intending real world researcher to make serious efforts to gain proficiency in harvesting these resources. And to be able to discriminate between the dross and the good stuff. See Chapter 3, p. 54.

Disclaimers

- *No single text could hope to cover all you need to carry out a worthwhile research project – particularly one relevant to practical real world issues.* This text is wide-ranging and tries to give the reader a feeling for the issues involved in designing, carrying out, analysing and reporting on different kinds of study so that you appreciate some of the many possibilities open to you. The intention has been to try to provide a clear overall structure, while seeking to address some of the complexities and controversies in current social research. We are interested in innovative approaches and feature several which we consider worth consideration. Each chapter has annotated suggestions for further reading in the website. This is particularly important in the case of specific methods and techniques of investigation and analysis, where it is highly likely you will have to go beyond what is provided here.
- *All the reading in the world won't make you into a skilled researcher.* There is the danger of the centipede problem (it never moved again after trying to work out which leg it moved first) and much to be said for jumping in, carrying out a project or two and developing skills through experience – using this text as a reference along the way. This is, in fact, an important feature of flexible design research; it is flexible in the sense that the design evolves as a result of your data-gathering experiences. Fixed designs (such as experiments and surveys) do call for considerable pre-planning before the main data collection, but you can, and should, gain experience through pilot work.

The use of language

- In order to avoid both the suggestion that all real world researchers and others involved are males (or females) and the clumsy 'she/he', the plural 'they' is used whenever feasible. If the singular is difficult to avoid, we use 'she' and 'he' in a fairly random sequence.
- The preferred term to refer to people who agree to be involved in social research is 'participants'. Other terms are used in some situations.

The main steps when carrying out a project

As a first step you are strongly recommended to:

• start your project journal.

To complete a project you need to:

• decide on a focus for the project;
• develop a set of research questions;
• choose a research design;
• select the method(s);
• arrange practicalities for data collection;
• collect data;
• prepare the data for analysis;
• analyse and interpret the data; and
• report and disseminate your findings.

Note: To carry out a purely desk-based study, your data are the reports of previous research and hence you need not worry about many of the data collection issues. See Chapter 5.

PART I

Setting the scene

Before leaping into a project, you need to have an idea about what you are letting yourself in for. Real world research, as discussed and explained at the beginning of Chapter 1, is often an 'away fixture' taking place on someone else's territory. As Shadish, Cook and Campbell (2002) put it: 'In such settings as schools, businesses, clinics, hospitals, welfare agencies, and homes, researchers have far from perfect control, are typically guests and not royalty, have to negotiate and not command, and often must compromise rather than get everything they would like' (p. xix). False moves can inoculate a firm, school or wherever against future involvements, not only with you, but with other potential researchers – and, possibly, against the whole idea of systematic enquiry as an approach to dealing with problems or understanding situations. Practitioners, such as nurses, teachers or social workers, when getting involved with research, commonly wish to research some aspect of the situation in which they work or are already involved in some way. Here you will have to live with any mess you make.

This is not to argue for things being cut and dried before starting. Any proposals you make for carrying out a project will benefit from discussing your ideas with others including 'stakeholders' – i.e. those likely to have an interest in the research either because it might involve them in some additional efforts or trouble, or who might be affected by the findings. Indeed there is much to be said in favour of collaborative ventures, where the 'client' and/or others involved have a substantial say in the enterprise.

Keeping your own project journal

It is good practice to keep a full and complete record of all the various activities with which you are involved in connection with the project. Some people limit this to the stages when they are collecting data. It is certainly invaluable then as it helps to keep in one place details of appointments and meetings, what data were actually collected, where, when, etc. However, there is much to be said for starting the journal on day one of planning the project. It can take a variety of formats but an obvious one is a large-size diary with at least a page for each day (they come very cheaply from about March each year!). Keeping it on your computer is attractive, providing you have good computer housekeeping habits.

The kinds of things which might be entered include:

- Notes of things you have read; references (get into good habits of taking full references – see Chapter 3, p. 52 – the effort now will save you pain later when you are trying to chase up missing references). You may find that you get an idea about A when working on B – if you don't make a note, it may get lost.
- Any thoughts relevant to the project, particularly when you decide to modify earlier intentions; reminders to yourself of things to be done; people to be chased up, etc.
- Appointments made, and kept, together with an aide-mémoire of where you have put anything arising from the meeting (one strategy is to include everything here in the diary).
- Taking stock of where you are in relation to each phase of the project; short interim reports of progress, problems and worries; suggestions for what might be done.

Knight (2002, p. 2) also recommends including reflections on how you, as researcher, are influencing the research findings and on the significance of that influence. Also warnings of things to avoid, such as helping out or giving advice when you are supposed to be simply observing.

The journal can be very valuable when you get to the stage of putting together the findings of the research and writing any reports. In particular, with some styles of research where it is expected that you produce an *audit trail* (a full record of your activities while carrying out the research) or a reflexive journal (an account reflecting on the process of the research), the research journal is indispensable.

CHAPTER 1

Introduction

> This chapter:
>
> - explains what is meant by focusing on the real world;
> - argues that design matters;
> - stresses that much real world research is concerned with evaluating something, and that there is often a concern for action or change;
> - reveals the authors' assumptions about what you are looking for in using this book;
> - attempts to give something of the flavour of real world research; and
> - concludes by arguing for knowing something about methodology (the fundamental principles on which the methods of social research are based) as well as the practicalities of doing a project.

What is real world research?

Real world research, as the term is used in this book, refers to *applied research* projects which are typically small in scale and modest in scope. Real world research looks to examine personal experience, social life and social systems, as well as related policies and initiatives. It endeavours to understand the lived-in reality of people in society and its consequences. A substantial amount of *research* of this type is carried out in universities or research institutes by both staff and students, particularly in applied fields such as business and management, criminology, education, and health-related areas such as nursing, social policy, social work and socio-legal studies. There is also applied work in academic social science disciplines including psychology and sociology. It also commonly takes place in local government, businesses, NGOs (non-government organizations) and community organizations, where it is carried out by professionals and practitioners, including practitioner-researchers.

This means that real world research can shape the world as well as explain to us why the world is in the shape that it is. Its focus is different from much *academic research* where the main concern is with developing and extending an academic discipline. The topics selected are those of current interest to social scientists in universities and other advanced institutions. Research of this type is of high prestige in those circles. Real world research is a mixed bag, with the common theme that the main interest lies elsewhere. This doesn't mean that there is a strict dichotomy between academic research and applied research with real world concerns. As Alan Baddeley puts it in a paper on applying cognitive psychology '. . . the combination of practical satisfaction and theoretical make the attempt to combine basic and applied research very rewarding' (Baddeley, 2013, p. 443). Not that this is easy though. Chelimsky (2013) is concerned that in the field of evaluation there is much current practice where *theory* is largely ignored, while theoretical writing fails to understand the problems of practitioners in the real world.

Much real world research focuses on problems and issues of direct relevance to people's lives, to help find ways of dealing with the problems or of better understanding the issues. There is no lack of such problems. A fairly random selection highlighted at the time of writing includes crime, austerity and social change, climate change, education, terrorism, gambling, anti-social behaviour, obesity and diet, child care and abuse, and provision for old age, amongst a host of other concerns. The faith is that research, in the sense of principled, careful and systematic enquiry, is one of the best tools available to address these issues.

This book focuses on problems and issues which have a 'people' dimension and relevant *research methods* and approaches. The focus is not overly restrictive as all the problems and issues listed above impinge on humans in some way. Many problems, particularly large-scale, global ones such as climate and environmental change, call for expertise in a range of *natural sciences* and technologies, but the effects on, and of, the way that people behave are an important part, both of the problems and of their solution. Hence, the book, and the examples used within it, is multi-disciplinary.

As indicated above, the main focus in *Real World Research* is on relatively small-scale research carried out by individuals or small teams. Again, this is not a major restriction as much real world research concerns problems and issues which are practical, local and grounded in a specific context, and where the need is for answers within a short time-scale. And even global problems have local implications so that sensible projects can be carried out with limited resources. For example, Serrao-Neumann, Di Giulio, Ferreira and Choy (2013) were involved with local-scale projects undertaken in urbanized coastal areas in Brazil and Australia, focusing on improving the dialogue between researchers and decision-makers to improve climate-change adaptation. This research provided suggestions for dealing with the issue studied and made recommendations for change.

In carrying out this type of research, a strong dose of humility is needed. It takes place in highly complex and often volatile situations where conclusions are necessarily tentative. These situations are almost inevitably political (with both a small and a large 'p') and there can be many reasons why even eminently sensible proposals arising from the research do not come to pass. For example, educational researchers have faced sustained criticism in the United Kingdom from politicians and others to the extent that the president of the British Educational Research Association claimed that because of a range of perceived shortcomings, 'educational research might not be missed (even gladly dismissed) by some practitioners and policy makers' (Mortimore, 2000), although he goes on to assert that, 'the work is essential if independent questioning and impartial evaluations of policy and practice are to take place' (p. 5).

The real world notion carries the suggestion of breaking out from the ivory tower and trying to deal with problems affecting people's lives directly. It can also be viewed as moving from the research laboratory into places such as schools, hospitals, businesses, shopping malls, street corners or any other setting where people work, play or go about their lives. There is ample evidence that findings from *laboratory research* are not necessarily replicated in other settings. Levitt and List (2006) discuss differences in the *data* from laboratory experiments and data generated in natural settings, pointing out that each approach has strengths and weaknesses, and a combination of the two is likely to provide deeper insights than either in isolation. It is similarly dangerous to generalize from studies with university student participants to other groups. Mintz, Redd and Vedlitz (2006) conducted an *experiment* with a group of military officers and replicated it with a group of students at a public university in the United States. In a scenario dealing with a decision problem in the area of counter-terrorism, the two groups gave widely differing results. However, while most real world research takes place in the 'field' (as non-laboratory settings are often referred to by social scientists) and with non-student groups, some researchers with a real world concern for current practical problems choose to work in laboratories and/or with student participants.

The purpose of this book is to give assistance, ideas and confidence to those who, for good and honourable reasons, wish to carry out investigations involving people which have this kind of real world focus; to draw attention to some of the issues and complexities involved; and to generate a degree of informed enthusiasm for a particularly challenging and important area of work.

Design matters

If you don't give serious attention to the *design* of a research project you are likely to end up with a mess. Catherine Hakim likens the designers of research projects to architects who are 'responsible for supervising all subsequent work to implement the design, including that done by quantity surveyors, builders and other specialists who are hired in to help turn the blueprint into a reality' (Hakim, 2000, p. 1). In small-scale real world research, it is common for researchers to combine the role of designer with responsibility for carrying out the project. This should not preclude seeking specialist assistance in areas such as the development of questionnaires or other data collection instruments, or from statisticians or other experts in data analysis.

Social research, that is research which focuses on people in a social setting, has been carried out in many different ways, the more important of which for carrying out real world studies are covered in later chapters. They fall traditionally into two very broad families, commonly referred to as *quantitative research* and *qualitative research*. As the label suggests, quantitative research typically relies on the collection of data in numerical form while in qualitative research data are typically non-numerical, often in the form of words. However, they are shorthand terms for research *paradigms*, each of which has a collection of typical features over and above the type of data collected. They are discussed in some detail in the next chapter.

In a very similar way, social research designs can be divided into two major types or styles. In one style the design of the study is fixed at an early stage of the research process. You have worked out what you are going to do and how you are going to do it in considerable detail before getting down to collecting data. We refer to them as *fixed designs*, and discuss them in detail in Chapter 6. The experiment and the survey, two strong traditions in social research, are the prime examples of this style of research. The second broad strategy is more flexible, in the sense that while there may be a considerable amount of preliminary planning, details of procedure are not fixed in advance and the focus is liable to change as the research proceeds. Here the detailed design evolves as a result of what is found out in the early stages. We refer to them as *flexible designs*, and discuss them in detail in Chapter 7. There are several popular designs of this type including ones taking an ethnographic approach or using grounded theory.

Many texts refer to what are here called fixed designs as quantitative designs, and flexible ones as qualitative designs. This is because fixed designs almost always depend on the collection of quantitative, numerical data and flexible designs typically rely heavily on the collection of *qualitative data*, usually in the form of words. However, there is no bar on flexible designs involving the collection of *quantitative data*. In practice many real world flexible designs involve the use of two or more data collection methods and it is common to collect at least a small amount of quantitative data. Similarly, there is a case for many fixed designs, while concentrating on the collection of quantitative data, also collecting some qualitative data. More generally, there is a growing interest in *multi-strategy designs*, discussed in Chapter 8, where there is substantial collection of both qualitative and quantitative data in different phases or aspects of the same project.

In some circles, particularly amongst those who are advocates of the increasingly widely advocated evidence-based approaches, there is a strong tendency to regard fixed designs as superior to flexible ones. Experiments, particularly those involving randomized controlled trials (RCTs), are viewed by many as the 'gold standard' for social research, though this view is by no means universal. This issue is discussed in some detail in Chapter 6, p. 117, where the notion of a universally applicable gold standard in the design of social research is questioned.

The requirement for a detailed design in fixed design research is well established. There are clear rules about what is needed in order to carry out the research to a professional standard. To a large extent this involves following tried and tested steps and procedures. Flexible designs are much more difficult to pin down. This is in part because it has only been relatively recently that researchers have given consideration to the design issues which they raise. There had been a tradition in the disciplines of social anthropology and sociology, from which these approaches largely derive, of an 'apprenticeship' model. Skill in their use was developed by working alongside someone already skilled. However, establishing principles for the design of this type of research has excited much interest and generated many publications recently.

At a more general level, quantitative research with its heavy reliance on numerical data and statistical analysis is considered by many of its proponents to be the way to do 'scientific' research. The scientific status of qualitative research is more in dispute. Some proponents of this style of research have no wish to have their research viewed as *science*. As discussed in the next chapter, there are strong arguments for characterizing both types of research as scientific – provided that they are carried out in a systematic, principled fashion.

Evaluation and change

Much research with a real world focus is essentially some form of *evaluation*. Is the organization of educational provision for children with special needs such as learning difficulties, or problems with sight or hearing, working effectively in a particular local authority area? Does a child abuse service actually serve the interests of the children concerned? Can a business improve its interviewing procedures for new sales staff? Evaluation brings to the fore a very different agenda of issues from those usually associated with 'pure' research. For example, issues to do with change (How can it be implemented? What are the barriers to implementation and how might they be overcome?) often loom large. There are influential approaches within applied social research which regard the support and engineering of change as an integral part of the research process (see Chapter 2, p. 34). However, as Stange and Phillips (2007) warn, in an introduction to a journal issue with a set of studies pointing to the difficulties of introducing change, 'Real change is real hard in the real world'.

Should you, as a researcher, get involved in these aspects? A possible stance is to say that the researcher's responsibility stops with achieving some understanding of what is going on, and then handing that information over to those directly concerned. An alternative is to say that it is part of the researcher's job to use this understanding to suggest ways in which desirable change might take place and perhaps to monitor the effectiveness of these attempts. There are no general solutions to these issues. The answers in each case depend to a considerable extent on the situation in which you find yourself. Certainly someone attempting to carry out research into the situation in which they themselves are working or living may find that the change aspects become virtually impossible to separate out from the research itself.

This mention of what amounts to 'self-evaluation' opens up a Pandora's box. At one extreme, some would doubt the feasibility of insiders taking part in any worthwhile, credible or objective enquiry into a situation in which they are centrally involved. Others advocate approaches such as 'participatory evaluation' (Cousins & Chouinard, 2012), 'participatory action research' (Chevalier & Buckles, 2013), 'collaborative ethnography' (Lassiter, 2005) or 'involving service users in research' (Lowes & Hulatt, 2005) and emphasize the benefits of participation, collaboration and involvement. These texts amply demonstrate the feasibility of such approaches, but the problems and stresses of doing this type of research, and the need for specialists in research and *methodology* have to be recognized. The role that such specialists should take on then becomes an important issue. One thing they need to be able to do is 'give away' skills, an important skill in its own right.

All of which carries with it the implication that the real world researcher needs to have knowledge, skills and expertise in areas outside the likely competence of most academic researchers. How change comes about in individuals and groups is itself an immense research area, some knowledge of which is likely to be helpful if you are involved in its implementation. (Hall & Hord, 2014 provide a practical introduction). For the activist researcher, working for social justice, change is a central concern (Lorenzetti, 2013). For all researchers, a very strong sense of audience is needed to guide the style, content and length of any report or other communication arising from the project. If an important objective is concerned with change, then a report which does not communicate to the decision-makers in that situation is a waste of time.

The audience for this book

Having just stressed the need for a sense of audience when writing, we should make clear for whom this book is written.

After several years teaching courses at both undergraduate and postgraduate level which try to deliver real world research skills, we both have been increasingly involved in assisting, through supervision and consultancy, individuals or small groups wishing to carry out some study, often one directly relevant to the setting in which they work. These have included teachers, social workers, health service professionals, NGOs and charities as well as others working directly with particular client groups (e.g. ex-offenders, vulnerable and disadvantaged populations) as well as professional psychologists and social scientists responsible for providing advice and support to others in both private and public sectors. In carrying out these studies, they are usually seeking to meet some perceived, often pressing, need. We have also been made conscious (partly through responses to the previous editions of this book) of the increasing call for practitioners and professionals in diverse fields such as accountancy, architecture and design, business and management, criminology, and development studies, to carry out empirically based projects, for which many feel inadequately prepared. Such groups form important target audiences.

However, a large section of this book's readership has always been students and academics, which we trust will remain true with the current edition. The book seeks to provide advice to students at all levels and across a range of disciplines. The focus is on the design, carrying out, analysing, interpreting and reporting findings, dissemination and application of real world research. Our aim is to help you get more 'bang for your buck' and produce research with an impact, not least by being picked up by policy-makers.

In part, this is an attempt to arm anyone wishing to use social research methods with tools and expertise that they can both use for themselves and 'give away' to others to use. We also have the hope, based on experience, that practitioners in the helping and caring professions, and others working with people, can usefully enquire into their own and others' practice, with a view to understanding, developing and changing it.

A word to those with a social science background

It is our strong impression that, for carrying out real world research, the exact social science discipline background of the potential researcher is not all that important. A psychology graduate is likely to have been well steeped in experimental design and to know relatively little about qualitative approaches (although such approaches are now being taken seriously by an increasing proportion of departments). A sociology graduate will be likely to have had the reverse experience. The approach taken in this book is deliberately promiscuous. Strategies and techniques which have tended to be linked to different disciplines have been brought together in an attempt to give researchers a range of options appropriate to the research questions they are asking. Hence it is hoped that those from a range of social science disciplines will find material which is both useful and accessible. This book's multi-disciplinary approach to methodology in the *social sciences* becomes more relevant for two reasons. Firstly, the expansion of the range of methods and methodological approaches explored by disciplines including criminology, politics and social work. Secondly, the encouragement of *stakeholders*, funding bodies and research councils to engage in cross-disciplinary research.

A word to those without a social science background

Our experience is that the approaches advocated here can be accessible to those without a background or training in the social sciences. The things that social researchers do are not all that different from those in a variety of other trades and professions. Northmore (1996) for example, writing for investigative journalists, reveals many similarities. The research task has been compared with that of the detective: information is gathered; a 'case' is made on the basis of evidence; comparisons are made with the *modus operandi* of suspects; decisions are made about the best explanation, etc. (Scriven, 1976; Smith & Davis, 2012). There are more obvious linkages with the helping professions such as therapists, counsellors, etc. and with humanities disciplines such as history.

A problem is that you 'know not what it is that you know not' and may rush in blindly or blithely without realizing the complexity of the situation. Our advice is that you seek to appreciate the implications of carrying out a *scientific* study. If you are not from a scientific background, or are 'anti-science', please try to keep your prejudices in check. The next chapter aims, among other things, to clear away some common misconceptions about the scientific approach. You won't be expected to wear a white coat, or, necessarily, to crunch numbers.

Associated with the scientific approach is the need for rigour and for rules or principles of procedure. However, as has already been stressed, many real world studies both permit and require a flexibility in design and prosecution which may well appeal to those with a background in the arts or humanities. Well-written flexible research designs based on people's accounts or other qualitative data can provide a compelling report. A major theme of this book is how to introduce rigour into all aspects of research so that we achieve a justified believability and *trustworthiness* in what we find and write up.

You will be at a disadvantage compared to those with a social science background in two main ways. First, the carrying out of systematic research calls for a set of skills – for example, in observing and interviewing, designing, analysing, interpreting and reporting. The development of these skills requires practice, which takes time. This can and should have taken place during training in most social science subjects but in the absence of these skills, you will have to learn 'on the job' or to sub-contract some or all of the tasks to others who do have the necessary skills.

Second, and more difficult to remedy, the social sciences have a substantive content of philosophical underpinning, theories, *models* and findings which in general you will not be aware of. It is difficult to assess how much of a disadvantage this puts you under. One obvious solution is to work in partnership, or on some kind of consultancy basis, with a professional social researcher. This practice is becoming more commonplace with numerous NGOs, organizations and individuals linking up with universities and academics to develop, as well as conduct, mutually beneficial research. If you are a practitioner or professional, trained and experienced in the field which is the subject of the research, then you will have a corresponding, and possibly more useful, set of theories, models, etc. to those deriving from the 'pure' social science disciplines. This is not to minimize the importance of theory. It simply makes the point that a theoretical or conceptual framework can be acquired by a variety of means (including interaction with, and analysis of, the data you have collected). When, as will often be the case, the intention is to assist individuals, groups or organizations to understand, and possibly develop or change, some aspect of themselves and the situation in which they find themselves, there is virtue in staying close to the concepts and language they use. Certainly, unassimilated jargon often accentuates the commonly acknowledged theory/practice divide.

The basic claim being made here is that principled enquiry can be of help in gaining an understanding of the human situation and its manifestations in an office, factory, school, hospital or wherever, and in initiating sensible change and development via evaluation or small-scale research. It is important not to claim too much, however. Common sense, management fiat, hunches, committee meetings, political considerations and the like are going to continue to form the main precursors to action. As Gerring (2001) reminds us, 'The cause of civil rights, for example, was advanced more by visual images – of peaceful protesters being sprayed with water cannons and beaten by police – than by social science' (p. 254). But getting research on the agenda as something likely to be of assistance if there is an important decision to be made or problem to be dealt with, would be a step forward. And if you can consult an experienced researcher for advice and support, you may well find that your efforts are more effective.

Returning to the real world

The proposal for a real world emphasis is reflected in several dichotomies – suggesting applied research rather than pure or *basic research*; *policy research*, not theoretical research. These dichotomies are probably not very helpful as they suggest absolute distinctions. Hakim (2000) sees these differences more in terms of emphasis. For her the main features that distinguish policy research from theoretical research are:

> an emphasis on the substantive or practical importance of research results rather than on merely 'statistically significant' findings, and second, a multi-disciplinary approach which in turn leads to the eclectic and catholic use of any and all research designs which might prove helpful in answering the questions posed (p. 213).

The emphases and priorities of the real world researcher differ in several ways from those of the traditional academic researcher. Box 1.1 suggests some of the dimensions involved. Not all of the aspects shown in the box will occur in any particular study, but they go some way to characterizing this approach to research. Kelly (2003) illustrates a range of tensions found in the fledgling field of community psychology when trying to meet the aim of carrying out research which is nested in, and relevant to, real life communities and also the expectations of their reference group of scientific psychologists.

Entering into this kind of real world research could, with some justice, be viewed as capitulation to the values of an enterprise culture. There are obvious dangers in being a 'hired hand'. You may, overtly or covertly, be serving the agendas of those in positions of power (Scheurich, 1997), perhaps being hired to seek sticking-plaster solutions to complex and intractable problems. As Lynd (1939, p. 178), quoted by Gerring (2001, p. 255), warned, 'when [a social scientist] pulls his scientific punch by pocketing more important problems and accepts a retainer to work as an expert for the partisan aims of a bank or an advertising agency, he is something less than a scientist'.

However, there is the advantage that letting society, in the guise of the client or sponsor, have some role in determining the focus of your research project makes it more likely that findings are both usable and likely to be used. And, as Lynd added, 'when the social scientist hides behind the aloof "spirit of science and scholarship" for fear of possible contamination, he is likewise something less than a scientist'.

Why do research in the real world?

Real world research is a cornerstone of applied learning, evidence based policy and informed decision-making. It means that important organizational, practice and policy decisions are made from an informed perspective, ultimately leading to evidence based policy and practice, not

BOX 1.1

Relative emphases of real world and academic researchers

Real world researcher	Academic researcher
Interest is in solving problems	*Interest is in gaining knowledge and advancing the discipline*
Getting large effects (looking for robust results) and *concern for actionable factors* (where changes are feasible)	*Establishing relationships and developing theory* (and assessing statistical significance in quantitative studies)
Almost always works in the 'field' (industry, hospital, business, school, etc.)	*Depends on the focus of the research but in some disciplines mainly in laboratories*
Strict time constraints	*As long as the topic needs* (but increasing time pressures).
Strict cost constraints	*As much finance as the topic needs* (or the work shouldn't be attempted)
Often little consistency of topic from one study to the next	*High consistency of topic from one study to the next*
Generalist researchers (need for familiarity with range of methods and approaches)	*Highly specialist researchers* (need to be at forefront of their discipline)
Oriented to client needs (generally, and particularly in reporting)	*Oriented to academic peers* (generally, and particularly in reporting)
Currently viewed as dubious by many academic researchers	*Carries high academic prestige*
Need for well-developed social skills	*Some need for social skills*

practice based policy and evidence. In the current climate of risk management, accountability and restricted funding, real world, applied research becomes more relevant; it's too expensive to make risky decisions and all decisions need to be potentially 'future-proofed'. From an academic perspective the importance of real world research in the UK is firmly embedded in funding guidelines from research councils and as part of the national Research Evaluation Framework (REF), which state that research should have an impact on society and not sit in isolation. Socially engaged research that has an impact upon people's lives is seen, in the social sciences anyway, as a gold standard for which we should all be aiming. However, the notion of socially engaged, accountable and transformative research means that researchers, policy-makers, stakeholders and gatekeepers need to be on the same page in terms of the importance of access and the role value of real world research. This is becoming more commonplace with the realization that *quid pro quo* agreements need to occur. Organizations should recognize that, by allowing access and giving up some control, they can get invaluable research done at a fraction of the commercial price. Academic institutions should accept that effective, impactful and high ranking research can be done without a huge external grant if they are willing to support staff by investing in research, by giving them access to resources (i.e. internal funds for research, funded PhDs, access to research support services), themselves.

Issues of access, accessibility and impact will vary with the organizations involved, the research question being asked and the *population* to be studied. All of which can have a significant impact on the viability of real world research. Getting access to certain organizations' (e.g. NHS Trusts, or police forces) classified or restricted information (e.g. health databases, as well as populations (e.g. sex offenders) means that some socially sensitive research can often be off the table without extensive negotiations and safeguarding procedures.

One of the biggest areas of debate within applied, real world social science research is how the findings are used, if at all. Often research is conducted for, or with, stakeholders, but because an organization commissions research, paid or otherwise, does not mean that they have to listen to the outcomes, or implement change. Hence, some real world research can vanish into a vacuum, which can be frustrating for researchers. It is important to realize that even though real world research is important and as a researcher you do the best job possible, ultimately the impact of the research is governed by the organization through which you do it. Doing research in the real world means that you have to be prepared for this.

Although there are these difficulties and issues with real world research, as long as there is a clear understanding of research ownership, accountability, independence and the roles of all involved from the outset, a lot of these can be mitigated. Real world research should be central to policy-making, effective practice and the management of societal change.

Website examples

The website gives references to a range of examples of real world studies.

There are similar website examples given in most chapters. Most are from journal articles; others are published reports of various kinds. You are strongly recommended to follow them up whenever the topic interests you. They have all been obtained directly from the Internet. As discussed in Chapter 3, p. 53, you will need access to a university or other academic library to get full-text versions of much of the material, although abstracts are often freely available and there are an increasing number of journals where access to the full text is also free.

Don't be concerned if you can't understand the more technical aspects of an article, particularly in these early chapters. You usually only need to get a general idea of what it is about. Don't be put off by the fact that most articles are multi-authored. Much real world research is a group activity. And it is not unusual for research students and junior researchers (who might have done most of the work) to have their name coupled with those of project directors, thesis supervisors or other senior staff.

Beginning the journey

One of the beauties and enduring strengths of books is that they are 'random access devices'. It is up to readers what they select or skip. In this book the marked pages, chapter headings and index are all ways of giving rapid and direct access to the more 'nuts and bolts' aspects of research, such as the choice and use of different methods of gathering evidence, of analysing different kinds of data, of writing a report appropriate to a particular audience, and so on.

Be warned though, that entering into any kind of investigation involving other people is necessarily a complex and sensitive undertaking. Many social scientists, particularly those teaching academic courses preparing students to carry out social research projects, argue that a thorough grounding in methodology (i.e. in the theoretical and philosophical background to social research) is an essential precursor. Whether the same prior methodological understanding is necessary to carry out real world research is the question at issue here. There are certainly counter-examples: novice researchers without a social science background who have produced competent pieces of research. However, it is a good general principle that it does help to know why you are doing what you are doing – and an important part of the 'why' comes from methodology. Hence the following chapter seeks to provide sufficient of this background to place the practical aspects of doing a social research project in a theoretical context.

There is a more specific reason for the inclusion of this material which should be made explicit. Advocating flexible designs as a serious possibility is still likely to be viewed as a radical and risky departure in some disciplines, especially those steeped in the statistical sampling paradigm. Justification is called for. Taking a stance that there are some circumstances where fixed designs are to be preferred, and others where flexible ones are more appropriate (and some where it helps to have both), and claiming that the whole can be regarded as a scientific enterprise is also likely to antagonize those of both scientistic and *humanistic* persuasion. There are strongly held views that there is an ideological divide between qualitative and quantitative approaches and that this particular twain should never meet. Bryman (1988; 2006b) and Teddlie and Tashakkori (2009) consider that many of these differences are more apparent than real and that there can be advantages in multi-strategy designs which combine qualitative and quantitative approaches.

Hence, before getting down to how you are going to design your research project in Part II of the book, Chapter 2 presents an overview of the methodology of social research.

Further reading

The website gives annotated references to further reading for Chapter 1.

CHAPTER 2

Approaches to social research

This chapter:

- explores what it means to be 'scientific' and argues for its advantages;
- rejects extreme relativist views of social science;
- introduces the two broad traditions commonly referred to as quantitative and qualitative social research;
- considers the positivist view of science (and social science) to be discredited;
- reviews the main current approaches to social research with particular focus on post-positivism and constructionism;
- considers the increasing popularity of multi-strategy research, which combines quantitative and qualitative aspects; suggests that both pragmatist and realist approaches have relevance to real world research; and
- concludes by stressing the practical value of the material covered in the chapter.

Introduction

There are many approaches to carrying out social research and a bewilderingly large set of ways of labelling these approaches. The starting point here is to restrict the field to approaches which can reasonably be viewed as scientific. To do this calls for consideration of what being 'scientific' means.

Science continues to get a bad press. There is a lack of public confidence in scientists and their pronouncements. Scientists are seen as providing information potentially biased to suit their sponsors or as being unwilling to consider the views of critics. Concerns about potential side-effects of science-based initiatives such as genetically modified crops, vaccination programmes or the cloning of animals are raised on a regular basis, suggesting lurking dangers from even the best efforts of scientists – see, for example, the discussion by Leach and Fairhead (2007) and Hobson-West (2007) on how recent controversies around vaccines exemplify anxieties thrown up by science-based technologies. Goldacre (2009; 2013), in deservedly popular polemical texts, castigates not only the misrepresentation of scientific findings and scaremongering by journalists, but also nutritionists, homeopaths, cosmetics companies and the pharmaceutical industry, who consistently disregard or distort scientific evidence.

Social science more rarely hits the headlines in this way. Some social researchers have strong reservations about being labelled as 'scientific'. This is commonly associated by them, and by the public at large to some extent, with doing particular types of study. Specifically, something which involves collecting 'hard' data, usually in the form of numbers which are subsequently analysed using statistics. Their preference is for 'softer' styles of research involving methods such as relatively unstructured interviews or participant observation which result in data typically in the form of words. And for which they would be unlikely to think of any form of statistical analysis. There have also been moves by governments and other agencies, particularly in the United States, to define science and science-based research in a very narrow, exclusive way effectively demoting, or even ruling out, this type of research (Christ, 2014; Lather, 2009). If the pressure to make all social research fit into the same methodological framework is not resisted it will reduce the types of research question that can be addressed. A major message of this text is that those doing research of this kind, traditionally labelled 'qualitative', need not shun being scientific. Qualitative researchers may wish to do so of course and that is their privilege. We hope that they will still find information and advice in this text which helps them to carry out their research.

What is science?

There is widespread agreement that science-based research has features such as the use of rigorous systematic procedures; that it is *empirical*, involving the collection of data or information of some type; that these data are analysed in ways that are adequate to justify whatever conclusions are drawn. There is less agreement about the *scientific method*. Is there a particular set of procedures which, if followed, give the seal of approval so that the result is 'science'? Contrary to common preconceptions, including those of many who regard themselves as scientists, and not a few of those who would be disturbed to be so labelled, it is not obvious what is meant by science or the scientific method. Chalmers (2013), for example, spends over 300 pages seeking answers to his own question: 'What is this thing called science?'

A scientific attitude

Sidestepping controversies about what is, or is not, science, we simply propose to assert that for much real world problem-based research, it is valuable to have a 'scientific attitude'. By this we mean that the research is carried out systematically, sceptically and ethically:

- systematically means giving serious thought to what you are doing, and how and why you are doing it. In particular you are explicit about the nature of the observations that are made, the circumstances in which they are made, and the role you take in making them;

- sceptically refers to subjecting your ideas to possible disconfirmation. It also involves considering alternative hypotheses and interpretations and subjecting the observations and preliminary conclusions made to scrutiny (by yourself initially, then by others); and
- ethically means that you follow a code of conduct for the research which ensures that the interests and concerns of those taking part in, or possibly affected by, the research are safeguarded.

The intention behind working in this way is to seek the 'truth' about whatever is the subject of the research. 'Truth' is a term to be approached with considerable caution and the intention can, perhaps, be best expressed in negative terms. You should not be seeking to promote or 'sell' some particular line, or to act simply and solely as an advocate. Some of these issues can become very problematic when carrying out real world research. For example, a part of your role may well be to act as an advocate for the sponsor of the research, or for a disadvantaged group whose cause you are seeking to assist. A commitment to carrying out the research in an ethically responsible manner, while it might not be viewed by some as a defining characteristic of a scientific attitude to social research, appears to us to be central. You are working with people and may do them harm. The widespread dubious practices in the promotion of health-related products, highlighted by Goldacre (2013), provide a salutary warning.

Why is it valuable to have this attitude? The main argument is that working in this way is likely to lead to better quality, more useful, socially responsible, research. In part this comes from working systematically and being explicit about all aspects of your study. It opens up what you have done to scrutiny by others, which forms part of addressing the need for scepticism or disbelief. But the ethical dimension is crucial. As Connelly (2007) puts it:

> Social responsibility in science is not an optional extra or an afterthought. To think it ever was is a consequence of our mystification of scientific work as apart from everyday life: a domain of value-free facts that are unsullied by considerations of subjectivity, emotion or appropriateness (p. 937).

The view of scientists as value-free, totally objective, machine-like automata, while still held by some researchers (even by some social researchers), is discredited. As discussed later in the chapter, it was the standard view of how science was done, but is now recognized as far from the truth. You can't leave your humanity behind when doing research.

For some small, straightforward, research projects where the questions to be answered are clearly specified initially, and the method of data collection self-evident, this scientific attitude will in itself take you a substantial way. Obviously skills in the use of the method chosen and in analysis of the resulting data are needed, but if you are working systematically, sceptically and ethically, you should be able to do something worthwhile.

However, in practice, very few actual real world studies turn out to be as straightforward as this. Worthwhile research typically calls not only for skills and an appropriate attitude, but also some knowledge and understanding of what others have done in the past, to avoid continually trying to reinvent the wheel. This book tries to provide a framework for designing and carrying out studies where things are not cut and dried, and where you need to take difficult decisions about how to proceed.

Postmodernism and extreme relativist approaches

The movement known as *postmodernism* has influenced thought about social research (Alvesson, 2002; Sim, 2011) as well as permeating the arts, literature and architecture. Although by no means a unified approach, several ideas figure prominently. Essentially, whatever *modernism* advocated is opposed by postmodernists. Modernism was linked to developments in Europe leading to the scientific revolution of the sixteenth century and later centuries, and the so-called 'Enlightenment' fully flowering in the eighteenth century. It sought to provide freedom from the irrationality, ignorance and superstition of the middle ages. Modernism's central belief was in rationality, and in progress through science. Postmodernism challenges the idea of progress through reason. Modernism seeks general truths. Postmodernism says there is no basis for such claims to truth. 'Objective criteria that are presented as a basis for distinguishing truth from falsity are seen to be nothing more than forms of persuasion that are designed to show that what is claimed is true' (Blaikie, 2007, p. 50). Critics of postmodernism are scathing. For example:

> The philosophical postmodernists, a rebel crew milling beneath the black flag of anarchy, challenge the very foundations of science and traditional philosophy. Reality, they propose, is a state constructed by the mind, not perceived by it. In the most extravagant version of this constructivism, there is no 'real' reality, no objective truths external to mental activity, only prevailing visions disseminated by ruling social groups (Wilson, 1999, p. 44).

As in many movements in social science, there are varying postmodernist positions, discussed by Maxwell and Mittapalli (2010, p. 151). They cite Ezzy (2002, pp. 15–18) who argues that, while some postmodernists deny that reality exists, others simply want to emphasize the complexity of our process of understanding it. While such moderate postmodernists would reject the idea of universal truth, they are likely to accept 'the possibility of specific, local, personal, and community forms of truth' (Kvale, 1995, p. 21).

Within social science there are influential relativistic approaches as well as postmodernism. They are variants of what is commonly referred to as qualitative research, discussed in the following section. Within this tradition there is almost invariably a rejection of the view that 'truths' about the social world can be established by using natural science methods. This is because of the nature of the subject matter of the social sciences – people. People, unlike the objects of the natural world, are conscious, purposive actors who have ideas about their world and attach meaning to what is going on around them. In particular, their behaviour depends crucially on these ideas and meanings. This central characteristic of humans has implications for doing research involving them. Their behaviour, what they actually do, has to be interpreted in the light of these underlying ideas, meanings and motivations. Davidson and Layder (1994), for example, cite the pattern whereby females typically do more housework than their male partners, fathers and sons:

> But since women are not drawn to the kitchen sink by some irresistible, physical force (they are not *compelled* to conform to this social convention in the same way that they would be compelled to obey the law of gravity if they jumped from a cliff), social scientists

cannot hope to formulate general laws on the basis of observing this pattern. Instead, they have to ask questions about the beliefs people hold and the meanings they attach to action. They have to concern themselves with the inner world of their subjects in order to understand why they act as they do (p. 31, original emphasis).

Rejection of the use of natural science methods need not carry with it a rejection of a scientific approach, appropriately modified to take note of the special subject matter of social research. Some qualitative researchers share the extreme *relativism* of the postmodernists, considering that there is no defensible basis for choosing one account over any other one. Most, however, take the view that there are reasonable grounds for making such a choice and would not demur from the claim that following the scientific attitude of working systematically, sceptically and ethically helps to do this.

While extreme relativists (including extreme postmodernists) are avowedly non-scientific and as such fall outside the scope of this book, more moderate relativists have made a central contribution to qualitative social research.

The two traditions: quantitative and qualitative social research

For many years there was a basic choice to be made when carrying out a piece of social research. The two alternatives were known as quantitative and qualitative social research. The quantitative route tried to follow essentially the same research path as researchers in the so-called 'natural' sciences such as physics, chemistry and biology. Advocates of qualitative approaches considered that, because the focus of social research is on human beings in social situations, you need a very different approach to the research task. Human consciousness and language, the interactions between people in social situations, the fact that both researcher and researched are human – and a host of other aspects – all were considered to require, and make possible, a radically different approach to research. Their criticisms of quantitative approaches as a basis for social research were influential, but many social researchers either chose to ignore these criticisms or attempted to come to terms with them rather than abandon quantitative research.

Warring tribes of quantitative and qualitative social researchers fought a good fight. The quantitative camp claimed that their scientific approach was the only way to conduct serious research and cast doubts on the value of qualitative research. Qualitative advocates countered that the dead hand of numbers and statistics was no way to understand anything worthwhile about people and their problems. Thankfully the new millennium appears to have brought a détente, though sniping across the trenches continues (Holosko, 2012 and Shaw, 2012 provide an example of a reasonably civilized interchange). There are still zealots proclaiming their version of the true faith, but several commentators (e.g. Bryman, 2006b; Walsh, 2012) now see this as a worn-out debate. This is in part because many researchers appear content to continue with their own prescriptions following well-worn paths, letting others follow their own, different, paths. This situation has been described as the 'two solitudes' (Stoppard, 2002). There remain problems, particularly when a researcher wishes to use qualitative methods in a field where quantitative methods are the norm (e.g. Yang, 2013). Encouragingly, however, there is a growing recognition of the value of combining elements of both quantitative and qualitative research styles, discussed below under the label of multi-strategy design.

Notwithstanding these developments there remain two, readily discernible, different ways of approaching social research. Box 2.1 summarizes typical features of the quantitative approach. Typical features of the qualitative approach to social research are summarized in Box 2.2. Comparison of Boxes 2.1 and 2.2 reveals that to a considerable extent they present mirror images of each other: numerical vs. non-numerical; decontextualized vs. context important; *objectivity* vs. subjectivity, etc. What is put forward as a positive feature for one side of the divide would represent a criticism from the other.

The features in these boxes are likely to be seen in much social research based on the collection of quantitative (numerical) and qualitative (non-numerical) data, respectively. Particular features are not always present. For example, in the design of experiments, a widely used form of quantitative research, it is rare to find a concern for generalizing the findings from the participants studied to a wider population.

Quantitative and qualitative research have traditionally been considered as different research paradigms (Kuhn, 1962; 2012) in the sense of distinctive belief systems carrying with them clear philosophical assumptions. However, as pointed out by Maxwell and Mittapalli (2010), either

BOX 2.1

Quantitative social research: typical features

- Measurement and quantification (i.e. turning the information or data obtained into numbers) is central. Accuracy and precision of measurement is sought.
- A focus on behaviour (i.e. on what people do or say).
- The scientific approach is adhered to, with the same general principles as natural science.
- A *deductive* logic is adopted where pre-existing theoretical ideas or *concepts* are tested.
- Design of the research is pre-specified in detail at an early stage of the research process.
- *Reliability* (consistency over time and with different observers) and validity (showing they measure what is intended) of measurements is important.
- Detailed specification of procedures is provided so that *replication* of the study is possible (i.e. it can be repeated so that the findings can be checked).
- Statistical analysis of the data is expected.
- *Generalization* of the findings is sought (usually in the form of statistical generalizability which requires the *sample* of participants studied to be representative of some wider population).
- Objectivity is sought and distance maintained between the researcher and participants.
- Standardization is sought in the interests of control and accuracy. This often involves decontextualization (i.e. stripping the situation researched from its context, or ignoring the possible effects of the context). Some artificiality may be needed to achieve the desired standardization.
- A neutral, value-free position is sought.

> **BOX 2.2**
>
> ## Qualitative social research: typical features
>
> - Accounts and findings are presented verbally or in other non-numerical form. There is little or no use of numerical data or statistical analysis.
> - An inductive logic is used starting with data collection from which theoretical ideas and concepts emerge.
> - A focus on meanings.
> - Contexts are seen as important. There is a need to understand phenomena in their setting.
> - Situations are described from the perspective of those involved.
> - The design of the research emerges as the research is carried out and is flexible throughout the whole process.
> - The existence and importance of the values of researchers and others involved is accepted.
> - Objectivity is not valued. It is seen as distancing the researcher from participants.
> - Openness and receptivity of the researcher is valued.
> - The generalizability of findings is not a major concern
> - It takes place in natural settings. Artificial laboratory settings are rarely used.
> - Both the personal commitment and *reflexivity* (self-awareness) of the researcher are valued.
> - It is usually small scale in terms of numbers of persons or situations researched.
> - The social world is viewed as a creation of the people involved.

type of research can be carried out from a range of philosophical stances. Moreover, the extent to which philosophical concerns of this kind actually influence the practice of social researchers is open to question (see below p. 26). The claim that they are paradigms in one of the many other ways the term has been used – namely as referring to the preferred ways of working of discernible 'tribes' of researchers – is easier to sustain. Historically subject discipline tribes often sought to inculcate students into the methodological ways of their tribe. Health, Psychology, Public Health, and Social Policy were primarily aligned to quantitative approaches; Criminology, Sociology and Social Work to qualitative ones. There is now much greater flexibility.

The quantitative paradigm

The quantitative research paradigm has been, historically, closely linked to *positivism*. Criticisms of positivism have made this link more problematic and it has been largely superseded by a post-positivist approach which seeks to maintain aspects of positivism while coming to terms with these criticisms.

Positivist research

Positivism had been, for many years, the standard philosophical view of natural science. Its main features are listed in Box 2.3. Many of the individual tenets of positivism have been subjected to severe criticism from a range of philosophical standpoints, summarized in Box 2.4. For

BOX 2.3

Positivistic science – the 'standard view'

- Objective knowledge (facts) can be gained from direct experience or observation, and is the only knowledge available to science. Invisible or theoretical entities are rejected.
- Science separates facts from values; it is 'value-free'.
- Science is largely based on quantitative data, derived from the use of strict rules and procedures, fundamentally different from common sense.
- All scientific propositions are founded on facts. Hypotheses are tested against these facts.
- The purpose of science is to develop universal causal laws. The search for scientific laws involves finding empirical regularities where two or more things appear together or in some kind of sequence (sometimes called a *constant conjunction* of events).
- *Cause* is established through demonstrating such empirical regularities or constant conjunctions – in fact this is all that causal relations are.
- Explaining an event is simply relating it to a general law.
- Is it possible to transfer the assumptions and methods of social science from natural to social science?

BOX 2.4

Critiques of positivist-based science

- Doubts about the claim that direct experience is a sound basis for scientific knowledge.
- Rejection of the view that science should deal only with observable phenomena, and not with abstract or hypothetical entities.
- Impossibility of distinguishing between the language of observation and of theory.
- Theoretical concepts do not have a 1:1 correspondence with 'reality' as it is observed.
- Scientific laws are not based on constant conjunctions between events in the world.
- 'Facts' and 'values' can't be separated.

(after Blaikie, 2007, p. 183)

example, the positivist notion is that science becomes credible and possible because every scientist looking at the same bit of reality sees the same thing. However, it has been amply demonstrated that what observers 'see' is not simply determined by the characteristics of the thing observed. The characteristics and perspective of the observer also have an effect. Research looking at how scientists actually go about their research through the interdisciplinary perspective known as 'science and technology studies' or STS (e.g. Hackett, Amsterdamska, Lynch, & Wajcman, 2008; Sismondo, 2010, and Kuhn's (1962; 2012) earlier review from a historical perspective), found it very different from the 'standard view' and marked a waning of the influence of positivism with philosophers and researchers with methodological interests (Proctor & Capaldi, 2006, pp. 33–8; Sheppard, 2014).

Haig (2014) considers that, whereas psychology students typically receive extensive research methods training, there is little or no training in depth about the nature of science, and of scientific method. This is a situation which can be generalized to that of many users of social research methods. His text makes an important contribution toward remedying this deficiency.

Post-positivist research

What is the way forward for quantitative social research if positivism is to be discarded? There are post-positivist approaches which seek to answer this question. *Post-positivism* is sometimes taken in a general sense to include the full range of current approaches following the demise of positivism, including anti-positivist views (e.g. O'Leary, 2004, pp. 6–8). It is restricted here to those who try to adapt the approach taken in the natural sciences to social science research. Common to all such attempts is a heavy reliance on quantitative methods.

As with positivism, post-positivism is not a unitary school of thought, but more a group of theorists who share some but not all of a range of views. While positivists held that the researcher and the researched person were independent of each other, there is an acceptance by post-positivists that the theories, hypotheses, background knowledge and values of the researcher can influence what is observed (Reichardt & Rallis, 1994). However, they have a continuing commitment to objectivity which they approach through recognizing the possible effects of these likely biases. Post-positivists believe that a reality does exist but consider that it can only be known imperfectly and probabilistically in part because of the researcher's limitations. Box 2.5 lists some characteristics found in post-positive approaches.

To a large extent their view about how you should go about social research follows a positivist agenda. They strive for general laws and theories through which we can understand the social world. They believe in taking a scientific approach, starting with a theory which is tested through collecting data, resulting in the theory being supported or shown to need revision, calling for further testing (for post-positivists, you can never be sure that your theory is correct; it may be shown to be incorrect by new research). They do this by putting forward a small number of detailed hypotheses or specific research questions tested through quantitative measures of a few carefully specified variables.

Post-positivist research aims to find the truth about something. It is accepted that any one study cannot do this, but if other related studies point in the same direction, you are progressively

BOX 2.5

Post-positive views of research

- Evidence in research is always imperfect and fallible.
- Although there is no absolute warrant for knowledge we should be guided by the best evidence we have at the time.
- Research is the process of making claims which are then refined or abandoned in the light of evidence.
- Methods and conclusions should be examined to reduce possible bias and establish reliability and validity.
- Research seeks to develop statements which can help explain situations or describe *causal relationships*.
- Sociopolitical factors (e.g. the relationships of power and influence that occur in all human groups – including groups of scientists) have an influence on the ways in which knowledge is shaped and on what beliefs are accepted.
- Knowledge construction is both a rational activity based on evidence and a social activity based on power, politics and ideology.

(based on Phillips & Burbules, 2000, pp. 29–43)

more confident in the conclusion. Post-positivists are realists in the sense that they believe that there is an external reality separate from our descriptions of it. However, they do not accept the naive realist view of positivists that we can know things in the world directly without taking into account the uncertainties and doubts referred to in Box 2.4. Realist approaches are discussed separately later in the chapter (p. 38).

Detailed prescriptions for research procedures have been developed to increase confidence in their assertions about this reality. This involves specifying precise hypotheses so that we can ask clear, unambiguous questions to get clear, unambiguous answers. Objectivity is sought together with precise control of the research situation.

All these characteristics are associated with the fixed type of research design discussed in Chapter 6. The evidence-based movement discussed in that chapter is very largely post-positivist (in some cases unreconstructedly positivist). Real world research presents severe challenges for those seeking to work within a post-positivist paradigm. The settings in which it takes place often make the degree of control which is called for impracticable. Design requirements, such as the use of randomization procedures, may be difficult or impossible to fulfil. It can be problematic to achieve the objectivity expected when you are working in real life settings where the researcher has, or develops, an emotional involvement. Practitioner-researchers may find the role they are expected to play in research based on post-positivist principles uncongenial.

Overview

Followers of the quantitative research tradition in social research fall into two main camps. There are those who continue on the old positivist path, and post-positivists who, recognizing the force of the criticisms of positivism discussed earlier, seek to come to terms with them. Both groups can be further divided into those who make their theoretical position clear and a substantial majority where (in published work) it is not made explicit. Relatively few now make an explicit statement of their adherence to positivist principles. Much more common is an apparent taken-for-granted belief in most, if not all, of the aspects of the 'standard view' of science listed in Box 2.3 while ignoring the criticisms in Box 2.4. For example, the assumption that the researcher is 'value-free' remains. Some observers detect a recent retrenchment where policy-makers and funders are privileging research which follows a positivist path (a controversy in the United States over recent federal initiatives to define quality education research in very narrow terms being particularly heated – see Baez and Boyles, 2009, Chapter 1 for a detailed review).

The qualitative paradigm

The philosophical underpinnings of qualitative research are various. Handbooks, such as Denzin and Lincoln (2011), provide the comprehensive coverage needed to survey the full field, though it is worth bearing in mind the comment from Hood (2006) that 'most researchers will not fit neatly into the categories of any given typology'. Social constructionism is highlighted here as a broadly based mainstream qualitative approach with affinities to *phenomenology* and *hermeneutics* approaches (see Chapter 7, p. 165).

Social constructionist research

Social *constructivism/constructionism* indicates a view that social properties are constructed through interactions between people, rather than having a separate existence. Meaning does not exist in its own right; it is constructed by human beings as they interact and engage in interpretation. Social constructivist is also used to describe this kind of approach but usually indicates a focus on the individual rather than the group, and is concerned with how individuals construct and make sense of their world. It becomes important within social and societal based research when, for example, talking about topics such as public attitudes to sexual abuse, obesity or cancer. Constructionist approaches are also sometimes referred to as *interpretive/interpretivist approaches*, indicating a focus on how the social world is interpreted by those involved in it. Burr (2003) and Gergen (2009) provide clear accounts.

This approach emphasizes the world of experience as it is lived, felt and undergone by people acting in social situations (Schwandt, 2007). Researchers with this theoretical orientation find grave difficulties in the notion of an objective reality which can be known. They consider that whatever the underlying nature of reality (there are differing views amongst them about this) there is no direct access to it. In principle there are as many realities as there are participants – as well as that of the researcher. They consider that the task of the researcher is to understand the multiple social constructions of meaning and knowledge. Hence they tend to use research methods such as interviews and observation which allow them to acquire multiple perspectives. The research participants are viewed as helping to construct the 'reality' with the researchers. Values of the researcher and others are assumed to exist and subjectivity is an integral part of the research. The social constructionist approach is very open in the sense that it does not proscribe or prescribe any specific or particular way of doing research or method of data collection – although almost all the research under this heading uses qualitative data collection methods. The central aim or purpose of research is understanding.

Real world research is concerned with problems and issues where the social dimension is important and approaches which take serious note of this aspect have a clear attraction. The phenomena of interest tend to be fluid social constructions, rather than firm facts. Alderson (1999b) contrasts the approach appropriate when developing an effective treatment for a medical condition such as tuberculosis with that appropriate for quasi-medical conditions such as attention deficit hyperactivity disorder (ADHD) or emotional and behavioural disturbance, difficulty or disorder (EBD). While some aspects of the treatment of a disease such as tuberculosis have a social dimension (such as its resurgence in developed countries following increased migration from developing countries), the use of quantitative methodology in the development of effective drug treatments for dealing with the medical condition is well established and non-controversial.

The 'disease', like EBD, is not visible or even clearly definable:

- diagnoses vary widely and are contested;
- 'predictions' that stigmatize and work as negative self-fulfilling prophecies risk increasing the incidences;
- there is no agreed treatment; and
- it is impossible to test such ill-defined, complex and elusive phenomena through rigorous trials (Alderson, 1999b, p. 55).

The key point is that EBD is a social construction in the way that it is identified, perceived and evoked by relationships and situations (Galloway, Armstrong & Tomlinson, 1994). Considering the problem behaviours associated with EBD without taking note of the context in which they occur, as would be usual in a typical quantitative *survey* or piece of experimental research, makes them difficult to understand or interpret.

Another example of this is when seeking to understand paedophilia. An individual may have fantasies and distorted attitudes to children, but may never act upon them; they only become a sexual offender the moment they download images from the Internet or (try to) commit a contact offence (McCartan, 2009). Therefore, there is a difference between the offence/act, the offender and the social response, which makes it difficult to prevent and police all aspects of child sexual abuse.

There are other contemporary qualitative perspectives which share features with social constructionism, including *phenomenological* and *hermeneutic* approaches, both of which have been used fairly extensively in recent years by applied social researchers (see Chapter 7, p. 165). Some approaches influential in academic research, such as *ethnomethodology*, have attracted little interest in applied research (see, however, de Montigny, 2007, who argues persuasively that it has characteristics making it worthy of consideration for social work research).

Paradigms and research questions

A mantra of this book is that the research question provides the key to most things when doing social research. The next chapter focuses directly on how you go about deciding on your research questions. Some kinds of research question appear to call for a quantitative approach, others for a qualitative one. You should use the appropriate methodology to answer your question. Don't simply use the most prevalent in your research area or discipline; or the 'flavour of the month' methodology currently doing the rounds. If your research questions seem to call for both qualitative and quantitative data collection methods (i.e. if you have one research question for which you need to 'go quantitative', and others where you need to 'go qualitative'), the answer is to follow a multi-strategy design. This has both quantitative and qualitative elements and is discussed below, and in detail in Chapter 8.

This degree of choice may not be open to you. In your field or discipline there may be an expectation on what constitutes an appropriate approach for your research question; so that you, say, carry out an experiment which puts you firmly in the quantitative box, or that you carry out a qualitative ethnographic study. The starkness of this choice is heightened by methodologists who hold the 'incompatibility thesis' (discussed in more detail in Chapter 8, p. 175). This is that qualitative and quantitative research are two distinct ways of viewing research that are incompatible with each other. As Sale, Lohfeld and Brazil (2002) put it, 'Because the two paradigms do not study the same phenomena, qualitative and quantitative methods *cannot* be combined' (p. 43, original emphasis).

- Inspection of features of the two traditions as listed in Boxes 2.1 and 2.2 certainly confirms the view that they are very different. The philosophical assumptions discussed in the previous section do appear to be incompatible. However, research reports, and discussions with social researchers about how they actually go about their research, reveal what is in some ways a more complex, and in others a simpler, picture. Many of the distinctions between qualitative and quantitative research appear to break down under this kind of scrutiny (Hammersley, 1992b). Brannen (2005) points out that: the claim that qualitative research does not use numbers and that quantitative does, is simplistic; counter-examples exist;
- the claim that qualitative studies focus on meanings while quantitative research is concerned with behaviour is not fully supported – both may be concerned with people's views and actions; and
- the association of qualitative research with an inductive logic of enquiry and quantitative research with hypothetico-deductive logic is often reversed in practice (both often involve both logics); and both quantitative and qualitative research can be concerned with making generalizations (although of different types).

While the philosophical assumptions made in the quantitative and qualitative traditions are undeniably incompatible, this does not mean that researchers when carrying out quantitative research (in the sense that their study collects numerical data which are then analysed using statistics, and has other features as given in Box 2.1) accept these assumptions. The same argument can be made in respect of qualitative researchers. Increasingly, researchers combine quantitative and qualitative research in the same project. The very existence of this type of project, and its rapid emergence in the past few years as a preferred alternative, casts serious doubts on the incompatibility thesis. Bryman (2006b) conducted a content analysis of recent articles in this field and reports that only 14 (6 per cent) of the 232 made any reference to compatibility or philosophical issues. In interviews with 20 UK social researchers he found virtually none of them were concerned about transgressing philosophical principles by conducting this type of research. As one of his respondents put it, 'I don't think you have to subscribe to all the sort of foundation or philosophical assumptions in order to do exciting and interesting things in your research practice, which I think is a sort of quasi autonomous realm from philosophy and so on' (p. 115). He did find that some of the researchers felt uneasy about their sidelining of philosophical issues. It should be pointed out that researchers carrying out research involving both qualitative and quantitative aspects may be unlikely to report incompatibility concerns. Sandelowski, Voils and Barroso (2007), reviewing attempts to synthesize the multi-strategy research literature, claim that it is difficult to find any actual difference between studies presented as qualitative as opposed to quantitative. Voils, Sandelowski, Barroso and Hasselblad (2008) raise similar concerns and point out the use of quantitative techniques to integrate qualitative findings as a further breakdown of the distinction.

Hence, claims such as 'the philosophy of the social sciences cannot be an optional activity, indulged in by those reluctant to get on with real empirical work. It is the indispensable starting point for all the social sciences' (Trigg, 2001, p. 255) can be refuted by the actual practice of researchers – many don't do this. It is more a question of whether or not concerning oneself with philosophical matters leads to better, more useful, research, and, crucially, what type of philosophical insights help to do this.

It might be argued that some practising social researchers have, without realizing it, been making the appropriate philosophical assumptions, just as Molière's 'Bourgeois Gentilhomme' was astounded to be told that he had been speaking prose all his life. We prefer not to get entangled with these metaphysical speculations and are supported in this by the increasing number of supporters of a pragmatic approach. According to Maxcy (2003), *pragmatism* 'seems to have emerged as both a method of inquiry and a device for the settling of battles between research purists and more practical-minded scientists' (p. 79). Bryman (2006b) suggests that 'in the new climate of pragmatism . . . issues to do with the adequacy of particular methods for answering research questions are the crucial arbiter of which methodological approach should be adopted rather than a commitment to a paradigm and the philosophical doctrine on which it is supposedly based' (p. 118).

In terms of research paradigms, a way forward is to be less concerned with 'paradigms as philosophical stance' and to adopt a notion of 'paradigms as shared beliefs among groups of researchers' (Morgan, 2007). This does not mean that establishing a philosophical stance is a waste of time and should just be ignored. It provides one way of thinking about which kinds of research questions are important, and what constitute answers to the questions. If you find this approach helpful, follow it. However, it inevitably tends to privilege philosophical issues over all other concerns and effectively sets unnecessary vetoes on certain types of research. Taking as a point of reference the practices of groups of researchers rather than maxims handed down by philosophers gives another way forward. Their views about which questions are important to study and which methods are appropriate for finding answers appear likely to fulfil the pragmatist's concern for usefulness.

A pragmatic approach

To be pragmatic, in the general use of the word, indicates a concern for practical matters; being guided by practical experience rather than theory. Such an approach will be likely to be congenial to real world researchers whose main concern is to get on with the job, i.e. to come up with answers to the problems they are trying to address. This pragmatism can also be enforced by, and pushed onto, the researcher by the funders or stakeholders involved in real world research projects. External pragmatism of this kind should be resisted as it can affect the independence, *credibility* and rigour of the research. While sympathizing with researcher and stakeholder or funder impatience, our position is that you are likely to do a better job if you appreciate something of the theoretical bases to social research. This is itself a pragmatic argument for the inclusion of the kind of material covered in the chapter!

In addition to this non-technical use of the term, pragmatism refers to a philosophical position with a respectable, mainly American, history going back to the work of Peirce, William James and Dewey (Cherryholmes, 1992; Howe, 1998) and revived in that of Richard Rorty (e.g. Rorty, 1999). Shook and Margolis (2009) provide a comprehensive review. Baert (2005) discusses the implications of pragmatism for empirical research.

Box 2.6 lists some of the main features of the pragmatic approach in the context of social research. The central idea is that the meaning of a concept consists of its practical implications. Hence, truth is simply defined as 'what works'. In relation to research, a pragmatist would advocate using whatever philosophical or methodological approach works best for the particular research problem at issue.

Pragmatists believe that values play a large role in conducting research and in drawing conclusions from studies, and they see no reason to be concerned about that influence. Cherryholmes (1992) claims that, 'For pragmatists, values and visions of human action and interaction precede a search for descriptions, theories, explanations, and narratives. Pragmatic research is driven by anticipated consequences . . . Beginning with what he or she thinks is known and looking to the consequences he or she desires, our pragmatist would pick and choose how and what to research and what to do' (pp. 13–14). In similar vein, Teddlie (2005) says that pragmatic researchers:

> decide what they want to research guided by their personal value systems; that is, they study what they think is important. They then study the topic in a way that is congruent with their value system, including variables and units of analysis that they feel are the most appropriate for finding answers to their research questions. They also conduct their studies in anticipation of results that are congruent within their value system. This general description of the way in which pragmatists conduct their studies portrays the manner in which many researchers in the social and behavioral sciences actually do conduct their studies, especially research with important social consequences (p. 215).

Mertens (2002) is not convinced that the values of the researcher are in practice the guide. She considers that it may be the values of clients, policy-makers and other in positions of power which prevail (see also House & Howe, 1999).

BOX 2.6

Some features of the pragmatic approach

- Seeks a middle ground between philosophical dogmatism and scepticism.
- Rejects traditional dualisms (e.g. rationalism vs. *empiricism*, facts vs. values) and generally prefers more moderate and commonsense versions of philosophical dualisms based on how well they work in solving problems.
- Recognizes the existence and importance of the natural or physical world as well as the emergent social and psychological world.
- Places high regard on the reality of, and influence of, the inner world of human experience in action.
- Knowledge is viewed as being both constructed and based on the reality of the world we experience and live in.
- Endorses fallibilism (current beliefs and research conclusions are rarely, if ever, viewed as perfect, certain, or absolute).
- Justification comes in the form of what Dewey called 'warranted assertability'.
- Theories are viewed instrumentally (they become true and they are true to different degrees based on how well they currently work; workability is judged especially on the criteria of predictability and applicability).
- Endorses eclecticism and pluralism (e.g. different, even conflicting, theories and perspectives can be useful; observation, experience, and experiments are all useful ways to gain an understanding of people and the world).
- Human enquiry (i.e. what we do in our day-to-day lives as we interact with our environments) is viewed as being analogous to experimental and scientific enquiry. We all try out things to see what works, what solves problems, and what helps us to survive.
- Endorses a strong and practical empiricism as the path to determine what works.
- Views current truth, meaning, and knowledge as tentative and as changing over time. What we obtain on a daily basis in research should be viewed as provisional truths.
- Prefers action to philosophizing (pragmatism is, in a sense, an anti-philosophy).
- Takes an explicitly value-oriented approach to research that is derived from cultural values; specifically endorses shared values such as democracy, freedom, equality, and progress.
- Endorses practical theory (theory that informs effective practice).
- Generally rejects *reductionism* (e.g. reducing culture, thoughts, and beliefs to nothing more than neurobiological processes).

(based on Johnson & Onwuegbuzie, 2004, p.18 who provide a more comprehensive list)

Multi-strategy research designs

As indicated above, research where qualitative and quantitative approaches are combined in the same project is becoming increasingly popular. Commonly labelled *mixed method research*, it is referred to here as multi-strategy research, for reasons explained in Chapter 8, which is devoted to this type of research design.

The rise of multi-strategy research is, at least in part, attributable to weariness with qualitative/ quantitative hostilities; the appreciation by practising researchers that it was actually possible to do research with both quantitative and qualitative elements without dire consequences; and the realization by both practising researchers and methodologists that pragmatism provided a highly compatible theoretical underpinning to mixing the two types of method in the same project.

There are difficulties in taking this path. Not least among them is the fact that the design strategies traditional with researchers favouring quantitative methods (discussed in Chapter 6) are very different from those traditional in qualitatively inclined research circles (Chapter 7). Because of this the training requirements and sets of skills needed differ widely. One solution is the research team, where different members complement each other, but this may cloak later difficulties in integrating findings from qualitative and quantitative methods. However, many undergraduate and postgraduate social science research methods courses, in both the UK and other countries, now teach quantitative, qualitative and multi-strategy designs regardless of discipline area. This means that researchers should be more methodologically multilingual than previously.

It is possible to overemphasize these differences. As discussed above, there are common aspects in using qualitative and quantitative methods which have been downplayed by partisans of the two traditions. And the more that new researchers are given an even-handed introduction to both approaches (even if they subsequently go on to specialize), the easier it will be to develop multi-strategy research projects.

Realism and real world research

Using a pragmatic approach, as discussed in the previous sections, provides one way of justifying bringing together qualitative and quantitative approaches. Pragmatism is almost an 'anti-philosophical' philosophy which advocates getting on with the research rather than philosophizing – hence providing a welcome antidote to a stultifying over-concern with matters such as *ontology* and *epistemology*. Suggesting that real world researchers might, with advantage, take note of developments in realist philosophy smacks of a return to matters which some pragmatists suggest are better left on one side – though others, such as Rescher (2000) provide a pragmatic justification for adopting a realist stance. We think it worthwhile to highlight just two features of the realist approach. First, a general issue. Research very commonly seeks to provide explanations. Answers to 'how' or 'why' questions – how or why did something happen? *Realism* addresses these issues directly, providing a helpful language for this task. Secondly, an issue which looms particularly large in real world research. This is that virtually all real world research takes place in 'field', rather than laboratory, situations. Realism provides a way of approaching such open, uncontrolled situations. Hence it can provide findings and responses that are directly related to the situations researched. This is likely to appeal to stakeholders and funders: directed research for direct concerns.

Realism has a long tradition in the philosophy of science, including social science (Manicas, 1987). Early forms of the approach, sometimes referred to as 'naive realism', attracted severe criticism, but more recent formulations have a strong current position in the philosophy of both natural and social science. Box 2.7 lists some of the main features of the realist view of science. The writings of Roy Bhaskar and Rom Harré have been particularly influential (e.g. Bhaskar, 2008; Harré, 1986) while the text by Ray Pawson and Nick Tilley (Pawson & Tilley, 1997) provided a stirring, though controversial (because of its polemical style), manifesto for its use in evaluation research. The 'new' realism is variously labelled as 'scientific realism', 'critical realism', 'fallibilistic realism', 'subtle realism' and 'transcendental realism' amongst other terms, each of which stress particular features. For example, fallibilistic realism focuses on:

the evident fallibility of our knowledge – the experience of getting things wrong, of having our expectations confounded, and of crashing into things – that justifies us in believing that the world exists regardless of what we happen to think about it. If by contrast, the world itself was a product or construction of our knowledge, then our knowledge would surely be infallible, for how could we ever be mistaken about anything? (Sayer, 2000, p. 2)

BOX 2.7

A realist view of science

- There is no unquestionable foundation for science, no 'facts' that are beyond dispute. Knowledge is a social and historical product. 'Facts' are theory-laden.
- The task of science is to invent theories to explain the real world, and to test these theories by rational criteria.
- Explanation is concerned with how *mechanisms* produce events. The guiding metaphors are of structures and mechanisms rather than phenomena and events.
- A law is the characteristic pattern of activity or tendency of a mechanism. Laws are statements about the things that are 'really' happening, the ongoing ways of acting of independently existing things, which may not be expressed at the level of events.
- The real world is not only very complex but also stratified into different layers. Social reality incorporates individual, group and institutional, and societal levels.
- The conception of causation is one in which entities act as a function of their basic structure.
- Explanation is showing how some event has occurred in a particular case. Events are to be explained even when they cannot be predicted.

(partly after House, 1991)

Realism is an attractive choice for those doing social research who wish to characterize what they are doing as scientific. It can provide a model of scientific explanation free of the problems encountered in positivist and relativist accounts. Its advocates claim that it is scientific, in a sense which is fully in accord with currently influential approaches to the philosophy of science.

The version known as critical realism incorporates features highlighted by an emancipatory approach, such as taking note of the perspectives of participants, and even of promoting social justice (House, 1991). Bhaskar's (1986) text entitled *Scientific Realism and Human Emancipation* elaborates his concern for 'emancipatory social practice' (Corson, 1991). However, Corson is concerned that it is primarily a critical exercise: 'The guiding assumptions here are that there will always be an overabundance of explanatory possibilities, that some of them will be mistaken, and that the primary task of social science is to be critical of the lay thought and actions that lie behind the false explanations' (pp. 18–19). Pawson allies himself with researchers seeking to develop realism as an empirical method. While realism has been seen as particularly appropriate for research in practice-based and value-based professions such as social work (Anastas, 1998; 1999), it is only recently that there has been a substantial amount of empirical research seeking to 'make realism work' (Carter & New, 2004). Ackroyd (2009) seeks to remedy the lack of consideration of the implications of a realist standpoint for research design. These practical issues are returned to in several of the later chapters in this book.

A note on realism and social constructionism

The mainstream qualitative approach of social constructionism (sometimes constructivism) discussed earlier in the chapter (p. 24) appears, on initial consideration, to be antithetical to realism. Indeed several of its advocates are avowedly 'anti-realist'. Clearly naive realism is ruled out, but few if any would defend it in any case. However, a rapprochement between what might be termed moderate social constructionism and more sophisticated versions of realism appears feasible. In suggesting that the real world is complex and multifaceted we need to take this into account in doing realistic and achievable research that can have an impact. Nightingale and Cromby (2002) present a strong case for a *critical realist* constructionism as more credible, with greater utility and closer to a 'truth' than a range of alternatives which they discuss (see also Collier, 1998 and Galloway, 2000).

Causation and realist explanation

Research may be carried out for several different purposes but it is commonly viewed as trying to find explanations. Why did something happen? Why does a particular public health initiative have the effects it has? How can we explain the pattern of events that we find? Another way of saying this is 'What caused it to happen?' Experiments, particularly those involving randomization such as *randomized controlled trials (RCTs)*, are frequently portrayed as the best way of establishing causation. The logic behind this claim is well established. It calls for a particular view of causation, usually called a *successionist view*. Essentially, A is considered to have caused B because the occurrence of A is regularly followed by the occurrence of B. The particular aspect of RCTs, and similar experimental designs, is that they are very good at ruling out alternative explanations of why B regularly follows A. Note, however, that their use and interpretation, particularly in the complex situations in which much real world research takes place, is controversial (see Chapter 6, p. 117).

This idea of what constitutes causation, which is central to the positivist view of science, does not give a direct answer to 'how' or 'why' questions. Something in addition, some theory of what is happening, is needed. The realist approach has a different view of causation, called *generative causation*. Here, the cause of A following B is because of the operation of one or more mechanisms. The standard simple example used by realists is the operation of gunpowder.

Does gunpowder blow up when a flame is applied? Yes, if the conditions are right. It doesn't ignite if it is damp; or if the mixture is wrong; or if no oxygen is present; or if heat is only applied for a short time. In realist terms, the outcome (the explosion) of an action (applying the flame) follows from mechanisms (the chemical composition of the gunpowder) acting in particular contexts (the particular conditions which allow the reaction to take place). This is illustrated in Figure 2.1.

Realist view of doing experiments

Experimenters need to have a very substantial knowledge of the phenomenon they are interested in before it is worth their while to set up a formal experiment. Through theory and observation, and as a result of previous experiments, they develop knowledge and understanding about the mechanism through which an action causes an outcome, and about the context which provides the ideal conditions to trigger the mechanism. There may well be several such mechanisms, as well as other mechanisms, which could have the effect of blocking the effect of the action. Disabling the latter mechanisms is known as experimental (or laboratory) control. The laboratory in the physical sciences is essentially a special space devoted to this kind of control where temperature, vibration, air quality, etc. are all carefully monitored to ensure that their variation cannot influence the outcome. Note that this has nothing to do with control groups.

The whole enterprise differs radically from the logic of experimental design as traditionally expounded in research methods texts. There the experimenter simply manipulates one variable and looks for resultant change in a second one. In positivist science the experimenter looks for this 'constant conjunction' (change in one variable reliably leads to a change in the second variable). If this is found, it constitutes a 'law'. The realist experimenter is engaged in a very different

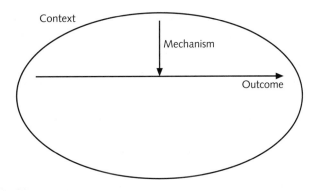

Figure 2.1 Representation of realist explanation.

kind of exercise. In Bhaskar's (1979, p. 53) terminology, you '[f]irst . . . must trigger the mechanism under study to ensure that it is active; and secondly must prevent any interference with the operation of the mechanism'. This is a more active task; it is to 'manipulate the entire experimental system, so as to *manufacture* the desired interrelationship between independent and dependent variable. The experimentalist is indeed a *system builder* and the crucial evidence is produced not by controlled observation but by *work'* (Pawson & Tilley, 1997, p. 60, original emphasis). Some realists are heavily critical of experimental designs. Pawson and Tilley (1997, Chapter 2), for example, consider the standard control group design to be fatally flawed. Byrne (1998) contends that '[b]y its own criteria experimentalism only works when the world is linear and when causes are simple and single' (p. 65). Nonlinearity and complex causation are not too difficult to demonstrate, particularly in real world settings.

Studies of the history of how physical scientists actually go about their trade (e.g. Koyré, 1968) reveal that it fits in well with this kind of realist explanation. Theory is gradually and hesitantly developed so that eventually experiments can be done which make clear the mechanisms in operation. The studies also reveal that the process bears little resemblance to the kind of logical positivist analysis derived from Hume and John Stuart Mill, which underpins traditional views of how experiments should be done.

Mechanisms in evaluation research

Pawson and Tilley (2004a) explain the role of mechanisms in simple terms:

> Mechanisms describe what it is about programmes and interventions that bring about any effects. Mechanisms are often hidden, rather as the workings of a clock cannot be seen but drive the patterned movements of the hands. This realist concept tries to break the lazy linguistic habit of basing evaluation on the question of whether 'programmes work'. In fact, it is not programmes that work but the resources they offer to enable their subjects to make them work. This process of how subjects interpret and act upon the intervention stratagem is known as the programme 'mechanism' and it is the pivot around which realist research revolves (p. 6).

They use the example of attempts to reduce car park crime through the introduction of closed-circuit television (Pawson & Tilley, 1997, pp. 78–82). Clearly the cameras do not in themselves make cars more difficult to break into. If they do work, it must be through processes in the minds of potential thieves, parkers of cars, car park attendants, police and others. From a knowledge of the situation, combined with observation in car parks, it is possible to put forward a range of suggestions for mechanisms. They suggest eight possibilities including:

(a) 'caught in the act' – offenders being more likely to be observed, arrested, punished and deterred;
(b) 'increased usage' – drivers feel that the car park is safer, leading to increased usage. As more people are around, potential offenders are deterred; and
(c) 'appeal to the cautious' – cautious drivers who lock their cars, use alarms and immobilizers are attracted to parks with CCTV, driving out more vulnerable cars.

More than one mechanism may be involved in a particular situation, and whether or not a particular mechanism operates will depend on the context. If, for example, much of the crime in a particular car park is committed by a single offender, then increasing the probability of appre-hension as in mechanism (a) will be likely to have a much more dramatic effect on car crime than if many thieves were involved. Mechanisms (b) and (c) will be largely inoperative in commuter car parks which already fill up early in the morning and remain virtually full until workers return in the evening. However, car parks which are currently little used, and where each parked car has a relatively high chance of being broken into, may provide an appropriate context for firing the 'increased usage' mechanism.

Pawson and Tilley point out that their list of mechanisms and contexts is speculative. As in much real world research, there is little social science background from which they might have been derived or, as they put it, 'there being no existing sociology of the car park' (p. 80). However, it may be worthwhile to search for existing studies in similar situations such as shopping malls, football stadiums and town centres where CCTV cameras are employed, and where similar mechanisms may occur (Brown, 1995).

These proposals help to focus the research effort. They may suggest avenues which were not initially obvious within your research area and discipline or outside of them. Some of the most original, interesting and impactful research is multi-disciplinary. Research into why people desist from offending, with roots in philosophy, psychology and sociology, has influenced research developments in criminology (Maruna, 2001). In the car park example, while data relat-ing to break-ins would almost certainly be routinely collected, assessing the operation of an 'appeal to the cautious' mechanism suggests examining unmolested cars. Are there changes in the numbers and proportions of cars left unlocked, or with visible stealable goods, or without an armed alarm? Similarly other mechanisms may suggest some attention to what is stolen, or to locations of the crimes, or to their timing, etc. You will also have to concern yourself with what is technically feasible; for example, it is only recently that CCTV pictures have been of suffi-ciently high definition to provide unequivocal identification of offenders, and hence potentially operate the 'caught in the act' mechanism.

This approach has inspired a substantial number of researchers to follow the realistic evalu-ation path, and Pawson and Tilley (1997) is extensively cited. See their Chapter 8, p. 178, for further details and examples.

Mechanisms in other types of real world research

The focusing power and general utility of seeking answers to the question of 'What mechanisms seem to be operating in this situation?' is by no means restricted to evaluation research.

In much real world research, it is not a difficult task for practitioners and others with a well-developed and intimate knowledge of the situation (and for researchers with whom they have shared this knowledge) to come up with a set of proposals for the mechanisms and contexts likely to be relevant. Box 2.8 gives an example of this process. Pawson and Tilley (2004a; Appendix 1 'Thinking it through', p. 36) present a similar exercise asking participants to brain-storm not only possible mechanisms, but also the contexts in which they might occur and possible outcomes for 'smoking cessation' and 'domestic violence' programmes.

Following up these leads fits in most appropriately with an initial exploratory phase which is common in a large proportion of real world research. In some situations this may have to be

BOX 2.8

Practitioner proposals for mechanisms

A client organization wished to know why some residents from a nearby centre for adults with learning difficulties attended their evening club whereas others did not. Some explanations were suggested by the key worker of the client organization and others by the students undertaking the project.

1. Perhaps some residents did not want to make the journey to the club or did not have adequate transport.
2. Perhaps the residents wanted to be accompanied on the journey.
3. Perhaps they did not have enough information (or any information) about the club.
4. Perhaps the club did not provide the kinds of activities which the residents liked.
5. Perhaps the club was not friendly enough.

Consideration of these suggestions indicates the possibility of the following mechanisms affecting club attendance:

- an accessibility mechanism (1 and 2);
- an information mechanism (3); and
- a needs and expectations mechanism (4 and 5).

Evidence about the operation of these mechanisms could then be sought in a project.

(example taken from Hall & Hall, 1996, p. 31. Note the original is not described in terms of mechanisms)

'virtual' exploratory work where, without further observation or other direct data gathering, you explore with those who are knowledgeable about the setting which mechanisms and contexts appear to be the 'bankers'; i.e. where there is consensus that they are the ones to concentrate on. Or you may be in the fortunate position where you are building on previous work (your own or that of other researchers), or even have a developed theoretical framework, which provide strong pointers to the mechanisms and contexts to work on in detail.

'Working on in detail' constitutes the main phase of your research. It can, in principle, follow any of the designs covered in the following chapters. The desirable end-state of this process for realists is that you come up with one or more postulated mechanisms which are capable of explaining the phenomena, and that from the research you have good reason to believe in their existence. And you need to be able to specify the contexts in which these mechanisms operate. This discussion has been couched in terms of mechanisms which operate to produce an outcome or effect, but there may also be mechanisms operating which block the outcome or effect. In particular, your research will be set in some social system or situation where existing mechanisms may be blocking the change or outcome you are seeking.

The website provides further discussion on mechanisms, with exemplars.

Working in open systems

An abiding complication when carrying out real world research is that it almost always takes place in non-laboratory situations. Research laboratories are devices intended to maximize the control of the experimenter over all aspects; effectively they are *closed systems*. Outside the laboratory we have to come to terms with much more *open systems*. One of the intentions behind using RCTs and similar experimental designs is to establish predictable regularities under these 'field' conditions. However, realists believe that even in the absence of the degree of closure needed to establish predictable regularities, the laws still apply. They seek to show how it is that in the particular situation in which the research took place, there was a particular causal configuration involving a set of mechanisms that had the particular pattern of results achieved. The task is to carry out an analysis of the possible causes which were in operation while eliminating alternatives which might have been involved.

In the open systems of real world research, the hospital ward, housing estate, business or whatever forms the focus of our research, cannot be hermetically sealed from external influences. People, information and all other aspects of the situation are likely to change in ways that may or may not have anything to do with the focus of our investigation. These are systems which are open in the sense that they can be entered and exited both literally and figuratively at any time. There is an arbitrariness about what we consider to be the context of our study and what is its actual content.

Manicas and Secord (1983) make the more general claim that social and psychological reality exists in inherently open systems. They stress the complexity of the task:

> The acts of persons in life settings are open-systemic events that involve an enormous range of codetermining structures and systems. One needs knowledge only of physics to account for the fall of a person from a precipice; one needs knowledge of biological structures and processes to comprehend birth or death; one needs psychology to have an understanding of the structures and processes that underlie performances – and of course this is made more difficult by the fact that the relevant intrinsic structures of persons are complexly related and causally codetermining (p. 407).

In open systems we can well be in a position to explain some event after it has occurred even though we were not able to predict it. In closed systems, explanation and prediction are symmetrical; if we can explain we can predict, and vice versa. But in open systems the actual configurations of structures and processes are constantly changing making definite prediction impossible. This means that while the future cannot be predicted, the past can be explained by establishing the particular configuration which was in existence. The form of logic typically used by realists, known as *abductive reasoning* (or retroductive reasoning) (Peirce, 1986), appears to be particularly suited to carrying out research in these circumstances. It is a process that instead of just moving from theory to the observations (as in *deduction*), or from observations to theory (as in *induction*), cycles between the two (see Chapter 3, p. 67). 'Theory' here refers to mechanisms postulated as being capable of producing the events observed. Initially highly tentative possible mechanisms become more firmly established with successive cycles.

Realism and replication

Replication in research – the attempt to repeat a study – is a major cornerstone of natural science. A finding is not regarded as secure unless it has been independently replicated on several occasions, and 'failure to replicate' has dealt a death blow to many promising lines of research. In real world research, and social science more generally, attempts to replicate are rare. Some researchers using qualitative methods consider it an impossibility; each study is to them essentially unique. Certainly it is just not feasible to repeat a study exactly with the same people in the same situation.

The realist views replication as an attempt to confirm the structures and mechanisms identified in the original study under similar contingent conditions. However, replication does not produce conclusive verification of their existence (or, put in other terms, of the theory). Similarly, a failure to replicate previous findings does not conclusively falsify the theory. As Tsang and Kwan (1999) put it:

> One explanation of this failure is that the structures and mechanisms as postulated in the theory are inaccurate: in this case we have a true falsification. However, another possible explanation is that, in the replicated study, there is a different set of contingencies that either modifies the postulated mechanisms or invokes previously inactive countervailing mechanisms. This results in a different set of events being observed (p. 769).

Given the relatively primitive stage of our understanding of what is happening in many real world situations, a sensible strategy, with some hope of progress in that understanding, would appear to attempt to capitalize on any studies where there are relatively strong findings giving support to a particular theory suggesting the operation of certain mechanisms in the contexts of the study. This would be done most effectively by trying to set up as exact a replication as feasible in the first instance. After that, and given some success in that replication, effort could be put into generalizing the findings.

Which brand of realism?

As is common to many philosophically minded methodologists, realists are a fractious bunch with long-running feuds both between and within the various brands of realism. It may be clear to any such readers that we favour what might be termed 'realism-lite', pragmatically selecting ideas and terminology from different realist approaches which appear likely to be useful for the real world researcher. We find some aspects of critical realism attractive, particularly its affinity to emancipatory styles of research, but others less so (e.g. its emphasis on theory and critical analysis rather than on empirical research). Similarly, as Nash (2005) points out, many critical realists reject quantitative statistical approaches, whereas:

> scientific realists maintain that quantification is necessary to science and that the conventional epistemological assumptions of applied statistics can be surmounted. Scientific realists, for example, argue that the assumptions of positivism, often implicit in statistical modelling, are not inherent to quantification itself and that statistical techniques may be used to enhance realist explanatory narratives (p. 186).

We just use the term 'realism' to flag the approach to science and social research introduced in this section. Realism, and its implications for designing, carrying out and interpreting research findings, is returned to at various points in the book.

The purposes of research

Three possible purposes of research are commonly put forward – to explore, to describe and/or to explain. Each of these might form the focus of a real world project. It is sometimes claimed that exploring or describing are inferior to explaining; that research worthy of the name should seek to provide explanations. This is a laudable aim, and it will be suggesting at various points in the book that, following the realist line, asking the 'why' question (in other terms – what is going on here, and how might I explain it?) is almost always on the agenda. However, for much real world research we are in relatively uncharted waters and the most useful thing to concentrate on is to explore. Similarly, achieving a clear description of a poorly understood area can reasonably be the priority. Certainly many real world research questions call for an exploratory or descriptive focus. While one purpose will usually be central to a project a particular study may be concerned with more than one purpose. The purpose may also change as the study proceeds, particularly in multi-strategy designs (Chapter 8).

Action, change and emancipation

The 'action' perspective present in many real world studies, where there is a concern not only to explore, describe or explain but also to facilitate action, to help change or make improvements, to influence policy or practice, suggests that an additional purpose is important in much real world research.

Several action approaches stress an emancipatory or *empowerment* purpose. It is a theme in much *feminist research* where an aim is to help members of an oppressed group take control of their own lives. This can be through direct action where the study itself leads to change, or indirect through influence on policy (Brown & Strega, 2005). Critical theorists such as Marcuse and Habermas follow Marx in considering that their task is not primarily to understand the world but to change it. Their criticism is not only of capitalist society but also of the natural sciences which, because of their success in dominating nature, have become an important source of authority and power in society (see Blaikie, 2007, pp. 135–40 for an extended account). Critical theory has had an impact as it:

- locates social welfare projects, programmes and practices, and people's understandings and evaluations of them, historically and in their social, political and economic contexts;
- reveals how dimensions of oppression such as social class, gender, race, age, disability and sexuality generate and maintain certain practices and understandings;
- deconstructs commonly accepted ways of doing things and understandings so that these are not taken-for-granted but are exposed for the extent to which they both influence and are influenced by prevailing ways of thinking;

- is informed by theories of democracy and social justice that help to guide both the processes of judgement-making and the judgements to be made; and
- is committed to provoking change in the direction of equality (based on Everitt & Hardiker, 1996, pp. 98–9).

There are related approaches which stress the active participation of all involved with the research, including not only the researchers but also participants and others. An advocacy role for the researcher is expected, which is very different from that of the detached, objective scientist. Key features, according to Kemmis and Wilkinson (1998, pp. 21–36), include:

- a focus on bringing about changes in practices;
- presentation of an action agenda for change by the researcher;
- concern for helping people free themselves from constraints (e.g. in power relationships or work practices);
- fostering self-development and self-determination;
- aiming to create debate and discussion so that change will occur; and
- participants being active collaborators in all aspects of the research process.

Some commentators express concerns about possible negative effects of this stance. Danieli and Woodhams (2005), for example, consider the field of disability research where, since the 1990s, something of a consensus appears to have been reached that *emancipatory research* is the most appropriate methodology. They question the wisdom of this view, querying the extent to which emancipatory research enables the removal of hierarchical relations during the research process. They consider that it potentially marginalizes some voices and potentially oppresses some disabled people and researchers. Hence that a more pluralistic and eclectic stance is preferable.

See Chapter 9, p. 188, for further discussion of types of action and evaluation research which focus on emancipation and empowerment. Having a purpose involving action or change is additional to the traditional exploring/describing/explaining purposes. You may need to achieve any or all of these purposes, depending on the situation and your research questions, to be in a position to achieve the action or change objective.

Practical value of the theoretical material covered in the chapter

This chapter has sought to give the flavour of a number of different theoretical approaches to social research. As already discussed, the extent to which this type of material is on a 'need to know' basis for real world research is a matter of dispute. As Gerring (2001) puts it, 'with a few exceptions . . . philosophy of science does not tell us much about how to improve work in the social sciences, or how to distinguish good work from bad; for most of it is written at a rather lofty ("philosophical") level' (p. 17). Because of this, philosophy of science has had rather limited effect on the practice of social science. It has had what Gerring describes as a 'centrifugal' effect on the methodology of social science, resulting in it being carved up into mutually incompatible schools and sects.

Certainly, problem-focused real world researchers in many cases appear to get by quite adequately giving little or no explicit attention to the philosophical underpinnings to social research. In more cynical mood there is a suspicion that the prime reason for authors of research methods texts devoting extensive space to philosophical material is to demonstrate their academic credibility and to satisfy the expectations of course tutors!

Why bother then with theoretical issues? Carter and Little (2007) suggest that:

> If Anna better understands the theoretical and disciplinary bases for her methodology, she is likely to use it in a more nuanced and flexible way and to feel personally confident in her practice rather than blindly following a recipe. This would enable Anna to become a reflexive and creative practitioner, capable of reinvention and evolution of her craft (p. 1324).

Discussion of the methodological bases to practice also helps make clear that there are several, very different, ways of thinking about the task of carrying out a real world project. Hopefully, this will inoculate against unthinking repetition of the familiar or docile acceptance of what others propose. Ignorance of alternatives helps perpetuate outmoded traditional approaches such as positivism. There are other more pragmatic reasons for discussion. Doctoral candidates, research students and others following courses will be expected to demonstrate their academic quality by a chapter or more on their methodology. Similar requirements are put on researchers both when seeking approval and/or funding for a project, and when trying to get the findings published.

Further reading

The website gives annotated references to further reading for Chapter 2.

PART II

Planning: selecting a strategy

The focus shifts in this part to the design of your own project. In this task it is useful to distinguish between the *strategy* and the *tactics* that you adopt when carrying out a research project. Strategy refers to the general broad orientation taken in seeking answers to research questions – the style, if you like. These strategic considerations are the main concern of this second part of the book. Before starting to collect data in earnest, you need to have given serious thought to the ethics of what you are proposing, discussed in the final chapter of Part II. Tactics, the specific methods of investigation, are dealt with in Part III, which concludes with a chapter on writing a project proposal.

PART II

Planning: selecting a strategy

CHAPTER 3

Developing your ideas

This chapter:

- helps you decide on the focus of your research, emphasizing the advantages of 'starting where you are';
- considers ways of researching the background to the research, including database and other literature searches;
- debates strategies for conducting and developing good literature reviews;
- examines the difference between a literature review as a preface to an empirical study and as a form of research in its own right;
- discusses how this focus can be refined into research questions; and the role of theory in this process.

Introduction

The task of carrying out a research project is complicated by the fact that there is no overall consensus about how to conceptualize doing social research. This shows in various ways. There are, for example, different views about the place and role of theory, also about the sequence and relationship of the activities involved. One model says that you need to know exactly what you are doing before collecting the data that you are going to analyse and that you collect all this data before starting to analyse it. A different approach expects you to develop your design through interaction with whatever you are studying and has data collection and analysis intertwined. These approaches were referred to in Chapter 1 as *fixed designs* and *flexible designs* respectively. The former have developed from the quantitative tradition of social research, the latter from the qualitative tradition (see Chapter 2).

Spradley (1980) compares these two research approaches to petroleum engineers and explorers respectively:

The [petroleum] engineer has a specific goal in mind; to find oil or gas buried far below the surface. Before the engineer even begins an investigation, a careful study will be made of the maps which show geological features of the area. Then, knowing ahead of the time the kinds of features that suggest oil or gas beneath the surface, the engineer will go out to 'find' something quite specific (p. 26).

To follow the fixed design route, you have to be in the position of knowing what you are looking for. However, those following flexible designs begin much more generally. They explore:

gathering information, going first in one direction then perhaps retracing that route, then starting out in a new direction. On discovering a lake in the middle of a large wooded area, the explorer would take frequent compass readings, check the angle of the sun, take notes about prominent landmarks, and use feedback from each observation to modify earlier information (p. 26).

For those interested in carrying out relatively small-scale real world investigations, each of these traditional models presents difficulties. A problem in following fixed designs is that one is often forced to work with sketchy maps at best. In other words, the firm theoretical base that is called for is difficult to get hold of. Similarly, free-range exploring is rarely on the cards. For one thing there isn't the time, and the reality is often that the real world researcher has some idea of the 'lie of the land', and is looking for something quite specific while still being open to unexpected discoveries.

This suggests that the real world researcher may need to be somewhat innovative in her approach, not automatically following research traditions when they do not seem to be appropriate for the research questions to which answers are sought. Fortunately researchers do already seem to be more eclectic in their actual research practice than methodologists urge them to be. As discussed in the previous chapter it seems that many of the differences between the two traditions are in the minds of philosophers and theorists, rather than in the practices of researchers. Undoubtedly there are situations and topics where a fixed design following a traditional quantitative approach is called for, and others where a flexible design following a constructionist or other traditional qualitative approach is appropriate. But there are others where a multi-strategy approach incorporating both quantitative and qualitative elements better fits the bill.

A reminder

It is important to remember that not all research is empirical, involving your collection of new data. So-called 'desk-bound' research based on already existing data has an important part to play in real world research (see Chapter 5). This type of research is already the norm in some disciplines and areas of study. As both time and money for funded research projects becomes scarcer, there is more expectation of reliance on existing data, and the greater use of in-depth rapid evidence reviews in policy and practice.

And a warning

The divide between qualitative and quantitative research methodology is not simply a methodological debate. It can sometimes be a fight for the soul of your academic discipline. Some disciplines and fields of study align themselves to quantitative research, others to qualitative; and yet others regard the norm as *desk-based research*, qualitative or desk-based methodologies over, or at the expense of, other methodologies. Experimental psychology was traditionally almost exclusively quantitative, although more recently qualitative research has established a strong position – much to the ire of some psychologists. In criminology the reverse applies.

Our stance is that the research question is the key. Different types of research question, as discussed later in the chapter, call for different methodologies.

Variance thinking or process thinking?

Talking in terms of fixed and flexible designs captures many of the procedural differences between traditional quantitative and qualitative research. It is, however, an essentially atheoretical approach and methodologists have sought more theoretically-based alternatives. The two types of causation, successionist and generative, discussed in the previous chapter (pp. 32–33), have been used to make the distinction. The successionist view traditionally predominant in quantitative research, where the focus is on establishing systematic relationships between inputs and outputs, deals with the contribution of differences in measured values of particular variables to differences in values of other variables. An alternative, traditionally predominant in qualitative research, is linked to the generative view of causation and deals with events and the processes that connect them. The task is to analyse the causal processes by which some events influence others.

Maxwell, personal communication, 21 July 2010, considers that the distinction between variance thinking and process thinking is '. . . a key aspect of the qualitative/quantitative divide, and one that it is essential for students to grasp. These are different "mental models" for thinking about the world, and an unconscious commitment to only one of these seriously handicaps students in their ability to appreciate or use the other.' See also Maxwell and Loomis (2003) and Maxwell and Mittapalli (2010).

Ragin (1987) makes the distinction as between variable-oriented (quantitative) and case-oriented (qualitative) approaches. He proposes a strategy known as qualitative comparative analysis (QCA) which seeks to integrate the two approaches, and which has gained considerable attention with methodologically oriented researchers (Rihoux & Ragin, 2008; Vaisey, 2009).

Deciding on the focus

The need for a focus

Before you can start, you obviously need to have some idea of what area you are going to deal with. This amounts to deciding on your focus (also referred to as a *research topic*). Our experience is that this tends either to be quite straightforward, almost self-evident (especially when you are told what to do!) or pretty problematic (when you have an open field).

Finding the focus involves identifying what it is that you want to gather information about. Until you have done this, further planning is impossible. If you are deciding for yourself, with few or no external constraints, the decision will be driven by what you are interested in and concerned about. Any research experience that you already have can be a legitimate influence on this decision, but you should beware of this having a strait-jacket effect (e.g. simply looking for topics where you might use your experience of carrying out surveys). Conversely, it is also legitimate to select a focus which leads you to branch out and gain experience of a strategy or technique not already within your 'toolbag'.

Sometimes the idea comes from your own direct experience or observation (see 'Starting where you are' below). Or it may arise from discussion with others about what would be timely and useful. Real world research often focuses on the solving of problems, and is frequently concerned with change and improvement in something to do with practice. For those carrying out a project as part of an academic award, at whatever level, your supervisor(s) are a key resource which you should make full use of, although any supervisor worth their salt should welcome you having your own ideas.

It is helpful to try to write down the research focus at this stage, even if you can only do this in a vague and tentative form. Later stages in the process will help to refine it and get it more clearly focused.

The website gives a varied set of examples of initial proposals for research foci.

Making a group decision

If you are proposing to carry out a group project[1] with colleagues or friends, it is valuable for each member to independently think about, and write down, their proposals for the research focus. The group then comes together to decide on an agreed focus. In this way all members of the group have some input into the process, and ideas of combining individual input with group collaboration and negotiation get built in at an early stage. Hall and Hall (1996, pp. 22–7) provide useful practical advice on working in groups, covering areas such as group development, unwritten contracts, team roles and leadership.

Having the decision made for you

In many cases the focus of a real world research project is given to the researcher(s) as a part of the job or as a commission or tender. That is not to say that the people giving the task to the investigators necessarily know what they want or that the researchers agree that this is what they should be wanting. The main task in this situation is clarificatory; translating the presenting problem into something researchable, and moreover 'do-able' within the parameters of time, resources and finance that can be made available.

---

[1] Most research is group research, although regulations often rule this out for students. Barnett (2012) makes a strong plea for group student projects, based on over 40 years' experience.

Starting where you are

If you do have some say in the choice of topic, there are several factors which might be taken into account. *Interest* is probably the most important. *All research involves drudgery and frustration and you need to have a strong interest in the topic to keep you going through the bad times.* Such interest in the focus of the research is not the same thing as having a closed and prejudged view of the nature of the phenomenon to be researched or the kind of outcomes that will be found, which is likely to affect the objectivity and trustworthiness of the research. All of these aspects, however, are a part of what Lofland, Snow, Anderson and Lofland (2006) call 'starting where you are'.

The website gives examples of 'starting where you are'.

As Kirby and McKenna (1989) put it:

> Remember that who you are has a central place in the research process because you bring your own thoughts, aspirations and feelings, and your own ethnicity, race, class, gender, sexual orientation, occupation, family background, schooling, etc. to your research (p. 46).

This open acknowledgement of what the researcher brings to the research is more common in some research traditions than others. However, even in traditional laboratory experimentation, the work of Robert Rosenthal and colleagues (e.g. Rosnow & Rosenthal, 1997) has led to a recognition of 'experimenter effects' of various kinds, although they tend to be viewed solely in terms of the difficulties they produce.

Researchers selecting their own foci make the choice for a variety of reasons. It may be, for example, to address a problem of 'practice'. That is, as professionals (psychologists, social workers, health service workers, teachers, managers, personnel officers, etc.) they wish to look at, perhaps evaluate or change, some aspect of practice that interests or concerns them. It may be their own, or colleagues', practice or professional situations, or those of others whom they have a responsibility to advise or support. Frequently encountered problems are obviously a sensible choice for a research focus as anything useful that you find out has a direct spin-off; and, importantly, there will be no shortage of instances to study.

In such situations you are also likely to know a lot about the topic even before starting the research, which can assist in planning. Maxwell (2013) comments:

> Traditionally, what you bring to the research from your background and identity has been treated as *bias*, something whose influence needs to be *eliminated* from the design, rather than a valuable component of it (p. 44, emphases in original).

Because of this, there is a tendency, particularly in proposals from students, to ignore what they can bring to the study from their own experience about the settings and issues to be studied. Maxwell's view is that such experiential knowledge can be profitably capitalized on. The potential for bias still exists of course and it will be necessary to seek to counter this by examining the assumptions and values you bring to the situation. One approach to this is to use an identity memo which articulates the expectations, beliefs and understandings you have from previous identity and experience. Maxwell (2013, pp. 46–8) provides examples.

Morse (2009) sounds a warning note. She accepts that:

> Obviously, researchers select a topic because the topic itself interests them. They have perhaps experienced it directly (such as feeling bereft following the death of a loved one, or being trapped in an abusive relationship). Perhaps as a result of that experience, the researcher may know first-hand the loneliness, or observed gaps in care, or whatever the experience is that will become the research topic (p. 1635).

While there are other undoubted benefits, Morse generally does not recommend choosing topics that researchers are close to: 'Research [is] not a method for working out your own problems, and if your problem was making you miserable, why dwell on it all day long?'

A working title

Once you have decided on a focus for your project, it is a good idea to try to come up with a working title. As you do further work, it can be reconsidered and possibly changed. A common style is to have a two-part title as in 'Measuring nursing workload in intensive care: An observational study' or 'Success for some: An evaluation of a success for all programme'. The title should encapsulate your focus in a short, stripped-down, form. Avoid the temptation to go for complex academic-speak. In general a good title should be no more than about ten words. The title helps when you are explaining to others what you propose to do. Some people have it written down in large letters in front of them to help keep focused.

Researching the background

The approach to deciding on the research focus suggested here differs from traditional views of the origins of research tasks. These see them as rooted in the academic discipline, revealed through the research literature and theoretical or methodological concerns. This places a considerable onus on researchers. They must have a thorough and up-to-date understanding of the 'literature'; detailed background knowledge of the relevant discipline; technical proficiency; and substantial time and resources. Bentz and Shapiro (1998, pp. 72–4) provide useful suggestions for getting started in more traditional research.

In many real world studies, the research literature, and the discipline, provide a *background resource* rather than the essential starting point for research designs. This change of view is important because of the change in power relationship between researcher and other interested parties that it suggests. The researcher does not set the agenda in isolation but acts in partnership with a variety of stakeholders.

One way in which this can be implemented is for those who have been, in the past, the *subjects* of research now to play a role in carrying out the research. This applies with particular force to the part of the project that is concerned with conceptualizing the task and deciding on the research questions. It is now considered good practice for those taking part, formerly referred to in some disciplines as *subjects*, to be termed *participants* (*see the Glossary*). If they can actually participate to some extent in designing the research, you may end up with a better project than one where you just 'subject' them to your ideas.

A good understanding about what is already known, or established, does not then have the absolutely central role in applied real world research that it does in academic, discipline-developing research. However, it can still be of considerable value. It may be possible to get background information from persons who have done related work, either directly or through the 'literature'. Unfortunately, for many real world topics, that literature tends to be somewhat inaccessible and fragmentary.

From researching the background in these ways, you go some way toward finding out what is known about the topic; what is seen as problematic; the approaches that have been taken; etc. It helps to get a good feel for this. However, it is all too easy to be imprisoned by what others have done into a particular way of looking at, and of investigating, the topic. Beware.

Acknowledging the constraints

Any real world study must obviously take serious note of real world constraints, which are particularly important at undergraduate level. Your choice of research focus must be realistic in terms of the time and resources that you have available. If you have a maximum of three weeks you can devote to the project, choose something where you have a good chance of 'getting it out' in that time. Access and cooperation are similarly important, as well as having a nose for situations where a project is likely to be counter-productive (getting into a sensitive situation involving, say, the siting of a hostel for adults with drug addictions when your prime aim is to develop community provision is not very sensible if a likely outcome is the stirring up of a hornets' nest). These are themes which will recur throughout our discussions and are particularly important when deciding on the kind of *research strategy* to be used and the practicalities of actually carrying out the study but they need to be at least in the background when considering the research focus.

Topics to avoid

There are several commonsense considerations worth noting. Avoid topics which are:

- Too ambitious. You need to focus on something feasible in the time you have available.
- Too trivial. Don't go to the opposite extreme.
- Unlikely to get support. For whatever reason (e.g. if you need financial or other assistance; or help in getting access).
- Calling for skills you don't have or can't acquire in time.
- Intractable. If there is an absence of research on a topic, it may be because it is too difficult.
- Unethical. Avoid topics likely to cause harm to anyone involved (physical, emotional, etc). See Chapter 10.

Searching and reviewing the literature

The 'literature' is what is already known, and written down, relevant to your research project. A traditional literature review 'involves systematically identifying, locating, and analyzing documents containing information related to the research problem. These documents can include articles, abstracts, reviews, monographs, dissertations, books, other research reports, and electronic media' (Gay & Airasian, 2003, p. 16). Note, however, that *systematic review* has recently gained a more specific meaning in the context of evidence-based approaches and the synthesis of research findings – see Chapter 5, p. 85. Many purposes of *literature reviews* have been proposed, some of which are listed in Box 3.1. At this stage, your main concern is to find material which helps you to design the project, including deciding on the research questions to which you will seek answers. Maxwell (2006) emphasizes the importance of *relevance* of the material for this task rather than striving for comprehensiveness – 'relevant works are those that have important implications for the design, conduct, or interpretation of the study, not simply those that deal with the topic, or in the defined field or substantive area, of the research' (p. 28).

If you are registered for a doctorate or other academic award, your supervisor or tutor should provide some initial leads, although this can vary from the detailed listing of key references to more general advice. Similarly if you are involved in a larger project, the project leader or colleagues should provide help and support.

Library searches

The first port of call in searching for yourself, as opposed to simply relying upon information provided by your tutor, is a university or other academic library. If you don't have membership of a library of this type, you are at a severe disadvantage when searching for research literature.

BOX 3.1

Purposes of the literature review

Puts together the literature on a topic of interest and:

1. Exposes main gaps in knowledge and identifies principal areas of dispute and uncertainty.
2. Helps identify general patterns to findings from multiple examples of research in the same area.
3. Juxtaposes studies with apparently conflicting findings to help explore explanations for discrepancies.
4. Helps define your terminology or identify variations in definitions used by researchers or practitioners.
5. Helps to identify appropriate research methodologies and instruments (e.g. interview schedules, validated tests and scales).

(based in part on Booth & Dixon-Woods, 2004, slides 3 and 4)

This is not solely because access to such libraries may be difficult (although you may be able to get in as a visitor) but also because library membership gives free access to many electronic journals and other material available from the Internet. Without it, your access, particularly to journal articles, will be restricted – or expensive.

Because libraries have been with us for a very long time, we tend to forget what jewels of civilization they are. If you have not already done so, you should ensure that you have a good understanding of both the print and electronic resources available and how to access them. The specialist librarian for your field of work is another invaluable resource. They are there to help. Grab any training workshops going – and do this early on in the life of your research. Even in the age of the Internet, there is much to be said for starting on the library shelves. Browse current issues of journals. Find those journals covering your research focus. Use the catalogue to find where relevant books are shelved. Don't despise older texts. Many are well worth studying.

Using electronic databases

Even if these first efforts result in useful candidates for key references likely to be important for designing your project (and certainly if they are pretty fruitless), you should, at an early stage, start exploring electronic resources.

The website lists a selection of electronic databases likely to be of interest for real world research.

Some databases cover specific fields of interest; others such as the Social Sciences Citation Index cover virtually all fields. Incidentally, citation indices are invaluable as they enable you to travel forward in time from a particular reference via later authors who have cited the initial work (Google Scholar, http://scholar.google.co.uk/ also has a useful 'cited by' link as part of the references resulting from a search). With real world research, there may be few really central references that you can get hold of and citations help you to see how others have made use of them. Subject librarians and supervisors, for those doing a student project or dissertation, can help you locate databases in your particular field or discipline.

It is well worthwhile becoming fully familiar with the relevant databases through use of help facilities and the examples they provide. They usually have 'advanced search' facilities which allow you to specify the material you are after in detail and avoid the situation where you have to trawl through several thousand 'hits'. Most allow searching using *keywords* and it is also a good idea to spend time developing a small set of keywords which describe central aspects of your research. This can be part of your task when doing the initial library search. Many journal articles include a list of keyword descriptors; use ones from relevant articles. An alternative is a *subject search* based on the descriptors used by the compilers of the database to categorize an article (these are listed in the thesaurus of the database). Databases also permit the use of 'and', 'or', and 'not' instructions and include features such as truncation (e.g. real* will select 'real', 'realist' and 'realistic' – note, however, that the marker for truncation differs from one database to another). Databases which include abstracts of the articles and not just citations are much more helpful in identifying relevant studies

It is highly likely that different databases will differ in the articles that they retrieve. Taylor, Wylie, Dempster and Donnelly (2007) compared seven databases (CINAHL; Medline; PsycInfo; SSCI; AgeInfo – a dedicated database for health and social welfare of older people; CareData – a UK social work database; and Social Services Abstracts – North American focus) by running equivalent searches for material relevant to social work practice with older people. They found substantial differences in their sensitivity (capacity to identify all the relevant material) and precision (proportion of relevant as against irrelevant material identified). Holden, Barker, Kuppens, Rosenberg and LeBreton (2014) report on multiple searches of the Social Work Abstracts database which show continuing sensitivity problems. The message from these, and similar studies, is that it is unwise to rely on searching just one database and searching more than one provides no guarantee that all relevant information will be found.

Using search engines

A useful complement to searching via databases is to use a web search engine. Google (available at http://www.google.com and also via many localized versions such as http://www.google.co.uk.) continues to be the most widely used search engine. It also incorporates Google Scholar, which describes itself as providing:

> a simple way to broadly search for scholarly literature. From one place, you can search across many disciplines and sources: peer-reviewed papers, theses, books, abstracts and articles, from academic publishers, professional societies, preprint repositories, universities and other scholarly organizations. Google Scholar helps you identify the most relevant research across the world of scholarly research.

The 'advanced search' facilities again help you to focus a search. 'Scholar preferences' can be set so that it gives a direct link to an academic library to which you have access, indicating whether or not a journal article (or any other material your search has found) is available to you. You may also be able to download references found in a search directly to bibliography managers (see below, p. 57).

Any general search engine should carry a health warning to the effect that it is up to you to assess the quality of the information provided. The Virtual Training Suite (http://www.vtstutorials.co.uk/) is a set of free Internet tutorials to help develop Internet research skills. They have been written as part of the (now sadly defunct) Intute initiative, by a national team of lecturers and librarians from universities across the UK. There are tutorials covering a wide range of disciplines and fields of study, as well as one on social research methods.

It can also be useful to use search engines developed by organizations such as government and other public sector bodies, as well as charities and others likely to be providing information resources in your field of interest. They can give you access to a wealth of relevant, specific research, policy and practice. Keep in mind, however, that it may be less objective and more value-laden than material in academic journals

Searching for qualitative research

There are problems in finding qualitative research by using systematic search strategies. Both sensitivity and precision have been found to be low and attempts to maximize the number of relevant records result in large numbers of false positives (i.e. selected items which are irrelevant on inspection). For example, Mackay (2007) encountered difficulties when searching for a social work topic where previous research is very fragmentary and key word searches unhelpful. Her strategy was to use what she termed 'qualitative searching', i.e. searching strategies that take into account the complexity of the literature by searching in-depth a fewer number of sources and identifying implicit ideas and concepts in social work *discourse*. This involved:

> spending the time systematically going through hardcopy books and journals, taking them off the shelves one by one and reading, starting at one shelf and continuing until I finished the section about social work. More relevant literature was found by going to different libraries and following the same procedure. Electronic journals were also used; the articles were accessed one by one and then read. I came upon the topic of hoarding in this way. After finding an article on hoarding using the manual method it was then easy to subject the topic to a search in the electronic databases and thus quickly find additional articles.
>
> Some of the literature was found by following hunches. For example I thought that the major social work theories would have some position on the physical space of practice even if it was not explicit. I used social work practice text books to follow up this hunch which proved to be correct. Using these search strategies I slowly but systematically identified pertinent ideas (pp. 236–7).

Mackay contrasts this with searching strategies that rely heavily on electronic databases searching a very large amount of literature. This produces a search of the surface discourse of the literature as mediated by those outside the profession. In-depth searching strategies of the type described are slow and labour intensive but useful when the topic being searched is not well conceptualized.

Saini and Shlonsky (2012a) and Finfgeld-Connett and Johnson (2013), in contributions focusing on systematic reviews (p. 96), cover strategies which are generally useful when searching the literature for qualitative research.

Obtaining material

From the information and abstracts in the databases and search engines, you then move on to the actual material in books and journals by getting hold of the titles using one means or another (the simple tactic of typing or pasting the full title of a journal article into Google will almost always find it). Increasingly, full-text journal articles are available for downloading through the Internet, although these may have to be paid for unless you have links to libraries which take out subscriptions to these journals. Some journals are only available in electronic format (e-journals). Inter-library loan services (for journal articles, reports, theses, etc. as well as books) can help you get hold of material not available in your home library.

The website lists a selection of open-access full content e-journals likely to be of interest for real world research.

You may find that when key words or a subject search have indicated a specific journal article, adjacent articles in the same journal turn out to be of greater interest or relevance (perhaps a variant of the dictionary phenomenon, where words next to the one you are looking up are often more interesting!). It is heartening to find that such serendipity ('the happy knack of making fortunate discoveries') when browsing library shelves for books is still with us in the virtual shelves of Amazon or the contents pages of e-journals.

If you are doing a funded research project that involves a sizeable literature review, or is a rapid evidence review, it is important to cost in the price of buying some journal articles that you may struggle to access via other means in the time available.

Copyright conditions for the use of electronic databases usually permit their free use for academic and non-profit-making research purposes, but exclude use for research, consultancy or services for commercial purposes which must be paid for. This will be an issue for some real world research.

Alternative approaches to literature review

There are ways of focusing a literature review other than providing a traditional narrative review of the research evidence on a topic (see Chapter 5). These include integrative reviews, theoretical reviews, methodological reviews and historical reviews. Kennedy (2007) groups these together as 'conceptual reviews', suggesting that they share an interest in gaining new insights into an issue or research topic. She cites a review by Goldhaber and Anthony (2003) on teacher qualifications and student achievement. Rather than asking which qualification had the greatest impact, their focus was on the nature of the issue. They examined problems with research methods, with how teachers' qualifications are distributed among student populations, and findings about whether these qualifications matter. These aspects would be unlikely to figure prominently in a tightly focused review based on key terms. The extent to which such theoretical and methodological issues are relevant to a particular real world study will obviously vary from one study to another, depending largely on your research questions. However, in those all too common real world areas where directly relevant research is sparse or of poor quality, they are likely to come to the fore. Recall the possible purposes of a literature review listed in Box 3.1. The identification of 'areas of dispute and uncertainty', 'apparently conflicting findings to' and 'explanations for discrepancies' will lead you into wider concerns which may have major implications for the design of your study.

Documenting your search

It is not too difficult to use these suggestions for the starting point of a hunt through what is currently in print which is relevant to your study. Getting hold of the material varies from the virtually instantaneous (as when you download a pdf of an article in an e-journal to which you have full-text access) to a matter of weeks or even a month or two (when you have made use of an inter-library loan).

As this proceeds, it is important to ensure that you keep a record of what you have found. Bibliographic information needs to be full and accurate. If you just jot down a name and a date you may have to spend hours later trying to find the full details. There are several styles for citing references (see Chapter 19, p. 505). A widely used one in social research is based upon the American Psychological Association's 'Publication Manual' (for additional help with APA style guidelines, visit the APA's online resource, http://www.apastyle.org.). The APA also provide recommendations for electronic reference formats (e.g. when citing a website, or a specific document from a website). Be warned that these recommendations may well change and hence that it is necessary to check for the latest version of their style guide.

When building up a database of the books and articles to which you have referred, a major decision is whether to follow the traditional route of paper index cards or to use bibliographic software (sometimes referred to as 'citation managers') such as Endnote, ProCite or Reference Manager. Bibliographic software is well worthwhile if you are going to build up big lists of references.[2] Many online journals allow you to download a reference directly into the bibliographic software, which saves much painstaking copying of the full reference details. Bibliographic software also permits automatic generation of reference lists in a variety of different formats when reporting on your research. You need to be careful to keep up good housekeeping practices, ensuring that you have up to date copies at all times. Losing a large list of references two days before you have to complete a report is no joke.

The reference itself can be supplemented with notes of what you have got from it. How you do this is very much up to you but there is little to be said for laboriously transcribing great chunks of material. Or for indulging in the displacement activity of routinely highlighting large chunks of photocopies of journal articles.

You may also wish to develop a data capture sheet. This is often used in bigger projects, for holding all the relevant information about the literature that you have accessed. It means that you can easily access and recognize your literature for writing-up purposes (likely to be some considerable time after the literature search). It will also help you to provide an *audit trail* for your project if this proves necessary (see Chapter 7, p. 172). Box 3.2 provides an example.

BOX 3.2

Example of a data capture sheet

Study	Population	Study methods
Study id:	Population:	Study design:
Study aim(s):	Country: Sample size: Type of offender:	Sample selection: Intervention: Comparator: Data collection: Dates/duration of study:
Results	Summary of main findings: Outcomes:	
Comments on quality and limitations of the study	Author affiliations:	

(literature review data collection tool (unpublished) used in McCartan *et al.*, 2014)

---

[2] Zotero is a free, open source extension for the Firefox browser, that enables users to collect, manage, and cite research from all types of sources from the browser. It is partly a piece of reference management software, used to manage bibliographies and references when writing essays and articles. On many major research websites such as digital libraries, Google Scholar, Google Books and Amazon, Zotero detects when a book, article, or other resource is being viewed and with a mouse click finds and saves the full reference information to a local file. If the source is an online article or web page, Zotero can optionally store a local copy of the source. Users can then add notes, tags, etc. Selections from the stored references can later be exported as formatted bibliographies – though they need careful checking.

Networking

Searching through databases and reading journal articles and texts can be supplemented by networking in various ways. People may already be doing work linked to what you are interested in. If your research is being supervised, perhaps for some award or qualification, then your supervisor or supervisors should be key resources. (If they are not, perhaps you should do something about it.) Networking through conferences and meetings of professional associations can give good leads. Internet discussion groups (the initial version known as 'Listservs' is still widely used but there are now other formats) form a virtual equivalent. They cover a wide variety of research related topics.

The website lists a selection of UK discussion groups.

Similar groups exist in most other countries and can be located with a little web-surfing. It is heartening to find how, in a list such as EVALTALK (the American Evaluation Association's discussion list devoted to discussions on evaluation research topics) senior figures in the field often take the time to respond to pleas for help and advice from novice researchers. Whatever means you use, communicating with people who have done some work in the area often turns up new sources, perhaps giving you access to unpublished material or to accounts of work in progress.

Other web-facilitated ways of interacting with researchers include *wikis*. A wiki is a collection of web pages designed to enable anyone who accesses it to contribute or modify content, using simple techniques. They can be used by researchers to provide collaborative websites. The encyclopedia Wikipedia is one of the best known wikis and has been the subject of controversy when students (and researchers?) have relied on it as a reference source. Head and Eisenberg (2010) provide an informative and well researched review of 'How today's students use Wikipedia for course related research'. Knight and Pryke (2012) give the experience of one UK university as a case study. Their conclusion is the common fear that students will adopt Wikipedia as 'the' information source appears to be unfounded; indeed, that 'an enlightened minority of academics have attempted to assimilate it into their teaching' (p. 649).

In personal contacts you should aim for a symbiotic relationship where you give as well as receive. It is discourteous, as well as likely to be counter-productive, to seek to pick others' brains on topics where you have nothing to contribute. If you are new to a field, or indeed to research in general, only network in this way after you have spent time researching the background and have at least some idea of what you might do. You are then less likely to waste others' time, and can throw your own ideas into the discussion. You may even get direct advice. For example, one research team doing a rapid evidence review (Horvath, Davidson, Grove-Hills, Gekoski, & Choak, 2014) put out a successful call to all members of their LinkedIn network to send material, research and recent findings that would be of use in their write-up.

Some researchers are very cautious about revealing what they are proposing, thinking that others are just waiting to steal their ideas. A colleague of the author (Robson), for example, found that when seeking permission to carry out a study with the cooperation of hospital consultants, one of them refused permission but then carried out a very similar study using the same test instruments. Such behaviour is clearly unethical and raises issues about 'whistle-blowing', i.e. whether and how it should be reported (see Chapter 10, p. 229). Obviously there are situations where you have to be careful, perhaps for reasons of organizational sensitivity, but openness usually pays dividends.

Research questions

A mantra of this book, here restated once more, is that research questions can provide the key to planning and carrying out a successful research project. Coming up with a small set of questions (or perhaps just a single question) to which the project will seek answers is a challenging exercise. It forces you to think.

However, reading published research articles in academic and professional journals you will find that a sizeable proportion have no mention of research questions. And, as White (2013) points out, 'Many well-known and widely read "general" texts on research methods simply do not broach the subject, or devote only a few paragraphs (or even lines) to the topic' (p. 214).

Bryman (2007) interviewed practising social researchers and found that several of them queried the view of research questions as central to the process of research. Others feel that having a set of research questions is too constraining. This applies particularly to those adopting flexible designs (see Chapter 7). In the original version of grounded theory (Glaser & Strauss, 1967) the advice was to approach the situation forming the focus of research with a totally open mind, which would be precluded by having a predefined set of research questions. Incidentally, it would also rule out an initial literature review (Dunne, 2011 provides suggestions for how and when to approach the literature review when using the grounded theory approach).

Some later versions of the grounded theory approach (e.g. Strauss & Corbin, 1998) do give the research question an important role even in the early stages of a project. However, real world research is concerned largely with problems and practical issues where some form of answer appears to be called for. To achieve this, there are clear advantages in keeping the search for answers to research questions to the fore throughout your journey through the project. Box 3.3 lists some of them.

Your initial set of research questions is provisional. With flexible designs this provisionality is maintained throughout the research process. It is probably greatest in the early, planning,

BOX 3.3

The value of research questions

They help to:

- *Define the project* A good set of questions summarizes in a few sentences what your project is concerned with.
- *Set boundaries* Stops you from spending time on things not relevant to the questions (*but*, particularly in flexible design research, be prepared to modify the questions in the light of your findings).
- *Give direction* Helps you focus your efforts (searching literature, data gathering, method selection, analysis).
- *Define success* Has your project resulted in credible answers to the research questions?

(based partly on O'Leary, 2005, p. 33)

stages of the project but, as the name suggests, it is expected that aspects of the research, including the research questions, will emerge or evolve as the work proceeds. This may even extend as far as the writing of the final report of the project. It may only be at this late stage that you appreciate *which* questions you have found answers to. In fixed designs the provisional research questions have to be firmed up after a *pilot study* phase and before the main data collection exercise.

Onwuegbuzie and Leech (2006) maintain that research questions are vitally important in multi-strategy design research involving both quantitative and qualitative aspects, where the research questions 'in large part, dictate the type of research design used, the sample size and sampling scheme employed, and the type of instruments administered as well as the data analysis techniques (i.e., statistical or qualitative) used' (p. 475).

Types of research question

You have considerable freedom in framing your set of research questions. Although some methodologists have tried to prescribe standard question formats they have not obtained general acceptance. Blaikie (2007, pp. 6–7) suggests a simple 'what', 'why', 'how' typology. In his view 'what' questions require a descriptive answer, describing the characteristics of something; 'why' questions suggest an interest in explaining or understanding something; and 'how' questions indicate a concern for change. More complicated schemes have been put forward. Knight (2002, pp. 9–10) considers that research questions tend to fall into one of five categories – 'descriptive', 'evaluative', 'narrative', 'causal', and 'effects'. For him 'descriptive' questions are flagged by 'what, who, where and when'; 'evaluative' by 'how good'; 'narrative' by questions about what happens and how it happens; 'causal' by 'why' questions; and 'effects'. Onwuegbuzie and Leech (2006) contrast quantitative research questions seen as mainly 'descriptive', 'comparative' or 'relationship' in type and very specific in nature, with qualitative research questions which are more open-ended and tend to address 'what' and 'how' questions.

It is common to link different types of question to the different purposes of research discussed in the previous chapter. Box 3.4 illustrates an example of this approach. Note, however, that it is often necessary to unpack a question, to consider its context and possible interpretation, before making the link. The link between research questions and your research design is also important (see Chapter 4, p. 76).

It is sometimes claimed that research questions must always be framed in terms of what can be directly observed or measured. This is linked to the idea of 'operational definitions', for which the classical example is that 'Intelligence is whatever intelligence tests measure' and forms part of the discredited positivist view of science discussed in the previous chapter. Maxwell (2013, pp. 79–82) discusses this in some detail and points out the risk of trivializing your study by restricting it to such directly observable questions. He argues for the use of realist-type questions which:

> do not assume that research questions and conclusions about feelings, beliefs, intentions, prior behavior, effects, and so on, need to be reduced to, or reframed as, questions and conclusions about the actual data one collects. Instead, they treat these unobserved phenomena as *real*, and their data as *evidence* about these, to be used critically to develop and test ideas about the existence and nature of the phenomena (Campbell, 1988; Cook & Campbell, 1979; Maxwell, 1992; 2011b) (p. 80) (emphases in original).

BOX 3.4

Linking research questions to purpose

In an evaluation of an innovatory reading programme for children with special needs, an *explanatory study* might focus on:

1. Do the children read better as a result of this programme?
   or
2. Do the children read better after following this programme compared with the standard programme?
   or
3. For what type of special need, ability level, class organization or school is the programme effective?
   Note: The 'as a result of' in (1) indicates that the concern is whether the programme caused the improvement. Questions (2) and (3) also imply a concern for causation, although this is not explicit. Question (3) is couched in terms of the realist concern for 'what works for whom in what context'.

   An *exploratory study* might focus on:
4. What is the experience of children following the programme?
   Note: With an established, rather than an innovatory, programme it may be that sufficient is known about this question for it to be approached as a *descriptive* task.

   A *descriptive study* might focus on:
5. What are teachers' views about the programme?
   and/or
6. To what extent are parents involved in and supportive of the programme?
   Note: This is a descriptive task if it is felt that sufficient is known about the dimensions of teachers' likely views, or of parents' involvement, etc. If not it is an *exploratory* task.

   The study could have an *emancipatory* role if it helps to extend the abilities, confidence or self-valuing of the children, or enriches their experience, or helps empower them, their parents or teachers.

   A study with adequate resources could target more than one purpose.
   (Box 4.3, p. 81, returns to this example when considering links between research questions and design strategy)

He accepts that there are risks by taking this stance in that there is an increased reliance on inference which may lead to drawing unwarranted conclusions, and stresses the need to address systematically and rigorously the validity threats that this approach involves (see Chapter 6, p. 109 and Chapter 7, p. 170).

In line with Maxwell's basic distinction between variance thinking and process thinking discussed earlier in the chapter, he talks in terms of 'variance questions' and 'process questions'.

BOX 3.5

Characteristics of good research questions

Good research questions:

- are clear and unambiguous;
- show the purpose(s) of your project (to explore, describe, explain, and/or empower);
- are answerable – and point to the type of data needed to provide answers;
- are not trivial; and
- form a coherent interconnected set (they are not an apparently random collection).

'Variance questions focus on difference and correlation: they often begin with "Does," "How much," "To what extent," and "Is there a relationship." Process questions, in contrast, focus on *how* things happen, rather than *whether* there is a particular relationship or how much it is explained by other variables' (p. 82, emphases original). Broadly speaking, variance questions point toward the use of a quantitative approach, process questions toward a qualitative approach. Van de Ven (2007, pp. 145–60) develops this distinction in detail.

Good research questions share some of the characteristics of questions in questionnaires, as discussed in Chapter 11. Box 3.5 lists desirable features.

Where do you get the research questions from?

There is no foolproof, automatic way of generating research questions. While the sequence envisaged here, of first deciding on a general research focus or area, and then refining that down into a small number of relatively specific research questions has an intuitive reasonableness, things may not work out like this. A question, or questions, may come first – perhaps stimulated by theoretical concerns. You then seek an appropriate context, a research focus, in which to ask the question.

Alvesson and Sandberg (2013) consider that the prevalent way of constructing research questions in social science is 'gap spotting'. This is 'to spot various gaps in the existing literature, such as an overlooked area, and based on that to formulate specific research questions' (p. 24). They present a detailed analysis and typology of how researchers construct research questions from the existing literature. The typology has three basic modes of gap-spotting – confusion spotting (where there are competing explanations of a phenomenon); neglect spotting (an overlooked area; an under-researched one; or a lack of empirical support; or lacking a specific aspect); and application spotting (extending and complementing existing literature) (see Alvesson & Sandberg, 2013, Table 3.1, p. 29 and Appendix 1, pp. 124–6).

This will be of value for those wishing to follow the same gap-spotting route. A couple of caveats though. Firstly, the main thesis of Alvesson and Sandberg's book is that the conventional approach of gap-spotting has been, at least in part, responsible for a perceived current emphasis on narrow, cautious research questions. They develop a 'problematization' methodology to challenge the assumptions underlying previous research, leading to more interesting and influential research.

Secondly, as discussed earlier (p. 50), the problem with much real world research is of finding a substantial relevant research literature in which to look for gaps! So, if you can find sufficient backgound research literature, you could spot gaps. If not, their text gives you a way forward. However, this need not be an either/or decision. The problematization methodology is essentially a call for thinking in terms of possible underlying theories which can help produce more imaginative empirical research. This will be a valuable exercise even if you go gap-spotting (see the following section on the place of theory).

Earlier work on the generation and development of research questions which are more likely to result in successful and productive enquiries than others supports this stance. Campbell, Daft and Hulin (1982) looked at these issues by using a range of empirical techniques, including contrasts between studies judged by their originators as being either successful or unsuccessful. Their remit was limited to research in industrial and organizational psychology, but many of their conclusions seem to have more general relevance. An idea that emerges strongly from their work is that the selection of innovative research questions is not a single act or decision. Significant research is a process, an attitude, a way of thinking. Significant research is accomplished by people who are motivated to do significant research, who are willing to pay the cost in terms of time or effort. They view the choice process for selecting the research questions as being often non-linear and involving considerable uncertainty and intuition. Research starting with mechanistic linear thinking, closely tied to the known and understood, may be clean and tidy but is unlikely to be of any significance. However, something that starts out as poorly understood, given considerable theoretical effort to convert it into something which is clearly defined, logical and rational, could well be of value.

Campbell *et al.* also conducted a relatively informal interview study with investigators responsible for what are considered important 'milestone' studies in the analysis of organizations and reached conclusions which supported their previous ones. Specifically, it did not appear that these milestone studies had arisen simply from seeking to test, or extend, an existing theory previously used in that field of research. In fact, in virtually all cases the relevant theory or knowledge was imported from some other field. What was clear was that these important studies were driven by some specific problem to be solved; that they were characterized by a problem in search of a technique, rather than the reverse. Each of the researchers was deeply involved in the substantive area of study, and it was interesting to note that many of them reported an element of luck in either the creation or the development of the research problem. However, it is well known in scientific creativity that Lady Luck is more willing to bestow her favours on the keenly involved and well prepared (Medawar, 1979, p. 89).

Developing your research question(s)

Think in terms of the purposes of your research

Clarifying the purpose or purposes of your research can go a long way toward sorting out the research questions. As discussed in the previous chapter (p. 39), three possible purposes of a research project are traditionally recognized, to *explore*, to *describe* and to *explain*.

A fourth possible purpose was seen to be important in real world research – to *emancipate*, reflecting the 'action' or 'change' perspective which is commonly present.

A particular study may be concerned with more than one purpose, possibly all four, but often one will predominate. *The purpose may also change as the study proceeds, particularly in multi-strategy designs.*

It is taken as given that all research is concerned with *contributing to knowledge*. Real world research also commonly seeks a potential usefulness in relation to policy and practice. To this end, essentially exploratory, descriptive or emancipatory studies often put forward some type of explanation for their findings although this is likely to be more tentative than from designs with an explicit explanatory purpose.

Know the area

It obviously helps to be really familiar with the area on which your research focuses, over and above the information you have gained from searching the literature. It is important to start from the perspective of what is unique to your project. Do not fall back on old ways of thinking about the topic, or the results of earlier literature searches. Start each project afresh! A good strategy is to 'go public' in some way – produce a review paper, do a seminar or other presentation with colleagues whose comments you respect (or fear).

Widen the base of your experience

You should not be limited by the research (and research questions) current in the specific field you are researching. Researchers in other fields and from other disciplines may well be wrestling with problems similar to yours, or from which useful parallels can be drawn. Time spent trawling through journals in cognate disciplines is one way of widening your view (it's another version of the anthropologists 'spending time in the next village').

Many university departments and research centres are now multi-disciplinary so a fresh perspective is not that far away. Don't be afraid to start a conversation with fellow students, academics or researchers. You may find that they have been waiting to have that conversation! Contact and discussion with practitioners and other stakeholders such as client groups may give a different perspective on what the questions should be.

Consider using techniques for enhancing creativity

There is a substantial literature on creativity and on methods of promoting innovation which is relevant to the process of generating research questions. Clegg and Birch (2007) and Vogel (2014), though business oriented, cover a range of generally relevant techniques to encourage individuals and groups to make the most of their creativity. Useful methods include the *nominal group* and *Delphi techniques* discussed in more detail in Chapter 15, p. 364.

Note: The techniques for enhancing creativity are primarily concerned with groups. Even if you are going to carry out the project on an individual basis, there is much to be said for regarding this initial stage of research as a group process and enlisting the help of others.

Consider, for example, the Delphi technique. In this context it might mean getting together a group of persons, either those who are involved directly in the project or a range of colleagues with interests in the focus of the research. Bear in mind the point made in the previous section, that there is advantage in including in the group colleagues from other disciplines and practitioners. Each individual is then asked to generate *independently* up to three specific research questions in the chosen area. They may be asked also to provide additional information, perhaps giving a justification for the questions chosen. The responses from each individual are collected, and all responses are passed on in an unedited and unattributed form to all members of the group. A second cycle then takes place. This might involve individuals commenting on responses made by the others, and/or revising their own contribution in the light of what others have produced. Third and fourth cycles might take place, either of similar form or seeking resolution or consensus through voting, or ranking, or categorizing responses.

Avoid the pitfalls of:

- *Deciding on the method(s) or design you will use before sorting out the research question(s).* It will restrict the kind of questions you can ask, possibly to ones which don't help with the problem you are trying to deal with. This is important for a real world researcher trying to deal with externally presented problems and issues. It is not unreasonable for a student, or for others selecting their own focus, to play to their own strengths and make pre-decisions on method or design.
- *Posing research questions that can't be answered.* Either in general or by the methods that it is feasible for you to use.
- *Asking questions that have already been answered satisfactorily.* Deliberate replication resulting from a concern about the status of a finding is different from ignorance of previous research.
- *Determining the findings or impact of the research before you have completed it.* Don't be tempted to 'oversell' likely benefits to the participants, stakeholders or other academics. If you are incorrect in your predictions you can look foolish and damage relationships.

Cut it down to size

Thinking about the focus almost always leads to a set of research questions that is too large and diffuse. Grouping questions together and constructing a hierarchy of sub-questions nested within more general ones helps to bring some order. It is important not to get premature closure, even on a list of questions threatening to get out of hand. What commonly happens is that something like a research programme emerges, which has within it several relatively separate research projects.

The time will come when you have to make hard decisions about where your priorities are. In particular what is feasible given the time and other resources you have available. In fixed designs you need to have done this to a very large extent even before you pilot. The role of the pilot is, amongst other things, to fine-tune the questions. In flexible designs (and in a flexible component of a multi-strategy design) you keep things much more open when starting data collection. Even here though it is wise to have a concern for feasibility at an early stage. The flexibility comes in modifying and developing the questions as data collection and analysis proceeds. An important criterion for such development is getting a better understanding of what is likely to be feasible as the research process continues.

Guidelines for the number of research questions you might be able to address in a single study vary from one to over ten. Obviously this depends on the nature of the specific research questions and the resources at your disposal. However, very few small-scale real world studies can cope adequately with more than six questions and three to six such questions is a fair rule of thumb.

The place of theory

As Kurt Lewin put it many years ago, when advising applied social psychologists 'there is nothing so practical as a good theory' (1951, p. 169). This view is contested. The pragmatic view that 'what works' is enough, discussed in Chapter 2 (p. 28), is currently influential in many areas. Thomas (2002; 2007), writing in the context of education research, advocates the abandonment of all theory because of its stifling effect on practice. Adams and Buetow (2014) consider that theory has the capacity to enhance the coherence and originality of academic works such as psychology theses. However, they acknowledge that 'General trends in academic environments are seen to play an important part in why students view theory as difficult, unnecessary, and unconnected with the real world' (p. 93). Hammersley (2012) supports Thomas's (2007) view that theory should not be treated as a sacred cow. He contends that whether or not theory is important for education researchers depends on which of the very different meanings of the term 'theory' is being used.

Certainly, theory can mean very different things to different people. In very general terms it is an explanation of what is going on in the situation, phenomenon or whatever we are investigating. Theories can range from formal large-scale systems developed in academic disciplines, to informal hunches or speculations from laypersons, practitioners or participants in the research. Obviously, there are advantages if links can be made to current formal theories. It provides some assurance that what you are doing is in tune with the attempts of other researchers to understand what is happening. And, as well as helping to carry out a higher quality study you may well be able to make some small contribution to the development of theory itself – there is no law that a real world project cannot make an academic contribution.

Typically, real world research (whether emprical or desk-based) begins in the outside world with a specific social problem. Either theory emerges through the research, or theories are brought to bear on the findings of these studies as a way of explanation. The aim here is not necessarily to establish the validity of a theory but rather to resolve some social problem or shed light on some issue, in part through developing a theoretical understanding of the problem or issue.

Admittedly, it may well not be feasible to make this kind of symbiotic connection between the research topic and existing theory in many real world studies. The topic may be novel and appropriate theories elusive. Time pressures may be such that there is not the opportunity to do the necessary delving into what is often quite difficult literature. Don't despair. In thinking about the focus of the research, you will develop what amounts to a personal theory about what might be going on and how it might be understood (what Argyris & Schön, 1974 describe as a 'theory-in-use' or 'tacit theory'). There are highly likely to be others around who can help: perhaps staff members, professionals, practitioners, clients who may have had a much longer experience with the situation and who, if asked, may have highly pertinent observations about how and why some approach will or won't 'work' (or, in realist terms, what are likely mechanisms). Again, it may be advantageous if you can move beyond this to more formal theory and concepts but this is by no means an essential feature of many real world studies.

A distinction is sometimes made between 'theory verification' and 'theory generation' research. Positivist methodology, which has traditionally formed the basis for fixed design experimental studies, starts with a theory, deduces formal hypotheses from it, and designs the study to test these hypotheses. The tradition in much flexible design research, quintessentially in grounded theory studies (see Chapter 7), is theory generation. Researchers do not start with a theory but aim to end up with one, developed systematically from the data collected. These connections are by no means universal. Fixed design research can be used for theory generation, qualitative flexible designs for theory verification (Hammersley, 1992a). The position taken here is that there is a place for both theory generating and theory verification approaches. Which is more appropriate will depend on the particular circumstances and context of your research. If an apparently serviceable theory relevant to your proposed study already exists, the sensible approach is to test its utility. If you are casting around for a plausible theory, then theory generation is indicated. What is important is that you have a theory on completion of the study, at least in the sense that you have achieved some understanding about what is going on.

Abduction and theory construction

The processes of deduction and induction, discussed in the previous chapter as typifying the approach taken in the quantitative and qualitative traditions respectively, are useful tools in research. However, they have been criticized as not properly representing the actual practice of researchers (e.g. Guttman, 2004) and inadequate when seeking to generate useful theories (Holcombe, 1998).

Abduction, abductive reasoning (Chapter 2, p. 37), has been proposed by realists and others as an alternative (e.g. Haig, 2014). Proctor and Capaldi (2006, Chapters 4 and 5) consider it to involve the following three interrelated ideas.

1. *Explaining patterns of data.* A number of phenomena are studied, their pattern observed, and a *hypothesis* or theory put forward to explain the pattern. They stress:

   . . . this is neither an induction nor a deduction. Induction is not involved as there may only be a small number of examples and the generalization is not about their shared properties but about their cause. Deduction is not involved either, for the generalization is not a derivation from the phenomena it applies to but rather is an explanation of them (p. 73).

2. *Entertaining multiple hypotheses.* Hypotheses are tested in the context of competing hypotheses or theories. In other words it is a matter of comparative theory evaluation. A theory may not explain all the facts (there are always likely to be anomalies) but to be acceptable there should only be anomalies affecting the competing theories.
3. *Inference to the best explanation.* Theories are not only evaluated in the context of other theories (i.e. it is preferable to the others) but, providing that there is judged to be sufficient evidence available, it is the best possible explanation given that evidence.[3]

---

[3] This approach has similarities to the grounded theory method (Chapter 7, p. 164). Ong (2012) provides an analysis of their differences.

Proctor and Capaldi put forward criteria for evaluating a theory which include *fruitfulness* (the ease with which it generates new predictions); *parsimony* (how few assumptions it makes); *scope* (the number of diverse phenomena it explains); *progressiveness* (the novelty of predictions and progress in understanding it leads to); and *consistency* (the extent which it is free of internal contradictions, and doesn't violate assumptions in other theories) (p. 77).

Conceptual frameworks

The theory about what is going on, of what is happening and why, is sometimes referred to as a *conceptual framework* (Miles, Huberman & Saldana, 2014):

> A conceptual framework explains, either graphically or in narrative form, the main things to be studied – the key factors, constructs or variables – and the presumed relationships among them. Frameworks can be rudimentary or elaborate, theory-driven or commonsensical, descriptive or causal (p. 20).

The term is sometimes defined rather more widely, e.g. 'the system of concepts, assumptions, expectations, beliefs, and theories that supports and informs your research' (Maxwell, 2013, p. 39).

Developing a conceptual framework forces you to be explicit about what you think you are doing. It also helps you to be selective, to decide which are the important features, which relationships are likely to be of importance or meaning and, hence, what data are you going to collect and analyse.

A *conceptual structure (or framework)* is commonly shown as a diagram though not necessarily so. Brathwaite (2003), for example, carries out a comparative analysis of six different frameworks put forward for guiding the design of an educational intervention in a narrative format. Leshem and Trafford (2007) provide a useful analysis of the role and function of conceptual frameworks in doctoral theses. They cite evidence that a thesis which has no conceptual framework is unlikely to be successful (Trafford, 2003). Berman (2013) discusses the issues involved from a researcher's perspective, reflecting on the usefulness of her doctoral conceptual framework. The paper includes an initial version of the framework and several later versions.

Box 3.6 gives some practical advice on how you might develop a conceptual framework diagram. Miles *et al.* (2014) provide examples. The concept maps approach fulfils a very similar function. Novak and Cañas (2008) discuss their underlying theory and how to construct and use concept maps.

⌨ *The website gives references to articles containing several types of conceptual framework.*

Replication studies

It is always worth considering the possibility of carrying out some form of replication study. This may be of an earlier study you have carried out, or (assuming you can find one) a relevant study by another researcher. Or, if you decide to carry out some form of case study, as discussed in Chapter 7, you can build replication into your design by having linked case studies which share important characteristics. Attempts to replicate are all too rare in the social sciences.

BOX 3.6

Developing a conceptual framework diagram

1. Get all of the diagram on one page. This helps you grasp the totality of the picture and to map relationships between the boxes.
2. Inputs to the framework come from a variety of sources, including:
   - previous research (your own, and other people's);
   - pilot studies;
   - theory that you think may be relevant;
   - your intuitions, hunches, etc.; and
   - views of others (professionals, practitioners, clients – anyone with experience of the research topic).
3. Try to map all the different inputs and ways of looking at the issues, so that you can see possible overlaps, inconsistencies, etc. The resulting framework can take on many forms (e.g. descriptive, theory-based) but should aim for internal consistency.
4. *You won't get it right first time.* There are likely to be several different ways in which you can represent the conceptual framework of the study. Go through several attempts or iterations. Discuss with friends and colleagues explaining why it is as it is. If this is a group project, it can be instructive to draw up frameworks independently initially. However, consensus on an agreed framework is crucial.
5. If you are unsure about including a particular feature or relationship include rather than exclude at this initial stage. However, don't play safe by including two-way links between just about everything in the diagram – try to justify each one.
6. Review the framework at an appropriate stage (after the pilot in a fixed design; at several points during data collection and analysis in a flexible design). It is highly likely that you will see the need to simplify the framework as you appreciate the reality of the time and resources available to you.

When they do take place, the dreaded 'failure to replicate' finding appears to be surprisingly frequent. Klein (2014) discusses the issue, detailing recent failures which have attracted publicity, not only in academic circles but also in the popular media such as *The New Yorker* and *Psychology Today*. He points out that replication failure is an 'accepted and anticipated aspect of scientific inquiry' (p. 327) citing, for example, Godfrey-Smith (2003) and Popper (2004). Nevertheless, it suggests the need for, and value of, replication studies. Brandt *et al.* (2014) have produced a set of rules which can be followed to produce a convincing close replication.

Their lack of attraction may, in part, be linked to the desire on the part of researchers to do something new and innovatory. The apparent unwillingness of some journals to publish replications, and the requirement in regulations for doctoral work to be innovatory, are also factors. A possible solution is what Bonett (2012) calls a 'replication-extension' study. This is the combination of:

results from a new study specifically designed to replicate and extend the results of the prior studies. Replication-extension studies have many advantages over the traditional single-study designs used in psychology: Formal assessments of replication can be obtained, effect sizes can be estimated with greater precision and generalizability, misleading findings from prior studies can be exposed, and moderator effects can be assessed (p. 409).

As argued in the previous chapter, p. 30, adoption of a realist perspective can provide a sound basis for the use of replication in the development and refinement of theories.

Hypotheses

Some readers, particularly those with a quantitative background, may be familiar with discussions of research couched in terms of *hypothesis testing*, with detailed definitions of null and alternative hypotheses. As discussed above, the approach favoured in this text (largely because of its wider applicability) is seeking answers to research questions. Put in these terms, a hypothesis is the predicted answer to a research question. A theory (whether expressed in terms of a conceptual framework and/or the mechanisms operating, or otherwise) explains why a particular answer is predicted. Talking in terms of hypotheses fits fixed design research best where we should be in the position to make predictions before the data are gathered. In flexible design research, we are only likely to be in this position as a result of the data gathering. The outcomes can be used to support the existence of particular mechanisms in the context studied even if they could not be predicted.

Further reading

The website gives annotated references to further reading for Chapter 3.

CHAPTER 4

General design issues

This chapter:

- develops a framework for designing a real world study linking purpose, conceptual framework, research questions, methods and sampling strategy;
- sensitizes the reader to the issues involved in selecting a research strategy;
- introduces experimental and non-experimental fixed design strategies;
- presents flexible design strategies seen as particularly appropriate for real world research including case studies, ethnographic studies, and grounded theory studies;
- covers a range of multi-strategy (mixed-method) designs;
- emphasizes that it is advisable to read the other chapters in Part II before making decisions about strategy; and
- concludes by considering the trustworthiness of research findings, and its relationship to research design.

Introduction

Design is concerned with turning research questions into projects. This is a crucial part of any research project, but it is often slid over quickly without any real consideration of the issues and possibilities. There is a strong tendency, both for those carrying out projects and those who want them carried out, to assume that there is no alternative to their favoured approach. Comments have already been made about disciplines preferring one methodology over another; the same is true in design terms. Traditionally, many psychologists assume that an experimental design is inevitably called for. Government funders in both the UK and US appear particularly interested in experimental designs using randomized controlled trials. For other social scientists, and for quite a few clients when commissioning studies, designs involving the statistical analysis of sample survey data are seen as the only possible approach.

As stressed in the previous chapter, the strategies and tactics you select in carrying out a piece of research depend very much on the type of research question you are trying to answer. Hakim (2000), in one of the few books which focuses on design issues across a range of social science disciplines, makes a comparison between designers of research projects and architects, and then goes on to extend this to suggest that those who actually carry out projects are like builders. For her:

> Design deals primarily with aims, purposes, intentions and plans within the practical constraints of location, time, money and availability of staff. It is also very much about *style*, the architect's own preferences and ideas (whether innovative or solidly traditional) and the stylistic preferences of those who pay for the work and have to live with the final result (p. 1, emphasis in original).

In small-scale research, the architect-designer and builder-researcher are typically one and the same person. Hence the need for sensitivity to design issues, to avoid the research equivalent of the many awful houses put up by speculative builders without the benefit of architectural expertise.

Such muddling through should be distinguished from the opportunity to develop and revise the original plan, which is easier in a small-scale project than in one requiring the coordination of many persons' efforts. Design modification is more feasible with some research strategies than with others – it is an integral part of what are referred to in this text as flexible designs. However, this kind of flexibility calls for a concern for design throughout the project, rather than providing an excuse for not considering design at all.

A framework for research design

Design, in the sense discussed above, concerns the various things which should be thought about and kept in mind when carrying out a research project. Many models have been put forward and Figure 4.1 is a simple one. The components are:

- *Purpose(s).* What is this study trying to achieve? Why is it being done? Are you seeking to describe something, or to explain or understand something? Are you trying to assess the effectiveness of something? Is it in response to some problem or issue for which solutions are sought? Is it hoped to change something as a result of the study?
- *Conceptual framework.* Your theory about what is going on, of what is happening and why. What are the various aspects or features involved, and how might they be related to each other?
- *Research questions.* To what questions is the research geared to providing answers? What do you need to know to achieve the purpose(s) of the study? What is it feasible to ask given the time and resources that you have available?
- *Methods.* What specific techniques (e.g. semi-structured interviews, participant observation) will you use to collect data? How will the data be analysed? How do you show that the data are trustworthy?
- *Sampling procedures.* Who will you seek data from? Where and when? How do you balance the need to be selective with that of collecting the data required?

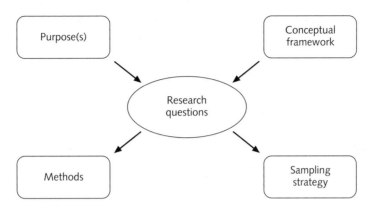

Figure 4.1 Framework for research design.

Ethical considerations, though not included in the design framework, inevitably arise when carrying out research involving people and should be taken into account both in the planning and carrying out of your project (see Chapter 10).

All these aspects need to be interrelated and kept in balance. In seeking funding for a project, you will have to make details of your proposed design clear to the funding body. There is a similar task when seeking access to an outside organization, and clearance from an ethics committee (or committees) for all projects whether or not funded.

The diagram suggests that there is some directionality about the whole process. Both your purposes and the conceptual framework feed in to, and help you specify, the research questions. When you know something about the research questions you want to be answered, then you are able to make decisions about the methods and the procedures to be used when sampling. However, unless you are dealing with a fixed design which is tightly pre-specified, this should not be taken to imply a once-only consideration of the different aspects.

In flexible designs there should be a repeated revisiting of all of the aspects as the research takes place. In other words, the detailed framework of the design emerges during the study. The various activities of collecting and analysing data, of refining and modifying the set of research questions, of developing theory, of changing the intended sample to follow up interesting lines or to seek answers to rather different questions, and perhaps even reviewing the purposes of the study in the light of a changed context arising from the way in which the other aspects are developing – are likely to be going on together.

This might suggest that a better representation of the relationship between these aspects in flexible designs would show two-way arrows between each of the components in the figure. Maxwell (2013, p. 5) approximates to this in a very similar diagram which he refers to as an 'Interactive' model of research design. Or even that one might revert to what Martin (1981) has called the 'garbage can' model of research design where such components are 'swirling around in the garbage can or decision space of the particular research project' (Grady & Wallston, 1998, p. 12). Lomi and Harrison (2012) present a set of readings illustrating the continuing interest in this type of model. However, for those who feel the need for a more structured approach, Figure 4.1 has the advantage of presenting a simple and logical structure.

Your design framework should have high compatibility between purposes, research questions, conceptual framework and sampling strategy. Some mismatches call for serious attention. For example:

- If the only research questions to which you can think of ways to get answers to are not directly relevant to the purposes of the study, then something has to change. Probably the research questions.
- If the methods and/or the sampling strategy are not providing answers to the research questions, something should change. Collect additional data and/or change the data collection method(s), extend the sampling or cut down on or modify the research questions.
- If there are research questions which do not link to the conceptual framework, or parts of the conceptual framework which are not represented in the set of research question, then one or other (or both) needs changing.

This is something of a counsel of perfection. Don't let it block any further progress if you can't get it quite right. You may not get an ideal solution with the time and resources you have available. Go for a practical solution that seems reasonably adequate (an example of the strategy of *satisficing* as advocated by Simon, 1979).

In fixed research designs you should get as much of this right as you can before embarking on the major phase of data collection. Hence the importance of pilot work, where you have the opportunity of testing out the feasibility of what you propose. In flexible research designs you have to get all of this sorted out by the end of the study. As Brewer and Hunter (2005, p. 45) put it, 'Once a study is published, it is in many ways irrelevant whether the research problem prompted the study or instead emerged from it'. This is not a licence to rewrite history. In many qualitative research traditions there is an expectation that you provide an account of your journey, documenting the various changes made along the way. However, you are definitely not bound to some form of 'honour code' where, say, you declare your initial set of research questions and then stick to them through thick and thin. Your aim is to come up with a final set of research questions, which are relevant to the purposes of the study (which may, or may not, have been renegotiated along the way); and which show clear linkage to the conceptual structure (from whatever source it has been obtained) and for which the sampling has been such that the data you have collected and analysed provides answers to those questions.

In the real world, of course, it won't be as neat and tidy as this. Some research questions may remain stubbornly unanswerable given the amount of sampling and data collection your resources permit. This is not a capital offence. Providing you have answers to some of the questions which remain on your agenda, then you have made worthwhile progress. And the experience will no doubt be salutary in helping you to carry out more realistically designed projects in the future. You could even claim this for a study where you ended up with no answers to relevant research questions, but this is not going to further your career as a researcher.

It may also be that you come up with unexpected findings which appear interesting and illuminative. These findings may well be assimilable into your framework by appropriate extension or modification of your research questions. There is nothing wrong with adding a further question providing it is relevant to your purposes and it can be incorporated within a (possibly modified) theoretical framework. If your ingenuity fails, and you can't link it in, then simply regard this as a bonus to be reported under the heading of 'an interesting avenue for further research'.

The central task is to design a research project that will enable you to get answers to the research question(s). If it does this, then don't be too concerned by disappointing findings.

Getting a feel for design issues

The shaded pages below give an overview of what is involved in choosing a research strategy, including a short description of the strategies you might consider.

   This might be a good time for you to get hold of the reports of a range of published studies (journal articles, research reports, dissertations, etc.) and to read them through to get a feel for different designs. Try not to get bogged down in the details, and don't be put off by complex analyses. When you get onto the detailed design of your own study and its analysis, you can seek assistance on such matters. The obvious sources are academic and professional journals close to your own concerns but, as previously suggested, there is a lot to be said for 'spending some time in the next village'. If your field is, say, social work, browse through a few health-related, educational or management journals. The purpose here is not so much to build up knowledge of directly relevant literature, or to find something you can replicate, although both of these are reputable aims in their own right. It's the overall design that you are after. The website gives details of a mixed bag of studies with fixed, flexible and multi-strategy designs worth chasing up and looking through. Note that they won't necessarily use the terminology adopted here of research questions, purposes, etc. (it is instructive to try to work these out as an exercise).

The website gives references to a selection of examples of research using fixed, flexible and multi-strategy designs.

   If you follow up these examples you will notice that several of them involve evaluating some practice, intervention or programme, or have an action perspective where they are concerned with change of some kind taking place. Chapter 9 covers the additional features to be considered in studies which have these purposes.

Choosing a research design strategy

This section seeks to sensitize you to the issues involved in choosing a research design strategy.

A. Is a fixed, flexible or multi-strategy design strategy appropriate?

A fixed design calls for a tight pre-specification before you reach the main data collection stage. If you can't pre-specify the design, don't use the fixed approach. Data are almost always in the form of numbers; hence this type is commonly referred to as a quantitative strategy. *See Chapter 6 for details.*

- A flexible design evolves during data collection. Data are typically non-numerical (usually in the form of words); hence this type is often referred to as a qualitative strategy. *See Chapter 7 for details.*
- A multi-strategy design combines substantial elements of both fixed and flexible design. A common type has a flexible phase followed by a fixed phase (the reverse sequence is more rare). *See Chapter 7 for details.*

Note: Flexible designs can include the collection of small amounts of quantitative data. Similarly, fixed designs can include the collection of small amounts of qualitative data.

B. Is your proposed study an evaluation?

Are you trying to establish the worth or value of something such as an intervention, innovation or service? This could be approached using either a fixed, flexible or multi-strategy design strategy depending on the specific purpose of the evaluation. If the focus is on *outcomes*, a *fixed design* is probably indicated; if it is on *processes*, a *flexible design* is probably called for. Many evaluations have an interest in *both outcomes and processes* and use a *multi-strategy design. See Chapter 9, p. 190 for details.*

C. Do you wish to carry out action research?

Is an action agenda central to your concerns? This typically involves direct participation in the research by others likely to be involved, coupled with an intention to initiate change. A *flexible design* is almost always used. See *Chapter 8 for details.*

D. If you opt for a fixed design strategy, which type is most appropriate?

Two broad traditions are widely recognized – *experimental* and *non-experimental designs*. Box 4.1 on p. 79 summarizes their characteristics.

E. If you opt for a flexible design strategy, which type is most appropriate?

Flexible designs have developed from a wide range of very different traditions. Three of these are widely used in real world studies. These are *case studies, ethnographic studies* and *grounded theory* studies. Box 4.2 on p. 80 summarizes their characteristics.

F. If you are considering a multi-strategy design strategy, which type is most appropriate?

It may well be that a strategy which combines fixed and flexible design elements seems to be appropriate for the study with which you are involved. One or more case studies might be linked to an experiment. Alternatively, a small experiment might be incorporated actually within a case study. *Issues involved in the carrying out of multi-strategy designs are discussed in Chapter 8.*

Note: The research strategies discussed above by no means cover all possible real world research designs. They are more of a recognition of the camps into which researchers have tended to put themselves, signalling their preferences for certain ways of working. Such camps have the virtue of providing secure bases within which fledgling researchers can be inculcated in the ways of the tribe, and, more generally, high professional standards can be maintained. They carry the danger of research being 'strategy driven', in the sense that someone skilled in, say, doing experiments assumes automatically that every problem has to be attacked through that strategy.

G. The purpose(s) help in selecting the strategy

The strategies discussed above represent different ways of collecting and analysing empirical evidence. Each has its particular strengths and weaknesses. It is also commonly suggested that there is a hierarchical relationship between the different strategies, related to the purpose of the research; that

- flexible (qualitative) strategies are appropriate for exploratory work;
- non-experimental fixed strategies are appropriate for descriptive studies; and
- experiments are appropriate for explanatory studies.

There is some truth in this assertion – certainly as a description of how the strategies have tended to be used in the past. There is a further sense in which a flexible strategy lends itself particularly well to exploration, a sense in which certain kinds of description can be readily achieved using non-experimental (typically survey) approaches and a traditional view that the experiment is a particularly appropriate tool for getting at cause and effect relationships (see, though, the discussion in Chapter 2, p. 18). However, these are not necessary or immutable linkages. Each strategy (fixed, flexible or multi-strategy) can be used for any or all of the purposes. For example, grounded theory studies aim to be explanatory through the development of theory; also there can be, and have been, exploratory, descriptive and explanatory case studies (Yin, 2003; 2012; 2013).

Real world studies are very commonly evaluations, i.e. their purpose is to assess the worth or value of something. A fixed, flexible or multi-strategy design may be appropriate depending on the specific focus of the evaluation (see B above).

If a purpose is to initiate change and/or to involve others, then an action research strategy may be appropriate. A flexible design is probably called for (see C above).

H. The research questions have a strong influence on the strategy to be chosen

While purpose is of help in selecting the research design strategy, the type of research questions you are asking is important. For example, questions asking 'how many' or 'how much' or 'who' or 'where' suggest the use of a non-experimental fixed strategy such as a survey. 'What' questions concerned with 'what is going on here?' lend themselves to some form of flexible design study. 'How' and 'why' questions are more difficult to pin down. They often indicate a flexible design. However, if the research can have control over events and if there is substantial prior knowledge about the problem and the likely mechanisms involved, then an experiment might be indicated.

Box 4.3 on p. 81 considers the research questions set out in Box 3.3 and discusses research strategies that might be appropriate.

I. Specific methods of investigation need not be tied to particular research strategies

The methods or techniques used to collect information, what might be called the tactics of enquiry, such as questionnaires or various kinds of observation, are sometimes regarded as necessarily linked to particular research strategies. Thus, in fixed non-experimental designs, surveys may be seen as being carried out by structured questionnaires and experiments through specialized forms of observation, often requiring the use of measuring instruments of some sophistication. In flexible designs, grounded theory studies were often viewed as interview-based and ethnographic studies seen as entirely based on participant observation.

However, this is not a tight or necessary linkage. For example, while participant observation is a central feature of the ethnographic approach, it can be augmented by interviews and documentary analysis. Similarly, there is no reason in principle for particular fixed design studies to be linked to specific data collection techniques. Non-experimental surveys could well be carried out using observation, the effect of an experiment assessed through questionnaire responses.

You should now have an appreciation of what is involved in selecting an appropriate research strategy. Before plunging in and making a decision, you need to know more about the issues involved in working within these strategies to help you get a feel for what might be involved. The rest of the chapters in Part II cover them in some detail.

Establishing trustworthiness

How do you persuade your audiences, including yourself, that the findings of your research are worth taking account of? What is it that makes the study believable and trustworthy? What are the kinds of argument that you can use? What questions should you ask? What criteria are involved?

In this connection validity and generalizability are central concepts. Validity is concerned with whether the findings are 'really' about what they appear to be about. Generalizability refers to the extent to which the findings of the enquiry are more generally applicable outside the specifics of the situation studied. These issues, together with the related one of reliability (the consistency or stability of a measure; for example, if it were to be repeated would the same result be obtained), were initially developed in the context of traditional fixed designs and there is considerable debate about their applicability to flexible designs. Hence trustworthiness is considered separately in each of the following chapters covering different types of research designs.

Further reading

The website gives annotated references to further reading for Chapter 4.

BOX 4.1

Experimental and non-experimental fixed design research strategies

Experimental strategy

The central feature of this strategy is that the researcher actively and deliberately introduces some form of change in the situation, circumstances or experience of participants with a view to producing a resultant change in their behaviour.

In 'experiment-speak' this is referred to as measuring the effects of manipulating one variable on another variable. The details of the design are fully pre-specified before the main data collection begins (there is typically a 'pilot' phase before this when the feasibility of the design is checked and changes made if needed).

Typical features:

- selection of samples of individuals from known populations;
- allocation of samples to different experimental conditions;
- introduction of planned change on one or more variables;
- measurement on very small number of variables;
- control of other variables; and
- testing of formal hypotheses.

Non-experimental strategy

The overall approach is the same as in the experimental strategy but the researcher does not attempt to change the situation, circumstances or experience of the participants.

The details of the design are fully pre-specified before the main data collection begins (there is typically a 'pilot' phase before this when the feasibility of the design is checked and changes made if needed).

Typical features:

- selection of samples of individuals from known populations;
- allocation of samples to different experimental conditions;
- measurement on a relatively small number of variables;
- control of other variables; and
- may or may not involve hypothesis testing.

BOX 4.2

Three widely used flexible design research strategies

Case study

Development of detailed, intensive knowledge about a single 'case', or of a small number of related 'cases'.

The details of the design typically 'emerge' during data collection and analysis.
Typical features:

- selection of a single case (or a small number of related cases) of a situation, individual or group of interest or concern;
- study of the case in its context; and
- collection of information via a range of data collection techniques including observation, interview and documentary analysis (typically, though not necessarily exclusively, producing qualitative data).

Ethnographic study

Seeks to capture, interpret and explain how a group, organization or community lives, experiences and make sense of their lives and their world.

The study typically tries to answer questions about specific groups of people, or about specific aspects of the life of a particular group.
Typical features:

- selection of a group, organization or community of interest or concern;
- immersion of the researcher in that setting; and
- use of participant observation.

Grounded theory study

The central aim is to generate theory from data collected during the study.

Particularly useful in new, applied areas where there is a lack of theory and concepts to describe and explain what is going on. Data collection, analysis and theory development and testing interspersed throughout the study.
Typical features:

- applicable to a wide variety of phenomena;
- commonly interview-based; and is
- a systematic but flexible research strategy which provides detailed prescriptions for data analysis and theory generation.

Notes: There are many other types of flexible design, some of which are summarized in Chapter 7. Many studies involving flexible designs focus on a particular 'case' in its context and can be conceptualized as case studies. Case studies can follow an ethnographic or grounded theory approach, but don't have to.

BOX 4.3

Linking research questions to research strategy

Consider the research questions discussed in Box 3.3:

1. Do the children read better as a result of this programme?
   or
2. Do the children read better in this programme compared with the standard programme?
   or
3. For what type of special need, ability level, class organization or school is the programme effective?

   If the interest is in quantitative outcome measures, and it is feasible to exert some degree of control over the situation (e.g. setting up different groups of children for the innovatory and standard programmes), these questions could be approached using an *experimental strategy*. If random allocation is used, this becomes a *true experiment*; if not, a *quasi-experiment*.

   If this control were not feasible, or not desired, but quantitative data were still sought, a *non-experimental fixed design* is possible.

   If there is a broader notion of what is meant by 'reading better' or of an 'effective' programme than that captured by a small number of quantitative variables, some type of *flexible strategy* is called for. This is likely to be a multi-method *case study*, and could also be *ethnographic* or *grounded theory* in style.

   A *multi-strategy* approach where the *case study* could incorporate, say, an *experimental* component, could be considered.
4. What is the experience of children following the programme?
5. What are teachers' views about the programme?
   and/or
6. To what extent are parents involved in and supportive of the programme?

   These questions could be approached using any of the flexible strategies, though (4) might particularly indicate an *ethnographic* approach.

   Questions (5) and (6) could, alternatively or additionally, follow a *non-experimental fixed design* if quantitative data are sought.

   The overall message is that, while the research questions help in deciding research strategy, much is still dependent on your own preferences and on the type of design and data which are going to speak most strongly to the stakeholders.

CHAPTER 5

Desk-based research

This chapter:

- covers research projects solely based on the review of existing research;
- considers the reasons why this type of research is becoming more common;
- reviews the different types of such desk-based research;
- gives suggestions for carrying out traditional literature reviews as a stand-alone project;
- accepts the need to do this in a systematic manner;
- discusses the rise in importance of a particular type of systematic review associated initially with the Cochrane Collaboration;
- gives suggestions for carrying out this type of review, emphasizing the need for substantial resources;
- introduces realist reviews; and
- provides a short overview of the current state of this field of research.

Introduction

Reviewing the literature (i.e. the existing research relevant to the topic you are interested in) is an essential part of the research process and for some can be the full research process in and of itself. While some social science disciplines and related applied fields require all student projects at undergraduate level to be empirical studies based on the collection of new data, for others the norm is to rely solely on an analysis and review of existing data. The latter are traditionally referred to as *desk-based* or *library* studies – now something of a misnomer as the work is often carried out using the Internet on laptop computers, not necessarily on desks or in libraries.

In some circumstances the collection of new data may not be feasible, or not ethical, or, perhaps, not appropriate. There is a trend for students in some disciplines where empirical work was the norm, now to be required to carry out a desk-based project. This can be for resource reasons, with larger student groups and faculty staff unable to cope with the supervisory commitment for students carrying out empirical projects. Owing to ethical issues surrounding data collection in some fields, including healthcare for example, students are no longer able to undertake their own empirical research.

Researchers may find that a client or funder wants something done quickly – and cheaply. Apart from such financial and timing issues, perhaps the people of interest are inaccessible; or there may be safeguarding issues for participants, or the researchers. In all such situations a review of existing evidence can be more appropriate. Desk-based studies are also planned as a precursor to empirical research or to complement it (e.g. Badcock-Walters & Kvalsvig, 2009).

Projects solely dependent on the review and analysis of existing data are not a soft option. Our mantra of work being carried out systematically, sceptically and ethically (Chapter 2, p. 15) applies to everything worthy of claiming to be research, including desk-based projects. You need to plan and conduct desk-based research with the same rigour and motivation that you would an empirical, primary-research orientated, project. This means setting aside sufficient time for the work, blocking out periods to search for data and to analyse it, as well making sure that you have left enough time to produce a professional standard report. Desk-based research is often done poorly. McKercher, Law, Weber, Song and Hsu (2007), in an analysis of 373 referees' reports of rejected journal submissions, found weak literature reviews in half of them.

It is worth repeating that, if a desk-based, literature-focused piece of secondary research is appropriate for your project, you need to approach it with the same academic rigour as an empirical, primary-research focused project. This means that it helps to clarify the task by starting with deciding what research question (or questions) you are trying to answer (see Chapter 3, p. 49). Admittedly, many desk-based projects, and their resulting reviews of research, do not provide explicit statements of the research questions they are addressing – which may be a partial explanation of their poor standard.

Traditional research reviews are sometimes referred to as narrative, or unstructured. This is to distinguish them from the term *systematic review*, which has a very specific meaning, discussed below. Such systematic reviews call for considerable time and resources, usually involving a team of researchers. They are not to be undertaken lightly. However, some of their features are worth incorporating into traditional reviews as a means of increasing their rigour and quality.

Types of desk-based research

Traditional literature reviews were very various, with little agreement on how they should be carried out. They were often unsystematic and unfocused. The rise of *evidence-based practice* in health-related areas in the late twentieth century was accompanied by a recognition of the need to improve the medical review articles supposed to provide the necessary evidence. Archie Cochrane, a prominent UK epidemiologist, sought to meet this need. The resulting Cochrane Collaboration (now a major international body) set out the rules for producing systematic reviews of randomized controlled trials (RCTs) relating to health care (http://www.cochrane.org). It has, more recently, widened its remit to cover other designs, including qualitative research. An offshoot, the Campbell Collaboration, extends the work to coverage of other areas of study (http://www.campbellcollaboration.org).

Their undoubted success has led to the situation where the term 'systematic review' is now usually taken to mean that it has been carried out following their rules. However, while a literature review benefits by being carried out systematically, as does virtually all research, there are many different ways of doing this.

For example, realists, led by Ray Pawson, took serious issue with both the assumptions and prescriptions of these developments, particularly when they sought to move from the relative simplicity of evaluating medical interventions to the greater complexity of reviewing social problems and issues (Pawson, 2006a). This has led to the development of *realist reviews* (sometimes referred to as a *realist synthesis*) which, while systematic, are very different.

Note: The terms for different types of review are not always used consistently. For example, reviews which are called 'literature reviews' here are sometimes referred to as 'systematic reviews' by their authors.

Literature reviews

While all the types of desk-based reviews covered in this chapter are *literature reviews*, the term is being used here to indicate that it is not a systematic review. It is sometimes referred to as a *traditional literature review* or a *narrative review* and is typically based on recent and current published materials. Examples vary widely in completeness and comprehensiveness. There will have been some process for selecting search material and criteria for which of the material to include (e.g. only research from peer-reviewed journals) but these processes are not necessarily made explicit. A summary then follows, either as text, or in tables, and an analysis is presented.

By being systematic in carrying out such a review and fully explicit in describing the process you have followed it is possible to carry out a very worthwhile review. The procedures developed to carry out Cochrane-type systematic reviews give valuable pointers for how you can do this, without necessarily following the specific features of their protocols.

The website gives references to examples of literature reviews.

Detailed suggestions on carrying out traditional literature reviews follow.

Critical literature reviews

The term 'critical' is sometimes affixed to 'literature review'. A *critical literature review* is one which goes beyond simply describing the articles identified, and both analyses them and seeks to critically evaluate their quality. All worthwhile literature reviews should be critical in this sense.

Some critical literature reviews go beyond seeking answers to research questions. They may produce a new model or theory or interpretation, or develop an existing one. Concentration on these more conceptual aspects may be at the expense of providing details about the search and analysis methods used, and sometimes a lack of formal quality assessment.

The detailed suggestions on carrying out traditional literature reviews (pp. 89–91) also cover critical literature reviews.

The website gives references to examples of critical literature reviews.

Note: A stand-alone critical review of a single article can form the basis for a desk-based review. See Chapter 3, p. 66 for details.

State-of-the-art reviews

These are essentially a subset of general literature reviews. Whereas literature reviews typically focus on both retrospective and current literature on a topic, state-of-the-art reviews tend to be limited to more current matters. They are useful for students, researchers and others who, by reading a single review article, can quickly get a feel for current issues in a topic area.

An 'annual review' of the literature in a wide range of disciplines and fields of study which should be available in academic libraries is perhaps the prime example of a state-of-the-art review. Most are produced, often by invitation, by established researchers with extensive experience of the area reviewed.

The limited time-scale that they cover is an obvious disadvantage. Important earlier developments, which may have shaped work on a topic, are likely to be omitted.

If you are interested in a carrying out a state-of-the-art review the advice given below for literature reviews (pp. 89–91) also applies.

The website gives references to examples of state-of-the-art literature reviews.

Systematic reviews

A full-blown Cochrane-style systematic review is a major enterprise, involving a team of researchers and many hours of work. *It is beyond the resources available for a student project at undergraduate level and much postgraduate work.* However, such reviews are becoming an important feature of funded projects, both in their own right and as a required precursor to one involving the collection of empirical data.

Petticrew and Roberts (2006) explain that:

> Systematic reviews are literature reviews that adhere closely to a set of scientific methods that explicitly aim to limit systematic error (bias), mainly by attempting to identify, appraise and synthesize all relevant studies (of whatever design) in order to answer a particular question (or set of questions). In carrying out this task they set out their methods in advance, and in detail, as one would for any piece of social research (pp. 9–10).

They view systematic reviews as being very similar to surveys. The difference being that while surveys are of people, systematic reviews are surveys of the literature.

As indicated earlier, the current interest in systematic reviews arose from a concern for assessing the effectiveness of interventions, particularly in the work of the Campbell and Cochrane Collaborations (see below). This has been linked to debates about the so-called 'gold standard' status of randomized controlled trials (RCTs), with fervent advocates and strong critics (see Chapter 6, p. 117).

See below (p. 93) for information on carrying out systematic reviews.

The website gives references to examples of systematic reviews.

Meta-analysis

Meta-analyses put together results from a number of individual quantitative studies to produce a single best estimate of the benefits or harm of an intervention. An American psychologist,

Gene Glass, coined the term and pioneered the use of the technique (Glass, McGaw & Smith, 1981; Glass, 2000). From being a rather esoteric aspect of educational statistics meta-analyses have recently gained prominence from their use in systematic reviews.

For a meta-analysis to be valid, all of the studies included must have similar characteristics such as the population studied, the type of intervention, and the comparison and measures being made. If these stringent conditions are met they are a means of effectively increasing the total sample size studied, and hence the likelihood of achieving statistical significance. Systematic reviews, which require the same conditions for validity, now typically include a meta-analysis.

The website gives references to examples of meta-analyses.

Qualitative meta-synthesis

Qualitative meta-synthesis attempts to do the same task as meta-analysis for qualitative studies. It is sometimes referred to as *meta-ethnography*, which is a confusing, and somewhat unfortunate, term as the approach is applicable to all types of research involving the collection of qualitative data.

The website gives references to examples of qualitative meta-synthesis.

The section below includes coverage of meta-analysis and meta-synthesis. See also Nordmann, Kasenda & Briel (2012) and Rice (2008) for accessible short introductions to meta-analysis and meta-synthesis respectively.

Umbrella reviews

Umbrella reviews, also referred to in the literature as *overviews* (or *overviews of research*), are systematic reviews of systematic reviews. They aim to address specific research questions by examining the findings of previous systematic reviews. Originally, they were put forward as a 'friendly front end' to the Campbell library of systematic reviews, enabling readers to get a quick overview of the reviews covering a particular topic area. They are dependent on the pre-existence of relevant systematic reviews. To date, the overwhelming number of systematic reviews are in the general area of health and based on reviews of RCTs. However, that situation is changing. The Campbell Collaboration has broadened its remit to cover other designs based on quantitative data, and also seeks to incorporate evidence from qualitative research, as well as reviews based on the synthesis of qualitative evidence (Higgins & Green, 2011, Chapter 20).

Umbrella reviews may appear attractive to students as the search task is straightforward and handleable. However, an acceptable standard of umbrella reviews calls for a clear understanding of the methodological issues involved. Journals increasingly publish reviews – see, for example an editorial by Conn and Sells (2014) which gives an explicit, and very helpful, welcome to umbrella reviews in a nursing journal.

The methods used for carrying out umbrella reviews are essentially the same as for any systematic review. Cooper and Kopenka (2012) and Smith, Devane, Begley and Clarke (2011) provide details of some specific issues that have to be addressed.

Recent overviews include topics in crime prevention, education, information technology, management and social work, in addition to those in health and medicine.

The website gives references to examples of umbrella reviews.

If you are interested in carrying out an umbrella review, the advice given below for systematic reviews (p. 93) also applies. You are also advised to consult the appropriate chapter of the Cochrane handbook (Becker & Oxman, 2011).

Systematic rapid reviews

Rapid reviews are systematic reviews carried out over a severely limited time period. They have gained some legitimacy in the UK in the form of Rapid Evidence Assessments (REAs) (http://www.gsr.gov.uk/professional guidance/rea toolkit/sitemap.asp). Similar initiatives have taken place in Canada (Khangura, Polisena, Clifford, Farraha & Kamela, 2014). Conducting systematic research reviews is typically a lengthy process which does not fit in with the needs of policy development. While aiming for the rigour of systematic reviews they are quicker and cheaper.

Harker and Kleinen (2012), after reviewing 49 health technology assessment rapid reviews, concluded that 'there is no agreed and tested methodology and it is unclear how rapid reviews differ from systematic review methods' (p. 397). They found a wide diversity of methodology in all aspects of the rapid reviews. Thomas, Newman, and Oliver (2013), following experience in carrying out several UK rapid reviews, give the approach a cautious welcome.

Grant and Booth (2009) identify several ways in which you can achieve a shorter timescale. These include:

> . . . carefully focusing the question, using broader or less sophisticated search strategies, conducting a review of reviews, restricting the amount of grey literature, extracting only key variables and performing only 'simple' quality appraisal. The reviewer chooses which stages to limit and then explicitly reports the likely effect of such a method (p. 100).

If you are interested in a carrying out a rapid review the advice given below for systematic reviews also applies. See also James Thomas's advice about the conditions under which a rapid review is likely to be feasible (Thomas, 2013).

The website gives references to examples of systematic rapid reviews.

Scoping reviews

Scoping reviews provide a preliminary assessment of the likely size and scope of the available research literature. They have been used by policy-makers to help decide whether a full systematic review would be worthwhile. They can also be used by researchers to decide whether to do further development work on a topic by carrying out a more extensive review, as a precursor for a project. Scoping reviews seek to be systematic along the lines of a systematic review.

They can make a worthwhile publication or student exercise in their own right. For example, see Connolly and Joubert (2014) who present a set of scoping reviews produced by social work students as a component of their research training at the University of Melbourne. However, they are not usually regarded by researchers or funders as a final output. This is partly because of their limited duration and, hence, scope and also because many scoping reviews simply focus on the existence of material, without attempting to assess its quality. Such reviews do not provide a good basis for policy or practice recommendations.

Pham *et al.* (2014) carried out a 'scoping review of scoping reviews' (!) – 344 published between 1999 and October 2012 – confirming that less than a quarter of them assessed the quality of the studies included in the reviews. They concluded that: 'Because of variability in their conduct, there is a need for their methodological standardization to ensure the utility and strength of evidence' (p. 371). Levac, Colquhoun and O'Brien (2010) make suggestions for how this could be done, extending a framework developed by Arksey and O'Malley (2005).

The advice given below for systematic reviews also applies for scoping reviews.

The website gives references to examples of systematic scoping reviews.

Realist reviews

Realist reviews, also referred to as realist synthesis, are certainly systematic, but they are very different from the Cochrane-type systematic review. As the term suggests, they are based on the realist approach introduced in Chapter 2, p. 30 and revisited in several later chapters. They are discussed in more detail, including coverage of carrying out this type of review, on p. 97.

Doing a literature review as a desk-based project

Desk-based projects based on a traditional literature review are very various. As for any type of research, the constraints and expectations of your particular situation are a central consideration. This covers issues like length and structure which must be clarified before you start. The basic requirement is for you to be systematic, that is, to think through what you are doing and why, and to make this clear to the reader. We would call this a systematic review, if the term had not already been appropriated with a more restricted meaning.

Important factors to keep in mind include:

- *Justification.* Why are you doing a desk-based project? Are there constraints either methodologically, practically or ethically that prevent you from doing a primary piece of research?
- *Data searching.* Have you considered the scale of your literature search? What databases will you use? What are your key search terms? How will you decide on the sample size?
- *Originality.* Are you asking an original, or adapted, research question (or questions)? You should be. Simply repeating what has been done already is not enough. Are you approaching the field in a new light? Perhaps a newly developed policy has turned everything on its head. Or are you developing an alternative perspective on past work?
- *Reporting.* Have you considered how you will structure the presentation of your desk-based study? This is important. *It is not simply an extended essay and should not be presented as one.*
- *Ethics.* Is ethics the main reason why you are doing the research in this way? Have you considered the ethics of reconsidering, or re-evaluating, others' primary data through your re-analysis of their data?

- *Data analysis.* How, exactly, will you analyse these data? Will you simply compare and contrast the findings of the individual pieces of research? Or are you going to use a more specialized technique (see Chapters 6, 7 and 8)? How much time will it take and have you planned appropriately? Details of the analysis, and any peripheral material, may be better placed in appendices.
- *Conclusions.* Can you make any concluding claims over and above simple descriptive statements? This is difficult with empirical research at the best of times, but can be more difficult with desk-based research; especially in small scale projects. Do not over emphasize the importance of these claims.

Anyone doing a project which solely consists of a desk-based literature review should not think that they can get away with just reading this chapter in preparation for their task. We can let you off Part IV, but the rest of the text is all potentially relevant.

The main steps when carrying out a literature review as a desk-based project

As a first step you are strongly recommended to:

- start your project journal.

  To complete a project you need to:

- decide on a focus for the project;
- develop the research question or questions;
- choose a search strategy;
- consider ethical issues;
- record search findings in the form of reviews of the research identified;
- prepare these data for analysis;
- analyse and interpret them; and
- report and disseminate your findings.

For material on project journals, see p. 89; on developing a focus, see p. 90; on deciding on research questions, see p. 90; on search strategies and recording findings, see p. 90; for data preparation, analysis and interpretation, see p. 91 (for quantitative data), or p. 91 (for qualitative data); and on reporting and dissemination, see p. 91.

Project journals

A project journal in the form of diary and *aide-mémoire*, recording what you have done and plan to do, noting ideas, etc. is the same whether you are collecting new data or carrying out a desk-based project.

Focus

Deciding on the focus for a review has somewhat different constraints. Many topics which would be ruled out because of difficulties in collecting new data, either from resource limitations, population inaccessibility, or ethical considerations, can form the focus of a review of existing research. The problem is more with the existence and accessibility of this material. Restricting your search to material of high quality (perhaps by limiting the search to articles in peer-reviewed journals) may result in a poor harvest. Casting the net wider to include other material such as conference, or 'grey' material of doubtful prove-nance, may be necessary. This then leads to both quality and other problems (you are likely to be unsure about the representativeness of the reports you have managed to get hold of).

Research question

The same issues apply to research questions. Ones that would be ruled out for empirical projects may be perfectly feasible in a literature review; and vice versa. It is notable that such reviews are typically limited to a single research question, possibly because of time, and other, resource limitations. The titles of reviews are typically a research question expressed in the form of a statement, but retaining the question format is one means of highlighting it. Box 5.1 gives examples.

Search strategy

Your search strategy needs to be detailed, specifying the kind of research you are after. It should include the search terms and databases and/or other sources you will use. Your criteria for which literature to include are important. Criteria could include 'literature in refereed journals in English over the last ten years'. The search is driven by the research question, which may call for a search for quantitative research, or qualitative research, or both. If an initial search reveals few items fulfilling your criteria, they will have to be widened.

Ethical issues

Ethical concerns about your treatment of participants in the data collection phase of a research project do not arise when carrying out a review of existing research. However, a desk-based study is not without ethical concerns. They include such things as the honesty, truthfulness and fairness with which you tackle the review task, referred to by Siu and Comerasamy (2013, p. 90) as *integrity*. For example, Box 5.2 lists aspects which may compromise the honesty of your efforts.

They also discuss the relevant ethical principles of *transparency* and *accountability*. To be transparent, you need to provide full details of the process you followed in carrying out the review. To be accountable, you need to consider its possible effects. You are responsible for the messages you give through publishing the review, particularly if you aim to influence practice, or make recommendations.

Recording

Your search strategy should also include details of the kind of information you are going to record for each of the reports you select for inclusion. Research reviews can be based on any type of existing research. Most use reports of empirical research, but they can be based on reviews of earlier reviews (as in umbrella reviews, p. 86), or theoretical, or conceptual, material.

Analysis and synthesis

Treatment of the identified reports can be narrative in form as in a traditional essay. This can be supplemented by, or even largely replaced by, the type of tables and matrices recommended for summarizing qualitative data (Chapter 18, p. 467), aiding its analysis and synthesis, as discussed there. An alternative is to make use of the procedures advocated within systematic reviews (see below, p. 93). However, the role given there to qualitative research (p. 95), is limited. The qualitative meta-synthesis approach discussed below (p. 96) is more flexible. Box 5.6 gives details.

Another possibility is to make use of the well-developed methodology of content analysis (Chapter 15, p. 349). The 'content' analysed is a set of existing research reports. Inman, Devdas, Spektor and Pendse (2014) provide an example. A very different approach is suggested by Wall, Stahl and Daynes (2014) who propose the use of discourse analysis as a methodology for some research reviews.

Reporting and disseminating

Reporting on literature reviews as a piece of desk-based research should cover the same bases as for research based on collecting new primary data. One message that can be profitably adopted from systematic research is in relation to *transparency*. This means being explicit and open about the process of your review. The principle of reporting experimental research, that you should provide sufficient detail for a reader to carry out an exact replication of your work, should be followed. This includes stating, in exact terms, what rules you followed when searching for papers to review. What databases did you use, what were the key terms, what criteria for inclusion in your review, etc., etc.

Literature reviews, particularly so-called 'critical' reviews, commonly seek to move beyond a review of the existing literature. They may, for example, make recommendations for the direction of future studies in the topic area (Brooker & Joppe, 2014; Kalibatseva & Leong, 2014; Seeck & Rantanen, 2014); suggest that there are unanswered questions (Natalicchio, Messeni Petruzzelli & Garavelli, 2014); attempt a synthesis of the literature (Carter, Dubois & Tremblay, 2014); or review the methodological assumptions of the research (Zak & Getzner, 2014). In some cases, the main aim appears to be to provide advice to policy-makers, with the review providing justification for the recommendations made (e.g. Diamond *et al.*, 2014).

Recommendations relevant to policy and practice can support the dissemination of your review and increase its potential impact. Additional types of report targeting different audiences should also form part of your dissemination strategy.

Box 5.3 suggests a possible structure for a literature review to be submitted to a journal.

BOX 5.1

Examples of review titles in question format

Intimate partner violence and the rural–urban–suburban divide. Myth or reality? A critical review of the literature (Edwards, 2014).

Where has all the psychology gone? A critical review of evidence-based psychological practice in correctional settings (Gannon & Ward, 2014).

What do we really mean when we talk about 'exit'? A critical review of research on entrepreneurial exit (Wennberg & DeTienne, 2014).

Do local enhanced services in primary care improve outcomes? Results from a literature review (Kumar *et al.* 2014).

Does smart home technology prevent falls in community-dwelling older adults? A literature review (Pietrzak, Cotea & Pullman, 2014).

But why do we need politicians? A critical review (Corbett, 2014).

(emphases added)

BOX 5.2

Integrity in literature reviews

Issues include:

- declaring your own biases and personal ambitions so as to ensure objectivity in posing research questions and selecting the appropriate methodology;
- attending to possible conflicts of interest, as well as financial obligations, personal relationships or affiliation with a third party;
- ensuring that you report all methodological issues honestly;
- respecting intellectual property by acknowledging the work of researchers quoted;
- not fabricating or falsifying or misrepresenting data; and
- endeavouring to avoid discrimination, particularly in selecting the criteria for evaluating the literature.

(based on Siu & Comerasamy, 2013, p. 91)

BOX 5.3

Possible structure for a literature review journal article

- *Background.* Setting the context for the review.
- *Objectives.* A clear description of the aim of the review.
- *Methods.* Describing the review process employed, including search strategy, any quality assessment, and approaches to synthesis and analysis.
- *Results.* Summarizing the main results, supported by any figures and tables where appropriate.
- *Discussion.* Analysis of the results, with particular reference to implications for the field covered by the journal.
- *Conclusions.* Main conclusions and suggestions for future research if appropriate.
- *Key messages.* Up to five implications for practice and up to three implications for policy.

(based on suggestions from the editors of *Health Information & Libraries Journal*; Grant & Sutton, 2011)

Doing a systematic review

If you don't already have a background in carrying out systematic reviews, you have a long and steep learning curve ahead of you before you are in a position to do so. This is, in part, because they are complicated, resource-intensive enterprises, but also because they are under the watchful eye of large institutions who act as gatekeepers of the rules of the game. Play it their way and you will be allowed to make a contribution. First in the field was the *Cochrane Collaboration*, formed in 1993, with the motto 'Working together to produce the best evidence for healthcare' and now a major non-profit international organization with over 30,000 volunteers in over 100 countries in 2014. The linked *Campbell Collaboration* seeks to extend the remit by promoting systematic reviews in fields more closely linked to social science, such as crime and justice, education, international development, social policy and social welfare.

Box 5.4 lists the steps to be followed when carrying out a systematic review. Petticrew and Roberts (2006) provide a very readable practical guide to the field which is strongly recommended. Following this, if you are seriously considering taking this route, the best advice is to follow the detailed handbooks available from the various organizations active in the field.

The website gives information about systematic review handbooks.

BOX 5.4

The systematic review process

1. *Define the research question.* The question that the review aims to answer.
2. *Decide on the parameters.* Specify the topic (e.g. effects of an intervention); the population and any sub-populations; outcomes of interest; time period; cultural and other contexts; proposals for dissemination.
3. *Discuss proposed review with stakeholders.* Do this while deciding on steps 1 and 2.
4. *Recruit a steering group.* To provide advice from persons representing a range of interests (e.g. practitioners, participants, service managers, experienced researcher, statistician).
5. *Write a protocol.* State the review question; methods to be used; study types and designs to be reviewed; criteria for inclusion and exclusion; ways they will be appraised and synthesized. Discuss with steering group and, if appropriate, present to Campbell Collaboration or other organization for comment.
6. *Carry out the search process.* Put the protocol proposals into action by searching for the types of studies needed to answer the research question.
7. *Screen the references.* Identify those references which appear worth detailed further consideration.
8. *Assess screened references against inclusion/exclusion criteria.* Obtain full-text versions of all possibles and exclude those not meeting inclusion criteria. Retain summary details of ALL identified studies, whether or not judged to have met the inclusion criteria.
9. *Extract relevant information from included studies.* Produce a table giving details covering all the parameters established in step 2 above, and specified in the agreed protocol.
10. *Quality appraisal.* Assess the soundness of the methodological aspects of all included studies.
11. *Synthesize included studies.* Integrate the studies using statistical techniques (e.g. by meta-analysis) and/or narrative accounts. Take into account variations in population (nature and size of sample); study design; outcomes; and likelihood of bias.
12. *Write a report.* To include full details of the review, including information about studies included at each stage. Details of what is required are available for Cochrane and Campbell reviews as well as from journals accepting systematic reviews. Other versions of the report, as well as summaries, should be prepared for different audiences as part of your dissemination strategy.

(based, in part, on Appendix 1, pp. 284–7, Pettigrew & Roberts, 2006)

Campbell Collaboration procedure

Box 5.5 shows what is involved when working with the Campbell Collaboration.

BOX 5.5

Producing a Campbell Collaboration systematic review

Title proposal. The process of producing a Campbell Collaboration systematic review starts with the presentation of a clear idea in the form of a proposal. They ensure that no one else is working on a similar project in order to avoid duplication of work. If the title proposal is accepted, they publish it in their library and you will be asked to develop a protocol.

Protocol. The next stage is to develop a project plan – the project's protocol. In this process, they clarify agreements about how the Campbell Collaboration can support this specific project.

Review. After the protocol is accepted and published in their library, the work of producing the review itself begins. They will support the work according to the agreements made in the previous stages.

Publishing the review. After the review is accepted, they will make sure that the review is presented in the Campbell design and that it includes all the information necessary for their electronic journal. When this is done, it will be published officially in the online Campbell Library and can be freely distributed as per their open access policy.

The promotion of the review is a responsibility shared between the authors, the supporting institutions and Campbell. Typically, they will write about the completed review on their website, in newsletters, and make other efforts to promote the review depending on capacity. Through the network of their Users' Group, they will normally try to develop a user abstract, which is a summary of the review written in easily accessible language.

(see Noonan & Guzda, 2014)

Specific issues

Qualitative research and systematic reviews

While Campbell systematic reviews now accept a role for qualitative research, it is seen as supporting, and supplementary to, findings from quantitative research:

> Although qualitative studies cannot be used as the primary basis for conclusions about intervention effects, this does not mean they should be excluded from Campbell reviews. Qualitative research and other forms of descriptive research can help paint a richer picture of the intervention, its effects, how or why it produces those effects (or not), and other such features that provide texture and explanatory context to a review. Where available, the applicable findings of such research should be incorporated into the review in summary form (Noonan & Guzda, 2014, p. 12).

It is clear that qualitative research is expected to be presented in a statistical form, with descriptive statistics, effect sizes and confidence intervals called for (p. 47).

Qualitative meta-synthesis (meta-ethnography)

This is a type of thematic *coding* analysis (Chapter 18, p. 467) and is a non-statistical approach to combining and synthesizing qualitative research. It is not limited to ethnographic studies and can be used with all types of qualitative research. It is systematic, but not in the Cochrane/ Campbell sense of systematic review. Box 5.6 shows what is involved in carrying out a qualitative meta-analysis. Monforte-Royo, Villavicencio-Chávez, Tomás-Sábado, Mahtani-Chugani, & Balaguer (2012) provide an example.

Saini and Shlonsky (2012a), in a very accessible short guide, provide an overview of the various approaches to the synthesis of qualitative studies.

Mixed method (multi-strategy) systematic reviews

The Evidence for Policy and Practice Information and Coordinating Centre (the EPPI-Centre) of the Institute of Education, University of London has been a pioneer in using mixed methods (multi-strategy) studies in systematic reviews. See Saini and Shlonsky (2012b) for an overview.

BOX 5.6

Steps in a qualitative meta-synthesis

1. Description of how the phenomena of interest were determined;
2. How relevant studies were selected;
3. Reading and review of the selected studies;
4. A description of how studies relate to each other while addressing assumptions of;
5. How the studies were comparable or 'reciprocal';
6. How the findings of the studies 'opposed' each other; and
7. How the findings lead to a 'line of argument' or position;
8. How the studies were 'translated' into one another to present a unified theme;
9. How the translations were developed and interpreted into a single theme; and
10. Presentation of the interpreted results.
11. How the investigator determined the similarity of the phenomena of the studies selected;
12. How inclusion criteria on the similarity of the studies were determined;
13. How methodological similarities of the studies were determined, i.e. phenomenological or ethnography; and
14. The methods used to identify the similarities and differences in the studies.

(steps 1–10 based on Noblit & Hare, 1988; 11–14 on Sandelowski, Docherty & Emden, 1997)

In the EPPI-Centre approach there is no attempt to convert the qualitative findings into numbers. Harden (2010) asserts that:

> Using a mixed-methods model is one way to answer a number of questions in the same systematic review. Rarely do decision makers have just one question to answer; they are more likely to have a series of questions. The mixed-methods model enables us to integrate quantitative estimates of benefit and harm with more qualitative understanding from people's lives. This integration helps determine not only the effects of interventions but also their appropriateness (p. 8).

She provides an example of the approach. Other examples are available from the EPPI-Centre website (http://eppi.ioe.ac.uk/EPPIWeb/home.aspx).

Single-case research designs and systematic reviews

As discussed in Chapter 6, p. 134, while single-case research designs are well established in some fields of study, notably within special education, they remain controversial methodologically. Horner *et al.* (2005) put forward a range of criteria by which the quality of such studies could be evaluated as a precursor to their inclusion in systematic reviews. Moeller, Dattilo and Rusch (2015) applied these quality indicators in an attempt to identify evidence-based practice in special education. They concluded that two-thirds of the single-case designs they reviewed did not meet Horner *et al.*'s quality criteria, suggesting that this is a field needing further development either in terms of quality criteria or study design.

Doing realist reviews

Realist review is a type of research synthesis designed to work with complex social interventions. It is based on the realist approach to evaluation (Chapter 2, p. 30). Ray Pawson has criticized the use of systematic reviews in this context:

> Evidence-based policy is a dominant theme in contemporary public services but the practical realities and challenges involved in using evidence in policy-making are formidable. Part of the problem is one of complexity. In health services and other public services, we are dealing with complex social interventions which act on complex social systems – things like league tables, performance measures, regulation and inspection, or funding reforms. These are not 'magic bullets' which will always hit their target, but programmes whose effects are crucially dependent on context and implementation. Traditional methods of review focus on measuring and reporting on programme effectiveness, often find that the evidence is mixed or conflicting, and provide little or no clue as to why the intervention worked or did not work when applied in different contexts or circumstances, deployed by different stakeholders, or used for different purposes (Pawson, Greenhalgh, Harvey, & Walshe, 2005, p. 21).

Realist reviews seek to remedy this deficiency by providing an explanatory focus for systematic reviews (Pawson & Bellamy, 2006). Protocols for realist review, in similar format to those for systematic reviews, have been devised (e.g. Westhorp, Walker & Rogers, 2012; Molnar *et al.*, 2015).

Spicer, Ehren and Bangpan (2014) present a case study on the process of developing a realist review of school accountability in developing countries. Jagosh *et al.* (2014) provide critical reflections on this process, focusing on participatory research where it appears particularly appropriate (see also Macaulay *et al.*, 2011). Saul, Willis, Bitz and Best (2013) make the point that they 'can require considerable and sustained investment over time, which does not always suit the time-sensitive demands of many policy decisions' (p. 1). They have developed a rapid review version which they claim is useful to policy-makers, while preserving the core elements of realist methodology. It could also be of interest to students, with limited resources and time, attracted to a realist approach. There are also examples of realist scoping reviews (e.g. Toohey & Rock, 2011).

While the majority of realist reviews focus on health-related issues, a range of other disciplines and fields of study have now been covered. They include business, education, social policy, social work, and sports studies.

Carrying out a realist review

Box 5.7 summarizes the key steps in a realist review. As ever, deciding on the review question starts off the process. It will be determined by the kind of intervention being reviewed, the context in which it occurs and any policy issues which have led to it.

The focus of the review can be on whether the intervention works as predicted. Such predictions come from theories about its operation, in realist terms what mechanisms are involved. Such theories come from what is already known, or hypothesized – possibly from prior knowledge of the research literature, or from professionals, practitioners or participants who have had experience of the intervention.

It can be concerned with outcomes as in a systematic review. However, it is more likely to be: 'How does it work in different settings or with different groups?' If the intervention is policy driven an issue is how it works, or doesn't work, in practice. At this stage you are likely to have several possible theories in the running which you need to spell out. You now need evidence to choose between them, or to synthesize them.

Decisions having been made as to which theory and mechanisms to concentrate on, this drives step 2, the search for evidence. In the light of a background search you confirm or change these decisions, exploring new hypotheses about what might be happening if this is where the search takes you. As this concludes you confirm the inclusion criteria for the primary studies you will focus on.

Next, in step 3, you appraise these studies, assessing their relevance to the theories being tested and the quality of the evidence they are providing. You can extract different data from the different studies under review anywhere they seem to provide evidence which will help to make decisions between the theories.

In step 4 you put all the evidence together in a synthesis which will help you to refine the theory in terms of the realist mantra of 'What works, for whom, and under what circumstances?' The pattern of evidence helps in filling out those groups for which the intervention is more, or less, effective, and similarly the favourable and unfavourable contexts for its operation.

BOX 5.7

Key steps in realist review

Step 1: Clarify scope
    (a) Identify the review question.
    (b) Refine the purpose of the review.
    (c) Articulate key theories to be explored.
Step 2: Search for evidence
    (a) Exploratory background search to 'get a feel' for the literature.
    (b) Progressive focusing to identify key programme theories, refining inclusion criteria in the light of emerging data.
    (c) Purposive sampling to test a defined subset of these theories, with additional 'snowball' sampling to explore new hypotheses as they emerge.
    (d) Final search for additional studies when review near completion.
Step 3: Appraise primary studies and extract data
    (a) Use judgement to supplement formal critical appraisal checklists, and consider 'fitness for purpose'.
    (b) Develop 'bespoke' set of data extraction forms and notation devices.
    (c) Extract different data from different studies to populate evaluative framework with evidence.
Step 4: Synthesize evidence and draw conclusions
    (a) Synthesize data to achieve refinement of programme theory – that is, to determine what works for whom, how and under what circumstances.
    (b) Allow purpose of review (see step 1b) to drive the synthesis process.
    (c) Use 'contradictory' evidence to generate insights about the influence of context.
    (d) Present conclusions as a series of contextualized decision points of the general format 'If A, then B' or 'In the case of C, D is unlikely to work'.
Step 5: Disseminate, implement and evaluate
    (a) Draft and test out recommendations and conclusions with key stakeholders, focusing especially on levers that can be pulled in here-and-now policy contexts.
    (b) Work with practitioners and policy-makers to apply recommendations in particular contexts.
    (c) Evaluate in terms of extent to which programmes are adjusted to take account of contextual influences revealed by the review: the 'same' programme might be expanded in one setting, modified in another and abandoned in another.

(summarized from Pawson *et al.* 2005; Box 5.1, p. S1:24)

    The final, very important, step is to share your conclusions with the different stakeholders. You are seeking to influence policy-makers and practitioners by providing useful and usable advice on what might be changed to improve effectiveness.

The website gives references to examples of realist reviews.

In summary

It is clear that there are different ways of doing desk-based research as a project in its own right. The choice for many students and lone researchers is limited. Full systematic reviews, whether of the Cochrane or realist type, call for a research team and substantial resources (although 'rapid' versions may be feasible). However, there is much to learn from the procedures followed to assure quality and objectivity in systematic reviews, when doing a literature review.

Systematic reviews are not without their critics. Some make a root and branch attack. For example Boell and Cezec-Kecmanovic (2011) answer their question, 'Are systematic reviews better, less biased and of higher quality [than traditional literature reviews]?' with a resounding 'no'. They claim that 'in contrast to systematic reviews which put importance on the literature identification and selection process [. . .] reading is central to reviewing literature. Reading enables academics to improve their understanding of the subject area and therefore to further advance their searches.'

Others take a more measured approach, warning about the considerable variability in their methodological quality (Pölkki, Kanste, Kääriäinen, Elo, & Kyngäs, 2014). Wilson (2009) is concerned about the difficulty of discovering 'grey' literature, which can be of high quality, from a search of databases. Moreover, the common use of bibliographic status as a proxy for quality in systematic reviews can cause problems. He cites 'evidence of publication selection bias [that] clearly establishes that peer-reviewed journal articles are more likely to show statistically significant results than less formally published studies' (p. 429). However, Ferguson and Brannick (2012), focusing on publication bias in meta-analysis aspects of systematic review, suggest that 'searches for unpublished studies may increase rather than decrease some sources of bias' (p. 1). A rejoinder from Rothstein and Bushman (2012) takes issue with their analysis, and reaches the opposite conclusion. Their view is that: 'Rather than exclude unpublished studies, we recommend that meta-analysts code study characteristics related to methodological quality (e.g., experimental vs. non-experimental design) and test whether these factors influence the meta-analytic results' (p. 129).

This turmoil is not uncommon in a newly developing field. It is a healthy self-correcting aspect of scientific research and is particularly valuable when bandwagons start rolling. Cochrane style systematic reviews are a welcome, and influential, part of the evidence-based movement but the scientific attitude advocated in this text (Chapter 2, p. 16) calls on us to proceed, not only systematically, but also sceptically.

CHAPTER 6

Fixed designs

This chapter:

- covers general features of fixed design research, typically involving the collection of quantitative data;
- discusses how the trustworthiness (including reliability, validity and generalizability) of findings from this style of research can be established;
- explores the attractions and problems of doing experiments in real world research;
- gives particular attention to the randomized controlled trial (RCT) and whether it can be legitimately viewed as the 'gold standard' of research designs;
- attempts to provide a balanced view of the ubiquitous evidence-based movement;
- differentiates between true experimental, quasi-experimental and single-case experimental designs;
- considers non-experimental fixed designs; and
- concludes by discussing how to decide on sample sizes in fixed design research.

Introduction

This chapter deals with approaches to social research where the design of the study is fixed before the main stage of data collection takes place. In these approaches the phenomena of interest are typically quantified. This is not a necessary feature. As pointed out by Oakley (2000, p. 306) there is nothing intrinsic to such designs which rules out qualitative methods or data. Murphy, Dingwall, Greatbatch, Parker and Watson (1998) give examples of purely qualitative fixed design studies, and of others using both qualitative and quantitative methods, in the field of health promotion evaluation.

It has already been argued in Chapter 3 that there can be considerable advantage in linking research to theory. With fixed designs, that link is straightforward: fixed designs are theory-driven. The only way in which we can, as a fixed design requires, specify in advance the variables to be included in our study and the exact procedures to be followed, is by having a reasonably well-articulated theory of the phenomenon we are researching. Put in other terms, we must already have a substantial amount of conceptual understanding about a phenomenon before it is worthwhile following the risky strategy of investing precious time and resources in such designs. This may be in the form of a model, perhaps represented pictorially as a conceptual framework as discussed in Chapter 3.

Such models help to make clear the multiple and complex causality of most things studied in social research. Hard thinking to establish this kind of model before data collection is invaluable. It suggests the variables we should target: those to be manipulated or controlled in an experiment and those to be included in non-experimental studies.

In realist terms, this means that you have a pretty clear idea about the mechanisms likely to be in operation and the specific contexts in which they will, or will not, operate. You should also know what kind of results you are going to get, and how you will analyse them, before you collect the data. If the study does deliver the expected relationships, it provides support for the existence of these mechanisms and their actual operation in this study. This does not preclude your following up interesting or unexpected patterns in the data. They may suggest the existence of other mechanisms which you had not thought of.

Large-scale studies can afford to draw the net relatively wide. Large numbers of participants can be involved, several subgroups established, perhaps a range of different contexts covered, more possible mechanisms tested out. For the small-scale studies on which this text focuses, and in real world settings where relevant previous work may be sparse or non-existent, there is much to be said for a multi-strategy design (see Chapter 8) with an initial flexible design stage which is primarily exploratory in purpose. This seeks to establish, both from discussions with professionals, participants and others involved in the initial phase, and from the empirical data gathered, likely 'bankers' for mechanisms operating in the situation, contexts where they are likely to operate and the characteristics of participants best targeted. The second fixed design phase then incorporates a highly focused survey, experiment or other fixed design study.

Even with a preceding exploratory phase, *fixed designs should always be piloted*. You carry out a mini-version of the study before committing yourself to the big one. This is, in part, so you can sort out technical matters to do with methods of data collection to ensure that, say, the questions in a questionnaire are understandable and unambiguous. Just as importantly, it gives you a chance to ensure you are on the right lines conceptually. Have you 'captured' the phenomenon sufficiently well for meaningful data to be collected? Do you really have a good grasp of the relevant mechanisms and contexts? This is an opportunity to revise the design: to sharpen up the theoretical framework; develop the research questions; rethink the sampling strategy. And perhaps to do a further pilot.

Although this may seem like overkill, in fixed design research piloting is essential for once you start collecting 'real' data (i.e. after the pilot work), and participants are engaged, it cannot be changed. This is especially salient in funded research, for if you are not delivering what the funder wants then there will be issues further down the line. Therefore, it's always sensible to discuss the outputs of your pilot with your funders.

Also, while the central part of what you are going to do with your data should be thought through in advance, i.e. you are primarily engaged in a confirmatory task in fixed designs, there is nothing to stop you also carrying out exploratory data analysis (see Chapter 17, p. 415). It may be that there are unexpected patterns or relationships which reveal inadequacies in your initial understanding of the phenomenon. You cannot expect to confirm these revised understandings in the same study but they may well provide an important breakthrough suggesting a basis for further research.

This chapter seeks to provide a realist-influenced view of fixed design research. There is coverage of *true experimental, single-case experimental, quasi-experimental* and *non-experimental fixed designs*. The differences between these types of design are brought out and some examples given. In the 'true' experiment, two or more groups are set up, with random allocation of people to the groups. The experimenter then actively manipulates the situation so that different groups get different treatments. Single-case design, as the name suggests, focuses on individuals rather than groups and effectively seeks to use persons as their own control, with their being subjected to different experimentally manipulated conditions at different times. Quasi-experiments lack the random allocation to different conditions found in true experiments. Non-experimental fixed designs do not involve active manipulation of the situation by the researcher. However, the different fixed designs are similar in many respects, as discussed in the following section.

General features of fixed designs

Fixed designs are usually concerned with aggregates: with group properties and with general tendencies. In traditional experiments, results are reported in terms of group averages rather than what individuals have done. Because of this, there is a danger of the *ecological fallacy* – that is, of assuming that inferences can be made about individuals from such aggregate data (Connolly, 2006; Harrison & McCaig, 2014). Single-case experimental designs are an interesting exception to this rule. Most non-experimental fixed research also deals with averages and proportions. The relative weakness of fixed designs is that they cannot capture the subtleties and complexities of individual human behaviour. For that you need flexible designs. Or, if you want to capture individual complexities, as well as group aggregates, then a multi-strategy design is a more appropriate route to take (see Chapter 8). Even single-case designs are limited to quantitative measures of a single simple behaviour or, at most, a small number of such behaviours. The advantage of fixed designs is in being able to transcend individual differences and identify patterns and processes which can be linked to social structures and group, or organizational, features.

Fixed designs traditionally assume a 'detached' researcher to guard against the researcher having an effect on the findings of the research. Researchers typically remain at a greater physical and emotional distance from the study than those using flexible designs. In experimental research, the *experimenter effect* is well known. It is now widely acknowledged that the beliefs, values and expectations of the researcher can influence the research process at virtually all of its stages (Rosenthal, 1976, 2003; Rosnow & Rosenthal, 1997; Kazdin, Rosenthal & Rosnow, 2009). Hence the stance now taken is that all potential biases should be brought out into the open by the researcher and every effort made to counter them.

There are often long periods of preparation and design preliminaries before data collection and a substantial period of analysis after data collection. This does not, of course, in any way absolve the researcher from familiarity with the topic of the research, which is typically acquired vicariously from others, or from a familiarity with the literature, or from an earlier, possibly qualitative, study. There will be involvement during the data collection phase, but with some studies such as postal surveys this may be minimal. Your personal preference for a relatively detached, or a more involved, style of carrying out research is a factor to take into account when deciding the focus of your research project and the selection of a fixed or flexible design.

It has been fashionable in some academic and professional circles to denigrate the contribution of quantitative social research. As Bentz and Shapiro (1998) comment, in a text primarily covering qualitative approaches:

> There is currently an anti-quantitative vogue in some quarters, asserting or implying that quantitative research is necessarily alienating, positivistic, dehumanizing, and not 'spiritual'. In fact, it is clear that using quantitative methods to identify causes of human and social problems and suffering can be of immense practical, human, and emancipatory significance, and they are not necessarily positivistic in orientation. For example, quantitative methods are currently being used in the analysis of statistics to help identify the principal causes of rape. Baron and Straus have analyzed police records on rape quantitatively to look at the relative roles of gender inequality, pornography, gender cultural norms about violence, and social disorganization in causing rape (1989). Clearly knowing the relative contribution of these factors in causing rape would be of great significance for social policy, economic policy, the law, socialization, and the criminal justice system, and it is difficult to see how one would arrive at compelling conclusions about this without quantitative analysis (p. 124).

Baron and Straus (1993) also point out that quantitative and experimental methods have been used to understand social problems and criticize prevailing ideologies in a way which contributes to social change and the alleviation of human suffering (i.e. for emancipatory purposes as discussed in Chapter 2, p. 32). However, a move to fixed designs in areas where, traditionally, flexible designs have been used can only work if relatively large data samples can be collected to allow statistical analysis.

Oakley (2000) suggests that this antipathy to quantitative, and in particular experimental, research derives in part from the influence of feminist methodologists who have viewed quantitative research as a masculine enterprise, contrasting it with qualitative research which is seen as embodying feminine values. She rejects this stereotyping and in her own work has made the transition from being a qualitative researcher to a staunch advocate of true randomized experiments.

Establishing trustworthiness in fixed design research

This is to a considerable extent a matter of common sense. Have you done a good, thorough and honest job? Have you tried to explore, describe or explain in an open and unbiased way? Or are you more concerned with delivering the required answer or selecting the evidence to support a case? If you can't answer these questions with yes, yes and no, respectively, then your findings are essentially worthless in research terms. However, pure intentions do not guarantee trustworthy findings. You persuade others by clear, well-written and presented, logically argued accounts which address the questions that concern them. These are all issues to which we will return in Chapter 19 on reporting.

This is not simply a presentational matter, however. Fundamental issues about the research itself are involved. Two key ones are *validity* and *generalizability*. Validity, from a realist perspective, refers to the accuracy of a result. Does it capture the real state of affairs? Are any relationships established in the findings true, or due to the effect of something else? Generalizability refers to the extent to which the findings of the research are more generally applicable, for example in other contexts, situations or times, or to persons other than those directly involved.

Validity

Suppose that we have been asked to carry out some form of research study to address the research question:

Is educational achievement in primary schools improved by the introduction of standard assessment tests at the age of seven?

Leave on one side issues about whether or not this is a sensible question and about the most appropriate way to approach it. Suppose that the findings of the research indicated a 'yes' answer – possibly qualified in various ways. In other words, we measure educational achievement, and it appears to increase following the introduction of the tests. Is this relationship what it appears to be – is there a real, direct, link between the two things?

Central to the scientific approach is a degree of scepticism about our findings and their meaning (and even greater scepticism about other people's). Can we have been fooled so that we are mistaken about them? Unfortunately, yes – there is a wide range of possibilities for confusion and error.

Reliability

Some problems come under the heading of reliability. This is the stability or consistency with which we measure something. For example, consider how we are going to assess educational achievement. This is no easy task. Possible contenders, each with their own problems, might include:

- a formal 'achievement test' administered at the end of the primary stage of schooling; or
- teachers' ratings, also at the end of the primary stage; or
- the number, level and standard of qualifications gained throughout life.

Let's say we go for the first. It is not difficult to devise something which will generate a score for each pupil. However, this might be unreliable in the sense that if a pupil had, say, taken it on a Monday rather than a Wednesday, she would have got a somewhat different score. There are logical problems in assessing this, which can be attacked in various ways (e.g. by having parallel forms of the test which can be taken at different times, and their results compared). These are important considerations in test construction – see Chapter 13 for further details.

Unless a measure is reliable, it cannot be valid. However, while reliability is necessary, it is not sufficient. A test for which all pupils always got full marks would be totally consistent but would be useless as a way of discriminating between the achievements of different pupils (there could of course be good educational reasons for such a test if what was important was mastery of some material).

Unreliability may have various causes, including:

Participant error

In our example the pupil's performance might fluctuate widely from occasion to occasion on a more or less random basis. Tiredness due to late nights could produce changes for different times of the day, pre-menstrual tension monthly effects or hay fever seasonal ones. There are tactics which can be used to ensure that these kinds of fluctuations do not bias the findings, particularly when specific sources of error can be anticipated (e.g. keep testing away from the hay fever season).

Participant bias

This is more problematic from a validity point of view. It could be that pupils might seek to please or help their teacher, knowing the importance of 'good results' for the teacher and for the school, by making a particularly strong effort at the test. Or for disaffected pupils to do the reverse. Here it would be very difficult to disentangle whether this was simply a short-term effect which had artificially affected the test scores, or a more long-lasting side-effect of a testing-oriented primary school educational system. Consideration of potential errors of these kinds is part of the standard approach to experimental design.

Observer error

This would be most obvious if the second approach, making use of teachers' ratings as the measure of pupil achievement, had been selected. These could also lead to more or less *random errors* if, for example, teachers made the ratings at a time when they were tired or overstretched and did the task in a cursory way. Again, there are pretty obvious remedies (perhaps involving the provision of additional resources).

Observer bias

This is also possible and, like participant bias, causes problems in interpretation. It could be that teachers in making the ratings were, consciously or unconsciously, biasing the ratings they gave in line with their ideological commitment either in favour of or against the use of standard assessment tests. This is also a well-worked area methodologically, with procedures including 'blind' assessment (the ratings being made by someone in ignorance of whether the pupil had been involved in standard assessment tests) and the use of two independent assessors (so that inter-observer agreements could be computed). Further details are given in Chapter 14, p. 331.

Types of validity

If you have made a serious attempt to get rid of participant and observer biases and have demonstrated the reliability of whatever measure you have decided on, you will be making a pretty good job of measuring something. The issue then becomes – does it measure what you think it measures? In the jargon – does it have *construct validity*?

There is no easy, single, way of determining construct validity. At its simplest, one might look for what seems reasonable, sometimes referred to as *face validity*. An alternative looks at possible links between scores on a test and the third suggested measure – the pupils' actual educational achievement in their later life (i.e. how well does it predict performance on the criterion in question, or *predictive criterion validity*). These and other aspects of construct validity are central to the methodology of testing.

The complexities of determining construct validity can lead to an unhealthy concentration on this aspect of carrying out a research project. For many studies there is an intuitive reasonableness to assertions that a certain approach provides an appropriate measure. Any one way of measuring or gathering data is likely to have its shortcomings, which suggests the use of multiple methods of data collection. One could use all three of the approaches to assessing educational achievement discussed above (achievement tests, teachers' ratings and 'certificate counting') rather than relying on any one measure. This is one form of triangulation – see Chapter 7, p. 171. Similar patterns of findings from very different methods of gathering data increase confidence in the validity of the findings. Discrepancies between them can be revealing in their own right. It is important to realize, however, that multiple methods do not constitute a panacea for all methodological ills. They raise their own theoretical problems; and they may in many cases be so resource-hungry as to be impracticable (see Chapter 15, p. 383).

Let us say that we have jumped the preceding hurdle and have demonstrated satisfactorily that we have a valid measure of educational achievement. However, a finding that achievement increases after the introduction of the tests does not necessarily mean that it increased because of the tests. This gets us back to the consideration of causation which occupied us in Chapter 2 (see p. 32).

What we would like to do is to find out whether the treatment (introduction of the tests) actually caused the outcome (the increase in achievement). If a study can plausibly demonstrate this causal relationship between treatment and outcome, it is referred to as having *internal validity*. This term was introduced by Campbell and Stanley (1963), who provided an influential and widely used analysis of possible 'threats' to internal validity.

These threats are other things that might happen which confuse the issue and make us mistakenly conclude that the treatment caused the outcome (or obscure possible relationships between them). Suppose, for example, that the teachers of the primary school children involved in the study are an industrial dispute with their employers at the same time that testing is introduced. One might well find, in those circumstances, a decrease in achievement related to the disaffection and disruption caused by the dispute, which might be mistakenly ascribed to the introduction of tests per se. This particular threat is labelled as 'history' by Campbell and Stanley – something which happens at the same time as the treatment. There is the complicating factor here that a case might be made for negative effects on teaching being an integral part of the introduction of formal testing into a child-centred primary school culture, i.e. that they are part of the treatment rather than an extraneous factor. However, for simplicity's sake, let's say that the industrial dispute was an entirely separate matter.

Campbell and Stanley (1963) suggested eight possible threats to internal validity which might be posed by other extraneous variables. Cook and Campbell (1979) have developed and extended this analysis, adding a further four threats. All 12 are listed in Box 6.1 (Onwuegbuzie and McLean, 2003, expand this list to 22 threats at the research design and data collection stage, with additional threats present at the data analysis and interpretation stages). The labels used for the threats are not to be interpreted too literally – mortality doesn't necessarily refer to the

BOX 6.1

Threats to internal validity

1. *History.* Things that have changed in the participants' environments other than those forming a direct part of the enquiry (e.g. occurrence of major air disaster during study of effectiveness of desensitization programme on persons with fear of air travel).
2. *Testing.* Changes occurring as a result of practice and experience gained by participants on any pre-tests (e.g. asking opinions about factory farming of animals before some intervention may lead respondents to think about the issues and develop more negative attitudes).
3. *Instrumentation.* Some aspect(s) of the way participants were measured changed between pre-test and post-test (e.g. raters in observational study using a wider or narrower definition of a particular behaviour as they become more familiar with the situation).
4. *Regression.* If participants are chosen because they are unusual or atypical (e.g. high scorers), later testing will tend to give less unusual scores ('regression to the mean'); e.g. an intervention programme with pupils with learning difficulties where ten highest-scoring pupils in a special unit are matched with ten of the lowest-scoring pupils in a mainstream school – regression effects will tend to show the former performing relatively worse on a subsequent test; see further details on p. 130.
5. *Mortality.* Participants dropping out of the study (e.g. in a study of an adult literacy programme – selective drop-out of those who are making little progress).
6. *Maturation.* Growth, change or development in participants unrelated to the treatment in the enquiry (e.g. evaluating extended athletics training programme with teenagers – intervening changes in height, weight and general maturity).
7. *Selection.* Initial differences between groups prior to involvement in the enquiry (e.g. through use of arbitrary non-random rule to produce two groups: ensures they differ in one respect which may correlate with others).
8. *Selection by maturation interaction.* Predisposition of groups to grow apart (or together if initially different); e.g. use of groups of boys and girls initially matched on physical strength in a study of a fitness programme.
9. *Ambiguity about causal direction.* Does A cause B, or B cause A? (e.g. in any correlational study, unless it is known that A precedes B, or vice versa – or some other logical analysis is possible).
10. *Diffusion of treatments.* When one group learns information or otherwise inadvertently receives aspects of a treatment intended only for a second group (e.g. in a quasi-experimental study of two classes in the same school).
11. *Compensatory equalization of treatments.* If one group receives 'special' treatment there will be organizational and other pressures for a control group to receive it (e.g. nurses in a hospital study may improve the treatment of a control group on grounds of fairness).
12. *Compensatory rivalry.* As above but an effect on the participants themselves (referred to as the 'John Henry' effect after the steel worker who killed himself through over-exertion to prove his superiority to the new steam drill); (e.g. when a group in an organization sees itself under threat from a planned change in another part of the organization and improves performance).

(After Cook and Campbell, 1979, pp. 51–5)

death of a participant during the study (though it might). Not all threats are present for all designs. For example, the 'testing' threat is only there if a pre-test is given, and in some cases, its likelihood, or perhaps evidence that you had gained from pilot work that a 'testing' effect was present, would cause you to avoid a design involving this feature.

In general design terms, there are two strategies to deal with these threats. If you know what the threat is, you can take specific steps to deal with it. For example, the use of comparison groups who have the treatment at different times or places will help to neutralize the 'history' threat. This approach of designing to deal with specific threats calls for a lot of forethought and is helped by knowledge and experience of the situation that you are dealing with. However, you can only hope to deal with a fairly small number of pre-defined and articulated threats in this way. In flexible design research it is feasible to address such threats to validity after the research has begun, as discussed in the following chapter.

The alternative strategy, central to the design philosophy of true experiments as developed by Fisher (1935, 1960), is to use randomization, which helps offset the effect of a myriad of unforeseen factors.

While true experiments are therefore effective at dealing with these threats, they are by no means totally immune to them. The threats have to be taken very seriously with quasi-experimental designs, and non-experimental fixed designs, and a study of the plausibility of the existence of various threats provides a very useful tool in interpretation. The interpretability of designs in the face of these threats depends not only on the design itself but also on the specific pattern of results obtained.

If you rule out these threats, you have established internal validity. You will have shown (or, more strictly, demonstrated the plausibility) that a particular treatment caused a certain outcome. Note, however, that while an experiment can be effective in doing this, it tells you nothing about the actual mechanisms by which it did so, except in so far as you have anticipated possible alternative mechanisms and controlled for them in your design. This can be the benefit of a multiple strategy design approach because it can enable you to get the what and the why. As Shadish, Cook and Campbell (2002) put it:

> The unique strength of experimentation is in describing the consequences attributable to deliberately varying a treatment. We call this *causal description*. In contrast, experiments do less well in clarifying the mechanisms through which and the conditions under which that causal relationship holds – what we call causal explanation (p. 9, emphasis in original).

This limitation of experiments is central to Pawson and Tilley's (1997) critique of randomized controlled trials (RCTs) discussed later in the chapter (p. 117).

It is important to appreciate that 'validity threats are made implausible by *evidence*, not methods; methods are only a way of getting evidence that can help you rule out these threats (Irwin, 2008)' (Maxwell, 2013, p. 121, emphasis in original). The view that methods themselves can guarantee validity is characteristic of the discredited positivist approach and is itself untenable. Whatever method is adopted there is no such guarantee. The realist assumption is that all methods are fallible: 'a realist conception of validity . . . sees the validity of an account as inherent, not in the procedures used to produce and validate it, but in its relationship to those things that it is intended to be an account of' (Maxwell, 1992, p. 281, emphasis in original). See also House (1991).

The whole 'threat' approach sits well with a realist analysis, which is not surprising as Campbell was an avowed realist. See, however, House, Mathison and McTaggart, 1989, which makes a case for his approach, particularly in Cook and Campbell (1979), as being essentially eclectic, taking aspects from a whole range of theoretical positions.

These threats tend to be only discussed in relation to experimental and quasi-experimental designs. However, validity is an important issue for all types of fixed designs and Onwuegbuzie and McLean (2003) have expanded Campbell and Stanley's framework for use with non-experimental fixed designs.

Generalizability

Sometimes one is interested in a specific finding in its own right. You may have shown, say, that a new group workshop approach leads, via a mechanism of increases in self-esteem, to subsequent maintained weight loss in obese teenagers at a residential unit. This may be the main thing that you are after if you are only concerned with whether or not the approach works with that specific group of individuals at the unit.

If, however, you are interested in what would happen with other client groups or in other settings, or with these teenagers when they return home, then you need to concern yourself with the *generalizability* of the study. Campbell and Stanley (1963) used the alternative term *external validity*. Both this and generalizability are in common use. Internal and external validity tend to be inversely related in the sense that the various controls imposed in order to bolster internal validity often fight against generalizability. In particular, the fact that the laboratory is the controlled environment *par excellence* makes results obtained there very difficult to generalize to any settings other than close approximations to laboratory conditions. This aspect is sometimes referred to in terms of a lack of *ecological validity*, i.e. when findings from research lack relevance to real world situations.

If your teenagers are a representative sample from a known population, then the generalization to that population can be done according to rules of statistical inference (note, however, that experimenters rarely take this requirement seriously). Generalizability to other settings or to other client groups has to be done on other, non-statistical, bases. LeCompte and Goetz (1982) have provided a classification of threats to external validity similar to that given for internal validity, which is listed in Box 6.2.

BOX 6.2

Threats to generalizability (external validity)

1. *Selection.* Findings being specific to the group studied.
2. *Setting.* Findings being specific to, or dependent on, the particular context in which the study took place.
3. *History.* Specific and unique historical experiences may determine or affect the findings.
4. *Construct effects.* The particular constructs studied may be specific to the group studied.

(After LeCompte and Goetz, 1982)

There are two general strategies for showing that these potential threats are discountable: direct demonstration and making a case. Direct demonstration involves you, or someone else who wishes to apply or extend your results, carrying out a further study involving some other type of participant, or in a different setting, etc. Making a case is more concerned with persuading that it is reasonable for the results to generalize, with arguments that the group studied, or setting, or period is representative (i.e. it shares certain essential characteristics with other groups, settings or periods and hence that the same mechanism is likely to apply in those also). This sorting out of the wheat of what is central to your findings from the chaff of specific irrelevancies can be otherwise expressed as having a theory or conceptual framework to explain what is going on.

Such a theory or conceptual framework may be expressed in formal and explicit terms by the presenter of the findings as discussed in Chapter 3 (p. 68). A study may be repeated with a different target group or in a deliberately different setting to assess the generalizability of its findings. There is a strong case, particularly with important or controversial findings, for attempting a replication of the original study. While in practice no replication is ever exact, an attempt to repeat the study as closely as possible which reproduces the main findings of the first study is the practical test of the reliability of your findings. Whether it is worthwhile to devote scarce resources to replication depends on circumstances. Replication is nowhere near as common as it should be in social research. In consequence, we may well be seeking to build on very shaky foundations. The argument is sometimes put that as validity depends on reliability then we should simply worry about the validity; if we can show that validity is acceptable then, necessarily, so is reliability. The problem here is that it becomes more difficult to disentangle what lies behind poor validity. It might have been that the findings were not reliable in the first place. Accurate replication also depends upon a full and clear explanation of the methodology in the report of the original study.

It is easy to guarantee unreliability. Carelessness, casualness and lack of commitment on the part of the researcher help, as does a corresponding lack of involvement by participants. Reliability is essentially a quality control issue. Punctilious attention to detail, perseverance and pride in doing a good job are all very important, but organization is the key.

While validity and generalizability are probably the central elements in establishing the value and trustworthiness of a fixed design enquiry, there are other aspects to which attention should be given. They include, in particular, objectivity and credibility.

Objectivity

The traditional, scientific approach to the problem of establishing objectivity is exemplified by the experimental approach. The solution here is seen to be to distance the experimenter from the experimental participant, so that any interaction that takes place between the two is formalized – indeed, some experimenters go so far as not only to have a standardized verbatim script but even to have it delivered via a tape-recorder.

To some, this artificiality is lethal for any real understanding of phenomena involving people in social settings. An alternative is to erect an objective/subjective contrast. 'Objective' is taken to refer to what multiple observers agree to as a phenomenon, in contrast to the subjective experience of the single individual. In other words, the criterion for objectivity is intersubjective agreement. This stance tends to go along with an involved rather than a detached investigator, and notions of *triangulation* (see Chapter 7, p. 171) where the various accounts of participants with different roles in the situation are obtained by investigators who, by combining them with their own perceptions and understandings, reach an agreed and negotiated account.

Formulated in terms of threats, objectivity can be seen to be at risk from a methodology where the values, interests and prejudices of the enquirer distort the response (experiment being for some the answer, and for others an extreme version of the problem). Relying exclusively on data from a single individual can similarly threaten objectivity. And again, a project carried out for an ideological purpose other than that of research itself clearly threatens objectivity.

Credibility

Shipman (1997) has suggested that we should go beyond the traditional concerns for reliability, validity and generalizability when considering the trustworthiness of research and also ask whether there is sufficient detail on the way the evidence is produced for the credibility of the research to be assessed. We cannot satisfy ourselves about the other concerns unless the researcher provides detailed information on the methods used and the justification for their use. This is a responsibility which has always been accepted by those using experimentation. The report of an experiment in a journal article carries an explicit requirement that sufficient detail must be given about procedures, equipment, etc. for the reader to be able to carry out an exact replication of the study.

This kind of requirement may be rejected as scientistic by some practitioners using flexible designs, relying largely on qualitative data. However, it could be argued that there is a strong case for such research calling for an even greater emphasis on explaining the methods used and the warrant for the conclusions reached, because of the lack of codification of the methods of data collection or of approaches to analysis. This need is increasingly recognized in the design of qualitative research (e.g. Marshall and Rossman, 2011). However, there is considerable debate about the applicability of concepts such as reliability and validity, and the possibility and appropriateness of objectivity, when assessing the trustworthiness of flexible qualitative research. The following chapter pays considerable attention to this issue.

Experimental fixed designs

> If, following your reading of the previous chapter, it appears possible that an experimental fixed design may be appropriate for your project and its research questions, then perusal of this section should help in choosing a specific experimental design. However, before confirming that choice, it will be necessary to read the chapters in Part III of this book to help select appropriate methods of collecting data, and Chapter 17 to establish how you will analyse the data after it has been collected.

To 'experiment', or to 'carry out an experiment', can mean many things. In very general terms, to be experimental is simply to be concerned with trying new things – and seeing what happens, what the reception is. Think of 'experimental' theatre, or an 'experimental' car, or an 'experimental' introduction of a mini-roundabout at a road junction. There is a change in something, and a concern for the effects that this change might have on something else.

However, when experimentation is contrasted with the other research designs, a stricter definition is employed, usually involving the control and active manipulation of variables by the experimenter.

Experimentation is a research strategy involving:

- the assignment of participants to different conditions;
- manipulation of one or more variables (called *independent variables (IVs)*) by the experimenter;
- the measurement of the effects of this manipulation on one or more other variables (called *dependent variables (DVs)*); and
- the control of all other variables.

Note the use of the term *variable*. This is widespread within the experimental strategy and simply denotes something which can vary. However, it carries within it the notion that there are certain specific aspects which can be isolated and which retain the same meaning throughout the study.

The experimental strategy is a prime example of a fixed research design. You need to know exactly what you are going to do before you do it. It is a precise tool that can only map a very restricted range. A great deal of preparatory work is needed (either by you or someone else) if it is going to be useful. An experiment is an extremely focused study. You can only handle a very few variables, often only a single independent variable and a single dependent variable. These variables have to be selected with extreme care. You need to have a well-developed theory or conceptual framework. The major problem in doing experiments in the real world is that you often only have, at best, a pretty shaky and undeveloped theory; you don't know enough about the thing you are studying for this selectivity of focus to be a sensible strategy. This need to know what you are doing before you do it is a general characteristic of fixed research designs, but experiments are most demanding in this respect because of their extreme selectivity. And you are sacrificing a great deal of control when carrying out experiments in real world *field research* outside the laboratory.

Laboratory experiments

Real world research seeks to address social problems and issues of current concern and to find ways of addressing such problems. Experiments typically take place in special places known as laboratories. In principle, just as certain kinds of academic research can be carried out in real world settings, which anthropologists and other social scientists refer to as 'field' settings, so research with a real world problem-solving focus might be carried out in a laboratory.

However, the necessary artificiality of laboratories can limit their value. Aronson, Brewer and Carlsmith (1985) have distinguished two senses in which laboratory experimentation may lack realism (incidentally, nothing to do with realist philosophy). One is *experimental realism*. In this sense an experiment is realistic if the situation which it presents to the participant is realistic, if it really involves the participants (then referred to as 'subjects'), and has impact upon them. In the well-known Asch (1956) experiment on conformity, subjects made what seemed to them to be straightforward judgements about the relative length of lines. These judgements were contradicted by others in the room whom they took also to be subjects in the experiment. This study showed experimental realism in the sense that subjects were undergoing an experience which caused them to show strong signs of tension and anxiety. They appeared to be reacting to the situation in the same realistic kind of way that they would outside the laboratory.

However, it might be argued that the Asch study lacks what Aronson *et al.* term *mundane realism* (see also Aronson, Wilson & Akert, 2007). That is, the subjects were encountering events in the laboratory setting which were very unlikely to occur in the real world. Asch, following a common strategy in laboratory experimentation, had set up a very clearly and simply structured situation to observe the effects of group pressure on individuals. The real life counterpart, if one could be found, would be more complex and ambiguous, and in all probability would result in findings which were less conclusive. (The ethics of Asch's study are a different matter – see Chapter 10.)

Notwithstanding worries about the realism of laboratory-based studies, they remain popular with researchers, including those with real world concerns. After a review of the two approaches, Levitt and List (2006) conclude that 'the sharp dichotomy sometimes drawn between lab experiments and data generated in natural settings is a false one. Each approach has strengths and weaknesses, and a combination of the two is likely to provide deeper insights than either in isolation' (p. i).

Bias in experiments

Simplification of the situation, which is central to the experimental approach, may lead to clear results, but it does not protect against bias in them. The effects of two types of bias have been investigated in some detail. These are the *demand characteristics* of the experimental situation, and experimenter *expectancy effects*. In a very general sense, these are the consequences of the participants and the experimenters being human beings.

Bias due to demand characteristics occurs because participants know that they are in an experimental situation, know that they are being observed, know that certain things are expected or demanded of them (Orne, 1962; Robinson, Kersbergen, Brunstromb & Field, 2014). Hence the way in which they respond is some complex amalgam of the experimental manipulation and their interpretation of what effect the manipulation is supposed to have on them. Their action based on that interpretation is likely to be cooperative but could well be obstructive. Even in situations where participants are explicitly told that there are no right or wrong answers, that one response is as valued as another, participants are likely to feel that certain responses show themselves in a better light than others. There is evidence that persons who volunteer for experiments are more sensitive to these effects than those who are required to be involved (Rosenthal & Rosnow, 1975; Rosnow, 1993). However, Berkowitz and Troccoli (1986) are not persuaded of the widespread existence of biasing effects from demand characteristics. Certainly, there appears to be little research evidence on their effects in non-laboratory settings (McCambridge, de Bruin & Witton, 2012).

The classic ploy to counteract this type of bias is deception by the experimenter. Participants are told that the experiment is about X when it is really about Y. X is made to appear plausible and is such that if the participants modify their responses in line with, or antagonistically to, what the experimenter appears to be after, there is no systematic effect on the experimenter's real area of interest. As discussed in Chapter 10 (p. 216) increasing sensitivity to the ethical issues raised by deceiving participants means that this ploy, previously common in some areas of social psychology, is now looked on with increasing suspicion.

Experimenter expectancy effects are reactive effects produced by the experimenters who have been shown, in a wide variety of studies, to bias findings (usually unwittingly) to provide support for the experimental hypothesis. Rosenthal and Rubin (1980) discuss the first 345 such studies! The effects can be minimized by decreasing the amount of interaction between participant and experimenter; e.g. by using taped instructions or automated presentation of materials. However, for many topics (apart from studies in areas such as human–computer interaction) this further attenuates any real world links that the laboratory experiment might possess. *Double-blind procedures* can also be used, where data collection is subcontracted so that neither the person working directly with the participants, nor the participants themselves, are aware of the hypothesis being tested.

Knowledge about determinants of laboratory behaviour (demand characteristics, etc.) can be of value in real life settings. For example, police identity parades can be thought of as experiments, and suggestions for improving them have been based on this knowledge and on general principles of experimental design (Wells *et al.*, 1998).

Experiments in natural settings

The laboratory is essentially a place for maximizing control over extraneous variables. Move outside the laboratory door and such tight and comprehensive control becomes impossible. The problems of experimentation discussed in the previous section remain. Any special conditions marking out what is happening as 'an experiment' can lead to reactive effects. The classic demonstration of such effects comes from the well-known series of experiments carried out at the Hawthorne works of the Western Electric Company in the USA in the 1920s and 1930s (Dickson & Roethlisberger, 2003), and hence called the *Hawthorne effect*. Their studies investigating changes in length of working day, heating, lighting and other variables, found increases in productivity during the study which were virtually irrespective of the specific changes. The workers were in effect reacting positively to the attention and special treatment given by the experimenters. Re-evaluations of the original study have cast serious doubt on the existence of the effect (Kompier, 2006) and the interpretation of the original study (Wickström & Bendix, 2000; Levitt & List, 2009). However, new, more strictly controlled, studies have demonstrated the existence of (relatively small) Hawthorne effects (McCarney *et al.*, 2007; Verstappen *et al.*, 2004).

Problems in carrying out experiments in natural settings are listed in Box 6.3. There are gains, of course. Notwithstanding some degree of artificiality, and related reactivity, generalizability to the 'real world' is almost self-evidently easier to achieve when the study takes place outside the laboratory in a setting which is almost real 'real life'. Note, however, that there are claims of good generalization of some findings from laboratory to field settings (Locke, 1986). Other advantages are covered in Box 6.4.

Experimental designs as such are equally applicable both inside and outside laboratories. The crucial feature of so-called 'true' experiments (distinguishing them from 'quasi-experiments' discussed below) is *random allocation of participants to experimental conditions*. If you can find a feasible and ethical means of doing this when planning a field experiment, then you should seriously consider carrying out a true experiment.

The advantage of random allocation or assignment is that it allows you to proceed on the assumption that you have equivalent groups under the two (or more) experimental conditions. This is a probabilistic truth, which allows you, among other things, to employ a wide battery of statistical tests of inference legitimately. It does not guarantee that in any particular experiment

BOX 6.3

Problems in carrying out experiments in natural settings

Moving outside the safe confines of the laboratory may well be traumatic. Particular practical difficulties include:

1. *Random assignment.* There are practical and ethical problems of achieving random assignment to different experimental treatments or conditions (e.g. in withholding the treatment from a no-treatment control group). Random assignment is also often only feasible in atypical circumstances or with selected respondents, leading to questionable generalizability. Faulty randomization procedures are not uncommon (e.g. when procedures are subverted through ignorance, kindness, etc.). For small samples of the units being randomly assigned, sampling variability is a problem. Treatment-related refusal to participate or continue can bias sampling.
2. *Validity.* The actual treatment may be an imperfect realization of the variable(s) of interest, or a restricted range of outcomes may be insensitively or imperfectly measured, resulting in questionable validity. A supposed no-treatment control group may receive some form of compensatory treatment, or be otherwise influenced (e.g. through deprivation effects).
3. *Ethical issues.* There are grey areas in relation to restricting the involvement to volunteers, the need for informed consent and the debriefing of participants after the experiment. Strict adherence to ethical guidelines is advocated, but this may lead to losing some of the advantages of moving outside the laboratory (e.g. leading to unnecessary 'obtrusiveness', and hence reactivity, of the treatment). Common sense is needed. If you are studying a natural experiment where some innovation would have taken place whether or not you were involved, then it may simply be the ethical considerations relating to the innovation which apply (fluoridation of water supplies raises more ethical implications for users than an altered design of a road junction). See Chapter 9 for further discussion.
4. *Control.* Lack of control over extraneous variables may mask the effects of treatment variables, or bias their assessment. Interaction between participants may vitiate random assignment and violate their assumed independence.

the two groups will in fact be equivalent. No such guarantee is ever possible, although the greater the number of persons being allocated, the more confidence you can have that the groups do not differ widely.

An alternative way of expressing this advantage is to say that randomization gets rid (probabilistically at least) of the selection threat to internal validity (see Box 6.1, p. 108). That is, it provides a defence against the possibility that any change in a dependent variable is caused not by the independent variable but by differences in the characteristics of the two groups. Other potential threats to internal validity remain and the discussion of some of the designs that follows is largely couched in terms of their adequacy, or otherwise, in dealing with these threats.

BOX 6.4

Advantages in carrying out experiments in natural settings

Compared to a laboratory, natural settings have several advantages:

1. *Generalizability*. The laboratory is necessarily and deliberately an artificial setting where the degree of control and isolation sets it apart from real life. If we are concerned with generalizing results to the real world, the task is easier if experimentation is in a natural setting. Much laboratory experimentation is based on student participants, making generalization to the wider population hazardous. Although this is not a necessary feature of laboratory work, there is less temptation to stick to student groups when experiments take place in natural settings.
2. *Validity*. The demand characteristics of laboratory experiments, where participants tend to do what they think you want them to do, are heightened by the artificiality and isolation of the laboratory situation. Real tasks in a real world setting are less prone to this kind of game playing. So you are more likely to be measuring what you think you are measuring.
3. *Participant availability*. It is no easy task to get non-student participants to come into the laboratory (although the development of pools of volunteers is valuable). You have to rely on them turning up. Although it depends on the type of study, many real life experiments in natural settings have participants in abundance, limited only by your energy and staying power – and possibly your charm.

Randomized controlled trials and the 'gold standard'

A randomized controlled trial (RCT) is a type of experiment where participants are randomly allocated, either to a group who receive some form of intervention or treatment, or to a control group who don't. Use of RCTs is a central feature of the evidence-based movement currently highly influential in many fields of social research. Proponents argue that it is the 'gold standard' – the scientific method of choice, primarily because they consider it to be the best means of assessing whether or not the intervention is effective.

There is a growing tendency in some circles to equate the doing of science with the carrying out of RCTs. For example, the US Department of Education's Institute of Education Sciences in 2003 made it clear that it would privilege applications for funding of applied research and evaluation which used RCTs (with a grudging acceptance of other experimental approaches when RCTs were not feasible) in the interests of using 'rigorous scientifically based research methods'. This has sparked a heated debate among applied social researchers on 'what counts as credible evidence in applied research and evaluation practice' (Donaldson, Christie & Mark, 2009).

Privileging RCTs in this way is a serious distortion of the nature of scientific activity. It is historically inaccurate and carries with it an inappropriately narrow view of what constitutes evidence. A review of practices in the natural sciences reveals the minor role played by RCTs. Phillips (2005) concludes that:

> One cannot help but be struck by the huge range of activities engaged in by researchers in the natural sciences, and the variety of types of evidence that have been appealed to: establishing what causal factors are operating in a given situation; distinguishing genuine from spurious effects; determining function; determining structure; careful description and delineation of phenomena; accurate measurement; development and testing of theories, hypotheses, and causal models; elucidation of the mechanisms that link cause with effect; testing of received wisdom; elucidating unexpected phenomena; production of practically important techniques and artefacts (p. 593).

He gives a wide range of illustrative examples. In his view, any attempt to give a simple, single account of the nature of science appears quite arbitrary. Relying on RCTs, or any other specific methodology, as the criterion of scientific rigour 'detracts from the main question at hand when one is assessing an inquiry, which is this: *Has the overall case made by the investigator been established to a degree that warrants tentative acceptance of the theoretical or empirical claims that were made?*' (original emphasis). RCTs, and other designs which make use of treatment and control groups, can also raise difficult ethical issues (see Chapter 10, p. 210).

While the methodology used in a particular study is an important consideration it is the convincingness of the argument that matters; how well the evidence is woven into the structure of the argument; how rigorously this evidence was gathered; and how well counter-arguments and counter-claims are themselves countered or confronted with recalcitrant facts or data.

The message here is not that RCTs should be avoided – they have an important role and many practising real world researchers will be expected to be able to carry them out competently. However, they are by no means the only show in town.

The website provides further discussion on the issues involved in social experimentation and the use of RCTs.

Realist critique of RCTs

Pawson and Tilley (1997, especially Chapter 2) elaborate the view that the methodology of the RCT is inappropriate for dealing with complex social issues. They consider that, as well as generating inconsistent findings, the concentration on outcomes does little or nothing to explain why an intervention has failed (or, in relatively rare cases, succeeded). Hence, there is not the cumulation of findings which would help to build up understanding.

Experimentalists acknowledge the practical and ethical problems of achieving randomization of allocation to experimental and control groups in applied field experiments. Pawson and Tilley add causal problems to these perils. Allocation of participants to experimental or control groups by the experimenter removes that choice from the participants but '*choice is the very condition of social and individual change and not some sort of practical hindrance to understanding that change*' (Pawson and Tilley, 1997, p. 36; emphasis in original).

In their discussion of correctional programmes for prison inmates, Pawson and Tilley make the undeniable point that it is not the programmes themselves which work, but people cooperating and choosing to make them work. The traditional solution to this problem is to run volunteer-only experiments. Volunteers are called for, then assigned randomly to one of the two groups. The assumption is that motivation and cooperation will be the same in each of the groups. The reasonableness of this assumption will depend on the specific circumstances of the experiment. You can undermine goodwill and participant engagement by not including them in an intervention group. Pawson and Tilley illustrate, through an example of what they consider to be high-quality experimental evaluation research (Porperino and Robinson, 1995), the way in which participants' choice-making capacity cuts across and undermines a volunteer/non-volunteer distinction:

> The act of volunteering merely marks a moment in a whole evolving pattern of choice. Potential subjects will consider a program (or not), volunteer for it (or not), co-operate closely (or not), stay the course (or not), learn lessons (or not), retain the lessons (or not), apply the lessons (or not). Each one of these decisions will be internally complex and take its meaning according to the chooser's circumstances. Thus the act of volunteering for a program such as 'Cog Skills' might represent an interest in rehabilitation, a desire for improvement in thinking skills, an opportunity for a good skive, a respite from the terror or boredom of the wings, an opening to display a talent in those reputedly hilarious role-plays, a chance to ogle a glamorous trainer, a way of playing the system to fast-track for early parole, and so on (p. 38).

They back up this intuitive understanding of how prisoners find their way on to programmes by a detailed re-analysis of the findings. Their overall conclusion is that such volunteer-only experiments encourage us to make a pronouncement on whether a programme works without knowledge of the make-up of the volunteers. The crucial point is the 'programs tend to work for some groups more than others, but the methodology then directs attention away from an investigation of these characteristics and towards . . . the battle to maintain the equivalence of the two subsets of this self-selected group' (p. 40).

However, the messages that come from RCTs are undoubtedly invested with considerable value by many audiences. As we appear to be approaching a situation where governments and other decision-making bodies claim that they are more receptive to evidence from research findings (perhaps more their rhetoric than reality), why not use RCTs? Unfortunately, the track record for RCTs in social research is very poor. Even Oakley (2000) in arguing for their use accepts the continuing equivocal nature of their findings, while putting some proposals forward for improving them. We are in danger of repeating the cycle of enthusiasm–disillusion found by educational experimenters in the 1920s and 1930s and evaluation research in the US in the 1960s and 1970s.

A possible way forward is via the realist mantra of establishing 'what works, for whom, and in which contexts', rather than looking for overall effects of social programmes, interventions, etc. By establishing the likely operative mechanisms for different groups or types of participants in particular situations and settings, it becomes feasible to set up circumstances where large effects are obtained. In other words, the experiment is retained as the tool for obtaining quantitative confirmation of something that we already know to exist (or have a strong intuition or hunch as to its existence).

How is this actually done? Pawson and Tilley (1997), discussing these matters largely in the context of large-scale evaluative research, advocate the use of subgroup analysis. With large numbers of participants, it becomes feasible to set up contrasts between subgroups illustrating and substantiating the differential effects of mechanisms on different subgroups. For small-scale studies, and in real world settings where relevant previous work may be sparse or non-existent, there is much to be said for a multi-strategy design with an initial flexible design stage primarily exploratory in purpose. This seeks to establish, both from discussions with professionals, participants and others involved in the initial phase, and from the empirical data gathered, likely 'bankers' for mechanisms operating in the situation, contexts where they are likely to operate, and the characteristics of participants best targeted. A second fixed design phase then incorporates a highly focused experiment or other fixed design study. An RCT may be the design of choice for this second phase if:

- the sponsor of the research, and/or important decision-makers consider the evidence from an RCT to be required (either for their own purposes or to help in making a case to others); *and*
- the establishment of randomized experimental and control groups is feasible practically and ethically; *and*
- it appears unlikely that there will be differential effects on the experimental or control groups unconnected to the intervention itself (e.g. persons within the control group become disaffected or disgruntled because of their non-selection for the experimental group).

Note that the subgroup for whom a particular mechanism is considered to be likely to be operative (as established in the initial phase) should form the basis for the pool of volunteers from whom the experimental and control groups are randomly formed. Where feasible, similar restrictions can be placed on the contexts so that they are equivalent for the two groups.

If one or other of the three circumstances listed above does not obtain, then other designs can be considered. If randomization can be achieved then a true experiment involving two or more comparison groups (rather than an experimental and control group) has attractions. For example, when the initial work indicates different contexts or settings where a particular enabling mechanism is likely to operate in one context but not in the second or a disabling mechanism operates in the second. This avoids problems in establishing 'non-intervention' control groups.

Where there are problems, of whatever kind, in achieving randomization, quasi-experimental designs remain feasible. A control group design might be used, with efforts being made to ensure as far as possible that the experimental and control groups are closely equivalent (particularly in aspects identified during the initial phase as being of relevance to the operation of the mechanisms involved; e.g. by using selected participants for the two groups for whom a particular mechanism appears salient).

Quasi-experimental designs (see p. 126) can be used in situations where a mechanism is considered to be likely to be operative with one set or subgroup of participants but not with a second subgroup. Or where an additional disabling mechanism is thought to be operative in the second subgroup. The initial exploratory phase is used not only to build up a picture of the likely enabling and disabling mechanisms, but also to find a way of typifying or categorizing the best ways in which participants might be grouped to illustrate the operation of these mechanisms. Randomized allocation of participants is, of course, not possible when a comparison between different subgroups is being made.

Single-case designs (p. 134) lend themselves well to a realist reconceptualization. The strategy of thoroughly analysing and understanding the situation so that reliable and reproducible effects can be achieved bears a striking resemblance to the methodology developed by the experimental psychologist B. F. Skinner (Sidman, 1960), even though the terminology and underlying philosophy are very different. Similarly the various non-experimental fixed designs can be viewed through realist eyes. In particular, they lend themselves to the type of subgroup analyses advocated by Pawson and Tilley (1997).

The designs discussed in the following sections of this chapter can be looked at using the realist perspective considered here. While they bear more than a passing resemblance to traditional positivist-based experimental and non-experimental designs (and can be used in this traditional manner by those who have not yet seen the realist light), there are major hidden differences. As discussed above, the participants involved in the different groups, the situations, circumstances and contexts and the aspects of an intervention or programme that are targeted, are all carefully selected and refined in the interests of obtaining substantial clear differential effects. This is simply a rephrasing of the injunction that fixed designs are theory-driven which opened this chapter. By an initial exploratory phase where hunches and hypotheses about the likely mechanisms and contexts and those participants for whom the mechanisms will operate (or by some other means such as modelling your approach on earlier work; or by yourself having an intimate experience of the working of a programme or intervention; or talking to those who have that experience and understanding), you set up a highly focused study. It is worth noting that this is the common approach taken in the natural sciences. The actual experiment to test a theory is the culmination of much prior thought and exploration, hidden in the textbook rationalizations of the scientific method and the conventions of experimental report writing.

A successful experiment with clear differential outcomes is supporting evidence for the causal mechanisms we proposed when designing the study and a contribution to understanding where, how and with whom they operate.

True experiments

A small number of simple designs are presented here. Texts on experimental design give a range of alternatives, and of more complex designs (e.g. Maxwell & Delaney, 2003; Shadish *et al.*, 2002).

> *Often those involved in real world experimentation restrict themselves to the very simplest designs, commonly the 'two group' design given below. However, the main hurdle in carrying out true experiments outside the laboratory is in achieving the principle of random allocation, and once this is achieved there may be merit in considering a somewhat more complex design.*

Box 6.5 provides an overview of the some commonly used true experimental designs.

BOX 6.5

Overview of simple true experimental designs

Note: The defining characteristic of a true experimental design is random allocation of participants to the two (or more) groups of the design.

1. *Two group designs*
   (a) *Post-test-only randomized controlled trial (RCT).* Random allocation of participants to an experimental group (given the experimental 'treatment') and a 'no treatment' control group. Post-tests of the two groups compared.
   (b) *Post-test-only two treatment comparison.* Random allocation of participants to experimental group 1 (given experimental 'treatment' 1), or to experimental group 2 (given experimental 'treatment' 2). Post-tests of the two groups compared.
   (c) *Pre-test post-test randomized controlled trial.* Random allocation of participants to an experimental group (given the experimental 'treatment') and a 'no-treatment' control group. Pre-test to post-test changes of individuals in the two groups compared.
   (d) *Pre-test post-test two treatment comparison.* Random allocation of participants to experimental group 1 (given experimental 'treatment' 1), or to experimental group 2 (given experimental 'treatment' 2). Pre-test to post-test changes of individuals in the two groups compared.
2. *Three- (or more) group simple designs*
   It is possible to extend any of the above two group designs by including additional experimental groups (given different experimental 'treatments'). The RCTs retain a 'no treatment' control group.
3. *Factorial designs*
   Two (or more) independent variables (IVs) involved (e.g. 'type of music' and 'number of decibels'). Each IV studied at two (or more) 'levels'. Random allocation of participants to groups covering all possible combinations of levels of the different IVs. Can be post-test only or pre-test post-test.
4. *Parametric designs*
   Several 'levels' of an IV covered with random allocation of participants to groups to get a view of the effect of the IV over a range of values. Can be post-test only or pre-test post-test.
5. *Matched pairs designs*
   Establishing pairs of participants with similar scores on a variable known to be related to the dependent variable (DV) of the experiment. Random allocation of members of pairs to different experimental groups (or to an experimental and control group). This approach can be used in several two group designs. Attractive, but can introduce complexities both in setting up and in interpretation.
6. *Repeated measures designs*
   Designs where the same participant is tested under two or more experimental treatments or conditions (or in both an experimental and control condition). Can be thought of as the extreme example of a matched pairs design.

Designs involving matching

In its simplest form, the *matched pairs design*, *matching* involves testing participants on some variable which is known to be related to the dependent variable on which observations are being collected in the experiment. The results of this test are then used to create 'matched pairs' of participants, that is, participants giving identical or very similar scores on the related variable.

Random assignment is then used to allocate one member of each pair to the treatment group and one to the comparison group. In this simplest form, the design can be considered as an extension of the simple two-group design, but with randomization being carried out on a pair basis rather than on a group basis. The principle can be easily extended to other designs, although of course if there are, say, four groups in the design then 'matched fours' have to be created and individuals randomly assigned from them to the four groups.

While the selection and choice of a good matching variable may pose difficult problems in a field experiment, it is an attractive strategy because it helps to reduce the problem of differences between individuals obscuring the effects of the treatment in which you are interested. Generally we need all the help we can get to detect treatment effects in the poorly controlled field situation, and matching can help without setting strong restrictions on important variables (which could have the effect of limiting the generalizability of your findings). To take a simple example, suppose that age is a variable known to be strongly related to the dependent variable in which you are interested. It would be possible to control for age as a variable by, say, only working with people between 25 and 30 years old. However, creating matched age pairs allows us to carry out a relatively sensitive test without the conclusions being restricted to a particular and narrow age range.

Designs involving repeated measures

The ultimate in matching is achieved when an individual's performance is compared under two or more conditions. Designs with this feature are known as *repeated measures designs*. We have come across this already in one sense in the 'before and after' design – although the emphasis there is not on the before and after scores per se, but on the relative difference between them in the treatment and comparison groups as a measure of the treatment effect.

The website discusses some methodological problems with designs using matching or repeated measures.

Choosing among true experimental designs

Box 6.6 gives suggestions for the conditions under which particular experimental designs might be used when working outside the laboratory. Cook and Campbell (1979) have discussed some of the real world situations which are conducive to carrying out randomized experiments. Box 6.7 is based on their suggestions.

BOX 6.6

Considerations in choosing among true experimental designs

1. *To do any form of true experimental design you need to be able to carry out random assignment to the different treatments.* This is normally random assignment of persons to treatments (or of persons to the order in which they receive different treatments, in repeated measures designs). Note, however, that the unit which is randomly assigned need not be the person; it could be a group (e.g. a school class), in which case the experiment, and its analysis, is on classes, not individuals.
2. *Use a matched design when:*
   (a) you have a matching variable which correlates highly with the dependent variable;
   (b) obtaining the scores on the matching variable is unlikely to influence the treatment effects; and
   (c) individual differences between participants are likely to mask treatment effects.
3. *Use a repeated measures design when:*
   (a) order effects appear unlikely;
   (b) the independent variable(s) of interest lend themselves to repeated measurement (participant variables such as sex, ethnic background or class don't – it is not easy to test the same person as a man and as a woman);
   (c) in real life, persons would be likely to be exposed to the different treatments; and
   (d) individual differences between participants are likely to mask treatment effects.
4. *Use a simple two-group design when:*
   (a) order effects are likely;
   (b) the independent variable(s) of interest don't lend themselves to repeated measurement;
   (c) in real life, persons would tend not to receive more than one treatment; and
   (d) persons might be expected to be sensitized by pre-testing or being tested on a matching variable.
5. *Use a before-after design when:*
   (a) pre-testing appears to be unlikely to influence the effect of the treatment;
   (b) there are concerns about whether random assignment has produced equivalent groups (e.g. when there are small numbers in the groups); and
   (c) individual differences between participants are likely to mask treatment effects.
6. *Use a factorial design when:*
   (a) you are interested in more than one independent variable; and
   (b) interactions between independent variables may be of concern.
7. *Use a parametric design when:*
   (a) the independent variable(s) have a range of values or levels of interest; and
   (b) you wish to investigate the form or nature of the relationship between independent variable and dependent variable.

BOX 6.7

Real life situations conducive to randomized experiments

1. *When lotteries are expected.* Lotteries are sometimes, though not commonly, regarded as a socially acceptable way of deciding who gets scarce resources. When done for essentially ethical reasons it provides a good opportunity to use this natural randomization for research purposes.

2. *When demand outstrips supply.* This sets up a situation where randomized allocation may be seen as a fair and equitable solution (however, using randomization to allocate places at oversubscribed schools in England has proved highly controversial). There are practical problems. Do you set up waiting lists? Or allow reapplication? Cook and Campbell (1979) advocate using the initial randomization to create two equivalent no-treatment groups, as well as the treatment group. One no-treatment group is told that their application is unsuccessful, and that they cannot reapply. This group acts as the control group. The second no-treatment group is permitted to go on a waiting list, they are accepted for the treatment if a vacancy occurs, but data from them are not used.

3. *When an innovation cannot be introduced in units simultaneously.* Many innovations have to be introduced gradually, because of resource or other limitations. This provides the opportunity for randomization of the order of involvement. Substantial ingenuity may be called for procedurally to balance service and research needs, particularly when opportunities for involvement arise irregularly.

4. *When experimental units are isolated from each other.* Such isolation could be temporal or spatial – or simply because it is known that they do not communicate. Randomization principles can then be used to determine where or when particular treatments are scheduled.

5. *When it is agreed that change should take place but there is no consensus about solutions.* In these situations decision-makers may be more susceptible to arguments in favour of a system of planned variation associated with random allocation.

6. *When a tie can be broken.* In situations where access to a particular treatment is based upon performance on a task (e.g. for entry to a degree or other course) there will be a borderline. It may be that several persons are on that border (given the less than perfect reliability of any such task, this is more accurately a border region than a line). Randomization can be used to select from those at the border who then form the treatment and no-treatment control groups.

7. *When persons express no preference among alternatives.* In situations where individuals indicate that they have no preference among alternative treatments, their random assignment to the alternatives is feasible. Note that you will be comparing the performance on the treatments of those without strong preferences, who may not be typical.

8. *When you are involved in setting up an organization, innovation, etc.* Many opportunities for randomization present themselves if you as researcher can get in on the early stages of a programme, organization or whatever. It would also help if guidelines for local and national initiatives were imbued with a research ethos, which would be likely to foster the use of randomization.

(after Cook and Campbell, 1979; pp. 371–86)

There are occasions when one starts out with a true experiment but along the way problems occur, perhaps in relation to assignment to conditions, or to mortality (loss of participants) from one or other group, or where you don't have the time or resources to carry out what you originally intended. Such situations may be rescuable by reconceptualizing what you are proposing as one of the quasi-experiments discussed below.

Quasi-experiments

The term *quasi-experiment* has been used in various ways, but its rise to prominence in social experimentation originates with a very influential chapter by Campbell and Stanley in Gage's *Handbook of Research on Teaching*. This was republished as a separate slim volume (Campbell and Stanley, 1963). For them, a quasi-experiment is '[a] research design involving an experimental approach but where random assignment to treatment and comparison groups has not been used'.

Campbell and Stanley's main contribution was to show the value and usefulness of several such designs. More generally, they have encouraged a flexible approach to design and interpretation, where the particular pattern of results and circumstances under which the study took place interact with the design to determine what inferences can be made. Their concern is very much with the threats to validity present in such studies (see Box 6.1), and with the extent to which particular threats can be plausibly discounted in particular studies. Quasi-experimental approaches have considerable attraction for those seeking to maintain a basic experimental stance in work outside the laboratory.

Quasi-experiments are often viewed as a second-best choice, a fall-back to consider when it is not possible to randomize allocation. Cook and Campbell (1979), however, prefer to stress the relative advantages and disadvantages of true and quasi-experiments, and are cautious about always advocating randomized experiments even when they are feasible. They recommend considering all possible design options without necessarily assuming the superiority of a randomized design – and with the proviso that if a randomized design is chosen then it should be planned in such a way as to be interpretable as a quasi-experimental design, just in case something goes wrong with the randomized design, as it may well do in the real world.

Box 6.8 provides an overview of the main types of quasi-experimental designs covered in the following section.

Quasi-experimental designs to avoid – the *pre-experiments*

Quasi-experimental designs are essentially defined negatively – they are not true experimental designs. They include several which are definitely to be avoided, although these so-called 'pre-experimental' designs (listed in Box 6.8) continue to get used, and even published. Details are presented here (in Boxes 6.9, 6.10 and 6.11) to enable you to recognize and avoid them, and also because the reasons why they are problematic present useful methodological points.

The 'pre-test post-test single-group' design is commonly found and it is important to stress that the deficiencies covered here concern its nature as an *experimental design* where you are trying decide whether the experimental treatment was responsible for the effects found. If the concern is simply to determine whether there is an increase of performance after a treatment, or

BOX 6.8

Overview of a range of quasi-experimental designs

Note: A quasi-experimental design follows the experimental approach to design but does not involve random allocation of participants to different groups. The following list outlines a few commonly used designs.

1. *Pre-experimental designs*
   (a) Single-group post-test-only.
   (b) Post-test only non-equivalent groups, i.e. use of groups established by some procedure other than randomization (e.g. two pre-existing groups).
   (c) Pre-test post-test single group design.
   These designs should be avoided owing to difficulties in interpreting their results (though they may be of value as part of a wider study, or as a pilot phase for later experimentation).

2. *Pre-test post-test non-equivalent group designs*
   Two (or more) groups established on some basis other than random assignment. One of these might be a control group. Interpretation of findings more complex than with equivalent true experimental designs.

3. *Interrupted time series designs*
   In its simplest (and most common) form, involves a single experimental group on which a series of measurements or observations are made before and after some form of experimental intervention. Requires a dependent variable on which repeated measures can be taken and an extended series of measurements.

4. *Regression-discontinuity designs*
   All participants are pre-tested and those scoring below a criterion value are assigned to one group (say an experimental group); all those above that criterion are assigned to a second group (say a control group). The pattern of scores after the experimental intervention provides evidence for its effectiveness.

even to assess its statistical significance (see the discussion in Chapter 17, p. 462), there are no particular problems. The difficulty is in possible validity threats. They may also be useful as pilot studies, to determine whether it is worthwhile to commit resources to carry out a more adequate experiment.

Quasi-experimental designs to consider

It is possible to get to a feasible quasi-experimental design by considering the main problems with the previous two designs – the 'post-test only non-equivalent groups' design, and the 'pre-test post-test single-group' design. With the former, we do not know whether or not the two groups differ before the treatment. With the latter, we do not know how much the group would have changed from pre-test to post-test in the absence of the treatment.

BOX 6.9

Designs to avoid, no.1: the one group post-test only design

Scenario: A single experimental group is involved in the treatment and then given a post-test.

Reasons to avoid: As an experiment, where the only information that you have is about the outcome measure, this is a waste of time and effort. Without pre-treatment measures on this group or measures from a second no-treatment control group, it is virtually impossible to infer any kind of effect.

Improvements: Either improve the experimental design or adopt a case study methodology.

Note: This is not the same thing as a case study. Typically the case study has multiple sources of data (usually qualitative, but some may be quantitative) extending over time, and there is also information about the context.

BOX 6.10

Designs to avoid, no. 2: the post-test only non-equivalent groups design

Scenario: As no. 1 but with the addition of a second non-equivalent (not determined by random assignment) group that does not receive the treatment, i.e.:

1. Set up an experimental and a comparison group on some basis other than random assignment.
2. The experimental group gets the treatment, the comparison group doesn't.
3. Do post-tests on both groups.

Reasons to avoid: It is not possible to determine whether any difference in outcome for the two groups is due to the treatment, or to other differences between the groups.

Improvements: Strengthen the experimental design by incorporating a pre-test or by using random assignment to the two groups; or use case study methodology.

One tactic used to strengthen the design is, effectively, to combine the two designs into a 'pre-test post-test non-equivalent groups' design. A second tactic is to make additional observations:

- over time with a particular group, leading to the 'interrupted time-series' design (p. 127); and/or
- over groups at the same time, leading to the 'regression-discontinuity' design (p. 127)

BOX 6.11

Designs to avoid, no. 3: the pre-test post-test single group design

Scenario: As no. 1, but with the addition of measurement on the same variable before the treatment as well as after it; i.e. the single experimental group is pre-tested, gets the treatment, and is tested again.

Reasons to avoid: Although widely used, it is subject to lots of problems. It is vulnerable to many threats to validity – including history (other events apart from the treatment occurring between measures), maturation (developments in the group between measures), statistical regression (e.g. choice of a group 'in need' in the sense of performing poorly on the measure used, or some other measure which correlates with it, will tend to show an improvement for random statistical reasons unconnected with the treatment – see below).

Improvements: Strengthen the experimental design, e.g. by adding a second pre-tested no-treatment control group.

Note: It may be possible on particular occasions to show that this design is interpretable. This could be because the potential threats to validity have not occurred in practice. For example, if you can isolate the group so that other effects do not influence it; or if you have information that there are no pre-treatment trends in the measures you are taking – although strictly that type of information turns this into a kind of time-series design (see p. 131).

to assess the effectiveness of the treatment. It is a general rule of quasi-experimental designs that it is necessary to consider not only the *design* of a study, but also the *context* in which it occurs, and the particular *pattern of results* obtained, when trying to decide whether a treatment has been effective. Note the similarities with the realist approach, e.g. in the emphasis on context and the importance of detailed analysis of what actually happens in a study, the stress on 'what works, for whom and in what circumstances'. This is not surprising as Cook and Campbell (1979, pp. 28–36) endorse a realist approach and seek to move beyond positivist notions of causation in their analysis.

Pre-test post-test non-equivalent groups design

The interpretability of the findings depends on the pattern of results obtained. If, for example, the experimental group starts lower and the outcome is an increase in the experimental group taking it above the comparison group at post-test, while there is no change in comparison group, the switching of the two groups from pre- to post-test permits many threats to validity to be ruled out. Other patterns can be more difficult to interpret.

The website gives an analysis of the interpretability of different patterns of outcomes.

A common strategy in this type of design is to use one or more matching variables to select a comparison or control group. This is different from the matching strategy used in true or randomized experiments where the experimenter matches participants and randomly assigns one member of the matched pair to either treatment or comparison group. Here the researcher tries to find participants who match the participants who are receiving a treatment. This approach is unfortunately subject to the threat to internal validity known as *regression* to the mean. While this threat is always present when matching is used without random assignment, it shows itself particularly clearly in situations where some treatment intended to assist those with difficulties or disadvantages is being assessed. Suppose that a comparison is being made between the achievements of a 'disadvantaged' and a 'non-disadvantaged' control group. The pre-treatment levels of the disadvantaged population will almost inevitably differ from those of the non-disadvantaged population, with the strong likelihood that those of the disadvantaged population tend to be lower. Hence in selecting matched pairs from the two populations, we will be pairing individuals who are pretty high in the disadvantaged group with individuals pretty low in the non-disadvantaged group. Figure 6.1 indicates what is likely to be going on.

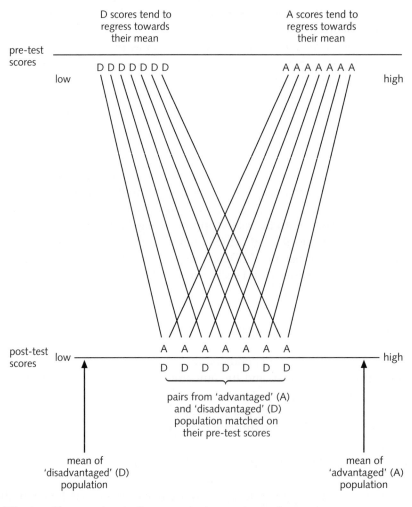

Figure 6.1 Effects of 'regression to the mean' when using extreme groups.

Because pre-test scores are not 100 per cent reliable (no scores ever are), they will incorporate some random or error factors. Those scoring relatively high in their population (as in the selected disadvantaged group) will tend to have positive error factors inflating their pre-test score. Those scoring relatively low in their population (as in the selected non-disadvantaged group) will tend to have negative error factors reducing their pre-test score. On post-test, however, such random factors (simply because they are random) will be just as likely to be positive as negative, leading to the 'regression to the mean' phenomenon – post-test scores of originally extreme groups tend to be closer to their population means.

As can be seen from the figure, the effect of this is to produce a tendency for the disadvantaged groups to score lower *even in the absence of any treatment effects*. Depending on the relative size of this effect and any treatment effect, there will appear to be a reduced treatment effect, or zero, or even a negative one.

Time-series designs

In the simplest form of this design, there is just one experimental group, and a series of observations or tests before and after an experimental treatment. The time-series approach is widely used in some branches of the social sciences (e.g. in economics) and has a well-developed and complex literature, particularly on the analysis of time-series data (Glass, Willson & Gottman, 2008). Textbooks covering this field suggest rules of thumb for the number of data points needed in the before and after time series, typically coming up with figures of 50 or more.

This extent of data collection is likely to be outside the scope of small-scale studies. However, there may well be situations where, although 50 or so observations are not feasible, it is possible to carry out several pre- and post-tests. Certainly, some advantages accrue if even one additional pre- and/or post-test (preferably both) can be added. This is essentially because one is then gathering information about possible trends in the data, which help in countering several of the threats to the internal validity of the study. Coryn, Schröter and Hanssen (2009) provide a detailed example. With more data points, say five before and five after, the experimenter is in a much stronger position to assess the nature of the trend – does the series appear to be stationary (i.e. show no trend to increase or decrease)? Or does it appear to increase, or decrease? And is this a linear trend, or is the slope itself tending to increase? Techniques for the analysis of such short time series are available, although not universally accepted (see Chapter 17, p. 462).

As with other quasi-experimental designs, interpretation is based on a knowledge of the design itself in interaction with the particular pattern of results obtained, and contextual factors. Figure 6.2 illustrates a range of possible patterns of results. Collecting data for a time-series design can become a difficult and time-consuming task. The observations must be ones that can be made repeatedly without practical or methodological problems. Simple, non-obtrusive measures (e.g. of play in a school playground) are more appropriate than, say, the repeated administration of a formal test of some kind.

If pre-existing archive material of some kind is available, then it may be feasible to set up a time-series design, even with an extended time series, at relatively low cost of time and effort for the experimenter. Increasingly, such material is gathered in conjunction with management information systems. However, it will require very careful scrutiny to establish its reliability and validity, and general usefulness, for research purposes. It will usually have been gathered for other purposes (although if, as is sometimes the case, you are in a position to influence what is

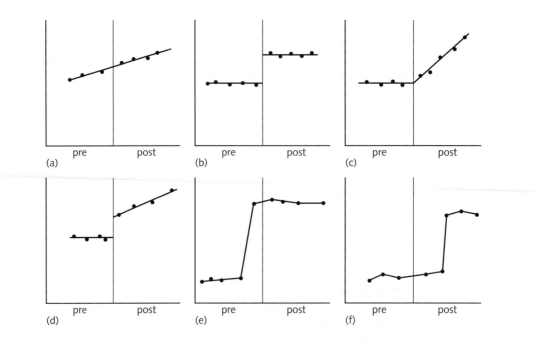

Figure 6.2 Patterns of possible results in a simple time-series experiment. (a) No effect. Note that making single pre- and post-tests (or taking pre- and post-test averages) would suggest a spurious effect. (b) Clear effect. Stable pre and post – but at a different level. Several threats to validity still possible (e.g. history – something else may be happening at the same time as the treatment). (c) Again, clear effect, but of a different kind (move from stability to steady increase). Similar threats will apply. (d) Combines effects of (b) and (c). (e) 'Premature' and (f) 'delayed' effects. Such patterns cast serious doubts on the effects being causally linked to the treatment. Explanations should be sought (e.g. may get a 'premature' effect of an intervention on knowledge or skill, if participants are in some way preparing themselves for the intervention).

gathered and how it is gathered, this can be very helpful), which may well mean that it is inaccessible to you, or is systematically biased, or is being collected according to different criteria at different times, or by different people, or is inflexible and won't allow you to answer your research questions.

While many time-series designs involve a single group before and after some treatment or intervention, more complex designs are possible. For example, a non-equivalent comparison group can be added with the same series of pre- and post-treatment tests or observations being made for both groups. The main advantage of adding the control group is its ability to test for the 'history' threat. A 'selection–history interaction' is still possible though, that is, that one of the two groups experiences a particular set of non-treatment related events that the other does not. In general the plausibility of such a threat will depend on how closely comparable in setting and experiences the two groups are.

One way of discounting history-related threats is to use the group as its own control, and to take measures on a second dependent variable which should not be affected by the treatment. In a classic study Ross, Campbell and Glass (1970) used this design to analyse the effect of the introduction of the 'breathalyzer' on traffic accidents. They argued that serious accidents should decrease following the introduction of new legislation in Britain which brought in the 'breathalyzer' *during the hours that pubs were open* (the 'experimental' dependent variable), but should be less affected during commuting hours when the pubs were shut (the 'control' dependent variable) – this was before the days of extended opening hours for British pubs. They were able to corroborate this view, both by visual inspection of the time series and by statistical analysis.

Other time-series designs involving the removal of treatment, and multiple and switching replications have been used. A lot of the interest in these designs has been in connection with so-called 'single-case' or 'single-subject' research, particularly in the behaviour modification field (e.g. Barlow, Andrasik & Hersen, 2006). Although having their genesis in a very different area of the social sciences, time-series designs show considerable similarities to single-case research designs (see below, p. 134).

Regression-discontinuity design

This rather fearsomely named design is conceptually straightforward. As in the true experiment, a known assignment rule is used to separate out two groups. However, whereas with the true experiment this is done on a random basis, here some other principle is used. In probably its simplest form, all those scoring below a certain value on some criterion are allocated to, say, the experimental group; all those scoring above that value are allocated to the control group (or vice versa). Trochim (1984, 1990) and Lesik (2006) discuss the use of the design.

It might be, for example, that entry to some compensatory programme is restricted to those scoring below a particular cut-off point on some relevant test; or conversely that entrance scholarships are given to those scoring above some cut-off. Figure 6.3 illustrates a possible outcome for this type of design. As with other quasi-experimental designs, the pattern of outcome, design and context must be considered when seeking to interpret the results of a particular experiment.

There is a superficial similarity between the graphs obtained with this design and those for the time-series design. Note, however, that whereas the latter shows time on the horizontal axis of the

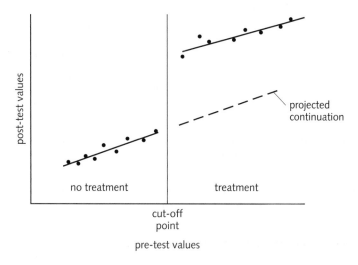

Figure 6.3 Illustrative outcome of a regression discontinuity design.

graph, the regression discontinuity design has pre-test scores along this axis. The issues are in both cases about trends in the data: are they present, do they differ and so on. 'Eyeballing' the data, i.e. visual inspection to assess this, forms a valuable part of the analysis, although most would argue that this needs to be supplemented by more formal statistical analysis. Conceptually the analyses for the two designs are equivalent, although different statistical techniques have to be used.

The website gives examples of studies using different quasi-experimental designs.

Concluding thoughts on quasi-experimental designs

Quasi-experimentation is more of a style of investigation than a slavish following of pre-determined designs. The designs covered above should be seen simply as suggestions for starting points. If you are not in a position to do true experiments, then with sufficient ingenuity you ought to be able to carry out a quasi-experiment to counter those threats to internal validity that are likely to be problematic.

Single-case experiments

A distinctive approach to carrying out experiments originated in the work of B. F. Skinner (e.g. Skinner, 1974). It has subsequently been developed by his followers, variously known as Skinnerians, Radical Behaviourists, or Operant Conditioners – among other labels. Sidman (1960) has produced a very clear, though partisan, account of this approach concentrating on the methodological issues and strategies involved. The work of Skinner arouses strong passions and, in consequence, his approach to experimental design tends to be either uncritically adopted or cursorily rejected.

There is much of value here for the real world investigator with a leaning to the experimental – mixed, as in Skinner's other work, with the unhelpfully polemical, the quirky and the rather silly. The approach is variously labelled, commonly as 'small-N', 'single-subject', or 'single-case' designs. This latter has the virtue, which would probably have been resisted by Skinner, of making the point that the 'case' need not necessarily be the individual person – it could be the individual school class, or the school itself, for example. It does, however, carry the possibility of confusion with 'case study', which as defined in this book is a multi-method enterprise (though this may incorporate a single-case experiment within it).[1] Skinner's search was for a methodology which produced meaningful, reliable data at the level of the individual – and which didn't require statistical testing to decide whether or not an effect was present. His view was that 'eyeballing' the data was all that should be needed. If such visual inspection did not produce clear results then, another, better, experiment should be designed, continuing until clear, unambiguous results are obtained. However, there is the difficulty that what may be viewed as a clear

---

[1] Single-case fixed designs are very different from *case studies*. The latter are almost always of flexible design using several data collection methods (see Chapter 7). However, it would be feasible to have a multi-strategy design which incorporated a single-case fixed design element within a case study.

result by one person may not be as clear to others. Which takes us back to using statistics, albeit ones appropriate for single-case data. Barlow, Nock and Hersen (2008) provide detailed discussions of the design and analysis (including statistical analysis) of single-case experiments. See also Chapter 17, p. 454.

Box 6.12 gives an overview of several types of single-case design.

A–B design

The simplest A–B design involves two experimental conditions (the terminology is different from that used in the previous designs of experiments, but is well established). The first condition (A) is referred to as the *baseline*; the second condition (B) corresponds to the treatment. Both

---

BOX 6.12

Overview of a range of single-case designs

Note: These designs call for a series of measures on a dependent variable (DV) (or, more rarely, on two or more such variables). Typically the study is repeated with a small number of participants to establish the replicability of the findings.

1. *A–B designs*
   Base-line phase (A) of a sequence of observations prior to intervention followed by a second phase where the intervention is introduced (B) and a further sequence of observations. Effectiveness of intervention shown by difference in observations made in B from those made in A (note similarity to interrupted time series design).
2. *A–B–A designs*
   As A-B but adding a third phase which reverts to pre-intervention baseline condition (A).
3. *A–B–A–B designs*
   Addition of a second intervention phase (B) to A–B–A design. Avoids possible ethical problems of finishing with a return to baseline.
4. *Multiple baseline designs*
   (a) *Across settings.* A DV is measured or observed in two or more situations (e.g. at home and at school). Change is made from a baseline condition (A) to the intervention (B) at different times in the different settings.
   (b) *Across behaviours.* Two or more behaviours are measured or observed. Change is made from a baseline condition (A) to the intervention (B) at different times for the different behaviours.
   (c) *Across participants.* Two or more participants are measured or observed. Change is made from a baseline condition (A) to the intervention (B) at different times for the different behaviours.

   Additional phases can be added leading to multiple baseline versions of the A–B–A and A–B–A–B designs.

conditions are 'phases' which extend over time, and a sequence of tests or observations will be taken in each phase.

The investigator looks for a clear difference in the pattern of performance in the two phases – this being an actual 'look' as typically the data are 'eyeballed' by Skinnerians with their principled antipathy to statistical analysis. A distinctive feature of the Skinnerian approach is that the baseline phase is supposed to be continued until stability is reached, that is, so that there is no trend over time. In practice, this is not always achieved. The restriction to a stable baseline obviously assists in the interpretation of the data, but even so, the design is weak and subject to several validity threats (e.g. history–treatment interaction). *Because of this the design is probably best regarded as 'pre-experimental', with the same strictures on its use as with the other pre-experimental designs* considered in the preceding section on quasi-experiments (p. 136). The design can be strengthened in ways analogous to those employed in quasi-experimental design – effectively extending the series of phases either over time, or cross-sectionally over different baselines.

It is also a pragmatic point as to whether the necessary baseline stability can be achieved, although Skinnerians would consider it an essential feature of experimental control that conditions be found where there is stability. As with lengthy time-series designs, this approach presupposes an observation or dependent variable where it is feasible to have an extended series of measures. Skinnerians would insist on the dependent variable being rate of response but this appears to be more of a historical quirk than an essential design feature.

A–B–A design

This improves upon the previous design by adding a *reversal phase* – the second A phase. The central notion is that the investigator removes the treatment (B) and looks for a return to baseline performance. Given a stable pre-treatment baseline, a clear and consistent shift from this during the second phase, and a return to a stable baseline on the reversal, the investigator is on reasonably strong ground for inferring a causal relationship.

The problems occur when this does not happen, particularly when there is not a return to baseline in the final phase. This leaves the experimenter seeking explanations for the changes that occurred during the second phase other than that it was caused by the treatment (B); or evaluating other possible explanations for the failure to return, such as carry-over effects from the treatment. The design is also open to ethical objections, particularly when used in an applied setting. Is it justifiable deliberately to remove a treatment when it appears to be effective? This is not too much of an issue when the goal is to establish or demonstrate some phenomenon, but when the intention is to help someone, many practitioners would have reservations about the design.

A–B–A–B design

A simple, though not entirely adequate, answer to the ethical problems raised by the preceding design is to add a further treatment phase. In this way the person undergoing the study ends up with the – presumed beneficial – treatment. All additions to the sequence of baseline and treatment phases, with regular and consistent changes observed to be associated with the phases, add to one's confidence about the causal relationship between treatment and outcome. There is no reason in principle why this AB alternation should not continue as ABABAB – or longer.

However, it does involve extra time and effort which could probably be better spent in other directions. The design does also still call for the treatment to be withdrawn during the sequence, and there are alternative designs which avoid this.

Multiple baseline designs

The approach in this design involves the application of the treatment at different points in time to different baseline conditions. If there is a corresponding change in the condition to which the treatment is applied, and no change in the other conditions at that time, then there is a strong case that the change is causally related to the treatment.

Three versions of the design are commonly employed: multiple baselines *across settings*, *across behaviours* and *across participants*.

- in the across settings design, a particular dependent variable (behaviour) of a participant is monitored in a range of different settings or situations and the treatment is introduced at a different time in each of the settings;
- in the across behaviours design, data is collected on several dependent variables (behaviours) for a particular participant and the treatment is applied at different times to each of the behaviours; and
- in the across participants design, data is collected on a particular baseline condition for several participants and the treatment is applied at different times to the different participants.

The general approach is illustrated in Figure 6.4.
Other designs have been used and are briefly explained here.

Changing criterion designs

A criterion for performance is specified as a part of the intervention. That criterion is changed over time in a pre-specified manner, usually progressively in a particular direction. The effect of the intervention is demonstrated if the behaviour changes to match the changes in criterion.

This design is attractive in interventions where the intention is to achieve a progressive reduction of some problem behaviour or progressive increase in some desired behaviour. It is

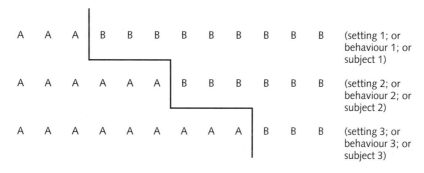

Figure 6.4 The multiple baseline design.

probably most useful for situations involving complex behaviours or where the intention is to try to achieve some major shift from what the person involved is currently doing. Certainly the notion of 'successive approximations' which is built into this design sits very naturally with the 'shaping of behaviour' approach central to Skinnerian practice and applicable by others.

Multiple treatment designs

These involve the implementation of two or more treatments designed to affect a single behaviour. So, rather than a treatment being compared with its absence (which is effectively what baseline comparisons seek to achieve), there are at least two separate treatments whose effects are compared. In its simplest form, this would be ABC, i.e. a baseline condition (A), followed in sequence by two treatment conditions (B and C). This could be extended in several ways: ABCA or ABACA or ABACABCA, etc. The latter gives some kind of assessment of 'multiple treatment interference' – the extent to which there are sequence effects, where being exposed to one condition has a subsequent influence on the apparent effect of a subsequent condition.

There are several more complex variants. In one (known as a *multiple schedule design*), each treatment or intervention is associated in a consistent way, probably for a substantial number of times, with a particular 'stimulus' (e.g. a particular person, setting or time) so that it can be established whether or not the stimulus has consistent control over performance. An alternative (known variously as a *simultaneous treatment* or *alternating treatment design*) is for each of the settings to be balanced across stimulus conditions (persons, settings or times) so that each of the settings has been associated equivalently with each of the stimuli. This then permits one to disentangle the effects of the settings from 'stimulus' effects. Barlow *et al.* (2006) give details.

These designs have several advantages. As the main concern is for differential effects on the two conditions, the establishment of a stable baseline becomes less crucial. In the two latter variants, there is no need for treatment to be withdrawn or removed, and the relative effects of the different conditions can be determined without the need for lengthy successive involvement with different phases. It is possible to generate what might be called 'combined designs' by putting together features from the individual designs considered above. For example an ABAB design could be combined with a multiple baseline approach.

The general approach taken to design in single-case experimentation bears some similarities to that taken in quasi-experimentation. There is concern for specific threats to validity which might make the study difficult or impossible to interpret, particularly in relation to causality. These are taken into account in developing the design. However, there is often substantially greater flexibility and willingness to modify the design than is found in other types of experimentation. It is common to review and possibly alter the design in the light of the pattern of data which is emerging. Decisions such as when to move from one phase to another are made in this way. The attraction of a combined design is that additional or changed design features (which can counter particular threats to validity) can be introduced reactively to resolve specific ambiguities.

This approach is foreign to the traditional canons of fixed design research, where a design is very carefully pre-planned and then rigidly adhered to. Interestingly, it has similarities to the flexible designs discussed in the next chapter.

There are also similarities between single-case experimentation and the way in which experiments are carried out in some branches of the natural sciences. Statistics play little part; the trick is to set up the situation, through control of extraneous variables that would cloud the issue (Ernest Rutherford, the eminent physicist, is widely quoted as saying, 'If your experiment needs statistics, you ought to have done a better experiment'). By doing this, the cause–effect relationship shines out for all to see, in realist terms ensuring the context is such that the mechanism(s) operate. It may be necessary to 'fine-tune' your study so that unforeseen eventualities can be accounted for. With sufficient experimental skill and understanding you should be able to find out something of importance about the specific focus of your study (whether this happens to be a person or a radioactive isotope). You will need to test it out on a few individuals just to assure yourself of typicality – which was not only Skinner's approach but also that of the supreme experimentalist Ivan Pavlov.

The website gives examples of a range of studies using single-case designs.

Passive experimentation

Several types of study which appear to be very similar to experiments do not have the active manipulation of the situation by the experimenter, taken here to be a hallmark of the experimental approach. They are sometimes called passive experiments but are discussed here under the heading of non-experimental fixed designs.

Non-experimental fixed designs

If, following your reading of the previous chapter, it appears possible that a non- experimental fixed design may be appropriate for your project and its research questions, then perusal of this section should help in choosing a specific non-experimental design. However, before confirming that choice, it will be necessary to read the chapters in Part III of this book to help select appropriate methods of collecting data (the survey is a very common type of non-experimental fixed design and hence Chapter 11 is particularly relevant), and Chapter 17 to establish how you will analyse the data after it has been collected.

This style of fixed design research differs from the experimental one in that the phenomena studied are not deliberately manipulated or changed by the researcher. Hence it is suitable in situations where the aspects of interest are not amenable to such changes for whatever reason. These include variables or characteristics which:

- are not modifiable by the researcher (e.g. personal characteristics such as gender, age, ethnicity);
- should not be modified for ethical reasons (e.g. tobacco smoking, alcohol consumption); or
- it is not feasible to modify (e.g. placement in a school or classroom).

As these constraints apply to a high proportion of the variables of likely interest in applied social research, these designs are of considerable importance to anyone intent on carrying out a fixed design study.

Dealing with things as they are, rather than as modified by the experimenter, has the advantage of not disturbing whatever it is that we are interested in. Byrne (2002) stresses that, 'It is important to realize that surveys are not experiments. They are fundamentally different and in my view much superior' (p. 62) – note, however, that he presents a radical critique of the traditional variable-oriented approach as presented here.

Non-experimental fixed designs are commonly used for descriptive purposes, and, because of their fixed, pre-specified nature are not well adapted to exploratory work. They can be used when the interest is in explaining or understanding a phenomenon. The designs have been rarely used by researchers with emancipatory concerns but there is no reason why, say, a descriptive study could not be useful for anti-discriminatory or other emancipatory purposes.

Working within the realist framework they can help establish cause in the sense of providing supportive evidence for the operation of mechanisms and for teasing out the particular situations and groups of people where enabling or disabling mechanisms have come into play. The specification of which mechanisms have operated in a *post hoc* (i.e. after the study has taken place) manner is viewed as entirely legitimate. While prediction of the exact pattern of results may not be feasible because of the open nature of the systems which social research studies, this does not preclude an explanation of the particular pattern obtained.

Measuring relationships

Non-experimental fixed designs are commonly used to measure the relationship between two or more variables. Do pupils from different ethnic backgrounds achieve differently in schools? Are there gender differences? What is the relationship between school characteristics and student achievement? They are sometimes referred to as correlational studies. However, this tends to suggest that a particular statistical technique (the *correlation* coefficient) is to be used whereas there is a range of possibilities for analysis which is discussed in Chapter 17.

The traditional approach is to start with a conceptual framework or other approach to theory, in some provisional form at least. In realist terms, this means having a pretty clear idea (e.g. from a previous study or from other sources) of likely mechanisms and the contexts in which they will operate. This theory is then used to identify the variables and possible relationships to be studied. Research questions are formulated prior to data collection. Similarly, decisions about the methods of data collection and analysis, and the sampling strategy determining who will be asked are all finalized before data collection proper starts. And it is expected that, when these decisions have been made, they are kept to throughout the study.

When all measures are taken at the same time (or, in practice, over a relatively short period of time), it is commonly referred to as a *cross-sectional* study, and is widely used in fixed design social research. It is often employed in conjunction with the survey method of data collection discussed in detail in Chapter 11. The pattern of relationships between variables may be of interest in its own right, or there may be a concern for establishing causal links. In interpreting the results of these studies, statistical and logical analyses effectively take the place of the features of experimental design which facilitate the interpretation of true experiments.

The variables to be included in the study are those needed to provide answers to your research questions. These questions will, as ever, be governed by the purposes of your study and by the theory or conceptual structure you have developed. Whereas the tradition in experimental research is to label these as independent variables (those which the experimenter manipulates) and dependent variables (those where we look for change), they are usually referred to here as *explanatory variables* and *outcome variables*, respectively.

It is possible to include more explanatory variables in this design than is feasible in experimental designs. However, this should not be taken as an excuse for a 'fishing trip' – just throwing in variables in the hope that something will turn up. To reiterate the principle – the variables are included because of their relevance to your research questions.

The choice of participants to make up the group is important. Again, your research questions effectively determine this. An issue is the homogeneity of the group. For example, while you may not be interested in this study in gender issues in themselves, you may consider it important to have both males and females in the group. It may be, however, that males and females are affected by different variables and hence there will be increased variability on the outcome variable. A solution here is to analyse the two genders separately; i.e. to perform a subgroup analysis.

When decisions have been made about the composition of the group, data can be collected. Typically quantitative, or quantifiable, data are collected often using a questionnaire, or some type of test or scale for both explanatory and outcome variables (see Chapters 11 and 13, respectively).

Analysis and interpretation

A variety of data analysis techniques can be used, including (but by no means limited to) correlational analysis. Chapter 17 gives examples. The techniques can be thought of as providing statistical control for factors controlled for in true experiments by employing a control group and randomization of allocation of participants to experimental and control groups. So, for example, a survey on attitudes to nuclear power might show gender differences. Frankfort-Nachmias and Nachmias (1996, p. 126) discuss an example from Solomon, Tomaskovic-Devey and Risman (1989) where 59 per cent of men and 29 per cent of women support nuclear power. This analysis of differences in percentages (produced by 'cross-tabulation'; see Chapter 17, p. 414) provides a kind of statistical equivalent to an experimental design which is of course not feasible due to the impossibility of randomly assigning individuals to be males or females!

Establishing the statistical significance of the relationship between gender and attitude does not enable us to conclude that these variables are causally related. Nor does it, in itself, help in understanding what lies behind this relationship. In realist terms, we need to come up with plausible mechanisms and seek evidence for their existence. As Frankfort-Nachmias and Nachmias suggest, it may be that 'the women in the study may have been less knowledgeable about technological matters and therefore more reluctant to support nuclear power. Or perhaps women's greater concern with safety would lead them to oppose nuclear power more than men' (p. 127).

Further subdivision of the group allows one to control statistically for the effects of such variables providing the relevant information (e.g. degree of knowledge in the above example) has been collected. Various statistical techniques such as path analysis can be used to analyse the data in more detail (Chapter 17, p. 437). However, the interpretation, particularly in relation to causation, remains a challenging task and is an amalgam of theoretical, logical and statistical considerations.

Making group comparisons

An alternative approach to seeking relationships in a single group is to have a second group and make comparisons between the two groups. The groups may be naturally occurring ones already in existence or may be created especially for the study. Group selection raises the same issues about threats to internal validity as in experimental (particularly quasi-experimental) design. The threat of *differential selection* will arise if the groups differ in some ways other than those indicated by the *explanatory variable(s)*. Assuming random allocation to the two groups is not feasible, some other approach must be taken to guard against this threat. Possibilities include:

- matching on variables likely to be relevant (see p. 123);
- using a statistical method of control for existing differences (see Chapter 17);
- using direct control, e.g. by only selecting participants from a particular ethnic or socioeconomic background; and/or
- analysing subgroups.

Measures will typically be made on other background or control variables (e.g. ethnicity) which may be of interest in their own right or as helping to understand what lies behind any differences found. They could then form the basis for subsequent subgroup analyses.

While the relational and group comparison approaches may seem very different, the difference is largely in the way the study is conceptualized. The example of gender differences in attitude to nuclear power was discussed above as a single group containing both males and females. The focus was on relations between gender and attitude. It could be viewed as based on separate groups of males and females. The focus is then on differences between the two groups.

Gender is a dichotomous variable (i.e. it only has two possible values). Other explanatory variables can take on a wide range of values. When they are involved, instead of talking about separate comparison groups differing on the variable of interest, there is a wide range of differences on that variable. Separate and distinct comparison groups (two or more) can be thought of as a special case of that general situation. This approach effectively brings together both relational and comparative studies within the same framework. It also paves the way to the use of statistical techniques such as analysis of variance (and particularly, in this context, analysis of covariance which permits the separating out of the effects of control variables) and multiple linear regression.

Category membership

The identification of membership of particular categories or groups in non-experimental fixed design research can be difficult and complex. This may appear straightforward for a variable such as age. However, there are situations where even age can be problematic, say, in a study of the drinking habits of young adults or in cultures where date of birth may not be recorded or remembered. Gender, as a social construct, can raise category difficulties in particular cases. An area such as ethnicity bristles with complexities, particularly in multi-cultural societies (see Stanfield, 1993).

In flexible design research where participant numbers are almost always small, it is usually feasible to achieve the depth needed to deal with the complexities but fixed design research, typically with much larger numbers, necessarily has to simplify. Notwithstanding the difficulties, it would be unfortunate if this put important topics out of bounds. As Mertens (2005) comments, 'Discontinuing such research based on the rationale that our understanding of race, gender, and disability is limited needs to be weighed against the benefit associated with revealing inequities in resources and outcomes in education, psychology, and the broader society' (p. 150).

Classification of non-experimental fixed designs

This is a murky area where a plethora of terms have been used including comparison and causal-comparative designs, correlational designs, natural experiments, *ex post facto*, available data designs, descriptive designs and surveys. Johnson (2001) has suggested that many of the designs used can be classified in terms of the purpose, or research objective, of the study as one aspect, and the time dimension as a second one.

Purpose (research objective)

The main non-experimental fixed designs are *descriptive, predictive* or *explanatory*:

- Descriptive designs are primarily concerned with describing something; with documenting its characteristics.
- Predictive designs are primarily concerned with predicting or forecasting some event or phenomenon in the future.
- Explanatory designs are primarily concerned with developing or testing a theory about something; to identify the causal factors or mechanisms producing change.

'Primarily' flags that a project may have more than one objective. Primarily descriptive and predictive designs often attempt some explanation of what is happening.

Time dimension

Three types are commonly found, *cross-sectional designs, longitudinal designs* and *retrospective designs*:

- In cross-sectional designs, the data are collected at a single point in time (practical considerations may extend this to a relatively brief period rather than a single point).
- In longitudinal designs, the data are collected at more than one point in time or brief period. Many such designs involve an extended series of data collections (as in experimental time-series designs, discussed earlier in the chapter, p. 131) but some just involve two data collections. Subtypes include trend designs (independent samples of participants at the different data collections) and *panel designs* (same participants).
- In retrospective designs, the researcher collects data at a point in time about the situation at some earlier point in time as well as the current situation (e.g. by asking questions about earlier behaviour). This is effectively a special case of a cross-sectional design which attempts to simulate a longitudinal design and obtain data relating to more than one point in time.

Longitudinal panel designs can avoid many of the difficulties in interpretation and threats to internal validity of much non-experimental fixed design research discussed above (see also Ruspini, 2002 and Menard, 2007). However, they are difficult and complex to run and typically call for considerable resources. Some of the problems include sample attrition (when participants are lost to the study), the need to devise measures which can be used repeatedly and for special methods of data analysis (see Menard, 2007).

The website gives examples of studies using cross-sectional, longitudinal and retrospective designs.

Sample size in fixed designs

One of the most common questions asked by a novice researcher is 'What size of sample do I need?' The answer is not straightforward, as it depends on many factors. In some real world research, the question is answered for you by the situation. You may be working in an organization where the obvious thing is to survey everybody or your resources may be so stretched that this sets the limits on the number of participants you can deal with. In such circumstances, it is particularly important to have thought through how your data are to be analysed before proceeding. There are minimum numbers for statistical tests and procedures below which they should not be used. Hence, if you plan to use a particular test or procedure then this sets minimum numbers for your design.

Following Borg and Gall (1989), Mertens (2005, p. 325) suggests 'rule-of-thumb' figures of about 15 observations per group for experimental, quasi-experimental and non-experimental designs involving group comparisons and about 30 observations for non-experimental designs involving relations in a single group. In *survey research*, which typically seeks to incorporate more variables than experimental and other non-experimental designs, they recommend somewhat larger numbers (see Chapter 11, p. 245). Cohen (1992) provides a similar set of rules for sample sizes for a range of commonly used statistical tests.

When the main interest, as in many surveys, is to generalize the findings to the population from which the sample is drawn, then issues such as the homogeneity of the population are important. If pilot work establishes considerable heterogeneity, this then indicates the need for a larger sample. Similarly, the more accurate you want the estimates from your study to be, the larger a sample is needed. There are statistical techniques for determining the relationship between sampling error and sample size. Formulae have been developed to assist in the choice of an efficient sample size when it is important to limit estimation errors to a particular level. Henry (1990, Chapter 7) and Czaja and Blair (2005, pp. 142–8) give introductions. Lipsey (1990) provides a more detailed account and a useful general treatment of power analysis which covers the factors that affect the sensitivity of a design in detecting relationships (see Chapter 17, p. 441). Clark-Carter (1997) provides power tables to help in choosing sample sizes. They should be treated with care, as you need to be clear about the assumptions on which they are based. This is a matter on which it is advisable to seek assistance from a statistician if it is of importance in your study.

Further reading

The website gives annotated references to further reading for Chapter 6.

CHAPTER 7

Flexible designs

This chapter:

- reiterates the rationale for referring to 'flexible' rather than the more usual 'qualitative' research design;
- covers some general features of flexible design research and the researcher qualities it calls for;
- concentrates on three traditions of flexible design research: case studies, ethnographic studies, and grounded theory studies;
- briefly reviews a range of other possible approaches including the narrative, phenomenological, hermeneutic and feminist research traditions;
- discusses how to determine sample size in flexible designs; and
- concludes by considering the place of reliability and validity in this type of research, and the ways in which researcher bias and threats to validity can be dealt with.

Introduction

It is now considered respectable and acceptable in virtually all areas of social research (including applied fields such as criminology, education, health, social work, and business and management) to use designs based largely or exclusively on methods generating qualitative data. There are still some isolated outposts, particularly in fields abutting medicine and in areas of experimental psychology, where such designs are considered illegitimate or inferior to traditional quantitative designs. However, within social psychology, and applied areas, including clinical, educational and forensic psychology, qualitative methodologies are becoming established. Other areas, such as educational research in the UK, appeared for some time to be in danger of espousing a new orthodoxy where anything other than qualitative research was viewed as deviant, but recent governmental support for quantitative evidence-based approaches in both the US and the UK has had its effects.

The position taken in this text is that for some studies and for certain types of research question, research largely or exclusively based on qualitative data is indicated. For others, research largely or exclusively based on quantitative data is needed. The qualitative/quantitative ways of labelling research *designs* are so well established that it risks miscommunication not to use them. However, as already pointed out in Chapter 2, their use is not entirely logical. In principle (and not uncommonly in practice) so-called qualitative designs can incorporate quantitative methods of data collection. All of these approaches show substantial flexibility in their research design, typically anticipating that the design will emerge and develop during data collection. As discussed in the previous chapter, so-called quantitative approaches call for a tight pre-specification of the design prior to data collection. Hence our preference for referring to them as *flexible* and *fixed designs* respectively.

It is worth stressing that whereas fixed design research is, typically, an 'off-the-shelf' process where the task is primarily one of choice from a range of well-defined alternative designs, flexible designs are much more 'do-it-yourself'. Although there are research traditions in flexible design research, covered in the chapter, your task is much more that of constructing a one-off design likely to help answer your research questions.

The following two chapters also cover designs likely to include some flexible elements. The multi-strategy designs in Chapter 8 are ways in which substantial fixed and flexible design aspects can be incorporated in the same study. The 'designs for particular purposes' in Chapter 9 run the whole gamut from strictly fixed experimental designs common in some types of evaluation research to the highly flexible designs typical of action research.

General features of flexible designs

We first provide a general specification for the design of a flexible study, followed by accounts of three influential design traditions within flexible design research which are commonly used for real world studies; *case studies*, *ethnographic studies*, and *grounded theory studies*.

The chapter also gives information about a range of other traditions within qualitative research which may be worth considering for some real world projects. Box 7.1 gives a flavour of the kind of characteristics to be found in a flexible design where serious attention has been given to the general norms and canons of this style of research. This should be seen in the context of the overall design framework developed in Chapter 4 (Figure 4.1; p. 73). In other words, thought and attention will have to be given to the *purpose(s)* of your research, to its *conceptual structure*, to the *research questions* to which you seek answers, to the *methods* of data collection and the *sampling strategy* which will be needed to get these answers.

You don't try to get all of this cut-and-dried before starting data collection. The purpose or purposes of the study are likely to be pretty clear from the outset, but flexible designs are a work in progress and therefore can adapt as the research evolves. However at this stage, you may not have much of an idea about what theoretical framework is going to be most helpful. Indeed, one version of the grounded theory tradition discussed below argues that you should seek to enter the field without theoretical preconceptions (something which many would regard as impossible to achieve). It is highly likely that your research questions will be initially under-developed and tentative. You obviously need to make some early decisions about methods of data collection,

BOX 7.1

Characteristics of a 'good' flexible design

1. Typically multiple qualitative data collection techniques (possibly some quantitative data also – if a substantial amount of quantitative data collection this becomes a multi-strategy design, see Chapter 8) are used. Data are adequately summarized (e.g. in tabular form). Detail is given about how data are collected.
2. The study is framed within the assumptions and characteristics of the flexible design approach to research. This includes fundamental characteristics such as an evolving design, the presentation of multiple realities, the researcher as an instrument of data collection, and a focus on participants' views.
3. The study is informed by an understanding of existing traditions of research, i.e. the researcher identifies, studies, and employs one or more traditions of enquiry.
4. This tradition need not be 'pure', and procedures from several can be brought together. The novice researcher is recommended to stay within one tradition initially, becoming comfortable with it, learning it, and keeping a study concise and straightforward. Later, especially in long and complex studies, features from several traditions may be useful.
5. The project starts with a single idea or problem that the researcher seeks to understand, not a causal relationship of variables or a comparison of groups (for which a fixed design might be indicated). Relationships might evolve or comparisons might be made, but these emerge later in the study.
6. The study shows a rigorous approach to data collection, data analysis, and report writing. The researcher has the responsibility of verifying the accuracy of the account given.
7. Data are analysed using multiple levels of abstraction. Often, writers present their studies in stages (e.g. multiple themes that can be combined into larger themes or perspectives) or layer their analyses from the particular to the general.
8. The writing is clear, engaging, and helps the reader to experience 'being there'. The story and findings become believable and realistic, accurately reflecting the complexities of real life.

(after Cresswell, 1998, pp. 20–2)

because if you don't, you never get started. However, in these designs you don't have to foreclose on options about methods. Ideas for changing your approach may arise from your involvement and early data collection. Or as you change or clarify the research questions, different means of data collection may be called for. Similarly, your sampling of who, where and what does not have to be decided in advance. Again, you need to start somewhere but the sampling strategy can and should evolve with other aspects of the design.

Realism and flexible design

Within the realist framework, it is held that theory, rather than data or the methods used to produce that data, is central to explaining reality. This is fully consonant with the view developed in this text that it is the research questions which drive the design of a study, whether it be flexible or fixed. And that these questions have to be linked to theory, whether pre-existing, which is tested by the research, or generated by the process of the research itself.

Hence a realist view has no problems with flexible design research nor with the use of qualitative data. As pointed out by Anastas (1999):

> Flexible or qualitative methods have traditionally included the researcher and the relationship with the researched within the boundary of what is examined. Because all any study can do is to approximate knowledge of phenomena as they exist in the real world (fallibilism) the process of study itself must be studied as well. Because all methods of study can produce only approximations of reality and incomplete understanding of the phenomena of interest as they exist in the real world, the findings of flexible method research can be seen as no more or less legitimate than those of any other type of study (p. 56).

Researcher qualities needed for flexible design research

Doing flexible design research calls for flexible researchers. This approach to research makes great demands on the researcher *while carrying out the study*. It is commonly said that it involves the 'researcher-as-instrument', i.e. that rather than being able to rely on specialist tools and instruments, to a large extent you have to do it all yourself. Certainly the quality of a flexible design study depends to a great extent on the quality of the investigator. It is not a 'soft' option in the sense that anyone can do it without preparation, knowledge of procedures or analytical skills. It *is* soft, however, in the sense that there are few 'hard and fast' routinized procedures, where all you have to do is to follow the formulae. This makes life harder rather than easier – though also more interesting.

Ideally this kind of research calls for well trained and experienced investigators but other aspects are also important. Personal qualities such as having an *open and enquiring mind*, being a *'good listener'*, general *sensitivity* and *responsiveness to contradictory evidence* are needed. You have to be adaptive and quick-witted in the field as new issues can arise and the research itself may have to change. All such qualities are commonly regarded as skills central to the professional working with people in whatever capacity. Relevant professional experience of this kind is also likely to provide you with a firm grasp of the issues being studied in a particular study.

The professional or practitioner working with people as their job has much to contribute both *as* an investigator or *to* an investigator. As an investigator, probably carrying out 'insider' research, she will need a firm grasp of the material in this book and experience (this can lead to 'Catch-22' problems – how do you get the experience without carrying out a study, and vice versa). Working in collaboration with someone who has the methodological skills and the experience is obviously one way forward. Box 7.2 tries to provide an indication of the skills needed to be an effective flexible design researcher.

BOX 7.2

General skills needed by flexible design investigators

1. *Question asking.* Need for an 'enquiring mind'. Your task includes enquiring why events appear to have happened or to be happening. This is something you ask yourself as well as others and is mentally and emotionally exhausting.
2. *Good listening.* Used in a general sense to include all observation and sensing, not simply via the ears. Also 'listening' to what documents say. '*Good*' means taking in a lot of new information without bias; noting the exact words said; capturing mood and affective components; appreciating context. You need an open mind and a good memory. (Taping helps but is not a panacea.)
3. *Adaptiveness and flexibility.* These studies rarely end up exactly as planned. You have to be willing to change procedures or plans if the unanticipated occurs. The full implications of any changes have to be taken on board, e.g. you may need to change the design. There is a need to balance *adaptiveness* and *rigour*.
4. *Grasp of the issues.* The investigator needs to *interpret* information during the study, not simply record it. Without a firm grasp of the issues (theoretical, policy, etc.), you may miss clues, not see contradictions, requirement for further evidence, etc.
5. *Lack of bias.* The preceding skills are negated if they are simply used to substantiate a preconceived position. Investigators should be open to contrary findings. During data collection, preliminary findings should be submitted to critical colleagues who are asked to offer alternative explanations and suggestions for data collection. See the discussions on researcher bias at various points in the chapter.

Research traditions in qualitative research

Box 7.3 provides an overview of the main approaches to flexible design research featured in this chapter.

BOX 7.3

Overview of three approaches to flexible design research

1. *Case study.* A well-established research strategy where the focus is on a case (which is interpreted very widely to include the study of an individual person, a group, a setting, an organization, etc.) in its own right, and taking its context into account. Typically involves multiple methods of data collection. Can include quantitative data, though qualitative data are almost invariably collected.

(continued)

2. *Ethnographic studies.* Another well-established strategy where the focus is on the description and interpretation of the culture and social structure of a social group. Typically involves participant observation over an extended period of time, but other methods (including those generating quantitative data) can also be used.

3. *Grounded theory studies.* A more recently developed strategy where the main concern is to develop a theory of the particular social situation forming the basis of the study. The theory is 'grounded' in the sense of being derived from the study itself. Popular in research on many applied settings, particularly health-related ones. Interviews are commonly used but other methods (including those generating quantitative data) are not excluded.

Case studies

In case study, the *case* is the situation, individual, group, organization or whatever it is that we are interested in. Case study has been around for a long time (Hamel, 1993 traces its history within social science). To some it will suggest the legal system, to others the medical one. Gerring (2006) gives references to case studies in areas as disparate as anthropology, archaeology, business studies, education, international relations, marketing, medicine, organizational behaviour, politics, psychology, public administration, public health, social work and sociology. The varying strategies developed for dealing with cases in different disciplines have useful lessons, suggesting solutions to problems with case study methodology, including the thorny one of generalizing from the individual case. There is some danger in using a well-worn term like case study. All such terms carry 'excess baggage' around with them, surplus meanings and resonances from these previous usages.

The intention here is to provide guidance in carrying out *rigorous* case studies. This involves attention to matters of design, data collection, analysis, interpretation and reporting which form a major part of later chapters. Before getting on with this, however, let us be clear as to what we mean by case study. Following the lead set by Robert Yin (2009), who has done much to resuscitate case study as a serious option when doing social research:

Case study is a strategy for doing research which involves an empirical investigation of a particular contemporary phenomenon within its real life context using multiple sources of evidence.

The important points are that it is:

- a *strategy*, i.e. a stance or approach, rather than a method, such as observation or interview;
- concerned with *research*, taken in a broad sense and including, for example, evaluation research;
- *empirical* in the sense of relying on the collection of evidence about what is going on;
- about the *particular*; a study of that specific case (the issues of what kind of generalization is possible from the case, and of how this might be done, are important);
- focused on a *phenomenon in context*, typically in situations where the boundary between the phenomenon and its context is not clear; and
- using *multiple methods* of evidence or data collection.

The central defining characteristic is concentration on a particular case (or small number of cases) studied in its own right. However, the importance of its context or setting is also worth highlighting. Miles, Huberman and Saldana (2014, p. 30) suggest that in some circumstances the term 'site' might be preferable 'because it reminds us that a "case" always occurs in a specified social and physical *setting*: we cannot study individual cases devoid of their context in a way that a quantitative researcher often does.'

While some commentators see case studies as being essentially qualitative (e.g. Stake, 1995; 2005), it is now widely accepted (e.g. Yin, 2009; Gerring, 2006) that they can make use of both quantitative and qualitative data collection methods. It is relatively rare to see case studies where any quantitative component has anything other than a minor role (hence they are viewed here as flexible, rather than multi-strategy, designs). However, one of us (K.M.) was recently involved in a case study based evaluation of two UK based projects with a substantial quantitative component (McCartan *et al.*, 2014).

Taking case study seriously

Valsiner (1986) claimed that 'the study of individual cases has always been the major (albeit often unrecognized) strategy in the advancement of knowledge about human beings' (p. 11). In similar vein, Bromley (1986) maintained that 'the individual case study or situation analysis is the bed-rock of scientific investigation' (p. ix). But he also notes, in an unattributed quotation, the common view that 'science is not concerned with the individual case' (p. xi). These widely divergent claims betray a deep-rooted uncertainty about the place and value of studying cases.

Case study was until recently commonly considered in methodology texts as a kind of 'soft option', possibly admissible as an exploratory precursor to some more 'hard-nosed' experiment or survey or as a complement to such approaches but of dubious value by itself. Campbell and Stanley (1963) presented an extreme version of this view:

> Such studies often involve tedious collection of specific detail, careful observation, testing and the like, and in such instances involve the error of misplaced precision. How much more valuable the study would be if the one set of observations were reduced by half and the saved effort directed to the study in equal detail of an appropriate comparison instance. It seems well-nigh unethical at present to allow, as theses or dissertations in education, case studies of this nature (p. 177).

However, Campbell subsequently recanted and in later publications (e.g. Cook and Campbell, 1979) viewed case study as a fully legitimate alternative to experimentation in appropriate circumstances. Cook and Campbell make the point that 'case study as normally practiced should not be demeaned by identification with the one-group post-test-only design' (p. 96). Their central point is that *case study is not a flawed experimental design; it is a fundamentally different research strategy with its own designs.*

It is useful to separate out criticisms of the practice of particular case studies from what some have seen as inescapable deficiencies of the strategy itself. As Bromley (1986) pointed out, 'case studies are sometimes carried out in a sloppy, perfunctory, and incompetent manner and sometimes even in a corrupt, dishonest way' (p. xiii). Almost 30 years later Hyett, Kenny and Dickson-Swift (2014), in a review of published case study reports, find that methodological flaws are still common.

Can case study be scientific?

As discussed in Chapter 2, the positivist 'standard view' of science (which found case study problematic) has been comprehensively demolished, although its ghostly presence lingers in the views and practices of many quantitatively inclined social researchers. Case study does not appear to present any special difficulties for the realist view of science, developed and defended in that chapter (see Box 2.7, p. 31). The study of the particular, which is central to case study, is not excluded in principle; it is the aims and intentions of the study, and the specific methods used, that have to concern us. Carr and Kemmis (1986) reach very similar conclusions: 'What distinguishes scientific knowledge is not so much its logical status, as the fact that it is the outcome of a process of enquiry which is governed by critical norms and standards of rationality' (p. 121).

Designing case studies

The 'case' can be virtually anything. The individual person as the case is probably what first springs to mind. A simple, single case study would just focus on that person, perhaps in a clinical or medical context where the use of the term 'case' is routine. More complex, multiple case studies might involve several such individual cases. Case studies are not necessarily studies of individuals, though. They can be done on a group, on an institution, on a neighbourhood, on an innovation, on a decision, on a service, on a programme and on many other things. (There may be difficulties in defining and delimiting exactly what one means by the 'case' when the focus moves from the individual person.) Case studies are then very various. Box 7.4 gives some indication of different types and of the range of purposes they fulfil. Yin (2004; 2012) gives details of a wide range of different case studies.

Stake considers that Yin's approach is more concerned with identifying general patterns than focusing on the case itself. He advocates what he terms *naturalistic* case studies concentrating on the particularities of the case showing how things worked for that particular case in a specific setting (Abma & Stake, 2014; Stake, 2006).

Whatever kind of case study is involved (and the list in Box 7.4 only scratches the surface), there is always the need, as in any kind of research, to follow a framework for research design such as that given in Chapter 4 (Figure 4.1, p. 73). The degree of flexibility of design will vary from one study to another. If, for example, the main purpose is exploratory, trying to get some feeling as to what is going on in a novel situation where there is little to guide what one should be looking for, then your initial approach will be highly flexible. If, however, the purpose is confirmatory, where previous work has suggested an explanation of some phenomenon, then there is a place for some degree of pre-structure. There is an obvious trade-off between *looseness* and *selectivity*. The looser the original design, the less selective you can afford to be in data selection. Anything might be important. On the other hand, the danger is that if you *start* with a relatively tight conceptual framework or theoretical views, this may blind you to important features of the case or cause you to misinterpret evidence. There is no obvious way out of this dilemma. Practicalities may dictate some pre-structuring, for example, if the project is on a very tight time-scale, as in much small-scale contract research.

BOX 7.4

Some types of case study

1. *Individual case study.* Detailed account of one person. Tends to focus on antecedents, contextual factors, perceptions and attitudes preceding a known outcome (e.g. drug user; immigrant). Used to explore possible causes, determinants, factors, processes, experiences, etc., contributing to the outcome.
2. *Set of individual case studies.* As above, but a small number of individuals with some features in common are studied.
3. *Community studies.* Studies of one or more local communities. Describes and analyses the pattern of, and relations between, main aspects of community life (politics; work; leisure; family life; etc.). Commonly descriptive, but may explore specific issues or be used in theory testing.
4. *Social group studies.* Studies of both small direct contact groups (e.g. families) and larger, more diffuse ones (e.g. occupational group). Describes and analyses relationships and activities.
5. *Studies of organizations and institutions.* Studies of firms, workplaces, schools, trades unions, etc. Many possible foci, e.g. best practice; policy implementation and evaluation; industrial relations; management and organizational issues; organizational cultures; processes of change and adaptation; etc.
6. *Studies of events, roles and relationships.* Focus on a specific event (overlaps with (3) and (4)). Very varied; include studies of police–citizen encounters; doctor–patient interactions; specific crimes or 'incidents' (e.g. disasters); studies of role conflicts, stereotypes, adaptations.
7. *Cross-national comparative studies.* Used for research on local and national governments and the policy process.

(after Hakim, 2000, pp. 63–72)

Holistic case studies

Yin (2013) differentiates between two versions of the single case study on the basis of the level of the unit of analysis. A study where the concern remains at a single, global level is referred to as *holistic*. This would typically (though not necessarily) be how a case study of an individual would be viewed but would also apply to, say, the study of an institution which remained at the level of the whole rather than seeking to look at and analyse the different functioning of separate sub-units within the institution.

Holistic case studies are appropriate in several situations. The *critical case* is a clear, though unfortunately rare, example. This occurs when your theoretical understanding is such that there is a clear, unambiguous and non-trivial set of circumstances where predicted outcomes will be found. Finding a case which fits, and demonstrating what has been predicted, can give a powerful boost to knowledge and understanding. This is the way in which experiment is used classically – the 'crucial experiment'. It is interesting to note that some of the most illustrious of this genre, for example, the verification of Einstein's theory of relativity by measuring the 'bending' of light from a distant star at a rare eclipse, are effectively case studies (being the study of a particular instance in its context) rather than experiments (in that no experimental manipulation of variables is possible).

The *extreme case* also provides a rationale for a simple, holistic case study. A former colleague now features as a case in an orthopaedic textbook because of the virtually complete recovery he made from horrific arm and leg injuries in a cycle crash, after skilled surgical and physiotherapy support, together with his own determination, confounded initial gloomy predictions. More generally, the extreme and the unique can provide a valuable 'test bed' for which this type of case study is appropriate. Extremes include the 'if it can work here it will work anywhere' scenario, to the 'super-realization' where, say, a new approach is tried under ideal circumstances, perhaps to obtain understanding of how it works before its wider implementation.

However, context can be crucial. Research into Project Dunkelfeld in Germany (http://www.dont-offend.org), a walk-in centre for individuals with sexual deviant fantasies (such as involving rape, or child sexual abuse) who have not committed an offence and who seek help, indicates that the project has helped to reduce sexual offending. In Germany there is not a requirement for medical practitioners to report this information to state authorities, so anonymity is guaranteed. In a context where there is an expectation of reporting, and therefore no guarantee of anonymity (as in the UK), a similar project would be unlikely to be effective.

Multiple case studies

In many studies it is appropriate to study more than a single case. A very common misconception is that this is for the purpose of gathering a 'sample' of cases so that generalization to some population might be made.

Mookherji and LaFond (2013) discuss the kinds of generalizations which can be made from multiple case studies, and how they can be maximized. Yin makes the useful analogy that carrying out multiple case studies is more like doing multiple experiments. These may be attempts at replication of an initial experiment or they may build upon the first experiment, perhaps carrying the investigation into an area suggested by the first study or they may seek to complement the first study by focusing on an area not originally covered. This activity, whether for multiple case studies or for multiple experiments (or for multiple surveys for that matter; or for multiple studies involving other research design strategies), is not concerned with *statistical generalization* but with what is sometimes referred to as *analytic* or *theoretical generalization*. The first case study will provide evidence which supports a theoretical view about what is going on; perhaps in terms of mechanisms and the contexts in which they operate. This theory, and its possible support or disconfirmation, guides the choice of subsequent cases in a multiple case study. Findings, patterns of data, etc. from these case studies which provide this kind of support, particularly if they simultaneously provide evidence which does not fit in with alternative theories, are the basis for generalization.

Put simply, cases are selected where *either* the theory would suggest that the same result is obtained *or* that predictably different results will be obtained. Given, say, three of each which fall out in the predicted manner, this provides pretty compelling evidence for the theory. This is an over-simplification because case studies and their outcomes are likely to be multi-faceted and difficult to capture adequately within a simple theory. Support for the theory may be qualified or partial in any particular case, leading to revision and further development of the theory, and then probably the need for further case studies.

Preparing a case study plan

An important feature of case study is that if more than one investigator is involved, they typically take on essentially similar roles. The tasks cannot be reduced to rigid formulae with division of function as in survey research. Whereas in fixed design research, different people can be involved with data collection, in case study research all the researchers needs to be fully integrated into the process. They all need an intelligent appreciation of what they are doing, and why. Hence, it is highly desirable that all are involved in the first stages of conceptualization and definition of the research questions. Similarly, they should all be involved in the development of the case study plan.

The plan contains details of the data collection procedures to be used and the general rules to be followed. Where there is a single investigator, the main purpose of the plan is to enhance the validity of the study but it also acts as an *aide-mémoire* for the investigator. When a team is involved, it also serves to increase reliability in the sense of assisting all investigators to follow the same set of procedures and rules. Box 7.5 gives suggestions for the organization of the plan.

BOX 7.5

The case study plan

It is highly desirable that an explicit plan is prepared and agreed by those involved *in the full knowledge and expectation that aspects of this may change as the work continues.*
The following sections may be helpful:

1. *Overview.* Covers the background information about the project; the context and perspective, and why it is taking place; the issues being investigated and relevant readings about the issues.
2. *Procedures.* Covers the major tasks in collecting data, including:
   (a) access arrangements;
   (b) resources available; and
   (c) schedule of the data collection activities and specification of the periods of time involved.
3. *Questions.* The set of research questions with accompanying list of probable sources of evidence
4. *Reporting.* Covers the following:
   (a) outline of the case study report(s);*
   (b) treatment of the full 'data base' (i.e. totality of the documentary evidence obtained); and
   (c) audience(s).*

Note: The plan should communicate to a general intelligent reader what is proposed. It forms part of establishing the validity of the study.

---

*There may be several audiences, for which different reports (in style and length) are needed. Consideration of reports and audiences at this stage, and during the study, helps to guide the study. See Chapter 19.

Pilot studies

A pilot study is a small-scale version of the real thing; a try-out of what you propose so that its feasibility can be checked. There are aspects of case study research which can make piloting both more difficult to set up and, fortunately, less crucially important. It may be that there is only one case to be considered or that there are particular features of the case selected (such as geographical or temporal accessibility, or your own knowledge of the case), such that there is no sensible equivalent which could act as the pilot.

In circumstances like these, the flexibility of case study gives you at least some opportunity to 'learn on the job'. Or it may be that the initial formulation leans more toward the 'exploratory' pole of case study design and later stages with the benefit of experience can have a more 'explanatory' or 'confirmatory' focus.

Yin distinguishes between 'pilot tests' and 'pre-tests'. He views the former as helping investigators to refine their data collection plans with respect to both the content of the data and the procedures to be followed. For him, the pilot is, as it were, a laboratory for the investigators, allowing them to observe different phenomena from many different angles or to try different approaches on a trial basis. We prefer to regard these as case studies in their own right with an essentially exploratory function where some of the research questions are methodological. What he calls the 'pre-test' is a formal 'dress rehearsal' in which the intended data collection plan is used as faithfully as possible and is perhaps closer to the usual meaning of a pilot study.

The website provides references to case studies of different types as used in a range of disciplines.

Many flexible design studies, even though not explicitly labelled as such, can be usefully viewed as case studies. They take place in a specific setting, or small range of settings, context is viewed as important, and there is commonly an interest in the setting in its own right. While they may not be multi-method as originally designed, the use of more than one method of data collection when feasible can improve many flexible design studies. Hence, even if you decide to follow one of the other flexible design traditions, you will find consideration of the above sections on case study of value.

Ethnographic studies

An ethnography provides a description and interpretation of the culture and social structure of a social group. It has its roots in anthropology, involving an immersion in the particular culture of the society being studied so that life in that community could be described in detail. The ethnographer's task was to become an accepted member of the group including participating in its cultural life and practices. Anthropologists initially focused on exotic cultures such as Trobriand Islanders in New Guinea. Sociologists, initially at Chicago University, adapted the approach to look at groups and communities in modern urban society (Bogdan & Biklen, 2007), and it is currently widely used in social research (e.g. Atkinson, Delamont, Coffey, Lofland & Lofland, 2007; Nahman, 2013).

A central feature of this tradition is that people are studied for a long time period in their own natural environment. Critics of the approach are concerned about researchers getting over-involved with the people being studied, perhaps disturbing and changing the natural setting, and hence compromising the quality of the research. However the argument is that 'in order to truly grasp the lived experience of people from their point of view, one *has* to enter into relationships with them, and hence disturb the natural setting. There is no point in trying to control what is an unavoidable consequence of becoming involved in people's lives in this way' (Davidson & Layder, 1994, p.165; emphasis in original). Hence it becomes necessary to try to assess the effects of one's presence.

The main purpose and central virtue of this approach is often considered to be its production of descriptive data free from imposed external concepts and ideas. Its goal is to produce 'thick description' (Geertz, 1973) which allows others to understand the culture from inside in the terms that the participants themselves used to describe what is going on. There is clear value in doing this for and about cultures where little is known or where there have been misleading presumptions or prejudices about the culture of a group.

Some ethnographists display a general distrust of theorizing. However, there seems to be no reason why an ethnographical approach cannot be linked to the development of theory (Hammersley, 1985). Working within the ethnographic tradition is not an easy option for the beginner, for the reasons given in Box 7.6.

Using an ethnographic approach

Using an ethnographic approach is very much a question of general style rather than of following specific prescriptions about procedure. In process terms, it involves getting out into 'the field' and staying there. Classically this meant staying there for a long period, of the order of two or more years. This is highly unrealistic for virtually all real world studies and hence this section focuses on the use of ethnographic techniques rather than on how to carry out a full-scale

---

BOX 7.6

Difficulties in doing an ethnographic study

1. To 'do an ethnography' calls for a detailed description, analysis, and interpretation of the culture-sharing group. This requires an understanding of the specialist concepts used when talking about socio-cultural systems.
2. For traditional ethnographies the time taken to collect data is very long, often extending over years. Some current approaches (sometimes referred to as 'mini-ethnographies') seek to cut this down drastically, but this creates a tension with the requirement to develop an intimate understanding of the group.
3. Ethnographies have typically been written in a narrative, literary style which may be unfamiliar to those with a social science background (conversely this can be an advantage to those with an arts or humanities background). This may also be a disadvantage when reporting to some real world audiences.
4. Researchers have been known to 'go native', resulting in their either discontinuing the study or moving from the role of researcher to that of advocate.

ethnography. However long you are in the field it is crucial that you have a full record of your involvement – you need high quality 'field notes' (Emerson, Fretz & Shaw, 2011). Box 7.7 lists features of the ethnographic approach.

Participant observation is very closely associated with the process of an ethnographic study. Chapter 14 considers the different types of role the observer might take. Whatever degree of participation you adopt (ranging from that of full group member to one where you are involved solely as a researcher) observation is difficult, demanding and time-consuming. Gill and Temple (2014) give a 'warts and all' account. Box 7.8 helps you to assess whether or not it is for you. If it isn't, you should probably rule out an ethnographic study. However, while it is undoubtedly true that virtually all ethnographic studies do use this type of observation, they can be eclectic in methods terms, making use of whatever technique appears to be feasible. The feature which is crucial is that the researcher is fully *immersed* in the day-to-day lives of the people being studied.

The focus of an ethnographic study is a group who share a culture. Your task is to learn about that culture, effectively to understand their world as they do. Initially such studies were carried out by cultural anthropologists who studied societies and cultures very different from their own. Even when some familiar group, or sub-group within one's own society is the focus, the ethnographic approach asks the researcher to treat it as 'anthropologically strange'. This is a very valuable exercise, particularly for those carrying out 'insider research'. It provides a means of bringing out into the open presuppositions about what you are seeing.

You should be aware though that ethnography presents certain additional dimensions of ethics, morality and risk (both for the researchers and for participants. Therefore it is not a methodology to be selected lightly. University, and other, ethics committees usually have a lot to say about ethnographic research!

BOX 7.7

Features of the ethnographic approach

1. The shared cultural meanings of the behaviour, actions, events and contexts of a group of people are central to understanding the group. Your task is to uncover those meanings.
2. To do this requires you to gain an insider's perspective.
3. Hence you need both to observe and study the group in its natural setting, and to take part in what goes on there.
4. While participant observation in the field is usually considered essential, no additional method of data collection is ruled out in principle.
5. The central focus of your study and detailed research questions will emerge and evolve as you continue your involvement. A prior theoretical orientation and initial research questions or hypotheses are not ruled out, but you should be prepared for these to change.
6. Data collection is likely to be prolonged over time and to have a series of phases. It is common to focus on behaviours, events, etc. which occur frequently so that you have the opportunity to develop understanding of their significance.

BOX 7.8

Using participant observation

Commit yourself to doing this only if the following fits you pretty closely:

1. You see interactions, actions and behaviours and the way people interpret these, act on them, etc. as central.
2. You believe that knowledge of the social world can be best gained by observing 'real life' settings.
3. You consider that generating data on social interaction in specific contexts, as it occurs, is superior to retrospective accounts or their ability to verbalize and reconstruct a version of what happened.
4. You view social explanations as best constructed through depth, complexity and roundedness in data.
5. You are happy with an active, reflexive and flexible research role.
6. You feel it is more ethical to enter into and become involved in the social world of those you research, rather than 'standing outside'.
7. You can't see any alternative way of collecting the data you require to answer your research questions.

(adapted and abridged from Mason, 1996, pp. 84–102)

Ethnography and realism

Classically, ethnography was seen as a way of getting close to the reality of social phenomena in a way which is not feasible with the experimental and survey strategies. The Chicago sociologist Herbert Blumer talked about using ethnography to 'lift the veils' and to 'dig deeper' illustrating his realist assumptions (Hammersley, 1989).

However, there is a tension within the ethnographic research community on this issue. 'Central to the way in which ethnographers think about human social action is the idea that people *construct* the social world, both through their interpretations of it and through the actions based upon those interpretations' (Hammersley, 1992a, p. 44, emphasis in original). Hammersley goes on to argue, persuasively, that this constructivist approach can be compatible with realism. This calls for an abandonment of the 'naïve' realism characteristic of early ethnography where it was assumed that the phenomena studied were independent of the researcher who could make direct contact with them and provide knowledge of unquestionable validity. He argues in favour of 'subtle' realism as a viable alternative to the relativist constructionist approach.

The key elements of subtle realism, elaborated in Hammersley (1992a, pp. 50–54) are:

• defining knowledge as beliefs about whose validity we are reasonably confident (accepting that we can never be absolutely certain about the validity of any claim to knowledge);
• acknowledging that there are phenomena independent of our claims about them, which those claims may represent more or less accurately; and

- an overall research aim of representing reality while acknowledging that such a representation will always be from a particular perspective which makes some features of the phenomenon relevant and others irrelevant (hence there can be multiple valid and non-contradictory representations).

This represents a reprise, using rather different terminology, of some of the issues discussed in Chapter 2 where the case was made for the adoption of a realist approach.

Designing an ethnographic study

The framework for research design given in Chapter 4 (Figure 4.1, p. 72) is applicable for an ethnographic study. As with other types of study, you need to give serious consideration to the purposes of your work and to establishing some (probably very tentative) theoretical or conceptual framework. This gives you an initial take on possible research questions, which in themselves assist in the selection of data collection methods and sampling – in the sense of who you observe, where, when, etc. While you can assume that participant observation of some kind will be involved, it may be that you have research questions which call for an additional approach or that additional methods will give valuable scope for triangulation.

An ethnographic approach is particularly indicated when you are seeking insight into an area or field which is new or different (and, paradoxically, in an area with which you are very familiar). It can help gain valuable insights which can then guide later research using other approaches. Remember that your initial research questions (and the other aspects of the framework you started out with) are highly likely to change and develop as you get involved.

There is no one specific design for an ethnographic study. Depth rather than breadth of coverage is the norm, with a relatively small number of cases being studied. Description and interpretation is likely to be stressed (Atkinson *et al.*, 2007; O'Reilly, 2009). This small number, whether of people, situations, places, times or whatever, is essentially a *convenience sample*, sometimes a *snowball sample* where one informant suggests someone else you should contact (Chapter 11, p. 280). Looked at in these terms it highlights potential concerns about the representativeness of your account. Duneier (2011), in an engaging paper on 'How not to lie with ethnography', discusses strategies for improving the reliability of findings. One is to:

> . . . imagine that I will stand trial for ethnographic malpractice. An attorney has brought a claim against me on behalf of my study's readers . . . witnesses who know about my subject will be called. The important thing about these witnesses is that they will be the ones I most fear hearing from because what they know is least convenient for the impressions I have given the reader. They may also have been the least convenient for me to get to know (p. 2).

He also suggests thinking about the 'inconvenience sample'. This includes people, observations, etc. not in the sample whose existence would have implications for the story being told.

References to studies from different areas and disciplines using an ethnographic approach are provided in the website.

While ethnography is a distinctive approach, it can be linked with either the case study or grounded theory approaches. A case study can be approached ethnographically or an ethnographic study can be approached by means of grounded theory.

Grounded theory studies

A grounded theory study seeks to generate a theory which relates to the particular situation forming the focus of the study. This theory is 'grounded' in data obtained during the study, particularly in the actions, interactions, and processes of the people involved. It is closely associated with two American sociologists, Barney Glaser and Anselm Strauss. Their highly influential text introducing this approach (Glaser & Strauss, 1967) has been followed by several more accessible introductions including Birks and Mill (2015), Glaser and Strauss (1999), and Corbin and Strauss (2008).

Their approach was in reaction to the sociological stance prevalent in the 1960s which insisted that studies should have a firm *a priori* theoretical orientation. It has proved particularly attractive in novel and applied fields where pre-existing theories are often hard to come by. The notion that it is feasible to discover concepts and come up with hypotheses from the field, which can then be used to generate theory, appeals to many.

Grounded theory is both a strategy for doing research and a particular style of analysing the data arising from that research. Each of these aspects has a particular set of procedures and techniques. It is not a theory in itself, except perhaps in the sense of claiming that the preferred approach to theory development is via the data you collect. While grounded theory is often presented as appropriate for studies which are exclusively qualitative, there is no reason why some quantitative data collection should not be included. Indeed, the first studies reported in Glaser and Strauss (1967) made extensive use of quantitative data. In later years, differences have built up between the two collaborators to the extent that Glaser (1992) takes vigorous exception to the direction in which Strauss (and other colleagues) has taken grounded theory. Rennie (1998), in developing a rationale for grounded theory which reconciles realism and relativism, argues that Strauss and Corbin's approach effectively reverts to the *hypothetico-deductivism* of traditional experimentalism, and that Glaser's procedures are more consistent with the objectives of the method.

Box 7.9 indicates some attractive features of grounded theory research; Box 7.10 some problems in carrying it out.

BOX 7.9

Attractive features of grounded theory research

1. Provides explicit procedures for generating theory in research.
2. Presents a strategy for doing research which, while flexible, is systematic and coordinated.
3. Provides explicit procedures for the analysis of qualitative data.
4. Particularly useful in applied areas of research, and novel ones, where the theoretical approach to be selected is not clear or is non-existent.
5. A wide range of exemplars of its use in many applied and professional settings is now available.

BOX 7.10

Problems in using grounded theory

1. It is not possible to start a research study without some pre-existing theoretical ideas and assumptions (as assumed in some versions of grounded theory research).
2. There are tensions between the evolving and inductive style of a flexible study and the systematic approach of grounded theory.
3. It may be difficult in practice to decide when categories are 'saturated' or when the theory is sufficiently developed.
4. Grounded theory has particular types of prescribed categories as components of the theory which may not appear appropriate for a particular study.

Carrying out a grounded theory study

A grounded theory study involves going out into 'the field' and collecting data. No particular type of 'field' is called for. Such studies have been carried out in a very wide range of settings. Glaser and Strauss initially worked in organizational contexts; interest in their studies of dying in hospitals (Glaser & Strauss, 1965; 1968) provided the stimulus for their first methodology text (Glaser & Strauss, 1967). El Hussein, Hirst, Salyers and Osuji (2014) provide an accessible short introduction.

Interviews are the most common data collection method. However, other methods such as observation (participant or otherwise) and the analysis of documents can and have been used. Similarly, although grounded theory is typically portrayed as a qualitative approach to research, there is no reason in principle why some form of quantitative data collection cannot be used.

Procedurally, the researcher is expected to make several visits to the field to collect data. The data are then analysed between visits. Visits continue until the *categories* found through analysis are 'saturated'. Or, in other words, you keep on gathering information until you reach diminishing returns and you are not adding to what you already have. (A category is a unit of information made up of events, happenings, and instances).

This movement back and forth – first to the field to gather information, then back to base to analyse the data; then back to the field to gather more information, then back home to analyse the data; etc. – is similar to the 'dialogic' process central to the hermeneutic tradition (see below, p. 165). It is very different from a traditional linear one-way model of research where you first gather all your data, then get down to the analysis. It is close to the common-sense approach which one might use when trying to understand something which is complex and puzzling. One of the real challenges of collecting data in this fashion is how to collate it while remaining in the field, to avoid being seen as an obvious outsider or researcher. Tactics that have been used include making periodic trips to a toilet or wash-room to write up notes; or memorizing all the day's activities, then writing it all up afterwards; or sending 'texts' to yourself with key information. All of which present their own challenges. This is something that has to be carefully thought through in the planning stages.

Sampling in grounded theory studies is *purposive* (see Chapter 11, p. 281). We do not seek a representative sample for its own sake; there is certainly no notion of random sampling from a known population to achieve statistical generalizability. Sampling of people to interview or events to observe is so that additional information can be obtained to help in generating conceptual categories. Within grounded theory, this type of purposive sampling is referred to as *theoretical sampling*. That is, the persons interviewed, or otherwise studied, are chosen to help the researcher formulate theory.

The repeated comparison of information from data collection and emerging theory is sometimes referred to as the *constant comparative* method of data analysis. Its most standardized form is given in Strauss and Corbin (1998) and Corbin and Strauss (2008) and is summarized in Box 7.11 (note however that Glaser, 1992 dissents quite violently from some of their prescriptions).

Further details of the analysis process are given in Chapter 18. A summary is presented here because of the intimate inter-relationship between design and analysis in a grounded theory study. It may also help you to appreciate that a grounded theory study is by no means an easy option and

BOX 7.11

Data analysis in grounded theory studies

The analysis involves three sets of coding:

1. *Open coding.* The researcher forms initial *categories* of information about the phenomenon being studied from the initial data gathered. Within each category, you look for several subcategories (referred to as *properties*) and then for data to dimensionalize (i.e. to show the dimensions on which properties vary and to seek the extreme possibilities on these continua).
2. *Axial coding.* This involves assembling the data in new ways after open coding. A *coding paradigm* (otherwise known as a *logic diagram*) is then developed which:
   - identifies a *central phenomenon* (i.e. a central category about the phenomenon);
   - explores *causal conditions* (i.e. categories of conditions that influence the phenomenon);
   - specifies *strategies* (i.e. the actions or interactions that result from the central phenomenon);
   - identifies the *context* and *intervening conditions* (i.e. the conditions that influence the strategies); and
   - delineates the *consequences* (i.e. the outcomes of the strategies) for this phenomenon.
   - *Selective coding* involves the integration of the categories in the axial coding model. In this phase, conditional *propositions* (or hypotheses) are typically presented.
3. The result of this process of data collection and analysis is a *substantive-level theory* relevant to a specific problem, issue, or group.

Note: The three types of coding are not necessarily sequential; they are likely to overlap.

While the terms 'axial coding' and 'selective coding' are well established they are somewhat confusing as 'coding' usually refers to applying categories to data.

should not be undertaken lightly. It is, of course, possible to design a study which incorporates some aspects of grounded theory while ignoring others. For example, you may feel that the approach to coding is too prescriptive or restrictive. However, as with other research traditions, by working within the tradition you buy shelter and support from criticism – providing that the ways of the tribe are followed faithfully. And, less cynically, the fact that a group of researchers and methodologists have worked away at the approach over a number of years makes it likely that solutions to problems and difficulties have been found. Wu and Beaunae (2014) present a set of 'Personal reflections on cautions and considerations for navigating the path of grounded theory doctoral theses and dissertations', which they characterize as 'a long walk through a dark forest'.

Realism and grounded theory

Disagreements within the grounded theory family, mentioned above, are mirrored in the stance taken about realism. Bryant and Charmaz (2007) claim that: 'The key weaknesses of Glaser and Strauss's statement of the GTM [Grounded theory method] resided in the positivist, objectivist direction they gave grounded theory' and, in particular, that: 'In seeking to provide a firm and valid basis for qualitative research their early position can be interpreted as justification for a naïve, realist form of positivism' (p. 33). This reading is not unreasonable, but it was appreciated at an early stage that such positivist shackles were not an intrinsic feature of the approach.

Certainly, grounded theory as practised has developed in more flexible ways, to the extent that: 'The postmodernist may see this style as objectivist, realist and scientific; the positivist may see it as disconcertingly literary' (Charmaz, 2003, p. 280). While this comment refers to reports of grounded theory studies, it reflects a more general perception that there are both objectivist and constructivist aspects to the ways of grounded theorists.

Of the two founding fathers, the position taken by Strauss (e.g. Corbin & Strauss, 2008) is the more constructivist, although considered by Annells (2006) to still reflect some aspects of positivist thought and language. Rennie and Fergus (2006) view the grounded theory method as an 'accommodation' of realism and relativism. For example, they consider that users of grounded theory:

> . . . are given the impression that social phenomena are external to the researcher and awaiting discovery, while being told that these phenomena are to be formulated creatively. They are encouraged to believe that with the correct procedures they will be able to access social phenomena grounded in reality, while being advised that the returns from the grounding will vary depending on the interests of the particular analyst (p. 484).

It is clear that there is no basic incompatibility between taking a realist view and using grounded theory. Grounded theory offers guidelines for building conceptual frameworks specifying the relationships among categories. If the guidelines are used as flexible tools rather than rigid rules, grounded theory gives researchers a broad method with distinct procedures that work in practice (Hallberg, 2006). As such it is suitable for pragmatic researchers of different methodological persuasions (or none).

A range of references to studies from different areas and disciplines using a grounded theory approach is provided in the website.

Other traditions

This section lists several other possible approaches which have been used. The main principle for their inclusion has been that they may be useful for answering particular kinds of research question.

- *Narrative research.* Based on 'stories'. Can refer to an entire life story, long sections of talk leading to extended accounts of lives, or even an answer to a single question.
- *Biographical and life history research.* A particular kind of case study where the 'case' studied is an individual person and the intention is to tell the story of a person's life.
- *Phenomenological research.* Focuses on the need to understand how humans view themselves and the world around them. The researcher is considered inseparable from assumptions and preconceptions about the phenomenon of study. Instead of bracketing and setting aside such biases, an attempt is made to explain them and to integrate them into the research findings. The research methodology, informed by what is often called 'interpretive phenomenology', seeks to reveal and convey deep insight and understanding of the concealed meanings of everyday life experiences.
- *Hermeneutics.* Originally concerned with the translation and interpretation of sacred texts such as the Bible. It continues to provide a useful method for the analysis of texts and other documents. It has also been extended to include seeking understanding of any human action, with an emphasis on the importance of language in achieving that understanding, and on the context in which it occurs. The focus is on how the understanding is achieved rather than what is understood.

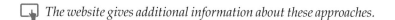 *The website gives additional information about these approaches.*

Feminist perspectives and flexible designs

Some researchers following a feminist perspective reject quantitative methods and designs, and both *positivism* and *postpositivism*. For them flexible, qualitative designs are the only option. There is certainly an emphasis in these design traditions on non-exploitative research seeking an empathetic understanding between researcher and participants which chimes closely with feminist views. However, as Davidson and Layder (1994, p. 217) point out, feminist methodologists are not the only, nor the first, to advocate such approaches. Reinharz (1992) also cautions against the assumption that research using qualitative methods is inherently feminist. She also describes the wide variety of viewpoints that feminists hold on the appropriateness of different methods and methodologies. Eagly and Riger (2014) present a balanced critique, focusing on psychology.

Hence the position taken here, following Davidson and Layder (1994), is that while the critique presented by feminist methodologists of traditional social science research has yielded important insights, and helped to strengthen the case for qualitative research, the claim for a distinctive feminist research methodology has not been substantiated.

Sampling in flexible designs

Determining an appropriate sample in fixed designs, as discussed in the previous chapter, is relatively straightforward. There is almost always a concern that the sample is representative of a known population, so that statistical generalization is possible. Given this, what we find out about the sample can be regarded as telling us something about that population, probabilistically at least. The size of the sample is largely determined by the requirements of the statistical analysis we intend to carry out. Such analyses typically assume representative sampling (although, as discussed in Chapter 17, p. 452, all too often the samples have not been selected in a way which ensures this).

The most important thing to appreciate about sampling in flexible designs is that one is playing a very different kind of game. The data are almost always non-numerical and hence conventional statistical analysis is not feasible. Aspects of the qualitative data may be amenable to conversion into a numerical form, or there may be some data collected directly as numbers, enabling summary or descriptive statistics to be calculated, but the sample sizes are likely to be below those needed for statistical testing. More fundamentally, the nature of the sampling makes such testing inappropriate. It is typically *purposive* or *theoretical*, rather than seeking to be *representative* of a known population (see Chapter 11, p. 282). In these circumstances statistical generalization is not possible.

Nevertheless, although there are situations where researchers using flexible designs simply want to say something sensible about the specific circumstances of their research, many wish to make generalizations of some sort. This may be in the form of a theoretical conceptualization of what they have found (the central aim of a grounded theory study). Or, in realist terms, that they have evidence for mechanisms operating in certain contexts. Or, in very general terms, that the findings from the study somehow 'speak' to what might be happening in other settings or cases.

Generalizability of findings from flexible design research

> *Resist the temptation to smuggle in the concepts and approach of statistical generalization. It won't work.*

Small (2009) emphasizes the basic incompatibility of statistical generalization and flexible design research. Box 7.12 summarizes one of the scenarios that he presents to illustrate his case (see also a second hypothetical scenario based on an ethnographic study of an 'average' neighbourhood).

An alternative, favoured by Small, is to view the scenario of Box 7.12 as akin to multiple case studies rather than a small sample study. As discussed earlier in the chapter, multiple case studies are effectively replications where each successive case adds to the understanding of questions at issue:

> The first unit or case yields a set of findings and a set of questions that inform the next case. If the study is conducted properly, the very last case examined will provide very little new or surprising information. The objective is *saturation*. An important component of case study design is that each subsequent case attempts to replicate the prior ones. Through 'literal replication' a similar case is found to determine whether the same mechanisms are

BOX 7.12

Incompatibility of statistical generalization and flexible design research

Scenario: Study of attitudes towards immigration of working-class African Americans
Approach: Lengthy open-ended interviews with 35 *respondents*.
Question: How to ensure that the findings are generalizable?
Plan: Find city with large working-class African American population.

Random selection of 100 people from telephone directory: 40 target population agree to an interview; 35 follow through (highly optimistic figures). Conduct high quality two-hour interviews.

From the perspective of statistical generalizability:

* *Problems of inbuilt and unaccounted for bias.* The 35 are those polite enough to talk, friendly enough to keep appointment based on cold call and extroverted enough to share feelings with interviewer. We know nothing about the 65 who weren't interviewed or about working class blacks in other cities.
* *Sample too small.* Not large enough to make confident predictions about complex relationships in the population.
Alternatives
* *Use a survey instead.* This would need to severely restrict the number of questions. With one simple yes/no question, to be confident statistically about the 1,000 working class blacks in one city you need an approximate sample of 300.
* *Use a different sampling technique.* Snowball sampling where interviewees recommend other interviewees will increase the number of respondents and possibly their openness. But this would be seen as increasing bias and reducing representativeness from the perspective of statistical generalization.

(abridged from Small, 2009, pp. 11–15)

in play; through 'theoretical replication' a case different according to the theory is found to determine whether the expected difference is found (p. 25).

Note, however, that while the scenario has a weak sample on a sampling logic basis, it is also weak on a case logic basis. It is possible that one might achieve saturation after the 35 interviews – or even with a much smaller number. Following the case logic, one starts with a single interview, not knowing how many are going to be sufficient. The choice of a second interviewee will be based on issues arising from the first, perhaps using snowball sampling or some other means to identify a person from a particular background, age or gender. The process is then repeated several times until saturation. Viewed in this light the 'How big a sample' question disappears. There are obvious variants of this process where, perhaps, a small set of interviews are set up and decisions made about what lines to follow up after they are completed.

Such a process would be viewed as horrendously biased if statistical generalization is the aim. Morse (2008) argues cogently that many of the problems of bias seen by critics of qualitative research designs and procedures arise from this inappropriate aim. For her, the following techniques of verification and saturation inherent in well-conducted qualitative research provide adequate safeguards:

- *Constantly evaluating the quality of data.* In a qualitative study, the quality of data is paramount. Investigators must attend to sampling adequacy (enough data), and sampling appropriateness (by interviewing 'good informants' who have experienced the phenomenon and who know the necessary information). If the proposed methods of data collection are not working and resulting in useful data, the investigator must change strategies – perhaps looking to a new study site, or types of participants, or even exploring whether the question itself is appropriate.

   Sampling for scope and variation. This is necessary to ensure that comprehensive data are obtained.

   Investigator sensitivity. Includes researcher reflexivity and techniques that enhance interpretation, including comparison with the literature, reflection on and comparison with known concepts, and the saturation of negative data.
- *Recognizing the progressive nature of inquiry.* Qualitative inquiry is a puzzle-solving activity. Ideas are initiated from one example, one instance or one participant, and the investigator is learning (gaining ideas) as the study progresses. Data from some participants may contribute more to the theoretical development of the study than others, some exemplars are better examples than others, and so on. This selection process is also reflected in the presentation of results, with the researcher's commentary describing the range and richness of the categories or themes, and the best (clearest case) exemplars used.

Establishing trustworthiness in flexible design research

The trustworthiness or otherwise of findings from flexible research is the subject of much debate. Fixed design researchers criticize the absence of their 'standard' means of assuring reliability and validity, such as checking inter-observer agreement, the use of quantitative measurement, explicit controls for threats to validity, the testing of formal hypotheses, and direct replication. Thus, for example, while the essential test of validity of a finding in the natural sciences is that it has been directly replicated by an independent investigator, this approach is not feasible when a flexible design is used (and is also highly questionable in real world fixed design research involving people). One problem is that identical circumstances cannot be re-created for the attempt to replicate. As Bloor (1997) pus it: 'Social life contains elements which are generalizable across settings (thus providing for the possibility of the social sciences) and other elements that are particular to given settings (thus forever limiting the predictive power of the social sciences' (p. 37).

Some researchers using flexible designs deny the relevance of canons of scientific enquiry (e.g. Guba & Lincoln, 1989). Others go further and reject the notion of any evaluative criteria such as reliability and validity (Wolcott, 1994). Taking an extreme relativist stance, it is maintained that using such criteria privileges some approaches inappropriately.

Altheide and Johnson (1994) argue that fields in the humanities such as history and literature employ evaluative criteria such as elegance, coherence and consistency which provide more appropriate standards for qualitative studies. While they may appear imprecise to traditional positivistically inclined researchers it is worth noting that even such a vague notion of elegance is used as a central criterion for the choice of one explanation over a rival in fields such as theoretical physics, the very heartland of natural science. More generally, accepting that social science researchers of whatever persuasion can benefit from some understanding of methodology in the humanities need not be at variance with the aspiration of remaining within the scientific fold put forward in Chapter 1. The problems of the relativist position outlined in Chapter 2 suggest a need for evaluative criteria in flexible designs. However, given the inappropriateness of the methods and techniques used in fixed design research, it is clear that different procedures for ensuring trustworthiness are called for (Kirk & Miller, 1986).

The terms *reliability* and validity are avoided by many proponents of flexible design. Lincoln and Guba (1985, pp. 294–301), for example, prefer the terms *credibility, transferability, dependability* and *confirmability*. However, this attempt to rename and disclaim the traditional terms continues to provide support for the view that qualitative studies are unreliable and invalid (Kvale & Brinkmann, 2009, p. 168). As Morse (1999) puts it in a forceful journal editorial entitled 'Myth #93: Reliability and Validity are not Relevant to Qualitative Inquiry':

> To state that reliability and validity are not pertinent to qualitative inquiry places qualitative research in the realm of being not reliable and not valid. Science is concerned with rigor, and by definition, good rigorous research must be reliable and valid. If qualitative research is unreliable and invalid, then it must not be science. If it is not science, then why should it be funded, published, implemented, or taken seriously? (p. 717)

While this argument goes over the top in apparently denying any value to non-scientific endeavours, it has force when we are seeking to characterize our research as scientific, following the arguments developed in Chapter 2.

The problem is not so much with the apple-pie desirability of doing reliable and valid research but the fact that these terms have been operationalized so rigidly in fixed design quantitative research. An answer is to find alternative ways of operationalizing them appropriate to the conditions and circumstances of flexible design research.

Validity

What do we mean by claiming that a piece of qualitative research is valid, that it has validity? It is something to do with it being accurate, or correct, or true. These are difficult (some would say impossible) things to be sure about. It is possible to recognize situations and circumstances which make validity more likely. These include the features of 'good' flexible design listed in Box 7.1. Conversely, it is pretty straightforward to come up with aspects likely to lead to invalid research. As with fixed, quantitative, designs they can be thought of as 'threats' to validity and are discussed below.

An alternative, though related, tack is to focus on the credibility of the research. The fact that some persons find it credible, or are prepared to trust it, is in itself a pretty weak justification. They may find it believable because it fits in with their prejudices. However, if the concern is with what might be appropriate bases for judging something to be credible, this returns us to consideration of what constitutes good quality research and possible threats to validity.

Threats to validity in flexible designs

Maxwell (1996) has presented a useful typology of the kinds of understanding involved in qualitative research. The main types are *description*, *interpretation*, and *theory*. Each of the main types has particular threats to its validity.

Description

The main threat to providing a valid description of what you have seen or heard lies in the inaccuracy or incompleteness of the data. This suggests that audio- or video-taping should be carried out wherever feasible. Note that, simply because you have a tape does not mean that it must be fully transcribed. Where taping is not feasible the quality of your notes is very important. These issues are discussed in detail in Chapter 12.

Interpretation

The main threat to providing a valid interpretation is through imposing a framework or meaning on what is happening rather than this occurring or emerging from what you learn during your involvement with the setting. This does not preclude a style of research where you do start with some kind of prior framework but this must be subjected to checking on its appropriateness, with possible modification. Mason (1996) shows how you might go about demonstrating the validity of your interpretation:

> In my view, validity of interpretation in any form of qualitative research is contingent upon the 'end product' including a demonstration of how that interpretation was reached. This means that you should be able to, and be prepared to, trace the route by which you came to your interpretation.
>
> The basic principle here is that you are never taking it as self-evident that a particular interpretation can be made of your data but instead that you are continually and assiduously charting and justifying the steps through which your interpretations were made (p. 150).

Note that Maxwell's notion of 'interpretation' refers specifically to interpretation of the meaning and perspective of participants, as in 'interpretive' research. He would consider the wider use of interpretation given here as not distinguishable from 'theory'.

Theory

The main threat is in not considering alternative explanations or understandings of the phenomena you are studying. This can be countered by actively seeking data which are not consonant with your theory. See the discussion of 'negative case analysis' below.

Bias and rigour

Issues of bias and rigour are present in all research involving people. However, the nature of much flexible design research is such that they are often particularly problematic. There is typically a close relationship between the researcher and the setting, and between the researcher and respondents. Indeed the notion of the 'researcher-as-instrument' (p. 173) central to many styles of qualitative research emphasizes the potential for bias. Padgett (2008, Chapter 8) presents a range of commonly used strategies to deal with these threats, which are discussed below.

Prolonged involvement

Involvement over a period of years was a defining characteristic of ethnography in its traditional anthropological version. Most current studies following the ethnographic approach have much more condensed fieldwork, but a period of weeks, or even months is still usual, a much more prolonged period than is typical in fixed methods research. This relatively prolonged involvement is also typical of other styles of flexible methods research and helps to reduce both reactivity and respondent bias. Researchers who spend a long time in the setting tend to become accepted and any initial reactivity reduces. Similarly, it permits the development of a trusting relationship between the researcher and respondents where the latter are less likely to give biased information.

There can, however, be greater researcher bias with prolonged involvement. A positive or negative bias may build up. It may be difficult to maintain the researcher role over an extended period of time (the 'going native' threat). Or developing antipathy might result in a negative bias.

Triangulation

This is a valuable and widely used strategy involving the use of multiple sources to enhance the rigour of the research. Denzin (1988b) distinguished four types of triangulation:

- *data triangulation:* The use of more than one method of data collection (e.g. observation, interviews, documents);
- *observer triangulation:* Using more than one observer in the study;
- *methodological triangulation:* Combining quantitative and qualitative approaches; and
- *theory triangulation:* Using multiple theories or perspectives.

Triangulation can help to counter all of the threats to validity. Note, however that it opens up possibilities of discrepancies and disagreements between the different sources. Thus, interviews and documents may be contradictory or two observers disagree about what has happened. Bloor (1997, pp. 38–41) argues that while triangulation is relevant to validity, it raises both logical and practical difficulties, for example, that findings collected by different methods differ to a degree which makes their direct comparison problematic. Such problems are a particular issue in multi-strategy (mixed methods) designs (Chapter 8, p. 184).

Peer debriefing and support

Peer groups (i.e. of researchers or students of similar status who are involved in flexible design research) can have a number of valuable functions. They can contribute to guarding against researcher bias through debriefing sessions after periods in the research setting. Such groups can also fulfil something almost amounting to a therapeutic function. This type of research can be extremely demanding and stressful for the researcher and the group can help you cope.

Member checking

Member checking involves returning (either literally or through correspondence, phone, e-mail, etc.) to respondents and presenting to them material such as transcripts, accounts and interpretations you have made. It can be a very valuable means of guarding against researcher bias. It also demonstrates to them that you value their perceptions and contributions. There are potential problems; perhaps your interpretation is challenged or a respondent gets cold feet and seeks to suppress some material. It is essential that you have a pre-agreed clear understanding with them about the rules governing such situations and that you respect both the spirit and the letter of such agreements. However a supine giving in to any criticism is not called for. Disagreements can usually be negotiated in a way which reflects both respondents' concerns and the needs of the study. Bloor (1997, pp. 41–8) discusses some of the complexities with examples.

Negative case analysis

The search for negative cases is an important means of countering researcher bias. As you develop theories about what is going on, you should devote time and attention to search for instances which will disconfirm your theory. This may be in data you already have or through collection of additional data. This is sometimes referred to as 'playing the devil's advocate' and you have a responsibility to do this thoroughly and honestly. Don't be too concerned that this procedure will lead to you ending up with a set of disconfirmed theories. In practice, it usually amounts to developing a more elaborated version of your theory.

Audit trail

The notion is that you keep a full record of your activities while carrying out the study. This would include your raw data (transcripts of interviews, field notes, etc.), your research journal (see Chapter 11, p. 273), and details of your data analysis.

Maxwell (1996; pp. 92–6), and Miles *et al.* (2014, pp. 317–21) provide alternative, but overlapping, sets of strategies which might be considered. Note, however, that while using such strategies will undoubtedly help in ruling out threats to validity, there is no foolproof way of *guaranteeing* validity. And that the strategies only help if you actually use them! Whereas in traditional fixed design research (particularly in true experimentation) threats to validity are essentially dealt with in advance as part of the design process, most threats to validity in flexible design research are dealt with after the research is in progress, and using evidence which you collect after you have begun to develop a tentative account.

Reliability in flexible designs

Reliability in fixed design research is associated with the use of standardized research instruments; for example, formal tests and scales as discussed in Chapter 13. It is also associated with the use of observation where the human observer is the standardized instrument. The concern is whether the tool or instrument produces consistent results. Thinking in such terms is problematic for most qualitative researchers. At a technical level, the general non-standardization of many methods of generating qualitative data precludes formal reliability testing. Nevertheless, there are common pitfalls to all types of data collection and transcription including equipment failure, environmental distractions and interruptions, and transcription errors. Easton, McComish and Greenberg (2000) suggest strategies to minimize the risk from these problems.

In a more general sense, however, researchers using flexible designs do need to seriously concern themselves with the reliability of their methods and research practices. This involves not only being thorough, careful and honest in carrying out the research, but also being able to show others that you have been. One way of achieving this is via the kind of audit trail described above.

Generalizability in flexible designs

Maxwell (1992) makes a useful distinction between *internal* and *external generalizability*. Internal generalizability refers to the generalizability of conclusions within the setting studied. External generalizability is generalizability beyond that setting. The former is an important issue in flexible designs. If you are selective in the people you interview, or the situations that you observe in a way which, say, excludes the people or settings which you find threatening or disturbing, this is likely to bias your account.

External generalizability may not be an issue. A case study might just be concerned with explaining and understanding what is going on in a particular school, drop-in centre or whatever is the focus of the study. It very rarely involves the selection of a representative (let alone random) sample of settings from a known population which would permit the kind of statistical generalization typical of survey designs. However, this does not preclude some kind of generalizability beyond the specific setting studied. This may be thought of as the development of a theory which helps in understanding other cases or situations (Ragin, 1987) sometimes referred to as *analytic* or *theoretical generalization*. For example, in realist terms, the study may provide convincing evidence for a set of mechanisms and the contexts in which they operate generalizable from, say, the particular intensive care unit studied to many other such units.

Further reading

The website gives annotated references to further reading for Chapter 7.

CHAPTER 8

Multi-strategy (mixed method) designs

This chapter:

- explains what multi-strategy designs are;
- rejects the incompatibility thesis which claims that this kind of research is not possible;
- discusses the mixed methods movement:
- presents a typology of multi-strategy designs;
- stresses the centrality of research questions to multi-strategy design;
- emphasizes its compatibility with both pragmatic and realist stances;
- suggests ways of dealing with discrepancies between the findings of quantitative and qualitative elements;
- provides examples of multi-strategy research; and
- concludes by warning that this increasingly advocated approach is no easy option.

Introduction

This chapter focuses on designs where there is a substantial element of qualitative data collection as well as a substantial element of quantitative data collection in the same research project. The term *mixed methods* is commonly used for these designs (sometimes 'multiple methods' – but see below). However, as they involve not only combining methods in some way but also using more than one research strategy they are referred to here as *multi-strategy designs* (a terminology also favoured by Alan Bryman who has published extensively in this area, e.g. Bryman, 2004). In the interests of communication both terms are included in the chapter title. Using both fixed and flexible design strategies in the same research project raises a number of issues, some theoretical, some very practical.

Using two or more methods of collecting qualitative data in a project is commonly done and non-controversial. Case studies have followed this approach for many years, typically combining two or more methods of collecting qualitative data. Multiple quantitative data collection methods are also common (e.g. where data from a structured observation schedule are linked to a questionnaire survey). See Chapter 14, p. 383, where these are referred to as *multiple methods* studies, for further discussion of the issues involved.

The last 20 years have seen a considerably increased interest in multi-strategy (mixed method) designs. Apart from a large handbook on the topic (Tashakkori & Teddlie, 2010), specialist texts include Creswell and Plano Clark (2011). Greene (2007) and Teddlie and Tashakkori (2009) concentrate on how to carry out this type of research. The *Journal of Mixed Methods Research* and the *International Journal of Multiple Research Approaches* both started in 2007 and are sources of published articles from a wide range of different fields. An annual UK conference on the topic has been held since 2005. Some advocates of multi-strategy (mixed method) designs are evangelical in their zeal. It is seen by them as an idea whose time has come, a 'third way' to do research, arising phoenix-like from the smoking ashes of the quantitative-qualitative wars.

The quantitative-qualitative incompatibility thesis

The 'incompatibility thesis' is that multiple strategy research is not possible because qualitative and quantitative research are associated with two distinct paradigms that are incompatible with each other. Sale, Lohfeld and Brazil (2002) assert that: 'Because the two paradigms do not study the same phenomena, quantitative and qualitative methods cannot be combined' (p. 43). Guba (1987) puts it more colourfully: 'The one [paradigm] precludes the other just as surely as belief in a round world precludes belief in a flat one' (p. 31).

Howe (1988) provides a comprehensive and convincing rebuttal of this thesis. He supports the view that, far from being incompatible, combining quantitative and qualitative methods is a good thing, and that 'there are important senses in which quantitative and qualitative methods are inseparable' (p. 10). A principle in the incompatibilist argument is that abstract paradigms should determine research methods in a simple one-way fashion. This principle was queried in Chapter 2 (p. 30) where an alternative, pragmatic, view was put forward. This is that there is a more complex two-way relationship between research methods and paradigms, where paradigms are evaluated in terms of how well they square with the demands of research practice. Crudely, if as is increasingly the case, research practitioners are successfully carrying out multi-strategy research, then the incompatibility thesis is refuted.

This is not to deny that there are major differences, particularly in research design and analysis, when dealing with quantitative and qualitative methods. The two preceding chapters discussed in detail the two research traditions of fixed and flexible design research which appear poles apart. However, as Howe (1988) points out, it is possible to overemphasize these differences, and fail to realize that there are many similarities.

The chief differences between quantitative and qualitative designs and analysis can be accounted for in terms of the questions of interest and their place within a complex web of background knowledge. Because quantitative research circumscribes the variables of interest, measures them in prescribed ways, and specifies the relationships among them that are to be investigated, quantitative data analysis has a mechanistic, non-judgemental component in the form of statistical inference. But, as Huberman (1987) notes, this component is small in the overall execution of a given research project, and it is far too easy to overestimate the degree to which quantitative studies, by virtue of employing precise measurement and statistics, are eminently 'objective' and 'scientific'. One gets to the point of employing statistical tests only by first making numerous judgments about what counts as a valid measure of the variables of interest, what variables threaten to confound comparisons, and what statistical tests are appropriate. Accordingly, the results of a given statistical analysis are only as credible as their background assumptions and arguments, and these are not amenable to mechanistic demonstration (p. 12).

In other words, fixed designs call for a complex web of qualitative judgments. Campbell (1978) goes so far as to argue that all research has a qualitative grounding. A further illustration of the blurring of the line between quantitative and qualitative research is a study by Gueulette, Newgent and Newman (1999), cited by Onwuegbuzie and Leech (2005), which analysed over 300 randomly selected studies labelled by their authors as representing qualitative research and found that over 40 per cent of the articles actually involved the blending of qualitative and quantitative methodologies.

It could still be argued that, despite the appearance that current research practice gives, quantitative and qualitative methods are in some sense incompatible. This view had greater force when methodologically minded researchers thought that they had to make a forced choice between a positivist and an interpretivist (or constructionist) approach. Positivist and interpretivist approaches are undoubtedly incompatible. Hence, if the positivist paradigm underpins quantitative methods, and an interpretivist paradigm underpins qualitative methods then, despite appearances, the two are incompatible. However, as discussed in Chapter 2, positivism has long ceased to be a viable option (though the message has still not got through to some researchers) and post-positivist approaches, including the more sophisticated variants of realism, as well as pragmatism, allow one to move beyond making the forced choice on which the incompatibility thesis relied. Howe (1988) concludes trenchantly:

> Questions about methodology remain, but they ought not be framed in way that installs abstract epistemology as a tyrant or that presupposes the moribund positivist-interpretivist split. The fact that quantitative and qualitative methods indeed might be historical outgrowths of incompatible positivist and interpretivist epistemologies no more commits present-day researchers to endorsing one or the other of these epistemologies than the fact that astronomy is an outgrowth of astrology commits present-day astronomers to squaring their predictions with their horoscopes (p. 15).

The mixed methods movement

The development of a movement where so-called mixed methods research evolved into a new research paradigm is commonly cited as an aftermath of the quantitative-qualitative *paradigm wars*. An early period in which the positivist quantitative paradigm was dominant between the 1950s and mid-1970s was followed by one in which the qualitative interpretivist/constructivist research paradigm became established as a viable alternative in the mid-1970s to the 1990s. Mixed methods, as a research paradigm, is seen as emerging from the 1990s onwards, establishing itself alongside the previous paradigms so that 'we currently are in a three methodological or research paradigm world, with quantitative, qualitative, and mixed methods research all thriving and coexisting' (Johnson, Onwuegbuzie & Turner, 2007). Its defining characteristics are typically cited as:

- quantitative and qualitative methods within the same research project;
- a research design that clearly specifies the sequencing and priority that is given to the quantitative and qualitative elements of data collection and analysis;
- an explicit account of the manner in which the quantitative and qualitative aspects of the research relate to each other; and
- pragmatism as the philosophical underpinning for the research (Denscombe, 2008).

However, not all mixed methods studies fit within this definition (see, for example, the very varied set of studies in Weisner, 2005).

Many researchers within the mixed methods movement do explicitly espouse a pragmatic approach (e.g. Morgan, 2007; Onwuegbuzie & Leech, 2005), but this is a controversial area – *see below*.

Referring to approaches of this kind as 'mixed methods' research is well established so while, as discussed above, we use 'multi-strategy designs' as a better descriptor, feel free to substitute 'mixed methods' if you prefer to vote with the current majority.

Types of multi-strategy designs

Research strategies and methods can be combined in a variety of ways. Box 8.1 presents a simple typology, based upon the order or sequence of the design elements and the priority that they are given. The two 'transformative' designs are typically used when there is a dedication to social change of some kind, reflecting an emancipatory or empowerment purpose. A very similar typology, with slightly different labels, has been put forward by Leech and Onwuegbuzie (2009).

Maxwell and Loomis (2003) accept the value of such typologies but stress their limitations. They consider that they do not capture the actual diversity of the designs researchers have used, and that typically they do little to clarify the actual functioning and interrelationship of the qualitative and quantitative parts of the design. Rather than viewing a research design as choosing from a set of possible arrangements or sequences they propose an interactive model with five components – purposes or goals, conceptual framework, research questions, methods and validity (Maxwell, 2005, p. 5). Their model is very similar to that developed in Chapter 4 (p. 72), but with the 'interactive' relationship between the components stressed by linking them using two-way arrows. It follows the mantra repeated throughout this book; that the research questions are at the heart of the design. Maxwell and Loomis advocate an integration of the typological and their interactive design approach. Typologies help in deciding on the *type of study*; in making broad decisions about how to proceed; in the sequencing and ordering of different approaches; and their relative dominance. The design model is a tool for designing and analysing an *actual study (see below)*.

A typology of multi-strategy designs focusing on the sequencing and status of data collection methods

1. *Sequential explanatory design.* Characterized by the collection and analysis of quantitative data followed by the collection and analysis of qualitative data. Priority is typically given to the quantitative data and the two methods are integrated during the interpretation phase of the study. The qualitative data function to help explain and interpret the findings of a primarily quantitative study.

2. *Sequential exploratory design.* Characterized by an initial phase of qualitative data collection and analysis followed by a phase of quantitative data collection and analysis. Priority is given to the qualitative aspect of the study. The findings are integrated during the interpretation phase. The primary focus of this design is to explore a phenomenon.

3. *Sequential transformative design.* One method precedes the other with either the qualitative or the quantitative method first. Priority may be given to either method. The results are integrated during interpretation. This design is guided primarily by a theoretical perspective (e.g. by the conceptual framework adopted).

4. *Concurrent triangulation design.* Qualitative and quantitative methods are used separately, independently and concurrently. Results are compared to assess their convergence.

5. *Concurrent nested design.* Involves the embedding or nesting of a secondary method within a study with one main or primary method. The primary method can be either quantitative or qualitative.

6. *Concurrent transformative design.* Guided primarily by the researcher's use of a specific theoretical perspective, as in the sequential transformative design above.

(based on Creswell, 2003, pp. 213–19)

Benefits of multi-strategy designs

Many benefits have been claimed for combining quantitative and qualitative data collection methods in a project. Box 8.2 lists some of them. Several of these benefits can accrue in multiple-method projects where the methods used are all quantitative, or all qualitative (see Chapter 15, p. 383). However, it will be clear that there is a greater variety of potential benefits when approaches associated with the two different paradigms of quantitative and qualitative research are brought together.

Complexities of multi-strategy designs

Bryman (2004) summarizes the results of interviewing a sample of 'mixed method' researchers. They cited a range of concerns, including:

- *Skills and training.* Skills and training is seen as a problem area. The skills and inclinations of many researchers are either quantitative or qualitative and they feel uncomfortable with the

BOX 8.2

Potential benefits of multi-strategy designs

1. *Triangulation.* Corroboration between quantitative and qualitative data enhances the validity of findings.
2. *Completeness.* Combining research approaches produces a more complete and comprehensive picture of the topic of the research.
3. *Offsetting weaknesses and providing stronger inferences.* Using these designs can help to neutralize the limitations of each approach while building on their strengths, leading to stronger inferences.
4. *Answering different research questions.* Multi-strategy designs can address a wider range of research questions than is feasible with single method fixed or flexible designs.
5. *Ability to deal with complex phenomena and situations.* A combination of research approaches is particularly valuable in real world settings because of the complex nature of the phenomena and the range of perspectives that are required to understand them.
6. *Explaining findings.* One research approach can be used to explain the data generated from a study using a different approach (e.g. findings from a quantitative survey can be followed up and explained by conducting interviews with a sample of those surveyed to gain an understanding of the findings obtained). This can be particularly useful when unanticipated or unusual findings emerge.
7. *Illustration of data.* Qualitative data can illustrate quantitative findings and help paint a better picture of the phenomenon under investigation. Bryman (2006a) refers to this as putting 'meat on the bones' of dry quantitative data.
8. *Refining research questions (hypothesis development and testing).* A qualitative phase of a study may be undertaken to refine research questions, or develop hypotheses to be tested in a follow-up quantitative phase.
9. *Instrument development and testing.* A qualitative phase of a study may generate items for inclusion in an instrument (e.g. questionnaire, test or scale, or structured observation schedule) to be used in a quantitative phase of a study.
10. *Attracting funding for a project.* Agencies funding research projects are showing increased interest in interdisciplinary research involving collaboration between disciplines traditionally using different approaches (e.g. in health-related areas where collaboration on projects between nursing, medical and other professionals is increasingly promoted and encouraged).

(based, in part, on Bryman, 2006a)

other tradition. Most commonly, this takes the form of qualitative researchers expressing unease about involvement in the more advanced forms of quantitative data analysis.

- *Timing issues.* Quantitative and qualitative components sometimes have different time implications. Most frequently, this takes the form of quantitative research being completed more quickly than the qualitative component.
- *Limits of multi-strategy research.* Multi-strategy research is not obviously beneficial when the rationale for combining quantitative and qualitative research is not made explicit. In such

cases, it is difficult to judge what has been gained by employing both approaches. In some studies, qualitative data are used only or mainly to illustrate quantitative findings. In such cases, the qualitative findings are largely ornamental and do not add a great deal to the study.
• *Lack of integration of findings.* Responses indicated that only a small proportion of studies fully integrate the quantitative and qualitative components when the research is written up.

Mason (2006), while acknowledging that they can have several benefits, is concerned that multi-strategy designs can produce disjointed and unfocused research, and can severely test the capabilities of researchers. Researchers 'need to have a clear sense of the logic and purpose of their approach and of what they are trying to achieve, because this ultimately must underpin their practical strategy not only for choosing and deploying a particular mix of methods, but crucially also for linking their data analytically' (p. 3). However, she admits that sometimes mixing methods and data can become possible more by accident than design, especially where existing data sets become available unexpectedly or serendipitously, or where access is available to a potential data source.

Mason stresses that, in the real world, practical, political and resource issues will establish certain constraints and contexts for those wishing to carry out multi-strategy research projects. These include:

• power, status and inequalities within and between teams, and for individual researchers, and between disciplines and fields of interest;
• constraints and opportunities of research funding; responsibilities to and expectations of funders and other stakeholders;
• access to and ownership of data; opportunities for collaboration, for sole working, for authorship;
• spread of skills and competencies; time, resources and capacity to learn new skills; and
• possibilities for strategic planning of outputs, e.g. for different purposes and audiences (pp. 11–12).

Mason concludes that 'it is just as important to recognize how these factors play out in one's own real life research, as it is to be clear about a desired strategy for mixing methods – since these are inextricably related and mixed methods research practice will involve dealing with both in tandem'.

Designing and carrying out multi-strategy research

The basic approach to research design discussed in Chapter 4 still applies. There is the additional task of clarifying and making explicit your rationale for, and the purpose of, using this type of design as discussed above. Essentially, why are you mixing quantitative and qualitative methods?

Hence, in the design framework of Figure 4.1 we have the elements of:

• purpose(s);
• conceptual framework;
• research questions;

- methods; and
- sampling procedures.

In multi-strategy research, consideration of purpose(s) has to be extended from the general issues covered in Chapter 4 to 'Why a multi-strategy design?' In a similar vein, the other elements (particularly the conceptual framework – see Greene, Caracelli and Graham, 1989) – have to take note of the particular issues raised by using both quantitative and qualitative methods of data collection. We are effectively marrying fixed and flexible design elements in the same overall project. Issues already discussed earlier in this chapter include:

- Implications for the overall design of likely difference in time scales for the qualitative and quantitative elements. Is the completion of one phase essential before a consequent phase can be started?
- As a sole researcher, do you have the necessary skill set to carry out both qualitative and quantitative elements? And to analyse and interpret both data sets? Can you get help where and when needed?
- In a research team, is there agreement about who does what? Are all team members in agreement about the design approach, etc.?

Research questions rule

The centrality of research questions for the research process has been the mantra of this text. This view enjoys considerable support in the research community active in multi-strategy social research. It is, in part, accounted for by the pragmatist stance taken by many of them which regards the research question(s) as the driver for carrying out research. However, there is not a necessary linkage between the two and researchers can, and do, approach multi-strategy research from other philosophical or theoretical standpoints – sometimes from none which is discernible.

Chapters 6 and 7 discussed research questions in the context of fixed design and flexible design strategies respectively. As multi-strategy designs necessarily include both fixed and flexible design elements or phases, they therefore call for the inclusion of a research question, or questions, covering both aspects. Keeping the focus on its being a single research project is helped by having a single main research question which to be answered properly needs both quantitative and qualitative data collection. Separate sub-questions, focusing on the different elements individually, can then be developed.

Onwuegbuzie and Leech (2006) present a detailed discussion of the development of research questions in this field and provide several examples of main research questions focusing on the concurrent/sequential distinction.

Examples of research questions for which a sequential design is appropriate

1. *What is the difference in perceived barriers to reading empirical research articles between graduate students with low levels of reading comprehension and those with high levels of reading comprehension?* Here, the quantitative research component would generate levels of reading comprehension

and the qualitative research element would generate the perceived barriers to reading empirical research articles. The overall research design is sequential because the quantitative phase of the study would inform the qualitative phase. The researcher would administer a test of reading comprehension, rank these comprehension scores, and then select students who attained scores that were in the top third and bottom third, say, of the score distribution. These students could then be interviewed and asked about their perceptions of barriers that prevent them from reading empirical research articles.

2. *What is the difference in the perceived atmosphere of the classroom between male and female graduate students enrolled in a statistics course?* To address this question, you would use qualitative techniques (e.g. interviews, focus groups, observations) to examine the experiences of students enrolled in a statistics course. On finding that the negative experiences of some of the study participants are extreme, relative to other members of the class, you might decide to compare statistically scores on the final statistics examination between these two sets of students. The overall research design would be sequential. A qualitative phase might involve a case study research design. The quantitative research phase would call for a descriptive, correlational, or causal-comparative research design.

3. *What are the characteristics of participants who do not fit the theory emerging from an initial phase of the design?* [A generic question type widely applicable when grounded theory is used.] Qualitative techniques (e.g. interviews, focus groups, observations) could be used to collect and analyse qualitative data using a grounded theory approach until theoretical saturation is reached. Cases which do not fit the emergent theory could be identified. Such negative and other non-negative cases could be compared with respect to one or more sets of existing quantitative scores. Alternatively, new quantitative data could be collected and the two groups compared with regard to the new data. The overall research design would be sequential with the qualitative phase represented by a case study or grounded theory design, and the quantitative research phase by a correlational or causal-comparative design (examples based on Onwuegbuzie & Leech, 2006).

Examples of research questions for which a concurrent design is appropriate

1. *What is the relationship between graduate students' levels of reading comprehension and their perceptions of barriers that prevent them from reading empirical research articles?* To answer this question information about both the levels of reading comprehension and the perceived barriers to reading empirical research articles must be obtained. Levels of reading comprehension would be gleaned from the quantitative component of the study, perceived barriers to reading empirical research articles from the qualitative part. The overall research design would be concurrent because the quantitative phase of the study did not inform or drive the qualitative phase or vice versa.

2. *What are the implications of the 'No Child Left Behind' Act on parents?* [A generic question type widely applicable to other legislation.] A research question such as this could lead to a descriptive research design for the quantitative component of the study (possibly with a variety of different data sets) and, say, a case study design for the qualitative element. Alternatively, the overall design could be thought of as a case study incorporating both quantitative and qualitative data collection. If both elements are essentially exploratory, a concurrent design will minimize the overall duration of the study (examples based on Onwuegbuzie and Leech, 2006).

Pragmatism, realism or 'anything goes'?

It has already been pointed out that many of the researchers who advocate 'mixed methods' designs couple this with an explicit endorsement of the virtue of a pragmatic stance. Interviews with them by Bryman (2006b, p. 124) found 'a tendency to stress the compatibility between quantitative and qualitative research and a pragmatic viewpoint which prioritizes using any approach that allows research questions to be answered regardless of its supposed philosophical presuppositions'. Bryman (2006b) provides support, viewing a pragmatic approach as providing a way of redirecting attention to methodological rather than metaphysical concerns.

Pragmatism can be seen as providing a licence to carry out multi-strategy research, safe in the knowledge that a body of leading researchers in the field have followed this path. For Onwuegbuzie and Leech (2005) what they term 'pragmatic researchers' are simply those who learn to utilize and to appreciate both quantitative and qualitative research. From this they consider that several advantages flow, including the following:

- researchers can be flexible in their investigative techniques;
- a wide range of research questions can be addressed;
- they are more likely to promote collaboration among researchers (including those of different philosophical orientations);
- they are more likely to view research as a 'holistic endeavour'; and
- as they have a positive attitude to both qualitative and quantitative approaches, they are likely to favour using qualitative techniques to inform the quantitative aspect of a study and vice versa (p. 383).

This could be seen as a pretty minimal theoretical underpinning to multi-strategy research, verging on an 'anything goes' philosophy where, by the fact of carrying out this kind of project, you qualify as a pragmatist. There is a danger of being open to the criticism of carrying out incoherent projects lacking a rationale and of dubious validity. The situation can be rescued by taking seriously the design task discussed in the previous section. Given clarity of the purposes of the study, a thought-through conceptual structure, and in particular a feasible research question or questions, as well as attention to the other aspects of the design framework, a convincing methodological rationale can be established.

It is, of course, possible to take on board the philosophical tenets of pragmatism, as discussed in Chapter 2, p. 28. Scott and Briggs (2009) develop a sophisticated 'pragmatist argument for mixed methodology' in the field of medical informatics, basing the argument on this eminently real world field's confluence of pragmatist clinical practice, empirical social science and information technology.

Notwithstanding the dominant pragmatic tendency in much multi-strategy research, other theoretical rationales have been put forward. While there are several possibilities, some are effectively ruled out if one takes the 'third way' argument seriously. Viewing multi-strategy research designs which are neither exclusively quantitative, nor exclusively qualitative, but a genuine attempt to develop a hybrid third way, restricts the choice. Post-positivists find much going under the banner of qualitative research deeply uncongenial. Interpretivists and constructionists are probably even less sympathetic to the ways in which essentially quantitative strategies such as experiments and surveys are conducted. Among the attractions of realist approaches is their capacity to embrace both quantitative and qualitative ways of carrying out social research, seized on by Lipscomb (2008) and by McEvoy and Richards (2006), who have argued for (critical) realism as a natural partner for multi-strategy research.

The view taken in this text is that realism (including critical realism) has much to offer the real world researcher. Adoption of realist terminology and associated concepts (e.g. and in particular, generative mechanisms) encourages a productive way of thinking about many of the issues which arise in designing a study, and interpreting and understanding its findings. Multi-strategy research, rather than introducing new and specific realist concerns, provides a context where they appear particularly apposite. Maxwell and Mittapalli (2010, p. 160–2), in a chapter advocating the use of 'realism as a stance for mixed methods research', review several examples of the explicit uses of realism in this field. They include realist approaches to evaluation research, a field where quantitative and qualitative approaches are often combined (Pawson & Tilley, 1997; Henry, Julnes & Mark, 1998) – see Chapter 9, p. 190; and several studies adopting a critical realist perspective (e.g. Clark, MacIntyre & Cruickshank, 2007; Lipscomb, 2008; Mingers, 2006; Olsen, 2004).

Dealing with discrepancies in findings

Findings from the qualitative and quantitative elements or phases of a project may, or may not, corroborate each other. If they do, fine. You have greater confidence in the findings and their validity. If they don't, all is not lost but you do have to do further work to try to establish the reason(s) for the discrepancy. Greene (2007), in her discussion of dealing with divergent findings, emphasizes their value for deepening understanding of the phenomena studied (see, especially, pp. 79–82). May (2010) extends this to suggest ways of dealing with contradictory data.

Moffatt, White, Mackintosh and Howel (2006) discuss different ways of dealing with apparent discrepancies between qualitative and quantitative research data in a study evaluating whether welfare rights advice has an impact on health and social outcomes. These include:

- *Treating the methods as fundamentally different.* A process of simultaneous qualitative and quantitative dataset interrogation enables a deeper level of analysis and interpretation than would be possible with one or other alone and demonstrates how multi-strategy research produces more than the sum of its parts. It is not wholly surprising that methods come up with divergent findings if they ask different, but related questions, and are based on fundamentally different theoretical paradigms. Combining the two methods for cross-validation (triangulation) purposes is only a viable option if both methods are examining the same research problem. Moffatt *et al.* approached the divergent findings as indicative of different aspects of the phenomena in question and searched for reasons which might explain these inconsistencies. They treated the datasets as complementary as each approach reflected a different view on how social reality ought to be studied.
- *Exploring the methodological rigour of each component.* It is standard practice at the data analysis and interpretation phases of any study to scrutinize methodological rigour. In this case, they had another dataset to use as a yardstick for comparison and it became clear that interrogation of each dataset was informed to some extent by the findings of the other. Possible reasons why there might be problems with each dataset were investigated individually but they found

themselves continually referring to the results of the other study as a benchmark for comparison. With regard to the quantitative study, the sample size had insufficient power to detect small differences in the key outcome measures. Other factors provided some explanation for the lack of a measurable effect between intervention and control group and between those who did and did not receive additional financial resources. The number of participants in the qualitative study who received additional financial resources as a result of this intervention was small but they argue that the fieldwork, analysis and interpretation were sufficient to claim that the findings were therefore an accurate reflection of what was being studied. However, there still remained the possibility that a reason for the discrepant findings was due to differences between the various sub-samples.

- *Exploring dataset comparability.* They compared the qualitative and quantitative samples on a number of social and economic factors. There were negligible differences in test scores between the groups at baseline, which led them to discount the possibility that the samples were markedly different on these outcome measures.
- *Collecting additional data and making further comparisons.* Quantitative and qualitative follow-up data verified the initial findings of each study.
- *Exploring whether the intervention under study worked as expected.* The qualitative study revealed that many participants had received welfare benefits via other services prior to this study, revealing the lack of a 'clean slate' with regard to the receipt of benefits, which was not anticipated.
- *Exploring whether the outcomes of the quantitative and qualitative components match.* The qualitative study revealed a number of dimensions not measured by the quantitative study, such as, 'maintaining independence', which included affording paid help, increasing and improving access to facilities and managing better within the home. Secondly, some of the measures used with the intention of capturing dimensions of mental health did not adequately encapsulate participants' accounts of feeling 'less stressed' and 'less depressed' by financial worries. The data demonstrated the difficulties of trying to capture complex phenomena quantitatively. They also demonstrated the value of having alternative data forms on which to draw whether complementary (where they differ but together generate insights) or contradictory (where the findings conflict). The complementary and contradictory findings of the two datasets proved useful in making recommendations for the design of a definitive study.

The strategies adopted in this study have general relevance to the further exploration of discordant results. They highlight the dangers of relying on the findings from any study which used a single method of data collection (including relying on mono-method RCTs when seeking to evaluate complex interventions with a social component).

The website gives further examples of dealing with divergent findings in multi-strategy research.

Examples of multi-strategy research

The Moffat *et al.* (2006) paper discussed in the previous section, although primarily methodological in focus, also provides a good example of a multi-strategy design. Practical UK examples (with interactive datasets) include the Crime Survey for England and Wales (http://www.crimesurvey.co.uk), the general Household Survey (http://data.gov.uk/dataset/general_household_survey) and the National Student Survey (http://www.thestudentsurvey.com/the_nss.html).

The website gives further examples of multi-strategy research.

Concluding comments

To carry out a multi-strategy research project, you are likely to have to call on material and suggestions from the other chapters of this book. In this sense, but not in others, it is similar to evaluation research (it is, of course, perfectly feasible for an evaluation to use a multi-strategy design).

You also need to cover the material in this chapter, giving particular attention to design aspects. So, a multi-strategy design is not to be selected lightly, particularly by a lone and/or new researcher. Not only do you need to have the requisite skills to use both qualitative and quantitative data collection techniques successfully but you also need the time to actually carry out at least two very different types of data collection – and to analyse and interpret the resulting data. Obviously experience, and the existence of a team of researchers, reduce many of these concerns. A lack of integration of findings from qualitative and quantitative analyses in much research is referred to throughout this chapter and is addressed at the end of Chapter 18, p. 484.

The mixed methods advocates make a strong case for this type of research design, and it appears likely to be of increasing importance in the next few years. However, a poorly designed and/or executed multi-strategy design is worse than a competent mono-method study.

Further reading

The website gives an annotated list of further reading.

CHAPTER 9

Designs for particular purposes: evaluation, action and change

This chapter:

- stresses the ubiquity and importance of evaluation;
- discusses different forms of evaluation research;
- covers the planning and carrying out of evaluations;
- emphasizes their political dimension;
- introduces needs assessment and cost-benefit analysis;
- explains the distinctive features of action research and other participatory approaches;
- considers the place of research in producing social change; and
- some of the problems associated with doing this.

Introduction

Much real world research is concerned with evaluating something. Real world researchers also often have an 'action' agenda. Their hope and intention is that the research and its findings will be used in some way to make a difference to the lives and situations of those involved in the study and/ or others. This takes us into the somewhat specialist fields of *evaluation research* and *action research*.

Researchers tend to bemoan the lack of influence that research has on practice. Some reasons for this ineffectiveness, and what might be done about it, are discussed later in the chapter.

Evaluation research

An evaluation is a study which has a distinctive purpose; it is not a new or different research strategy.

The purpose of an evaluation is to assess the effects and effectiveness of something, typically some innovation, intervention, policy, practice or service. It is sometimes referred to as program evaluation (the spelling reflecting that it started out as a largely North American activity). Fixed, flexible or multi-strategy designs can be used, and either qualitative or quantitative methods.

A high profile is being given to evaluation in many different settings. There is an increasing expectation that real world researchers will be able to carry out evaluation research.[1] Carrying out such studies undoubtedly highlights and brings to the fore the 'real worldness' of the enterprise. Issues concerning clearances and permissions, negotiations with 'gatekeepers', the political nature of an evaluation, ethics, and the type of report, are not in themselves design issues but they set an important context for the choice of design. Evaluation is intrinsically a very sensitive activity where there may be a risk or duty of revealing inadequacy or worse. Your intentions may be misconstrued and your findings misused or ignored. There are also signs of 'evaluation fatigue' – a weariness and wariness on the part of those being evaluated (Dahler-Larsen, 2006, p. 154) which Imrie and Raco (2003) warn may 'render findings statistically unrepresentative or even wholly insignificant' (p. 215). The implication for the design of an evaluation is that you have to think through very carefully what you are doing and why. For example, you are more likely to get a positive response if the evaluation research is with and for those involved, rather than something done to them. You will queer the pitch for later researchers if any promises you make (e.g. to share findings with participants and to respect their confidentiality) are broken.

The importance of evaluation

Accountability is now a watchword in the whole range of public services involving people, such as education, and health and social services. This concern in the United Kingdom arises in part from political and ideological considerations, where it forms part of a drive to place public services within a framework similar to that governing private profit-making businesses. Parallel moves in other parts of Europe, and particularly within the United States, suggest a more general phenomenon. Irrespective of its origins, the notion that we should seek to understand and critically assess the functioning of services and programmes has much to commend it. The contentious issues are: who does this, for whom, in what way, and for what purposes?

Much of the research that social scientists get involved with in the real world can be thought of as some kind of evaluation. While evaluation is not necessarily research, it profits from the kind of principled, systematic approach which characterizes research. Evaluation of this type is commonly referred to as *evaluation research*. It is a field which has grown rapidly since the 1960s, helped by the US government setting aside a proportion of the budget of the many social programmes initiated at that time for evaluation. Evaluations of such large-scale programmes have not been very conclusive but have tended to show that they did not achieve their aims. There has been widespread criticism of the quality of many evaluations. Nevertheless, discussion of the problems and issues in carrying out large-scale evaluations has thrown up much of value for use in more manageable small-scale studies. Oakley (2000, Chapters 9 and 10) provides a detailed and balanced account of these issues.

---

[1] Evaluation research has suffered in the UK with a lack of recognition by the academic community and in research assessment exercises. Arthur and Cox (2014) explore the similarities between research and evaluation and present recommendations to help remedy this discrimination.

The characteristics of real world research discussed in the first chapter are present in evaluations in a very clear-cut way. For example, they are commonly commissioned by a client or sponsor, who will often have a direct interest in the thing evaluated. Hence, rather than deciding on the topic that interests them, evaluators have this determined by others, although the approach taken is likely to be the subject of negotiation between evaluator and client. Ethical issues abound. Whose interests are being served by an intervention? Who is the real client (is it the person funding the study, or those whom the service is intended to benefit)? How are vested interests taken into account? The evaluation, its results and how they are presented may affect people's jobs, education, health and sanity. Political issues are similarly inescapable. The type and style of evaluation chosen, as well as the criteria used, may mean a choice of the perspectives, values and goals of some parties or participants rather than those of others.

Evaluations also highlight issues to do with change. The service, programme or other subject may well seek to produce or encourage change in those involved. A positive side of a topic having been chosen by the client or sponsor is that evaluation findings are more likely to influence the real world (or at least that bit of it represented by the programme or innovation being evaluated) than traditional research. This aspect is discussed in more detail in later sections on action research and change. The evaluation may indicate that changes are needed in the programme if it is to be effective. However, evaluation findings are likely to be just one of a complex set of influences on the future development of the programme. Evaluators need to communicate the results and their implications not so much to their peers in the scientific and evaluation community, who are likely to be both knowledgeable about and sympathetic to empirical enquiry, but to clients and decision-makers who are less likely to be. This means that considerable thought has to be given to the communication process, and to the style and nature of evaluation reports. These topics are picked up again in the final chapter of the book.

The practical problems of doing real world research also loom large. Evaluation tends to work to short time-spans and tight deadlines. Participants may be difficult to contact, perhaps because they are busy, perhaps because they are keeping out of your way. 'Gatekeepers', such as middle management in a firm or a deputy head teacher in a school, may be obstructive. Administrators may decide to alter the system or context in important ways during the study. External events ranging from national strikes to floods, blizzards or other extremes of weather may intervene.

A note on possible subjects for an evaluation

The list is endless. Once one gets involved with evaluation, you appreciate the force of the 'Law of the Hammer' – give someone a hammer and it transforms their environment into a set of things to be hammered (Kaplan, 1964). Get into evaluation and everything seems to be a candidate for an evaluation.

The website gives references to examples of evaluation.

The discussion in the rest of this chapter is couched mainly in terms of the evaluation of a 'programme' (American readers, do feel free to translate). This is for simplicity of presentation. Change it into terms appropriate to whatever it is that you are called upon to evaluate. The concentration in this text is of course on the 'people' aspects of the evaluation. In specific cases it may be necessary to supplement this in various ways; for example, software evaluation will have a substantial additional technical agenda.

Defining evaluation research

The position taken here is that evaluation research is essentially indistinguishable from other research in terms of design, data collection techniques and methods of analysis.

A realist approach is applicable to evaluations, particularly when the concern is for the 'how' and the 'why' of programme effectiveness (Pawson & Tilley, 1997; Henry, Julnes & Mark, 1998). So-called 'theory-based' or 'theory-driven' evaluation has similar concerns (Donaldson, 2007). Although the terminology sometimes differs, both approaches seek to identify the underlying causal mechanisms and the contextual elements that generate the observed effects. They focus on the sources and barriers to behaviour change at different levels (individual, household, community and environmental) and seek to identify why programmes have an impact and how they can be improved.

Evaluation research can, and does, make use of flexible, fixed and multi-strategy design strategies including virtually all of the variants discussed in the previous three chapters. It is sometimes claimed that the strongest evaluation studies follow an experimental strategy in making comparisons between at least two groups (one of which has received the new programme, service or whatever, while another has not). However, while the study of outcomes in this comparative way is often important, evaluations can sensibly target other aspects such as whether or not a programme meets the needs of those taking part. Also, in practice, there are often severe problems in finding an appropriate control group, or in achieving random allocation to the different groups, and in securing effective isolation between them to avoid cross-contamination. There are also more fundamental critiques of the use of control group methodology in evaluation research (Pawson & Tilley, 1997), although it still has strong advocates (e.g. Oakley & Fullerton, 1996).

The flexibility in design and execution of the case study, together with the fact that most evaluations are concerned with the effectiveness and appropriateness of an innovation or programme in a specific setting (i.e. that it is a 'case' rather than a sample), make the case study strategy appropriate for many evaluations.

Evaluation is often concerned not only with assessing worth or value but also with seeking to assist in the improvement of whatever is being evaluated. Michael Quinn Patton, a prolific American evaluator, who writes more entertainingly than most in a field littered with turgid texts, considers that:

> the practice of evaluation involves the systematic collection of information about the activities, characteristics and outcomes of programs, personnel and products for use by specific people to reduce uncertainties, improve effectiveness, and make decisions with regard to what those programs, personnel, or products are doing and affecting (Patton, 1982, p. 15).

This definition would not be universally accepted but is helpful in drawing attention to:

- the need for *systematic* information collection;
- the *wide range of topics* to which evaluation has been applied;
- the point that, to be effective, the evaluation has to be *used* by someone; and
- the *wide variety of purposes* of evaluations.

It also helps in broadening out the view of evaluation from an exclusive concern for the extent to which someone's objectives have been met. This is likely to continue to be an important aspect of the evaluation of many planned programmes with explicit objectives but is clearly only a part of what an evaluation might concern itself with. Unplanned or unanticipated outcomes or processes may be very important and would not be looked for. For example, McCord (2003) describes five types of crime prevention programmes whose rationale, design, and execution seemed promising, but which caused harmful effects. Analyses of the programmes show how they can contribute to crime, as well as reduce it; they can also increase illness and reduce the ability of clients to cope with life challenges. Some programmes may prevent some types of crime but promote other types, and some may reduce crime while contributing to mental illness and alcohol abuse. In a similar vein, Evans, Scourfield and Murphy (2014) found that identifying students for an intervention to promote social and emotional learning (SEL) could lead to unintended consequences:

> 1) identification may be experienced as negative labelling resulting in rejection of the school (2) the label of SEL failure may serve as a powerful form of intervention capital, being employed to enhance students' status amongst peers . . . (3) targeting of discrete friendship groups may lead to the construction of intervention 'outsiders' . . . (4) students may seek to renegotiate positioning within targeted friendships groups by 'bragging' about and reinforcing anti-school activities.

Purposes of evaluation research

Box 9.1 lists a range of purposes, together with some questions associated with those purposes. This by no means exhausts the possibilities. Patton (1987) lists over a hundred types of evaluation. He has also pointed out that evaluators may indulge in less than reputable types of activity, such as *quick-and-dirty evaluation* (doing it as fast as possible at the lowest cost); *weighty evaluation* (a thick report); *guesstimate evaluation* (what do we think is happening without collecting proper data); and *personality-focused evaluation* (are the programme staff nice, friendly, helpful, etc.).

Suchman (1967) produced a similar list of 'pseudo-evaluations' incorporating some possible covert motives of those funding evaluations. These include *eyewash* (emphasis on surface appearances); *whitewash* (attempts to cover up programme limitations or failures that have been discovered); *submarine* (the political use of evaluation to destroy a programme); *posture* (the ritualistic use of evaluation research without interest in, or intention to use, its findings – occurs when evaluation was a requirement for funding the programme); and *postponement* (using the need for evaluation as an excuse for postponing or avoiding action). While expressed in jocular fashion, these latter possibilities illustrate the care that one should take before getting into the political situation which virtually all evaluations represent – see the later section on 'Carrying out an evaluation'.

Formative and summative evaluation

The distinction between formative and summative evaluation is emphasized in several texts and is covered here as experience suggests that clients with some knowledge of the jargon may tend to express their preferences in these terms. The distinction is primarily one of purpose.

BOX 9.1

Some purposes of evaluation: likely questions posed by sponsor or program staff

	To find out if client needs are met	To improve the program	To assess the outcomes of a program	To find out how a program is operating	To assess the efficiency of a program	To understand why a program works (or doesn't work)
Likely questions posed by sponsor or program staff	What should be the focus of a new program? Are we reaching the target group? Is it what we provide actually what they need?	How can we make the program better (e.g. in meeting needs; or in its effectiveness; or in its efficiency)?	Is the program effective (e.g. in reaching planned goals)? What happens to clients as a result of following the program? Is it worth continuing (or expanding)?	What actually happens during the program? Is it operating as planned?	How do the costs of running the program compare with the benefits it provides? Is it more (or less) efficient than other programs?	They are unlikely to seek answers to this – but such understanding may assist in improving the program and its effectiveness.

Note: For 'program' read 'service'; or 'innovation'; or 'intervention'; (or 'programme') as appropriate. (from Robson, 2000; Table 1.1, p. 10)

Formative evaluation is intended to help in the development of the programme, innovation or whatever is the focus of the evaluation. *Summative evaluation concentrates on assessing the effects and effectiveness of the programme*. This is likely to cover the total impact of the programme, not simply the extent to which stated goals are achieved but all the consequences that can be detected. The distinction is not absolute. In particular, summative evaluation could well have a formative effect on future developments, even if it is presented after a particular 'run' of a programme or intervention. Evaluations are rarely totally negative or totally positive, and typically carry within them strong implications for change.

Formative evaluation needs to be carried out and reported on in time for modifications to be made as a result of the evaluation. There is a tension between doing something 'cheap and nasty' (and quick), of likely low reliability and validity, and better-quality work where the findings are too late to meet important decision points in the development of the project. This is one aspect of 'real world' working; you are also in 'real time'. The pace tends to be out of the control of the researcher and in the hands of someone else. In all aspects of carrying out an evaluation, great attention has to be paid to feasibility. The design must take note of constraints of time and resources, of how information is to be collected, of the permissions and cooperation necessary to put this into practice, of what records and other information are available and so on.

Outcome and process evaluation

Similar aspects to those highlighted by the formative/summative distinction are sometimes expressed in terms of *process* and *outcome* respectively. The traditional view of evaluation restricted the questions asked to those concerning outcome. The task was seen as measuring how far a programme, practice, innovation, intervention or policy met its stated objectives or goals. This approach, while still considered a central feature by many, is now more commonly seen as only covering a part of what is needed.

Process evaluation is concerned with answering a 'how', or 'what is going on' question. It concerns the systematic observation and study of what actually occurs in the programme, intervention, or whatever is being evaluated. This may well be a crucial part of an evaluation as, without this kind of examination, the nature of what is being evaluated may be obscure or misunderstood. The discrepancy between the 'official' view of what should be going on, and what is actually taking place, may be substantial. A new programme for, say, teaching reading, may have timetabled daily individual sessions. Exigencies of the school's working, and a possible low priority accorded to the programme by a head or deputy, might mean that the majority of such sessions never take place. Or a school's emphasis on reading may be at the expense of time spent on writing; an unintended consequence of the programme. Generally, relying on an official account or label is dangerous.

Process evaluation provides a useful complement to outcome evaluation of either the *systems analysis* or *behavioural objectives* variety. The latter are essentially 'black box' approaches, concentrating on what goes into the box (i.e. the programme), and in particular what comes out. A study of the intervening processes may help to shed light on this, and assist in determining the causal links involved. Such study of the processes involved may well be valuable in its own right, as well as in giving a better basis for the evaluation of outcomes. In some circumstances, the experiences and interactions provided by the programme may legitimately be the focus of interest and prime criteria for judging its value.

BOX 9.2

Features of evaluation

Any evaluation should meet the following criteria:

1. *Utility.* There is no point in doing an evaluation if there is no prospect of its being useful to some audience.
2. *Feasibility.* An evaluation should only be done if it is feasible to conduct it in political, practical and cost-effectiveness terms.
3. *Propriety.* An evaluation should only be done if you can demonstrate that it will be carried out *fairly* and *ethically*.
4. *Technical adequacy.* Given reassurance about utility, feasibility and proper conduct, the evaluation must then be carried out with technical skill and sensitivity.

Carrying out an evaluation

Evaluations are things to avoid unless you have a good chance of doing them properly. Box 9.2 lists four criteria that should be satisfied before you commit yourself. The *utility* criterion emphasizes that usefulness is at the heart of an evaluation. Otherwise it becomes an essentially pointless activity. The aphorism that 'the purpose of evaluation is not to prove but to improve' expresses this view in strong terms.

Similarly, you have better things to do with your life than to get locked into a study where the results would be suppressed and not acted upon because of political sensitivity or to accept a commission where the time and resources available preclude a serious and responsible study. You should similarly beware the 'submarine' – the study set up to legitimate the closure of a programme or service, or otherwise provide support to some already decided course of action. Obviously anything which prejudices your position in this way is to be avoided.

And finally, a point also tied up with ethics, you have no business in getting involved in studies unless you can deliver as a technically adequate evaluator. Box 9.3 presents a checklist of some of the things that need to be thought about in planning an evaluation. Box 9.4 lists some of the relevant skills, and it will be clear that they mirror closely many of the topics covered in this text. Hence, although this section of the chapter is itself quite short, it is fair to say that virtually all of the book is concerned with what to do when carrying out evaluations. The last skill, 'sensitivity to political concerns', looms particularly large in evaluations and is expanded upon below.

The politics of evaluation

While political considerations are never far from real world research (see Chapter 10, p. 235), *all* evaluations have a political dimension. Innovations, policies and practices will have their sponsors and advocates. Most will have critics and sceptics. Staff running programmes may have much to gain or lose from particular outcomes of an evaluation. Jobs may be on the line.

BOX 9.3

Checklist for planning an evaluation

1. *Reasons, purposes and motivations*
   - Is the evaluation for yourself or someone else?
   - Why is it being done?
   - Who should have the information obtained?
2. *Value*
   - Can actions or decisions be taken as a result?
   - Is somebody or something going to stop it being carried out?
3. *Interpretation*
   - Is the nature of the evaluation agreed between those involved?
4. *Subject*
   - What kinds of information do you need?
5. *Evaluator(s)*
   - Who gathers the information?
   - Who writes any report?
6. *Methods*
   - What methods are appropriate to the information required?
   - Can they be developed and applied in the time available?
   - Are the methods acceptable to those involved?
7. *Time*
   - What time can be set aside for the evaluation?
   - Is this adequate to gather and analyse the information?
8. *Permissions and control*
   - Have any necessary permissions to carry out the evaluation been sought and received?
   - Is participation voluntary?
   - Who decides what goes in any report?
9. *Use*
   - Who decides how the evaluation will be used?
   - Will those involved see it in a modifiable draft version?
   - Is the form of the report appropriate for the designated audience (style/length)?

And remember:

- *Keep it as simple as possible* – avoid complex designs and data analyses;
- *Think defensively* – if it can go wrong it will, so try to anticipate potential problems.

(adapted from Robson, Sebba, Mittler and Davies, 1988, p. 85)

A positive evaluation may lead to the expansion of a programme and to inflows of money and resources which can make major differences to the lives of clients involved.

Evaluations tend to focus on programmes or initiatives which are in the political arena, whether at national or local level, or simply of concern in an individual business, school or other

BOX 9.4

Skills needed to carry out evaluations

There are many different kinds of evaluation which call for different mixes of skills. The following seem fundamental to many evaluations:

- writing a proposal;
- clarifying purposes of the evaluation;
- identifying, organizing and working with an evaluation team;
- choice of design and data collection techniques;
- interviewing;
- questionnaire construction and use;
- observation;
- management of complex information systems;
- data analysis;
- report writing, including making of recommendations;
- fostering utilization of findings;
- sensitivity to political concerns.

unit. Because of these policy implications, the existence and outcomes of an evaluation are likely to be of interest and concern for a whole range of 'stakeholders' – national and local government, both politicians themselves and bureaucrats; the agencies and their officials responsible for administering the programme or policy; persons responsible for direct delivery; the clients or targets of the programme, and groups such as unions responsible for looking after their interests; possibly taxpayers and citizens generally. It would be highly unlikely for the interests of all of these groups to be identical, and one can usually guarantee that, whatever the results and findings of an evaluation, some will be pleased and others not.

This means, among other things, that carrying out an evaluation is not an activity for those particularly sensitive to criticism or disturbed by controversy. Criticism may be both methodological (of the way the study has been carried out) or political (of the findings) or the latter masquerading as the former. The main implication is that it pays to give meticulous attention to the design and conduct of the study, and to ensuring that the legitimate concerns of gatekeepers have been taken into account.

Needs assessment

An innovatory programme or new service is usually set up because of a perceived need which is not being met by current provision. Logically, the assessment of such needs should take place before the programme is set up and organized and it would appear reasonable for it to be the responsibility of the programme planners. However, it is quite common for evaluators to be asked to advise on, or even carry out, the needs assessment themselves. Similarly, there are situations where those involved both run and evaluate the programme. Hence a note on the topic might be useful.

Needs assessment is the process whereby needs are identified and priorities among them established. It is fairly clear what is meant by 'needs' at a common-sense level but it may help to regard them as arising when there is a discrepancy between the observed state of affairs and a desirable or acceptable state of affairs. Griesbach, Hopkins, Russell and Rich (2004) have produced a-useful guide which describes the needs assessment process step-by-step and gives examples of how to do a needs assessment for specific areas of work. Box 9.5 is based on a detailed checklist from their guide for use when carrying out a needs assessment.

BOX 9.5

Needs assessment checklist

1. Identify key individuals to be involved in a Steering Group.
2. Define the target population for the needs assessment.
3. Ensure their needs are the focus of the needs assessment.
4. Communicate the aims of the needs assessment to service providers.
5. Decide who will carry out the needs assessment (e.g. partner agencies or an external contractor).
6. Consider whether additional assistance may be needed (e.g. with data collection, data entry and analysis, and/or report writing). Get a commitment from the relevant staff as soon as possible.
7. Estimate the cost and identify the source of funding for the needs assessment.
8. Identify the appropriate overall approach to your needs assessment.
9. Gather existing sources of information about the needs of your target population and consider what this information tells you about their needs.
10. Identify existing services in your area that are already available to meet the needs.
11. Consider the ways in which you will obtain the views of your target population about their needs, and whether ethical approval is needed.
12. Consider the ways in which you will obtain the views of service providers about the needs of the target population. Think of ways to engage busy staff in your needs assessment and how to allay people's fears (e.g. of closure) or concerns (e.g. that no action will be taken as a result of the needs assessment).
13. Ensure that information is analysed and interpreted, and that conclusions are drawn.
14. Consider how those who gathered the information can be involved in the analysis, and how the results can be relayed back to all those who contributed to the process.
15. Once you have identified the needs of your target population, prioritize them, consider all the options for meeting them, and develop an implementation plan. Consider how the views of service users could be taken into account in the prioritization and option appraisal process and how to ensure service providers are involved in the development of the implementation plan.
16. Once agreement is reached on the changes to make, consider how to monitor and evaluate them.
17. Consider the most appropriate methodology for the evaluation and whether it can be done internally or by an external consultant.

(adapted and abridged from Griesbach et al., 2004, p. 37)

See also Wild, Rush and Epping-Jordan (2000) who have developed a very accessible workbook for the World Health Organization covering the 'what, how and why' of needs assessment, together with detailed case examples.

The danger of concentrating on 'accessible' needs must be acknowledged. As Judd, Smith and Kidder (1991, p. 408) point out, such technical decisions have ideological consequences. They cite crime prevention programmes. Considering the events leading to crime as a long causal chain, intervention at any point along that chain might reduce crime. This could range from intervening in the childhood experiences of potential delinquents, through providing job skills for the unemployed, to promoting better home security measures. Programmes focusing on the installation of door locks, security lighting and burglar alarms are much more accessible, with clear outcome measures, but they carry the ideological implication that reducing crime is about protecting potential victims.

The website gives references to examples of needs assessments.

Cost-benefit and cost-effectiveness evaluation

There is an increasing call for measuring the effectiveness of programmes in financial terms. Cost-benefit analysis attempts to compare the costs (the various inputs to a programme, such as staff, facilities, equipment, etc.) with the benefits accruing, measuring both in monetary terms. If the benefit to costs ratio exceeds one this provides support for its continuation or expansion. Other things being equal, a programme with a higher benefit to costs ratio is to be preferred to one with a lower ratio. The main difficulties in such an analysis are in deciding what to include in both costs and benefits and then how to determine the amounts of money involved. Cost-effectiveness analysis is similar but the benefits are expressed in non-monetary terms (e.g. in terms of academic qualifications for an educational programme). Providing that an appropriate means of assessing non-monetary benefit is available, this can provide a simpler way of making relative judgments about programmes.

These analyses are complex and call for skills within the province of economics. A brief introduction is provided in Robson (2000, pp.136–40). There is more detailed coverage in Layard and Glaister (2008), and Gray, Clarke, Wolstenholme and Wordsworth (2010).

The website gives references to examples of cost-benefit and cost-effectiveness analyses.

What an evaluator needs

As already pointed out, virtually the whole of this book is relevant to the potential evaluator. You need to have an understanding of the issues involved in the initial development of a proposal, in the selection of a general research strategy and of specific methods and techniques of collecting data. There has been a tendency in small-scale studies to equate evaluations with the use of questionnaires (as the sole method) but evaluation is a complex field where the benefits of multi-strategy designs and using multiple methods are particularly clear. Many evaluations collect both qualitative and quantitative data and you need to know appropriate analysis and interpretation techniques. Reporting in a way that is understandable and helpful for those who have to act on the findings is crucial.

This section has sought to give some indication of where the young science of evaluation research is at, and in particular to encourage an appreciation of the complexity and sensitivity of the evaluator's task. Your job is to select a research strategy and a method of data collection and analysis (probably, in most evaluations, more than one method). A thorough knowledge of the programme being evaluated is an essential precursor to your selection and subsequent sensitive use of the methods.

An open-minded exploration of the most suitable strategy and best methods for the task in hand is needed. *However, it is the usefulness of the data for the purposes of the evaluation, and not the method by which it is obtained*, which is central. As Jones (1985) puts it:

> If you can find out something useful about a program by talking to a few disgruntled employees, then talk to them. If the only way you can get the data you need is by participant observation, then participate and observe (and do not forget to take good notes). If you need a time series design with switching replications, then set it up and switch when the time comes. If you need archival data, then locate the necessary records and extract whatever you require. Use whatever you have in your toolbox that will get the job done (p. 258).

Rigour and systematic data collection are important. Unfortunately, the quality of many evaluations is suspect. See, for example, McCulloch's (2000) analysis of the weaknesses of five different evaluations of the same community regeneration project.

Realist evaluation

As discussed in Chapter 2, p. 34, Pawson and Tilley's (1997) *Realistic Evaluation* has been influential with workers in the field of evaluation research and represents a clear example of realism's influence on research practice. Pawson and Tilley (2004b) presents an updated summary of the approach; see also Pawson and Tilley (2001) and Pawson (2006b).

The website gives references to examples of realist evaluations.

Action research

As with evaluation research, *action research* is primarily distinguishable in terms of its purpose, which is to influence or change some aspect of whatever is the focus of the research. In this sense it is concerned with the emancipatory purpose of research, discussed in Chapter 2. It adds the promotion of change to the traditional research purposes of description, understanding and explanation. *Improvement* and *involvement* are central to action research. There is, firstly, the improvement of a *practice* of some kind; secondly, the improvement of the *understanding* of a practice by its practitioners; and thirdly, the improvement of the *situation* in which the practice takes place.

Collaboration between researchers and those who are the focus of the research, and their participation in the process, are typically seen as central to action research. One version, known as *participatory action research* (Chevalier & Buckles, 2013; Kindon, Pain & Kesby, 2010; Ponciano, 2013) highlights this aspect. An active, involved, role for participants can facilitate the emancipatory role of research. See below, p. 199, for further discussion of this issue.

Kurt Lewin first used the term action research (Lewin, 1946). He viewed it as a way of learning about organizations through trying to change them. It has continued to be used to promote organizational change and development (e.g. Argyris, Putnam & MacLain-Smith, 1985). Action research has been a popular approach to research in a variety of settings, particularly educational (e.g. Koshy, 2005; Schmuck, 2006; Somekh, 2005). Its protagonists maintain that practitioners are more likely to make better decisions and engage in more effective practices if they are active participants in educational research. Action research developments in education were initially largely stimulated by professional researchers, but there has subsequently been a tendency to de-emphasize the role of the external researcher and to stress the value of groups of practitioners carrying out their own enquiries into their own situation, though linked for mutual support in a loose network. More recently there has been a welcome coming together of professional and practitioner-researchers in the UK through organizations such as the Collaborative Action Research Network (http://www.did.stu.mmu.ac.uk/carnnew/index.php).

Lewin, writing and working just after the Second World War, saw action research as a tool for bringing about democracy (it is interesting to note, as pointed out by Bentz and Shapiro, 1998; p. 128, that his initial studies were aimed at convincing homemakers through group discussions to use less meat in wartime, which is perhaps democratic in a somewhat limited sense). Later action researchers see action research more as an embodiment of democratic principles in research. Merging activism and research with the aim of empowering women has been central to the agenda of many feminist researchers (Reinharz, 1992). Stringer (2014) provides an accessible introduction to conducting action research focusing on social change.

The close and collaborative relationship between researcher and researched central to action research fits well with the approach of flexible design research and is alien to that of fixed design research. However, the joint concern for action and research, particularly when this is carried through at all stages of the research, can cause serious problems. For example, if notions of collaboration and participation are taken seriously, then some power of decision about aspects of the design and data collection is lost by the researcher. This may well be a price worth paying, particularly if you have the social skills to head them off from non-feasible designs and inappropriate method.

As with evaluation research, the technical aspects of action research do not differ in essentials from social research in general in that the same range of methods of data collection are potentially available. While evaluation research can follow either fixed, flexible or multi-strategy design strategies, depending on the purposes of the evaluation, there are, as indicated above, affinities between action research and the flexible strategy. These lie in the close links between researcher and participants. The particular stress in both ethnographic and grounded theory on the 'researcher-as-instrument', and the consequential central role of the researcher's perceptions, is at some variance with the collaborative, democratic stance of action research. Case studies have the flexibility of design and approaches, as well as in the use of method, which encourage their use as a model for action research.

Links between evaluation research and action research

The focus of a piece of action research can be, and often is, an evaluation. Conversely, there are particular variants of evaluation which aspire to the same kind of goals as action research. These include *participatory evaluation* (e.g. Campbell *et al.*, 2014; Cousins & Earl, 1995) and *empowerment evaluation* (e.g. Cummings, 2013: Pinto, Rahman & Williams, 2014).

The action research cycle

A widely adopted version of action research views it as a spiral, or cyclical, process (Kemmis and Wilkinson, 1998, p. 21). This involves planning a change, acting and then observing what happens following the change, reflecting on these processes and consequences and then planning further action and repeating the cycle. Bassey (1998) presents a more detailed specification of the various stages involved, given here as Box 9.6. If, following these stages, the change is deemed insufficient, then the whole process could be repeated. As with most representations of what happens in research, this is an idealization and in practice unlikely to be as neat and linear as suggested.

BOX 9.6

Stages of action research

1. *Define the inquiry*. What is the issue of concern? What research question are we asking? Who will be involved? Where and when will it happen?
2. *Describe the situation*. What are we required to do here? What are we trying to do here? What thinking underpins what we are doing?
3. *Collect evaluative data and analyse it*. What is happening in this situation now as understood by the various participants? Using research methods, what can we find out about it?
4. *Review the data and look for contradictions*. What contradictions are there between what we would like to happen and what seems to happen?
5. *Tackle a contradiction by introducing change*. By reflecting critically and creatively on the contradictions, what change can we introduce which we think is likely to be beneficial?
6. *Monitor the change*. What happens day-by-day when the change is introduced?
7. *Analyse evaluative data about the change*. What is happening in this situation now – as understood by the various participants – as a result of the change introduced? Using research methods what can we find out about it?
8. *Review the change and decide what to do next*. Was the change worthwhile? Are we going to continue it in the future? What are we going to do next? Is the change sufficient?

(slightly modified from Bassey, 1998, pp. 94–5)

It might be argued that a participative collaborative style is more important than sorting out the complexities of various feedback loops in the cycle. As Fuller and Petch (1995) point out, it:

> involves collaboration with others more traditionally thought of rather demeaningly as the 'subjects' of research in the development of ideas about what to study; it may also include their active participation in carrying out the study and in interpreting results. Thus initial thoughts about researchable topics and priorities may have been developed collectively in formal or informal discussions with professional colleagues or with groups of users or carers. The latter may then be involved in collecting and analysing data, or (perhaps more often) in discussions about the interpretations of findings and their dissemination. In this way, both the choice of topic and the processes of research are democratized, the research has wider ownership than the researcher alone, and there is an extra level of commitment both to its successful completion and to acting on the findings (p. 6).

There are clear advantages of working in this way, and of a move toward practitioner research when there is an action agenda. However Stoecker (2009), in presenting an analysis of applications sent to a community-based research funding pool, showed that:

> most proposed research emphasized neither participation nor action. Grassroots community members, or organizations controlled by them, were rarely involved at the crucial decision stages of research, and instead limited to participation in collecting data. In addition, most research was proposed to produce papers, presentations or websites, rather than directly support action (p. 385).

A not uncommon gap between rhetoric and reality. Greenbank (2013) gives a clear account of the practical and ethical challenges involved in implementing an action research project.

Realism and action research

In common with most social psychologists at that time, the approach of the founding father of action research, Kurt Lewin (1946), was underpinned by positivist realist assumptions. It followed the tradition of experimentation while he sought to bridge the gap between establishing general laws and the diagnosis of specific social problems. The position taken by many current action researchers is based in social constructivism (e.g. Gergen, 2003; Gustavsen, 2004) to the extent that Hilsen (2006) claims that this seems to be almost taken for granted.

However, as discussed in Chapter 2, p. 28, realist and constructivist approaches are not necessarily incompatible. Several researchers have argued for the use of critical realism in this context. For example, Coghlan and Brannick (2005) in a text on doing action research in your own organization identify critical realism as the approach most in accord with carrying out this type of action research. Sæther (2007) proposes that critical realism and notions of a pragmatic action research can provide a common framework for research in economic geography. Beckinsale and Ram (2006) provide a practical example of the use of Pawson and Tilley's realistic evaluation in an action research project on the delivery of ICT (Information Communications

Technology) to ethnic minority businesses. Finally, Alton-Lee (2006) gives an interesting account of her doctoral and related research which used a scientific realism framework for an action research project.

⌨ *The website gives references to examples of action research projects.*

Intervention and change

Fullan (2007), in the fourth edition of a deservedly popular and influential text on educational change, points out that following the failings and shortcomings of many attempts, we now know a considerable amount about what we should and should not do when seeking to implement change. He provides a useful general framework for both understanding and effecting change, stressing that *change is a process, not an event*. His original maxims, which have stood the test of time, are presented in abridged form as Box 9.7.

BOX 9.7

Assumptions for those wishing to initiate change

1. Don't assume that your version of what the change should be is the one that could or should be implemented. You have to exchange your reality of what should be through interaction with others concerned.
2. Change involves ambiguity, ambivalence and uncertainty about the meaning of the change. Effective implementation is a process of clarification.
3. Some conflict and disagreement are not only inevitable but fundamental to change.
4. People need pressure to change (even in directions they desire) but it is only effective under conditions that allow them to react and interact. Resocialization is at the heart of change (otherwise you need to replace the people involved!).
5. Effective change takes time. It is a developmental process that takes at least two years.
6. Lack of implementation isn't necessarily because of rejection or resistance. There are many other reasons, including insufficient resources or time elapsed.
7. Don't expect all, or even most, people or groups to change. Progress occurs by increasing the number of people affected.
8. You need a plan based on these assumptions and underpinned by a knowledge of the change process.
9. Change is a frustrating, discouraging business. If you are not in a position to make the above assumptions, which may well be the case, don't expect significant change, *as far as implementation is concerned.*

(adapted and abridged from Fullan, 1982, p. 91)

Researchers and practitioners

Practitioners such as nurses, social workers and teachers will not necessarily have expertise in the strategies, methods and analytic techniques needed to carry out research. Notwithstanding the obvious benefits that research skills and experience bring, the common-sense core to the practice of social research, as highlighted in previous chapters, is not difficult to grasp. Such a grasp enables the interested practitioner to be directly involved in carrying out worthwhile studies – to become a 'practitioner-researcher'. Involving practitioners in research, whether through following an action research model or otherwise, provides an obvious means of facilitating change (Fox, Martin & Green, 2007).

It could well be that researchers have much to learn from practitioners. Smedslund (2009) has argued that there is a mismatch between current research methods and the nature of psychological phenomena. And that practitioners in their professional work can acquire an understanding of these phenomena. He goes on to advocate a *bricoleur*[2] model as more appropriate than the standard researcher-practitioner model (Smedslund, 2012).

See the section of the website on 'The relative roles of practitioner-researchers, researchers and consultants in carrying out real world research', which gives practical advice on fulfilling these roles.

Further reading

The website gives annotated references to further reading for Chapter 9.

---

[2] 'A bricoleur is a resource person who is enlisted when ordinary established procedures in daily life fail to work, and who utilizes whatever is at hand in the given situations to effect a solution. As a bricoleur, the psychologist is one who works in innovative ways with people in their life-situations, relying on knowledge of human nature, language and culture, and specific individuals' (Smedlund, 2012, p. 644).

CHAPTER 10

Ethical and political considerations

This chapter:

- stresses the importance of carrying out real world research ethically, warning that unethical research has been all too common;
- discusses ethical codes and guidelines;
- lists questionable practices to avoid;
- explains why *informed consent* is an important principle – and how it can be obtained;
- warns about the use of deception and of covert observation – and when this might be justified;
- discusses *anonymity* and *confidentiality*;
- advocates giving serious attention to researcher risk and safety;
- reviews the particular ethical problems when working with vulnerable groups;
- considers some of the ethical dilemmas common in real world research;
- gives attention to scientific fraud and dishonesty;
- reviews the role of ethical boards and committees, and suggests how best to deal with their concerns; and
- concludes with a reminder that political influences on real world research are inevitable.

Introduction

It should be self-evident that there are ethical considerations when carrying out real world research involving people. There is a potential for harm, stress and anxiety, and myriad other negative consequences for research participants. This is exacerbated when the topic of research is socially sensitive (e.g. topics relating to crime, social vulnerability, or victimization) or the participants are vulnerable (e.g. victims of crime, or socially disadvantaged groups). Few would now think that judgments about such possible effects should be left solely in the hands of the researcher.

Classical cases of unethical research involving people are well known but merit repetition both as warnings and because of their influence on the present situation. The shocking story of research abuse by German doctors during World War II, where physicians carried out unethical medical experiments on Jews, gypsies, and political prisoners, led directly to the post-war development of international codes of *ethics* written to protect research participants. These include the Nuremburg and Helsinki codes, which cover social research in medical settings (Eby, 2000), and the European Declaration of Human Rights (Sprumont, 1999).

The American Tuskegee Syphilis study also ranks high in the history of unethical research. Conducted by the United States Public Health Service (USPHS), it began in 1932 and continued for four decades until exposure in the national media prompted its termination. The study examined the development of untreated syphilis in a sample of nearly 400 black males from Tuskegee in Alabama, who already had the disease. Unethical aspects of the study included an absence of informed consent, together with active misinformation about the purpose of the research. To observe the 'natural course' of the disease, they were not given the standard treatment for syphilis available in the 1930s nor, when effective treatment with antibiotics became available in the 1940s, was this provided. The study demonstrates the disregard for human rights that can take place in the name of science. It is worth stressing that the researchers involved were respected scientists and that the findings from the study were published in reputable journals. Sprumont (1999, pp. 83–6) provides a detailed account together with discussion of the ethical lessons to be learned from this study.

This is not an isolated study, although extreme in its disregard for the rights and welfare of the participants. Polit and Beck (2008, pp. 167–8) list more recent examples from the medical and nursing field. Plomer (2013) covers the law and ethics in relation to medical research and human rights.

Other disciplines contribute studies with controversial ethical aspects. An often cited experiment, carried out in the early 1960s, is by Milgram, a psychologist from Yale University. His study was on the conflict between obedience toward authority and one's personal conscience. Milgram was interested in the justification for acts of genocide offered by those accused at the World War II Nuremberg War Criminal trials where their defence was based on 'obedience' – that they were just following orders. The aim of Milgram's experiment was to investigate what level of obedience would be shown when participants were told by an authority figure to administer electric shocks to another person (an extended discussion is in Milgram, 2004a; 2004b). Although widely criticized on ethical grounds (e.g. Baumrind, 2013), Milgram mounts a spirited defence of his study. The main issues are:

- *Use of deception.* Participants were deceived as to the exact nature of the study for which they had volunteered, and by making them believe they were administering real electric shocks to a real participant. However Milgram could not have found results that truly reflected the way people behave in real situations if he had not deceived his participants, all of whom were thoroughly debriefed afterwards.
- *Possible harm to participants.* It has been argued that Milgram did not take adequate measures to protect his participants from the stress and emotional conflict they experienced. His defence was that he and the students and psychiatrists (who had been asked to predict the results of the first experiment) – did not expect the results he obtained. He suggested that such criticisms are based as much on the unexpected results as on the procedure itself. There could be long-term

effects on the participants. Before the experiment they might have considered themselves incapable of inflicting harm on another person. Their behaviour in the experiment suggested they could do this. Milgram argued that such self-knowledge was valuable. Participants, including those who had experienced extreme stress during the experiment, were interviewed a year later by an independent psychiatrist who found no evidence of psychological harm or of traumatic reactions.

- *Right to withdraw.* Although Milgram stated at the start that participants could withdraw and still receive a promised financial reward, the pressures during the experiment suggested that withdrawal was not possible.

Burger (2014) suggests that, irrespective of ethical considerations, the very high rates of obedience in these studies, which many have found surprising. were to be expected given 'the incremental nature of the task, the novelty of the situation and the kind of normative information made available, the opportunity to deny or diffuse responsibility, and the limited opportunity to ponder decisions' (p. 489).

Sociologists have also made contributions to the roll-call of studies controversial on ethical grounds. Humphreys, also in the 1960s, sought to challenge stereotypical beliefs about men who committed impersonal sexual acts with one another in public toilets. He sought to gain a better understanding of who these men were and what motivated them to seek quick, impersonal sexual gratification, using participant observation. Humphreys stationed himself in toilets and offered to keep an eye out for the police and give warning if a stranger were approaching the area. By observing hundreds of acts, he gained the confidence of some of the men involved. After disclosing his role as a researcher, he persuaded them to tell him about their personal lives and motives. His findings that a majority of the men were married and that most of them were successful and well educated went against stereotypes (see Humphreys, 1975).

The research has been strongly criticized on ethical grounds, not least by his colleagues at Washington University. Charges included lack of initial consent to be involved, invasion of privacy and threats to the social standing of those involved. Humphreys' defence rested on the impossibility of obtaining the findings other than by the approach he took and their importance in challenging inaccurate stereotypes.

The Milgram and Humphreys examples illustrate some of the ethical complexities in carrying out research involving people. There can be inescapable ethical dilemmas when carrying out research in sensitive areas. Total prohibition of risky research might itself be considered unethical. An approach which seeks to evaluate the relative costs (i.e. negative consequences) and benefits (i.e. positive consequences) of research is needed. The benefits should be judged to outweigh the costs before the research is carried out. Questions that then arise include: Which costs and benefits are taken into account? On whom do the costs fall? To whom do the benefits accrue? Who makes the judgements?

Following these ethical calamities and controversies, it is now accepted that the researcher should have neither the power to make, nor the responsibility of making, such judgements. Which is why we are in the era of *ethical review* boards and committees. The problematic research in the 1970s and 1980s that helped to create them means that no researcher should be ignorant of the realities of unethical research and its consequences. It also forces researchers to think very carefully about the implications of researching sensitive questions, intrusive methodologies, or vulnerable populations. Being ethical does not prevent socially sensitive research; it requires responsible research.

Unintended consequences

Merton's article on 'The unanticipated consequences of planned social action' (Merton, 1936) first highlighted what is now commonly referred to as the 'law of unintended consequences'. This can mean that research, carried out with the best of intentions, becomes unethical because of such effects. For example, Pires (2014) evaluated a Brazilian project which was intended to help families, with a clear focus on empowering women. However, children became considered responsible for continued access to the aid. Consequently the children bore the responsibility for the financial survival of the family. Evans, Scourfield and Murphy (2014) reviewed recent school-based social and emotional learning (SEL) interventions and found that they could result in unintended effects. In a case study they identified four negative processes at work:

> (1) identification may be experienced as negative labelling resulting in rejection of the school (2) the label of SEL failure may . . . enhance students' status amongst peers . . . (3) targeting of discrete friendship groups may lead to the construction of intervention 'outsiders' . . . (4) students may seek to renegotiate positioning within targeted friendships groups by 'bragging' about and reinforcing anti-school activities . . .

In general, such effects are difficult to anticipate in the complex systems in which many interventions take place. However, a thorough pre-analysis can identify some likely problems. Certainly, small-scale pilot interventions before rolling out major programmes are indicated on ethical grounds.

Ethical codes and guidelines

It is vital that, at a very early stage of your preparations to carry out a research project, you give serious thought to the ethical aspects of what you are proposing. Ethics is a process and not an endpoint, meaning that it should be reviewed throughout the research process and should be done in tandem with others, not as a stand-alone, one time only, pursuit.

Ethics refers to rules of conduct; typically to conformity to a code or set of principles (Israel, 2014). There are a number of different approaches to research ethics. In medical and health related research, approaches tend to be used in which ethical decisions are made either on the basis of the consequences or outcomes of research participation (Long & Johnson, 2007) or on the basis of principles such as autonomy, non-maleficence, beneficence and justice (Beauchamp & Childress, 2013). Social researchers have argued that the ethical dilemmas that arise in social research are context-specific. The bases for ethical decision-making in social research are commonly considered to include a commitment to participants' rights and to respect for participants; a commitment to knowledge (or the right for others to know, e.g. how specific organizations operate); a commitment to the promotion of respect for social science (e.g. to avoid 'spoiling the field'); and, protecting the researcher (e.g. from litigation) (Wiles, Heath, Crow & Charles, n.d.; c).

Elements of all these approaches are enshrined in the various codes and guidelines produced by organizations whose members use social research methods. UK examples include those of the Association of Social Anthropologists, British Psychological Society, British Society of Criminology,

British Sociological Association, British Association of Social Workers, British Educational Research Association, and the Social Research Association. US equivalents include the American Anthropological Association, American Psychological Association, American Sociological Association, and the American Educational Research Association. The website 'Codes of Ethics Online' at http://ethics.iit.edu/research/other-codes-ethics includes a very extensive set of codes of ethics of professional societies, corporations, government, and academic institutions. An interesting feature is the inclusion of earlier versions of codes of ethics of some organizations represented so that it is possible to study the development of their codes. See also Kimmel (2007) who provides an international survey of codes of ethics (p. 328) together with a list of web links to them (p. 323). Some emerging areas of research may not have their own ethical codes and frameworks (e.g. Socio-legal Studies). This does not mean that they are 'ethics?-free'; rather that researchers in such fields need to look at ethical codes in related fields for support and guidance.

Commentaries are available for several of the codes. For example, Banyard and Flanagan (2006, Chapter 3) provide a commentary on the BPS ethical guidelines. Sales and Folkman (2000) and Barnett and Johnson (2008) are useful publications from the American Psychological Association covering related ethical issues.

Several of the codes and guidelines are relatively vague, leaving researchers able to interpret them in ways fitting the needs of the specific research that they are undertaking. This allows social researchers to adopt a 'situational relativist' approach in which ethical decisions are made on the basis of issues applicable to specific research projects.[1]

You should familiarize yourself with the code or codes most relevant to your work and ensure that you follow the code scrupulously.

Unfortunately, it is not unknown for students, and others, when presenting a research proposal, to regard the claim that, say, 'I have followed the BPS Ethical Code for Research with Human Participants' as a full discharge of all ethical responsibilities. Having read the code, you should consider its specific implications for your research project and make clear what you are doing to meet your ethical obligations.

Ethical issues

A distinction is sometimes made between ethics and morals. While both are concerned with what is good or bad, right or wrong, ethics are usually taken as referring to general principles of what one ought to do. Morals are usually taken as concerned with whether or not a specific act is consistent with accepted notions of right or wrong. The terms 'ethical' and 'moral' are used interchangeably in this text to refer to 'proper' conduct, except where the context makes codified principles relevant. Ethical and moral concerns in scientific studies have come to the fore alongside the changing views of the nature of science discussed in Chapter 2. A traditional view was that science was *value-free (value-neutral)* and the task of the scientist was simply to describe what is in an objective manner. This can be harder to achieve when your research involves people, particularly when there is an emotional aspect, or value-laden issues, or interactive

---

[1] However, as discussed later in the chapter, institutional ethical review boards and committees may not be sympathetic to such an approach, nor necessarily knowledgeable about ethical issues in the context of social research. See p. 211.

situations. It is a different task from determining what ought to be done to behave ethically. If objectivity cannot be guaranteed when doing research, and the values of the researcher are inevitably involved in the research, the worlds of 'is' and 'ought' become much more difficult to disentangle.

Carrying out experiments involving people poses ethical problems in sharp forms. Control over what people do obviously has a moral dimension. While this is self-evident in experimental situations where subjects are explicitly manipulated, ethical dilemmas lurk in any research involving people. In real world research, we may not be able, or wish, to control the situation but there is almost always the intention or possibility of change associated with the study. This forces the researcher, wittingly or not, into value judgements and moral dilemmas. Suppose we are looking at a new approach to the teaching of reading. It is highly likely that we start with the premise that this looks like being a 'good thing', probably an improvement on what is currently on offer. Life – your own and the participants' – is too short to waste it on something which does not appear to have this 'prima facie' value. A possible exception would be where the latest educational fad was sweeping the schools and a demonstration of its drawbacks might be a useful inoculation for the system – although even in this case, my experience has been that the conclusion ends up as something like, 'If you want to take on this new approach, these are the conditions under which it seems to be most effective.'

Reverting to consideration of the likely 'good' intervention, an immediate issue becomes: 'Which schools are to be involved?' Do you choose the fertile soil of a friendly, innovative school? Or the stony ground of a setting where there is probably a greater, though unacknowledged, need for something new? These are partly research issues but they have a clear ethical dimension.

Ethical issues arise from the very beginning of a study. For example, it may appear unethical to select certain foci for research because of the likely exacerbation of an explosive situation, simply by carrying out research in that area. A particular experimental design (such as an RCT) might be preferable in design terms to a weaker one (say, using matched samples) but the latter may be preferable from an ethical perspective. Issues continue throughout the whole of a study, up to and including the reporting, and disseminating, of your findings. For example:

- Is the giving of necessary additional resources of staff, equipment or whatever to the places where the research takes place simply part of the deal, the investigator showing good faith by giving as well as taking? Or is it unfair coercion to take part, reminiscent of prisoners gaining food or an early release for taking part in trials of potentially dangerous drugs?
- Do individuals have the right not to take part? And even if they do, are there any overt or covert penalties for non-participation ('It will look good on your reference if you have taken part in this study')?
- Do they know what they are letting themselves in for?
- Is their consent 'fully informed'?
- Will individuals participating be protected, not only from any direct effects of the intervention, but also by the investigator ensuring that the reporting of the study maintains confidentiality?
- On the other hand, is confidentiality always appropriate? If people have done something good and worthwhile, and probably put in extra effort and time, why shouldn't they get credit for it?
- Conversely, if inefficiency or malpractice is uncovered in the study, should the investigator let the guilty ones hide?

- What responsibility do investigators have for the knowledge that they have acquired? Are they simply the 'hired hand' doing the bidding of the paymaster? Or – changing the metaphor to one used by Carl Rogers – are they simply ammunition wagons, loaded with powerful knowledge just waiting to be used, whether the users are the 'good guys' or the 'bad guys'? Incidentally, Rogers' (1961) view is, 'Don't be a damn ammunition wagon, be a rifle.' That is, those doing applied studies have to target their knowledge and take responsibility for what they 'hit'.

Each of these issues is complex. Although general guidelines can be given as in the various codes discussed above, the issues must be carefully thought through in each specific situation. The issues which arise when you are involving participants and collecting data are discussed below. However, ethical issues can arise throughout the research process, from selecting a topic right through to reporting your findings, and are covered in the appropriate chapters.

Note: In any research situation someone must be ultimately responsible for the tone and direction of the research project, including the ethics involved. For students at whatever level, this is the supervisor (or supervisors if more than one. For researchers it is the team leader (often referred to as the Principal Investigator). This does not let the individual student or researcher off the hook. You are accountable for any, and all, decisions which you make on your own initiative.

Ethical issues when involving participants and collecting data

Box 10.1 presents a list of questionable practices which you might be tempted to indulge in. All of them can be applied to any methodology, but are likely to be more salient for some over others (e.g. point 1 in respect to ethnography; point 9 for RCTs). The presumption is that you do not succumb to temptation, unless in a particular study you can convince yourself, and an appropriate ethical review board or committee, that the benefits accruing outweigh the costs. Kimmel (2007, Chapters 6 and 7) discusses in detail the particular ethical problems associated with applied research.

BOX 10.1

Ten questionable practices in social research

1. Involving people without their knowledge or consent.
2. Coercing them to participate.
3. Withholding information about the true nature of the research.
4. Otherwise deceiving the participant.
5. Inducing them to commit acts diminishing their self-esteem.
6. Violating rights of self-determination (e.g. in studies seeking to promote individual change).
7. Exposing participants to physical or mental stress.
8. Invading their privacy.
9. Withholding benefits from some participants (e.g. in comparison groups).
10. Not treating participants fairly, or with consideration, or with respect.

Carrying out research involving vulnerable groups (e.g. children; persons with learning difficulties) raises difficult ethical issues – see the section below on p. 222).

Informed consent

Should people always be asked in advance whether they are prepared to take part and know in detail what it will involve? It may not be possible or practicable to do this. You may have good grounds for believing that telling them would alter the behaviour you are interested in. But not telling them means that you have taken away their right not to participate.

There are several questions you can ask to help decide. Will the study involve people doing things they would not otherwise do? If not, it is less of an infringement. So, an observational study of naturally occurring behaviour is less questionable than a field experiment where you contrive something which would not otherwise happen. Not that all experiments are equivalent. One which involved you stalling a car when the traffic lights turn green to study the effects on driver behaviour, while questionable in its own right, is probably less so than a simulated mugging on a tube train to study bystander behaviour. Reasonable things to take into account are the degree of inconvenience, and of likely emotional involvement, to participants. In studies where the judgement is made that prior permission must be sought, it is increasingly the practice to present all potential participants with an 'informed consent' form.

However, even this apparently highly ethical procedure can have its pitfalls. In research on socially sensitive topics such as AIDS, drug abuse, or crime prevention, it is possible that the investigator would be under legal pressure to disclose all research information including such signed forms. American investigators have been served with a subpoena to appear in court, and in a similar situation two journalists have faced prison rather than reveal their sources. Hence, in such situations it might be preferable to proceed informally, while still ensuring that participants have been fully informed, and that you have their consent.

Tyldum (2012) argues that applying pressure to be involved in a project can be defended in some circumstances, even if this reduces the opportunity to give consent freely. Research based solely on volunteers could be biased. She claims that: 'In order to get access to all respondent groups, various forms and degrees of institutional, economic and emotional pressure are widely used to recruit respondents' (p. 199).

Box 10.2 provides an example of an informed consent form. Details of the form will differ for different types of research (Kimmel, 2007, Appendix 3 gives several examples). Note the emphasis on the participant's right to withdraw *at any time*. While this may be annoying and inconvenient from the researcher's perspective (particularly when random or matched samples have been selected in fixed design studies), it is unethical to set up psychological barriers to withdrawal mid-study (as in the Milgram experiment). It may well be that their involvement has proved stressful in some way that could not have been reasonably anticipated.

Box 10.3 suggests the steps you might take when obtaining consent. Boynton (2005, pp. 91–103) covers a range of issues involved when seeking voluntary informed consent, illustrated by examples from her own research. She also describes group exercises useful in sensitizing researchers to aspects of the process.

Even when procedures to elicit informed consent are scrupulously followed, there is evidence that participants may have only limited understanding of a project and their involvement in it. For example, Walker, Hoggart and Hamilton (2008) suggest that the amount of information

BOX 10.2

Example of consent form

Address
(use headed paper from your institution/project)

Informed Consent Form
Title of Project:
Name of Researcher:

1. I have read and understood the attached information sheet giving details of the project.
2. I have had the opportunity to ask the researcher any questions that I had about the project and my involvement in it, and understand my role in the project.
3. My decision to consent is entirely voluntary and I understand that I am free to withdraw at any time without giving a reason.
4. I understand that data gathered in this project may form the basis of a report or other form of publication or presentation.
5. I understand that my name will not be used in any report, publication or presentation, and that every effort will be made to protect my confidentiality.

Participant's signature: Date:
Participant's name (in CAPITALS)

Researcher's signature: Date:

Attachment (information sheet)
_____

Notes: 1. Details of the form will differ depending on the project and the circumstances. For example, in some situations it may be advisable to make it clear that a participant will suffer no adverse consequences from withdrawing from involvement.

2. Give the participant a signed copy of the consent form and attached information sheet. This may be useful if there are later issues about consent.

that can be conveyed, and absorbed, prior to consent, is limited. Crow, Wiles, Heath and Charles (2004) sought to identify and disseminate best practice in relation to informed consent in research by interviewing researchers working with 'vulnerable' people. The researchers who took part in their project came up with a set of suggestions to help ensure that participants understand what they are consenting to, which forms the basis for Box 10.4.

Crow *et al.* also make the point that in institutional settings, such as schools, participants are sometimes allocated to a researcher by a gatekeeper without them knowing what the research will involve (i.e. they have not consented to participate). Their suggestion is that, rather than

BOX 10.3

Steps in obtaining consent

1. Explain to participants what the study involves. An information sheet is useful as it provides a permanent record for the participant and can be attached to the consent form as suggested in Box 10.2. It may also be instructive if your study involves participants reading questionnaires or some similar task, since those who struggle with reading an information sheet may not be suitable for your study overall. With some groups (e.g. children or persons with learning difficulties – see below, p. 222) it may be necessary to explain verbally.

2. Let them know they can have time to think about participation. A minimum of 24 hours is advised and may be required by ethics committees. In situations where this is not possible, clear instructions and time to reflect on participation are still required.

3. Provide participants with a consent form. Other formats from that suggested in Box 10.2 can be used (e.g. checklist, letter, cover sheet on a questionnaire, or a page in an Internet-based study). In medical and some other contexts there is an expectation that you provide contact details of an independent person the participant can call to discuss the research (e.g. in a hospital study this could be a doctor who is not involved in the design or completion of the research).

4. Check and double-check with participants that they fully understand the research, their role in the study, and any implications it has for them. Ask if they have any questions or concerns. It is good practice to continue to check their well-being even after getting consent, during the study itself, and after the study has finished (particularly in research on sensitive topics, or where there is an indication that participants have been, or are, subject to stress – not necessarily from their involvement with the research).

(based on Boynton, 2005, Table 5. 10, p. 93)

having persons involved in the research who have not given their consent, researchers take along newspapers, magazines or wordsearch books to research sessions so that, should this case arise, the individual can spend the time in another non-research activity without the gatekeeper knowing this has occurred.

The suggestions in Box 10.4 will, no doubt, help to achieve the objective of making sure that participants fully appreciate what they have consented to, and are given multiple opportunities to reconsider and, possibly, withdraw. However, maximizing withdrawal rates makes the researcher's task somewhat more difficult, perhaps calling for the recruitment of additional participants. More importantly it may reduce the quality of the research through compromising aspects of the design (e.g. if participants withdraw at a late stage where replacement is not possible and the reduced sample size unbalances the design or makes it impossible to carry out planned analyses). Crow *et al.* (2006) make the more general point that the new patterns of research governance, including the operation of ethics review boards and committees, are likely to affect the quality of data collected. They discuss an 'optimistic' scenario where more ethical

BOX 10.4

Ensuring participants understand what they are consenting to

- Ask participants to repeat back to a researcher what a project is about and what participation will involve to check that information has been absorbed;
- Repeat the consent procedure with participants after data have been collected. Once someone has participated in the data collection, they will know whether or not they want to continue to participate, or consent to their data being used;
- Ensure consent is obtained at each point of data collection (and perhaps also ahead of the point of publication of reports, articles and books);
- In observational settings, wear a badge saying 'Researcher' to remind people being observed that research is in progress;
- Use pictures and graphics in information about a study that illustrates what participation will involve and includes a photo of the researcher;
- Use a video to demonstrate what participation will involve;
- Use different words, graphics and layouts for different age groups;
- Keep information to a manageable length, if possible no more than a page (excessively detailed information sheets can overwhelm participants); and
- Allow time for participants to talk to others (e.g. parents, teachers, carers) about the information provided about a project before a decision to participate is made. This time period may be one or two days or a week.

(based on Wiles, Heath, Crow and Charles, n.d.; b)

research practice will lead to better-quality data and a more 'pessimistic' scenario where the unintended outcome is poorer quality data. Within the 'optimistic' scenario:

> The trend towards researchers paying more careful attention to the issue of informed consent is contributing to better research than that undertaken in the less closely monitored and regulated past. The key elements of the argument are that it does so because it helps to prepare researchers for the data collection process; because it helps to prepare research participants for the data collection process; and because it establishes a more equal relationship between researchers and research participants in which the latter can have confidence, as a result of which research participants will be more open and frank about the aspects of their lives that are being researched. There is a further argument that greater confidence on the part of people approached to participate in research ought to improve participation rates and thereby the ability to generalize findings (p. 85).

In a more 'pessimistic' scenario:

> Data quality is held to suffer as a result of the processes put in place to gain informed consent. The key elements of this argument are that informed consent has an adverse

effect on participation rates (in the extreme making some groups of people or some topics unresearchable); that the processes of gaining informed consent inhibit the development of the rapport necessary for the collection of authentic data; and that the quality of the data collected suffers as a result of the practical arrangements for gaining consent (p. 88).

They feel that a synthesis of the two positions is possible, in which ethical research practice is treated neither as an automatic guarantee of, nor as an inevitable obstacle to, the collection of good-quality data. A balance is needed between 'research participants being provided with too little information (which risks participants being deceived or manipulated) and of too little attention being paid to consent issues (which risks participants being coerced)' (p. 94) on the one hand, and 'problems associated with participants being provided with too much information (which risks research being delayed, participants' thinking being moulded, and participants becoming alienated) and with too much attention being paid to consent procedures (which risks narrowing of research agendas if certain social groups or topics become unresearchable)' (p. 95) on the other hand.

Crow *et al.* (2006) conclude that the rigidity of standardized regulation will need to be tempered by a degree of flexibility according to the characteristics of specific research contexts. The discussion below on ethical review boards and committees takes up this point.

Deception

The use of deception has been widespread in social research, notably though by no means exclusively, in experiments by social psychologists. Milgram's study on obedience discussed above is one of a whole host of examples. A widely quoted example is the classic study by Festinger and Carlsmith (1959) on their theory of 'cognitive dissonance', where a whole repertoire of deceptions was used. Participants were deceived about the purpose of the study; they were told it was over when it wasn't; they were encouraged to lie to someone about the experiment; and they were not told that this 'someone' was an accomplice of the researcher. The crowning deception was that, while they were told that they would be paid for their involvement, they were asked to return their earnings at the end of the study! One of the positive features of the use of students studying psychology as participants in psychological experiments is that they almost routinely expect deception to take place which, while posing problems in regarding their responses as typical, eases some ethical concerns.

There has been no lack of criticism of such deception. Kelman (1967), for example, considered that it undermined what should be a mutual trust between researcher and participant, revealing a lack of respect by the researcher for those who were helping them with the research. There is widespread unease about the use of lying and deceit in the service of psychology, with worries that it may have negative effects on the participants, the profession of psychology and on society as a whole (Christensen, 1988). Justification for deception is based on a cost-benefit approach to ethics – that the benefits (e.g. in terms of the knowledge gained) outweigh the costs to participants of the deceit – on the understanding that it would not have been possible to carry out the study without using deception, and that safeguards such as debriefing participants about the true situation and that all possible means of keeping them from harm are used.

However, it is increasingly called into question and some commentators call for the complete outlawing of all forms of deception (e.g. Ortmann & Hertwig, 1997). Barrera and Simpson (2012) conducted experimental tests of the empirical effects of deception, concluding that it did not significantly affect the results.

The issue is complex and it appears likely that deception is likely to be with us for the foreseeable future. For example, the well-known *placebo effect* (e.g. where an inactive substance such as a sugar pill, perhaps used as a control in a study, has positive effects) is an important and, as yet, not fully understood phenomenon. Deception of research participants is considered necessary to understanding the placebo effect, but has received little ethical attention (Justman, 2013; Miller, Wendle & Swartzman, 2005). Participants' expectations for improvement are seen to be a major driving force behind the placebo effect. Researchers argue that a necessary feature of research aimed at elucidating placebo mechanisms is the use of deception in experimental manipulation of participants' expectations (e.g. about whether or not they will receive a 'powerful painkiller' or a 'sugar pill'). If so, there is a clear tension between the methods needed to understand the placebo effect and ethical norms for conducting research involving human participants.

Miller *et al.* discuss possible ways in which deceptive research can be made compatible with informed consent. They propose using 'authorized deception' where 'participants can be informed prior to deciding whether to volunteer for a study that the experimental procedures will not be described accurately or that some features of these procedures will or may be misleading or deceptive' (p. 856). This allows them to decide whether they wish to take part in research involving deception and appears compatible with the spirit of informed consent. A potential problem with this approach is that informing participants that deception will occur may make them suspicious and wary, possibly leading to biased data.

Covert observation

Observing people as part of a research project without letting them know what you are doing is clearly at odds with the principle of informed consent. The Humphreys study discussed on p. 207 is probably the one most widely cited in discussions of research ethics but many studies have used covert participation by researchers in gangs, religious cults and deviant communities (Lauder, 2003). The use of covert methods in general has always been contentious, as they may involve the deliberate misleading of people (Lugosi, 2006). Their attraction to researchers is that they can provide access to information that is otherwise unavailable.

Non-participative observation can have the advantage of being an unobtrusive method of data collection (i.e. non-reactive, in the sense of not affecting or influencing whatever is being observed – see Chapter 13, p. 322). Covert observation of behaviour in public places, without actually taking part, raises fewer ethical issues providing that such observation has no negative consequences for those observed. The widespread availability of technologies such as CCTV security cameras, webcams, mobile phone networks, radio frequency identification tags, supermarket loyalty cards, and other sensing devices, although with considerable potential for research purposes (e.g. Diminescu, Licoppe, Smoreda & Ziemlicki, 2007; Evans, 2007) gives cause for concern about the erosion of privacy in public places (Nissenbaum, 1998). Box 10.5 lists some of the issues involved.

BOX 10.5

Arguments for, and criticisms of, covert research

Arguments for covert research:

- Some areas of social life cannot be researched unless the research is covert – once people are told they are taking part in a study, their behaviour will change and it then becomes impossible to conduct the research. Many studies in psychology follow this model (although researchers may still gain consent for participation even though participants may not be made aware of the actual focus of the research). In some cases, consent from 'gatekeepers' to conduct a covert study of a group may be sought.
- Some areas of social life/organization *should* be researched in that it is in the interests of the general public to expose how such organizations or institutions operate but the only way this can occur is through covert means.
- In some types of observational research, it is not possible to obtain consent from all participants in that a researcher does not know who will enter the area that is observed.

Criticisms of covert research:

- Covert methods are generally not necessary and the same objectives can be achieved by open methods. It is argued that most groups will accept and agree to collaborate with research once they know that they can trust the researcher involved.
- It violates the principle of informed consent and invades privacy for no good reason.
- It is a betrayal of trust and once participants realize that they have been used for research purposes (as they are likely to do when the research is published) they will feel used and upset.
- It makes further research in that area or topic or with that particular group very unlikely (i.e., it 'spoils the field').
- It brings all social science into disrepute. It makes social science no different from journalism.

(based on Wiles, *et al.*, n.d.; c)

Petticrew *et al.* (2007) discuss the practical lessons learned about collecting covert observational data from an evaluation of the prohibition of smoking in public places in Scotland. These include:

- The difficulty of achieving and maintaining concealment.
- The difficulty of 'fitting into' a bar they had never previously visited and of discreetly observing smoking.
- The experience of being an observer. There was undoubtedly an impact on the researchers themselves. Researchers often reported feeling somewhat paranoid, partly because of risk of being recognized, but also in cases where the noise of their air sampler seemed obtrusive in a quiet bar, though this could be masked.

Collecting covert observational data poses unique practical challenges, in particular in relation to the health and safety of the researcher (*see below*).

Anonymity and confidentiality

Giving anonymity to participants when reporting on research is the norm. It is regarded as good practice by ethical research boards and committees and expected in legal frameworks such as the UK's Data Protection Act (1988). The responsibilities of researchers in respect of the Act are detailed in http://www.recordsmanagement.ed.ac.uk/InfoStaff/DPstaff/DP_Research/ResearchAndDPA.htm, from the University of Edinburgh. Stratford and Stratford (1998) discuss differences between American and European approaches to personal privacy in an online environment. Box 10.6 provides a useful statement from a journal, covering many of the issues involved.

BOX 10.6

Anonymization and ethical practice

A Statement of Ethical Practice from the Journal *Social Research Online:*

The anonymity and privacy of those who participate in the research process should be respected. Personal information concerning research participants should be kept confidential. In some cases it may be necessary to decide whether it is proper or appropriate even to record certain kinds of sensitive information. Where possible, threats to the confidentiality and anonymity of research data should be anticipated by researchers. The identities and research records of those participating in research should be kept confidential whether or not an explicit pledge of confidentiality has been given. Appropriate measures should be taken to store research data in a secure manner. Members should have regard to their obligations under the Data Protection Act. Where appropriate and practicable, methods for preserving the privacy of data should be used. These may include the removal of identifiers, the use of pseudonyms and other technical means for breaking the link between data and identifiable individuals such as 'broadbanding'* or micro-aggregation.** Members should also take care to prevent data being published or released in a form which would permit the actual or potential identification of research participants. Potential informants and research participants, especially those possessing a combination of attributes which make them readily identifiable, may need to be reminded that it can be difficult to disguise their identity without introducing an unacceptably large measure of distortion into the data.

Statement of Ethical Practice, Social Research Online
http://www.socresonline.org.uk/welcome.html

Note: * 'broadbanding' is combining different identifying variables.

   ** 'micro-aggregation' is grouping observations and replacing with a single mean.

Invasion of privacy is regarded as a serious matter and the giving of informed consent does not imply that you consent to your privacy being invaded. Confidentiality should extend beyond not naming participants to not revealing personal details which might give away a participant's identity. As well as the loss of privacy itself it is possible that negative consequences of some kind may result if participants are identified in a report or publication. From a narrow research perspective, participants may be less willing to provide information about themselves if they worry, concerned that they may be identified.

There is, however, evidence that participants may not always want to be anonymized. For example, working with children with special needs, we found that some would have liked to have their own names used. It could also be argued that when the research has revealed some particularly praiseworthy conduct, it is churlish not to give personal credit.

Participants need to be made aware that their identity may have to be shared depending on what they say and the topic at hand (e.g. in connection with criminal or illegal activity). However, if made aware of this at the start of the research process, they can make an informed decision about participation.

Grinyer (2002) provides a useful review of the issues involved in anonymization.

Researcher safety and risk

While discussion of ethical principles rightly stresses the potential risks to the participants in the research, researchers themselves, in common with other professionals, can be at risk. This is particularly problematic when researching sensitive topics or working in difficult environments. For example, Stoler (2002) discusses the effects on the researcher of researching childhood sexual abuse, while Belousov *et al.* (2007) review the difficulties faced by fieldworkers in ensuring personal safety when working in conditions characterized by danger and crisis. Lee-Treweek and Linkogle (2000) include contributions from researchers who describe the risks they encountered while carrying out fieldwork, while Dickson-Swift, James, Kippen and Liamputtong (2008) and Craig (2004) provide helpful suggestions of ways of minimizing the risk for researchers when studying sensitive topics.

Concerns are not limited to obviously sensitive or dangerous situations. Kenyon and Hawker (1999) report on an exploratory e-mail survey of social researchers experienced in one-to-one interviewing or lone observation in field settings. Despite an acknowledgement that the chance of a dangerous encounter is low, many of the respondents stated that fears about their personal safety do arise during fieldwork periods and that these fears can affect the quality of their data collection.

Boynton (2005, Chapter 6) provides a detailed and highly practical discussion of how to safeguard researcher safety and well-being. It is grounded in her experience as a community researcher studying prostitution. Her analysis of risk assessment for researchers forms the basis for Box 10.7. It is couched in terms of the responsibilities of researchers and of managers (supervisors for student researchers). Third (2001 pp. 91–2) gives a practical example of assessing risk for student researchers in a project studying homelessness. While much research does not present more than a minimal risk to the researchers involved, it is worth considering each of the aspects in the assessment for all projects, particularly those taking place in fieldwork situations.

BOX 10.7

Risk assessment for researchers

- *Buildings*. Access from the street/car park to buildings – is it well lit? Are there clear paths, ramps or steps, etc., or any machinery or other features that could present a safety problem?
- *Your property*. Keep your bags and belongings in a safe place, even when visiting someone in their home. Ensure you know where your belongings are at all times. Don't take anything valuable with you unless you have to. Managers should be clear about staff safety when staff are responsible for equipment such as mobile phones or laptops.
- *Well-being*. Do you know where fire escapes, the nearest phone or the security office/ number is? (If you are directly at risk call 999.) Have you had a health check and is this supported in your job? If there are any risks posed to your physical or psychological health, have these been planned for in the project?
- *Equipment*. Have you been trained in the correct use of equipment and been given inoculations if appropriate? If you have to carry equipment for work, has it been checked so you avoid back strain?
- *People*. Anticipate and know how to respond to potential racist/sexist/homophobic remarks or abuse from participants and others. If you are likely to encounter participants who are drunk, on drugs or have severe mental health problems, are you trained in how to deal with them appropriately? Do you know the difference between someone who is ill and someone who is being inappropriate? Do you have the confidence to leave any situation that feels uncomfortable? Are other people around who could come to your assistance should you need it? Are you able to control and leave an interview? Do you have a policy on how to deal with participants who become a nuisance or who won't 'let go'? Managers should check that staff are aware of their boundaries and are not promising participants too much or overstepping their role as researcher.
- *Environment*. Are you likely to have to work or travel in adverse weather conditions? Can you plan your route and avoid getting lost? Is there any risk of assault? Have you had, or do you require, training in self-defence or assertiveness? Do you know the area where you'll be working, or can you find out about it? Are you wearing appropriate clothing? Is there a place of safety you can go to if working in the field?
- *Lone working*. Can you summon help if necessary? Is the risk posed to you high, medium or low? If possible, work in pairs and avoid dangerous buildings/situations. Never allow a person to work in a dangerous situation without training or support. Ensure you record your location, route and expected time of return. Have a check-in system with your buddy. Train and empower staff in raising the alarm if necessary. Get advice from local services (police, council, etc.) on any dangerous locations.
- *Setup*. Have you designed your study to avoid cold-calling? Are researchers equipped with identification badges? Are you regularly checking on the training and emotional needs of researchers?

(based on Boynton, 2005, Table 6.1)

Working with vulnerable groups

Consent issues for groups considered to be 'vulnerable' are particularly sensitive. One issue is that the individuals concerned are likely to have difficulties in giving informed consent because of problems in understanding what is involved. Groups who are perceived as vulnerable include children, people with learning difficulties or disabilities, those who are cognitively impaired including persons with Alzheimer's disease, and people with mental health problems. Participants can also be seen as vulnerable because of their social, economic, religious or cultural background. Wiles, Heath, Crow and Charles (n.d.; a) provide an extensive literature review on the topic of informed consent concentrating on issues relevant to vulnerable groups. Holland, Williams and Forrester (2014) explore the issues involved in a project researching substance abuse with parents and their children. They demonstrate 'how ethical decisions were made through, by or alongside participants, drawing on examples of access, consent, protection from harm and negotiating the presence of others in interviews' (p. 411).

Ethical review boards and committees, for understandable reasons, give particularly careful scrutiny to proposals to conduct research involving such groups. However, it may have the unintended consequence of inhibiting research focusing on vulnerable persons or of excluding them from the sample to be selected for a project. This is clearly both undesirable and unethical. A clear example of this, in the UK, was avoidance for many years of research with black and minority ethnic communities on sexual abuse, because of issues around cultural sensitivity. In the light of recent cases in Cleveland and Oxford, it seems that this avoidance did not help the communities in question.

The whole notion of categorizing groups as 'vulnerable' is considered suspect by some researchers and organizations representing their interest.

Wiles *et al.* (n.d.; c) suggest that:

> the onus is on researchers to find ways of obtaining consent from individuals that is meaningful to them, regardless of their abilities. This means identifying ways to explain the purpose and nature of the research clearly and unambiguously, which may involve using a range of media, and identifying ways in which individuals can indicate their wish to discontinue participating, which is likely to involve becoming familiar with the ways in which individuals convey assent and dissent. In relation to both of these points the ways in which this can be achieved is likely to be different for different groups and individuals. Researchers need to be sensitive to the needs of the specific groups, and the individuals within their sample, in achieving this (p. 5).

The legal position regarding research differs depending on the group and varies from country to country. In the UK there is no legal framework underpinning research practice although the Research Governance Framework (Department of Health, 2005b) has attempted to bring together various guidelines and statutes in the field of health research.

Access to these groups has often to be negotiated through a range of gatekeepers. In several areas of research people have to be accessed through organizational settings, such as schools, health and social care settings. Gatekeepers in these contexts include professionals who run organizations, service providers, care-givers, parents, relatives or guardians. They often have the power to refuse access and even when this hurdle has been passed can adversely affect potential participants' willingness to be involved. Wiles *et al.* (n.d.; a) discuss two related problems:

> The first concerns an over-protectiveness of gatekeepers which may result in people being denied the opportunity to participate in research (Heath *et al.*, 2005). The second concerns a failure of gatekeepers to provide opportunities for potential participants to exercise choice in participating in research (Miller and Bell, 2002). In relation to the first of these issues, some gatekeepers may deny access to researchers for a range of reasons, one of which may be an assumed lack of competency on the part of the potential research participant. Even where access is agreed the gatekeeper may seek consent from relatives alongside the consent of the individual concerned (especially in the case of children). This often means that even if the person wants to participate their wishes may be overridden by refusal from a relative (Heath *et al.*, 2005). The issue of seeking parental consent in relation to research focusing on sensitive issues such as drug use and sexual behaviour is particularly problematic (Allen, 2002; Valentine *et al.*, 2001). In most cases researchers are not in a position to influence an organisation's decision to deny access or to seek additional consent from relatives (p. 21). (*Note*: Reference is Heath *et al.*, 2004 not 2005.)

Children and young people

It is now widely recognized that children from an early age can be competent witnesses to speak for themselves about their experiences of, and their views on, the social worlds in which they live (James, Jenks & Prout, 1998). If they are to be directly involved in research, there is an expectation that they are given an understandable explanation of what will happen and a clear choice about whether they want to get involved or not (Cohen and Emanuel, 1998). Box 10.8 covers the main issues to consider and Box 10.9 gives an example of a student consent form used in schools.

The need to ask permission from 'parents or other gatekeepers' in all circumstances has been questioned by some researchers. A principle cited has been that of so-called 'Gillick competence', established following a legal ruling in England. This enabled a person under 16 to give consent to medical treatment without parental knowledge or consent if they were deemed to be 'of sufficient age, maturity and understanding' to understand what is proposed and thus to make an informed decision (see Balen *et al.*, 2006, pp. 32–3 for details). This ruling does not apply to interventions such as social research which are not potentially of direct benefit to the health of the child but the UK Department of Health's interpretation of its implications (Department of Health, 2001b) is that a person aged under 18 is able to consent to participate in research if they have sufficient understanding and intelligence to understand fully what is involved in the proposed research. In this situation, parental consent is not legally required but it is normally regarded as good practice.

A distinction is sometimes made between 'assent' and 'consent'. 'Assent' is usually understood as an agreement to participate in research without necessarily understanding its purpose. It has been suggested in the medical context that most children aged 14 have the necessary competence to give consent and most children aged 7 or over understand enough to be able to give or refuse assent (see Nicholson, 1987). However, Rossi, Reynolds and Nelson (2003) consider that acceptance of 7 for the age of assent has little empirical support. It appears clear that if a child is able to give their assent, but not yet competent to give informed consent, then the

BOX 10.8

Informed consent for research involving children and young people

1. The following questions should be addressed:
   - Have they been given all the information about the research that they need to make a decision to participate?
   - Do they understand the information they have been given – in particular, how are very young children, those with learning disabilities, or with communications problems to be informed and their consent gained?
   - Are they clear that they can agree or refuse to take part – without any adverse consequences?
   - Are they clear that they can withdraw at any point without adverse consequences?
   - Have you agreed a signal with a child or young person to enable them to withdraw easily?
2. While they themselves must give their consent to participate, it may be necessary to ask permission from parents or other gatekeepers to approach the child. When seeking permission from gatekeepers it is important that they too are provided with all relevant information about the research.
3. Where gatekeepers' permission to approach children and young people is granted, it is important to remember that the informed consent of individual children and young people must still be sought. This is of particular importance when carrying out research within institutions like schools or residential units. It should not be assumed that the approval of a head teacher or unit manager for the research to take place equates to the consent of individual children and young people. Complete disclosure of relevant information should always be given to children and young people and informed consent sought.
4. All children and young people participating in research studies should be given written information, in understandable language and appropriate format, for them to keep. This will include a contact telephone number should they wish to get back in touch with the researchers at a later date.

   (based, in abridged form, on 'Guidelines for Research', National Children's Bureau, 2006 – Informed consent, pp. 2–3)

informed consent of parents, or others acting in their stead, is essential. The situation where children are able to give informed consent is more complex.

Balen *et al.* (2006) are concerned that ethical guidelines for social research and the practices of ethical review boards and committees are essentially adult-centred and continue to view children and young people as dependent, and in need of protection from issues and questions that might arise in the research. They give an example where competent children have consented to

BOX 10.9

Example of consent form for students in schools

Your parents/guardians gave you permission to take part in a study about gambling.

The goals of this study are to find out (1) more about teenage gambling, and (2) why some teenagers gamble a little and others gamble a lot.

You should know that the survey is totally anonymous. This means no one — not your parents, your teachers, not even your friends — will know what you wrote on the survey. And when the results of the study are reported, everyone's answers will be grouped together so no one can trace your answers back to you.

You should also know that your involvement in this study is completely voluntary, which means you can skip questions or stop doing the survey at any time.

If you agree to be in this study, you will be given a paper-and-pencil survey. The survey will ask questions about your gambling behaviours, school work, after-school activities, substance use and risk-taking behaviours. It will take you about 20 minutes to complete.

If you have any questions or concerns about the study, you may contact <insert contact name>.

Thank you for your help!

This study has been approved by your school and by the <insert name of university ethics review committee and file number>.

If you want to do the survey, read this, then sign your name.
Any questions I had about the study have been answered and I understand that:

- I am agreeing to be in this study, which asks questions about gambling, school and other behaviours (like drinking and smoking).
- My answers on the survey are anonymous; so *no one*, except me, knows what I wrote.
- My answers on the survey will be kept strictly confidential (this means private).
- My participation in this study is completely voluntary. Therefore, I can skip any questions, or even stop doing the study at any time for any reason.
- My answers will be grouped with other students' answers, then used to develop prevention and treatment programs for teenagers in the *<insert name of region>*.

Signature _____ **Date** _____

(from McPhee and Canham, 2002; Appendix A)

participate in research but their parents have not given consent, and the children have been excluded from the research (Goodenough, Williamson, Kent & Ashcroft, 2003; see also Alderson, 1999a, p. 61). They cite examples from their own research where seeking parental consent has been problematic, including a study with children whose parents are drug and/or alcohol users. Balen and colleagues acknowledge that parents have rights and responsibilities to protect their children, and the need for ethical review, but conclude that 'researchers need to engage with the gatekeepers of research to ensure that the laudable effort to protect potentially vulnerable participants avoids overprotection, paternalism and the further disenfranchisement of already marginalized young people'.

Bray (2007) discusses the practical issues faced by researchers gaining consent from children prior to involvement in research. After reviewing a variety of approaches to aid the process, including audiovisual presentations using videos or DVDs, written information leaflets, computer assisted information, and visual information using pictures, she describes an 'activity board' approach. Multiple images illustrating relevant concepts such as 'confidentiality' formed part of a matching task which the researcher went through with each child. She stresses the need for flexibility and adapting the task and its presentation for different ages and abilities. The importance of keeping written information to a minimum and seeking alternative approaches is also stressed by Alderson (2004).

School-based research

Homan (2002) describes the situation in school-based research where it has not been unusual for researchers to focus on getting approval from head teachers and class teachers. Parental approval might be sought but the children were not involved in this process. Rather than informed consent on their part, he describes this as the 'principle of assumed consent'. Schoolchildren may be told that they are participating in a research project by teaching staff. Sometimes the research activity may be presented as part of overall class work. Researchers may not be given enough time to explain the study so children have little opportunity to decide whether or not they want to participate.

A review of relevant journals suggests the situation has not changed significantly more recently. For example, the British Educational Research Journal, the official journal of BERA (the British Educational Research Association), has produced ethical guidelines for educational research (available at http://www.bera.ac.uk/publications/guidelines/). The guidelines have a section on informed consent which states: 'Researchers must take the steps necessary to ensure that all participants in the research understand the process in which they are to be engaged, including why their participation is necessary, how it will be used and how and to whom it will be reported' (para. 11). However, inspection of recent volumes of the journal reveals that very few of the published articles dealing with school-based research mention obtaining informed consent from the children involved. The situation is similar in the United States and Canada where the main concern appears to be the effects of a move from 'passive parental consent' in which parents exclude their children from research participation by returning a signed form declining participation, to 'active parental consent' where written permission from the parent or guardian must be obtained. This has had the effect of substantially reducing participation rates and increasing selection bias (Esbenson, Melde, Taylor & Peterson, 2008).

While there are types of research where child consent may be inappropriate (e.g. secondary analysis of existing data, or studies making use of data already routinely collected), there appears to be little justification on ethical grounds for such consent not to be a routine requirement for much school-based research (and an expectation that this is included in reports of the research). Abrams, Allen and Markowitz (n.d.) list what aspects their Institutional Review Board look for when children are being asked for their agreement to take part in school-based research:

- Participation in research must be voluntary, without coercion or manipulation.
- Alternatives to participation in the research should be comparable in time, effort, and 'appeal'.

- There is sensitivity to the amount and type of attention directed toward children participating in research in comparison to those who are not participating. The following should be considered: research/non-research setting, presence of adults, the emotional effect on children of participation or non-participation.
- Any credit/compensation offered for research participation should be comparable to that offered for completing the non-research alternative.
- Investigators should adopt methods that keep students' decisions for participation in research activities private.

University and college students

An expectation that students act as participants in research carried out in their department (common in psychology), raises somewhat different ethical issues. More generally, whenever anyone takes part in a study for a 'consideration' of some kind, whether financial or as an explicit or implicit part of their duties or position, there are ethical implications. The situation can lead to researchers and participants taking on employer and employee roles respectively. The employer has to guard against the notion that payment justifies placing the participant at risk. On the employees' side there is the likely tendency to 'give them whatever I think that I am being paid for'.

Other vulnerable groups

These include people with mental health problems, learning disabilities and cognitive impairments (including those with dementia), people who are disadvantaged because of their role, or place, in society (including black and minority ethnic communities, religious affiliation, or economic position). Prisoners and others in institutions also present ethical problems, not so much in relation to informed consent but more concerning the issues just discussed with students – the need to ensure that their consent is freely given and not as part of an expectation of more favourable treatment.

In healthcare settings, consent to treatment lies at the heart of the relationship between patient and professional. In order for people with mental health problems, learning disabilities or cognitive impairments to have equity of access to healthcare, they need to be able to give informed consent to health interventions, or be assessed as incompetent to give consent. In England and Wales the Mental Capacity Act (Department of Health, 2005a), which attempts to clarify issues of consent and capacity, includes the following key principles:

- presumption of capacity;
- the right for individuals to be supported to make their own decisions; and
- the right for individuals to make what might be seen as eccentric or unwise decisions.

Similar presumptions are made in the United States (Gunn, Wong, Clare & Holland, 1999).

Goldsmith, Skirton and Webb (2008) make the point that whether or not capacity to consent is achieved may depend on the effort made to 'tailor' the relevant information to the abilities and needs of the individual concerned. As discussed in relation to obtaining informed consent with children, you should consider using a range of ways of providing information to meet these needs, including the use of pictures, graphics, photos, video and computers (e.g. Connors & Stalker, 2003; Dunn, Lindamer, Palmer, Schneiderman & Jeste, 2001). Objective screening tools to assess capacity to consent have been devised (e.g. the Mental Alternations Test (MAT), used by Nokes and Nwakeze, 2007 to assess the cognitive capacity of older persons who are HIV positive).

If people do not have the capacity to consent to their participation in a project a difficult ethical dilemma has to be faced. Are they to be automatically excluded from research which could have a direct benefit to themselves and others? In the UK, the Mental Capacity Act 2005 (see Dobson, 2008) has opened up the possibility that people not able to consent could no longer be excluded from participation in research, enabling access to experiences and potential treatments and care for which they may not hitherto have been considered. However, as listed in Box 10.10, strict safeguards are needed. Researchers are required to consult with others not involved in the project and there is full scrutiny by an appropriate ethics board. Approval will also be required from persons with the responsibility of safeguarding the interests of the individuals concerned.

BOX 10.10

Conducting research with people not having capacity to consent to their participation

The researcher must ensure that the project meets the following requirements:

- The research project is associated with the condition which impairs the participant and/or any treatment of the condition. An 'impairing condition' is one which causes or contributes to any disturbance of the mind or brain (and on which the assessment of lack of capacity is based).
- The research project could not be undertaken as effectively solely with participants who have capacity to consent.
- The research must be intended to provide knowledge of the causes, treatment or care of people affected by the same or similar impairing condition or concern treatment or care of the condition.
- The participant is likely to benefit from undertaking the research and the benefit is not disproportionate to any burden in taking part.
- If there are no benefits to the person and if the research concerns the gaining of knowledge about the condition, then there should be negligible risk to the participant.
- Participation in the project should not interfere with the participant's freedom of action or privacy in a significant way, or be unduly invasive or restrictive.

(based, in abridged form, on a summary from the Mental Capacity Act, 2005 by Dobson, 2008, p. 25)

General ethical responsibilities

Real world research can lead to the researcher finding out about some practices or conduct which present ethical dilemmas. These include:

Discovery of illegal behaviour

If you discover something you know or suspect to be illegal, such as sexual or physical abuse of children, this must be reported to the police or other appropriate authority. As a student or junior researcher, this should be discussed with your supervisor or project director, who may feel it is their responsibility to contact the authorities. The requirement to report overrides any confidentiality agreements you have made (in situations where it is known that laws may be broken, it may be sensible to make it clear at the outset that you will have to report illegal acts).

Whistle-blowing situations

Other situations, while not revealing illegal or unlawful activities, may cause concern. Suppose that in an office, school or hospital setting, you observe serious and persistent bullying by someone in a position of power. Or that people are being put at physical or other risk by someone's dereliction of duty. There are no general rules applying to all such situations. In the first instance, they should be discussed with research supervisors or colleagues. If they concur with your assessment of the seriousness of what you have found, and with the need for action, then this will have to be taken up formally with your contacts in the organization or an appropriate senior figure. This may mean that you will have to withdraw from any involvement with the people involved. McNamee (2002) discusses the general issues involved together with particular problems which can occur in action research and educational ethnographic studies.

Differing perceptions about what is ethical

It may be that something which you find disturbing on ethical grounds is accepted and commonplace in the setting with which you are involved. Perhaps you are seeking to impose your own values and expectations. Once again, it is advisable to seek help and advice. Following this, you may consider that the ethical course is to try to seek an understanding of what is going on by 'telling it as it is'. Remember that while you have particular ethical responsibilities as a researcher, this does not mean that you have a privileged voice on what constitutes ethical behaviour in others.

Ethical reporting of research

A further agenda of ethical issues arises in connection with the research report, discussed in Chapter 19.

Values in research

Values and value judgements are closely linked to morals and moral judgements. Traditional positivist science views science and scientists as 'value-free'. The position is that facts and values are fundamentally different and scientific research which is based on facts arising from empirical data has no role in making value judgements.

As discussed in Chapter 2 (p. 21), the positivist position has been largely discredited. This is in part because of successful critiques of the notion of value-free science by philosophers of science as well as feminist and critical theorists. Where this leaves the position of values in social research is disputed. Even positivist researchers would accept that the actual choice of a research project and the kind of research questions asked involves value judgements. A topic is chosen because it is viewed as more worthwhile than another. Defining, say, the use of soft drugs as a social problem with high priority for research resources indicates a particular set of values. The recommendations for action or practice arising from evaluation research similarly contain value judgements.

The argument is more about the position of values in the actual conduct, analysis and interpretation of social research. Some regard the attempt to differentiate facts and values as misconceived. Others, while accepting the value-laden nature of what are taken to be facts, seek to establish and get out into the open when value judgements are being made.

Fraud

Scientific fraud, a very serious type of misconduct by researchers, is an intentional effort to deceive the scientific community and others about the nature of research results (Schaffner, 1992). According to Schaffner, the definition of scientific fraud includes fabrication of results, fudging of results by changing them to fit in with the story the researcher wants to tell and suppression of results – leaving out the results that don't fit. Other serious types of scientific misconduct include *plagiarism* and the suppression of scientific findings. The latter is a particular problem in real world research where the *sponsor* of a project may seek to forbid publication of some inconvenient results.

📝 *The website includes a discussion of some well-documented examples of scientific fraud.*

Academic dishonesty by students

Much attention has been focused in recent years, heightened by the possibilities of 'cut and paste' of material from the Internet and the availability of essays for purchase, on the problem of plagiarism (see Chapter 19, p. 489). This applies with equal force to dissertations and research reports as to library type assignments. Other aspects of academic dishonesty relevant to research projects include the fabrication of information, references or results.

Lambert, Hogan and Barton (2003) review literature which claims that academic dishonesty is epidemic across most US college campuses and that the majority of students have engaged in it to some degree at some point in their academic careers. Such dishonesty cuts to the heart of the purpose of higher education and is unlikely to be specific to the American context. A specific example concerns a California State University criminology professor, who was responsible for a survey regarding potential juror bias. Following publicity which suggested that the results of the survey might affect the outcome of a trial, a number of students came forward and admitted that they had carried out the survey rather than the professor and had falsified the results (Murphy, 2004). At least six students admitted making up every answer they submitted, despite having to include respondents' phone numbers as a failsafe against cheating. While the professor concerned deserves serious censure for breaches of ethical guidelines which might have been expected to be picked up by an institutional review board, the students' dishonesty is clear.

> *Each instance of research dishonesty, misconduct and/or fraud has the potential to pervert the research process, compromise the safety and interests of participants and/or lead to a loss of public confidence in social and other research. You can only justify carrying out real world research involving people if you are prepared to subscribe to the highest ethical standards ruling out such behaviour.*

Ankier (2002) provides a useful discussion of these issues in the context of clinical research and reviews the legal and regulatory frameworks in different countries focusing on the Nordic countries, France, Germany, the US and the UK.

Ethical review boards and committees

The development of ethical review boards and committees, whose approval has to be sought, and received prior to the start of a research project, is now a prominent feature of the landscape for anyone seeking to carry out research. For those working in universities, or other institutions with a research function (e.g. research councils, charities, and government bodies) there will be an institutional board or committee to deal with. There may well also be a board or committee linked to the context in which the research is to take place. For example, in the UK research carried out within the National Health Service (NHS) has to be approved by Research Ethics Committees (REC) (Department of Health, 2001a). The volume, degree and length of scrutiny by ethics boards and committees depends on several factors, including who funds the research, the application process, and whether more than one of them is involved.

The NHS has produced a useful leaflet on 'Defining Research' (available at http://www.hra.nhs.uk/documents/2013/09/defining-research.pdf) to help decide if a project is research, which normally requires review by an REC, or whether it is some other activity such as audit, service evaluation[2] or public health surveillance, which doesn't.

It is your responsibility (or the responsibility of your research supervisor or project director) to find out the expectations of both bodies about the order in which they should be approached and whether they have an agreement about their relative roles. If you have been asked to carry out a project, either on an individual basis as an outside consultant, or as an insider within a firm or business where this kind of research is a one-off, it is advisable to join a professional organization for advice and support on ethical issues. In any case adherence to the ethical guidelines for your discipline or area of work (see p. 208) is essential.

Ethical review and social research

The formal review system, with an emphasis on approval by a committee, rather than on self-regulation and acceptance of personal responsibility in research has resulted 'in a common view of research ethics as a troublesome barrier to negotiate before the real business of doing research

---

[2] The concept of 'service evaluation' here is much narrower than that of evaluation research as discussed in Chapter 9. Much evaluation research would appear to require review.

can begin' (Long & Fallon, 2007, p. 1399). There is concern amongst users of social research methods about the operation and effects of ethical boards and committees, seen particularly strongly by qualitative researchers and, more generally, by anyone wishing to use innovatory methods and methodologies (Nind, Wiles, Bengry-Howell & Crow, 2013), or when researching sensitive topics (Noland, 2012). Van den Hoonaard (2011) and Monaghan, O'Dwyer and Gabe (2013) provide scathing analyses of university Research Ethics Committees' practices and effects in Canada and Ireland respectively.

The website includes a discussion of problems and issues with ethical review and qualitative research.

In the real world, ethics boards and committees will not go away. Nor should they. The examples of unethical research discussed in this chapter help explain their necessity. The challenge is to find ways in which their operation can be influenced so that research of whatever type is dealt with fairly and equitably, and that good research is supported. This important issue is addressed below (p. 234).

Interacting with ethical review boards

The roles and responsibilities and composition of ethics committees are 'givens' as far as you are concerned. It is reasonable to expect that general institution-wide committees include at least one member who has knowledge of, and current experience in, the use of both qualitative and quantitative social research methods and the particular ethical issues that this involves. If this is not the case, the committee should be prepared to provide details of how it will seek appropriate advice by co-option or other means.

All committees develop their own internal culture, which has a bearing on how they function, the ways they interpret the guidelines and the values and views expressed in the committee. Melville (2005) suggests that developing skills in preparing ethics applications depends in part on understanding the culture and functional operation of the committee. Social researchers and committee members can hold widely divergent views about each other, especially the motives and roles of the other party, which can create unnecessary obstacles in negotiating the ethics review process. In addition to the view of some social science researchers that ethics committees do not have the expertise or skills to assess their research, Melville notes the following misunderstandings:

- In a fluid environment of changing standards of privacy among the public and legislators, litigation and risk management, ethics committees often exhibit a strong culture of ethical sensitivity and caution. Professionals who feel they are better equipped to deal with ethics, given their profession's commitment to ethical codes and practices, can interpret this as overzealous and unnecessary.
- Ethics committees may be more conscious than researchers of abusive and fraudulent research practices and the potential for these to occur whether through deception, inexperience or incompetence.

- A lack of understanding by committees of the time and expertise required by researchers to complete ethics review protocols.
- Conflicts over which set of standards to apply to individual cases, for example, whether a legal or ethical standard is to be applied (if both a legal requirement and an ethical guideline apply, the legal requirement will prevail; where guidelines prescribe a standard that exceeds that required by law, this higher standard should apply).
- Researchers can feel aggrieved that this is an unnecessary scrutiny. They will have already undergone a peer review process when applying for competitive funding or, as students, satisfied these requirements by going through faculty or school confirmation processes.

With greater experience of the process of ethical review, by both researchers and committees, it is likely that a greater degree of mutual understanding will be reached on many of these issues. Committees composed of multidisciplinary teams can be expected to acquire considerable knowledge through assessing large numbers of proposals. Researchers of all kinds will have to accept that ethical review is here to stay and that the onus is on researchers to ensure they provide sufficient detail (regardless of the methodology chosen) on all relevant aspects of the study in plain language to the committee.

Review boards are typically required to assess the 'scientific merit' of a proposal, and to satisfy themselves that the skills and experiences of the researchers are such that the aims of the proposal can reasonably be expected to be achieved. Poor quality research has ethical implications. It is wasteful of resources and can needlessly put participants at risk. This remit for an ethical board is entirely reasonable providing that the view of 'scientific' is not narrowly positivistic.

An approach taken in some countries, notably the United States, has been to regard certain types of empirical study involving people as not requiring submission to ethical review boards – effectively saying that they don't count as research. This may be good news to those who need not trouble the board and can just get on with their projects. However, it has two unfortunate effects. Firstly, a narrowing of the definition of research, and an effective downgrading of some types of study. Secondly, the possibility that a study with unethical features is carried out.

This text has argued for a relaxed view of what constitutes science (Chapter 1, p. 8), including within the fold a wide range of both qualitative and quantitative methodologies. Accepting this view does mean that it is incumbent on review boards to develop the expertise necessary to give fair and equitable treatment across this range. Let us hope that the active involvement of real world researchers familiar with different methodologies in ethical review will help to bring this about. Volunteers needed!

National systems for ethical review

Researchers need to be familiar with the system operating in their own country. In the UK, universities have what are usually referred to as Research Ethics Committees, typically at both institutional and school, or departmental, levels. The latter system, where powers are delegated to school or departmental level, can avoid some of the problems discussed in the previous section, but then calls for a way of ensuring that common standards apply across the university. For research in the field of health and social care, there is a national Research Governance Framework (Department of Health, 2005b) which covers a wide range of relevant issues – similar frameworks exist in Scotland and Wales. Boynton (2005, pp. 57–60) gives details and useful advice.

Oakes (2002) discusses the system in the United States, focusing on the work of Institutional Review Boards (IRBs). In his view, researchers must accept the legitimacy of IRB review, learn more about IRB regulations, imperatives, and the pressures on them and educate IRBs about social scientific methodologies and empirically demonstrable risks. Melville (2005) provides a similar account of the Human Research Ethics Committee system in Australia. Both authors provide practical suggestions for ways to approach the ethical review task.

Getting your application approved

It may help to approach the task bearing in mind that research is not a right but a privilege and that the process is a form of peer review. Perhaps also, that ethical review boards and committees did not spontaneously appear to frustrate you but are a direct consequence of many documented violations of very basic ethical principles. Box 10.11 makes some suggestions to gain approval. Many committees welcome the degree of involvement suggested here. Some don't.

The type of research that you are doing may also have an impact on the degree and volume of research committee involvement. Research committees will, understandably, pay more attention to what is considered high risk research (for instance, research with vulnerable participants, or on socially sensitive issues) as there is more potential harm to the participants, researcher and the institution involved.

BOX 10.11

Some suggestions on how to get your application approved

1. Plan the ethical aspects of your study from the very beginning.
2. Try to start a dialogue with the chair of the committee (or an administrator, or member with responsibilities for dealing with research involving human participants) at an early stage.
3. If allowed, attend one or more meetings of the committee. All committees develop their own internal culture, which has a bearing on how they function, the ways they interpret the guidelines and the values and views they express in the committee. Such observation, and the dialogue mentioned above, can be invaluable in helping to shape your application, and to sensitize you to issues they are likely to find problematic.
4. If the committee regulations allow this, attach a covering letter to your application summarizing your study, giving special attention to issues relating to using human participants (informed consent, debriefing, anonymity and confidentiality, data protection, etc.).
5. Know the timetable for meetings and the deadlines for submission prior to the meeting. Approval may be conditional, possibly requiring further discussion at a later meeting.
6. If possible, attend the meeting at which your application is discussed, and be prepared to answer questions or concerns.
7. If you disagree with a decision, seek a personal meeting with the chair to discuss things.
8. If this does not resolve the situation, or if you feel (after discussion with experienced colleagues) that the committee has shown bias or otherwise dealt inappropriately with your case, there should be a formal appeal process.

Politics and real world research

Acknowledging that values and value judgements are involved in various ways in the process of real world research provides a basis for the argument that such research is inevitably political (see also the discussion in Chapter 9, p. 194 on the political nature of evaluation research). Hammersley (1995; Chapter 6) provides a clear and detailed analysis of the question, 'Is social research political?' He discusses four ways in which values are implicated in research:

- Through the research commitment to producing knowledge; i.e. knowledge is preferred to ignorance. This presupposition shows that in a fundamental sense research cannot be value-free or politically neutral.
- Research requires resources. Given that they could be used for other purposes, allocating them to research represents a political and value choice.
- Research is founded upon presuppositions reflecting the values of the researcher; which may derive, for example, from their gender and ethnicity.
- Research has effects on people's lives through their being involved in the research and/or being in a context affected by the research findings. Ethical concerns about such possible consequences provide another route whereby the researcher's values influence the research.

Such features are not specific to research. They are characteristic of many human activities which therefore have a similar political dimension. The point is worth stressing, however, when views of science as value-free or value-neutral still linger.

A second way in which social research may be considered as political arises from the view of politics as to do with the exercise of power. Whether or not researchers were ever autonomous, simply following their own noses uninfluenced by any external forces, is questionable. In the current climate in many countries those with power influence virtually all aspects of the research process from the choice of research topic (controlled by which projects get funding or other resources) to the publication of findings. This is typically viewed as a malign, corrupting influence. The line taken in this text (see Chapter 1, p. 4) is that, while there are undoubtedly dangers in this situation, if it is unavoidable don't waste time and effort trying to avoid it.

It has been argued that traditional styles of social research primarily serve the interests of planners and the scientific community itself (Scott, 1999, p. 91). A more inclusive participatory style of research involving the participants directly, and working to an agreed shared agenda with sponsors and others in positions of power, increases the possibility of research being more useful and more widely used. Singh (2010, Chapter 5) presents a critical discussion of relationships between social research and black and minority ethnic groups. He develops a model 'that is more responsive to oppressed groups whilst remaining committed to methodological rigour' (p. 87).

Box 10.12 covers some of the political influences on real world research. While some of these influences may not affect the technical adequacy of a research project, they can introduce biases of various kinds. For example, Terrre Blanche and Seedat (2001), discussed in Terre Blanche, Durrheim and Painter (2006), reviewed the work of the South African Institute for Personnel Research (NIPR) during the apartheid era and concluded that, in the main, the work was technically sound in that it was properly collected, analysed and interpreted. However, the researchers were strongly influenced by the political context at that time to ask only certain kinds of question, e.g. 'How can black workers be assigned to different job categories to make industrial

BOX 10.12

Political influences on real world research

The person(s) or agencies sponsoring, funding or otherwise providing resources, access or facilities for the research may influence some or all of the following:

1. *Selection of research focus*. Not a problem providing that you consider the project feasible and ethical.
2. *Selection of research design* (research questions, strategy, methods, etc.). Again not a problem providing that you consider the design feasible and ethical. It may be important to fall in with their preferences as this could influence the utilization of findings.
3. *Granting of access*. A problem only when access is refused, which may be due to fear of exposure, general dislike or distrust of research and researchers, previous unfortunate experiences with projects. Rare when funded by the organization involved.
4. *Publication of findings*. Can cause severe problems. It is important that this is clarified in the contract or agreement made when starting the project. This should cover both their and your rights of publication (including who has final control over the content and whether they can prohibit your separate publication). You must decide at the outset whether the conditions are acceptable. Jenkins (1984) provides a graphic example of how things can go wrong.
5. *Use made by sponsor of findings*. This is likely to be outside your control. Findings may be misrepresented, used partially or suppressed totally. Providing this falls within the terms of the contract or agreement, you just put this down to experience. Or you may even get a publication discussing what happened!

Note: Such influences can introduce biases of various kinds – see Box 10.13.

companies more efficient?' rather than 'How can companies be transformed so as to employ more black managers?' (Terre Blanche *et al.*, 2006, p. 13).

Knowledge that a research project has been sponsored by a particular agency may affect the credibility of its findings (e.g. a study funded by a pharmaceutical company on the environmental effects of genetically modified organisms will have low credibility with some audiences). There is undoubtedly the possibility that funded researchers will, wittingly or unwittingly, produce 'favourable' results. If you consider the project worthwhile and can live with criticism, your responsibility if you proceed is to guard against bias and generally observe all ethical considerations. Box 10.13 lists some sources of potential bias arising from political influences.

Some view research as a means of achieving political ends. Choices made in selecting a research topic and research questions, design, analysis, interpretation, and presentation of findings can all be manipulated to serve a political purpose. The codes of practice and systems of ethical review, discussed earlier in the chapter, discourage such attempts to bias research practice. However, the actual power wielded by researchers themselves is limited, although care has to be taken that it is not abused. For example Forster (2003), discussing the ethics and politics of classroom research, reflects that for her dissertation research 'I imposed the research on my

BOX 10.13

Potential bias from political influences

1. Some types of research may be supported, others suppressed. Decisions about the topics which will receive funding are strongly influenced by policy and ideological considerations.
2. Researchers opt for types of research which they consider are more likely to be funded and to have their findings published.
3. Reviewers of grant applications favour proposals which fall in with their personal, methodological or ideological preferences.
4. Reviewers of journal articles and other publications favour proposals which fall in with their preferences. Journal publication is strongly influenced by dominant ideologies and powerful interest groups.
5. Decision-makers in government departments favour policy-based research projects directly relevant to their current policy concerns.
6. Undesirable findings are suppressed through removal of consent to publish or indirect pressure.

class, which can be seen as an abuse of power as a teacher. Further, although students had the right not to comply with my research requests such as being interviewed, some might have felt unable to object because of the hierarchical teacher–student power relation'.

The claim is that because researchers have specialist expertise, their voice and their findings should be taken note of. This privileged position is disputed by constructivists and others taking a relativist stance (see Chapter 2, p. 17). As discussed in that chapter, the realist position is that researchers can claim some limited and fallible authority in relation to the production of knowledge (see also Hammersley, 1995; p. 107). Hammersley and Scarth (1993) discuss instances of researchers exceeding the boundaries of their authority.

Their power is also limited by the fact that research findings are not a major contributor to the development of public policy. As de Forest (2006) puts it when describing the history of an educational project on teacher selection: 'Political reality trumps educational research.' Policy is often based on ideology. The policy is decided and then the search is for evidence to support that policy. Effectively we have 'policy-based evidence' rather than 'evidence-based policy'.

More sophisticated approaches attempt to take political sensitivities into account (e.g. Morrison, 2006) or to develop approaches to public policy experiments which are more robust in the political interventions that have ruined some or all parts of similar previous efforts (King *et al.*, 2007).

Political pressures on researchers

Political sensitivities within organizations worried that researchers might portray them in ways which might result in adverse publicity can lead to them exerting pressure on researchers in various ways. Hence, it is important to be aware throughout the research process, but especially at the start, who 'owns' the research project. Just because you are the main researcher or team leader does not mean that you have full control over what happens during, or after, the research process. If you are doing funded research, do those who pay own the data? Have you looked at the intellectual copyright clauses in the research agreement? Is there a time lag between your submission of the final report and its publication? Who has the final say on the type of dissemination of your research? More importantly, who has final veto? You need to get answers to all of these questions. There should be experience in your institution to guide you in these issues.

Box 10.14 provides an anonymized version of a new researcher's recent experience. The lessons are clear. Make sure that you have all the necessary approvals and agreements. Keep

BOX 10.14

A cautionary tale from a new researcher

My research involved a study of an aspect of the working of a major UK government initiative. I did several presentations about my research around and about, including both abroad and in the UK. When I got my PhD, the local paper did a piece on me and focused on what my research was about. It duly appeared and the day after I received an email from the initiative's national R&D manager wanting information about the research, had I had the proper approvals, etc. I rang the person concerned and explained it was part of my PhD and that, of course, I had had the proper approvals. I emailed the manager details of when and from whom I had received the different approvals needed. I explained how and when I collected the data and the formal arrangements made in order to so. The manager seemed happy with this and I heard nothing more.

Nearly a year later, someone else from the initiative contacted me asking for all the information again, a copy of my raw data, all the consent forms, a copy of my thesis and details of pending publications. On top of this, they reported that it was known that I had used pictures of the inside of the place where I had carried out the research, and other material, and questioned if I had permission to do this. I explained that anything that I had used was freely available on the Internet, including on their own website.

I told them my thesis was publically available and they could access that through the normal channels. I scanned all my original approvals and sent those. I had already told the manager details of my publication plans. I was not prepared to send them the raw data or the consent forms, in part because this would have jeopardized confidentiality undertakings I had made.

I was put under severe pressure to give them additional information. I discussed this situation with an experienced researcher in another institution who had carried out research involving the same national initiative. The researcher said that this was normal behaviour on their part and that they were especially defensive. The researcher supported the position that I had taken and recommended that I ignore these additional demands.

As a very novice researcher, had I not also had access to experienced colleagues in my own institution to advise me about how to respond, I would have been really put off about doing anything ever again!

them safe. New researchers, whether students or junior researchers, need to have someone with experience they can turn to if they are put under pressure.

Sexism, racism and social research

Sexism

Feminist commentators and researchers have made a convincing case for the existence of sexist bias in research. This is seen in all areas of science, including the natural sciences (Harding & Hintikha, 2013) but is obviously of great concern in the social sciences where the human, in one or both genders, is the researcher and the researched-upon. The substantial literature on feminist research methods and methodology provides detailed coverage of the issue (e.g. Brisolara, Seigart. & SenGupta, 2014; Hesse-Biber, 2014).

Eichler (1988), in a clear and readable analysis applicable to all social science disciplines, suggests that sexism in research arises from four 'primary problems': androcentricity, overgeneralization, gender insensitivity and double standards. She also argues that there are three further problems, which while logically derived from and falling within the primary problems, occur so frequently as to merit separate identification – sex appropriateness, familism and sexual dichotomism. Box 10.15 gives an indication of the meaning of these terms. This analysis covers a much wider range of issues than the use of sexist language. It is now generally accepted that such language should be avoided when reporting research, as discussed in Chapter 19 (p. 490).

Problems arising from sexism can affect all aspects and stages of the research process, and both female and male readers and researchers are urged to be on their guard. Eichler (1988, pp. 170–5) provides a comprehensive 'Nonsexist Research Checklist' giving examples of how the various problems arise in the concepts employed in the research, its design, methods, data interpretation, etc.

Racism

Racism can also be problematic across the research experience. Much research is westernized and 'white' in nature, in the same way that research tends to be gendered. Researchers often research and write from the dominant cultural experience, which tends to be white. This means that when findings from research are generalized, especially in fields like criminology, psychology, or social work, they are not representative. Many of the research issues surrounding race mirror those of sexism listed in Box 10.15, but can also involve issues of vulnerability and the capability of researchers to cross a cultural divide. This is partly why some research on or with black and minority ethnicity is avoided, even when conducted by the BME population in question themselves.

For real world research to be effective and generalizable we have to get past issues of race and gender, difficult though this may be. Problems arising from these issues can affect all aspects and stages of the research process. All readers and researchers are urged to be on their guard.

BOX 10.15

Sexism in research: sources of bias

1. *Androcentricity.* Viewing the world from a male perspective: e.g. when a test or other research instrument is developed and tested on males, and then assumed to be suitable for use with females. Note that gynocentricity (viewing the world from a female perspective) is, of course, also possible, though relatively rare.
2. *Overgeneralization.* When a study deals with only one sex but presents itself as generally applicable: e.g. a study dealing solely with mothers which makes statements about parents. Overspecificity can also occur when single-sex terms are used when both sexes are involved; e.g. many uses of 'man', either by itself or as in 'chairman'.
3. *Gender insensitivity.* Ignoring sex as a possible variable: e.g. when a study omits to report the sex of those involved.
4. *Double standards.* Evaluating, treating or measuring identical behaviours, traits or situations by different means for males and females: e.g. using female-derived categories of social status for males (or vice versa). This may well not be inappropriate in a particular study but nevertheless could lead to bias which should be acknowledged.
5. *Sex appropriateness.* A commonly used and accepted form of 'double standards': e.g. that child-rearing is necessarily a female activity.
6. *Familism.* A particular instance of 'gender insensitivity'. Consists of treating the family as the smallest unit of analysis when it would be possible and appropriate to treat an individual as the unit.
7. *Sexual dichotomism.* Another instance of 'double standards': treating the sexes as two entirely distinct social groups rather than as groups with overlapping characteristics.

(adapted from Eichler, 1988)

Further reading

The website gives annotated references to further reading for Chapter 10.

PART III

Tactics: the methods of data collection

Having decided on a focus for the research, the research questions to which you seek answers, and the overall research strategy that is appropriate for getting those answers, you now need to give thought to methods. How will you actually go about what a detective would call 'making enquiries'? In fact, when carrying out real world research, our options are essentially the same as those available to the detective. We can *watch* people and try to work out what is going on; we can *ask* them about it; and we can look out for fingerprints (as well as any other evidence they leave behind them).

Put in the more usual research language, watching becomes *observation*, asking becomes *interviewing*, using *questionnaires* and administering *tests*. Interviewing is usually taken as implying personal, face-to-face (or in the case of the increasingly commonly used, telephone interviewing), voice-to-voice interaction. Questionnaires and tests may be administered in an interview, face-to-face situation or the researcher's questions can be presented without direct, personal, interaction – as in a postal survey. 'Looking for other evidence' covers a variety of methods including *documentary analysis*.

Chapter 11 covers the development and use of questionnaires in the context of the sample survey. Interviews are covered in Chapter 12, and observation in the following chapter. Chapter 14 covers tests and scales. Chapter 15 brings together a wide range of other methods, including the possibilities opening up for Internet-based research.

A realist stance permeates how one views the data obtained by the use of any and all of these methods. Realists claim that it is possible to make judgements about the value of such data on rational grounds, although the judgements are fallible and prone to error. One way of increasing confidence in findings is method triangulation (Olsen, 2004) i.e. by the use of multiple methods, which is discussed and advocated towards the end of Part III, p. 383. Realists treat data, such as participants' accounts in interviews and responses in questionnaires and test situations, as indicative of their lived 'reality' although recognizing that the meanings attached to experiences are mediated by socio-cultural contexts (Willig, 1999). It is only by collecting, and subsequently analysing and interpreting the data, that we have evidence for the existence of mechanisms, and the contexts in which they operate, central to realist explanation.

Selecting the method(s)

The selection of a method or methods is based on what kind of information is sought, from whom and under what circumstances. It is decided at an early stage in a fixed design project, although it may be feasible to add supplementary methods during the project.

Even in flexible designs, there is a need to make some initial decisions about how to collect data (or you never get started). However, in flexible designs the nature and number of methods used can change as data collection continues.

A rational choice?

The rational approach is to ask, given your research questions, and a decision on research strategy, what methods are most suitable? However, in practice, the choice of particular methods may well precede the choice of a research problem. As Walker (1985) puts it:

> Just as an instrumentalist will not change from playing the clarinet to playing the trumpet because a particular piece demands it, but will usually turn to another piece of music, searching for pieces that suit both the instrument and the player, so researchers generally give a lot of time and thought to the formulation of possible and potential research problems, looking for those that appear to fit their interests and preferred methods (p. 47).

This phenomenon of 'methods in search of problems' rather than the reverse is a genuine one. In one sense it does not matter providing that the methods fit the problem chosen. However, it can cause difficulties in real world research where the problem is presented to you, and the choice might be between using an inappropriate method or turning the work away. The moral is to seek to get a broad grounding in all strategies and a broad range of methods, so that you are in a position to make a rational choice.

What methods are available?

Many interviews and questionnaires, and direct observation of different kinds, tend to be the most popular. Experiments also commonly use some form of controlled observation but the actual technique is often specific to the particular field of study.
   The following are simple rules of thumb for selecting methods:

- To find out what people do in public, use *direct observation*.
- To find out what they do in private, use *interviews* or *questionnaires*.
- To find out what they think, feel and/or believe, use *interviews*, *questionnaires* or *attitude scales*.
- To determine their abilities, or measure their intelligence or personality, use *standardized tests*.

Consider practicalities

Anything you propose to do must be within the constraints of available time and resources. You may wish to carry out a participant observation study, but if it would take three months for you to be accepted and fully involved, then it is impracticable for a one-month maximum study period. A second-best alternative involving interviews may be called for.
   Business confidentiality, or the stress it might cause, may rule out direct observation. Ethical considerations will similarly rule out some methods in some situations.

CHAPTER 11

Surveys and questionnaires

This chapter:

- discusses the use of questionnaires in surveys and elsewhere;
- compares self-completion, face-to-face, telephone and Internet versions;
- explains the various stages involved in carrying out a sample survey;
- stresses the professionalism needed to carry out a high-quality survey;
- covers practical issues in the design, development and use of questionnaires; and
- concludes with a discussion on the why and how of sampling.

Introduction

Questionnaires and interviews are very widely used social research methods of collecting data from and about people. Competence in their design and implementation can reasonably be expected from a real world researcher. This chapter focuses on the issues raised in using questionnaires in the context of a survey. However, they are also used in many other contexts both as the primary method of data collection and as a secondary method. Using a questionnaire as a primary, or single, method of collecting data in a project raises many of the issues which arise when it is set within a survey. So, even if you do not think of the project in survey terms it will be useful to work through the following sections of the chapter.

Considered as a secondary method, perhaps administering a questionnaire after participants have been involved in an experiment, or as part of the experiment itself, your central concern may be with the nuts and bolts of questionnaire design as covered on p. 258.

The ubiquity of surveys

Surveys are common. You will have to have led a very hermit-like existence not to have been asked to take part in some form of survey – which brand of washing powder or lager do you buy, and what other brands do you know? Who would you vote for if there were a national election next week? Do you think the government is doing a good job? And so on, and on. Similarly, the results of surveys of one form or another pepper the pages of newspapers and radio and television output.

Surveys have been with us for a long time. The Domesday Book, and efforts to assess the effects of the plague in London in the seventeenth century, provide notable landmarks. Tonkiss (2004) highlights their importance in the development of a science of society in the late eighteenth and early nineteenth centuries. Marsh (1982, Chapter 1) gives a detailed and fascinating account as part of her defence against critics of the use of surveys within sociology.

Much current use of surveys is highly instrumental, undertaken in the interests of better marketing and higher sales of some service or product. A worrying trend is the use of 'pseudo-surveys' as a sales ploy which is likely to further increase a growing unwillingness to participate in genuine surveys. However, a substantial amount is academic in the positive sense of seeking to find out something about what is going on in society today. In either case there is a high premium on 'getting it right', that is, on getting an accurate and unbiased assessment of whatever it is that is being measured. In some fields, most notably in political polling, error can be glaringly obvious – when the predicted winner loses, or there is wide discrepancy between polls purporting to measure the same thing. Often, however, there is no obvious reality test and judgements of reliability and validity have to fall back on an analysis of how the survey was carried out.

Large-scale surveys are big business and require substantial time, effort and a range of personnel to carry out. Even the relatively small-scale survey likely to be feasible for readers of this text can't be completed quickly due to the various stages which have to be completed, as indicated in Box 11.1. This refers to the situation where a small sample of, say, 200 or 300 people are involved in the main study. Rough estimates of 'person-days' have been given so that if, say, several interviewers are available, the actual period of time taken in the main data collection can be reduced (although time will be needed to train interviewers). Coding of data can take place as soon as some interviews have taken place.

A period of three to four months for the whole process is probably a realistic minimum. However, if you don't have that amount of time available, it's surprising what can be done by burning the midnight oil. Just don't try to leave out any of the activities; they are all important if you are to do a worthwhile study. This timetable assumes that no problems will occur (and they will – you just don't know in advance what they are going to be – bad weather, school holidays, industrial disputes, flu or other epidemics, and computer breakdowns are not unknown).

A survey using questionnaires sent by mail will have a rather different time schedule. The need for repeat mailings, reminders, etc., central to getting satisfactory response rates in a postal survey, takes up a substantial period of time. Internet-based surveys are increasingly popular and can cut down the period of time needed, although they have their own problems (see p. 253).

BOX 11.1

Steps in carrying out a small-scale interview-based questionnaire survey

Activity	Estimated number of days (likely minimum)
1. Development of research questions, study design (including sample selection for pretests and main study), and initial draft of questionnaire.	20
2. Informal testing of draft questionnaire.	5
3. Revise draft questionnaire.	3
4. Pretest of revised draft using interviews.	3
5. Revise questionnaire again (possible revision of design and main study sample).	3
6. Carry out main data collection interviews.	30*
7. Code data and prepare data files.	10
8. Analyse data and write report.	20

*Depends on size of sample, whether telephone or face-to-face (and, if latter, on travelling time between interviews).

Designing surveys

There is a sense in which surveys are a research strategy (i.e. an overall approach to doing social research) rather than a tactic or specific method. In those terms a survey is a non-experimental fixed design, usually cross-sectional in type (see Chapter 6, p. 140). However, many of the concerns in doing a survey are not so much questions of overall strategic design but more to do with highly practical and tactical matters such as the detailed design of the instrument to be used (almost always a questionnaire, largely or wholly composed of fixed-choice questions), the sample to be surveyed, and obtaining high response rates.

Box 11.1 is couched in terms of a survey carried out by *interviewers*: those persons armed with clipboards, and a questionnaire, who stop you in the street or knock on the front door and ask if you would mind answering a few questions. Other forms of survey are possible including the self-administered *postal (mail) questionnaire*, and, increasingly commonly, *telephone* and *Internet surveys*. Indeed, surveys are not necessarily restricted to the use of questionnaires. A traffic survey may be exclusively observational; a survey of the working life of lecturers in universities may rely on a weekly diary (leaving on one side for the moment the likely trustworthiness of such information if it is to be used to seek to demonstrate to their paymasters how hard-working they are).

Because of the ubiquity of surveys, it is likely that you will have a good common-sense appreciation of what the term means. It is, however, difficult to give a concise definition, precisely because of the wide range of studies that have been labelled as surveys. The typical central features are:

- the use of a fixed design;
- the collection of a small amount of data in standardized form from a relatively large number of individuals; and
- the selection of representative samples of individuals from known populations.

While this captures the large majority of surveys, there are examples where a considerable amount of data is collected from each individual, where the 'unit' involved is not an individual but some form of organization such as a school, firm or business; and, particularly in the latter case, where the number of 'units' sampled gets down to single figures. Most surveys attempt to give a 'snapshot' of the situation at a particular point in time. However, as indicated in Box 11.1, practicalities dictate that data are collected over a period of time. They are, nevertheless, treated as if collection were simultaneous, i.e. as a cross-sectional design. There is, however, nothing in principle to stop the use of surveys in longitudinal designs.

The most common form of survey is the *sample survey*. Here, the participants in the sample are selected as being representative of some larger group, known as the *population* (this can be an actual population, say the people living in a town, or any group such as the workers in a factory). As discussed below (p. 282), a major issue in survey research is the representativeness of the sample, how it is achieved and assessed. It is sometimes possible to survey everybody in the population of interest. This is known as a *census* and avoids all sampling problems. Developments in information technology have made censuses increasingly feasible in some areas – it is as easy to contact several thousand people via the Internet as a dozen (though there are other problems in carrying out Internet-based surveys, discussed below on p. 253).

Advantages and disadvantages of the survey

Researchers tend to have strong, frequently polarized, views about the place and importance of surveys. Some see the survey as *the* central real world strategy. It may be that in non-laboratory situations where experiments are often neither feasible nor ethically defensible, surveys give that reassuring scientific ring of confidence. Associated with surveys is a satisfyingly complex set of technological concerns about sampling, question-wording, answer-coding, etc. Others view surveys as generating large amounts of data, often of dubious value. Falsely prestigious because of their quantitative nature, the findings are seen as a product of largely uninvolved respondents whose answers owe more to some unknown mixture of politeness, boredom, desire to be seen in a good light, etc. than their true feelings, beliefs or behaviour. As is often the case, such caricatures are not without foundation. Surveys have also suffered from being viewed as necessarily positivistic, a view comprehensively demolished by Marsh (1982, especially Chapter 1).

Nevertheless much survey research has a strong positivistic flavour. Mishler (1991, Chapter 1) stresses the differences between asking and answering in naturally occurring, contextually grounded conversations and the question-response process in survey interviews. His view is that many of the routine procedures of this kind of research represent efforts to bridge this gap. An essential feature of survey interviewing is that it is organized social discourse, but, 'by adopting an approach that is behavioral and anti-linguistic, relies on the stimulus-response model, and decontextualizes the meaning of responses, researchers have attempted to avoid rather than to confront directly the inter-related problems of context, discourse and meaning' (p. 27).

The reliability and validity of survey data depend to a considerable extent on the technical proficiency of those running the survey. If the questions are incomprehensible or ambiguous, the exercise is obviously a waste of time. This is a problem of *internal validity* where we are not obtaining valid information about the respondents and what they are thinking, feeling or whatever.

The problem of securing a high degree of involvement by respondents to a survey is more intractable. This is particularly so when it is carried out by post or the Internet, but is also still difficult when the survey is carried out face-to-face (remember that nearly all surveys carried out by interviewers involve fleeting interactions with total strangers – it is asking a great deal of the interviewer to establish a rapport with each and every respondent so that they are fully involved). Securing involvement is in part also a technical matter (a poorly designed and printed, lengthy questionnaire administered just before Christmas to workers in an organization who are currently trying to meet a seasonal deadline is unlikely to get a good response), but it has to be accepted as a likely hazard in almost all surveys.

If the sampling is faulty, this produces a *generalizability* or *external validity* problem. Generalization, from the sample surveyed to the wider population it is meant to represent, is at risk. Another type of external validity problem occurs if we seek to generalize from what people say in a survey to what they actually do. The lack of relation between attitude and behaviour is notorious (Erwin, 2001). Reliability is more straightforward. By presenting all respondents with the same standardized questions, carefully worded after piloting, it is possible to obtain high reliability of response.

Notwithstanding all these caveats, a good, competently run survey is something which all generalist real world social researchers should be able to offer. Surveys provide the sort of data which are not difficult for an intelligent lay audience to understand, particularly an audience which is scientifically literate. Lindblom and Cohen (1979) make a strong case that, of the various forms of 'usable knowledge' those carrying out professional social research might provide, the humble survey may well be the most influential. Hakim (2000) makes a related point in referring to one of the main attractions of the sample survey as its *transparency* (or *accountability*): In other words that:

> the methods and procedures used can be made visible and accessible to other parties (be they professional colleagues, clients, or the public audience for the study report), so that the implementation as well as the overall research design can be assessed (p. 77).

To this end, a standardized language is used to refer to the sampling procedures employed. Questionnaires, codebooks, introductory letters, analyses of non-response, etc. are expected to be included in the report. Increasingly, raw survey data are deposited in data archives (e.g. the UK Data Archive at Essex University, http://www.data-archive.ac.uk), permitting both checking and further analysis by other workers. This standard of professionalism found in quality survey work now mirrors that traditionally expected in experimental studies.

Box 11.2 lists some of the advantages and disadvantages of the questionnaire-based survey.

BOX 11.2

Advantages and disadvantages of questionnaire-based surveys

Disadvantages
General to all surveys using respondents

1. Data are affected by the characteristics of the respondents (e.g. their memory, knowledge, experience, motivation and personality).
2. Respondents won't necessarily report their beliefs, attitudes, etc. accurately (e.g. there is likely to be a social desirability response bias – people responding in a way that shows them in a good light).

Postal, Internet and other self-administered surveys

3. Typically have a low response rate. As you don't usually know the characteristics of non-respondents, you don't know whether the sample of respondents is representative.
4. Ambiguities in, and misunderstandings of, the survey questions may not be detected.
5. Respondents may not treat the exercise seriously and you may not be able to detect this.

Interview surveys

6. Data may be affected by characteristics of the interviewers (e.g. their motivation, personality, skills and experience). There may be interviewer bias, where the interviewer, probably unwittingly, influences the responses (e.g. through verbal or non-verbal cues indicating 'correct' answers).
7. Data may be affected by interactions of interviewer/respondent characteristics (e.g. whether they are of the same or different class or ethnic background).
8. Respondents may feel their answers are not anonymous and be less forthcoming or open.

Advantages
General to all surveys using respondents

1. They provide a relatively simple and straightforward approach to the study of attitudes, values, beliefs and motives.
2. They may be adapted to collect generalizable information from almost any human population.
3. High amounts of data standardization.

Postal, Internet and other self-administered surveys

4. Often this is the only, or the easiest, way of retrieving information about the past history of a large set of people.
5. They can be extremely efficient at providing large amounts of data, at relatively low cost, in a short period of time.
6. They allow anonymity which can encourage frankness when sensitive areas are involved.

(continued)

Interview surveys

7. The interviewer can clarify questions.
8. The presence of the interviewer encourages participation and involvement (and the interviewer can judge the extent to which the exercise is treated seriously).

Notes: Advantages 4 and 5 may be disadvantages if they seduce the researcher into using a survey when it may not be the most appropriate strategy to answer the research question(s).

Postal and Internet surveys have rather different advantages and disadvantages (see p. 251).

The telephone survey is a variation of the interview survey which does not involve face-to-face interaction and has rather different advantages and disadvantages (see p. 251, 269).

Why a survey?

Surveys are almost always carried out as part of a non-experimental fixed design. While this can be for *any* of the research purposes, whether exploratory, descriptive, explanatory, or emancipatory, surveys are not well suited to carrying out exploratory work. There is nothing to stop you asking a wide range of largely open-ended questions in an attempt to explore some area but it is likely to be an inefficient and ineffective procedure taking a great deal of time to analyse. Surveys work best with standardized questions where we have confidence that the questions mean the same thing to different respondents, a condition which is difficult to satisfy when the purpose is exploratory. The requirement is that you know what kind of information you want to collect.

Many, probably most, surveys are carried out for descriptive purposes. They can provide information about the distribution of a wide range of 'people characteristics', and of relationships between such characteristics. For example, a political party might be interested in voters' views about their policies, and on how such views are related to, say, age, gender, income, region of the country, etc. At a local level, there may be a need to find the relative degree of support or opposition to alternative development plans.

It is possible to go beyond the descriptive to the interpretive; to provide explanations of the phenomena studied and the patterns of results obtained. Details of possible approaches to analysis are provided in Chapter 17. Surveys can be used to get at causal relationships but this is not an easy or a straightforward undertaking, partly because of the non-experimental design used, but also because the information is typically in the form of correlations. And as will no doubt be burned into the brain of anyone who has followed even an elementary course in statistics, correlation does not imply causation. What is required is a sophisticated analysis of the detailed pattern of correlations.

Suppose we are interested in the jobs that pupils from different ethnic backgrounds go into after leaving school and that we want not only to see who goes to what kind of job but also to interpret this information. When we try to explain why there is a differential involvement of, say, Pakistani, Afro-Caribbean and white youths in particular types of employment, we might find from a survey that there are differences in educational attainment in the groups from different ethnic backgrounds and, further, that this attainment is related to occupational type. It is not legitimate simply to make the connection that differences in educational attainment are the cause of the differential pattern of occupation for the pupils from different educational backgrounds. Leaving aside practical problems such as how jobs can be classified, and the more intractable measurement problem of ensuring that tests of educational attainment are 'culture-free' (that is, that they do not introduce biases related to ethnic background – which itself constitutes a threat to the internal validity of the study), it is patently obvious that the different ethnic groups are likely to differ in a host of other ways apart from their educational attainment. Differential encouragement from the home, family income, parental and friends' occupations, careers advice (or the lack of it) and attitudes of potential employers are just a few of the possibilities.

Explanation and interpretation depend on incorporating into the study information on a substantial number of such variables and then analysing the pattern of correlations, seeing where relationships are strong and where they are weak or non-existent. From this you seek to tell the most convincing story that you can; in realist terms, what mechanisms are operating in which contexts. What goes into the pot, that is, which variables you seek information on, is determined by pilot work where potential mechanisms are suggested (perhaps involving semi-structured interviews, focus groups or other methods of data collection) and by previous studies, as well as any theoretical framework or contenders for mechanisms that you have developed.

Approaches to survey data collection

Most surveys involve the use of a questionnaire. There are three main ways in which questionnaires have been administered:

- *Self-completion.* Respondents fill in the answers by themselves. The questionnaire is often sent out by post (or, increasingly, using the Internet) permitting large samples to be reached with relatively little extra effort.
- *Face-to-face interview.* An interviewer asks the questions in the presence of the respondent, and also completes the questionnaire.
- *Telephone interview.* The interviewer contacts respondents by phone, asks the questions and records the responses.

However, increasingly the Internet is being used to carry out surveys – see below.

Responses are usually sought from individuals, although that individual might be responding on behalf of a group or organization. Self-completion survey questionnaires can be administered on a group basis (e.g. gathering all students in a school into a hall and asking them to complete the survey at the same time). This is essentially for administrative convenience and efforts should be made to ensure that individual responses were received.

The format and appearance of the questionnaire will vary depending on the method of data collection selected. Box 11.3 summarizes features of the different approaches.

Resource factors

While all forms of data collection call for a substantial amount of time and effort in developing the questionnaire, the self-completion version is substantially lower in cost to administer than face-to-face interviews. In its usual postal version the costs are essentially that of postage (though this does involve the provision of stamped addressed envelopes, reminders, etc. – see below, p. 265).

BOX 11.3

Comparison of approaches to survey data collection

Aspect of Survey	Postal Questionnaires	Internet Surveys	Face-to-Face Interviews	Telephone Interviews
Resource Factors				
Cost	Low	**VERY LOW***	High	Low/ Medium
Length of data collection period	Long	**SHORT**	Medium/ Long	**SHORT**
Distribution of sample	**MAY BE WIDE**	**MAY BE WIDE**	Must be clustered	**MAY BE WIDE**
Questionnaire Issues				
Length of questionnaire	Short	Short	**MAY BE LONG**	Medium
Complexity of questionnaire	Must be simple	**MAY BE COMPLEX**	**MAY BE COMPLEX**	**MAY BE COMPLEX**
Complexity of questions	Simple to moderate	Simple to moderate	**MAY BE COMPLEX**	Short & simple
Control of question order	Poor	Poor/Fair	**VERY GOOD**	**VERY GOOD**
Use of open-ended questions	Poor	Fair/Good	**GOOD**	Fair
Use of visual aids	Good	**VERY GOOD**	**VERY GOOD**	Not usually possible
Use of personal/ family records	**VERY GOOD**	**VERY GOOD**	Good	Fair
Rapport	Fair	Poor/Fair	**VERY GOOD**	Good
Sensitive topics	GOOD	Variable	Fair	Fair/**GOOD**
Data-Quality Issues				
Sampling frame bias	Usually low	Variable	**LOW**	**LOW** (with RDD**)
Response rate	Poor/Medium	Poor/Medium	Medium/ VERY HIGH	Medium/ High
Response bias	Medium/High***	Medium/ High***	**LOW**	**LOW**

(continued)

| Control of response situation | Poor | Poor | **GOOD** | Fair |
| Quality of recorded response | Variable | Variable | **GOOD** | **GOOD** |

*Entries in bold capitals indicate the type of survey which has an advantage for a particular aspect
**Random Digit Dialling (see p. 269)
***Favours more educated respondents

(abridged and adapted from Czaja and Blair, 2005, Exhibit 3.1, p. 35. Blair, Czaja and Blair, 2014, Exhibit 4.2, pp. 50–1 gives a reformulated version)

If the questionnaires are being administered in a group setting you don't even have the cost of stamps. Interviews involve an interviewer for the whole time; in a face-to-face situation travel time can add very substantially to the time and cost involved.

The data collection period is shortest in Internet surveys and telephone interviews. It is feasible to carry out a substantial number of these per interviewer on each working day, though some repeat calls will be needed. A substantial amount of time is taken up in postal questionnaires by the necessity of sending out reminders and repeat questionnaires to non-respondents. However, in the situation where a self-completion questionnaire is administered in a group setting and all members of the sample are present, this can be completed in an hour or so. The geographical distribution of the sample can be wide for both self-completion questionnaires and telephone interviews but to make face-to-face interviews feasible in resource terms, it is necessary to limit the study to a particular area.

Questionnaire issues in surveys

The questionnaire length, and hence the time taken to complete it, can be greatest in face-to-face interviews. Its complexity has to be kept to a minimum when self-completion questionnaires are used. You also lose control of question order in this situation; respondents can answer the questions in any order, which may have effects on the answers given.

Although surveys rely very largely on closed questions (where there is a choice between a number of fixed alternatives) some open-ended questions (where respondents are free to answer as they wish) can be successfully introduced in face-to-face interviews, and to a lesser extent in telephone interviews. It is also feasible, when in the face-to-face situation, to include the use of visual aids, for example cards with lists from which the respondent chooses. It may be necessary for some surveys to obtain information about personal or family records, perhaps ages of family members. Self-completion questionnaires, particularly when completed in the family setting, permit respondents to seek out the information before completing the question.

A skilled interviewer should be able to achieve good rapport with nearly all interviewees in the face-to-face situation. This is somewhat more difficult when the telephone is used and the self-completion questionnaire has to rely on the quality of its presentation. Conversely, the lack of direct contact means that self-completion questionnaires, and to a somewhat lesser extent telephone interviews, can be better at dealing with sensitive topics.

Data-quality issues

There are not major differences in bias in the list of the people from which a sample is drawn (sometimes referred to as the *sampling frame*) between the different approaches, although both telephone and face-to-face interview situations make it relatively easy to check that the respondent falls within the population of interest. A low response rate is a serious and common problem with self-completion questionnaires and, as discussed below, every effort should be made to get this to an acceptable level. Self-completion questionnaires can be subject to response bias, for example, people with reading and/or writing difficulties are less likely to respond. These skills are not called for in the interview situation.

The interviewer has good control of the response situation particularly when across the table from the respondent. However, there is essentially no control of this with self-completion questionnaires; we don't even know for certain whether the person completing the questionnaire is who they say they are. Similar considerations apply to the quality of recorded response.

Computer-assisted approaches

Computers are now increasingly used in a variety of ways to support survey researchers. Computer-Assisted Interviewing (CAI) refers to the way in which computers can be used in the development and administering of survey questionnaires. It has also been known as Computer-Assisted Survey Information Collection (CASIC). Rather than using a paper questionnaire, interviewers carry laptops from which questions are read out and responses to the survey questions are entered. The data can then be transmitted back to the field centre via modem. All of the social surveys carried out by the Office for National Statistics in the UK have used this method since 1995. Several software packages are available including Blaise, which was developed by Statistics Netherlands (http://www.blaise.com).

The website gives details of different versions of computer-assisted interviewing.

Box 11.4 lists some of the advantages and disadvantages of this approach.

The website gives references to examples of research using computer-assisted interviewing.

Internet surveys

These are a relatively new and increasingly popular development (see Chapter 15, p. 377 for discussion of general issues in the use of the Internet for research purposes). The two main forms are e-mail and website based. E-mail surveys commonly use text messages as part of the e-mail or as an attachment. Website based surveys permit a high degree of creativity in the design of the survey. Various response options are possible, and pictures, audio and film clips can be included. A major disadvantage is the fact that, despite the rapid growth of Internet use, access remains limited. For example, in 2008, about two-thirds of UK households had some form of Internet access. Adults under 70 years of age who had a degree or equivalent qualification were most likely to have access to the Internet in their home, at over 90 per cent, compared with fewer than 60 per cent of individuals who had no formal qualifications (Office for National Statistics, 2008). Response bias is also a concern with highly educated computer-literate persons

BOX 11.4

Advantages and disadvantages of computer-aided interviewing (CAI)

Advantages

1. *Cost savings can be made:*
   - There is no need for any data entry to be done at the field centre.
   - Reliable results can be obtained quickly.
   - Paper does not need to be printed (and thus no costs involved).
2. *Questionnaires can be improved:*
   - More complex routing and checking is now possible.
   - Data can be checked as interview proceeds, allowing inconsistencies to be detected.
3. *Fieldwork savings can be made:*
   - Data can be downloaded quickly.
   - Typing in responses and coding data is much less time-consuming.
4. *The data are ready to analyse very soon after the fieldwork is carried out* (although some data cleaning is necessary).

Disadvantages

1. *Despite there being cost savings associated with CAI, there can also be high costs involved:*
   - Large numbers of interviewers, laptop computers and software can cost a lot of money, thus CAI may be too expensive for a small-scale survey carried out outside large agencies.
2. *Problems associated with IT can be encountered:*
   - Computer programmers are needed who are familiar with both survey research and IT – these are not usually easy to come by.
   - Time that is saved at the end of the survey process (see Fieldwork savings above) is needed at the beginning to programme and code the questions.
3. *Interviewers can also encounter problems:*
   - Respondents may be wary of a machine; this may either prevent them from taking part in the survey at all or may affect their responses.
   - There may be problems with power, for example, if the laptop's battery fails or if the laptop needs to be plugged in.
   - They would need extra training in how to use the CAI software and laptops, for example, the interview may take longer if the interviewer is slow at typing.
4. *Problems encountered by researchers:*
   - It can be very difficult to decipher CAI questionnaires on paper (particularly with regard to the interpretation of the codes, routing and interviewer instructions that are separate from the questions themselves).
   - This extra information means that there is a rapidly expanding volume of documentation.

(based on the Question Bank Fact Sheet 8: Computer Assisted Learning, Centre for Applied Social Surveys. http://surveynet.ac.uk/sqb/)

more likely to respond. Box 11.5 summarizes some of the advantages and disadvantages of Internet surveys.

IF (and this is a big 'if') you are carrying out a survey where it is known that the population of interest has Internet access AND there is a good population list give serious consideration to using an Internet survey instead of a postal survey. A well-designed website survey is preferable to an e-mail based survey.

BOX 11.5

Advantages and disadvantages of Internet surveys

Disadvantages

1. A substantial proportion of households in all countries do not have Internet access. Even with current trends and national policies, the proportion seems unlikely to reach that of households with telephone access.
2. Large response bias effects appear likely with poorer households and persons with lower educational attainment tending to have less computer experience, older equipment, poorer and slower connections and hence less likely to complete online questionnaires.
3. There is a lack of good population lists (sampling frames) even for those who do have Internet access. Probability sampling is only possible in situations where there are adequate lists (in organizations such as schools, universities, hospitals, some businesses, etc.).
4. While postal questionnaires are uniform in the sense that all respondents get exactly the same form, many factors affect the appearance of online questionnaires (screen size, operating system, the browser used, loading speed, etc.).
5. They need to be relatively short to avoid high rates of non-response and refusal, non-reponse to individual items and non-completion.
6. They need to be self-explanatory as there is no interviewer to explain instructions or questions. Note, however, that it is easy to set up e-mail or other links back to you for queries on a website based or e-mail survey.
7. You have no control over the order in which questions are answered. This is technically possible in website based surveys but is inadvisable as forcing participants to give a response before proceeding is likely to lead to them not continuing. Neither can you control who actually completes it, whether it is an individual or group response, nor the situation in which it is completed – at home, or at work, or wherever.

Advantages

1. Low cost. You cut out not only interviewer costs, but also the paper, printing, postage and data entry costs of postal surveys. Sample size and geographical distribution of the sample have little effect on costs. Follow-up costs are also small.

(continued)

2. Speed of data collection. Typical data collection periods are less than 20 days. Additional time is needed for follow-up contact to maximize response rates.

3. Website based surveys can easily incorporate complex skip patterns which are automated and invisible to the person completing the survey. These would be confusing in a paper-based questionnaire.

4. Visual aids including pictures and diagrams, video- and audio-clips, animation, pop-up instructions, drop-down lists can be designed into website based surveys. Care must be taken to avoid problems for those with less sophisticated computer systems and/or poorer or slower connections to the Internet (see disadvantage 4 above).

5. Website based surveys can be adapted to make them more accessible to particular populations. For example, persons with disabilities such as blindness, severe physical disabilities and hearing impairment may be able to respond more effectively to an appropriately designed website based survey. (Mertens, 2005 p. 206).

Note: Disadvantages 5, 6 and 7 are also present in postal surveys.

Dillman, Smyth and Christian (2014, pp. 301–50) discuss the issues involved in carrying out Internet surveys. To counter the bias likely to be caused in the many situations where coverage is a problem, owing to some groups you would wish to be properly represented in your sample having limited Internet access, they recommend using postal and interview-based approaches in addition to using the Internet in a project. As one might expect, there are several websites giving useful information about relevant developments, including http://www.websm.org which is devoted to web survey methodology. Software to design and develop such a survey is widely available (e.g. from Creative Research Systems at http://www.surveysystem.com/ and Bristol Online Surveys at http://www.survey.bris.ac.uk).

'SurveyMonkey' (http://www.surveymonkey.com) is a private American company that enables users to create their own web based surveys. The basic product is free but an enhanced paid product and services are also available. It has been widely used and comes with glowing testimonials from their website and elsewhere on the web. There are dissenting voices (e.g. http://www.news.software.coop/get-the-survey-monkey-off-your-back/878/).

The website gives references to examples of Internet surveys.

Carrying out a sample survey

The most straightforward task for a survey is to answer questions of the 'how many', 'how much', 'who', 'where' and 'when' types. It can provide an estimate of the number or proportion of people who hold a certain belief (e.g. physical punishment of children by parents should be illegal) or engage in a particular behaviour (e.g. who have, as a parent of a child under five years, punished the child physically during the past 12 months).

This kind of descriptive information can be of value in its own right in helping to gauge public opinion, perhaps as a precursor to introducing or changing legislation. It can also be used to answer research questions or test hypotheses derived from theories. For example, the hypothesis that 'Non-parents are more likely than parents to support all physical punishment of children by parents being made illegal' arising from a 'realities of parenting' mechanism that the experience of parenting leads to an awareness of the need for physical punishment in particular contexts. Again, this is in principle something which can be addressed by means of a survey.

Here, as in many surveys, it would be necessary to collect information about specific sub-groups in the population, in this case parents and non-parents. Showing, even from a well-designed and carried out survey, that a higher proportion of non-parents support legislation (and even if it is statistically significant) does not in itself provide convincing evidence for the 'realities of parenting' mechanism. Collecting additional information on the gender of the respondent, their actual amount of involvement in the bringing up of young children (some non-parents may have substantial involvement; some fathers who believe that 'bringing up the children is the job of the mother' may have very little); age, number and gender of children; attitude of parents to this issue before they were parents – permits more sophisticated analyses and tests of causal models.

The importance of a theoretical framework or conceptual structure for surveys seeking to move beyond description to explanation cannot be overestimated. Whether expressed in terms of a set of possible mechanisms and the contexts in which they operate, or in other terms, they prevent the survey questionnaire degenerating into a fishing trip where questions are added simply because 'it seemed a good idea at the time'.

While most surveys target the individual, this is not an essential feature. We may be interested in groups, organizations or other units. Schools, hospitals, social services departments, etc. in the United Kingdom are surveyed to assess aspects of their performance (e.g. school attendance rates; hospital waiting lists) to generate league tables of various kinds and to 'name and shame' those whose performance is judged unsatisfactory.

Population

An early design decision concerns the population from which the sample of respondents is to be drawn. An important consideration is the geographical area to which we wish to generalize the results. This is governed largely by the research questions and the resources available. It may be necessary to modify your research questions, perhaps making them more geographically specific to make the survey feasible within the resources available. As indicated in Box 10.3 this is only a major issue with surveys where the questionnaire is administered by interviewers.

For many surveys, the target age range of participants requires consideration. An 'adult' population could be 21 years or older, but depending on the particular focus of the survey younger eligible ages might be appropriate. Obviously, the wider the age range covered in the population, the fewer of each age for a given sample size. As the confidence that can be placed in a finding increases with the number of persons on which it is based, it is sensible to use a restricted age range (e.g. 20 to 29 years inclusive) if this ties in with your research questions – or if the questions can be modified without doing violence to your overall aims.

Population list

This is a list of those in the population from which the survey sample is drawn. Survey researchers refer to it as the *sampling frame*. For a survey of people in an organization, this could be all those on the payroll. For general population surveys, telephone directories have often been used, though a moment's thought will reveal some of their inadequacies. These include not everyone having a phone, that it is usually based on households rather than individuals, people may be ex-directory and the rise in the number of cell phone-only individuals not listed in directories. Random-digit dialling (RDD) techniques, discussed below on p. 269, overcome some of these difficulties although they obviously can't reach those without a telephone. Voters' lists are sometimes used but are likely to be both dated and incomplete.

If a reasonably adequate list of those in the population can be obtained, this puts you in the position of being able to draw a (reasonably adequate) *random sample*; i.e. a sample where all members of the population have an equal chance of being selected for the sample. The advantages of doing this are substantial and are discussed below.

When there is not a perfect match between the list you can get hold of and the population of interest, questions arise about the size and nature of the discrepancy between them and how this will bias the estimate of the variable(s) we are interested in. With low percentages who cannot be reached by telephone, little bias will be introduced by their exclusion from a telephone survey. However, even in countries such as the United States where the percentage without telephones is overall very low, there is considerable demographic variability. Households with lower incomes are less likely to have phones and hence bias may be introduced on questions where poverty is of relevance. While it would be possible to visit households to contact sufficient non-telephone households to obtain an estimate of the likely bias, this is likely to be difficult, time-consuming and expensive.

Modern technology suggests possible solutions. For example, Zuwallack (2009) piloted the use of mobile or cell phones for survey purposes and found a higher percentage of young adults and minorities than a comparative landline sample. Şahin and Yan (2013) carried out a systematic review of 171 studies in various disciplines of their use in data collection. Galvez, Mankowski, Braun, and Glass (2009) describe the development of an iPod audio computer-assisted self-interview to increase the representation of low-literacy populations in survey research. Chauchard (2013) used an audio self-administered questionnaire with a basic MP3 player when collecting data about sensitive caste-related data in rural India.

Designing and using a questionnaire

This section covers general issues of questionnaire design in both surveys and other contexts. Issues specific to the design of self-completion and interview-based (both face-to-face and telephone) data collection are covered at the end of the section.

It is worth stressing that the questions for the questionnaire are *not* produced by your sitting down and trying to think of some interesting things to ask or even of getting a group together to do this. The questions should be designed to help achieve the goals of the research and in particular to answer the research questions. Blair, Czaja and Blair (2014, p. 183) present a model (based upon Tourangeau and Rasinski, 1988: and Presser and Blair, 1994) of how the survey questions fit into the overall survey process which is shown as Figure 11.1. The model is useful because it not only emphasizes the researcher's task of linking research questions to survey questions (their 'analytic use') but also stresses the respondent's tasks, which involve interpreting the question, recalling information which is relevant to it, deciding on an answer, and reporting

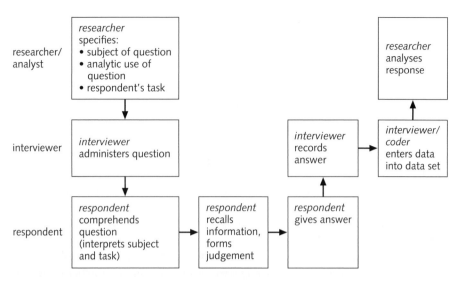

Figure 11.1 Model of the survey data collection process.

that answer to the interviewer (who may or may not be the same person as the researcher). This helps us to appreciate that a good questionnaire not only:

- provides a valid measure of the research questions; but also
- gets the cooperation of respondents; and
- elicits accurate information.

Respondents must be able to understand the questions in the way that the researcher intends, have accessible the information needed to answer it, be willing to answer it, and actually answer in the form called for by the question. A major part in the art and craft of producing a questionnaire is in writing it in such a way that respondents understand what you want from them, and are happy to give it to you, while the questions at the same time remain faithful to the research task.

The researchers' task

The researchers' central task is to link research questions and the questionnaire questions. Returning to the example about physical punishment of children, the research question:

Are non-parents more likely than parents to support all physical punishment of children by parents being made illegal?

is clearly inappropriate as one of the items in the questionnaire. If we were to ask the question getting, say, 57 per cent agreeing, 23 per cent disagreeing and 20 per cent 'don't know' responses, it provides a very dubious assessment. Respondents cannot very well report about the views of parents and non-parents in general. Even if they could, it is indirect, asking for their views about the views of others.

An obvious improvement is to ask:

Should all physical punishment of children by parents be made illegal?

1. *Yes*
2. *No*
3. *Don't know*

targeting the question on a sample of parents and non-parents. In this form, they are asked what they think rather than judging the opinions of others. Reflecting further on this, or doing some type of pre-testing, might raise possible criticisms of this form of the question:

- Respondents may not understand what is meant by 'physical punishment', nor even by the exact meaning of 'made illegal'.
- Respondents may have different views of what is meant by 'physical punishment'.
- Respondents may consider that, under some specific circumstances, particular forms of physical punishment should be legal.
- 'Don't know' is not appropriate here; they are asked about their views or opinions, not their knowledge ('no opinion' or 'not sure' would be preferable).

These illustrate common issues in drafting questionnaires. The language of the question may have to be changed so that it is both understandable and unambiguous to respondents.

Suppose the question is rephrased as:

Should parents be allowed to smack their children?

This certainly gets rid of the relatively complex and possibly ambiguous terms 'physical punishment' and 'made illegal'. However, in trying to ensure that it is clear and understandable, we have moved a long way from the research question. It also limits and restricts; smacking is only one form of punishment.

Criticisms of initial attempts at questions often result in an appreciation that the single question won't do, that multiple questions may have to replace it. In this example, it may be necessary to include coverage of different forms of punishment and different circumstances. The exercise of writing questions may lead to you revisiting your research questions. When you get down to working out exactly what you are going to ask people, it may become clear to you that you are really interested in something rather different from what you originally thought. Here, for example, mature reflection may suggest that you should focus on the morality of physical punishment rather than its legality.

The respondents' task

As shown in the model in Figure 11.1, the respondent has to first understand the question, which is why its wording is so important. When the self-completion format is used, they are on their own; you can't help them other than by the written instructions and the questions themselves. Many questionnaires ask respondents to remember and report things; 'How many times during the last month have you . . .', 'When did you last . . .', etc. An important part of pre-testing is to find out whether they can remember the information you are asking for. If you make the task too difficult, not only will the quality of the answers be low but you are likely to make the task uninviting, leading to low response rates.

The set of possible fixed-alternative responses should be *accurate, exhaustive, mutually exclusive* and *on a single dimension*:

- 'accurate' means that they link to the central point of the question; if the question relates to the value of something, you don't have responses of 'very interesting', etc.;
- 'exhaustive' means that all possible options are covered (include 'other' if necessary, but try by pre-testing to include most possibilities so that its use is kept to a minimum);
- 'mutually exclusive' means that only one of the possible responses applies (note, however, that a format is sometimes used where respondents are asked to select each of the responses that apply; e.g. the newspapers that they read regularly); and
- a set of responses including 'very useful', 'useful', 'boring' and 'very boring' relates to more than one dimension.

A wide variety of ways of presenting the response alternatives have been used. Perhaps the most common is the numerical scale as in Figure 11.2 below, question 14. Graphic responses can be used. The simplest form is a line joining two opposing adjectives, say 'bad' and 'good', the respondent indicating the strength of their response by a mark on the line. The distance of the mark from an end of the line can then be measured. An alternative graphic approach uses a set of 'smiley' faces spaced in a line, with the mouth line at one extreme a 'U' shape indicating happiness and the other an inverted 'U' for sadness. Respondents indicate their feelings to the question by marking or indicating the relevant face.

Various techniques and approaches including Likert scales and the semantic differential used in connection with the development of tests and scales can also be used in survey questionnaires. For more details see Chapter 13.

The questions

The central part of the questionnaire is devoted to the questions which derive from your research questions. Their wording, as has already been pointed out, is crucially important. Box 11.6 provides suggestions for avoiding the most obvious problems. Further details are given in more specialized texts (e.g. de Vaus, 2014; Saris & Gallhofer, 2014).

Designing self-completion questionnaires

Figure 11.2 gives a simple example of a self-completion questionnaire. It is worth stressing the need to cut down open-ended questions to a minimum with this type of questionnaire unless you can afford to spend a lot of time on analysis or only have a small number of responses to deal with. The desire to use open-ended questions appears to be almost universal in novice researchers but is usually rapidly extinguished with experience. Pilot work using interviews

Consumer behaviour and green attitudes

First some facts about you

1. Sex   Male ☐   Female ☐

2. Age group

    16–24 ☐   25–34 ☐   35–49 ☐   50–64 ☐   65+ ☐

Now some questions about the things you buy

3. Of the following household items, which brands do you normally buy?

Toilet roll	
Washing powder	
Washing-up liquid	
Household cleaners/polishes	
Nappies	

4. With regard to the goods just mentioned, which of the following things would you say influenced you when choosing what to buy?

    Quality ☐   Reliability ☐

    Reputation ☐   Advertising ☐

    Presentation/Packaging ☐   Brand name ☐

    Cost ☐   'Environmental friendliness' ☐

    Ethics (e.g. animal testing) ☐

5. Do you have any insulation in your home?

    None ☐   Loft ☐   Cavity ☐

6. Does anyone in your household run a car?

    Yes ☐   No ☐

    If Yes, do any of them run on unleaded petrol?

    Yes ☐   No ☐

7. How often do you use any of the following?

	Always	Sometimes	Never
Bottle banks	☐	☐	☐
Recycled paper	☐	☐	☐

8. Does the use of artificial additives and preservatives affect what foods you buy?

    Yes ☐   No ☐

9. With reference to any issues have you, during the past 5 years, done any of the following?:

    Signed a petition ☐   Been a member of a political party ☐

    Written to an M.P. ☐   Been part of a demonstration ☐

    Been a member of a pressure group ☐

    P.T.O

Figure 11.2 Example of a self-completed questionnaire.

Now some opinions about the following statements

10. The following is a set of statements about attitudes to green issues.
For each statement please say whether you agree strongly, agree, are neutral,
disagree or disagree strongly with it. Tick the appropriate box.

	Strongly agree	Agree	Neutral	Disagree	Strongly disagree
Britain should not allow its air pollution to cause acid rain in Scandinavia.	☐	☐	☐	☐	☐
There is too much panic about running out of resources.	☐	☐	☐	☐	☐
Manufacturers shouldn't make things that are harmful to the environment.	☐	☐	☐	☐	☐
Recycling is just a fad.	☐	☐	☐	☐	☐
Countries with rain forests are entitled to chop them down to sell their timber.	☐	☐	☐	☐	☐
Live for today. Don't worry about tomorrow.	☐	☐	☐	☐	☐
Industries should stop damaging the countryside, even if prices must rise to pay for it.	☐	☐	☐	☐	☐
Being 'Green' is just another youth craze.	☐	☐	☐	☐	☐
The government should invest more money into looking at alternatives to nuclear power.	☐	☐	☐	☐	☐

Just a few more facts about you

11. What is your occupation? Please give details

☐
☐

12. What is the income level of your household?

£5,000–9,999 ☐   £10,000–14,999 ☐   £15,000–19,999 ☐   £20,000 and over ☐

13. Educational qualifications

None ☐   GCSE ☐   A-levels ☐   Degree ☐   Other (please give details) ☐

☐
☐

14. What point in this scale best indicates your political views?
Circle the appropriate number.

Left 1 2 3 4 5 6 7 **Right**

Thank you very much for your cooperation

Source Gibbs, nd

Figure 11.2 (*Continued*)

BOX 11.6

Checklist to help avoid problems in question wording

1. *Keep the language simple.* Avoid jargon. Seek simplicity but avoid being condescending.
2. *Keep questions short.* Long and complex questions are difficult to understand.
3. *Avoid double-barrelled questions.* Double-barrelled questions ask two questions at once (e.g. 'Is your key worker caring and supportive?'). Split into separate questions.
4. *Avoid leading questions.* Leading questions encourage a particular answer (e.g. 'Do you agree that . . .?').
5. *Avoid questions in the negative.* Negatively framed questions are difficult to understand, particularly when you are asked to agree or disagree (e.g. 'Marijuana use should not be decriminalized'; Agree/Disagree. 'Marijuana use should remain illegal' avoids the problem).
6. *Ask questions only where respondents are likely to have the knowledge needed to answer.* 'Do you agree with the government's policy on foreign aid?' is unsatisfactory if respondents don't know what it is. Either tell them or ask a preliminary filter question to establish whether they know what the policy is. Then only ask those who said 'yes'.
7. *Try to ensure that the questions mean the same thing to all respondents.* Meanings and terms used may vary for different age groups, regions, etc.
8. *Avoid a prestige bias.* This occurs when a view is linked to a prestigious person before asking the respondent's view.
9. *Remove ambiguity.* Take great care with sentence structure.
10. *Avoid direct questions on sensitive topics (in interview situations).* Several indirect strategies are possible (e.g. using numbered cards with the alternatives; respondent gives relevant number).
11. *Ensure the question's frame of reference is clear.* When asking for frequency of an event specify the time period.
12. *Avoid creating opinions.* Respondents don't necessarily hold opinions on topics. Allow a 'no opinion' alternative.
13. *Use personal wording if you want the respondents' own feelings, etc.* Impersonal wording gives their perception of other people's attitudes (use it if that is what you are after).
14. *Avoid unnecessary or objectionable detail.* It is unlikely that you will want precise income or age; use income or age groupings.
15. *Avoid prior alternatives.* Give the substance of the question first, then the alternatives. Not the reverse.
16. *Avoid producing response sets (particularly in interview situations).* With 'agree/disagree' questions, some people tend to agree regardless of their real opinion ('acquiescence response set') or provide answers making themselves look good ('social desirability response set'); e.g. inflate their income or decrease their alcohol consumption. Seek to put people at their ease and avoid giving the impression that some answers are normal or unusual.

(adapted and abridged from de Vaus, 2002; pp. 118–21)

and open-ended questions can provide suggestions for closed alternatives. Although postal questionnaires typically have low response rates, there is much that one can do to increase the likelihood of getting a high response rate, as set out in Box 11.7. Note the emphasis given to the covering letter and to the various follow-up activities. The latter are crucial in achieving an acceptable response rate.

Response rate

Unfortunately, there is little agreement on what constitutes an adequate response rate. For a survey most commentators consider a minimum of 60 per cent as acceptable (e.g. Mangione, 1995), while others raise the bar to at least 75 per cent (e.g. Fowler, 1993). However, Baruch (1999), who reviewed 175 surveys in a range of reputable journals, found a mean reponse rate of 55 per cent, with a decline in the later studies. Recent published papers with substantially smaller response rates are not difficult to find.

BOX 11.7

Factors in securing a good response rate to a postal questionnaire

1. The appearance of the questionnaire is vital. It should look easy to fill in, with plenty of space for questions and answers.
2. Clarity of wording and simplicity of design are essential. Give clear instructions (e.g. 'put a tick').
3. Arrange the contents to maximize cooperation, e.g. ensure that early questions don't suggest to respondents that the survey is not for them. If there are attitude questions interpose them throughout the questionnaire to vary the response required.

Design and layout

4. Coloured pages (e.g. different colour for instructions) can clarify the structure.
5. Answering by putting ticks in boxes is familiar to most respondents. Circling pre-coded answers can confuse.
6. Sub-lettering questions (e.g. 5a, 5b, etc.) can help in grouping questions on a specific issue.
7. Repeat instructions if confusion is possible.
8. Initial questions should be easy and interesting. Middle questions cover the more difficult areas. Make the last questions interesting to encourage return of the questionnaire.
9. *Wording of questions is of crucial importance. Pre-testing is essential.*
10. A brief note at the end can:
    (a) ask respondents to check that they have not accidentally omitted to answer any questions;

(continued)

(b) solicit an early return of the questionnaire;
(c) thank them for their help; and
(d) offer to send an abstract of the findings.

Initial mailing

11. Use good-quality envelopes, typed and if possible addressed to a named person.
12. Use first class postage, stamped not franked if possible.
13. Enclose a stamped addressed envelope for return of the questionnaire.
14. For 'home' surveys, Thursday is the best day for sending out; for organizations, Monday or Tuesday.
15. Avoid a December mailing.

Covering letter

16. This should indicate the aim of the survey and convey its importance, assure confidentiality and encourage reply. If serial numbers or other codings are used, say why.
17. Tailor it to the audience (e.g. a parent survey might stress its value for child-care).
18. Give the name of the sponsor or organization carrying out the survey on the letterhead and in the body of the letter.
19. Pre-survey letters, advising respondents of the forthcoming questionnaire, can increase response rate.

Follow-up letter

20. This is the most productive factor in increasing response rates. All the above suggestions apply.
21. Emphasize the importance of the study and the value of the respondent's participation.
22. Conveying disappointment and surprise at non-response can be effective.
23. Don't suggest that non-response is common.
24. Send a further copy of the questionnaire and another stamped addressed envelope.

Further follow-ups

25. These are subject to the law of diminishing returns but are worthwhile. Three reminders are commonly recommended. They can increase response rates by a further third.

Use of incentives

26. Incentives accompanying the initial mailing appear to be more effective than rewarding the return of completed questionnaires (e.g. through a prize draw).

Note: Dillman *et al.* (2009) provide a more detailed discussion of non-response and ways of increasing response rates.

A systematic review by Pit, Vo and Pyakurel (2014) of survey response rates by general practitioners (a difficult audience), found that the following strategies had positive results:

[providing] monetary and nonmonetary incentives, larger incentives, upfront monetary incentives, postal surveys, pre-contact with a phonecall from a peer, personalised packages, sending mail on Friday, and using registered mail. Mail pre-contact may also improve response rates and have low costs (p. 1).

Non-response bias

The bias in findings resulting from the absence of data from those who do not respond is more important than non-response itself (obviously, if non-responders would have given the same results as responders, even a very low response rate would not introduce bias). It is generally accepted that a higher response rate makes it more likely that the sample is representative (Baruch & Holtom, 2008). Singer (2006) reviews the relationship between non-response rates and non-response bias, concluding that the rate of non-response alone is not a good predictor of non-response bias. She suggests various ways in which non-response can lead to biased survey estimates and offers practical suggestions for coping with them. See also Stoop (2006), who gives a highly entertaining presentation (something of a rarity in the usually serious world of survey research) entitled, *The Hunt for the Last Respondent: How to decrease response rates and increase bias.*

Decline in willingness of people to participate

A widespread finding in developed countries is a trend for decreasing response rates to surveys and other questionnaires. More people, for a variety of reasons, are not prepared to take part (Tourangeau, 2006).

The website includes more detailed discussions on the topics of 'Response rate' and 'Decline in willingness of people to participate in surveys'.

Designing interview-based questionnaires

Much of the general advice on interviewing covered in the following chapter is relevant to those involved in the use of interview-based questionnaires, either face-to-face or telephone based. The distinctive feature of these interviews is that they are highly structured. In effect they involve you using essentially the same type of instrument as that for a self-completion questionnaire. There is a fixed set of questions with pre-specified and standardized wording. The response alternatives are also typically fixed and pre-specified although it is common to have a small number of questions where the answer is open-ended (typically of the 'any other comment on this that you would like to make' variety).

The questionnaire in an interview-based study is more usually referred to as the *interview schedule*. It covers:

- what the interviewer says by way of introduction;
- introductions to particular questions, or groups of questions;

- the questions (word for word);
- the range or set of possible answers (sometimes referred to as 'prompts');
- response codes;
- possible 'skips' in sequence (e.g. where a 'yes' answer is followed by a particular question; a 'no' answer by a 'skip' to a different question);
- closing comments; and
- reminders to the interviewer about procedure.

It is helpful to distinguish those parts of the schedule which are an *aide-mémoire* for the interviewer from those which are to be said to the respondent (e.g. by having them in different colours, or by having one group in lower case and the other in CAPITALS).

The codes for different responses are usually circled directly, during the interview, by the interviewer to assist in subsequent analysis. Any apparently open-ended questions are often provided with a set of pre-categorized responses, and it is the interviewer's responsibility to decide in which of these categories the response lies. Either this is done during the interview, or a verbatim response is recorded during the interview and the coding carried out as soon as possible afterwards. The set of pre-categorized responses is developed during pilot work, as discussed below on p. 278. The self-completion questionnaire shown above as Figure 11.2 could be used, with minimal adaptation, for an interview-based survey.

When specialist interviewers are used in a project, it is helpful to have a separate *interview guide*. This gives detailed instructions on procedure, to try to ensure that this is standardized across different interviewers. Often there will also be training sessions with the same aim. For the relatively small-scale project on which this text focuses, and in particular where the researcher(s) are also doing the interviewing, a separate interview guide may not be necessary. Sufficient procedural instructions can be incorporated in the interview schedule. However, it is crucial that these details of procedure are not lost and are incorporated in the report eventually arising from the interviews. Box 11.8 gives general advice appropriate for all structured interviews, whether for surveys or for other purposes.

BOX 11.8

General advice for interviewers carrying out structured interviews

1. *Appearance.* Dress in a similar way to those you will be interviewing. If in doubt err on the side of neatness and neutrality.
2. *Approach.* Be pleasant. Try to make the respondent comfortable.
3. *Familiarity with questionnaire/interview schedule.* View yourself as an actor, with the interview schedule as your script. Know it thoroughly.
4. *Question wording.* Use the exact wording of questions and keep to their sequence.
5. *Fixed-alternative response questions.* Only allow the standard alternatives.
6. *Open-ended response questions.* Either code immediately or record the answers exactly for later coding. Don't make cosmetic adjustments, correct or fabricate.

Comparing self-completion and interview-based questionnaires

The crucial procedural difference between self-completion and interview-based questionnaires is of course that while the respondent fills in the self-completion questionnaire, the interviewer completes the interview schedule. This may seem a straightforward difference but it has complex ramifications. The presence of the interviewer opens the door for factors to do with the interviewer: skills, experience, personality, and degree of involvement in, or alienation from, the research, to name but a few. When several interviewers are employed in a project, it is easy to show that factors such as these can have major effects on the responses of interviewees. With single interviewers, such effects are still present but their influences are virtually impossible to gauge. Interactions between interviewer and interviewee can also be influential; differences or similarities in class, ethnic origin, gender, age and status can affect rapport and the extent to which the interviewee seeks to please, or reacts against, the interviewer.

The self-completion questionnaire has its own problems. The researcher is ignorant of many of the factors influencing the choice of response to a question. While there are ways of assessing a respondent's consistency, for example, by including different forms of the same question at different points in the questionnaire, these are themselves problematic as it is well documented that small and seemingly innocuous changes in wording can sometimes have substantial effects on response. It is virtually impossible to determine whether or not the respondent is giving serious attention to the questions, or regarding the exercise as a tedious chore to be completed in a perfunctory manner. An interview permits the assessment of this type of factor, and gives the possibility of differentiating respondents on this basis. Also, because of the fact of person-to-person interaction in the interview, involvement, and hence the quality of data, is likely to be greater than with the impersonal self-completion questionnaire (Hazel & Clark, 2013; Hillier, Cannuscio, Griffin, Thomas & Glanz, 2014).

The refusal rate for interviews (particularly personal face-to-face ones) is typically very much smaller than the non-response rate for postal questionnaires. As pointed out above, good planning can increase the response rate for questionnaires but this remains a major problem.

Issues specific to telephone-based survey interviews

Telephone based surveys are becoming increasingly common. They provide a means of capitalizing on many of the advantages of interview-based surveys while substantially reducing the time and resources involved in running face-to-face interviews by cutting out the travel requirement. With more people choosing to have ex-directory phone numbers, problems arise in the use of telephone directories to establish the sampling frame (p. 277). This increases the attractiveness of random digit dialling (RDD) techniques. This is a way of selecting numbers for a telephone survey where some of the last digits of the phone number are generated randomly. It is, technically, complicated. Czaja and Blair (2005, Chapter 8) provide a detailed discussion of its use in the US context with examples. See Nicolaas (2004) for an example of its use in the UK context. General discussion of the issues involved is provided in a special journal issue edited by Lavrakas (2007).

Box 11.9 lists some of the aspects to consider in carrying out a telephone survey.

BOX 11.9

Planning and conducting telephone surveys

1. It is usually a good idea to send an advance letter (unless you are using an RDD strategy, in which case you would not necessarily know the names and addresses of respondents).
2. Provide a brief explanation of your purpose, who you are, and what your expectations are.
3. Make sure that you are talking to the right person! You may find that your initial contact would prefer to refer you to someone else who would be more appropriate for your purposes.
4. Once you know that you are talking to the right person, make sure that this is a good time to talk. If not, schedule an appointment for a follow-up call. And be sure to return the call at the appointed time.
5. Try to keep the phone time to a short duration. Based on pilot testing, you should be able to give the respondent a rough estimate of the amount of time that the survey will take.
6. Establish rapport and move quickly. Be organized.
7. Use an appropriate tone of voice (friendly and conversational). Sound enthusiastic, fresh, and upbeat. If you get tired, take a break. (No one wants to continue in a survey if you are asking questions with your head down on the desk from fatigue.)
8. Speak at an appropriate speed (sometimes, matching the respondents' speed will increase their comfort level).
9. Keep a log of calls made and their outcomes (e.g. busy, no answer, completed, follow-up appointment made) and date and time your notes.
10. Before conducting the survey, be sure to rehearse.
11. Set hour-by-hour goals (e.g. I want to make 5, 10, or 20 phone calls each hour). With a large telephone survey, it is easy to start feeling that you are not getting anywhere, so set your goals and you will see that you are making progress if you keep with it.
12. You can tape-record a phone call but you must inform the respondent that you are doing so.

(abridged and adapted from Mertens, 2005, pp. 198–9)

Pre-testing

The draft questionnaire is best pre-tested informally, initially concentrating on individual questions. Colleagues, friends and family can usually be cajoled into reading them through and providing (hopefully) constructive comments on wording. Are the questions clear, simple, unambiguous?

A second stage uses respondents from the groups of interest. This can be done on an individual basis where they are asked to give any thoughts that occur to them when the question is read out. The intention is to help understand the meaning of the question to the respondent and how they arrive at their response to help improve the wording. It is an approach widely used by cognitive psychologists, known as *protocol analysis* – see Chapter 15, p. 363. An alternative is to use *focus groups* to help improve not only question wording but other aspects of running the project (e.g. length of questionnaire, wording of covering letter). Details on the size, composition and running of such groups are given in Chapter 12, p. 298.

A formal pre-test can now be run as a miniature pilot version of the real thing; i.e. your best shot at the procedures, questionnaire and covering materials. The number of respondents to aim for in a survey depends on a variety of factors, including the sub-groups you are interested in (e.g. males and females; ethnic groups; ages), and resources you have available, but you should aim for at least 20 per sub-group. It is highly likely that you will need to revise both questionnaire and procedures as a result of this exercise. If there is anything other than very minor changes, a second formal pre-test should be run. Even with limited resources, you should allow for the possibility of this second pre-test. If the first pre-test throws up major problems, it is back to the drawing board and further informal testing before a second pre-test. You keep on with this process until you have overcome any problems that have arisen.

With self-completion postal surveys (where it is usually feasible to have a relatively large pre-test) a low response rate to the first pre-test rings warning bells. It is worthwhile expending considerable time and effort to do something about this. You may be able to find out what lies behind this by contacting non-respondents. Or run focus groups to try to find what the obstacles are and how they might be overcome. If a second pre-test also gives low rates, you should consider changing to an interview-based (probably telephone) approach.

Final design and planning

After implementing the suggestions from pre-testing, your main task with the questionnaire is editorial. Make sure there are no spelling mistakes, that the layout is professional with appropriate spacing and clear presentation.

At this stage you make final decisions about the sampling plan and the coding procedures to be used. You should also ensure that you know the main analyses of the data that you are going to use. It is foolish in the extreme to spend considerable resources in designing and running the survey if you don't analyse it in a way that is both technically acceptable and helps to answer your research questions. If you haven't checked this in advance, you are likely to end up with something unanalysable.

Data collection

Your main task here is to keep on top of things, making sure that the practicalities are being attended to and the carefully worked out plan followed. Book-keeping should be meticulous so that you know when the various things have happened. In postal surveys, this includes dates of posting of materials and follow-ups, recording of return questionnaires, etc. In interview-based studies, this includes dates on all contacts and resulting action, etc. This monitoring role lets you see if problems are arising so that you can do something about it early.

The returned questionnaires should be checked immediately. If sections have been missed by, say, turning over two pages, or entries are illegible or inconsistent (e.g. if someone replies to both the questions following 'If YES please . . .' and 'If NO please . . .') then this is picked up and a second contact made to try to resolve the problem.

The section on 'Arranging the practicalities' on p. 395 covers further issues relating to this phase.

Coding of responses

Codes are symbols, usually numbers, which are used to identify particular responses, or types of response, in questionnaires and similar instruments. They help in organizing, quantifying and analysing your data (see Chapter 18, p. 461). For example, the answer to a question about a respondent's sex might be coded as '1' for female, and '2' for male. The numbers are arbitrary; they could be reversed or different ones used, providing the coding is consistent.

Closed questions

With closed questions, and other items such as attitude and other scales, there should be little difficulty in coding. The range of possible responses will have been checked and, if necessary, modified during piloting. Numerical symbols are assigned to the various answer categories and analysis can proceed directly. From the point of view of analysis, it is preferable to include the codes on the questionnaire. For example:

*At which of the following ages did your **father** finish his full-time education?*

Please tick the appropriate box		Official use only
14 or younger	☐	1
15	☐	2
16	☐	3
17	☐	4
18	☐	5
19	☐	6
20 or over	☐	7

(The code is included in the box to help the analyst; the code of the box ticked is written by the analyst in the right-hand column.)

You are free to assign any meaning that you wish to a coding digit (or digits) – *providing that the meaning is consistent within a particular coding scheme.* The code can be arbitrary (e.g. yes = 1; no = 2) or can be the actual number (e.g. age in years = 27 or whatever). It is preferable to have a code for non-response (e.g. '0' or '1') rather than leaving a blank. Whether or not this needs to be discriminated from (and hence separate codes used for) 'don't know', 'not sure', etc., will depend on the particular survey.

Open questions

Coding of responses here involves combining the detailed information contained in the response into a limited number of categories that enable simple description of the data and allow for statistical analysis. The main purpose is to simplify many individual responses by classifying them into a smaller number of groups, each including responses that are similar in content. *This process inevitably involves some loss of information.*

Coding of open questions in a survey should be based on a substantial, representative sample (say 50 cases) selected from the total set of responses. It should not be based solely on early responses, as these may well be unrepresentative and it may prove necessary subsequently to develop a revised set of coding categories, which leads to wasteful recoding of those already analysed.

The standard procedure has been to copy all the responses to a particular question on a (large) sheet of paper, headed by the text of the question, and with each response preceded by the case number (i.e. the code given to that person's questionnaire). The object is then to try to develop a smallish set of categories (say 8 to 10) into which these responses can be sorted. This is not an easy exercise; it is largely driven by the nature of the responses and the themes and dimensions they suggest. However, one should also bear in mind the purposes of the survey in general and of that question in particular, and try to ensure that the coding categories are such that a minimum of relevant information is lost. The number of categories that it is sensible to use is in part dependent on the overall number of cases in the sample and on the detail of the statistical analysis you wish to carry out.

This process has the effect of turning the answers to open questions to a defined set of standard responses. It is sometimes used at the pilot stage of a questionnaire study to produce a set of categories for closed questions.

Diaries

A diary, considered as a research tool, is a kind of self-administered questionnaire. As such, it can range from being totally unstructured to a set of responses to specific questions. Diaries are tantalizingly attractive because they appear, on the surface, to provide the means of generating very substantial amounts of data with minimal amount of effort on the part of the researcher. They can also serve as a proxy for observation in situations where it would be difficult or impossible for direct observation to take place, as with Coxon's (1988) use of sexual diaries for mapping detailed sexual behaviour, or Waddington's (2005) study of gossip in the workplace.

The diary, however, places a great deal of responsibility on the respondent. Unstructured diaries leave the interpretation of the task very much with the pen of the respondent. Using a specific set of questions which ask about the respondent's activities at given times simplifies and structures the task but still produces data which are prone to bias. The kind of enthusiastic involvement that one would seek carries with it dangers of misreporting (perhaps to please the researcher) or even of changing the behaviour to be reported on (perhaps to show the diarist in a good light). These are phenomena potentially present whenever the respondents know they are involved in a research study but they are sufficiently bothersome here to cast doubt on the use of the diary as the *sole* method in an investigation. Lee (1993, p. 116), while agreeing that diaries provide an appropriate method to study activities over time and that they have a role to play in the study of sensitive topics, concluded that problems of sample bias, changed behaviour and sample attrition (i.e. participants dropping out of the research) limited their usefulness.

Hence, it is recommended that if a diary approach is used, it is combined with a second data collection method so that cross-checks can be made with diary entries to give confidence about the reliability and validity of the diary method in the situation in which it is being used. Crosbie (2006) supplemented their main form of data collection (which was face-to-face interviews) with self-administered activity diaries and questionnaires. Not untypically, they had considerable difficulty with response rate and had to change from their initial strategy of postal administration of the activity diaries and the questionnaire where the response rate was 3 per cent for the diary and 25 per cent for the questionnaire (suggesting that the diary appeared more demanding than the questionnaire). Asking interviewees to fill in an activity diary at the end of the face-to-face interviews and return it by post in a pre-paid envelope increased the response rate to almost 50 per cent. Johnson and Bytheway (2001) also combined use of a diary with interviews in a study of medication in later life. They made extensive efforts to maximize completion of the diaries through piloting. In early interviews a fieldworker gave assistance, enlisting the aid of a 'scribe' to complete the diary if necessary. Continuing assistance was given if there were problems. Following these efforts, 56 fully completed diaries were obtained from a final sample of 77 participants.

The website gives references to examples of research projects using diaries as a data collection method.

The type of question asked in the diary (or other requests for information made) will, as with other techniques, be dictated by the purpose of your study. Box 11.10 gives suggestions for the development of a diary form (see Gullan, Glendon, Matthews, Davies & Debney, 1990; Crosbie, 2006; and Johnson & Bytheway, 2001 for examples). The instructions given to participants are very important. Box 11.11 gives an example.

BOX 11.10

Notes for guidance in developing a diary form

1. Think of it as a questionnaire (even though you may not cast it in question format). You need to devote the same amount of care and preparation (and piloting) as you would for other questionnaires.
2. Piloting of the form, and the instructions to go with it, are essential.
3. Because the diary involves self-completion of a series of forms, cooperation is vital. You need to ensure that respondents know *what* they have to do, *why* and *when*.
4. As with other questionnaires, include an item only if you know what you are going to do with it. You should be clear, before you start the study proper, how the items relate to your research questions, and how you will analyse them subsequently.
5. In a study extending over time, do not assume that 'things are going on all right'. Check, preferably by a personal contact.
6. General considerations about confidentiality, anonymity, feedback of results, permissions, etc. apply.

BOX 11.11

Example of instructions to accompany the diary form

Think of this as an ordinary diary. There are 14 pages, one page for each day of the fortnight. We have divided the day up into hours, and we have given you boxes to tick and a space at the top and bottom for you to make notes.

According to the time, we want you to tick a box whenever:

1. you take your medicines;
2. you feel symptoms or pains;
3. you have a meal or snack;
4. you have or make a phone call;
5. visitors call; and
6. you go out visiting or shopping.

When we come back to check the diary, we would like to ask you about these things. We are specially interested in when you take your medicines and whether anything out of the ordinary upsets your routines.

So whenever you tick a box, make a note of what the symptom was, what medicines you took, who visited you, or whatever. Just enough to help you remember.

Try to fill the diary in whenever it's convenient. At some point each morning, you should think back over the previous 12 hours and check that the diary is up-to-date. Likewise you should do the same in the evening.

We hope you find this an interesting – or even helpful – exercise. We will keep in touch with you during the fortnight and will come to collect the diary when it is over.

Many thanks for your help.

(from Johnson and Bytheway, 2001, pp. 186–8)

Variants of the diary method have been used. One attempts to combine the keeping of a diary with the 'critical incident' approach (Butterfield, Borgen, Amundson & Maglio, 2005; Schluter, Seaton & Chaboyer, 2008). This tries to separate out, and to get people to notice, specific happenings that they consider to be important (see Chapter 15, p. 366). Thus, in a managerial context, these might be whatever is crucial or critical in achieving a satisfactory outcome in a particular task. Respondents are then asked to rate these incidents according to their difficulty and importance to the job.

The 'reflective journal', where participants are asked to provide an account of their experiences in a particular setting or situation and a reflection on that experience, can be viewed as an unstructured variant of a diary. It is commonly used in professional training courses as an assessment and development tool (e.g. in clinical psychology courses – see 'Writing a Reflective Journal: Personal Development', 2007).

Sampling in surveys – and elsewhere

Sampling is an important aspect of life in general and social research in particular. We make judgements about people, places and things on the basis of fragmentary evidence. Sampling considerations pervade all aspects of research and crop up in various forms no matter what research strategy or investigatory technique we use. This discussion focuses on survey sampling where it is closely linked to the *external validity* or *generalizability* (see Chapter 6, p. 110) of the findings: the extent to which what we have found in a particular situation at a particular time applies more generally.

The idea of 'sample' is linked to that of 'population'. *Population refers to all the cases*. It might be, for example, all adults living in the United Kingdom, or all children attending schools in Texas, or all privately run homes for the elderly in Paris. The last example illustrates that 'population' is being used in a general sense – it isn't limited to people. The concept can be further stretched to include units that are not 'people-related' at all, for example, populations of situations (e.g. all possible locations in which someone might be interviewed) or of events or times. It is unusual to be able to deal with the whole of a population in a survey, which is where sampling comes in. *A sample is a selection from the population*.

Non-'people-related' sampling is in practice very important (e.g. sampling places and times – deciding, for example, where, when and how interviews take place), and has already been discussed in the context of flexible designs (see Chapter 7, p. 166). However, particular attention needs to be given to the selection of the 'people sample' in planning a survey. This is because the dependability of a survey is crucially affected by the principles or system used to select respondents – usually referred to as the 'sampling plan'.

There are some circumstances where it is feasible to survey the whole of a population. A national census attempts to do just that, of course, and while it hardly qualifies as the small-scale study targeted in this book, there are occasions when the population of interest is manageably small – say, the line managers in an organization, or the pupils in a particular school, or patients in a hospital, or clients of a particular local social service. It should not be assumed, however, that a full census is necessarily superior to a well thought-out sample survey. There are trade-offs requiring careful thought. Will you actually be able to carry out the full set of interviews or would it be preferable to do a smaller number of longer, more detailed ones? Can you in fact reach (virtually) everybody? The 'hard-to-get' may differ from the rest in important ways that you should know about. If you are sampling, you might be able to devote more time and resources to chasing them up.

The various types of sampling plan are usually divided into ones based on *probability samples* (where the probability of the selection of each respondent is known), and on *non-probability samples* (where it isn't known). In probability sampling, statistical inferences about the population can be made from the responses of the sample. For this reason, probability sampling is sometimes referred to as *representative sampling*. The sample is taken as representative of the population. In non-probability samples, you cannot make such statistical inferences. It may be possible to say something sensible about the population from non-probability samples – but not on the same kind of statistical grounds.

What size of sample in surveys?

While probability samples allow you to generalize from sample to population, such generalizations are themselves probabilistic. The larger the sample, the lower the likely error in generalizing. As a rule of thumb, Borg and Gall (1989) recommend about 100 observations for each of the major subgroupings in a survey, with 20 to 50 for minor subgroupings. Chapter 6, p. 144 discusses the relationship between sample size and sample error and refers to sources of tables which provide estimates for the sample sizes needed to guarantee a particular margin of error.

Probability samples

Simple random sampling

This involves selection at random from the population list – sometimes called the *sampling frame* – of the required number of persons for the sample. Traditionally a lottery method or random number tables (as found in many statistics books) has been used. Computer programs now make this task very straightforward and can be accessed from several websites. For example 'Research Randomizer' (http://www.randomizer.org) provides an easy way of performing random sampling (a tutorial is provided). Each person in the sampling frame has an equal chance of being included in the sample, and all possible combinations of persons for a particular sample size are equally likely. Note that *each* person is chosen at random, as compared with systematic sampling where only the first one is (see below). You can't produce a simple random sample without a full list of the population.

Detailed examples of procedures for this, and the other forms of probability sampling discussed below, are given in Groves *et al*. (2009) and Lohr (2010).

Systematic sampling

This involves taking every nth name from the population list. After deciding on the sample size needed, you divide the total number of names on the list by this sample size. So, if a sample of 50 is required from a population list of 2,000 then every 40th (i.e. 2000/50) person is chosen. You then randomly choose a number that is less than n (i.e. less than 40 in the example) to start and take every nth name from the list until you have the required sample.

For the sample to be representative, this method relies on the list being organized in a way unrelated to the subject of the survey. Although this may seem to be a simple and straightforward way of drawing a probability sample, it has certain statistical peculiarities. Whereas the initial chance of selection of any person is the same, once the first person has been chosen, most persons will have no chance of inclusion and a few will be automatically selected. Similarly, most combinations of persons are excluded from the possible samples that might be chosen. This might be important if the ordering in the list is organized in some way (possibly unknown to you). Working in schools, where class lists are arranged alphabetically, you could find that a sample is almost exclusively made up of students sharing a relatively common surname.

Both random and systematic sampling require a full list of the population. Getting this list is often difficult. Hence, if there is any possibility of ordering in the list messing up your systematic sample, you may as well go for a random sample as the extra effort is minimal.

Stratified random sampling

This involves dividing the population into a number of groups or *strata*, where members of a group share a particular characteristic or characteristics (e.g. stratum A may be females; stratum B males). There is then random sampling within the strata. It is usual to have *proportionate sampling*, that is, where the numbers of the groups selected for the sample reflect the relative numbers in the population as a whole (e.g. if there are equal numbers of males and females in the population, there should be equal numbers in the samples; if 80 per cent of the population are from one ethnic group and 20 per cent from another group, then one sample should be four times the other in size). It may sometimes be helpful to have *disproportionate sampling*, where there is an unequal weighting. This would allow you to 'oversample' a small but important stratum or to ensure that there is at least some representation of certain 'rare species' even to the extent of including all examples of them. Also, if it is known (perhaps from pilot work) that there is greater variation in response from one particular stratum, then this is an indication to include a disproportionately large number from that stratum in the overall sample.

Sampling theory shows that in some circumstances stratified random sampling can be more efficient than simple random sampling, in the sense that for a given sample size, the means of stratified samples are likely to be closer to the population mean. This occurs when there is a relatively small amount of variability in whatever characteristic is being measured in the survey *within* the stratum, compared to variability across strata. The improvement in efficiency does not occur if there is considerable variability in the characteristic within the stratum. So, for example, if females tend to give similar measures, ratings or whatever in a particular survey and males also tend to give similar ratings to other males but show overall differences from females, there would be advantage in stratifying the sample by gender.

It is possible to combine stratification with systematic sampling procedures. However, the same criticisms apply to systematic sampling as discussed above and there seems little or no reason to prefer them to stratified random samples.

Cluster sampling

This involves dividing the population into a number of units, or *clusters*, each of which contains individuals having a range of characteristics. The clusters themselves are chosen on a random basis. The sub-population within the cluster is then chosen. This tactic is particularly useful when a population is widely dispersed and large, requiring a great deal of effort and travel to get the survey information. Random sampling might well generate an extremely scattered sample, and as usual it is likely to be the most distant and difficult to reach who are not there when you call, necessitating a second difficult visit. It may also be that permission has to be negotiated to interview respondents and doing this on what is effectively a one-to-one basis for all respondents will be particularly time-consuming.

An example might involve schoolchildren, where there is initially random sampling of a number of schools, and then testing of all the pupils in each school. There are problems in generalizing to the population of children. Strictly, statistical generalization is limited to the population of schools (i.e. the clustering variable). This method has the valuable feature that it can be used when the sampling frame is not known (e.g. when we do not have a full list of children in the population, in the above example). The procedure is widely used, not only in educational research but also with hospitals and medical practices, businesses and other situations where there are groups of a similar nature.

Multi-stage sampling

This is an extension of cluster sampling. It involves selecting the sample in stages; i.e. taking samples from samples. Thus one might take a random sample of schools, then a random sample of the classes within each of the schools, then from within the selected classes choose a sample of children. As with cluster sampling, this provides a means of generating a geographically concentrated sampling. The generalizability issue is the same as for cluster sampling but judicious use of sampling at appropriate stages enables one to tailor the scale of the project to the resources available.

It is possible to incorporate stratification into both cluster and multi-stage sampling. Judgement about the relative efficiencies of these more complicated forms of sampling, and their relationship to the efficiency of simple random sampling, is difficult, and if you are expending considerable resources on a survey, it is worth seeking expert advice.

The website gives step-by-step instructions for the selection of different types of probability samples.

Non-probability samples

In probability sampling, it is possible to specify the probability that any person (or other unit on which the survey is based) will be included in the sample. Any sampling plan where it is not possible to do this is called 'non-probability sampling'.

Small-scale surveys commonly employ non-probability samples. They are usually less complicated to set up and are acceptable when there is no intention or need to make a statistical generalization to any population beyond the sample surveyed. They can also be used to pilot a survey prior to a probability sample approach for the main survey. They typically involve the researcher using her judgement to achieve a particular purpose, and for this reason are sometimes referred to as *purposive samples*, although it is perhaps more useful to restrict the use of the term as indicated below.

A wide range of approaches has been used. The first two, quota and dimensional sampling, are basically trying to do the same job as a probability sample, in the sense of aspiring to carry out a sample survey which is statistically representative. They tend to be used in situations where carrying out a probability sample would not be feasible, where for example there is no sampling frame, or the resources required are not available. Their accuracy relies greatly on the skill and experience of those involved.

Quota sampling

Here the strategy is to obtain representatives of the various elements of a population, usually in the relative proportions in which they occur in the population. Hence, if socio-economic status were considered of importance in a particular survey, then the categories 'professional/managers and employers/intermediate and junior non-manual/skilled manual/semi-skilled manual/unskilled manual' might be used. Interviewers would be given a quota of each category (with examples to assist them in categorization). Within the category, convenience sampling (see below) is normally used. The interviewer will, for example, seek to interview a given number of unskilled manual workers, a given number of semi-skilled manual workers, etc. by, say, stopping passers-by, and will continue until his quota for the day is complete. The common use of the term 'representatives' in quota sampling has to be looked at with some care. They are representative only in number, not in terms of the type of persons actually selected.

All such means of gathering quota samples are subject to biases. Careful planning, experience and persistence can go some way to addressing obvious biases. If, for example, home visits are involved, avoiding houses where there is a Rottweiler or other large dog, or sounds of a ghetto-blaster, or there are no curtains, or apartments where the lift is out of order, etc. may be understandable behaviour on the part of the sensitive interviewer, but mitigates against representativeness in householders in the sense of all householders having an equal chance of appearing in the sample.

Quota sampling is widely used by market researchers and political and other opinion pollsters. It is in their interest, particularly in situations where the accuracy of their survey findings can be checked (as in election polling) to devote considerable resources to the training of their staff. For non-specialists in the field it is best avoided if possible.

Dimensional sampling

This is an extension of quota sampling. The various dimensions thought to be of importance in a survey (perhaps established by pilot work) are incorporated into the sampling procedure in such a way that at least one representative of every possible combination of these factors or dimensions is included. Thus a study of race relations might identify ethnic group and length of stay in this country as important dimensions. Hence the sampling plan could consist of a table or matrix with 'ethnic group' and 'length of stay' constituting the rows and columns. Refinements of this approach involve selection of particular combinations of the dimensions (e.g. 'Kenyan Asians' with '10–15 years' residence') either because of their particular importance, or because of an inability through lack of time and resources to cover all combinations.

The critical comments made about quota sampling apply with equal force to dimensional sampling.

Convenience sampling

This involves choosing the nearest and most convenient persons to act as respondents. The process is continued until the required sample size has been reached.

Convenience sampling is sometimes used as a cheap and dirty way of doing a sample survey. You do not know whether or not the findings are representative.

It is probably one of the most widely used and least satisfactory methods of sampling. The term 'accidental sample' is sometimes used but is misleading as it carries some suggestion of randomness whereas all kinds of largely unspecifiable biases and influences are likely to influence who gets sampled. Appropriate uses of convenience sampling include gaining a feeling for the issues involved or initial piloting for a proper sample survey.

Purposive sampling

The principle of selection in purposive sampling is the researcher's judgement as to typicality or interest. A sample is built up which enables the researcher to satisfy their specific needs in a project. For example, researchers following the grounded theory approach (Chapter 7, p. 161) carry out initial sampling, and from analysis of the results extend the sample in ways guided by their emerging theory (this is sometimes referred to as *theoretical sampling*). The rationale of such an approach is very different from statistical generalization from sample to population. It is an approach commonly used within other flexible designs.

Snowball sampling

Here the researcher identifies one or more individuals from the population of interest. After they have been interviewed, they are used as informants to identify other members of the population, who are themselves used as informants, and so on. This is a useful approach when there is difficulty in identifying members of the population, e.g. when this is a clandestine group. It can be seen as a particular type of purposive sample. As well as its value in identifying a sample it has also been used to shed light on social and other networks (Browne, 2005; Farquharson, 2005). However, Waters (2014) suggests, with an example, that it can be prone to failure in obtaining a sample, and that caution should be used in considering its adoption.

Other types of sample

Other types of sample may be used for special purposes in a variety of research situations. They include the following:

- *Time samples.* Sampling across time, for example in a study of the characteristics of the persons who use a particular space at different times of the day or week (can be probabilistic or non-probabilistic, depending on how it is organized). Commonly used in observational studies (see Chapter 14).
- *Homogeneous samples.* Covering a narrow range or single value of a particular variable or variables.
- *Heterogeneous samples.* A deliberate strategy to select individuals varying widely on the characteristic(s) of interest.

- *Extreme case samples.* Concentration on extreme values when sampling, perhaps where it is considered that they will throw a particularly strong light on the phenomenon of interest.
- *Rare element samples.* Values with low frequencies in the population are overrepresented in the sample; similar rationale to the previous approach.

Representative sampling and the real world

The exigencies of carrying out real world studies can mean that the requirements for representative sampling are very difficult, if not impossible, to fulfil. Population lists may be impossible to obtain. A doctor may not be prepared to provide you with a list of patients or a firm a list of employees. Or what you get hold of may be out-of-date or otherwise incorrect. This leads to 'ineligibles' – persons on the population list who are not part of your target population. Conversely, 'eligibles' may not get onto the list. This slippage between what you have and what you want causes problems with representativeness and lowers your sample size.

Non-response can be a very serious problem and it is worth giving considerable time and effort to reducing it (see the suggestions on p. 269). The basic issue is that those who do not participate may well differ from those who do, but it is extremely difficult to allow for this. It is worth stressing that even if you get everything else right (perfect random sample from perfect sampling frame), anything other than a high response rate casts doubts on the representativeness of the sample you actually achieve. And once below that rate, it is not so much a question of the rate you get but the (unknown) degree of difference between responders and non-responders that matters. It would be entirely feasible for a response rate of 30 per cent to lead to a more representative sample than one of 60 per cent.

There are things that you can do. In a postal survey it is possible to compare late returners of questionnaires with earlier ones or those responding after one, or two, reminders with those responding without prompting. If you know some characteristics of the population, you can check to see whether the sample you obtained is reasonably typical of the population on these variables. In any survey where there is differential responding between categories (say a particularly low rate from Asian females or top executives), you can compare their responses with those from other categories. Or you can make a real effort with a random sub-set of the non-respondents and try to turn them into respondents, then compare these with previous respondents. However, these are only palliatives and the real answer is that if representativeness is crucial for you, then you so set up your study that virtually everyone responds.

This may be something of a counsel of perfection. Commentators point out deficiencies in published research. Bryman (1989, pp. 113–17) showed that in practice few instances of survey research in organization studies are based on random samples. He quotes from Schwab:

> Of course we all know that almost all of the empirical studies published in our journals [organizational studies] use *convenience*, not probability samples . . . Thus if one took generalization to a population using statistical inference seriously, one would recommend rejecting nearly all manuscripts submitted (Schwab, 1985, p. 173).

The situation does not appear to have improved more recently. Williamson (2003) carried out a systematic review of recent research published in a reputable nursing journal between 1995 and 2002 and claimed that misrepresentation was rife, with almost two-thirds of the papers reviewed using statistics appropriate for representative samples with convenience samples. Although rarely referred to as such, many experiments use what are effectively convenience samples. It is common practice, particularly in laboratory experiments, to use people who are prepared to volunteer, or whom the experimenter can persuade to be involved.

As it looks, in the real world of research, as though there will continue to be widespread use of convenience and other non-random samples, this issue should be taken seriously. There are statistical approaches which can be used with non-random samples (see Chapter 17, p. 451). An alternative is to move away totally from statistical generalization and use the kind of theoretical generalization discussed in the context of case study research (see Chapter 7, p. 154).

Further reading

The website gives annotated references to further reading for Chapter 11.

CHAPTER **12**

Interviews and focus groups

This chapter:

- discusses different types of interviews, differentiating them in terms of amount of structure;
- considers the circumstances under which the different types are appropriate;
- reviews the advantages and disadvantages of interviews;
- provides general advice for interviewers including the kinds of questions to avoid;
- covers the phases of an interview;
- gives particular attention to semi-structured interviews including interview schedules;
- reviews issues involved in running focus groups and other group interviews; and
- concludes by reviewing the skills needed by interviewers.

Introduction

Interviewing as a research method typically involves you, as researcher, asking questions and, hopefully, receiving answers from the people you are interviewing. It is very widely used in social research and there are many different types. A commonly used typology distinguishes between structured, semi-structured and unstructured interviews. This can link to some extent to the 'depth' of response sought. The extreme example of a highly structured format is the survey interview discussed in the previous chapter. This is effectively a questionnaire with fixed questions in a pre-decided order and standardized wording, where responses to most of the questions have to be selected from a small list of alternatives. Less structured approaches allow the person interviewed much more flexibility of response, an extreme version being the 'depth interview' where the respondent is largely free to say whatever they like on the broad topic of the interview, with minimal prompting from the researcher. Interviews are commonly one-to-one and face-to-face, but they can take place in group settings and, as discussed in the previous chapter, the telephone and the Internet are increasingly being used because of the savings in time and resources they permit.

Interviews are commonly put forward as the method of choice for researchers favouring qualitative approaches in the disciplines of both psychology and sociology (Potter and Hepburn, 2005). However, the validity of interview data has been queried. For example, following detailed analysis of the interaction between interviewers and respondents in standardized social survey interviews, Houtkoop-Steenstra (2000) suggests that interview results can only be understood as products of the contingencies of the interview situation, and not, as is usually assumed, the unmediated expressions of respondents' real opinions.

The website includes further discussion on critiques of the validity of interview data.

Interviews can be used as the primary or only approach in a study, as in a survey or many grounded theory studies. However, they lend themselves well to use in combination with other methods, in a multi-strategy design or multi-method approach. An ethnographic approach can combine participant observation with interviews. Lofland, Snow, Anderson and Lofland (2006, p. 17) suggest that an ethnographic study almost always includes both observation and asking questions; sometimes just short informal interviews, possibly with 'intensive interviews' playing a major role. A case study might employ some kind of relatively formal interview to complement observation or other methods. An experiment could often usefully incorporate a short post-intervention interview to help incorporate the participant's perspective into the findings, possibly helping to explain them.

The last chapter covered interview-based survey questionnaires almost exclusively based on closed choice questions. This chapter focuses on a range of other types of interview where the questions are largely, if not exclusively, open-ended. A typical scenario envisaged is the small-scale research project where you, working as a student, teacher, social worker, applied social researcher or whatever, are wanting to carry out a study with limited resources and time, perhaps alone, perhaps with a colleague or some part-time assistance, possibly concerned with some situation in which you are already an actor. In these situations, such interviews can be a powerful tool, though not without problems – practical, theoretical and analytical, among others.

Types and styles of interviews

A commonly made distinction is based on the degree of structure or standardization of the interview:

- *Fully structured interview.* Has pre-determined questions with fixed wording, usually in a pre-set order. The use of a greater number of open-response questions is the only essential difference from an interview-based survey questionnaire.
- *Semi-structured interview.* The interviewer has an interview *guide* that serves as a checklist of topics to be covered and a default wording and order for the questions, but the wording and order are often substantially modified based on the flow of the interview, and additional unplanned questions are asked to follow up on what the interviewee says.
- *Unstructured interview.* The interviewer has a general area of interest and concern but lets the conversation develop within this area. It can be completely informal.

Semi-structured and unstructured interviews are widely used in flexible designs. A variety of other terms are used to describe the types of interview used in such designs, including *qualitative interviews*, *depth interviews* (sometimes referred to as *in-depth interviews*) and *focused interviews* (where open-ended questions are asked about a specific topic or issue. When carried out in a group setting, these are known as *focus groups*, see p. 298). Semi-structured and unstructured interviews are also used in life history and oral history research – see Chapter 15, p. 373.

Question focus

A distinction is commonly made between seeking to find out what people know, what they do, and what they think or feel. This leads, respectively, to questions concerned with *facts*, with *behaviour*, and with *beliefs* or *attitudes*.

Facts are relatively easy to get at, although errors can occur due to lapses in memory or to response biases of various kinds (e.g. age may be claimed to be less than it is by the middle-aged, inflated by the really aged). The best responses are obtained to specific (as against general) questions about important things in the present or recent past. The same rules apply to questions about behaviour and, of course, the respondent is often in a uniquely favourable position to tell you about what they are doing or have done. Beliefs and attitudes form a very important target for self-report techniques but are relatively difficult to get at. They are often complex and multi-dimensional and appear particularly prone to the effects of question wording and sequence. These problems point to the use of multiple questions related to the belief or attitude and can be best attacked by the construction of appropriate scales (see Chapter 13).

Advantages and disadvantages of interviews

The interview is a flexible and adaptable way of finding things out. The human use of language is fascinating both as a behaviour in its own right and for the virtually unique window that it opens on what lies behind our actions. Observing behaviour is clearly a useful research technique but asking people directly about what is going on is an obvious short cut when seeking answers to research questions.

Face-to-face interviews offer the possibility of modifying one's line of enquiry, following up interesting responses and investigating underlying motives in a way that postal and other self-administered questionnaires cannot. Non-verbal cues may give messages which help in understanding the verbal response, possibly changing or even, in extreme cases, reversing its meaning. To make profitable use of this flexibility calls for considerable skill and experience in the interviewer. The lack of standardization that it implies inevitably raises concerns about reliability. Biases are difficult to rule out. There are ways of dealing with these problems but they call for a degree of professionalism which does not come easily. Nevertheless, although the interview is in no sense a soft option as a data-gathering technique (illustrating once more that apparently 'soft' techniques resulting in qualitative data are deceptively hard to use well), it has the potential for providing rich and highly illuminating material.

Interviewing is time-consuming. The actual interview session itself will obviously vary in length. Anything under half an hour is unlikely to be valuable; anything going much over an hour may be making unreasonable demands on busy interviewees and could have the effect of reducing the number of persons willing to participate, which may in turn lead to biases in the sample that you achieve. Above all, don't say that it will take half an hour and then keep going for an hour and a half. It is up to you to terminate the interview on schedule and you have the professional responsibility of keeping this as well as all other undertakings that you make. The reverse phenomenon is not unknown: that of the interviewee so glad to have a willing ear to bend that you can't escape. How you deal with this depends very much on your own skills of control and closure. Remember that, just as you are hoping to get something out of the interview, it is not unreasonable for the interviewee to get something from you.

In some fields it appears to be increasingly difficult to obtain cooperation from potential interviewees. Hart, Rennison and Gibson (2005) discuss this problem in the context of a national survey. Longer interviews can produce 'respondent fatigue' where participants are unwilling to continue with not only highly structured survey interviews but also unstructured and semi-structured types (Axinn & Pearce, 2006, p. 42).

All interviews require careful preparation – making arrangements to visit, securing necessary permissions – which takes time; confirming arrangements, rescheduling appointments to cover absences and crises – which takes more time. Notes need to be written up. Tapes if used require whole or partial transcription (allow something like a factor of ten between tape time and transcription time unless you are highly skilled; i.e. a one hour tape takes ten hours to transcribe fully). Subsequent analyses are not the least of your time-eaters. As with all other techniques, time planning and time budgeting is a crucial skill of successful research in the real world.

General advice for interviewers

The interview is a kind of conversation, something that we have all had experience of. However, interviewing does demand rather different emphases in the social interaction that takes place from those in ordinary conversation. Your job as interviewer is to try to get interviewees to talk freely and openly. Your own behaviour has a major influence on their willingness to do this.

To this end you should:

- *Listen more than you speak.* Most interviewers talk too much. The interview is not a platform for the interviewer's personal experiences and opinions.
- *Put questions in a straightforward, clear and non-threatening way.* If people are confused or defensive, you will not get the information you seek.
- *Eliminate cues which lead interviewees to respond in a particular way.* Many interviewees will seek to please the interviewer by giving 'correct' responses ('Are you against sin?').
- *Enjoy it (or at least look as though you do).* Don't give the message that you are bored or scared. Vary your voice and facial expression.

It is also essential that you *take a full record of the interview*. This can be from notes made at the time and/or from a recording of the interview. Experienced interviewers tend to have strong preferences for one or other of these approaches. McDonald and Sanger have given a detailed account of their relative advantages and disadvantages (Walker, 1985, pp. 109–16 provides a summary). The literature, and common sense, suggest that various kinds of questions should be avoided – summarized in Box 12.1.

BOX 12.1

Questions to avoid in interviews

Long questions. The interviewee may remember only part of the question, and respond to that part.

Double-barrelled (or multiple-barrelled) questions, e.g. 'What do you feel about the current popular music scene compared with that of five years ago?' The solution here is to break it down into simpler questions (e.g. 'What do you feel about the current popular music scene?'; 'Can you recall the popular music scene from five years ago?'; 'How do you feel they compare?').

Questions involving jargon. Generally you should avoid questions containing words likely to be unfamiliar to the target audience. Keep things simple to avoid disturbing interviewees; it is in your own interest as well.

Leading questions, e.g. 'Why do you like Huddersfield?' It is usually straightforward to modify such questions, providing you realize that they are leading in a particular direction.

Biased questions. Provided you are alert to the possibility of bias, it is not difficult to *write* unbiased questions. What is more difficult, however, is not (perhaps unwittingly) to lead the interviewee by the manner in which the question is asked or the way in which you receive the response. Neutrality is called for and in seeking to be welcoming to and reinforcing the interviewee, you should try to avoid appearing to share or welcome their views.

Content of the interview

In structured and semi-structured interviews, the content, which can be prepared in advance, consists of:

- a *set of items (usually questions)*, often with alternative subsequent items depending on the responses obtained;
- suggestions for so-called *probes* and *prompts* (see below); and
- a proposed *sequence for the questions* which, in a semi-structured interview, may be subject to change during the course of the interview.

The items or questions

Three main types are used in research interviews: *closed* (or *'fixed-alternative'*), *open*, and *scale* items. Closed questions, as the fixed-alternative label suggests, force the interviewee to choose from two or more given alternatives. Open questions provide no restrictions on the content or manner of the reply other than on the subject area (e.g. 'What kind of way do you most prefer to spend a free evening?'). Scale items, which may well not be in question form, ask for a response in the form of degree of agreement or disagreement (e.g. strongly agree/agree/neutral/disagree/strongly disagree). Logically they are the closed or fixed-alternative type, but are sometimes regarded as a separate type. Closed questions and scale items were discussed in the previous chapter in the context of surveys (p. 272).

The advantages of open-ended questions when used in interviews are that they:

- are flexible;
- allow you to go into more depth or clear up any misunderstandings;
- enable testing of the limits of a respondent's knowledge;
- encourage cooperation and rapport;
- allow you to make a truer assessment of what the respondent really believes; and
- can produce unexpected or unanticipated answers.

The disadvantages lie in the possibilities for loss of control by the interviewer, and in particular in being much more difficult to analyse than closed ones.

Probes

A probe is a device to get the interviewee to expand on a response when you have the feeling that he has more to give. The use of probes is something of an art form and difficult to transmit to the novice interviewer. Sometimes the interviewer may be given instructions to probe on specific questions. There are obvious tactics, such as asking, 'Anything more?' or 'Could you go over that again?' Sometimes when an answer has been given in general terms, a useful probe is to seek a personal response, e.g. 'What is your own personal view on this?' There are also very general tactics, such as the use of:

- a period of silence;
- an enquiring glance;
- 'Mmhmm . . .'; and
- repeating all or part of what the interviewee has just said.

Zeisel (2006, pp. 230–43) gives an extended analysis of different types of probe.

Prompts

Prompts suggest to the interviewee a range of possible answers that the interviewer expects. The list of possibilities may be read out by the interviewer, or a 'prompt card' with them on can be shown. (e.g. a list of names of alcoholic drinks for a question on drinking habits). All prompts must be used in a consistent manner with different interviewees (and with different interviewers, if more than one is involved), and form part of the interview record.

The sequence of questions

A commonly used sequence is as follows:

1. *Introduction.* Interviewer introduces herself, explains purpose of the interview, assures of confidentiality, asks permission to tape and/or make notes.
2. *'Warm-up'.* Easy, non-threatening questions at the beginning to settle down both of you.
3. *Main body of interview.* Covering the main purpose of the interview in what the interviewer considers to be a logical progression. In semi-structured interviewing, this order can be varied, capitalizing on the responses made (ensure 'missed' topics are returned to unless this seems inappropriate or unnecessary. Any 'risky' questions should be relatively late in the sequence so that, if the interviewee refuses to continue, less information is lost.
4. *'Cool-off'.* Usually a few straightforward questions at the end to defuse any tension that might have built up.
5. *Closure.* Thank you and goodbye. The 'hand on the door' phenomenon, sometimes found at the end of counselling sessions, is also common in interviewing. Interviewees may, when the recorder is switched off or the notebook put away, come out with a lot of interesting material. There are various possible ways of dealing with this (switch on again, reopen the notebook, forget about it) but in any case you should be consistent, *and* note how you dealt with it.

Carrying out different types of interview

Structured interviews

In virtually all respects the procedures and considerations for carrying out structured interviews are the same as those discussed for survey interviews in the previous chapter. However, you do need to ensure that responses to open-ended questions are captured word for word. The easiest way of ensuring this is by taping the interview. As always, consent of the interviewees is needed and practicalities of recording have to be sorted out (check batteries, microphone, audibility of voices, etc.).

Structured interviews of this kind do not fit easily into flexible design studies. They are more likely to be contributing to a fixed or multi-strategy design alongside other methods. While no one form of data analysis is called for, content analysis (which effectively transforms the data into quantitative form) is commonly used. See Chapter 15, p. 349.

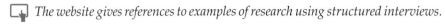 *The website gives references to examples of research using structured interviews.*

Semi-structured interviews

This type of interview is widely used in flexible and multi-strategy designs. Interviewers have their shopping list of topics and want to get responses to them, but they have considerable freedom in the sequencing of questions, in their exact wording, and in the amount of time and attention given to different topics. It is most appropriate when the interviewer is closely involved with the research process (e.g. in a small-scale project when the researcher is also the interviewer) rather than just given a short training session. Interviews described as 'semi-structured' can vary greatly in their degree of structure, ranging from being almost fully structured to allowing the interviewer much greater freedom. Accounts of the research should clarify this.

The *interview schedule* can be simpler than the one for a structured interview (Chapter 11, p. 267). It will be likely to include the following:

• introductory comments (probably a verbatim script);
• list of topic headings and possibly key questions to ask under these headings;
• set of associated prompts; and
• closing comments.

It is common to also include some more highly structured sequences (e.g. to obtain standard factual biographical and other material). One strategy is to have the different topics and associated questions and prompts on a series of cards. The interviewer will have an initial topic but will then be to some extent guided by the interviewee's responses as to the succeeding sequence of topics. Cards can be put on one side when they have been covered. Notes should be made during the interview, even if it is also being taped (in part as a fail-safe for when there is a taping problem). Allow a substantial amount of space for each topic as you won't know in advance how much material you will obtain in any particular area. The prompts may not be necessary but they provide a useful structure for organizing your notes. Box 12.2 gives an example of an interview schedule for a semi-structured interview (note that it is being used as a follow-up to a survey). Weiss (1994) gives a detailed and very readable account of qualitative interviewing including the semi-structured type. Drever (2003) presents a short, clear account of its use in small-scale research.

BOX 12.2

Example of interview schedule for semi-structured interview

Thank you for being willing to take part in a follow-up interview to the previous survey. Can I first of all assure you that you will remain completely anonymous and no records of the interview will be kept with your name on them.

1. Can I first ask you if you are now in employment?
   If *yes* take details of:

   (a) Job.
   (b) How person came to hear of job.
   (c) Application procedure.
   (d) Selection procedure.
   (e) Why this one was successful in contrast to previous attempts?
   (f) What problems did the person experience in previous attempts?

   (Probe until topic exhausted.)

   (g) Advance to 2.

(continued)

If *no* take details of:

(a) Last job applied for.
(b) How person came to hear about job.
(c) Application procedure.
(d) Selection procedure.
(e) Why was this one unsuccessful?
(f) If person not interviewed, ask above questions about the last job that got as far as interview. If none, ask above questions about the one they felt they got nearest to.
(g) What problems does the person in general experience in relation to finding work.

   (Probe until topic exhausted.)

(h) Advance to 2.

2. What careers advice have you received:
   (a) At school?
   (b) From local careers service?
   (c) From any other source including informal sources?

3. How would you evaluate that advice? (Ask in relation to all sources identified in 2.)
4. Have you taken part in any of the services for the unemployed provided locally? (Probe this and explain but do not prompt with examples at this stage.)
5. How would you evaluate these services? (Ask in relation to all sources identified in 4.)
6. Take respondents through the following list and ask them if they are aware of the service, what is provided, if they have had direct experience, and if they have, how they would rate that experience. (Omit from the list any services already covered in 4 and 5 above.)
   (a) Adult Training.
   (b) Youth Training.
   (c) Training Access Points.
   (d) Worklink.
   (e) Kirklees Community Enterprise Training Agency (KCETA).
   (f) Start-up Business Units.
   (g) Business access Scheme.
   (h) Workers Co-operatives.
   (i) Careers and Education Advice Service for Adults (CEASA).
   (j) Careers Service.
   (k) Redundancy Counselling.

7. What kinds of services could be provided that would help you personally to get a job (or would have made it easier if in employment)? Probe and direct to less obvious areas such as child minding and transport – pick up on factors mentioned in 1 and 2 above – but do not neglect more obvious direct services.
8. Have you been helped by any informal organizations? Probe on community-based initiatives, job clubs, local support networks, etc. Do not neglect simply the help and advice of relatives, friends and neighbours.
9. How do the factors identified in **8** compare to help received through formal services? Probe in what ways better, similar, worse or different.

(continued)

10. Do you have a regular routine to organize your time for the week? Probe the extent to which this includes finding employment or perhaps precludes it. NB if now employed ask in relation to time when unemployed.

11. Do you find your present income adequate and fair? If in employment contrast with time when out of employment.

12. Some people see the society we live in as a ladder to climb to greater rewards: others see it as divided between the haves and have-nots. How do you see society? Probe on social imagery.

13. Thank you very much for helping us and giving up your time. Can I finally ask you if you think there is any aspect of your experience of looking for work that has not been covered in this interview?

(*Source*: Cliff, Sparks and Gibbs, n.d.)

The website gives references to examples of research using semi-structured interviews.

Unstructured interviews

One type of unstructured interview is non-standardized, open-ended and in-depth. It has been compared to a lengthy intimate conversation but, as a research tool, it is not an easy option for the novice. Seidman (2006) provides a detailed review. His focus is on a phenomenological approach to depth interviewing, but the principles and methods can be adapted to a range of unstructured approaches.

Lofland *et al.* (2006), who prefer the term 'intensive interviewing', stress the importance of an *interview guide* when working in this way. This is not as extensive or detailed as used in more structured interviews but includes a list of things to be sure to ask about when talking to the person being interviewed. What you want is for interviewees to speak freely in their own terms about the set of concerns you bring to the interaction, plus anything else they wish to talk about. They provide a wealth of practical advice and suggestions for anyone carrying out this type of interview (pp. 99–107) and also reproduce an excellent set of self-instructions for introducing oneself prior to an intensive interview – see Box 12.3.

McCracken (1988) discusses a version of the intensive interview which he terms the *long interview*. By this he means not simply an interview which takes a long time, but an approach which can be substituted for participant observation in situations where the latter is not possible because of time or other constraints.

A further type of unstructured interview is the *informal interview*. This is where one takes an opportunity that arises to have a (usually short) chat with someone in the research setting about anything which seems relevant. In an ethnographic style study this might arise after a period of observation to try to seek clarification about the meaning or significance of something that took place. It is not appropriate as the main data collection method but, used in conjunction with other methods, can play a valuable part of virtually all flexible design research. It is not usually feasible to tape-record such interviews (getting out the recorder, asking permission, etc. is highly

BOX 12.3

Introducing yourself: a list of self-instructions

1. Explain purpose and nature of the study to the respondent, telling how or through whom they came to be selected.
2. Give assurance that respondent will remain anonymous in any written reports growing out of the study, and that their responses will be treated in strictest confidence.
3. Indicate that they may find some of the questions far-fetched, silly or difficult to answer, the reason being that questions that are appropriate for one person are not always appropriate for another. Since there are no right or wrong answers, they are not to worry about these and do as best they can with them. We are only interested in their opinions and personal experiences.
4. They are to feel perfectly free to interrupt, ask clarification of the interviewer, criticize a line of questioning, etc.
5. Interviewer will tell respondent something about herself – her background, training, and interest in the area of inquiry.
6. Interviewer is to ask permission to tape-record the interview, explaining why she wishes to do this.

(based on Lofland *et al.*, 2006, p. 104; original source Davis, 1960)

likely to get rid of the spontaneity and informality) but it is important that you make a detailed note of the interaction as soon as possible afterwards.

 The website gives references to examples of research using unstructured interviews.

Non-directive interviews

This is a term used for interviews where the direction of the interview and the areas covered are totally in the control of the person interviewed. Carl Rogers (1945) used this approach widely in therapeutic settings and it has had a considerable influence on interviewing style. However, there are important differences between clinical and research purposes. In Rogerian therapy, the interview is initiated by the client, not the therapist; the motivation, and hence the purpose of the interview, is to seek help with a problem and the extent to which it is helpful is the index of success. Because of this, a genuine non-directive interviewing approach of this type does not appear appropriate for research. Powney and Watts (1987, p. 20) suggest that Piaget's type of clinical interviewing, as used in his studies of cognitive development (e.g. Piaget, 1929), where he is insistent that the child must determine the content and direction of the conversation, fits better into research purposes. There is a certain irony here, as experimental psychologists, while recognizing Piaget's theoretical contributions, have been very dismissive of his methodology.

Focused interviews

An approach which allows people's views and feelings to emerge but which gives the inter-viewer some control, is known as the *focused interview* (Merton, Fiske & Kendall, 1990). It can be used where we want to investigate a particular situation, phenomenon or event (e.g. a youth training programme, an X-ray unit, or a TV programme). Individuals are sought who have been involved in that situation (e.g. they are all in an open prison and have been subjected to a 'short, sharp shock' treatment).

The first task is to carry out a *situational analysis*, by means of observation, documentary analysis or whatever. Typically this covers:

- the important aspects of the situation to those involved;
- the meaning these aspects have for those involved; and
- the effects they have on those involved.

An interview guide is then developed covering the major areas of enquiry and the research questions. The interviews concentrate on the subjective experiences of those involved. This approach demands considerable experience and skill on the part of the interviewer and great flexibility. In particular, the probe is a crucial aspect. Zeisel (2006, pp. 227–56) provides detailed and useful suggestions. The approach is widely used in a group setting; see the section on focus groups below.

The website gives references to examples of research using focused interviews.

Telephone interviews

Using the telephone for interviewing can be substantially quicker and cheaper than face-to-face interviews. Box 12.4 reviews the relative advantages and disadvantages of the two approaches. Telephone interviews are relatively rarely used by researchers apart from those working in com-mercial fields such as market research. However, they appear to be worth considering seriously in situations where lack of resources precludes carrying out an adequate sample of personal interviews and you can live with the disadvantages of telephone interviewing. Gwartney (2007) covers all aspects of the telephone interviewing process in some detail.

The website gives references to examples of research using telephone interviews.

Internet-based interviewing

The Internet has been increasingly used recently, not only for surveys as discussed in the previous chapter, but also for semi-structured and other types of interviews (see also Chapter 15, p. 377 for further discussion of the general issues involved). The most commonly used approach to date has been through e-mail. Box 12.5 lists some of the advantages and disadvantages of using e-mail in this way.

BOX 12.4

Face-to-face vs. telephone interviews

Advantages of telephone interviewing

1. Much cheaper and quicker, particularly if face-to-face interviewing would call for substantial travel.
2. Use of computer-assisted telephone interviewing (CATI) simplifies the task.
3. Supervision of interviewers' performance is easier, particularly if the interviews are recorded (raises ethical issues, e.g. in relation to confidentiality and informed consent – see Chapter 10).
4. Possible reduction of bias due to interviewer characteristics on responses.

Disadvantages of telephone interviewing

1. Potential for bias from problems in making phone contact with all members of the population of interest.
2. They need to be relatively short (usually less than 30 minutes); face-to-face interviews can be up to an hour in many cases.
3. The lack of visual cues can be a handicap (e.g. observation of non-verbal responses can provide helpful information, perhaps suggesting further exploration of a topic, or the need to change the topic).
4. It is not possible to gather contextual information (e.g. from observation of the respondent, neighbourhood, etc.).

BOX 12.5

Advantages and disadvantages of e-mail interviews

Note: E-mail interviews can be conducted in a variety of ways. The simplest is appropriate for structured survey-type questionnaires and involves a full set of questions being posted in a single e-mail to which a participant responds when they find it convenient. This is effectively equivalent to a postal questionnaire and to a large extent shares the same advantages and disadvantages of postal questionnaires discussed in the previous chapter while avoiding the costs and delays of using the postal system.

An alternative approach is closer to a dialogue, where a single question (or possibly a small number of related questions) is asked initially to which the participant responds. This allows for researchers to seek clarification and/or amplification of the response, and

(continued)

to vary the sequencing of later questions. As such it is closer to a semi-structured interview, although fully unstructured, depth-type variants are possible. The advantages and disadvantages listed below are discussed in terms of this latter style.

Advantages of e-mail interviews

1. *Cost.* An e-mail interview requires no travelling, no hire or purchase of recording equipment, and no transcribing costs. Several e-mail interviews can be posted at the same time.
2. *Range of participants.* Face-to-face interviewing involves travelling to meet participants or asking participants to travel to where you are. With e-mail interviewing, it is possible to interview people with access to e-mail anywhere with no travel costs.
3. *Time for reflection.* Face-to-face and telephone interviews occur in real time. The e-mail interview enables the participant to reflect on their responses before replying. Assuming that the full set of questions and responses are retained in the e-mail interchanges, it is feasible for participants to modify earlier responses. Researchers can similarly modify their questions in the light of the responses obtained.
4. *Concurrent interviewing is possible.* The interviewer can conduct several e-mail interviews over the same period of time. It is feasible to modify the set of questions based on the types and nature of responses obtained.
5. *Rapport.* The time taken to conduct the dialogue style e-mail interview can enable a good rapport to develop between the interviewer and the participant. The situation is similar to a series of multiple face-to-face interviews taking place over several days or weeks rather than a single interview of one or two hours.
6. *Saying things that would not be said face-to-face.* The impersonal nature of the e-mail interview may help people say things that they would not be willing to say face-to-face.
7. *Overcoming interviewer effects.* Face-to-face interviews can be affected by the personal visual characteristics of the interviewer.

Disadvantages of e-mail interviews

1. *Problems with the sample.* A generic problem for any web-based study (see Chapter 15, p. 378). There can be great difficulties in obtaining a representative sample and in ensuring that the person responding is who you think they are.
2. *The interview can take too long.* E-mail interviews of this type usually take place over several days, sometimes longer. This can result in a loss of involvement and problems in completion.
3. *Ethical issues.* Participants may fail to continue the interview because they have decided to withdraw from the interview but have not told the interviewer this. You have to make a decision whether or not to request the information again.
4. *Missing nonverbal cues.* Conducting an interview by e-mail means that a number of possible relevant visual cues are missing.
5. *Impersonality.* Cyberspace is an impersonal world, and possible effects on the conduct and outcome of an interview are not currently well understood.

(based, in abridged form, on Hunt and McHale, 2007, pp. 1416–18)

Other techniques have been exploited, including text messaging and Voice over Internet Protocol (VoIP) transmission technologies for delivery of voice communications over the Internet and other networks. VoIP products such as Skype offer the ability to employ both voice and video links for individual and group interviewing (e.g. Georgieva & Allan, 2008; Vandagriff & Nitsche, 2009).

Kazmer and Xie (2008) and Opdenakker (2006) have made detailed comparisons between different approaches to collecting qualitative semi-structured interview data using face-to-face, telephone, e-mail and instant messaging (e.g. MSN Messenger) methods. Their general conclusion is that all four methods of data collection can produce viable data. However:

- Using face-to-face interviews for collecting information is preferred when social cues of the interviewee are very important information sources, the interviewer has enough budget and time for travelling and standardization of the interview situation is important;
- Using telephone, text messenger or e-mail interviews for collecting information is preferred when social cues of the interviewee are less important information sources for the interviewer, the interviewer has a small budget and less time for travelling, when seeking access to people on sites with closed or limited access, standardization of the interview situation is not important and some *anonymity* is appropriate;
- Using text messenger or e-mail interviews for collecting information is preferred when both the interviewer and the interviewee are competent in typing and have access to computers; and
- Using e-mail interviews for collecting information is preferred when it is necessary that the interviewee takes time to respond to the developing dialogue, and/or when the interviewer and interviewee live in different parts of the world separated by several time zones (the other approaches would mean either the interviewer or interviewee interviewing at night).

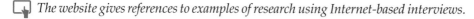 *The website gives references to examples of research using Internet-based interviews.*

Focus groups

Interviews can take place in a group context as well as one-to-one. They can follow any of the types previously discussed and, in particular, may be highly structured, semi-structured or unstructured. The more common versions have a substantial degree of flexibility and are effectively some form of hybrid with characteristics of a discussion as well as of an interview. Even though general topics, and sometimes specific questions, are presented by the researcher, the traditional interview format of alternate question and answer is both difficult to maintain and eliminates the group interaction which can be a particular strength of the group interview.

The generic term 'group interview' has tended recently to be used interchangeably with 'focus group' because of the latter's popularity, even though it has specific characteristics. Focus groups originated in market research in the 1920s, arising from the recognition that many consumer decisions were made in a social, group context (Bogardus, 1926). They are now widely used by political parties seeking to assess the likely response to proposed policies, and are currently a very popular method of data collection in many fields of applied social research. Part of their popularity is ascribed to the fact that 'they do not discriminate against people who cannot read or write and they can encourage participation from people reluctant to be interviewed on their own or who feel they have nothing to say' (Kitzinger, 1995, p. 299) and have found a place in fields such as disability research (Gates & Waight, 2007; Kroll, Barbour & Harris, 2007).

Possibly because of its historical background in market research the method has often been used for what might be called low-involvement topics. However, Överlien, Aronsson and Hydén (2005) demonstrate its use as an in-depth method in more high-involvement topics such as the promotion of safe sex.

Focus groups show signs of taking over from questionnaires as the automatic stock response to the question, 'What method should we use?' This is in part because they share with postal questionnaires the advantages of being an efficient way of generating substantial amounts of data and of apparently being easy to carry out. As with questionnaires, these perceived advantages are offset by considerable disadvantages. For example, it is difficult or impossible to follow up the views of individuals and group dynamics or power hierarchies affect who speaks and what they say. A common problem is when one or two persons dominate. Dealing with this, and more generally running the group sessions, calls for considerable experience, tact and sensitivity. Box 12.6 lists some of their advantages and disadvantages.

BOX 12.6

Advantages and disadvantages of focus groups

Advantages

1. A highly efficient technique for qualitative data collection since the amount and range of data is increased by collecting from several people at the same time.
2. Natural quality controls on data collection operate; for example, participants tend to provide checks and balances on each other and extreme views tend to be 'weeded out'.
3. Group dynamics help in focusing on the most important topics and it is fairly easy to assess the extent to which there is a consistent and shared view.
4. Participants tend to enjoy the experience.
5. The method is relatively inexpensive and flexible and can be set up quickly.
6. Participants are empowered and able to make comments in their own words, while being stimulated by thoughts and comments of others in the group.
7. Contributions can be encouraged from people who are either reluctant to be interviewed on their own, feel they have nothing to say or who may not usually participate in surveys.
8. People who cannot read or write or who have other specific difficulties are not discriminated against.
9. Facilitation can help in the discussion of taboo subjects since less inhibited members may break the ice or provide mutual support.

Disadvantages

1. The number of questions covered is limited. Typically fewer than ten major questions can be asked in an hour.

(continued)

2. Facilitating the group process requires considerable expertise.
3. The interview process needs to be well managed or the less articulate may not share their views, extreme views may predominate and bias may be caused by the domination of the group by one or two people.
4. Conflicts may arise between personalities. Power struggles may detract from the interview and status may conflict within the procedure.
5. Confidentiality can be a problem between participants when interacting in a group situation.
6. The results are difficult to generalize as they cannot be regarded as representative of the wider population.
7. The live and immediate nature of the interaction may lead a researcher or decision-maker to place greater faith in the findings than is actually warranted.

(adapted and abridged from Robinson, 1999, pp. 909–10)

A focus group (sometimes referred to as a *focus group interview* – which emphasizes the fact that this is a particular type of interview) is a group interview on a specific topic which is where the 'focus' comes from. It is an open-ended group discussion which the researcher guides, typically extending over at least an hour, possibly two or more.

Group size and composition

Opinion varies on the optimum size of the group. Stewart and Shamdasani (1990) suggest eight to twelve, whereas Morgan (1997) opts for six to ten. Krueger and Casey (2000) are critical of the widespread use of convenience samples and pre-existing groups. They urge caution when using groups of people who know and work closely with each other. Not only will such groups have their own well-established dynamics but also current relationships and hierarchies will influence contributions. There is debate about whether the groups should be homogenous (e.g. a study of the client perspective on the working of a health service might consist of a group of people who have recently used the service) or heterogeneous (e.g. a study within a firm might include shop-floor workers, secretarial staff, managers, etc.). Halcomb, Gholizadeh, Digiacomo, Phillips and Davidson (2007) review the literature on undertaking focus group research with culturally and linguistically diverse groups. The pros and cons of the two approaches are presented as Box 12.7. Market researchers traditionally brought together groups of strangers on the assumption that this would lead to a greater focus on the designated topic. However, this is neither feasible nor appropriate for many real world research projects.

Uses of focus groups

Focus groups can be, and have been, used in a wide variety of ways by researchers. They can be used in an initial phase to help prepare for the main data collection phase, for example, as a precursor to the development of a more structured instrument. They can be the *primary data*

BOX 12.7

Homogenous or heterogeneous groups?

Homogenous groups

Have a common background, position or experience which:

- facilitates communication;
- promotes an exchange of ideas and experiences;
- gives a sense of safety in expressing conflicts or concerns; and
- may result in 'groupthink' (unquestioning similarity of position or views).

Heterogeneous groups

Differ in background, position or experience which:

- can stimulate and enrich the discussion;
- may inspire other group members to look at the topic in a different light;
- may risk power imbalances;
- can lead to lack of respect for opinions expressed by some members; and
- can lead to a dominant participant destroying the group process.

(derived from Brown, 1999, p. 115)

collection method in a study. They are, however, commonly used in conjunction with other methods, for example, with observation and individual interviews, or with questionnaires. One approach is to use focus groups to amplify and understand the findings from a survey. Complex studies can have several different focus groups.

Focus groups have also been used within evaluation research, and to help bring about change in the group and its members.

The website gives references to examples of projects using focus groups.

The moderator role

The person running a focus group is usually referred to as the *moderator* (sometimes the *facilitator*). The terms signal two aspects of their role: to moderate in the dictionary sense of regulating, or keeping within measures or bounds; to facilitate in the sense of helping the group to run effectively.

These are not easy tasks and call for considerable skills and experience if they are to be done well. A balance between an active and a passive role is needed. 'The moderator has to generate interest in and discussion about a particular topic, which is close to his or her professional or academic interest, without at the same time leading the group to reinforce existing expectations or confirm a prior hypothesis' (Sim, 1998, p. 347). Acting as a moderator for a focus group run for research purposes may be particularly difficult for some professional groups. Those from helping and caring professions must appreciate that it is not being run for therapeutic purposes. They are not running a support group, although it may be that participants get a great deal from the experience (Marmoreo, Brown, Batty, Cummings & Powell, 1998).

There are considerable advantages in having a second researcher or other person involved in the running of the group. These include the following:

- it provides coverage of both the substantive area of interest and focus group experience (often not possible to combine these in a single person);
- a second person can make notes on who is speaking (difficult to determine if audio-taping is used; video-taping can be obtrusive);
- the second person can note non-verbal interactions; and
- can give feedback on the moderator's performance (e.g. talking too much, over-prompting; inhibiting discussion, allowing one person to dominate, etc.).

Data collection in focus groups

Audio-taping is generally recommended although there are some situations where this may affect the working of the group (perhaps because of the sensitivity of the topic, or the characteristics and expectations of group members). It is good practice to have written notes made even if the session is recorded. Groups are notoriously difficult to get good recordings from; recorders fail, etc. This is a task for the second researcher. Keeping the session going well is a sufficiently demanding task for the moderator.

Data analysis and interpretation

This should follow the general principles and processes for qualitative data analysis discussed in Chapter 18. Rabiee (2004) concentrates on the analysis of focus group data. As with other flexible designs generating qualitative data, analysis and interpretation of data from focus groups must take account of the context and circumstances in which the data are gathered.

The group context leads to some issues which are relatively specific to focus groups. Group dynamics obviously play a major part in what happens during the session and hence in the data you obtain. In particular it is dangerous to interpret an absence of dissenting voices as indicating consensus. Silence may indicate consent but it could reflect an unwillingness to express dissent. In this connection, advantages have been claimed for computer-mediated focus groups – see below.

Problematic methodological issues

Much of the literature on focus groups is methodologically naive. This perhaps reflects its roots in market research where concerns have tended to be highly practical and the literature focuses on how to do it, rather than worrying overmuch about the warrant for the assertions and conclusions made. Critical reviews of the focus group as a research method, including Hydén and Bülow (2003) and Wilkinson (1998; 1999), have pointed out that even though interaction between

BOX 12.8

Methodological issues arising from focus groups

1. The skills and attributes of the moderator and the manner of data recording will exert a powerful influence on the quality of the data collected in a focus group.
2. Focus groups explore collective phenomena, not individual ones. Attempts to infer the latter from focus group data are likely to be unfounded.
3. Focus group data may be a poor indicator of a consensus in attitudes, though they may reveal a divergence of opinion and the extent to which certain issues recur across groups.
4. Focus groups can reveal the nature and range of participants' views but less so, their strength.
5. Generalization from focus group data is problematic. If feasible, it will be theoretical generalization (see p. 284) rather than empirical or statistical generalization.
6. Focus groups tap a different realm of social reality from that revealed by one-to-one interviews or questionnaire studies. Each of these methods should be selected in terms of their relative appropriateness for the research question concerned and should not be expected to fulfil objectives for which they are methodologically unsuited.

(derived from Sim, 1998, p. 351)

participants is considered to be central to focus group research, this has rarely been explored in and of itself. Wibeck, Dahlgren and Oberg (2007) seek to remedy this by linking it to research studying interaction in other group settings.

Some issues needing consideration from a research perspective are listed in Box 12.8.

The website includes further discussion on the methodological background to focus group research.

Internet-based focus groups

Conducting focus groups via the Internet is becoming an increasingly popular method for collecting data. The main benefits of Internet-based focus groups include lower cost, no travel expenses, automatic capture of the discussion data, and the ability to reach remote populations for participation. Underhill and Olmsted (2003) carried out an experimental comparison of the quantity and quality of the information obtained from traditional face-to-face focus groups and different types of computer-based focus groups. Their results indicated that different groups produced similar amounts of information, and in particular that the quality of the information obtained from computer-based focus groups is not significantly different from information obtained from face-to-face groups. Walston and Lissitz (2000), in a similar study, found that the computer-based environment, in comparison to face-to-face, may lessen members' concern about what the moderator thinks of them and may discourage participants from withholding embarrassing information.

Internet-based focus groups not only adapt methodological approaches to take advantage of advances in communication technology but also provide a means of doing research with individuals who are unable or unwilling to engage in conventional face-to-face focus groups. So-called 'asynchronous' groups which do not function in real time (e.g. involving discussion groups, where messages are posted to the group and then responded to by other participants) have typically been used. Fox, Morris and Rumsey (2007), while accepting that they have advantages similar to those discussed above in relation to the use of e-mail for interviews, feel that they lose important features of focus groups including dynamic and immediate group interaction. They advocate the use of synchronous, real-time exchanges and provide an example of the use of this form of on-line communication in a research project with young people.

An on-line forum hosted by their university was created:

> The intention was to reassure participants and their parents that the research was linked to a reputable institution rather than to an unknown source. Security was achieved by the installation of password-protected access for both moderator and participants. The forum was tested first informally and then through a pilot focus group with faculty postgraduates. Feedback identified areas for alteration, including a scroll-back feature to allow participants to look back at previous threads of conversation (p. 542).

Fox *et al.* provide helpful discussion of methodological issues as well as consideration of the practical, ethical, and personal aspects involved in organizing, hosting, and moderating these virtual discussions. Tates *et al.* (2009) conclude that:

> online focus groups have considerable potential for gathering high quality data within a relatively short period of time from respondents who are unable or unwilling to engage in traditional group discussions. As such, the methodology offers access to respondents from understudied or marginalized populations that were previously hard to include (p. 6).

They opt for an asynchronous style and also provide full details of the procedures involved.

The website gives references to examples of research using Internet-based focus groups.

Other types of group activities used for research purposes

As discussed above, focus groups are a special kind of group where the prime purpose is data collection. The goal of a focus group is not necessarily to reach consensus, though this may happen. Focus groups do not vote on decisions, plan programmes or decide on a course of action. Other group activities used for research purposes include:

- *Brainstorming.* Used to generate and select alternative solutions (e.g. as discussed in Chapter 3 for developing ideas about aspects of a project rather than as a research method itself).
- *Delphi groups.* Successive rounds of questionnaires are used to collect data from experts who form a panel. Each questionnaire is followed by a summary of the replies received from the previous round. Often used to estimate the impacts of trends or develop scenarios of future outcomes.

- *Nominal groups.* Individual ideas are gathered (usually through some type of brainstorming) and combined. Generally round robin feedback is used from each individual on ideas and then they are prioritized by voting.

Delphi and nominal groups techniques are discussed further in Chapter 15, p. 364.

Dealing with interview data

The ways in which research interviews have been reported have not in general been noteworthy for their standards of rigour or detail. Typically, accounts are strong on content and its interpretation, much weaker on providing sufficient information to judge the trustworthiness of those accounts.

Note: Many of the issues involved in dealing with interview data, including assessing reliability and expectancy effects, are the same as those encountered with observational data (see Chapter 14, p. 343).

Taping and transcribing

Whenever feasible, there is considerable advantage in audio-taping a research interview (exceptions include informal interviews where taping is likely to be intrusive). The tape provides a permanent record and allows you to concentrate on the conduct of the interview. Whether or not you make a full transcript of the tape depends on the resources at your disposal, the number of tapes to be transcribed and the way in which you propose to analyse the data.

Kvale and Brinkmann (2009, Chapter 11) discuss what they call the '1,000 Page Question' – 'How shall I find a method to analyze the 1,000 pages of interview transcript?' Their answer is simple. The question is posed too late. As discussed earlier in relation to fixed designs (Chapter 6), it is too late to start thinking about analysis after the interviewing is done. In flexible and multi-strategy design research, the implications for analysis of amassing large amounts of interview (or any other) data have to be thought through before you commit yourself to the data collection. It makes little sense to have mounds of data that you have neither the time nor resources to deal with. Kvale and Brinkmann reformulate the 1,000 page question in various ways, including:

- How shall I conduct my interviews so that their meaning can be analysed in a coherent and creative way?
- How do I go about finding out what the interviews tell me about what I want to know? and
- How can the interviews assist in extending my knowledge of the phenomena I am investigating?

An alternative to full transcription is to be selective, picking out relevant passages, and noting the tape counter numbers where there are particular quotations, examples, etc.

Skills in interviewing

You don't become a good interviewer just by reading about it. Skills are involved which require practice, preferably under 'low risk' conditions where it is possible to receive feedback on your performance. The skills involved in structured interviews are relatively low level. Is the script being kept to? Are standard questions being asked in the same way to all interviewees? Are the 'skips' depending on particular answers carried out correctly? Are all interviewees responded to in the same way? And so on. The less the degree of structure in the interview, the more complex the performance required from the interviewer.

It is highly desirable that the pilot (or a pre-pilot) stage includes explicit interviewer assessment and training. Clearly if you are totally alone as a researcher, this causes problems, but you can ask the interviewees in the pilot to comment on your performance as well as on the interview schedule. A recording (audio or video) will facilitate the interviewer's evaluation of their performance.

If you are working with colleagues, then mutual (constructive) assessment of each other's interview performance is feasible. This type of feedback information is not only helpful for training purposes but also helps in the general task of viewing the interview situation as a complex social interaction whose characteristics have to some extent to be captured by the analysis. Roulston, de Marrais and Lewis (2003) investigated how novice researchers developed their interview skills, reporting on postgraduate students' experiences and reflections during an intensive training course. Challenges faced by their novice interviewers included unexpected participant behaviours, dealing with the consequences of the interviewers' own actions and subjectivities, constructing and delivering questions, and handling sensitive research topics. They provide recommendations for developing interview skills including close, guided analysis of interview tapes and transcripts.

Further reading

The website gives annotated references to further reading for Chapter 12.

CHAPTER 13

Tests and scales

> This chapter:
>
> - discusses the use of measurement scales and tests;
> - focuses on the measurement of attitudes as an example;
> - reviews the Likert, Thurstone, Guttman and semantic differential approaches to scaling;
> - stresses the advantages of using existing tests whenever feasible;
> - briefly reviews a selection of widely used tests; and
> - warns about the difficulties in developing your own test.

Introduction

Psychologists and other social scientists have developed a substantial range of self-report measuring instruments to assess people's abilities, propensities, views, opinions and attitudes – to name but a few. Most widely known by the lay public is the IQ or intelligence test but there are also tests of attainment, of creativity and of personality. They are, in many cases, versions of structured interviews or of self-completion questionnaires, though not usually referred to as such.

Technically, such tests provide a *scale* on which we can assess, usually quantitatively, the individuals' performance or standing on the attribute in question. There are other measurement scales where the function is not to test but to gain some insight into what people feel or believe about something.

Measurement scales

Many researchers are interested in the measurement of attitudes; people's views about issues such as the environment, global warming, abortion, gun and knife crime, child abuse, etc. Because of this, the following discussion is couched in terms of attitude measurement. The same principles apply to the development of scales measuring other aspects such as aptitudes, performances, personalities.

The term 'attitude' is somewhat slippery. It falls in the same kind of sphere as opinion, belief or value, but opinions vary as to how these different terms are interrelated. Lemon (1973) provides a clear analysis and suggests that the term's widespread usage derives in part from this very fuzziness; each worker has been able to tailor it to suit their own purposes.

There is a substantial technology and associated mystique about attitude measurement. Central to this is the belief that it is not possible to assess something like attitude by means of a single question or statement. For example, suppose someone strongly disagreed with the statement: 'Economic aid should be given to countries in Sub-Saharan Africa.' By itself this could not be taken as indicating an unsympathetic attitude to those countries' plight. The respondent might feel that such assistance would act against their interests, perhaps by inhibiting necessary changes in their economy. Answers to a range of statements can help in teasing out such issues. Having a set of 10 or 20 items is another form of triangulation; the response to each gives something of a 'marker' on the respondent's attitude. Putting the responses together enables us to build up a much fuller picture. The problems arise in selecting the items or statements and in working out how to put together the responses.

Arbitrary scales

It is still distressingly common to see attitude scales cobbled together by assembling an arbitrary group of statements which sound as if they would be relevant, with similar 'off the top of the head' ratings assigned to different answers, and a simple addition of these ratings to obtain some mystical 'attitude score'. Put like this, the deficiencies are obvious. We need some form of systematic procedure so that we can demonstrate that the different items are related to the same attitude. Similar justification is needed for the assignment of numbers of some kind to particular answers.

The summated rating (or Likert) scale

The summated rating approach is very widely used – and has the added advantage of being relatively easy to develop. It was originally devised by Likert in the 1930s (Likert, 1932) and scales developed by this method are commonly termed *Likert scales*. Box 13.1 gives a summary of the procedure and Box 13.2 provides an example. Maranell (2007, Part 4) gives full details.

The website gives references to further examples of Likert scales.

Items in a Likert scale can look interesting to respondents and people often enjoy completing a scale of this kind. This can be of importance, not only because if they are interested they are likely to give considered rather than perfunctory answers, but also because in many situations people may, not unreasonably, just not be prepared to cooperate in something that appears boring. However, even though the items may look arbitrary and similar to those in magazine self-rating exercises, the systematic procedures used do help to ensure that the scale has internal consistency and/or the ability to differentiate among individuals.

BOX 13.1

Developing a summated rating (Likert) scale

1. *Gather together a pool of items that appear to be related to or important to the issue.* This can be done by reading round the issue, borrowing from existing scales and 'brainstorming'. Items should reflect both a positive and a negative stance to the issue. Extreme positive and extreme negative statements should be avoided as they may be insensitive to individual differences in attitude (we want to discriminate between individuals – extreme statements may get everyone giving the same response). There should be about the same number of positive and negative statements.

2. *Decide on a response categorization system.* The most common is to have five fixed alternative expressions, labelled 'strongly agree', 'agree', 'undecided', 'disagree', and 'strongly disagree'.[a] Weights of 1, 2, 3, 4 and 5 are assigned to these alternatives, with the direction of weighting depending on whether the statement is positive or negative (e.g. 5 for a 'strongly agree' with a positive statement, and 'strongly disagree' with a negative statement).

3. *Ask a large number of respondents to check their attitudes to the list of statements.* The list should be in random order with positive and negative statements intermingled. The respondents should be a representative sample from the population whose attitude you wish to measure.

4. *Obtain a total score for each respondent.* This is done by summing the value of each of the responses given (e.g. 'agree' to positive item scores 4; 'strongly disagree' with negative item scores 5; 'neutral' to either scores 3; 'agree' to negative item scores 2; etc.). Rank the respondents according to total score obtained.

5. *Select items for final scale using 'item analysis'.* Each item (i.e. statement) is subjected to a measurement of its *discriminative power* (DP), that is, its ability to discriminate between the responses of the upper quartile (25 per cent) of respondents, and the responses of the lower quartile (25 per cent) – see worked example below. Items with the highest DP indices are chosen for the final scale. A typical scale would consist of 20 to 30 items.

Notes: There are alternative techniques for selecting the items for the final scale (e.g. each statement can be correlated with the overall score – those items with the highest correlations are retained).

Scales can be tested for validity and reliability using the methods covered in Loewenthal (2001; pp. 119–52).

---

[a] Alternatives are possible (e.g. 3, 4, 6 or 7 alternatives – odd numbers permit a neutral mid-point which is usually considered desirable); different labels for the alternatives may be used where appropriate (e.g. 'almost always', 'frequently', 'occasionally', 'rarely', and 'almost never').

(continued)

Calculating the discriminative power (DP) of items

1. Suppose the scale is tested on a sample of 60 respondents. The upper quartile will thus consist of the 15 respondents (25 per cent of 60) with the highest total scores; the lower quartile the 15 respondents with the lowest total scores.
2. The distribution of scores (i.e. number of 1s, 2s, 3s, 4s and 5s) for the upper quartile group is tabled for each item.
3. The distribution of scores (i.e. number of 1s, 2s, 3s, 4s and 5s) for the lower quartile group is tabled for each item.
4. Weighted totals and means are calculated separately for the upper and lower quartile groups, for each item:

    Example for one item

Weighted group	Number in group	Item scores					Weighted total	Weighted mean
		1	2	3	4	5		
Upper	15	0	1	2	7	5	$(1.2) + (2.3) + (7.4)$ $+ (5.5) = 61$	$61/15 = 4.07$
Lower	15	3	8	3	1	0	$(3.1) + (8.2) + (3.3)$ $+ (1.4) = 32$	$32/15 = 2.13$

5. The index of discriminative power (DP) for an item is the difference between the weighted means.

    For the example above, $DP = 4.07 - 2.13 = 1.94$.

BOX 13.2

Example of Likert scale – generalized expectancy for success scale

Highly improbable   1 2 3 4 5   Highly probable

In the future I expect that I will:

1. find that people don't seem to understand what I am trying to say.
2. be discouraged about my ability to gain the respect of others.
3. be a good parent.
4. be unable to accomplish my goals.
5. have a successful marital relationship.
6. deal poorly with emergency situations.
7. find my efforts to change situations I don't like to be ineffective.
8. not be very good at learning new skills.
9. carry through my responsibilities successfully.
10. discover that the good in life outweighs the bad.

11. handle unexpected problems successfully.
12. get the promotions I deserve.
13. succeed in the projects I undertake.
14. not make any significant contributions to society.
15. discover that my life is not getting much better.
16. be listened to when I speak.
17. discover that my plans don't work out too well.
18. find that no matter how I try, things just don't turn out the way I would like.
19. handle myself well in whatever situation I'm in.
20. be able to solve my own problems.
21. succeed at most things I try.
22. be successful in my endeavours in the long run.
23. be very successful in working out my personal life.
24. experience many failures in my life.
25. make a good impression on people I meet for the first time.
26. attain the career goals I have set for myself.
27. have difficulty dealing with my superiors.
28. have problems working with others.
29. be a good judge of what it takes to get ahead.
30. achieve recognition in my profession.

(from Fibel and Hale, 1978)

The equal appearing interval (or Thurstone) scale

This type of scale has been relatively widely used. However, the development of a Thurstone scale is considerably more cumbersome and difficult than the development of a Likert scale. There are also serious objections on theoretical grounds, reviewed by Kline (2000, p. 94). His advice is that 'there are sufficient problems to render its use dubious'.

The cumulated (or Guttman) scale

Critics of both Thurstone and Likert scales have pointed out that they may contain statements which concern a variety of dimensions relating to the attitude. For example, a scale on attitudes to nuclear power stations could include ethical and moral statements, concerning the economic consequences of developing nuclear power, a health dimension, an environmental aspect, etc. Combining statements relating to several dimensions on the one scale may well reflect the underlying structure of the attitude, but will make it difficult to interpret cumulative scores.

Approaches to determining the structure of attitudes fall into two broad categories: *phenomenological* – such as repertory grid technique (see below p. 363); and *mathematical* – as in factor and cluster analysis (see Chapter 17). The Guttman approach (Guttman, 1944) overcomes this complexity by seeking to develop a unidimensional scale.

In this type of scale, items have a cumulative property. They are chosen and ordered so that a person who accepts (agrees with) a particular item will also accept all previous items. An analogy is sometimes made with high-jumping. If someone has cleared the bar at 2 metres, we can be confident that she would also do so at 1.8 metres, 1.60, 1.40, 1.20 etc. Box 13.3 summarizes the steps needed to develop a Guttman scale and Box 13.4 shows how the analysis is carried out. Additional details can be found in Maranell (2007, Part 3).

BOX 13.3

Developing a cumulated (Guttman) scale

1. *Collect a large number of apparently relevant and usable statements.*
2. *Administer the statements to a standardization group.* Members of the group have to answer in a yes/no (agree/disagree) fashion.
3. *Carry out a scalogram analysis of the standardization group's responses.* This involves attempting to arrange the responses into the 'best' triangular shape – as demonstrated in Box 13.4.
4. *Apply the scale to respondents.* The attitude measure is usually the total number of items accepted or agreed to.

BOX 13.4

Guttman's scalogram analysis – example

In practice, the analysis will be based on a substantially greater number of items and participants in the standardization group than those included here. The principles are the same.

1. *List items and participants in order of the total number of 'agrees'* (x = agrees; o = disagrees).

Participant	3	6	7	1	9	8	10	2	5	4	Total for item
Item 5	x	x	x	x	x	x	x	x	x	x	10
Item 7	o	x	x	x	x	x	x	x	x	x	9
Item 8	o	o	x	o	x	x	x	x	x	x	7
Item 9	o	x	o	x	x	x	x	x	x	x	7
Item 12	o	o	x	x	o	x	x	x	x	x	7
Item 1	o	o	o	o	x	x	x	x	x	x	6
Item 15	o	o	o	x	o	x	x	o	x	x	5
Item 2	o	o	o	o	x	o	x	x	x	x	5
Item 11	o	o	o	o	x	o	o	x	x	x	5
Item 6	o	x	o	o	o	o	o	x	o	x	3
Item 14	o	o	o	o	o	o	o	x	x	x	3
Item 10	o	o	o	x	o	o	o	o	o	x	2
Item 3	o	o	o	o	o	o	o	o	x	x	2
Item 4	o	o	o	o	o	x	o	o	o	o	1
Item 13	o	o	o	o	o	o	o	o	o	x	1
Total for participant	1	4	4	6	7	8	8	10	11	13	

2. *Select those items which give the closest approximation to a triangular shape, i.e. to this pattern*:

```
x x x x x
o x x x x
o o x x x
o o o x x
o o o o x
o o o o o
```

This will involve some trial and error, and possible reorderings of the columns (i.e. the participants) when rows are removed.

Participant	3	6	7	1	8	10	9	2	5	4	Total
Item 5	x	x	x	x	x	x	x	x	x	x	10
Item 7	o	x	x	x	x	x	x	x	x	x	9
Item 8	o	x	o	x	x	x	x	x	x	x	8
Item 9	o	o	x	o	x	x	x	x	x	x	7
Item 1	o	o	o	o	x	x	x	x	x	x	6
Item 2	o	o	o	o	o	x	x	x	x	x	5
Item 11	o	o	o	o	o	o	x	x	x	x	4
Item 14	o	o	o	o	o	o	o	x	x	x	3
Item 3	o	o	o	o	o	o	o	o	x	x	2
Item 13	o	o	o	o	o	o	o	o	o	x	1
Total for participant	1	3	3	3	5	6	7	7	9	10	

Assess the reproducibility of the responses (i.e. the extent to which the participants' pattern of responses is predictable from their total score. This amounts to the same thing as the divergence from the perfect triangular shape. Guttman proposes a 'coefficient of reproducibility' which he suggests should be at least 0.9 if the scale is to be used. The coefficient $R = 1 - e/nk$, where

e = number of errors
n = number of respondents
k = number of items

In the example, there are 2 errors (both with subject 7; with a score of 3 the subject would have been expected to agree with item 8 and disagree with item 9). Hence $R = 1 - 2/100 = 0.98$.

3. *Administer the test to a fresh set of respondents and replicate the results to an acceptable degree of reproducibility.* This step is important (and unfortunately often omitted) as the initial selection of a relatively small set of items from a long list will inevitably capitalize on chance to some extent. It may be necessary to incorporate substitute items at this stage, which then necessitates further replication.

There are obvious attractions in the simplicity of a scale which gives a unidimensional assessment of attitude, so that one feels that the score obtained gives much firmer ground for subsequent interpretation and analysis than the multidimensional complexity of the other approaches we have discussed. The other side of this is that it is best adapted to measuring a well defined and clear-cut dimension, so that items reflecting unidimensionality can be generated without undue difficulty.

The website gives references to examples of Guttman scales.

Semantic differential scales

A widely used type of scale, the *semantic differential scale* (Osgood, Suci & Tannenbaum, 1957), takes a very different approach. It is concerned with assessing the subjective meaning of a concept to the respondent, instead of assessing how much they believe in a particular concept. The scale is designed to explore the ratings given along a series of bipolar rating scales (e.g. bad/good; boring/exciting). Factor analyses have shown that such ratings typically group together into three underlying dimensions – activity, evaluation, and potency. In this sense it provides a kind of attitude scale.

Activity refers to the extent to which the concept is associated with action (dimensions might be 'fast', 'active', 'exciting', etc.). *Evaluation* refers to the overall positive meaning associated with it ('positive', 'honest', 'dependable', etc.). *Potency* refers to its overall strength or importance ('strong', 'valuable', 'useful', etc.). A list of appropriate adjective pairs is generated for the particular concept you are trying to measure. However, broadly similar lists can be used in many contexts. Sources of lists include Osgood *et al.* (1957) and Valois and Godin (1991). Box 13.5 gives an example of a semantic differential scale.

The website gives references to further examples of semantic differential scales.

Using the scale

The scale is administered to the chosen sample of respondents in a standard fashion. It is scored simply by summing the ratings given to each adjective pair on a 1–7 scale (or whatever the number of alternatives that have been given). Average ratings can be computed and comparisons between sub-groups in the sample are feasible. To take it further, it is necessary to carry out a factor analysis (see Chapter 17, p. 436) to assess the relationship of the different adjective pairs and link them to the evaluative dimensions.

Comparison of Likert and semantic differential scales

Friborg, Martinussen and Rosenvinge (2006) suggest that: 'In measuring positive psychological constructs, Likert scales may introduce an acquiescence bias. To reduce this, items usually are transformed into negations of the concept. Such transformations may introduce errors, as negations of positive constructs may appear contra-intuitive' (p. 873). They suggest that the

BOX 13.5

Example of a semantic differential scale

Instructions: for each pair of adjectives place a cross at the point between them which reflects the extent to which you believe the adjectives describe police.

clean	:	:	:	:	:	:	:	dirty
honest	:	:	:	:	:	:	:	dishonest
kind	:	:	:	:	:	:	:	cruel
helpful	:	:	:	:	:	:	:	unhelpful
fair	:	:	:	:	:	:	:	biassed
delicate	:	:	:	:	:	:	:	rugged
strong	:	:	:	:	:	:	:	weak
stupid	:	:	:	:	:	:	:	intelligent
unreliable	:	:	:	:	:	:	:	reliable
heavy	:	:	:	:	:	:	:	light
foolish	:	:	:	:	:	:	:	wise
passive	:	:	:	:	:	:	:	active
energetic	:	:	:	:	:	:	:	lazy
boring	:	:	:	:	:	:	:	exciting
valuable	:	:	:	:	:	:	:	useless
impulsive	:	:	:	:	:	:	:	deliberate

semantic differential format may be an alternative to negations for reducing the effect of this tendency to agree with statements. Using a scale measuring resilience as an example of a positive psychological construct, they compared a Likert and a semantic differential response format with respect to psychometric properties. Their conclusion was that in measuring positive psychological constructs, a semantic differential format may effectively reduce acquiescence bias without lowering psychometric quality.

Other scaling techniques

There are several other scaling possibilities, including the following.

Q-sorts

A technique used to measure the relative position or ranking of an individual on a range of concepts. Q-sorting is a process whereby a person indicates their view of an issue (or whatever) by rank-ordering items into 'piles' along a continuum defined by a certain instruction. A basic principle of the Q-sort technique is that items are evaluated relative to each other. It is usually accomplished by providing the items on cards which the subject lays out and sorts into horizontally ordered category piles on a desk. It is particularly useful for exploring subjective issues such as perceptions and relationships. See Chapter 15, p. 368 for further details.

Sociometric scales

A technique used to describe relationships between individuals in a group. In its simplest form, it requires members of a group to make choices among other members of a group (e.g. whom they like). It is a versatile technique and has been used with groups ranging from pre-school children to prisoners. The technique is straightforward and results can be displayed in the form of 'sociograms' which give a diagrammatic representation of the choices made. Bukowski and Cillessen (1998) discuss the conceptual foundations of the approach and recent methodological advances in sociometric techniques. White (2007) has reservations, claiming that it takes far too long in its entirety; and 'is a blunt instrument, lacking the richness of nuance, ambivalence and possibility'.

Using existing tests and scales

The development of tests for assessing some aspect or other of human functioning is a complex and burgeoning enterprise. It could well be that a useful measure for a research study is provided by scores on an attainment test (e.g. in relation to reading) or that other indices (such as scores on a test of intelligence) provide valuable supplementary evidence. Considerable use is also made of tests seeking to assess aspects of personality, such as the Eysenck Personality Questionnaire (EPQ), Minnesota Multiphasic Personality Inventory (MMPI), and Sixteen Personality Factor test (16PF).

It is crucial that any such tests are professionally competent. One way to achieve this is by picking an existing test 'off the shelf'. The prime source of information on existing British and American tests is the series known as the *Mental Measurement Yearbooks*. These are available commercially in a consolidated form covering yearbooks from 1985 from the Buros Institute from the Internet or on CD (http://www.ovid.com/site/catalog/DataBase/120.jsp). It contains the most recent descriptive information and critical reviews of new and revised tests and covers over 2,000 commercially available tests in categories including personality, developmental, behavioural assessment, neuropsychological, achievement, intelligence, aptitude, speech, hearing and education. It is updated every six months, providing access to new test information and reviews. Details on the reliability and validity of the tests, and the test norms (i.e. the results of standardizing the test by using it with a given sample) are provided, so that you have a comparative baseline to assist in interpreting the scores you obtain.

Goldman and Mitchell (2008) have produced a useful directory of unpublished tests under the auspices of the American Psychological Association. They identify and describe non-commercial scales and tests from the fields of psychology, sociology, and education that have been devised by researchers and published in high ranking journals. A Canadian website from York

University (http://www.yorku.ca/rokada/psyctest/) provides student researchers with easy access to a number of psychological tests. Some are in the public domain, others are in copyright, but the test authors have given their permission to have them downloaded and used by student researchers.

Other strategies you might use in finding an appropriate test include:

- asking colleagues and others working in the same field if they know of anything suitable;
- searching the Internet; and
- consulting the catalogues of test publishers (listed in the *Mental Measurement Yearbooks*). You will have to pay for such tests, including the manual, and there may be restrictions on who can use them.

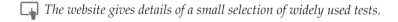 *The website gives details of a small selection of widely used tests.*

The use of computers to cover both the administration of a test and its analysis has become widespread (e.g. Domino & Domino, 2006). Tests with a cumbersome or complex scoring procedure which has previously inhibited their use (such as the MMPI) become much more feasible with computer analysis. It is unlikely to be cost-effective for you to do the development work necessary to use a computer-assisted test for a small one-off research project but there may be opportunities for making use of facilities developed for other purposes. Naglieri *et al.* (2004) give a detailed review of uses of the Internet for psychological testing.

Developing your own test

An alternative is, of course, to develop your own test. Don't do this unless you are prepared to devote considerable time and resources to the exercise. It also means that you lose the opportunity of making comparisons with other studies, which may be feasible when using an existing test. The further reading for the chapter gives references to texts which explain what is involved.

The middle way is to change an existing instrument so that it better fits your needs. This involves less work than starting from scratch but you should remember that the existing reliability, validity and norms will not then apply and will have to be re-established. If the material is copyright, modification will require the permission of the copyright holder. The easiest and most common modification is to shorten the test by omitting items. If data are available from the original development of the test, it may be possible to use them to re-establish validity and reliability. You may alternatively wish to change the response options (e.g. from seven to five alternatives, perhaps to fit in with other questionnaire items). Changes of question wording are tricky, because of the major effects that apparently minor changes can have on responding, but there may be justification in moving from general questions to more specific ones or in modifying a test targeted for one professional group to be appropriate for a different one. In this connection, the use of a sample very different from the one on which the test was standardized will call for new validation of the test.

Tests and scales based on observation rather than self-report

We have dealt in this chapter with a very similar agenda of issues to those faced in the development of a structured direct observation instrument (Chapter 14, p. 332). There are considerable overlaps. In a self-report situation, respondents are effectively acting as observers of their own behaviour. Direct observation by the researcher reduces potential biases and distortions arising from this process but it is obviously limited to those things that can be directly observed. Thoughts and feelings, beliefs and attitudes need self-report. Low-frequency and private behaviours are best approached in this way as they would be expensive and obtrusive to observe directly.

Further reading

The website gives annotated references to further reading for Chapter 13.

CHAPTER 14

Observational methods

> This chapter:
>
> - discusses the advantages and disadvantages of direct observation;
> - considers its role in real world research;
> - focuses on the very different approaches of structured observation and participant observation;
> - analyses different participant observer roles and their implications;
> - considers how to get started as a participant observer;
> - reviews observational biases which have to be taken into account;
> - discusses structured observation and coding schemes;
> - recommends the use of an existing coding scheme whenever feasible;
> - considers the practicalities of recording; and
> - concludes by describing ways of assessing the reliability of structured observation.

Introduction

As the actions and behaviour of people are a central aspect in virtually all real world research, a natural and obvious technique is to watch what they do, to record this in some way and then to describe, analyse and interpret that we have observed. Much research with people involves observation in a general sense. The typical experiment, whether in the laboratory or in the field, incorporates a form of controlled observation. However, we use a rather more restricted definition here, sticking primarily to *direct observation* as carried out by the human observer.

Fundamentally different approaches to the use of observational methods in research have been employed. Two polar extreme types are *participant observation* – an essentially qualitative style, originally rooted in the work of anthropologists and particularly associated with the Chicago School of sociology: and *structured observation* – a quantitative style which has been used in a variety of disciplines. Participant observation is a widely used method in flexible designs, particularly those which follow an ethnographic approach. Structured observation is almost exclusively linked to fixed designs, of both experimental and non-experimental types. Both styles call for a heavy investment of time and effort and should not be used without careful consideration of their resource implications in a real world study.

Concentrating on these two approaches has tended to eclipse a third one which may be styled *unobtrusive observation*. Its defining characteristic is that it is non-participatory in the interests of being *non-reactive*. It can be structured observation but is more usually unstructured and informal.

Advantages of observation

A major advantage of observation as a technique is its directness. You do not ask people about their views, feelings or attitudes; you watch what they do and listen to what they say. Thus, for example, when focusing on the road safety of children at pedestrian light-controlled crossings, observation is the obvious method to use (Zeedyk & Kelly, 2003).

Data from direct observation contrasts with, and can often usefully complement, information obtained by virtually any other technique. Interview and questionnaire responses are notorious for discrepancies between what people say that they have done, or will do, and what they actually did or will do. For example, Auge and Auge (1999) found that the scale of drug use by professional bodybuilders assessed by direct observation substantially exceeded estimates from earlier surveys. In a similar vein, Bendall (2006) reports on a project carried out to test the assumption that there is a relationship between a student nurse's description, on paper, of how she would care for a patient, and the actual observed behaviour. No relationship was found in more than two-thirds of student nurses in 19 hospitals.

As Montaigne, over 400 years ago, observed, 'saying is one thing; doing is another'. These inherent difficulties in the reliability and validity of such data, arising from deficiencies in memory and the wish to present oneself in a favourable light (the 'social desirability response bias') among many other factors, were discussed in Chapter 11, p. pp. 248, 264.

Observation also seems to be pre-eminently the appropriate technique for getting at 'real life' in the real world. It is, of course, possible to observe through one-way glass in a laboratory or clinic or set up some other situation and observe that, but direct observation in the field permits a lack of artificiality which is all too rare with other techniques. It can also reveal substantial differences from observations carried out in more contrived settings (e.g. Handen, McAuliffe, Janosky, Feldman & Breaux, 1998).

Disadvantages

Observation is neither an easy nor a trouble-free option. There is a major issue concerning the extent to which an observer affects the situation under observation, a phenomenon referred to as *reactivity*. McCall (1984, p. 273) considers it to be a common but far from universal feature of observational studies. There are acknowledged tactics for reducing the effect – for example, by seeking to ensure that the observed are unaware of being observed, at one extreme, or by them being so accustomed to the presence of the observer that they carry on as if she were not there, at the other extreme (see Lee, 2000, pp. 46–9 for a discussion of the evidence on this issue).

Gittelson, Shankar, West, Ram and Gnywali (1997), in a study of childcare and feeding practices in rural Nepal, provide empirical evidence on the size of reactivity effects and how they can be controlled.

There is a logical problem here. How do we know what the behaviour would have been like if it hadn't been observed? And, moreover, whether one takes on a very detached or very involved role as an observer, or something in between, there are related methodological and ethical problems. Virtually total detachment can come across as antisocial and itself cause reactions from those observed. To be highly involved risks compromising your researcher role.

A practical problem with observation is that it tends to be very time-consuming. The classic participant observation study, deriving from social anthropology, demands an immersion into the 'tribe' for several years. There is a trend toward a more 'condensed' field experience based on observation (Stenhouse, 1982) which has become popular in applied fields such as education, but this still requires a substantial time commitment. More structured approaches, normally requiring the use of some kind of observation schedule, can reduce the actual observation time substantially, but there is a correspondingly increased time investment required in developing such an instrument from scratch. Even on those rare occasions when an existing observation schedule developed by a previous worker is suited to your task, acquiring proficiency in its use can take much time and effort.

Observation in real world research

Observation, in part because it can take on a variety of forms, can be used for several purposes in a study. It is commonly used in an *exploratory phase*, typically in an unstructured form, to seek to find out what is going on in a situation as a precursor to subsequent testing out of the insights obtained. This could be in one of the multi-strategy designs discussed in Chapter 8 where a second phase collects quantitative data or a flexible design case study where further qualitative data collection follows.

Observation can be used as a *supportive* or *supplementary method* to collect data that may complement or set in perspective data obtained by other means. Suppose that the main effort in a particular study is devoted to one method of data collection, observation might then be used to validate or corroborate the messages obtained by that method. For example, in a study by Marroto, Roos and Victor (2007) of performance in an orchestra, the primary tools of data collection were journals and semi-structured interviews. The first author kept an electronic journal of his observations and reflections following every rehearsal, class and concert, and, in addition, observed and video-taped every rehearsal and concert.

It is not unusual, however, for observation to be the *primary method* in a particular study. When observation is used as the primary method, it is common to support this through interviews (e.g. Andrews & Andrews, 2003; Banks, Shaw & Weiss, 2007; Martin, 2002).

Observation can be combined on an equal footing with a second method as in Weiss, Feliot-Rippeault and Gaud (2007) where, in a study of a French Antarctic station, observation was used together with the administration of a series of structured questionnaires over the period of a year. It can also be used in multi-method case studies or other types of flexible design, where there are additional methods to supplement the observational data. Examples include Burack, Irby, Carline, Root and Larson (1999) in a study of physicians which combined participant observation of rounds, in-depth semi-structured interviews, a structured task involving thinking aloud, and patient chart review; and a case study by Casey (2007) with both structured observation sessions and semi-structured interviews.

Unobtrusive observation also has a potential role in experimental research. By watching what participants do in the experimental situation, it may be possible to gain valuable insights. The use of observation as a technique in survey and other types of non-experimental fixed design research is fairly unusual. Simple structured observational techniques could be used to substitute for, or complement, the widely used interview or questionnaire in some situations.

Approaches to observation

In prospect it may seem very straightforward, but the actual experience of being put in a situation with the instruction: 'Observe!' is daunting even to the experienced researcher. There seems to be either so much, or so little, going on. And how does one characterize and capture it?

As with all research, the driving force behind the use of observation is the research question or questions, even though these may be very broad, general and loosely phrased in an exploratory study. Leading on from this is the type of information which will be most helpful in answering these research question(s). There is a major divide here between *narrative accounts* and *coded schedules*. The former, discussed in Chapter 15, p. 373, are traditionally almost exclusively dependent on single-method qualitative approaches but need not be so. A narrative account can be constructed from quantitative, structured schedule data (see Fetterman, 1998). Coded schedules are covered in detail later in this chapter.

Classifying observational methods

The preceding discussion highlights one important dimension of difference in approaches to observation: the degree of *pre-structure* in the observation exercise. This can be dichotomized as *formal* or *informal observation*. Informal approaches are less structured and allow the observer considerable freedom in what information is gathered and how it is recorded. They would include note-taking and generally gathering information from informants. This kind of information is relatively unstructured and complex and requires the observer to perform difficult tasks of synthesis, abstraction and organization of the data. Formal approaches impose a large amount of structure and direction on what is to be observed. The observer has only to attend to these pre-specified aspects; everything else is considered irrelevant for the purposes of the study. High reliability and validity are easier to achieve with these latter formal approaches but at the cost of a loss of complexity and completeness by comparison with the informal route.

A second dimension, in practice by no means independent of the formality/structure dimension, concerns the *role* adopted by the observer in the situation observed. Specifically, this relates to the extent of *participation* in that situation. As indicated above, we will concentrate here on the two extreme positions on this dimension, where the intention is either to participate fully, effectively to become a part of the group or whatever is being studied, or to be a 'pure' observer, seeking to be an unnoticed part of the wallpaper. These two 'ideal types' carry with them very different methodological and philosophical views about the nature and purposes of observation.

The participant observer will tend to use flexible designs and qualitative, unstructured approaches. The pure observer might use qualitative approaches but has tended towards fixed designs and quantitative, structured methods. The basic difference is – *the pure observer typically uses an observation instrument of some kind, the participant observer is the instrument*.

Participant observation

A key feature of participant observation is that the observer seeks to become some kind of member of the observed group. This involves not only a physical presence and a sharing of life experiences but also entry into their social and 'symbolic' world through learning their social conventions and habits, their use of language and non-verbal communication, and so on. The observer also has to establish some role within the group.

This may sound warning bells of subjectivity and general 'bad science' to those trained in traditional views of experimental design and quantitative analysis. However, it can be argued persuasively that, when working with people, scientific aims can be followed by explaining the meaning of the experiences of the observed through the experiences of the observer. This arises from a perspective that the social world involves subjective meanings and experiences constructed by participants in social situations. The task of interpreting this can only be achieved through participation with those involved.

Whether or not one is prepared to accept this view as recognizably science, it is still possible to use the touchstones established in Chapter 2 as typifying the scientific approach. In particular, the necessary basis of trustworthiness can be achieved. Similarly, objectivity can be approached through a heightened sensitivity to the problem of subjectivity and the need for justification of one's claims. Admittedly, by no means all of the studies published which use participant observation pay serious attention to these canons. Several are more appropriately judged in terms of journalism or literature. This is not intended as a dismissive statement. If the intention is polemical, or to throw light on the human condition, then it would be crass scientific hegemony to claim that science is the only, or the best, means of persuasion or illumination.

There are, however, particular benefits from playing the science game, as already rehearsed. The claim made here is that by giving particular attention to trustworthiness, participant observation, along with other essentially qualitative techniques, can be scientific.

Participant observation, even in an abbreviated version where the involvement is measured in weeks or even days rather than the years of the classical anthropological model, places a considerable burden on the shoulders of the observer. Richards and Postle (1998) discuss these challenges in relation to social work settings. It can be extremely involving as graphically illustrated by Waddington (2004) in a candid account of his doctoral study of a five-month brewery strike.

The primary data are the interpretations by the observer of what is going on around him. The observer *is* the research instrument and hence great sensitivity and personal skills are necessary for worthwhile data. With participant observation, it is difficult to separate out the data collection and analysis phases of an enquiry. Analysis takes place in the middle of data collection and is used to help shape its development. This kind of approach revisits, at the level of method or technique, the issues raised at the level of research strategy when flexible designs were discussed in Chapter 7. Box 14.1 gives an indication of situations where you might consider using participant observation in a small project.

When participant observation might be useful in a small project

1. *With small groups.* You need to be able to get to know virtually all the people involved in a way that would not be feasible in a large group.
2. *For events/processes that take a reasonably short time.* That is, unless you can afford to give up a major slice of your life to the study. Even then the 'information overload' would be horrendous.
3. *For frequent events.* Participant observation is in general more easily handled in situations where there is repetition of the central activities fairly frequently (e.g. it's easier to study an office with a daily routine than a merger between two businesses – though the latter could well incorporate some participant observation within a multi-method case study).
4. *For activities that are accessible to observers.* This is an obvious point, but don't forget that direct observation can be supplemented by interviews or informal discussions with group members.
5. *When your prime motivation is to find out what is going on.* The wealth of information available in a participant observation study is such that you can probably find supporting evidence for virtually any initial hypothesis. Hence it is a dangerous (though seductive) technique for those simply wishing to confirm their prejudgements.
6. *When you are not short of time.* Even a small participant observation study takes up a lot of time, both day-to-day (writing up adequate field notes) and in terms of the 'immersion' you need to get anywhere. It is difficult to budget this time in advance.

For some people, what is referred to in this book as flexible design would be termed participant observation (or even field studies, or qualitative research). My quarrel with these usages is that their 'participant observation' is likely to include other methods in addition to observation, such as interviews and the use of documents and other artefacts; that 'field study' appears to refer to where the study takes place rather than to the kind of study it is; and similarly that 'qualitative' appears to refer to the kind of data collected rather than the methods or strategies used in their collection. However, tradition may well be stronger than logic.

Participant observers can either seek to hide the fact that they are carrying out some kind of research or make it clear from the start what their purpose is in participating. Both roles have their problems, as discussed below.

The complete participant

The complete participant role involves the observer concealing that she is an observer, acting as naturally as possible and seeking to become a full member of the group. Festinger, Riecken and Schachter (1956), in a widely known study, infiltrated a group of persons who believed a prediction of the imminent destruction of the world on a known day. Similar studies have been carried out of criminal fraternities and military training units. Clarke (1996) describes such covert observation in a mental health secure unit claiming to be a therapeutic community and found conflicts between 'carers' and 'controllers' (who saw their role as custodial). In each case a justification for keeping the group in ignorance of the researchers' real purposes was made in terms of the group's likely refusal to cooperate if these purposes were revealed. A subsidiary consideration was that the behaviour under observation would change if it were known that someone was prying into it.

There are obvious and strong ethical objections to this stance. Entering into a situation with the deliberate and planned intention to deceive is regarded as indefensible by many researchers and it is becoming increasingly rare. There are enough problems in carrying out real world research without being saddled with that particular guilt. There are also methodological problems with the complete participant role. The tendency to 'go native' (a problem shared by anthropologists and colonial administrators) is probably greatest when observation and recording have to be covert activities. This refers to the situation where the role you have adopted in the group takes over to the extent that the research perspective is lost. Great care has to be taken that your activities are appropriate to the role or suspicions and consequent distortions may be produced. Postponing recording until one is safely alone heightens the danger of seriously incomplete and selectively biased accounts and there is always the risk that your true purpose will be discovered.

Increasingly, the position taken by Kirby and McKenna (1989) is being adopted:

> It is essential that as a participant who is also a data gatherer, the researcher recognise the obligation to inform those in the setting about the research (i.e. what sort of research it is, for what purposes, and who is involved). Research from a *covert* or *manipulative* perspective is not generally acceptable (p. 78, emphasis in original).

> *These considerations suggest that you should avoid taking on the 'complete participant' role. If it appears impossible to carry out the research were your research purpose revealed, you are strongly recommended to seek the advice of experienced participant observers, and to ensure that your study falls within the appropriate code of conduct (see Chapter 10, p. 208).*

The participant as observer

A feasible alternative is the participant-as-observer role. The fact that the observer *is* an observer is made clear to the group from the start. The observer then tries to establish close relationships with members of the group. This stance means that as well as observing through participating in activities, the observer can ask members to explain various aspects of what is going on. It is important to get the trust of key members of the group (key either because of their position or because of personal qualities such as openness or interest in the ways of the group). Maintaining the dual role of observer and participator is not easy, and acceptance will be heavily dependent on the nature of the group and the interaction of particular features of the observer with the group. Your age, class, gender and ethnic background can be important in particular circumstances.

Intuitively it would appear that this role would have more of a disturbing effect on the phenomena observed than that of the complete participant and several experienced participant observers have documented this (e.g. Whyte, 1984). However, one such effect is that members of the group, particularly key informants, are led to a more analytic reflection about processes and other aspects of the group's functioning. There are situations, for example, in the evaluation of an innovatory programme, where this can be of positive benefit.

One possible strategy for the participant as observer is to *evoke* a particular situation or behaviour from members of the group. Essentially, this involves setting up a situation which has meaning for the group and then observing what happens. There are potential ethical problems here and also the danger of artificiality. The group may perhaps do something, or do something in a different way, to please or placate the 'important' observer. This kind of active involvement borders on carrying out an informal field experiment or, if viewed in a different light, can be seen as a kind of simulation or role play exercise.

It may also be possible to take advantage of the roles ascribed to one in a situation to gather information in a more active fashion. For example, working as a participant observer in some schools, particularly those for younger children or for children with special educational needs, the children commonly view you as something akin to a teacher. They then are not surprised to be quizzed by you on any and every aspect of their school life. Similarly, the researcher in hospitals is likely to be classified as some sub-species of the 'helping and caring' staff, providing potential insights into patient relationships with such staff.

The special case of observing a group of which you are already a member carries obvious advantages and disadvantages. Your knowledge of the group's ways may well be extensive but there is a corresponding problem in achieving anything approaching objectivity if you are already a native. Similarly, existing relationships with individuals can short-circuit a lengthy process of development of trust but it may prove difficult for others to see you in your new role as observer and there may be an artificiality and hesitancy in seeking to get shared understandings explicit and out into the open. In settings where there is a strong hierarchical structure, such as a school or hospital, a higher-status member may look askance at being observed or questioned by a lower-status member.

The marginal participant

In some situations, it may be feasible and advantageous to have a lower degree of participation than that envisaged in the preceding sections. This can be done by adopting the role of a largely passive, though completely accepted, participant – a passenger in a train or bus, or a member of the audience at a concert or sports meeting. Your likely familiarity with such roles helps, but it can also get in the way of the observer role. Conscious attention to active and open-minded observation is needed. Roles permitting note-taking are advantageous (e.g. student in a library, lecture theatre or seminar). Zeisel (2006) warns against assuming that while *you* know what role you are playing, others automatically come to the same conclusion: 'the marginal observer assumes when watching an informal football game in the park that he is taken to be a casual spectator. Meanwhile the football players think he is a park attendant about to tell them to stop playing on the grass' (p. 198).

Careful attention to dress and behaviour can help with such problems. 'Props' can be useful, such as bringing along your own child if you are observing in a children's playground (an increasingly sensitive context for carrying out a research project given concerns about lurking paedophiles). Zeisel also suggests that you can test assumptions about how you are perceived by others by slightly changing your normal behaviour to see how people in the situation respond.

Some marginal roles are effectively indistinguishable from that of the 'complete observer' – someone who does not take part in the activity, and whose status as a researcher is unknown to the participants.

The observer-as-participant

This is someone who takes no part in the activity but whose status as researcher is known to the participants. Such a state is aspired to by many researchers using systematic observation. However, it is questionable whether anyone who is known to be a researcher can be said not to take part in the activity – in the sense that their role is now one of the roles within the larger group that includes the researcher.

Getting started as a participant observer

Actually getting into, and getting to be a part of, the group that you are interested in can loom large as a problem. There is a real worry that you might 'blow it' by unintentional insensitivity or crassness. Anthropology abounds with horror stories of choosing as one's sponsor someone disliked or mistrusted by the rest of the group. Barley (1989) provides an engaging account of these issues. If, as may well be the case, you already have links with the group, there may be pre-existing trust which gets you in.

There are differing views as to how much work you should have done before starting observation. The classic view of many researchers using participant observation, typified by Whyte (1951), is that the theory should emerge from the observation and that hence you need a minimum of initial theoretical orientation. In participant observation, our central research questions are likely to be 'hows': How does the teacher control the class? How does a committee come to decisions? Clues about these things should be gathered during and as a result of the observation. The 'whats' and the 'whys', primarily factual things like the context, details of the setting and its history, can profitably be found out ahead of time.

The immersion process of actually getting 'into' the group can be both confusing and stressful. Have faith – what may initially seem to be total chaos will, with time, reveal pattern, structure and regularity. The tinted pages in *Part IV* on 'Arranging the practicalities' (p. 395) cover, in general terms, some of the things you need to sort out before getting started on data collection.

Collecting data

The basic task of the participant observer is to observe the people in the group, unit, organization or whatever is the focus of the research, while being involved with them. Accounts may also be collected from informants. However, to give form and precision to the data, the observer often has to *ask questions* about the situation and the accounts that are given. These are both questions to oneself, and, more sparingly, explicit questions to group members.

This may seem to go against the notion of direct observation and be more akin to interviewing. The distinction is blurred but in participant observation you are much less likely to have 'set piece' interviews and much more likely to have opportunistic 'on the wing' discussions or informal interviews with individuals. None the less, interviewing skills are very useful to the participant observer (see Chapter 12).

It is common practice to start with *descriptive observation*. The basic aim here is to describe the setting, the people and the events that have taken place. Spradley (1980) distinguishes nine dimensions on which this descriptive data may be collected, explained below in Box 14.2. An early task is to develop a detailed portrait using this descriptive approach. This is the initial *story* or *narrative account* based on the events with which you have been involved. There is a similarity here to the approach of the investigative journalist who is after the 'story'. The Chicago School, which pioneered the serious use of participant observation within sociology, had direct roots in journalism. The big difference between the researcher and the journalist (assuming that the latter is wanting to do a responsible job and trying to get to the bottom of the story) is that the researcher has to go beyond the story. This next stage involves developing a set of concepts, a theoretical framework, properly grounded in the detail of the story, which helps you to understand, and explain to others, what is going on.

Particular dimensions may loom large in some studies. Considering these dimensions, in the light of the research questions which led you to choose this group or setting in the first instance, is likely to lead to a greater focusing of the questions. This *focused observation* might be on a specific dimension or dimensions or on themes which cross the dimensions. For example, Burgess (1983), in a study of a comprehensive school, used his descriptive observations, within a general theoretical framework derived from symbolic interactionism, to focus his questions on such topics as:

How do teachers define the Newsom course? How do pupils define and re-define the course? What strategies, negotiations and bargains are used by the teachers and pupils? To what extent do activities in the Newsom department influence work within the core courses which Newsom pupils attend? (p. 209)

BOX 14.2

Dimensions of descriptive observation

1. *Space*. Layout of the physical setting; rooms, outdoor spaces, etc.
2. *Actors*. The names and relevant details of the people involved.
3. *Activities*. The various activities of the actors.
4. *Objects*. Physical elements, furniture, etc.
5. *Acts*. Specific individual actions.
6. *Events*. Particular occasions, e.g. meetings.
7. *Time*. The sequence of events.
8. *Goals*. What actors are attempting to accomplish.
9. *Feelings*. Emotions in particular contexts.

(after Spradley, 1980)

The terms, such as 'negotiation', 'strategy' and 'bargain', led him to an understanding of the concepts which were used by the participants to come to terms with the situations in which they were located (see Burgess, 1983, pp. 115–35 for an extended discussion).

Stated in somewhat more formal terms, the process involved in participant observation has been regarded as an example of *analytic induction* (Johnson, 2004). This is summarized in Box 14.3.

> *Observation and analysis are intertwined here. This is characteristic of flexible designs (which are likely to use participant observation) as discussed in Chapter 7. There is more detailed coverage of the analysis of the qualitative data produced through participant observation in Chapter 18.*

Recording in participant observation

In principle, the fact that one is a participant does not preclude or prescribe any approach to recording, providing that the group knows and accepts that you have this role and the task of observer. However, some approaches, for example, the use of taping, could inhibit the group and your participation in its activities. It may be the case that a group *for its own purposes* wishes to have its activities observed and analysed (possibly stimulated in this desire by your presence in their midst as a researcher – a beneficial 'Hawthorne'-like effect). In this case your role in participating is that of observer.

By the nature of the activity, it is not possible to be prescriptive about the recording of unstructured observation, even if this were desirable. Issues to do with the use of recording devices (audio cassette recorders and, possibly, video cameras, mobile phones and video recorders) are the same as those discussed in the context of interviews in Chapter 12. Box 14.4 discusses some of the issues involved.

BOX 14.3

The process of analytic induction

1. Formulate a rough definition of the phenomenon of interest.
2. Put forward an initial hypothetical explanation of this phenomenon.
3. Study a situation in the light of this hypothesis, to determine whether or not the hypothesis fits.
4. If the hypothesis does not fit the evidence, then *either* the hypothesis must be reformulated *or* the phenomenon to be explained must be redefined so that the phenomenon is excluded.
5. Repeat with a second situation. Confidence in your hypothesis increases with the number of situations fitting the evidence. Each negative one requires either a redefinition or a reformulation.

Note: Situations should be selected to maximize the chances of discovering a decisive one. In this way weaknesses are more quickly exposed. 'Situation' is used as a general term to indicate an instance, phenomenon, case, aspect (or whatever) that is observed.

BOX 14.4

Issues in recording participant observation

1. Even with the most unstructured observation, it is crucial to have a system which allows you to capture information unambiguously and as faithfully and fully as possible.

2. Where possible, records are made of observations *on the spot, during the event*. These may be very condensed, using abbreviations, etc. Their main purpose is to remind you of what happened when you are writing up detailed notes. They function as what are known in life history research as 'memory sparkers': who was there; any unusual details of the physical scene; important/interesting verbatim comments; incongruencies (it may help to ask yourself questions: 'Why did he do that?' etc.).

3. The record must, as a matter of routine, be gone through shortly afterwards to add detail and substance and to ensure that it is understandable and says what you intended it to say.

4. Getting this full record right may take as long as the original observation did. Lofland, Lofland, Snow, Anderson and Lofland (2006, pp. 112–15) suggest the following guidelines:
   - *Be concrete.* Give specific, concrete, descriptions of events – who is involved, conversations, etc; and when they occurred. Keep any inferences out (e.g. A was trying to get B to . . .).
   - *Distinguish comments from members.* Not only who made the comment but also whether it is an exact recall or you are just giving the substance.
   - *Recalls of forgotten material.* Things that come back to you later. Anything you forgot or later realize as meriting a record.
   - *Interpretive idea.* Notes offering an initial analysis of the situation as they occur to you. You need both notes addressing the research question and ones which will add supportive or elaborative material.
   - *Personal impressions and feelings.* Your subjective reactions.
   - *Reminder to look for additional information.* Reminder to check with A about B, take a look at C, etc.

   You will need a system to mark and separate out these different types of material (e.g. round brackets, square brackets, double brackets, etc.).

5. 'Lap-top' or 'palm-top' computers can be very effective in producing these records actually in the field. In any case, there is considerable advantage in getting the record on to a computer using word-processing or specialist text analysis software. This enables multiple copies of typescripts to be generated easily, for recording and analysis purposes, or the computer file can be analysed directly.

6. If you feel that this on-the-spot recording interferes with your observation or alternatively when your participating role gets in the way, then notes should be made as soon as feasible afterwards. It may be worthwhile developing facility in the use of a mnemonic system (e.g. Evans, 2007; Higbee, 2001) which can have a dramatic effect on the number of items recallable. Inevitably, however, notes made after the event are subject to greater distortion, particularly when there are intervening events.

7. A good basic rule is that you should always prepare the detailed notes of the full report within 24 hours of the field session and certainly never embark on a second observation session until you are sure that you have sorted out your notes for the first one.

Observational biases

The human instrument as used in participant observation has a lot going for it. It is very flexible and can deal with complex and 'fuzzy' situations which give even powerful computers a headache. It does have deficiencies as an instrument, though. Knowing what distortions and biases we are likely to introduce in our observation should help in counteracting them.

Such effects are the stock-in-trade of many psychologists in the fields of memory, perception and social interaction, although the extent to which there is transfer of this knowledge to colleagues engaging in observational tasks is questionable. The following is very much a layperson's guide to a complex area:

- *Selective attention.* All perceptual processes involving the taking in of information by observation and its subsequent internal processing are subject to bias. Attention – the concentration on some aspects of our surroundings rather than others – is an essential feature of coping with the overwhelming complexity of those surroundings. Our *interests, experience* and *expectations* all affect what we attend to. Features of the situation we are observing will also have differential salience, i.e. some are likely to stand out and be more likely to be attended to. At a simple level, if you can see a person's face, then you are more likely to attend to what they say than to someone with their back to you. The basic message is to *make a conscious effort to distribute your attention widely and evenly.* There are sampling techniques, commonly used in systematic observation, which can assist you to do this and which could be used in some participant observation situations without doing violence to the approach.
- *Selective encoding.* Expectations inevitably colour what you see, and in turn affect the encoding and interpretation of this. This is a rapid, usually unconscious, set of processes and hence difficult to guard against. Related to this is the 'rush to judgement' where something is categorized on the basis of initial and very partial information. Later information, which might have been used to modify the judgement, is as a result not taken into account. Hence, *try to start with an open mind – and keep it open.*
- *Selective memory.* The longer you wait after the event in constructing a narrative account, the poorer such an account will be in terms of its accuracy and completeness; and the more it will be in line with your pre-existing schemas and expectations. The moral is clear. *Write up field notes into a narrative account promptly.*
- *Interpersonal factors.* In the early stages of a participant observation, because of your own insecurity and other factors, you may focus on, and interact with, only a few of the group members, probably those who seem welcoming and easy to get on with. This is probably inevitable but carries with it the potential for bias. Those who welcome you may do so because they don't get on with other members of the group. Perhaps they are marginal or disaffected members. As you get to know more about the group, you should be able to avoid this but there is still the danger of your developing relationships with the more friendly and helpful members affecting your picture of the whole. There are still the likely biasing effects of your own presence. The general strategy is to *seek to recognize and discount all biases.*

Smith (1982) suggests ways in which new field workers may be trained to recognize and reduce such biases.

The website gives references to examples of research using participant observation.

Structured observation

Readers who worry about such things will appreciate that making the divide in this chapter between 'participant' and 'structured' observation lacks a little in logic. The former covers the dimension of the observer's participation in the situation, the latter the degree of structure that is used in observation. As discussed previously, participant observers have primarily used qualitative techniques, and in some senses their work could be labelled unstructured or unsystematic. However, to our ears at least, this carries a somewhat pejorative tone which we consider to be unwarranted. In fact, good participant observation *is* systematic but more in terms of the logical inference system used than the degree of pre-structure of observational categories. It is, of course, possible to have non-participant observation which is unstructured. The *ethological approach* (Tinbergen, 1963; Burkhardt, 2005), for example, starts with careful, exploratory, observation seeking a detailed and comprehensive description of the animal's (or human's) behaviour.

Structured observers tend to take a detached, 'pure observer', stance. For them, structured observation is a way of quantifying behaviour. There have been important developments in the use of quantitative systematic observation which deserve wider recognition (e.g. Sackett, 1978; Bakeman & Gottman, 1997).

Coding schemes

Coding schemes contain predetermined categories for recording what is observed. They range from simply noting whether or not a particular behaviour has occurred, to complex multi-category systems. Other forms of structured observation are possible – you can, for example, ask observers for global ratings of what they have seen over the whole of a session (or even based on an extended period). Barlow, Hayes and Nelson (1984, pp. 134–8) give examples. Such global ratings are effectively rating scales, and are dealt with in Chapter 13, p. 307.

> *The key features of much structured observation are the development of a coding scheme, and its use by trained observers.*

The start is, as always, from some research question. Researchers then need to define important concepts and devise ways in which they can be measured. And of course they need to concern themselves with reliability and validity. An essential feature is that the reliability of the measuring instrument used, the coding scheme, depends crucially on the skills of the observer. Hence a major, and often very time-consuming, task is to train observers so that they produce essentially the same set of codes when confronted with a particular instance or sequence of behaviour.

Achieving adequate inter-observer reliability is primarily a technical matter, calling for a knowledge of the characteristics of a usable coding scheme and adequate time spent in training observers. It may be worth stressing the likely congeniality of structured observational work to the frustrated experimentalist, yearning for the relative certainties and simplified complexities of laboratory-based experimental work and thwarted by the exigencies of the real world. The 'instrument makers' have now developed this type of observational methodology to a fine art, particularly in connection with sequential interaction.

Checklists and category systems

A distinction is sometimes made between observation systems based on checklists and those based on category systems. Rob Walker (1985) uses the term 'category system' for 'systems that, unlike checklists, use a relatively small number of items, each of which is more general than a typical checklist item, but which attempts to use the system to maintain some sort of more-or-less continuous record' (p. 136). Checklists are seen as providing a long series of items which can be recorded as present or absent. The distinction is blurred in many cases and the general term 'coding scheme' will be used here.

Experimentation and coding schemes

Structured observation is commonly used in experiments, particularly in obtaining measures on the dependent variable(s). Simple coding schemes are likely to be used. It is not unusual for the 'observation' to be carried out by an automatic device (e.g. a microswitch which detects a par-ticular kind of behaviour, such as whether or not a child is sitting at a desk).

Possible bases for a coding scheme

We have to decide what type of activity is going to be observed. A widely used system, which seems to be adaptable to a range of research questions, is derived from Weick (1968). It is summarized in Box 14.5.

BOX 14.5

Possible bases for the development of codes

There is a wide range of possibilities, including:

1. *Non-verbal behaviours*. Bodily movements not associated with language.
2. *Spatial behaviours*. The extent to which individuals move towards or away from others.
3. *Extra-linguistic behaviours*. Covers aspects of verbal behaviour other than the words themselves. This includes speaking rates, loudness and tendency to interrupt or be interrupted.
4. *Linguistic behaviours*. Covers the actual content of talking and its structural characteristics.

(Smith, 1991, pp. 298–306, provides examples of the use of these dimensions.)

Observer effects

Moving away from the laboratory, with its comforting screens and one-way mirrors, tends to leave the observer exposed to the observed. The extent of this exposure depends on the setting, the group involved and the research task. It is probably not too difficult to carry out unobserved systematic observation in the stands of a soccer ground, if one can select a good vantage point, even without access to the high-definition police video camera carrying out its own observation task. It is well-nigh impossible to achieve the same degree of invisibility in a secondary school classroom.

However, even when it is possible to carry out a study without the knowledge of the observed, ethical issues could well be involved once more. These are largely a matter of common sense and of consideration of the principles underlying 'codes of practice' (see Chapter 10, p. 208). If a multi-strategy design or multi-method approach is used, where structured observation is supplemented by the use of other methods, then, given that the other available methods tend almost always to depend on the knowledge and cooperation of the persons involved, we have a practical reason for disclosure to support the ethical one.

Once the observed persons know that this is happening, then the observer is, inevitably, to some extent a participant in the situation and the observation becomes potentially reactive (i.e. potentially changing the thing observed). The two main strategies used to minimize such 'observer effects' are *minimal interaction* with the group, and *habituation* of the group to the observer's presence. Minimal interaction is achieved through such obvious strategies as avoiding eye contact, the use of simple behavioural techniques such as not reinforcing attempts at interaction from the group (e.g. by smiling or otherwise responding positively when they do this) and planning your position in the environment to be 'out of the way'. Habituation involves one's repeated presence in the setting so that, particularly when you are an unrewarding, minimal interactor, it is no longer noticed.

It is never logically possible to be completely sure that your presence has not in some way changed what you are seeking to observe but there are several indicants which provide some reassurance:

- The pattern of interaction stabilizes over sessions.
- Different observers code essentially identical patterns for different sessions.
- Members of the group appear to accept your presence to the extent that they do not seek interaction.
- Group members say that your presence doesn't affect what is going on. It is helpful here to check this with different 'constituencies' present. A teacher may say that nothing has changed whereas pupils may claim that lessons are better prepared.

It is worth noting that in some circumstances an essentially non-interacting observer may be of more continuing interest and disturbance than one who gives a friendly smile or nod from time to time. It may also be more 'natural' and less disturbing to take up an explicit role in the situation. In work in special school classrooms, for example, we have found it profitable sometimes to take the role of 'teaching assistant', thus providing a natural entrée to interaction with the child about events in the classroom, while not precluding periods of busy, non-interacting, systematic observation.

Deciding on a coding scheme

As with participant observation, it is likely that the first phase of a study which ends up using structured observation will be exploratory and that this exploration will occur prior to the choice of a coding scheme. The need for a coding scheme arises when it has been decided (at least tentatively) that structured observation, probably alongside other techniques, is to be used. The research question(s) will (after a period of unstructured observation and, probably, gathering supporting information from other sources such as interviews and questionnaires) suggest how the processes you wish to study might be captured by various observational categories.

In certain circumstances it may be appropriate to start, as it were, even further back than this: that is, to regard the initial exploratory observation sessions as essentially fulfilling a *hypothesis generation* function. The style advocated for this phase is essentially the 'analytic induction' approach (see above, p. 329).

The use of existing coding schemes

Given that the development of a coding scheme is a difficult and time-consuming task and that there are already in existence a multiplicity of such schemes, one solution seems obvious: take one off the shelf. Furthermore, the concern sometimes expressed that researchers often seem more interested in paddling their own canoes rather than doing their bit by adding another brick to the grand collective scientific enterprise indicates that more replication of studies would not go amiss.

However, the position advocated here, which is the mainstream methodological view, is that the research question comes first. Sort that out, and refine it through pilot work; that then leads you to the specification of the coding scheme. You may well find considerable difficulty in getting hold of an existing coding scheme that does the job you want it to.

This should not, however, stop you from seeking one using the search techniques discussed in Chapter 3, p. 52. Even if any instruments you come across are not directly usable, you are likely to get valuable ideas about different possible approaches. Box 14.6 shows the widely used system devised by Flanders (1970) for analysing teacher and pupil behaviour in the classroom. Of the ten categories, seven refer to aspects of teacher talk, and two to student or pupil talk, with the tenth being a 'residual' category. An interval coding system is used where coders are expected to code every three seconds. Figure 14.1 shows a typical recording sheet. Each row represents one minute of time (20, 3-second intervals) and hence the sample would allow for 10 minutes of coding. The first 5 minutes have been completed, illustrating the fact that the appropriate category has to be inserted in the matrix for each coding interval. This obviously requires the coder to have fully memorized and internalized the coding system.

This system has been used in a very large number of studies (see examples in Wragg, 1999; also Atkinson, 1975, which illustrates some of its disadvantages) and attempts have been made to categorize classrooms through a variety of indices which can be derived from the analysis. These include proportions of teacher talk to student talk, the extent to which pupils initiate interactions (category 9 as a proportion of all pupil talk), etc. The very short time interval makes this what is termed a 'quasi-continuous' schedule; 3 seconds is seen as short compared with the

BOX 14.6

Categories used in Flanders' Interaction Analysis (IA) System

1. *Teacher accepts student feeling.* Accepts and clarifies an attitude or the feeling tone of a pupil in a non-threatening manner. Feelings may be positive or negative. Predicting and recalling feelings are included.
2. *Teacher praises student.* Praises or encourages pupil action or behaviour. Jokes that release tension, but not at the expense of another individual; nodding head, or saying, 'Mm hm?' or 'Go on' are included.
3. *Teacher use of student ideas.* Clarifying, building or developing ideas suggested by a pupil. Teacher extensions of pupil ideas are included but as the teacher brings more of his ideas into play, switch to category 5.
4. *Teacher questions.* Asking a question about content or procedure, based on teacher ideas, with the intention that a pupil will answer.
5. *Teacher lectures.* Giving facts or opinions about content or procedures; expressing *his* own ideas, giving *his* own explanation, or citing an authority other than a pupil.
6. *Teacher gives directions.* Directions, commands or orders to which a pupil is expected to comply.
7. *Teacher criticizes student.* Statements intended to change pupil behaviour from non-acceptable to acceptable pattern; bawling someone out; stating why the teacher is doing what he is doing; extreme self-reference.
8. *Student response.* Talk by pupils in response to teacher. Teacher initiates the contact or solicits pupil statement or structures the situation. Freedom to express own ideas is limited.
9. *Student-initiated response.* Talk by pupils which they initiate. Expressing own ideas; initiating a new topic; freedom to develop opinions and a line of thought, like asking thoughtful questions; going beyond the existing structure.
10. *Silence or confusion.* Pauses, short periods of silence and periods of confusion in which communication cannot be understood by the observer.

(from Flanders, 1970, p. 34)

Minute																							
1	5	5	5	5	5	5	5	5	4	4	4	8	8	2	3	3	3	3	5				
2	5	5	5	6	6	6	6	8	8	1	1	6	6	0	0	7	7	7	7	7			
3	5	5	5	5	5	5	5	5	5	5	5	5	5	5	5	5	5	5	5	5			
4	5	5	0	0	0	0	7	7	0	0	7	7	4	4	4	4	8	8	3	3			
5	4	4	4	8	8	2	2	2	3	3	3	5	5	5	5	9	9	7	7	7			
6																							
7																							
8																							
9																							
10																							

Figure 14.1 Sample recording sheet for Flanders interaction analysis.

processes that go on in classrooms. A particular use has been the study of 'interaction matrices' looking at pairs of observations, where the matrix shows how many times a particular type of utterance is followed by other types.

Developing your own scheme

The use of an initial exploratory observational stage in helping to clarify and focus your research questions has been described above. The first version of the coding scheme which emerges from this process should incorporate those behaviours and distinctions which you think are important in providing answers to these questions. It is not possible to give a 'cook book' set of procedures for this process. However Box 14.7 suggests a number of things which may be of help, and Box 14.8 gives an example.

BOX 14.7

Considerations in developing a coding scheme

If there is an existing scheme which appears appropriate, consider using or adapting it.
    The categories should be devised to provide information relevant to the research questions in which you are interested (your preliminary exploratory observation should help in clarifying the question). To be straightforward and reliable in use it will help if they are:

1. *Focused.* Only looking at carefully selected aspects of what is going on. Simply because you can observe it doesn't mean that you have to code it. Ask yourself, 'What use will the data be?'
2. *Objective.* Requiring little inference from the observer.
3. *Non context-dependent.* The observer's task is more difficult if the category to be used in coding an event depends on the context in which it occurs (however, if such contextual information is essential to answer the research question, then the observer will have to live with it).
4. *Explicitly defined.* Through a detailed definition of each category, with examples (both of what falls within the category and what doesn't).
5. *Exhaustive.* Covering all possibilities so that it is always possible to make a coding (to be compatible with (1) above it may be necessary to have a large 'residual' or 'dump' category).
6. *Mutually exclusive.* A single category for each thing coded (if the system has both (5) and (6) characteristics it is commonly referred to as an MEE system – a Mutually Exclusive and Exhaustive System). Note, however, that in some situations it may be simpler to have an event categorized multiple times.
7. *Easy to record.* Just ticking a box rather than requiring recall of which of a large number of categories to use. Observers will, though, need to be completely familiar with the category system if they are to use it properly.

BOX 14.8

Example of use of observational schedule

Barton, Baltes and Orzech (1980) studied naturally occurring interactions between staff and residents in a home for the elderly. They developed an observational schedule with five categories:

Independent behaviour. A resident's carrying out of *bathing, dressing, eating, grooming or toileting tasks (or parts of such tasks) without assistance. Can be self-initiated or initiated by others.*

Dependent behaviour. A resident's request for, or acceptance of, *assistance in bathing, dressing, eating, grooming or toileting.*

Independence-supportive behaviour. Staff verbal encouragement of, or praise for, a resident's execution of personal maintenance tasks without help; *and* staff discouragement of, or scolding for, a resident's request for assistance or non-attempts of execution of self-maintenance tasks.

Dependence-supportive behaviour. Staff assistance in a resident's personal maintenance, praise for a resident's acceptance; *and* discouragement of a resident's attempts to execute personal maintenance tasks without help.

Other behaviour. Staff or resident behaviour that is not related to personal maintenance tasks.

(*Source*: Barton *et al.*, 1980)

It may be useful to have more than one coding scheme in a study. Bryman (1989, pp. 207–9) describes an influential study of managerial work by Mintzberg (1973) which used three: a *chronological record*, categorizing the types of activities in the manager's working day, and their beginning and end times; a *mail record*, covering the nature of mail received, how it is dealt with, and the mail generated (this is largely a documentary analysis but involves observational coding of the kind of attention given to each item of mail – read, skimmed, etc.); and a *contact record*, detailing the meetings, calls and tours of the chronology record, categorizing their purposes and initiators.

 The website gives references to examples of research using structured observation schedules.

Coding sequences of behaviour

Your use of the scheme depends on the type of data you wish to collect. This in turn depends on the research questions you are seeking to answer.

It may be that simple frequency measures will suffice. This is adequate if all that is necessary is to compare frequencies, say, the relative frequencies of staff's 'dependence-supportive' and 'independence-supportive' behaviours when using Barton *et al.*'s (1980) schedule. However, in many studies the concern is when, and under what circumstances, different behaviours occur. Is residents' independence behaviour followed by staff independence-supportive behaviour? Is staff reliance on dependence-supportive behaviour associated with trends in residents' behaviour? Because of this common need for sequence information, the rest of this section focuses on the use of coding schemes for observing behaviour sequences.

A central issue concerns the 'unit' which is to be coded. The two main alternatives are to base this either on *time* or on an *event*. In the former, a particular time interval is coded (e.g. as 'child talking to mother'). In the latter, observers wait for a particular event to occur and note what type of event it was. One can also distinguish between 'momentary events' and 'behavioural states'. Momentary events are relatively brief and separate events (such as a child's smile) and the likely interest is in when they occur, and how frequently. Behavioural states are events of appreciable duration (such as a baby sleeping) and in addition to 'when', and 'how often', the likely concern is with 'for how long'. Obviously there is not a strict dichotomy between the two – all events take some time to complete. Technically it is now straightforward, using event recorders, or computers effectively functioning as event recorders, to store the times of occurrence of momentary events, and the start and end times of behavioural states.

Event coding

Events can be recorded in a variety of ways. Essentially the observer responds whenever the event occurs, using either pencil and paper, or some more complex recording instrument. Alternatives are shown in Figure 14.2. Tallying events with a simple checklist will often be sufficient. It provides frequency data, both in absolute terms (i.e. how many times each event has occurred) and relatively (i.e. the relative frequency of different events). The sequence record adds the order in which different events occur, hence providing information about transitions (i.e. which events follow which). Adding a time line gives information about the time interval between similar events and times for the various transitions. It obviously contains within it the

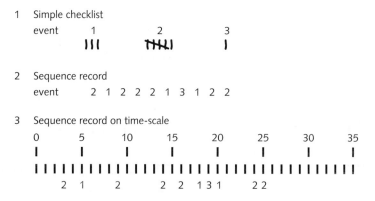

Figure 14.2 Alternative ways of coding events.

simple sequence information, and the frequency information can be computed from both the last two records so it could be argued that there is virtue in always recording both sequence and time. However, this does give the observer a more complex task and the general principle is still that the type of recording should be determined by what information is needed to answer the research questions.

State coding

While simple checklists and sequence records (usually indicating 'change of state' – e.g. from 'asleep' to 'awake') may sometimes be useful, it is usual to include time information giving the duration of particular states. Electronic recording devices make it straightforward to record start (onset) and finish (offset) times for the states being coded. This information produces a record equivalent to that shown in Figure 14.3. In practice, the onset of a particular state will probably be coded by pressing a key or button on a keyboard, and its offset in a similar way.

Many coding schemes have codes which are *mutually exclusive and exhaustive (MEE)*. This means that the definitions of states are such that if one state occurs, it is not logically possible for this to be so at the same time as any other state occurs (mutual exclusion); and that the total set of possible states covers all eventualities (exhaustiveness). Such MEE schemes have considerable advantages when it comes to analysis. Box 14.9 gives a simple example.

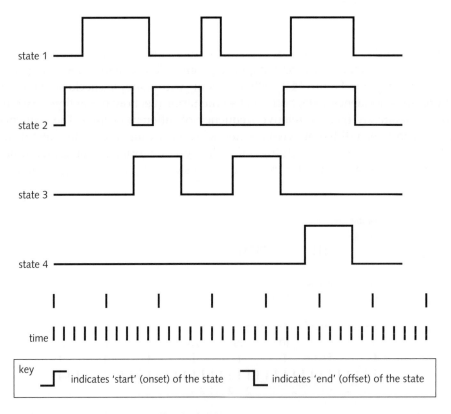

Figure 14.3 Record of 'onset' and 'offset' of states.

BOX 14.9

Example of a simple mutually exclusive and exhaustive coding scheme

State 1: child 1 talks; child 2 silent
State 2: child 1 silent; child 2 talks
State 3: both child 1 and child 2 talk
State 4: both child 1 and child 2 silent

For recording, there is also the practical advantage that only 'onset' times need be recorded – as each 'onset' necessarily means the 'offset' of some other state (illustrated in Figure 14.4).

Interval coding

Interval coding is triggered by time rather than by events. The observation period is divided into a number of intervals, say of 10 or 15 seconds in duration. The job of the observer is to note down information about what happened during the interval. This can be done in various ways, but a common strategy is to code with the category which best represents what occurred during that

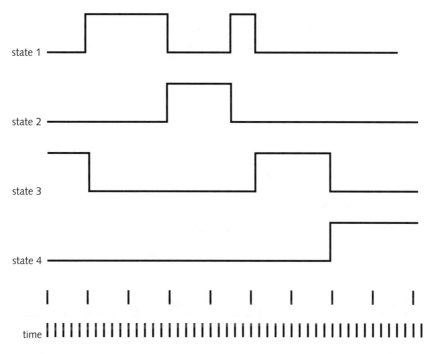

Figure 14.4 Record of 'onset' and 'offset' of mutually exclusive and exhaustive states.

interval (e.g. the most frequent event, or the dominant state – the state present during the greater part of the interval). This can be coded with pencil and paper using a simple sequence record (as in Figure 14.2 above) or a specially designed sheet incorporating the time intervals can be used (as in Figure 14.5 below). More complicated schemes may be called for. A commonly used variation is to have different types of coding for different time intervals. For example, general coding is carried out for five successive 10-second intervals, and the next 10 seconds is used is a different way (say, counting the number of children in the group who are 'on task').

This type of interval coding can be made easier to carry out by means of a 'bug in the ear'. That is, a simple device which gives a click audible only to the observer at the end of each interval. Special pieces of equipment are available for this purpose, but it is a simple matter to use a cassette recorder on which the time intervals have been recorded, together with an earpiece. It is also possible to record additional *aide-mémoire* information on the tape to help the observer.

Interval coding, though widely used, is not without its critics. Distortion can be introduced into the data if the interval chosen is not shorter than the shortest duration typically encountered for a codable state. Bakeman and Gottman's advice is that:

> when simplicity and low cost of instrumentation matter more than accuracy, or when the interval is shorter than most codable events and observers prefer checking or categorizing intervals to recording onset times, then an interval coding strategy probably makes sense. For all other cases, some variant of event coding should probably be used (Bakeman & Gottman, 1997, pp. 48–9).

Time sampling

In time sampling, some principle is used to select the time intervals during which coding takes place. These are interspersed with intervals where there is no coding (or a different form of coding, as in the example given in the preceding section). The principle may be random – random

time interval

category	1	2	3	4	5	6	7	8	9	10	11	12	13	14	15
1											✓	✓	✓	✓	✓
2	✓				✓										
3		✓	✓	✓											
4						✓	✓	✓							
5										✓					
6															
7									✓						
8															

Figure 14.5 Coding sheet for interval coding (pencil and paper).

number tables, or some other system (see p. 341) can be used to select the time intervals in seconds, minutes or whatever, from, say, the end of one coding interval to the start of the next. Or some regular sequence may be used – say 5 minutes 'on' followed by 15 minutes 'off'. This approach is sometimes used when the 'off' non-observing intervals are used actually to make the recording.

Careful thought must be given to assessing whether the type of sampling used leads to a representative picture of the phenomenon under observation. General sampling principles, as discussed in Chapter 11, p. 276, apply. Time sampling can be a useful and efficient way of measuring how much time is spent within the various categories of the coding scheme. It is likely to be a poor way of collecting sequential information, however, because of the gaps between observation periods.

Cross-classifying events

In situations where you have acquired a substantial appreciation of what is going on and hence are in a position to focus your observation sharply on certain kinds of events, an alternative approach to classification may be valuable.

Suppose you are interested in what happens when a child misbehaves in the classroom – say when he takes something from another child. Observers might be asked to note not only the occurrence of this behaviour, but specific aspects of what the two children were doing immediately before the incident; what kind of a disturbance occurred; and how it was settled. If mutually exclusive and exhaustive sets of codes can be devised for each of these phases, it becomes possible to *cross-classify* this event. Analysis can then subsequently show what is likely to lead to what and hence aid in its understanding.

Reliability and structured observation

When using structured observation, the observation schedule *as used by the observer* is the instrument and an important question is: 'How good an instrument?' Reliability and validity raise their heads once more. Validity concerns are essentially similar to those raised by any method of investigation (as discussed in Chapter 6, p. 105), but an assessment of the reliability of data obtained from structured observational schedules has attracted particular specialist approaches.

Problems occur if the observer-instrument shows variation at different times, or if different observer-instruments vary from each others. Hence there are two kinds of reliability; *intra-observer reliability* (sometimes called *observer consistency*) and *inter-observer reliability* (or *inter-observer agreement*).

Observer consistency

This is the extent to which an observer obtains the same results when measuring the same behaviour on different occasions (e.g. when coding the same audio- or video-tape at an interval of a week).

Inter-observer agreement

This is the extent to which two or more observers obtain the same results when measuring the same behaviour (e.g. when independently coding the same tape).

It is highly desirable to have more than one observer in any study involving structured observation. With a single observer, even if she shows high consistency, it may be that she is using the observation schedule in a totally idiosyncratic fashion. Demonstrating good inter-observer agreement defends against this and indeed goes some way towards showing validity. Even if a study is predominantly single-observer, it is often possible to enlist the help of a colleague who will devote the time necessary to learn to use the schedule and observe a proportion of the sessions to be coded.

Both observer consistency and inter-observer agreement are measured by the same means. Several indices have been developed. They involve the calculation either of the degree of correlation between the two sets of measurements or of the agreement (sometimes called concordance) between them. Bakeman and Gottman (1997) feel that this kind of agreement is generally valuable, particularly in sequential analyses involving coding over time. They advocate the use of concordance measures, such as Cohen's Kappa, which correct for chance agreement. There would be advantages in comparing results obtained in different studies and with different instruments if there were some standardization in this area. Bakeman and Gottman (1997, pp. 62–4) give an extended discussion with examples and further references.

Construction of a 'confusion matrix' showing the pattern of agreements and disagreements between two observers on a two-dimensional matrix shows very clearly where the two observers are differing in their judgement. This can be valuable at the training stage to highlight these confusions. It may be that further training is needed or that some attention has to be given to the definitions of the categories.

The website provides detailed instructions for measuring inter-observer agreement.

With some coding schedules, the 'units' being coded are non-problematic and different observers will have no problems in recognizing them. Suppose you simply have to categorize each complete contribution that a child and an adult make to a conversation. It is easy to determine whether it is the child or the adult speaking – the difficulty comes when you have to decide how to code that utterance. However, if you have a scheme where each of the contributions they make has to be split up into different sequential units ('gives instruction', 'provides model', 'gives praise', etc.), the transition points between the units may well be a source of disagreement between observers. In this situation it is necessary first to establish satisfactory inter-observer agreement on the unit boundaries (which can be done in a similar way to that for the coding schedule itself – Bakeman and Gottman, 1997, pp. 68–71) before going on to the main task of assessing agreement on the categories.

Reactivity of assessing inter-observer agreement

Just as there is the problem that the observer may change the thing observed, so the observer's observing may be affected by testing for inter-observer agreement. Taplin and Reid (1973) looked at the effects of different ways of monitoring the reliability of observation. They monitored observers continuously but told different groups different things. The poorest performance in terms of reliability was from observers who did not think that they were being monitored. Intermediate performance came from those who knew that they were being monitored on specific occasions. The best performance came from those under the impression that they were being monitored covertly on randomly selected occasions. The implications are clear. It is desirable not only to have inter-observer agreement checks but also for observers to know this but not know which sessions will be checked. This is, of course, easier to organize when analysis takes place via a video or other tape than when sessions are coded live.

'Observer drift'

The kinds of threats to validity discussed in Chapter 6 in the context of fixed designs (see p. 108) rear their head again when structured observation is used. 'Instrumentation' is a particular problem. This is caused by possible changes in the measuring instrument and refers here to changes in the way that the observer uses the schedule, and is usually termed 'observer drift'. Increased familiarity with its use may well make it easier to 'see' examples of particular categories or there may be subtle differences in the ways in which category definitions are interpreted over time. Inter-observer agreement checks go some way to minimizing these effects as the drift is likely to be individual and idiosyncratic. Intra-observer checks, perhaps by returning periodically to the rating of training examples, can also be used.

Expectancy effects

Observers coding behaviour after some intervention may well expect to see 'positive' changes compared to the pre-intervention situation. This is a classic Rosenthal-type expectancy situation (Blanck, 1993; Rosenthal, 1976; Rosenthal & Rubin, 1980; Blanck, 1993), particularly so when the observer is also the person with a stake in the outcome of the study. Again, inter-observer agreement tests will give some safeguard, although (unconscious?) collusion can occur. 'Blind' coding of various kinds should be considered. If there are comparison groups, observers may not be told to which group the individual observed belongs. It might be feasible for observers to be 'blind' as to whether they are watching a pre- or post-session. A system where one observer is closely involved in that particular trial and knows exactly what is going on but a second trained observer (who may be closely involved in another trial) is 'blind' to these features can sometimes be set up.

The use of video-tape provides other solutions. Pre- and post-treatment sessions can be coded in a random sequence after all the data have been collected. However, even if considerable care is taken, it is virtually impossible to eliminate all clues (clothing, decorations, leaves on trees, etc.). Taped material has other advantages, particularly in giving the opportunity of multiple viewing, but its use should be carefully thought through, piloted and time-budgeted. The tape necessarily captures only one perspective of the events and it is very seductive to accumulate large quantities of to-be-coded tapes.

Further reading

The website gives annotated references to further reading for Chapter 14.

CHAPTER 15

Additional methods of data collection

This chapter:

- covers a group of methods known variously as unobtrusive measures or indirect observation – including documentary analysis, content analysis and archival analysis;
- provides an introduction to a range of other more specialized techniques;
- considers the opportunities that the Internet presents for research;
- provides warnings about using methods which call for an in-depth understanding of their theoretical background; and
- concludes by recommending the use of more than one method of data collection whenever feasible.

Introduction

This chapter covers a very mixed bag of methods. The first part covers an important group, here considered under the heading of unobtrusive measures. Their common characteristic is that they are based on the study of already existing material. Collecting data using direct observation, discussed in the previous chapter, always runs the risk that it can in some way alter whatever is observed. Using material already available, independent of your research, removes that risk.

Brief coverage of a wide range of other methods follows. Several are quite specialized, useful for particular tasks or situations, others – while relatively widely used in social research – are not obvious candidates to use in a real world research project. The usual principle applies. If one of these methods provides a means of getting answers to a research question you are interested in, give it serious consideration. Some are only appropriate for certain types of data (e.g. visual methods and narrative analysis). Others (such as repertory grids, conversational and discourse analyses) carry with them theoretical and methodological baggage which makes it dangerous to view them as 'off-the-peg' techniques usable without buying into the theory. Others, while regarded by some commentators as methods of investigation, might be better thought of as different research strategies (e.g. simulation) or as analytic techniques (e.g. meta-analysis). Some (such as the use of protocols, vignettes, scenarios, critical incidents, Delphi and nominal groups) are useful techniques for specific purposes.

The Internet has become a part of our lives and has already been mentioned at several points in this text, mainly as a tool to assist in carrying out research. However, its importance also makes it an obvious candidate for a research topic itself. Both aspects are covered in the chapter.

Unobtrusive measures

We are becoming increasingly conscious of the effects that humans have on their environment, particularly in relation to pollution: 'ozone holes', radioactive waste and so on. One particular class of such effects covers the artefacts that people make and leave behind them; things created 'on purpose', ranging in time from prehistoric cave paintings, through medieval cathedrals to styrofoam containers for take-away pizzas. There is a general case to be made that humans reveal something of themselves through such productions; that such things contain clues about the nature of society's lifestyles.

Whether unintended outcome or intentional creation, the 'things' that people produce provide opportunities for the real world researcher. Eugene Webb, Donald Campbell and colleagues (Webb, Campbell, Schwartz, Sechrest & Groves, 1981; Webb, Campbell, Schwartz & Sechrest, 2000) have sensitized social scientists to a wide range of what they term *unobtrusive measures* (see also Lee, 2000): that is, of things which might, through ingenuity and inference, be considered as indices of some aspect of human behaviour. Their most often-quoted example is of the floor tiles around the hatching-chick exhibit at Chicago's Museum of Science and Industry, which needed replacing at six-weekly intervals, while tiles in other parts of the museum did not need to be replaced for years. This 'selective erosion' provided an index of the relative popularity of exhibits.

They distinguished between such *erosion measures* and *accretion measures*. The latter, for example, might be counting empty spirit bottles in rubbish bins as a measure of the level of home consumption of alcohol in a town that was officially 'dry'. Both types are trace measures – the physical effects of interaction which remain after that interaction. They are commonly referred to as 'behavioural by-products'. For example, weight as a by-product of eating is an obvious measure in studies of obesity (e.g. Blackburn, 2008). Box 15.1 gives a range of examples, illustrating the wide variety of possibilities. In each of the examples there are likely to be problems in making the inferences suggested.

Accretion measures

Accretion is something extra or added, the build-up of a product or residue. Apart from analyses of different types of garbage (Rathje & Murphy, 1992; Strasser, 2000) – particularly popular with archaeologists but less so with social scientists (could it be to do with the stench dissipating over

BOX 15.1

A variety of unobtrusive measures

- The diameter of a circle of children as an index of fear induced by a ghost-story-telling session.
- Dilation of the pupil of the eye as an index of fear or interest.
- Degree of clustering of white and black students in lectures as an index of racial attitudes.
- Distortion in the size of drawings of Santa Claus as an index of children's interest in Christmas.
- Time spent in front of a display as an index of its popularity.
- Number of times books are borrowed from a library (or bought from bookstores) as indices of their popularity.
- Weight of food left on plate compared to initial weight as an index of acceptability of food in an institution.
- Settings of car radios when brought in for service as an index of relative popularity of different stations.
- Amount and type of graffiti in pairs of male and female public toilets as an index of gender differences.
- Differences in amount of litter as an index of the relative effectiveness of different anti-littering strategies.

(taken, in part, from Webb *et al.* 2000; pp. 2–3)

time?) – examples include litter and graffiti. Litter has been used as an index of usage patterns in public places. Graffiti have been related to territoriality, for example, in areas of Belfast. Usage is a popular focus for accretion measures – the number of date stamps in a library book; or mileage logged by a car or van; or persons through a turnstile. However, some evidence on virtually any phenomenon is there for the taking. For example, the 'internal mail' envelopes that land in university pigeon holes, with their sequentially completed and crossed out addressees in little boxes on the envelopes, suggest a potential tool for getting at communication patterns within an institution.

Erosion measures

Erosion refers to deterioration or wear, something being worn down or removed totally. Again usage is the most obvious focus, with wear giving measures of interaction patterns, relative popularities, etc.

Box 15.2 lists some advantages and disadvantages of 'trace' measures of either type. It is probably a fair assessment that physical trace measures have only a small part to play in research involving humans; certainly few social scientists make serious use of them currently. They do

BOX 15.2

Advantages and disadvantages of 'trace' measures

Advantages

1. They are unobtrusive and non-reactive. The researcher does not need to be in direct contact with the person(s) producing the trace and hence there is no reason why the behaviour should be influenced by the research.
2. They can provide valuable cross-validation of other measures, either in support or disconfirmation of them.
3. They encourage ingenuity and creativity on the part of the researcher.

Disadvantages

1. The person(s) responsible for the trace and/or the population from which they come may be difficult or impossible to specify.
2. Similarly, it may not be reasonable to assume that all persons involved make equivalent contributions to the trace (a single person may make a substantial contribution through repetitive involvement).
3. Apparent links between cause and effect (e.g. usage and trace) may be mediated by other factors (e.g. softness of ground).
4. Ethical difficulties of researching without people's knowledge or consent (likely to depend on the case – a study of whisky bottles or letters in rubbish bins is more ethically dubious than footpath wear patterns).

have, though, a strong potential contribution as a second, additional, method. Looked at in this light, many of their disadvantages dissolve and their non-reactivity can provide useful validation for other, more central, methods.

The website gives references to examples of research using unobtrusive measures.

Content analysis of documents

Although the use of physical trace measures has never achieved much more than curiosity value in applied social research, there has been substantial interest in the analysis of a particular kind of artefact: the *document*. By this is meant, primarily, the written document, whether this be a book, newspaper or magazine, notice, letter or whatever, although the term is sometimes extended to include non-written documents such as films and television programmes, pictures, drawings and photographs.

A common approach to documentary analysis is *content analysis*, the quantitative analysis of what is in the document. It differs from the techniques that we have considered so far in that it is indirect. Instead of directly observing, or interviewing, or asking someone to fill in a questionnaire for the purposes of our research, we are dealing with something produced for a different purpose. It is an *unobtrusive measure* (see preceding section) which is non-reactive, in that the document is not affected by the fact that you are using it. *It is, of course, possible to analyse the contents of documents or other materials which have been collected directly for the purposes of your research. In this case it is not an unobtrusive technique.* The fact that a person is filling in, say, a diary for the project may in some way alter their behaviour; in other words, there is a possible reactive effect.

Content analysis has been defined in various ways. Neuendorff (2002) defines it as 'the systematic, objective, quantitative analysis of message characteristics' (p. 1). Krippendorff (2013) considers that 'content analysis has evolved into a repertoire of methods of research that promise to yield inferences from all kinds of verbal, pictorial, symbolic, and communication data' (p. 23). He also stresses the importance of the contexts of their use.

The focus on texts, including not only written material but data such as works of art, images, maps, sounds, signs, symbols, and even numerical records, is the key feature of content analysis. The context includes the purpose of the document as well as institutional, social and cultural aspects.

It is possible to do other things with documents over and above analysing their contents. Such approaches, for example focusing on the authenticity of the document, or the intentions of the writer, are derived from the methods of historians. They are essentially concerned with the problems of selection and evaluation of evidence. Barzun and Graff (2003) provide a view of research from the perspective of the historian which constitutes a very valuable extension to the methodological education of anyone using social research methods.

The checklist of criteria suggested by Gottschalk, Kluckhohn and Angell (1945), in relation to the use of personal documents for research purposes, is still a useful summary of important concerns relevant to the accuracy of all documents:

- Was the ultimate source of the detail (the primary witness) *able* to tell the truth?
- Was the primary witness *willing* to tell the truth?
- Is the primary witness *accurately reported* with regard to the detail under examination?
- Is there any *external corroboration* of the detail under examination? (p. 35)

Other important questions when using any document include: 'Who produced it, for what purpose, and from what perspective or mindset?' (See the discussion by the historian E. H. Carr in his classic text, *What is History?*, Carr, 1961.)

Content analysis is in several senses akin to structured observation. This similarity is particularly evident when structured observation is carried out on a recording of the situation observed. A video-recording of such a session appears to be a very similar kind of artefact to, say, a video-recording of a television programme. The main difference is that in the former case the intention is to obtain a closely equivalent picture to that which the 'live' observer would have seen in the situation. Selectivity of focus and direction will be made with the needs of the observer in mind. The edited picture making up the TV programme appears under the direction of the programme maker who has her own agenda, which is unlikely to include the needs of the content analyst.

This illustrates a general problem in content analysis. The material to be analysed is not only unstructured, or at least not structured with the needs of the observer in mind; it will in general be a document with a purpose. And that purpose is important in understanding and interpreting the results of the analysis. A distinction is sometimes made in documentary analysis between *witting* and *unwitting* evidence. Witting evidence is that which the author intended to impart. Unwitting evidence is everything else that can be gleaned from the document.

Qualitative analyses of documents

Documents are typically text-based – i.e. made up of words. We have already covered research designs and data collection methods which produce qualitative data, usually in the form of words. While the traditional approach to the content analysis of documents is essentially quantitative, measuring the number and type of various features present in the text, it is perfectly feasible to use virtually any of the approaches to the analysis of qualitative data detailed in Chapter 18. Several of the methods discussed later in the chapter, including the study of discourse, conversations, narratives, biographies and oral histories, typically involve the qualitative analysis of some type of text-based document. Miller and Alvarado (2005) suggest several different qualitative approaches.

Note, however, the warnings given in the previous section still apply. If a document has been produced outside the research context, there are serious concerns about its accuracy and potential biases resulting from the purpose of the document. With documents produced directly for research purposes, likely biases, etc. are easier to assess though still present.

Uses of content analysis

Content analysis came to prominence in the social sciences at the start of the twentieth century, in a series of quantitative analyses of newspapers, primarily in the US. In a debate prefiguring current concerns in the UK about the tabloid press, campaigns against 'cheap yellow journalism' were bolstered by statistical studies showing how 'worthwhile' news items were being increasingly dropped in favour of gossip, sports and scandals (Krippendorff, 2013). This type of content analysis was subsequently extended to radio, and then to television, and continues unabated in, for example, studies of advertising, and of pornography and violence in the media.

Similar studies have attempted to assess bias in school textbooks and the depiction of favourable or unfavourable attitudes to blacks, females and homosexuals both in texts and other publications. While the main interest has probably continued to be in the field of mass communications, content analysis has more recently been used in a wide variety of social sciences. In particular, the approach discussed here can be readily adapted for use in the analysis of qualitative interview and questionnaire data (e.g. in the coding of open-ended questions in surveys) and of direct observation (typically through coding of tapes and transcripts).

Documents themselves cover a very wide range, including for example:

- minutes of meetings;
- letters, memoranda, etc.;
- diaries;
- speeches;
- newspapers; and
- magazine articles.

Particular contexts generate specific types of document. In social work and health settings various types of case record can be of importance. Studies involving schools or other educational establishments might include:

- written curricula;
- course outlines, and other course documents;
- timetables;
- notices;
- letters; and
- other communications to parents.

The website gives references to examples of content analyses of text-based documents.

Material appearing on the Internet forms the subject of recent content analyses. Franzosi (2007, Vol. 3, Part 8) has several examples, including studies of 'Global Activism in Virtual Space'; 'The European Women's Lobby in the Network of Transnational Women's NGOs on the Web'; 'Hyperlinking as Gatekeeping'; 'Online Newspaper Coverage of the Execution of an American Terrorist'; 'Personal Home Pages and Self-Presentation on the World Wide Web'; and 'A Content Analysis of 64 Disaster Relief Home Pages'.

The term 'document' is now taken to include such non-written forms as:

- films;
- television programmes;
- comic strips and cartoons; and
- photographs.

These require somewhat different approaches to analysis from those discussed below, although the basic principles remain the same.

The website gives references to examples of content analyses of non-text-based 'documents'.

The main focus in this text is on the use of content analysis as a secondary or supplementary method or in multi-method designs. This does not preclude carrying out a study based solely on content analysis but there are substantial difficulties and deficiencies (see Box 15.4 below on 'Advantages and disadvantages of content analysis'). It is often possible to 'acquire' copies of documents of a variety of types in conjunction with interviews and observations. One useful attribute for a real world researcher is a jackdaw mentality where you are always on the lookout for such things; you need to seek and get permission for this unless they are clearly intended for general distribution but it is rarely refused. They can be used for triangulation purposes, or to provide something of a longitudinal dimension to a study when a sequence of documents is available extending back in time.

How to carry out a content analysis

As with virtually all the techniques covered in this text, content analysis is codified common sense, a refinement of ways that might be used by laypersons to describe and explain aspects of the world about them.

Start with a research question (or questions)

Once again, the effective starting point for the process is the research question. Perhaps, 'Is there a greater emphasis on sex and violence in the mass media now than there was ten years ago?' A different research question might derive from the comment, commonly heard in listeners' responses to radio programmes, that there is political bias in radio programmes. For example, the BBC Radio 4 *Today* programme seems particularly adept at generating near apoplexy in politically committed listeners. Note here that, while the communication here is initially live, in practice any study of the programme's content will be likely to be based on a transcript of what is heard. It is likely, however, that an audio recording will also be helpful, enabling you to judge from intonation whether a particular comment is to be taken in a sarcastic or ironic sense.

There may be occasions when you have documents but no properly formulated notion of what you are looking for (e.g. at an early, exploratory, phase of the study when the research questions have not been properly developed). In some methodology texts, this so-called 'fishing trip' is severely frowned on; for example: 'content analysis cannot be used to probe around a mass of documents in the hope that a bright idea will be suggested by probing. Content analysis gets the answers to the question to which it is applied' (Carney, 1973, p. 284). However, in the context of a *flexible design* this can be an entirely appropriate strategy. Note that this would be an example of a flexible design where the resulting data are essentially quantitative. It is in the tradition of *exploratory data analysis* discussed in Chapter 17, p. 415. Obviously, the choice of data is determined by what you want to know, your tentative research questions. But to suggest that there is a difference in value between the research of someone who starts out with the question and that of another who gets the idea for the question from peeking at the data, verges on the metaphysical. Either there is good evidence about the question from the data or there isn't.

Decide on a sampling strategy

It is usually necessary to reduce your task to manageable dimensions by *sampling* from the population of interest. General principles of sampling apply, as discussed in Chapter 11, p. 276. Thus, in the case of the *Today* programme, it might be considered appropriate to take a random sample of, say, 20 programmes from those transmitted over a three-month period. Or, possibly, some form of stratification might be considered – perhaps ensuring that all presenters of the programme are equally represented in the sample. A different approach would be to have as one's sample all the programmes transmitted over an extended period but to focus, from the point of view of the analysis, on a small part of the content, say, on references to a particular incident or type of incident.

There may be situations where the relevant documents are so rare or difficult to get hold of that sampling in this sense is inappropriate.

Define the recording unit

In addition to deciding on categories, it is necessary to select a *recording unit*. The unit most commonly used is probably the *individual word*. In the simplest version, all occurrences of the word would be treated as equal and counts of them made and compared. A somewhat more sophisticated approach would differentiate between the different senses of words that have multiple meanings (e.g. 'right' as 'correct'; or as 'non-left') and code phrases constituting a semantic unit (e.g. 'ice cream' or 'Houses of Parliament'). It is also possible to use *themes*, *characters* (i.e. the actors or individuals mentioned in the document, as in the analysis of the fiction example in Box 15.3 below), *paragraphs* or *whole items* as the recording unit.

Other possibilities suggest themselves for particular tasks. For example, when analysing newspaper or magazine content these might be:

- number of stories on a topic;
- column inches;
- size of headline;
- number of stories on a page;
- position of stories within the page or paper as a whole; or
- number and/or type of pictures.

It may be necessary to examine the context in which a recording unit is set in order to categorize it. Although you may have fixed on the word as recording unit, if you are interested in coding whether a treatment is positive or negative, favourable or unfavourable, it is likely that you will have to take into account the sentence in which the word appears.

There is some argument in content analysis circles about the degree of inference which coders should be called upon to make when categorizing items. This is sometimes expressed in terms of *manifest* and *latent content*, corresponding essentially to low- and high-inference items respectively. Manifest items are those which are physically present (e.g. a particular word); latent content is a matter of inference or interpretation on the part of the coder. At its simplest this may just require a judgement of warmth, favourableness, etc., but some might require use of a complex typology. As with other techniques of data collection, it is obviously likely to be more straightforward to achieve reliable results with low-inference systems. However, the research question should determine the type of system you are using and it may well be that a high-inference system is appropriate. This then puts greater stress on ensuring that you can demonstrate reliability through the use of independent coders or by some other means such as triangulating with data obtained through other sources.

Construct categories for analysis

It is difficult to give helpful general comments here, as there is such a wide range of possible types of research question for which content analysis might be used. Holsti (1969) lists several types of categories. Thus, in looking at what is said in the document, categories might be concerned with:

- *Subject matter*. What is it about?
- *Direction*. How is it treated, e.g. favourably or not?
- *Values*. What values are revealed?
- *Goals*. What goals or intentions are revealed?
- *Methods*. What methods are used to achieve these intentions?
- *Traits*. What are the characteristics used in describing people?
- *Actors*. Who is represented as carrying out the actions referred to?
- *Authority*. In whose name are statements made?
- *Location*. Where does the action take place?
- *Conflict*. What are the sources and levels of conflict?
- *Endings*. In what way are conflicts resolved (e.g. happily)?

As with structured observation systems, it is highly desirable that these categories are exhaustive and mutually exclusive. With exhaustive categories, you ensure that everything relevant to the study can be categorized (even if you have to resort to a 'dump' category for things that you don't know how to deal with). With mutually exclusive categories, anything to be analysed can only be categorized in one way; if it is categorized in one particular way, it can't also be categorized as something else.

The categories also have to be operationalized: that is, an explicit specification has to be made of what indicators one is looking for when making each and any of the categorizations. Sorting out the categories is the most crucial aspect of the content analysis. As Berelson (1952) pointed out, 'since the categories contain the substance of the investigation, a content analysis can be no better than its system of categories'. Box 15.3 gives two examples of category systems.

BOX 15.3

Examples of category systems

1. To answer research questions about characteristics of heroines in fiction targeted at adolescents

Physical characteristics	Social characteristics	Emotional characteristics
height	ethnic background	warm
weight	socio-economic class	aloof
'vital statistics'	occupation	stable
age	housing	anxious
hair colour	income	hostile (etc.)
eye colour (etc.)	religion (etc.)	

2. To answer research questions on trends in contents of newspapers

Domestic news	Foreign news	Cultural
political	European	music
ecological	American	theatre
crime	Russian	art
transport (etc.)	Chinese	opera (etc.)
	Third World (etc.)	

Sport
Business and financial
Television and radio
Children's and young people's items
Women's items
Cartoons
Advertisements (etc.)

(all of the above could be sub-categorized.)

A coding system of this kind can be combined with more qualitative approaches. For example Taylor (2008) discusses the witness statements given to the inquiry into the death of Victoria Climbié, a child who died as a result of months of appalling ill-treatment at the hands of those who were supposed to be caring for her. She makes a case for the need to incorporate more grounded theory techniques, research reflexivity and subjective interpretation, alongside the 'objective' coding frame being used, to highlight the kind of issues that lay beyond the codes and which cannot be effectively grasped by them.

Test the coding on samples of text and assess reliability

This is the best test of the clarity and lack of ambiguity of your category definitions. It is highly likely that this process will lead to the revision of your scheme. With human (as against computer) coding, at least two persons should be involved at this stage. When the scheme appears workable, tests of reliability should be made (these are formally equivalent to the tests carried out when assessing the inter-observer agreement of structured observation schedules – see Chapter 14, p. 332). If the reliability is low, further practice is necessary and it may also be necessary to revise the coding rules. The process should be repeated until the reliability is acceptable. If computer coding has been used, it is necessary to check for errors in computer procedures (see Chapter 17, p. 344).

Carry out the analysis

The analysis is equivalent to the set of activities you carry out when using and analysing a structured observation schedule. The statistical analysis of the data obtained can follow exploratory data analysis procedures or more conventional hypothesis testing approaches (see Chapter 17). The most common approach is to relate variables from the content analysis to other 'outside' variables (e.g. gender of the persons producing the documents or type of school from which they come). More complex procedures involve the use of factor analysis, as either an exploratory or a confirmatory tool, to identify themes in texts and the subsequent use of techniques such as analysis of variance to outside variables.

Box 15.4 lists some of the advantages and disadvantages of content analysis.

Computers and content analysis

Content analysis can be extremely laborious and time-consuming. It is a field where computerization has led to substantial benefits. Analyses which would have been beyond the resources of small-scale research can now be completed routinely given access to a computer and specialized software. The text can be easily manipulated and displayed in various ways (e.g. showing all sentences, or other units, containing a particular word or phrase). Using optical character recognition (OCR) devices can transform a document directly into a computer file without the necessity for typing, although the output needs close checking.

A major methodological bonus if you are using computer-aided content analysis is that the rules for coding the text have to be made completely explicit or the computer will not be able to carry out the task. Once these rules have been established and written into the software (itself no mean task) then it is possible to work through a range of documents and achieve results which

BOX 15.4

Advantages and disadvantages of content analysis

Advantages

- When based on existing documents, it is unobtrusive. You can 'observe' without being observed.
- The data are in permanent form and hence can be subject to re-analysis, allowing reliability checks and replication studies.
- It may provide a low-cost form of longitudinal analysis when a run or series of documents of a particular type is available.

Disadvantages

- The documents available may be limited or partial.
- The documents have been written for some purpose other than for the research and it is difficult or impossible to allow for the biases or distortions that this introduces (note the need for triangulation with other accounts/data sources to address this problem).
- It is very difficult to assess causal relationships. Are the documents causes of the social phenomena you are interested in, or reflections of them (e.g. in relation to pornography and/or violence in the mass media)?

are formally compatible with each other. At the same time, once the development stage has been completed and any 'bugs' removed from the system, the computer provides perfect coder reliability in applying the rules built into the program.

This does not mean that all problems have been solved. Little matters of validity, interpretation and explanation remain. You also still face the inescapable fact that content analysis is concerned with data reduction. You throw away much of the information in a document to see the wood for the trees. West (2001) reviews ways in which the computer can help in carrying out content analysis. Neuendorf's 'Content Analysis Guidebook Online' also gives details of programs for the qualitative analysis of documents and the analysis of audio, video and image data (http://academic.csuohio.edu/neuendorf_ka/content/).

The website gives details of several computer aids to content analysis.

Using data archives

An archive is simply a record, or set of records. Some records are in the form of documents containing text, as covered in the preceding section. Others may contain quantitative statistical information. Such archives share an important feature with the documents just discussed in that they have been produced for some other purpose than for your use as a researcher. They will have been collected and paid for by someone else (though there is also the possibility of revisiting a study you carried out previously, with a view to carrying out a different or extended analysis).

The ten yearly UK National Census is an archetypal example but there are many recurrent and one-off surveys (e.g. the Current Population Survey, General Household Survey, British Social Attitude Survey, American General Social Survey, British Workplace Industrial Relations Survey, British Crime Survey, and others; Hakim, 2000, Chapter 7, provides details). A recent development in UK government open data sharing is http://www.data.gov.uk, which provides a single access point to over 2,500 central government data sets that have been made available for free re-use.

There are clear advantages and disadvantages associated with such data. It is possible to tap into extensive data sets, often drawn from large representative samples, well beyond the resources of the individual researcher. Recent data sets should have good documentation, including full code-books describing the variables and codes that have been used, and easily accessible recording methods. The disadvantages flow from the fact that even those surveys carried out for research purposes are unlikely to be directly addressing the research question you are interested in. Useful on-line sites include the UK Data Archive (http://www.data-archive.ac.uk) which is a centre of expertise in data acquisition, preservation, dissemination and promotion and is curator of the largest collection of digital data in the social sciences and humanities in the UK. The Question Bank (http://surveynet.ac.uk/sqb/) focuses on quantitative survey methods and helps users locate examples of specific research questions and see them in the context within which they have been used for data collection. It is a good source of data for secondary analysis and also assists with the design of new survey questionnaires.

The UK Data Archive also provides links to a range of archives in other countries. See also the Council of European Social Science Data Archives (CESSDA) (http://www.cessda.org), an umbrella organization for social science data archives across Europe, which provides access to data collections including sociological surveys, election studies, longitudinal studies, opinion polls, and census data.

In the US, the Harvard-MIT Data Center (HMDC) (http://data.fas.harvard.edu/), originally the US Government Data Center, is an important source of quantitative social science data from major international data consortia. The Inter-University Consortium for Political and Social Research (ICPSR) (http://www.icpsr.umich.edu/) claims to be the world's largest archive of digital social science data.

Other data archives present greater problems and challenges for researchers. A prime example is the so-called 'Guildford Depository'. This contains the documents of British American Tobacco (BAT), which was housed in a depository in Guildford, UK and run by the company itself. As a result of litigation against the tobacco industry, the company has been obliged to provide public access to this collection of approximately eight million pages of documents, all relating to tobacco. Lee, Gilmore and Collin (2004) detail some of the difficulties:

> Visitors must access the BAT collection on-site, inconvenient for UK residents and prohibitive for those living outside the country, notably researchers from the developing world. Visits to the depository must be booked on a weekly basis in advance, and at times delays of up to 5 months have been experienced to obtain a booking. Once inside the depository, visitors can use a crude database to search the collection of approximately 43,000 files, with each file consisting of up to several hundred pages. As the database is indexed only at the file level, it is impossible to identify the subject of individual documents except by searching manually page by page. All the while, visitors are subjected to intensive video surveillance, with three video cameras trained upon the small reading room. Research is hindered further by delays of up to 1 year for photocopy requests to be processed by BAT (pp. 394–5).

As of July 2008, the BAT documents were integrated into the Legacy Tobacco Documents Library (LTDL) which also includes other US companies. Access is via the British American Tobacco Documents Archive (http://bat.library.ucsf.edu/) and is now easier.

Crow and Edwards (2012) provide an introduction to a set of papers discussing some of the particular, and rather different, methodological issues raised by archival research.

The website gives references to further examples of research involving a data archive.

Secondary data analysis

This is defined by Hakim (2000) as 'any reanalysis of data collected by another researcher or organisation' (p. 24). Data archives lend themselves to secondary analysis as they are readily available and, typically, there is information available about details of the data and of how they were collected. However, any existing data can be the subject of a secondary analysis. If you are carrying out a project as a course requirement or for a research degree do check that a project based entirely on the analysis of existing data falls within regulations as it is common for the collection of new data to be a requirement. *Secondary data analysis* can be an attractive strategy as it permits you to capitalize on the efforts of others in collecting the data. It has the advantage of allowing you to concentrate on analysis and interpretation.

Hakim (1982, 2000, pp. 24–7) discusses the issues involved and presents examples. They include:

- re-analysis of case study reports;
- additional analyses of case study, and other, reports to extend or re-assess the findings of a main report;
- reuse of a single data set, either to replicate the original findings, or to address different research questions;
- merging several years' data from a regular or repeated survey to achieve a sufficiently large sample to study a sub-group in a population;
- using a single data set extended by the addition of data from other sources; and
- using multiple data sets to provide an overall assessment of findings on a topic (as in systematic reviews of the evidence on a topic – see Chapter 5, p. 85).

Qualidata, a section within the UK Data Archive, is a repository of many useful qualitative data sets (http://www.esds.ac.uk/qualidata/about/introduction.asp). Fielding and Fielding (2000) argue that as qualitative data are costly to collect and analyse and commonly only a small proportion of such data are the subject of final analysis and publication, secondary analysis could be used with advantage. They demonstrate this approach by using secondary analysis to evaluate classic studies of crime and deviance. Savage (2005) points out that, particularly in the case of classic published studies, any secondary re-analysis should be not only of the archived data, but also of the published work itself, which raises a host of complex methodological and ethical issues. Corti, Witzel and Bishop (2005) discuss the general issues involved in the secondary analysis of qualitative data.

Using administrative records and management information systems

Many small-scale real life studies concern organizations, such as an office, school or hospital. A feature they all have in common is the collection of records and other information relating to their function. Such records can form a valuable supplementary resource and it is often possible to obtain access to them. The usual ethical principles apply in relation to confidentiality, and there may be particular problems associated with information collected for one purpose being used for a different one.

The records are, however, unlikely to provide direct answers to the questions we are interested in when carrying out research. Indeed, they may form a tempting distraction, with pages of descriptive statistics on individual measures and cross-tabulations between measures, amassed to little or no purpose. Simply to know that there are 73 per cent of males on an innovatory programme or that 23 per cent of the males and 48 per cent of the females are from low-income families, carries little meaning in its own right. The issue is: *What light can this information throw on our research questions?* We may be interested in answering questions on recently introduced crèche facilities or different access arrangements and this kind of routine data may in such circumstances be of direct value. Nevertheless, a thorough exploratory study of existing data may suggest questions or act as a starting point for unforeseen lines of enquiry. It is well worthwhile spending a fair amount of time looking at and playing with data from record systems. Patterns may suggest themselves and trends emerge which had not previously occurred to you.

Simon (2014) discusses the issues involved in using administrative data held by the UK Department for Work and Pensions to enhance surveys that they carry out, and to avoid duplication. This approach has been used successfully in several countries. While attractive in principle, in practice little overlap was found.

Typically it will be necessary to rearrange the data in various ways, so that, for example, you can compare data over different time periods. Your research questions assist in selecting from what can easily be a data mountain. If, as is increasingly the case, these routine systems have been computerized, your task *may* be simplified. It is, for example, usually relatively easy to provide suitably anonymized extracts from computer records. Previously it would have been necessary to go through filing cabinets and record cards to obtain the information you need. This has the possibility of introducing transcription errors and may also require that the researchers have access to confidential or private records. Access to computer records should be subject to strict controls and any necessary clearances must be obtained. Remember, however, that there is no guarantee at all that the computer system designed to cope with routine data collection has the flexibility to deliver the comparisons or selections that you need.

Hakim (2000, Chapter 4) discusses the design of studies based exclusively on administrative records. She makes the point that they have to be designed 'back to front'. That is, instead of designing the study and then collecting the data, the researcher starts by finding out what data are available in the set of records and then identifies a possible research design. The situation is rather different in a multi-method case study. If administrative records are available, they are examined to see what additional corroboration they can throw on the case. If they don't help with your research questions, then either don't use the administrative records or consider whether it makes sense to modify what you are after in the light of what they can tell you.

Box 15.5 lists some issues to be taken into account when using administrative records from management information systems. Caputo (1988) provides useful background on their use.

BOX 15.5

Issues in using administrative records for research purposes

1. *The quality of the data must be assessed.* Generally, information central to the activities of an organization will be of better quality than more peripheral items. Check on what actually happens (e.g. are large batches of forms filled in cursorily long after the event?). Find the views of the persons entering the data. If they think that 'the yellow form always goes into the dustbin' (actual quotation from a social worker) then they are unlikely to fill them in conscientiously.

2. *Careful study of existing record systems may allow you to avoid unnecessary duplication in data collection.* Informants in studies are often busy people and it is highly desirable to minimize the extra load you put on them for the purposes of research. Even though an existing question may not be asking for exactly what you had in mind, it may provide you with a close enough approximation of the information you need. It is sometimes feasible to add temporary 'research' questions to standard administrative forms.

3. *Sampling from administrative records may well be needed.* A variety of approaches may be possible (e.g. time samples, sampling of individuals, sampling of items).

   Note: As administrative records often give information on a rigidly defined set of topics over considerable periods of time, they lend themselves to some form of time-series analysis (see Chapter 6, p. 131).

Haldar and Waerdahl (2009) describe their research use of 'teddy diaries'. Norway uses teddy bears and 'teddy diaries' to help bridge the transition between family and school for pupils entering the first grade. Each school class is provided with a teddy bear which carries a diary that will visit each child's home. The diary is used to record the teddy bear's experiences during these visits. These stories are shared with the others in class, and with families who, in turn, receive the teddy's visits. Typically, children and parents write the family entry together. The intention of the exercise is educational rather than a management tool. Haldar and Waerdahl used the diaries to gain access to family representations of themselves and their lives. They obtained permission from the teachers and the schools involved, adhering to rules of anonymity for the families providing entries and their communities, viewing the teddy diaries as being publicly available material, in similar fashion to a school newspaper.

The website gives references to further examples of research using administrative records.

Introduction to a range of more specialist techniques

This section provides information about several approaches to data collection which, while not commonly used in real world research, are well worth considering in some contexts or to address particular research questions. Some, such as the use of simulation, or of verbal protocols, or of vignettes are relatively straightforward to use without a great deal of prior reading or support. Others, such as repertory grids, and phenomenological and hermeneutic techniques, are embedded in particular philosophical viewpoints and the extent to which they can, as it were, just be picked of the shelf and used without knowing that background is debatable.

There is an attempt to give sufficient information so that you get some feeling for what each method involves. However, further reading, following up the suggestions and references here will be essential if you wish to use one of the techniques.

Simulation

Simulations attempt to carry over the essential structural elements of some real world phenomenon into a relatively well controlled environment. They imitate the processes of a system to try to see how it works. Although some experiments in which a few variables are manipulated are sometimes thought of as simulations, the more common usage tries to capture the whole of the pattern which is likely to involve a myriad of variables. The focus is on what happens when the phenomenon, one hopes with all its essential characteristics, is transposed to a more controlled setting. In this sense they represent a halfway house between the decontextualized artificiality of the laboratory setting and sometimes intractable and inaccessible real world setting.

Suppose one is interested in the working of juries in legal cases. This is very difficult to examine in a real 'real life' setting which is not open to the investigator. Simulation of the jury room, and the task, is feasible – though much work in this field has been criticized because of its artificiality in following the experimental approach of manipulating single variables such as the attractiveness of the defendant.

Simulations commonly require participants to play an explicit role. This calls attention to our expectations about how someone fulfilling a particular role will behave. As Harré and Secord (1972) put it, humans in social situations are 'rule-following agents'. A notorious example is the simulated prison cell block investigated by Zimbardo and his colleagues (Haney & Zimbardo, 1998). Students were paid to role-play 'prisoners' and 'guards' under very realistic conditions. Prisoners, for example, were actually arrested by local police; handcuffed, searched, cautioned, etc. The study was terminated less than halfway through its planned duration because of the strong effects that it had on both prisoners (including extreme depression and anxiety) and guards (enjoyment of the power in their roles). Ethical criticisms are obvious, as well as the concern about the adequacy of the simulation in representing the reality of prison life. Note that this is a different issue from whether or not the participants take the situation seriously and are fully involved, which is a common problem in simulations. This feature can be employed with advantage when the simulation is used as a teaching tool and in intervention studies where the intention is to modify behaviour.

Simulation can be viewed as an alternative research strategy or as a means of implementing a case study, as it can involve different methods of investigation. The Zimbardo study, for example, used various checklists and personality tests, diaries, questionnaires and direct observation.

The website gives references to examples of simulation studies.

Repertory grid techniques

George Kelly proposed a theory of personality based on the notion of personal constructs (Kelly, 1963; 1970; Butt & Burr, 2004). Personal constructs are the dimensions we use to make sense of, and extend, our experience of the world. He views humans as effectively acting as scientists in their day-to-day activities, seeking to understand the course of events in which they are involved. We evaluate the phenomena making up our world through a limited number of constructs which we have found helpful in creating our personal view.

Kelly suggests that these personal constructs are bipolar (e.g. on a dimension from 'good' to 'bad'; or from 'makes me feel angry' to 'makes me feel pleased'). Repertory grid techniques are ways of eliciting these constructs and have been widely used, both by followers of Kelly and by others who simply find them useful. Kelly's use of the technique required a participant to complete a set of cards showing the names of a number of significant persons in their life (e.g. 'mother', 'best friend'). They were then asked to provide an important way in which two of the persons differed from the third – perhaps that two were 'kind' and one was 'cruel'. This was repeated several times to elicit a range of such constructs, which then constituted how that subject interpreted the behaviour of people important in her life. A grid could then be constructed, displaying the matrix of constructs against 'elements' (persons).

A continuing debate concerns how far it is necessary to stay with 'elicited' constructs which are necessarily idiosyncratic to the individual and often difficult to deal with in research or whether it is possible to work with 'provided' constructs. Although this seems to go against the basic tenet of the Kellian approach, it has been advocated by some of his followers (e.g. Bannister & Mair, 1968 – who do, however, point out the dangers of provided constructs).

A range of different types of grid has been developed. Approaches such as 'laddering', which look at the location of individual constructs within the overall construct system, have also been used (Bannister & Mair, 1968). A tension can increasingly be detected between the technology of 'gridding' (for which several computer packages are now available) and the philosophical roots of Kelly's view of personality.

Grids have been used extensively in clinical and counselling sessions and are increasingly found in research studies (Fransella, 2005; Caputi, Foster & Viney, 2006).

The website gives references to examples of the use of repertory grids.

Verbal protocols

A verbal protocol (or 'think aloud') is the name given to a self-report by a person about 'what they are doing, what they are about to do, what they hope to achieve, etc. with respect to a particular task or behaviour' (Johnson & Briggs, 1994). Gilhooly and Green (1996) cover the theoretical background to the approach. It provides a means of gathering information about how people approach a problem or task and the mental processes they adopt when doing this. The technique can provide rich, qualitative information about how people conceptualize their actions in specific situations. Ericsson (2006) discusses its use in studying the performance of experts in a variety of tasks – see for example Brooks and Gugerty (2004) who studied the directional judgement of experienced pilots.

It can be considered as an alternative to the more usual questionnaire or focus groups for some purposes. Cotton and Gresty (2006), following experience of using it in a study of e-learning, raise a number of concerns about the method including the level of guidance given to participants, observer influence, and the complexity of data analysis. They conclude, however, that the richness of the data collected outweighs these constraints.

'Think aloud' has been popular in fields such as ergonomics and human factors (Walker, 2004) and in software evaluation where there is increasing concern about the usability of materials This is partly because it can provide rapid feedback in a cost-effective manner. Two main variants have been used; in one participants are asked to verbalize about the task while carrying it out, in the other this is done immediately after it. If the former, the demands of the technique should not be so onerous that they interfere with performance of the task. This type is best suited to tasks which the person can complete at their own pace. Difficulties can arise in getting participants to produce a detailed commentary. The instructions given to them, and the type and amount of any prompts to be used need careful consideration. Haak, De Jong and Schellens (2003) provide a comparison of the two approaches.

The technique has been somewhat controversial, possibly because it has been used in fields more accustomed to quantitative data. It is likely to be of particular use where people interact with complex systems, as in human – computer interaction and software design, but is worth considering in any situations where greater insight and understanding of what is going on will be gained by having those involved tell you about it (for example as a supplementary method in psychological and other experiments).

The website gives references to examples of the use of verbal protocols.

Nominal and interacting groups – and the Delphi method

These are methods or techniques for eliciting subjective estimates from experts (or, more widely, individuals who have relevant knowledge about, or experience of, a topic of interest) – see Delbecq, Van De Ven and Gustafson (1986) for an overview. In the interacting group approach, an initial group discussion on the topic or issue is followed by a group assessment. In the nominal group approach, respondents make their initial estimates individually, followed by a group discussion on the subject and estimates, and the revision or confirmation of the individual views to reach a group view (Lock, 1987). Delphi techniques involve individuals making independent estimates or giving views about the issue in question. These are aggregated by a central group who then provide feedback on the group results to the individuals. The individuals subsequently confirm or revise their estimates until either a group consensus is reached or an acceptable range of views achieved (Adler & Ziglio, 1996).

The nominal group approach (Dunham, 1998; MacPhail, 2001; Allen, Dyas &Jones, 2004) has been shown to be superior to the interacting group in several studies (e.g. Van de Ven & Delbecq, 1971; Herbert & Yost, 1979). However, in their traditional form they both depend on individuals being brought together to discuss the issue concerned and to provide estimates or views. When experts are involved the high expense and impracticality of getting them all together in a group setting can make these approaches unfeasible (technical developments such as video-conferencing can obviate the requirement for their physical presence in one place).

These considerations may account for the apparent greater popularity of the Delphi approach (Keeney, Hasson & McKenna, 2006), which does not actually require individuals to be brought together. In a review of evidence on the use of the Delphi method in the context of nursing research (where the Delphi has been popular), Powell (2003) concludes that its major strengths are the likelihood of achieving consensus in areas and contexts in which empirical knowledge is required and the process of controlled feedback. The approach is seen as democratic and structured and as helping to consolidate collegial knowledge in the profession, thus facilitating interprofessional communication. The lack of clarity in the consensus-reaching process is regarded as the method's foremost methodological weakness. The findings are opinions and the validity and credibility of the research depends on the accuracy of conducting and reporting in the study. Achieving a high response rate is important for the validity of the results and a full description of the background and experience of the panel members is needed to assess their credibility (Kennedy, 2004).

The website gives references to examples of research using the Delphi and nominal group techniques.

Hybrids of the different approaches are possible. Adams (2006), in a study of risks in construction projects, combined an individual assessment method, a revised Delphi group approach and a vignette technique (this involves presenting short stories about hypothetical characters in specified circumstances to which participants are asked to respond – see below). The vignette used in this research consisted of a brief description of a construction project to provide a background to the set of questions that the experts were invited to respond to.

The responses sought were the experts' estimates of the relative likelihood of occurrences of risk on a set of projects similar to the one described in the vignette. The revised Delphi approach included mailing a semi-structured questionnaire. The experts were encouraged to consult other colleagues or experts in clarifying their opinions about the probabilities of risk. They were free to complete and mail or fax their responses if they so preferred. This was followed by a phone discussion to provide detailed information and explanation of the research to ensure that each expert had a depth of understanding similar to what they would have in a traditional Delphi approach and to ensure that each expert actually did reflect on the issues.

The individual expert opinions were aggregated to form a group opinion and fed back to them. To achieve group consensus in the absence of bringing all respondents together in one place, each respondent was asked, after completion of their questionnaire, how they would view their own responses in the light of the group aggregate that would emerge from the study. The options were for the experts to maintain their original individual estimates, adjust the estimates in view of the group aggregate or accept the group aggregate as being more accurate estimates about the risks. They all indicated that they would accept the group aggregate as the best reflection of their collective experience about the risks.

Research integration

This is the process of improving the understanding of real world problems by synthesizing relevant knowledge from diverse disciplines and stakeholders. Delphi and nominal group techniques have been used in this connection. McDonald, Bammer and Deane (2009) provide details and also cover another 12 techniques that have been used, including citizens' juries (Wakeford,

2002), consensus conferences (Hendriks, 2005), scenario planning (Bradfield, Wright, Burt, Cairns & Van Der Heijden, 2005) and soft systems methodology (Checkland & Poulter, 2006).

Although several of the techniques have tended to focus on stakeholder involvement in the interests of democratic participation, McDonald *et al.* (2009) make a strong case for their use in the investigation of real world problems by bringing together the insights of different disciplines. They argue, for example, that:

> examination of the impacts of the encroachment of housing on farm and bushland on the fringes of cities can benefit from the expertise of ecologists, economists, hydrologists, sociologists, soil scientists, demographers and so on. Similarly, to comprehensively model the impact of the covert release of an infectious disease agent on a major city requires input from, among others, communicable disease epidemiologists, statistical modellers, urban geographers, psychologists and legal experts (p. 1).

Such multi-disciplinary exercises, bringing together researchers from natural and social science disciplines, appear to have considerable potential.

The critical incident technique

The Critical Incident Technique (CIT) was first used as a research technique by Flanagan (1954). His work was carried out as part of the Aviation Psychology Program of the United States Army Air Forces during World War II, where he conducted a series of studies focused on differentiating effective and ineffective work behaviours. It has subsequently been used as a method to identify job requirements, develop recommendations for effective practices, and determine competencies for a vast number of professionals in various disciplines. Although initially based within the then dominant positivist paradigm, it has always been viewed as flexible, requiring modification for specific situations. These modifications include both the means of collecting data (such as observations or interviews) and the subsequent analysis of the data. By focusing on 'critical' incidents, this technique commonly elicits very effective or very ineffective practices.

Flanagan (1954) originally defined an incident as 'any observable human activity that is sufficiently complete in itself to permit inferences and predictions to be made about the person performing the act' (p. 327). These incidents may be events, activities or role behaviours. They are 'critical' because they affect the outcomes of the system or process and are memorable to those involved in the system. This predictive focus of the technique is useful in providing findings that are 'highly focused on solutions to practical problems' (Kemppainen 2000, p. 1265).

CIT has become a widely used research method and today is recognized as an effective exploratory and investigative tool (Chell, 2004), although there are critics of inconsistencies in its use and terminology (Bradbury-Jones & Tranter, 2008). Its influence ranges far beyond its industrial and organizational psychology roots. Butterfield, Borgen, Amundson and Maglio (2005), in a review of 50 years of the use of the technique, list studies in many disciplines including communications, nursing, job analysis, counselling, education and teaching, medicine, marketing, organizational learning, performance appraisal, psychology and social work. Schluter, Seaton and Chaboyer (2008) provide a detailed 'user's guide' which, though aimed at nurse researchers, is of general relevance.

The website gives references to examples of research using the critical incident technique.

Vignettes

Vignettes consist of text, images or other material to which research participants are asked to respond. They can be presented to participants in many different forms, ranging from short written prompts to live events. They are frequently based on simulations of real events, where participants are presented with vignettes of a fictional situation and invited to comment on how it makes them feel, or what they might do in that situation. The advantages and pitfalls of using vignettes were explored by Hughes and Huby (2002), who concluded that 'vignettes, used alone or in conjunction with other research techniques, can be valuable research tools in the study of people's lives, their attitudes, perceptions and beliefs'(p. 385). Gould (1996) suggests that the recent popularity of vignettes stems from an increasing recognition of the limitations of questionnaires in studies of these aspects.

They have been used in both fixed designs (Finch, 1987) and a variety of flexible designs (Barter & Renold, 1999), and in several ways. These include eliciting views from people receiving or providing a service. Ouslander, Tymchuk and Krynski (1993), for example, presented cartoons and accompanying text to elderly patients to explore their views on different treatment options. Vignettes have been used in research to conceptualize the attitudes of the general population (e.g. Denk, Benson, Fletcher & Reigel, 1997 who explored end-of-life medical decision-making in a general population using ten randomly assembled vignettes). Their use has also been advocated by Ely, Vinz, Downing and Anzul (1997) when analysing, interpreting and presenting qualitative data.

Vignettes have also been widely used in multi-strategy design and multi-method research (Hughes 1998) either to enhance existing data or to generate data not tapped by methods such as observation or interviews. MacAuley (1996) explored children's perceptions and experiences of long-term foster care, using vignettes, unfinished sentences, postal boxes, response cards, games and other visual stimuli to achieve an 'insider' position on children's perceptions and value systems. Wade (1999) used vignettes following individual interviews in her study about children's perceptions of the family, using selected stories on topics that had not been covered in the interview or which called for further exploration (see also Smart, Neale & Wade, 2001).

They are typically less expensive and quicker to carry out than observational studies and can easily generate considerable amounts of data from a large participant group. Vignettes provide a useful focus for discussion during individual interviews and can act as a stimulus for group discussions. Standardized information contained within the vignettes means all participants are responding to the same material.

Vignettes are recognized as being particularly useful in the study of potentially difficult or sensitive research topics of inquiry. The style of questions and the means by which participants are invited to respond can help to distance participants from sensitive topics. Participants can be asked to assume the role of a vignette character rather than answering questions from their own personal viewpoints, which also appears to reduce the 'social desirability effect' (see pp. 248, 264) in responding (Bendelow, 1993). Barter and Renold (2000), following a review of the research literature, suggest a set of principles to follow when using vignettes.

The website gives references to examples of research using vignettes.

Scenarios

The term 'scenario' is frequently found in planning contexts. It is usually taken to refer to alternative views of the future. Scenarios identify some significant events, main actors and their motivations and are used to explore possible developments in the future and to test strategies against those potential developments. They are widely used by governments, businesses and voluntary organizations to inform strategy and policy development. They can be done on a large or small scale; as part of a wider body of work or as a discrete exercise; as a way of gathering expert opinion from external bodies and individuals; or as a method to develop internal thinking. Snoek (2003; 2003a) discusses the use and methodology of scenario making and provides a typical example from a project on the use of scenarios about the future of teacher education in Europe.

Scenarios are also commonly used in software design (e.g. Bengtsson, Lassing, Bosch &Van Vliet, 2004). The technique is not restricted to uses about the future, or in development work. For example, Groves, Kucharewski and Longsdorf (2006) explored ethical issues related to research and publication within the leisure services profession through a survey to relevant faculty members assessing 21 scenarios addressing issues relating to current practices such as authorship, conflicts of interest, plagiarism, fraud, and duplication.

Q methodology

Q methodology was first developed by William Stephenson (1935; 1955) and is most often associated with quantitative analysis due to its dependence on factor analysis. However, Brown (1996) suggests that:

> what Stephenson was interested in providing was a way to reveal the subjectivity involved in any situation – e.g. in aesthetic judgment, poetic interpretation, perceptions of organizational role, political attitudes, appraisals of health care, experiences of bereavement, perspectives on life and the cosmos, et cetera ad infinitum. It is life as lived from the standpoint of the person living it that is typically passed over by quantitative procedures, and it is subjectivity in this sense that Q methodology is designed to examine and that frequently engages the attention of the qualitative researcher interested in more than just life measured by the pound (p. 561).

Q methodology is seen by its advocates as combining the strengths of both the qualitative and quantitative research traditions (Dennis & Goldberg, 1996, p. 104). An official organization is committed to the ideas and concepts of Q methodology as enunciated by Stephenson (The International Society for the Scientific Study of Subjectivity) – see http://www.qmethod.org/about.php. Whereas his view of Q Methodology as a privileged pathway to human subjectivity is highly debatable, the techniques it employs have been applied within other schools of thought (e.g. Carl Rogers, 1954; 1945) and form the basis for standard psychometric instruments (e.g. the California Q-sort – Block, 1961).

It calls for quite complex data analyses with lengthy calculations if done by hand. However, several software packages are now available, which removes one of the obstacles to the wider use of Q methodology (see section on analysis below).

Q-sort technique

This typically involves the rank-ordering of a set of statements from 'agree' to 'disagree', but can also be composed of pictures, recordings, and any other stimuli amenable to appraisal. It is sometimes followed by a focused interview during which participants are invited to discuss their choices. The statements are matters of opinion only (not fact) and the fact that the Q sorter is ranking the statements from her own point of view is what brings subjectivity into the picture. The rankings are subject to factor analysis, and the resulting factors, inasmuch as they have arisen from individual subjectivities, indicate segments of subjectivity which exist. Participants can be asked to sort the same items using two or more different criteria. Rogers (1954), for example, asks for 'real self' and 'ideal self' assessments. Or, for example, in a study of political perceptions, the task could be to sort the sample items according to either a conservative or liberal point of view.

A Q-sample (or Q-set) consists of a set of stimuli each printed on a separate card. Typically, the stimuli are statements expressing different opinions on a certain issue, and the number of statements is somewhere between 30 and 60. Van Exel and de Graaf (2005) provide a detailed worked example including a set of cards and score sheet.

Reliability issues

Thomas and Baas (1992) point out that, as it is a small sample investigation of human subjectivity based on sorting of items of unknown reliability, results from Q methodological studies can be criticized for their reliability and hence the possibility for generalization. Van Exel and de Graaf (2005) review the evidence and conclude that:

> The most important type of reliability for Q is replicability: will the same condition of instruction lead to factors that are schematically reliable – that is, represent similar viewpoints on the topic – across similarly structured yet different Q samples and when administered to different sets of persons. According to Brown (1980) an important notion behind Q methodology is that only a limited number of distinct viewpoints exist on any topic. Any well-structured Q sample, containing the wide range of existing opinions on the topic, will reveal these perspectives. Based on the findings of two pairs of tandem studies, Thomas and Baas (1992) concluded that scepticism over this type of reliability is unwarranted. The more common notion of statistical reliability, regarding the ability to generalise sample results to the general population, is of less concern here. The results of a Q methodological study are the distinct subjectivities about a topic that are operant, not the percentage of the sample (or the general population) that adheres to any of them (p. 3).

Analysis

Analysis of the Q sorts is a purely technical, objective procedure. First, the correlation matrix of all Q sorts is calculated. This represents the level of (dis)agreement between the individual sorts, that is, the degree of (dis)similarity in points of view between the individual Q sorters. Next, this correlation matrix is subject to factor analysis, with the objective to identify the number of natural groupings of Q sorts by virtue of being similar or dissimilar to one another, that is, to examine how many basically different Q sorts are in evidence. People with similar views on the topic will share the same factor. A factor loading is determined for each Q sort, expressing the extent to which each Q sort is associated with each factor (see Chapter 17).

Brown (1980; 1993) provides a comprehensive overview of the analysis of the Q sorts. Because of the tediousness of the analysis the use of a software package is strongly advised. Examples include PQMethod, QUANAL, PCQ for Windows, and WebQ (which permits Q-sorting of items online). Details and links are available from Peter Schmolck's website at http://schmolck. userweb.mwn.de/qmethod/.

The website gives references to examples of research using Q methodology.

Visual research methods

There has recently been a substantial growth in interest in visual research methods as the potential of image-based methodologies is increasingly being appreciated. Visual images can play a useful role in the research process in a variety of ways. Weber (2008, p. 47) lists the following possibilities:

- Images can be produced by participants as data;
- Found or existing images can be used as data or springboards for theorizing;
- Images and objects are useful to elicit or provoke other data;
- Images can be used for feedback and documentation of the research process; and
- Images are useful as a mode of interpretation and/or representation.

Visual images can be used as stimulus material in many research contexts, including interviews and questionnaires. Such uses of images are relatively non-problematic.

However, carrying out a project where visual images and their analysis have a central role is a different matter. It is not an easy choice and should only be attempted with an understanding of the complexities involved. Visual images contain a great deal of information and are difficult to analyse. As Knight (2002) comments: 'It takes a great deal of thought, discussion and persistence to find a way of sustaining a systematic gaze upon large sets of images, and that leaves aside questions about how the set is selected in the first place. This research is so new in social science that there is little to guide the researcher, which compounds the difficulties' (p. 102). There appears to be no general consensus for dealing with visual material, with solutions being put forward on an *ad hoc* or improvised basis.

Photographs have probably been the most widely used form of visual material. Their use illustrates some of the problems. While they have been lauded as being based on objectivity and accuracy of representation, it has long been appreciated that they only provide a particular view of reality, and that the possibilities of manipulation of the photographic image add further complexities. The view that 'all photos lie' is widely held (Goldstein, 2007). Films and video-tapes, taken by and widely used by anthropologists and other ethnographers, have also been considered to be flawed as research evidence (e.g. Emmison & Smith, 2000; Winston, 1998).

A general issue concerns the relative merits of researcher-generated as against participant-generated visual material. A popular example of the latter is the use of family photography and, particularly, family albums, to elicit individual and family memories (e.g. Kuhn, 2002; 2007).

Working with images produced by participants is consonant with the participatory approaches discussed in Chapter 9. Using researcher-generated material tends to be associated with realist approaches to image-based research, using participant-generated material with interpretivist approaches. The realist-interpretive divide is particularly evident in visually based research (Wagner, 2007).

Prosser and Loxley (2008) provide an excellent, detailed and balanced introduction to the use of visual methods, giving good coverage of both realist and interpretivist approaches, with examples. Their review is strongly recommended to anyone considering the use and analysis of visual material. They are clearly convinced about the value and growing importance of image-based research, seeing it as offering 'a range of alternative, diverse and creative possibilities that will expand and support the shifting orientation of social science research and ultimately advance knowledge' (p. 3). However, they warn that inherent complexities in the use of visual material, and unresolved theoretical conflicts, will cause problems if visual methods become fashionable.

Encouragingly, they argue that an applied, real world, approach is of advantage when carrying out visual research. The applied researcher's

focus on a problem and its resolution and . . . willingness to adopt and adapt whatever approach may help resolve that problem. Practitioners draw on a creative or esoteric mix of techniques, methods, perspectives and theoretical frameworks as necessary in order to arrive at resolutions. In contrast, we argue, visual researchers, like many other academics, tend to reapply their knowledge and skills to similar sets of problems within their 'comfort zone'. Of course applied researchers have similar tendencies but they are inventive out of necessity since their funding is often based on their past record in resolving everyday problems that affect people's lives. Applied researchers attempt to answer what could be considered concrete problems and demonstrate (hopefully) successful solutions in the everyday world whereas theoretical research focuses on abstract problems and their primary audience is the academic community. (p. 37).

This points to the desirability of career real world researchers gaining experience in this field. Nevertheless, and despite such encouragement, and the undoubted attractions and likely growth of interest in the field of visual research, the warnings remain. This is not a soft option. Visual research is a specialist field not to be approached without preparation.

The website gives references to examples of research using visual methods.

Discourse analysis

This is a widely used qualitative method based on the detailed examination of language. Taylor (2001) gives as a short definition the 'close study of language in use' (p. 5). While much research using qualitative methods relies on language as providing the means of communication between researchers and participants, in discourse analysis the language itself is the focus of research interest. To the outsider this might appear as a topic area rather than a method in itself but it is claimed that language has such a central role in social life that its study provides the key to understanding our social functioning. In discourse analysis, it is not only the substance of what is said (which forms the basis for conventional analyses) that is important but the styles and strategies of the language users – how they say things.

Unfortunately there is little agreement as to the usage of the term *discourse analysis*. This lack of clarity is inevitable, given its wide range of applications, ranging from purely linguistic analyses, through social psychological approaches, to sociological enquiries into social practices. The notion of 'discourse' itself is the subject of heated debate. As the Centre for Discourse Studies at Denmark's Aalborg University (http://diskurs.hum.aau.dk/english/discourse.htm) puts it:

> It has become one of the key critical terms in the vocabulary of the humanities and the social sciences, so it is not surprising that it is contentious. Discourse encompasses the use of spoken, written and signed language and multimodal/multimedia forms of communication, and is not restricted to 'non-fictional' (e.g. stylistics) nor verbal (e.g. gesture and visual) materials. Although early linguistic approaches judged the unit of discourse to be larger than the sentence, phenomena of interest can range from silence, to a single utterance (such as 'ok'), to a novel, a set of newspaper articles or a conversation.

Typically, it calls for a very detailed analysis of relatively small amounts of discourse. The variants likely to be of greatest value in the type of research covered in this text are not primarily linguistic but more social-psychological.

Virtually any social text can be used as a basis for this type of analysis, including existing documentation or naturally occurring talk, individual and group discussion and interview transcripts. Note, however, that the perspective differs from the traditional one in important respects. With interviews, for example:

> the interview is no longer seen as a means of measuring the genuine views of a participant but as a means of exploring the varied ways of making sense, or accounting practices, available to participants. The concern is at the level of language or discursive practices, rather than with the individual interviewee (Marshall, 1994, p. 95).

Discourse analysis has been concerned with a wide range of topics including gender relations and issues of social control. Research focusing on such topics has clear real world relevance, particularly in relation to policy issues. However, carrying out a discourse analysis calls for specialist expertise and an appreciation of the underlying theoretical background of the particular type of discourse analysis selected.

Jonathan Potter has developed a popular approach (Potter & Wetherell, 1987; Potter, 1997). The theoretical background to his approach is discussed in Potter (1996), and a detailed example of its use in practice is presented in Hepburn and Potter (2006). A variant known as critical discourse analysis based upon the work of Foucault has been proposed by Fairclough (1992). Dick (2004) provides a short, accessible, account together with an example of its application. She points out that it is extremely time-consuming and requires considerable expertise. The 'critical' flags that there is a concern for political issues with a focus on situations that oppress or advantage groups in society, leading into contentious areas (see Chapter 10, p. 355).

These approaches to discourse analysis are seen as falling within the relativist, social constructionist, view of social research (Chapter 2, p. 24). However, there are attempts to develop a critical realist approach. See Sims-Schouten, Riley and Willig (2007) who also provide a detailed example.

The website gives references to examples of research using discourse analysis.

Conversation analysis

The borderline between *conversation analysis* and discourse analysis is somewhat fuzzy. A simple distinction is that discourse analysis embraces the study, not only of conversations (typically as texts, in the form of transcripts), but also of texts from other sources. More fundamentally, most researchers using conversation analysis see it as underpinned by the sociological approach known as *ethnomethodology* (Garfinkel, 1984; 2002). Ethnomethodology is not known for its accessibility and conversation analysis has been similarly criticized, a frequent complaint being that its practitioners tend not to make their methodology and procedures comprehensible to researchers from other disciplines (e.g. Seedhouse, 2004). Kitzinger (2007), in a spirited defence of the value of conversation analysis (CA), rehearses some of these criticisms:

> It is dismissed as jargon-ridden and impenetrable, and (despite its claims to fidelity to participants' own orientations) as divorced from speakers' own understandings of what is going on in interactions. Feminist linguist Robin Lakoff (2003: 168–9) asks acerbically: 'who is aware that a TRP . . . is approaching as they speak?' and 'who realizes that they are producing a dispreferred second or a presequence?' Finally, CA – say the critics – is no fun! It is a method that is 'devoid of pleasure' (Hegarty, 2007: 55) (p. 133).

Notwithstanding these barriers, the approach has strong advocates, including those with applied interests (Barnes, 2005; Have, 2005; Housley & Fitzgerald, 2000). Kitzinger's students, in a set of papers on feminist conversation analysis in the same issue of the journal, provide a practical rebuttal – in particular stressing their enjoyment and involvement in carrying out the analyses.

The advice given above in relation to discourse analysis applies with equal force to conversation analysis.

The website gives references to examples of research using conversation analysis.

Narrative research

Narrative research (often referred to as narrative analysis) is a family of approaches which focus on the stories that people use to understand and describe aspects of their lives. It incorporates *biographical, autobiographical, life history* and *oral history* approaches. The term *narrative* carries many meanings and is used in a variety of ways by different disciplines. It is often used interchangeably with 'story-telling', although a distinction is made by some researchers between narrative as an account by an individual of their own experience and story-telling as its retelling by others.

Riessman and Quinney (2005) review some definitions used in different disciplines:

> In social history and anthropology, narrative can refer to an entire life story, woven from threads of interviews, observations, and documents . . . At the other end of the continuum lies the very restrictive definition of sociolinguistics. Here a story refers to a discrete unit of discourse: an answer to a single question, topically-centered and temporally-organized . . .

Resting in the middle on a continuum of definitions is work in psychology and sociology. Here, personal narrative encompasses long sections of talk – extended accounts of lives in context that develop over the course of single or multiple interviews (p. 394).

The common feature distinguishing narrative from other forms of discourse is *sequence* and *consequence*. Events are selected, organized, connected, and evaluated by the narrator as meaningful for a particular audience (Riessman, 2004).

First person narratives provide much of the material used by researchers. Holloway and Weaver (2002) warn that the content of such narratives necessarily emerges from memory, which is selective. However, they emphasize that 'the remembered events, as well as the experiences people choose from their vast store of memory, focus on the significant aspects of their social reality' (p. 202). See also Koch (1998) who defends the legitimacy of using narratives for research purposes. Notwithstanding the advocacy by narrative researchers such as Riley and Hawe (2005), the research use of narratives remains problematic. Atkinson (1997), while broadly endorsing a narrative approach, is worried that its new-found popularity might be a blind alley for qualitative research. He criticizes claims that narratives offer the analyst privileged access to personal experience. He also suggests that an appeal to narratives too often includes inappropriate assumptions about human actors and social action. Atkinson and Delamont (2006) broaden this criticism, suggesting that too many qualitative researchers are complicit in the general culture of what they term 'the interview society' and are too ready to celebrate narratives and biographical accounts, rather than subjecting them to systematic analysis.

There does not appear to be a standard set of procedures for actually carrying out narrative analysis. Narrative research has been carried out in several different methodological frameworks including ethnographical and phenomenological approaches, each of which has different traditions of analysis. As with much analysis of qualitative data (see Chapter 18), the main tasks are producing a verbatim transcript of the narrative and then proceeding with data reduction. Holloway and Weaver (2002, p. 213) suggest that the approaches can be divided into *holistic analysis* (i.e. analysing the narrative as a whole) or *sequential analysis* (where the text is broken down into segments which are coded and then collapsed into categories which are clustered into themes).

Musson (2004) discusses the use of life histories in organizational research. She provides examples of how general medical practitioners (GPs) in the UK experienced and understood health care reforms affecting their practice. Interestingly, Musson (p. 38) admits that she was not initially intending to use life histories but that, during the course of the research, it became clear that their use was central to her research concerns – an example of a not uncommon feature of research in practice.

Life histories, and other narratives, can be the main or sole method in a research project or combined with other methods. Musson (2004), for example, used participant observation, semi-structured interviews, group discussion and documentary analysis – as well as informal interviews which focused on the collection of individual life histories. The triangulation obtained by the use of several methods helps to ease some of the concerns about the trustworthiness of data from narrative research discussed above.

The advice given above in relation to discourse and conversation analysis applies with equal force to narrative research.

The website gives references to examples of research using narrative analysis.

Meta-analysis

Meta-analysis is a process used in summarizing the results of a number of different studies (Lipsey & Wilson, 2000; Littell, Corcoran & Pillai, 2008). As such, it is commonly linked with *systematic reviews* (discussed in Chapter 5, p. 93) popular within the evidence-based movement. However, systematic reviews represent one particular version of meta-analysis.

It is a general term for the analysis of analyses (hence a meta-analysis). It can be viewed as a method of doing research although it is more usually regarded as an analytic technique. It may well be a sensible use of the time and resources of even a small-scale researcher to put together findings from previous work in a heavily researched area, rather than carry out one more empirical study.

Many journals encourage researchers to submit meta-analyses that summarize the body of evidence on a specific topic. Meta-analyses are replacing the traditional narrative or literature review in some fields. They can also play a variety of other, supporting, roles. For example:

- A paper that reports results for a new study might include a meta-analysis in the introduction to synthesize prior data and help to place the new study in context.
- When planning new studies, a meta-analysis can help identify which questions have already been answered and which remain to be answered, which outcome measures or populations are most likely to yield useful results and which variants of a planned intervention are likely to be most powerful.
- When writing a project proposal, meta-analyses can be used to justify the need for a new study. The meta-analysis puts the available data in context and shows the potential utility of the planned study. Funding agencies commonly require a meta-analysis of existing research as part of the grant application to fund new research.

Most work has been carried out on the meta-analysis of quantitative studies, particularly of randomized controlled trials and other true experiments (using quasi-experimental studies raises additional issues, reviewed by Colliver, Kucera and Verhulst, 2008).

The aim is to provide an integrated study of research results on a specific question, giving particular attention to the size of effects and to statistical significance (see Chapter 17, p. 440). Rosenthal and Rubin's study, summarizing the first 345 studies on experimenter expectancy, is a classic example (Rosenthal & Rubin, 1980). In a similar vein, Milton and Wiseman (1999) analysed mass-media tests of extrasensory perception representing over 1.5 million trials in eight studies and gave an overall cumulative outcome which didn't differ from chance expectation.

Sophisticated statistical methods have been developed which go beyond a simple summing of significant and non-significant results, although they do have quite restrictive assumptions. The technique is also reliant on material from all relevant studies being published and available. The bias in favour of positive results in the publication policies of some journals also causes problems. Finally, the quality of the studies included is obviously of importance – garbage in, garbage out! Egger, Smith and Phillips (1997), and Sutton and Higgins (2008) provide comprehensive reviews of issues in this type of meta-analysis. Software is available to help carry out analysis including Meta-Stat and CMA. Rudner, Glass, Evartt and Emery (2002) is a users' guide to Meta-Stat (available as a free download at http://echo.edres.org:8080/meta/metastat.htm.) with step-by-step instructions on the design, coding, and analysis of meta-analytic studies. The commercial program CMA ('Comprehensive Meta-Analysis') is obtainable from http://www.meta-analysis.com/index.php.

Some attempts have been made to extend meta-analysis to studies incorporating qualitative data. Roberts, Dixon-Woods, Fitzpatrick, Abrams and Jones (2002) describe a meta-analytic approach including both qualitative and quantitative study evidence and give an example from the uptake of childhood immunization. Waight, Willging and Wentling (2002) carried out a purely qualitative meta-analysis of 15 major e-learning reports to establish recurrent themes. Finfgeld-Connett (2010) is concerned that findings from a large number of qualitative research investigations have had little impact on practice and policy formation. Because single qualitative investigations are not intended to produce findings that are directly applicable to practice and simple literature reviews of qualitative studies are poor at developing cumulative knowledge, more sophisticated methods of synthesizing qualitative findings are needed. She advocates a systematic meta-synthesis, which 'involves the qualitative aggregation and interpretation of non-quantitative findings that have been extracted from topically related study reports. This process results in the summation of findings and/or the inductive development of abstracted theory' (p. 247). Variants include meta-summary (Sandelowski, Barroso & Voils, 2007), meta-ethnography (Noblit & Hare, 1988) and grounded theory approaches (Finfgeld-Connett, 2006).

Once again cautionary notes have to be called. Meta-analysis of quantitative data calls for relatively sophisticated statistics and requires choices to be made between different statistical models of the process. The effort involved in carrying out a meta-synthesis of qualitative findings is considerable.

The website gives references to examples of research using meta-analysis.

Phenomenological and hermeneutic methods

Phenomenology and hermeneutics have been discussed in Chapter 7 (p. 165) as general approaches to carrying out flexible design research. They earn their place at that point in the text as they are usually viewed as methodologies with a considerable philosophical and theoretical underpinning. However, it is not unusual to find them treated not only as methodologies but also as methods of data collection.

As with several of the additional methods covered in this chapter, warnings are given about trying to use the method without a previous understanding of its theoretical basis. However, Porter (2008), writing in the context of nursing research where the approaches have achieved popularity, suggests the following:

So we need to ask whether these difficult theories really add that much to the quality of qualitative research. I want to suggest that they do not add much; that it is possible to jettison the baroque intricacies of high phenomenology and just use its simple basic assumptions, without any significant compromise to the integrity of research . . . To my mind, its essence is about trying to uncover, and possibly explain, people's experiences of health, illness, and care. Beyond arguing for the importance of those experiences over and above the objective manifestations of disease, disability, and treatment, what more do we need by way of philosophical foundation? (p. 268)

While somewhat heretical, these arguments chime with the pragmatic ones put forward in Chapter 2, querying the necessity for establishing one's philosophical position (particularly in respect of epistemology and ontology) before venturing into real world research.

De Witt and Ploeg (2006), in a review of ten years of interpretive phenomenological research in this field (other variants include descriptive and dialogic phenomenology) cover many of the issues involved in carrying out this type of research. Whitehead (2004) performs a similar function for hermeneutic research. Both of the studies focus particularly on issues to do with the rigour and trustworthiness of findings (see also Giorgi, 2005).

The usual cautionary note – carrying out some form of phenomenological or hermeneutic study and rooting it in the philosophical foundations of the approach calls for you getting to grips with difficult material to justify your choice and a thorough understanding of the variety you choose. If your concern is primarily to study people's lived experience in some situation, following Porter's suggestion, the philosophy may be superfluous. Read through the examples given and seek others. Following this, if you feel reasonably confident that you can see a way of answering your research questions, you could at least give it a trial. There may, of course, be other constraints. A journal, or the requirements of an academic award, may require discussion of the theoretical background.

 The website gives references to examples of research using phenomenological and hermeneutic methods.

Internet-based research

The value of the Internet for bibliographic-type tasks such as finding and gaining access to previous research both in journals and other publications, and in getting advice in developing a proposal from discussion groups, etc. was highlighted in Chapter 3, pp. 53, 55 and 58. Its usefulness in getting advice and support from such groups not only on project design, but also on the selection and use of methods, on analysis and on virtually all aspects of the process was also discussed in that chapter.

Lee (2000, pp. 117–18) covers several other features of the Internet which may be useful:

- It provides a potentially large pool of participants in surveys and other forms of social research;
- Cross-national research is feasible without the costs of travel;
- Researchers in remote or poorly resourced settings can have access to wider populations than would otherwise be available;
- A degree of anonymity for both researchers and research is possible, hence reducing possible demand characteristics (see Chapter 6, p. 114);
- It is well adapted to methods such as questionnaires and surveys where materials are circulated in written form;
- It holds promise for researching sensitive topics, such as gathering information on drug users and dealers; and
- It can provide, through specialist discussion groups and other Internet forums, access to groups with particular interests, lifestyles, etc.

A useful distinction can be made between using the Internet as a resource or as a topic which can be studied in its own right. Help in finding sources and getting support, mentioned above, is an extremely valuable example of the first type of use. Use of the Internet to carry out online surveys falls into the same category and was discussed in Chapter 11. General issues arising in and from the use of the Internet for data collection are discussed here. Taking aspects of the Internet itself as a research topic has become increasingly popular and provides a second focus for this section.

Using the Internet for research purposes raises important ethical issues. While the agenda of such issues is essentially the same as for any research project, some occur with particular force in this context and the relative novelty of Internet-based research risks inadvertent unethical practices simply because the implications have not been thoroughly explored.

Internet-based data collection in a research project

Researchers can now create studies (i.e. surveys, experiments, etc.) online without needing a knowledge of computer programming. Using e-mail to present a questionnaire needs consideration of the same design and presentation issues as a paper-based postal questionnaire. With the tools now readily available for the development of web pages in Hyper Text Markup Language (HTML), an HTML version of a paper questionnaire is not difficult to produce (applications such as Google Sites greatly simplify the task and do not call for any HTML expertise).

As a vehicle for data collection, the Internet promises increased sample size, greater sample diversity, easier access and convenience, lower costs and time investment, and many other appealing features. Research comparing traditional manual data collection with the use of the Internet generally shows small differences in the type of respondent recruited or the quality of data that they provide (e.g. Manfreda, Batagelj & Vehovar, 2002; Sethuraman, Kerin & Cron, 2005; Carini, Hayek, Kuh, Kennedy & Ouimet, 2003).

Computer skills and familiarity with the input devices affect a respondent's ability to complete an electronic survey. A relevant difference between paper-and-pencil and electronic formats is the level of rapport possible with the respondent. The impact of such rapport may be unpredictable. For some respondents, the signed letter accompanying a paper-and-pencil format may be more persuasive than an e-mail from a stranger, commonly sent with the electronic format. It is uncertain whether face-to-face interaction with a person or the relative anonymity of the Internet produces more authentic responses. The manual paper-and-pencil method might be expected to produce higher-quality data compared to the Internet-based method as it is more tangible, more personal and, generally, more credible to the respondents, especially if the research staff are in the room with them (Nosek, Banaji & Greenwald, 2002). However, Internet-based data collection can reduce costs and yield larger samples, making unfunded projects feasible.

Consumer researchers and marketing firms have created dedicated websites and electronic mailing lists designed to send out surveys to the willing public (e.g. VIP Voice – an online consumer panel of over 2.5 million registered members with offices in 60 countries – http://www.npdor.com/). Researchers using the Internet can recruit participants (e.g. psychologists' traditional quarry of students; or a specific occupational, religious or social group) by either mass e-mailing the survey to the target group or sending out the survey website link to community leaders or organizations that interact with the target group.

Despite the large potential participant pool, the actual number of respondents in an Internet survey can be quite low. For example, Benfield and Szlemko (2006), in a project concerning health behaviours and activity, e-mailed details of a website for the survey to all 25,000 students on campus. A second e-mail was sent out two weeks later with a reminder and the link. One month after the original recruitment e-mail, they had only 509 respondents (i.e. a 2 per cent response rate). They also provide a chastening account of the wide range of technical snags that can beset Internet-based data collection. Despite these problems they remain enthusiastic about its potential, concluding that:

> The single most appealing advantage of the electronic method of data collection is the elimination of the tedious data entry process. With the electronic method the data are entered into a database at the same time as the respondent completes the survey. If a researcher plans on collecting large amounts of data or having a large sample size, electronic data collection can be invaluable. It is a solution in itself when facing mountains of data and weeks' worth of data entry. An additional advantage is that typing errors by the researcher are avoided. The data file is an exact replica of the responses received (section 6).

What they refer to as 'electronic data collection' includes surveys, etc. carried out in computer labs as well as via the Internet.

Box 15.6 summarizes some of the advantages and disadvantages of using Internet data collection.

BOX 15.6

Advantages and disadvantages of Internet data collection

Advantages

1. Increasing computer literacy in many groups who are more comfortable with online presentation of material than completing paper questionnaires.
2. Some groups are more easily reached via the Internet (e.g. geographically widely dispersed, groups with special interests or concerns).
3. Economies of scale – the effort of contacting large samples is not much greater than contacting small samples.
4. A wide variety of recruitment strategies is available including e-mail contact, use of discussion and social networking groups.
5. The drudgery of data entry by the researcher can be eliminated (possibility of instant online data capture).

Disadvantages

1. Some groups and individuals are unfamiliar with computers (e.g. old persons, socially disadvantaged).
2. Some groups and individuals are unable to interact with computers without adaptation (e.g. visually and physically handicapped)
3. Development, piloting and testing of the electronic system including checking of data capture are not cost-effective for small samples.
4. There are likely problems in securing a representative sample and/or an acceptable response rate.

Recruitment strategies

Researchers have had to show ingenuity and persistence when recruiting samples for Internet-based studies. In a study of appearance-related concerns of young people who have chronic skin conditions, Fox (reported in Fox, Murray & Warm, 2003) recruited online, partly to increase the likelihood that participants had access to and some experience of using the Internet. Skin care charities and support organizations advertised a link to her website on their pages designed for young people. Young people sought further information about the study and chose to participate at their own discretion.

Benfield and Szlemko (2006), discussed above in relation to their severe recruitment woes, had further problems when seeking a community sample of driving behaviours. Their original recruitment procedure, involving placing leaflets on parked vehicles, resulted in a 0.5 per cent response rate. They then adopted a snowball sampling technique in which the survey was sent out to friends, family, and colleagues. This recruitment e-mail contained study information, the link to the survey, and instructions to forward the e-mail to friends, family, and colleagues. Using this approach, 60 initial e-mails yielded three times as many responses within the first month.

Cichy, Cha and Kim (2007) carried out an online survey of leaders in the private club industry. They targeted members of the Club Managers Association of America (CMAA) who were listed in the CMAA e-mail lists. To encourage members' participation in the online survey, an invitation e-mail was sent directly from the CEO of the CMAA to members. Two reminder e-mails were sent to those who had not responded, resulting in a 20 per cent response rate.

Hamilton and Bowers (2006) discuss recruitment issues and provide useful suggestions on a research design for a study employing both Internet recruitment and e-mail interviewing.

Sampling issues

Low response rates pose problems if representative samples are required (Chapter 11, p. 282). Although a wide population uses the Internet and has access to it, both nationally and internationally, this does not mean that they are all inclined to take part in research because of, potentially, language barriers, free time, skills in using technology and/or browsing habits.

Authenticity of response

The so-called 'cheaters and repeaters' problem, in which unqualified persons participate in the research or qualified persons participate more than once, can also affect the quality of Internet-based research. Steps should be taken to check that all participants are members of the target population (e.g. if working with a professional group to require details of their professional affiliation). It is feasible to ensure that multiple surveys completed by the same individual are weeded out before the data set is analysed (note that this could be a mistake rather than a deliberate attempt to repeat, if the participant is able to send a response before completing the survey and then makes a second attempt). These problems can occur in traditional paper-based market

BOX 15.7

Practical advice on Internet-based data collection

- If a single question is posted on a full computer screen, it is harder to skip a question than on a paper copy with 20 questions on a page.
- A large font and clearly delineated buttons for each response make questions easier to read for persons with visual difficulties.
- Online surveys eliminate the need for data entry by the researcher and less error is expected.
- Requiring responses to all questions and re-asking skipped questions may decrease response rates because some questions may be sensitive to answer or may not be understood by respondents.
- Plain web pages provide better results than fancier versions.
- Acknowledgement of a respondent's participation in a study should occur seconds after they have completed the survey.
- To ensure anonymity, online surveys should be e-mailed to a neutral party, such as an established website.
- Internet data must be properly secured when stored on a server or computer.
- Informed consent must be provided and respondents made aware of the risks and benefits of electronic records.
- When recruiting participants online, a posting of a précis of the research proposal, an outline of how the results will be used and invitation to participate should be included in the advertisement of the study.
- Include information about where individuals can obtain more information; for example, the researcher's e-mail address or WWW page should be provided.
- A questionnaire embedded in a WWW page is easier for a participant to complete.

   (abridged from Table 1, Cantrell and Lupinacci, 2007. Original sources: Hanscom, Lurie, Homa and Weinstein, 2002; Klein, 2002; and Lakeman, 1997.)

research of course, and are probably less expensive and time-consuming to safeguard against in Internet-based studies.

Practicalities of Internet-based data collection

The principles of questionnaire design, and generally the use of data collection methods discussed in previous chapters (and the earlier sections of this chapter) apply with equal force when using the Internet to collect data. Some specific things to take note of in web-based data collection are listed in Box 15.7.

The website gives references to examples of research using the Internet for data collection.

The Internet as a topic for research

The Internet is undeniably a world-wide phenomenon with major effects not only on communication but also, more generally, on society and its functioning. Phippen (2007) eloquently reviews these effects:

> The impact of the World Wide Web . . . is undoubtedly as significant as it was unpredictable. In some cases we can see entirely new forms of social interaction, from small, initial virtual communities . . . (Rheingold 2000), to today's massive, entirely virtual world such as Second Life. The advent of Web 2.0 sites such MySpace, Bebo, and Flickr and their relative population sizes (a recent measure claimed 25 million users of Bebo and over 70 million users of MySpace) show how people wish to use the web to facilitate social interactions, to form communities and to share experiences with people whom they have never physically met. Blogging provides the facilities for anyone with a web connection to expose their inner most thoughts to the world (and in a lot of cases, they seem very happy to do so!). While the immediate reaction of many to blogs is that they serve as a channel for narcissists, when one begins to examine the language and behaviour in blogs, one realises while the reasons for blogging may be broad and varied (from marketing and transparency within businesses to reflections on everyday life in a changing word for individuals) there is commonality in that they exist as a means of communication for people who wish to reach beyond their geographical constraints (para. 1).

It is therefore not surprising that researchers from many disciplines have made it a focus for research projects. Hine (2005) reviews the substantial body of work on how the Internet can be used as a focus for research. Phippen (2007) characterizes the existing research as being traditional in nature and, while acknowledging the value of such research, argues that greater use could be made of technical information generated when users interact with the web. For example, every time a link is clicked or a web resource request is typed into an address bar, details are written to a web server log file. The analysis of these files has been prevalent in the commercial world for a number of years. He provides examples of how this information could be used for research purposes. A wealth of technical data of this kind is available from contexts other than the Internet. For example, Evans (2007) discusses possible research uses for the 'transactional' data available from supermarket loyalty cards and the radio frequency identification tags attached to merchandise (and used by some US health care providers). In a similar vein Diminescu, Licoppe, Smoreda and Ziemlicki (2007) describe a project which makes use of the technical data on the position and usage of mobile phones. Each of these possible uses raises formidable ethical issues (see Chapter 10).

The website gives references to examples using the Internet as a topic for research.

Feminist research methods

Chapter 2 covered the contribution of feminist approaches to methodology (p. 39). The feminist view is that accepted ways of carrying out research (particularly positivistic, quantitative approaches) are dominated by males and miss many of the issues specific to women. Such research is regarded as a form of exploitation arising from the differential relationship between the researcher and respondent, particularly when the former is male and the latter female (Oakley, 1981). Theories, which influence the way in which questions are framed and data are collected and analysed, even if not inherently male, distort the experiences of women in the accounts that are collected.

This is also taken as support for specific feminist research methods that are qualitative and non-positivist (e.g. Roberts, 1981). Reinharz (1992) has, however, taken the view that, while there are distinct methodological practices that have been associated with feminist research, there is no one method that is solely owned by feminist researchers, nor is there a method that is in principle unusable by feminist researchers. Similarly, Mason (1997), in the context of social work research, rejects the view that there is a 'best' method for upholding feminist principles. Oakley (1998; 2000) has sought to rehabilitate quantitative methods and to integrate a range of methods in the task of creating an emancipatory social science. Landman (2006) takes a similar stance, agreeing that research that recognizes feminist precepts is not necessarily exclusively qualitative, pointing out that it can be argued that 'quantitative instruments, properly designed, could be potentially less harmful to respondents and more useful to policy makers' (p. 432). She also cites the view of Letherby (2004) that the use of qualitative research is not the only legitimate feminist approach. Letherby advocates variety and diversity in feminist methods, warning that the myth that feminists 'only do interviews' persists, which compounds sexist views about women as good listeners and men alone having numerical skills.

Reinharz (1992) has produced a useful compendium focusing on the diversity of methods actually used by feminist social scientists. She includes chapters on quantitative 'feminist survey research and other statistical research formats' and 'feminist experimental research' as well as the more qualitative approaches such as semi-structured and unstructured interviewing which are undoubtedly central to much feminist research practice.

The aim of feminist research to end the marginalization of women's lived experience in social science has facilitated other developments. Social research informed by feminist methodology with oppressed groups, whose lives and experiences would otherwise be rendered invisible or only partially rendered, has focused on ethnic groups such as Maori in New Zealand (Bishop, 1998) and gay and lesbian groups (Plummer, 1994).

The stance taken in this book, while not accepting the full feminist critique, is that there is considerable virtue for real world research in taking on board feminist proposals – particularly in acknowledging the emotional aspects of doing real world research and the value of emphasizing commitment as against detachment. While feminist research may not have a distinguishable set of methods for collecting data, it has undoubtedly had a strong influence on research practice, particularly in developing and popularizing innovative methods.

Using multiple methods

Using multiple (i.e. two or more) methods of data collection in a project is a common practice. Semi-structured interviews might be combined with participant observation in a flexible design or a questionnaire with the administration of some type of test in a fixed one. These examples would result in both methods producing qualitative data, or both quantitative data, respectively. In other situations, one method might produce qualitative data, a second quantitative data.

When carrying out an experiment (resulting in quantitative data), following up with informal interviews (resulting in qualitative data) can assist its interpretation. Quantitative data from a structured questionnaire can strengthen the findings in many flexible design studies. The most common pattern is to buttress a main method with a relatively minor second one.

The multiple-strategy designs discussed in Chapter 8 use more than one method, but represent a special case where there is a deliberate juxtaposition of both fixed and flexible design elements in the same project, and a substantial amount of time and effort is devoted to each of these aspects of the design. They are a relatively new, somewhat controversial, development.

Using more than one method in an investigation can have substantial advantages, even though it almost inevitably adds to the time investment required. The main advantage is commonly cited as permitting triangulation. Multiple methods can also be used to address different but complementary research questions within a study. This focuses on the use of different methods for alternative tasks. A common example occurs when initial exploratory work is done by means of unstructured interviews and subsequent descriptive and explanatory work employs a sample survey.

The complementary purposes notion can be used to assess the plausibility of threats to validity of the primary research technique used. This is a tactic used particularly in the context of quasi-experimental designs (see Chapter 6). The basic notion is that the particular pattern of findings and context of a specific quasi-experimental design may leave its interpretation open to particular 'threats'. So, for example, in a time series design, some persons may drop out of a treatment group during the course of a study (the 'mortality' effect). Interviews might be undertaken, both from this group and from those continuing, to assess whether there are differences between those who drop out and those who continue.

The message is that you need not be the prisoner of a particular method or technique when carrying out research. There is much to be said for using more than one method of data collection in a project. The main disadvantage (apart from the possibility that the methods produce conflicting results which need interpretation as discussed in Chapter 7, p. 184) is the time and resources needed to use each of the methods to a professional standard.

If you have reached this page, at the end of Part III of the book, and you are still not sure which general approach or method (or methods) of data collection best fits your research questions, and your personal preferences, Shamus Khan and Dana Fisher's The Practice of Research *(Khan & Fisher, 2013) might help. They invited researchers, covering a wide range of approaches and methods, to present a published article and then to give a candid account of what it was really like to carry out the research.*

Further reading

The website gives annotated references to further reading for Chapter 15.

CHAPTER 16

Writing a project proposal

This chapter:

- considers the characteristics of a good project proposal;
- lists the typical content of a project proposal;
- addresses the problem of pre-specifying flexible design proposals;
- reviews the shortcomings of unsuccessful project proposals; and
- suggests possible sources of funding.

Introduction

A research project could be an entirely private activity which you carry out by yourself, and for yourself alone, but it rarely is. By reading a text like this, you are signalling that you are trying to take note of what others have done and what they have learned about how to carry out research effectively. We don't have to reinvent the wheel for each new project – although there is something to be said for not being a prisoner of current orthodoxies about how things should be done.

Carrying out the project is rarely a totally solo exercise. Much real world research is a group activity. While research for a doctorate or other formal qualification is normally expected to be on an individual basis, supervisors are in the background providing advice and support. Using social research methods in your project almost always calls for the active involvement of research participants. It also usually involves access to, and the use of, public resources. Given this, there is an onus on researchers to make their findings available through some form of publication (i.e. 'making public').

It is, therefore, appropriate that any proposed research should be laid out for inspection and comment by others, and, in many cases, that it should be approved by others. Any student certainly requires her proposal to be formally approved. Those seeking funding require the approval of the funding agency to which they apply or they will not receive support. In both these cases, there will almost always be a specified format to the proposal. It is an obvious part of the professional approach advocated here that this should be strictly adhered to. If a maximum of 2,000 words is required for 1 May, you do not send in 3,000 on 8 May.

The main concern here is for general issues appropriate to all relatively small-scale real world research proposals. A useful analogy has been made between researchers and architects (Hakim, 2000, p. 1). Planning is the main link. The architect plans buildings. The researcher draws up plans to investigate issues and solve problems. In each case these plans must say something about structure, about how the task is conceptualized, and about the methods to be used in carrying out the plans.

For both the researcher and the architect, it is insufficient simply to present the concept of the problem and its suggested mode of solution (tower block or ranch house; survey or experiment). Factors like the resources needed to carry out the work; the qualifications and experience of those involved; previous work that has already been carried out by the applicant and others; computer facilities; obtaining of any necessary permissions and clearances – all these and many other matters are important.

> *The research proposal is your opportunity to persuade the 'client' that you know what you are talking about. That you have thought through the issues involved and are going to deliver. That it is worthwhile to take the risk and give you licence to get on with it.*

There is a temptation to think of writing the research proposal as merely an irksome formality, a hurdle that has to be jumped before you can get on with the real work of research. Viewed in this light, it is likely to be a waste of time. It is probable that you will produce a skimped and unconvincing proposal which, quite rightly, gets turned down. It is much more helpful to see it as an important and integral part of the research process. The work that you do at this stage may not produce the definitive proposal which gives an accurate account of what you are going to do in the research and what will come out of it. Little research has that degree of certitude. But if you can persuade experienced and disinterested judges that what you are proposing looks interesting and do-able within the constraints of resources and time that you have available, you should take heart. Remember that you are the one who has most to lose if you get into a situation where the research is a failure and that you want the best insurance policy that you can get. Viewed in that light, it is well worth investing in a good research proposal.

How to recognize a good proposal

A good proposal is direct and straightforward

It tells what you are proposing to do; and why you are proposing to do it. The former is concerned with aims and the research questions to which you will seek answers. Make sure that they are clear and explicit. For the latter, you will have to show why it is interesting and timely, which will involve a demonstration of your awareness of the empirical and theoretical context.

Good research demands clarity of thought and expression in the doing and the reporting. The proposal provides good evidence of this. If it is muddled, it deserves rejection.

A good proposal communicates well

The basic purpose is to communicate your intentions. Anything that gets in the way of this should be cut out. Complex mega-sentences illustrating the complexity and subtlety of your thought processes should be avoided. Fine writing with arcane vocabulary (such as 'arcane') does not help. Unless it is specifically asked for, you do not seek to impress by gargantuan book lists illustrating what you have read or hope to read. If the reader gains the impression that you are stuffing it with references for effect, you are in danger of losing their sympathy. The few key works central to your proposal are more appropriate. Incidentally, if you are referring to a specific point in a book or long journal article, give the page reference – it shouldn't be the reader's job to search for it.

As with any research-related writing, the question of audience is important. Appropriate assumptions may vary for different kinds of proposals but it is often helpful to regard the reader not as an expert in the exact sub-field of your research but more as a cross between an intelligent layperson and a generalist in the discipline.

A good proposal is well organized

The structure of your proposal should be simple and self-evident. It helps to have a consistent system for indicating and, if you need to, lettering or numbering, headings and sub-headings. The expected style is usually standard paragraphing and continuous prose. Don't produce a minutely sectionalized, note-form proposal.

Remember that research demands organization above virtually everything else. A poorly organized proposal does little for your cause.

The content of a research proposal

If you have to work to a standard format on a proposal form or grant application, this obviously determines how you set things out. Try to get hold of a few recent successful applications and study them. There is substantial overlap between many of the formats and it is likely that you will have to provide the following.

Abstract or summary

This should be brief, clear, and informative, giving a flavour of what is intended and why. It will be the first thing read so you want to give a good impression. Don't exceed any word limit which is specified. As with research reports it can be a good idea to write this as the final task after completing the other sections. If you prefer to write it first, do return to the abstract at the end to ensure that it does summarize what is in the proposal.

Aims, objectives, research questions and hypotheses

The format may specify how to deal with this aspect (e.g. you may be required to specify an overall aim and some more specific objectives). Inspection of successful proposals using a similar methodology to the one you propose will help. The general approach favoured in this text is to work using a small set of research questions. However, if they expect hypotheses (e.g. in experimental designs), give them hypotheses.

Background and purpose

A major section where you impress by your commitment and professionalism. It will include a short review of relevant work done by others. It is crucial that you unearth and include any very recent work. Its presence will be reassuring to a specialist reviewer and its absence potentially damning. You want to show that there is a gap to be filled, or a next step to be taken, or a concern arising – and that you have a good idea how this should be addressed.

Relevance is very important. Don't show off by displaying ideas or knowledge which do not contribute directly. It helps to get a sympathetic critic to read your draft. If you have been preparing this for some time, you will be so close to it that you find it difficult to put yourself into the position of someone reading it for the first time. Complex constructions may need unpacking, the implicit made explicit.

Dissertation proposals may require a substantial literature review, together with details of your methodological stance and a justification for its selection and, possibly, a conceptual framework (see the chapters in Part II of this text). A proposal seeking approval and funds from management to carry out a study in your workplace will be unlikely to need it. Other funding bodies usually make their expectations clear.

For all proposals, your aim is to lead the reader inexorably towards the conclusion you have reached: that this is the work that must be done, now, with these aims, and in this way. And that you are the person to do it.

The plan of work

Here you go into some detail about the general approach, methods and procedures to be used. The detail which is necessary or possible will vary according to the nature of the research. A traditional experiment will require close specification of the design to be used, how variables are to be operationalized and details of chosen tests or measures (justifying the specific choice if alternatives are possible). If more flexible strategies are used, you still have to demonstrate that you know what is involved (see below).

It is often helpful, and reassuring to the reader, if you have carried out some previous work to prepare the ground for the study. This may have been part of an earlier study or project which inspired you to develop it further. Or you might have carried out specific pilot work, perhaps to demonstrate the feasibility of what you are now proposing. This can get you out of a common 'Catch-22' situation. If you are, say, simply repeating a procedure that others have used, this does not constitute novel research; if you go for a novel procedure, how do you know that it is going to work?

You need to be clear where the research will take place and who will be involved. Will you be doing all the work or is it in some sense a group exercise? If the latter, how is your contribution to be demarcated from the larger enterprise? If it is at all feasible, the scale of the research should be stated (e.g. size of any samples). Any necessary permissions for access, cooperation or involvement will have to be negotiated prior to presenting the proposal and statements about this made here (possibly with documentation, such as confirmatory letters, as well).

The plan will also need to specify how data will be analysed. You should, once again, convince the reader that you have thought through the issues. Above all, you have to guard against the impression that you are going to gather the data and then think about analysis afterwards. Or that you will simply subject the data to an unspecified barrage of computer-generated analyses. You should indicate the nature and extent of any computer support needed and how the need will be met.

The format for a research proposal may require you to produce a timeline showing what happens when. A popular project management tool for doing this is known as a Gantt chart. In its simplest form, it is a horizontal bar chart where each bar shows the planned start and end times of tasks or activities as they occur across time. Specialist software is available but they can be produced using Excel (see https://www.projectsmart.co.uk/creating-a-gantt-chart-using-excel.php for a video presentation which provides a step-by-step guide). Even if you are not required to do this, it is a useful exercise to help you meet crucial deadlines and to tie yourself down to realistic plans.

Financial aspects

Any proposal which involves financial implications should spell these out and indicate who is going to pay. For a student, this may involve equipment, computer time, photocopying, printing, telephone, etc. A member of staff, or a practitioner or professional doing work for his own organization, may also have to include a sum to cover for the time he is involved and for any additional staff time (whether secretarial, technical or research assistance). Bids for external funding would include all these headings and substantial amounts for overheads. Different institutions and different funding bodies each have their own interpretations of what is admissible and you obviously have to play the game according to their rules.

Box 16.1 lists headings to consider when drawing up a budget forecast. It is all too easy to forget some aspect of what you will need to complete the project and very difficult to add in further expenditure once funding has been agreed.

There is a general tendency to underestimate the financial implications of any research, particularly when times are hard and money scarce. The best advice is to be as realistic as you can. Research is, by definition, problematic and unforeseen circumstances inevitably tend to increase costs. Cutting corners and skimping financially is a false economy. It may slightly increase your chances of getting approval (though not necessarily; experienced assessors might regard it as an indication of a lack of professionalism) but it will almost certainly decrease your chances of delivering satisfactorily on time. If you find that you do not have the time or resources to complete the project as envisaged, the situation can sometimes be rescued by 'trading down' to a simpler design (see Hakim, 2000, pp. 150–2).

BOX 16.1

Headings in a budget forecast

1. *Personnel*. To include salaries and overheads for the Project Director and any other staff and/or research assistants (perhaps on a proportionate basis). Standard scales will usually apply.
2. *Equipment*. Not usually a major item in social research projects but items such as video or other cameras, specialist computer systems, if essential and not otherwise available, are included. Regulations may require multiple quotations from different suppliers.
3. *Materials and supplies*. Likely to include computer supplies, software, printing and publication costs. Check whether you need to include library and inter-library facilities, telephones, etc.
4. *Secretarial and administrative support*. Specify whether whole or part time and salary grade.
5. *Travel and subsistence*. Split according to costs associated with data collection (e.g. in connection with field visits), attendance at conferences and workshops (e.g. training courses for research assistant to acquire specialist skills), and visits to other institutions (e.g. for discussions, library study).
6. *Consultancy*. May be needed if specialist advice is called for.
7. *Other costs*. Any costs specific to the project which do not fall under the previous headings. Must be specified in detail.

Note: Follow closely the format required by the body from whom you seek funding. Note in particular what is allowable and their expectations about what you (or your institution if you are approaching an outside body) will cover. Finance departments will have extensive experience of what is needed and should be consulted at an early stage. Institutions typically apply standard percentage mark-ups to some or all items; include where appropriate.

Ethical implications

Projects using social research methods will require ethical vetting or a statement explaining why this is considered not to be needed. See Chapter 10 for details. This may involve seeking approval from more than one board or committee. It is usually sensible to seek clearance from them at an early stage of the preparation of the proposal, when its main features have been settled. The formal proposal then simply certifies that approval has been granted.

There may also be legal implications of certain kinds of research. One which potentially affects much UK research arises from the Data Protection Act; other countries are likely to have corresponding legislation (see Chapter 10, p. 219). They are designed to protect individuals from having personal data stored on computer and other files without their knowledge, agreement and access. If any such data are stored in your research, you need to seek advice on your responsibilities.

A final note

Przeworski and Salomon (2004) conclude their excellent short paper on *The art of writing proposals: some candid suggestions for applicants to Social Science Research Council competitions* with the advice:

> To write a good proposal takes a long time. Start early. Begin thinking about your topic well in advance and make it a habit to collect references while you work on other tasks. Write a first draft at least three months in advance, revise it, show it to colleagues. Let it gather a little dust, collect colleagues' comments, revise it again. If you have a chance, share it with a seminar or similar group; the debate should help you anticipate what reviewers will eventually think. Revise the text again for substance. Go over the language, style, and form. Resharpen your opening paragraph or first page so that it drives home exactly what you mean as effectively as possible.

The problem of pre-specifying flexible design studies

In the flexible design studies discussed in Chapter 7, it is not feasible to pre-specify many of the details of the research project. The design, and much of the specific features of the project, is typically viewed as emerging and evolving during the project.

Proposals for this type of research must convince that the research questions are best dealt with in this way. It must also convince, through its argument and referencing, that you are competent to carry out this style of research and capable of using the proposed methods. Marshall and Rossman (2011) and Morse (2004) provide helpful suggestions for the development and description of this kind of proposal. Krathwohl and Smith (2005, Chapter 11) give an annotated example of a successful dissertation proposal using this type of methodology.

Multi-strategy designs

As these designs, discussed in Chapter 8, necessarily incorporate a substantial flexible design element or phase involving methods resulting in qualitative data, the issues discussed in this section also apply. They can, in fact, be exaggerated if reviewers of the proposal expect a similar specificity in the description of this flexible design phase to that presented in the fixed design element or phase. It may be advisable to meet this issue head-on by explaining that such specificity is not feasible in this part of the project's design.

Shortcomings of unsuccessful proposals

There are, of course, an almost unlimited number of ways in which to present an unsatisfactory research proposal which would justifiably be unsuccessful. Leedy and Ormrod (2013, Chapter 5) examine the matter thoroughly. They cite analyses of American grant applications which,

BOX 16.2

Ten ways to get your proposal turned down

1. Don't follow the directions or guidelines given for your kind of proposal. Omit information that is asked for. Ignore word limits.
2. Ensure that the title has little relationship to the stated objectives; and that neither title nor objectives link to the proposed methods or techniques.
3. Produce woolly, ill-defined objectives.
4. Have the statement of the central problem or research focus vague or obscure it by other discussion.
5. Leave the design and methodology implicit; let them guess.
6. Have some mundane task, routine consultancy or poorly conceptualized data trawl masquerade as a research project.
7. Be unrealistic in what can be achieved with the time and resources you have available.
8. Be either very brief, or, preferably, long-winded and repetitive in your proposal. Rely on weight rather than quality.
9. Make it clear what the findings of your research are going to be and demonstrate how your ideological stance makes this inevitable.
10. Don't worry about a theoretical or conceptual framework for your research. You want to do a down-to-earth study so you can forget all that fancy stuff.

although they relate to applications for external funding, have considerable relevance to all research proposals. Four major factors come out as shortcomings of poor applications:

- the problem being of insufficient importance, or unlikely to produce any new or useful information;
- the proposed tests, methods or procedures being unsuited to the stated objective;
- the description of the research being nebulous, diffuse or lacking in clarity, so that it could not be adequately evaluated; and
- the investigator not having adequate training, or experience, or both, for the research.

Box 16.2 gives a list of things you might like to think about when appraising your own research proposal. It is not exhaustive.

Sources of funding

Registered students

As a student registered on a research degree or carrying out a project as part of a formal qualification, this should not be your problem. Your supervisor(s) should accept the responsibility of providing you with the resources necessary to complete the project. Obviously this does not mean that you can expect unlimited funding. The design agreed between you should acknowledge financial realities. Many small-scale real world student projects call for minimal resources over and above your own time and efforts. Access to libraries, inter-library loans, the Internet, computer facilities, and support from specialists such as statisticians should be provided for all registered students. Research students should also be able to attend appropriate conferences and workshops. Other students who would like to carry out a project for which it would not be reasonable to expect their institution to meet the cost (perhaps a few weeks' fieldwork in an exotic location, or another project needing extensive travel) should not be barred from seeking sponsorship of some kind from an outside agency.

Shoestring projects

Carrying out a project on any basis other than as a registered student almost always calls for additional resources of some kind which you will have to fund. Projects can be, and have been, carried out on a purely voluntary basis where those involved give their own time and effectively fund themselves. They often give not only their time but pick up the bill for transport, printing, computing, libraries, etc. If this seems the only way forward to get a project up and running, why not go for it?

Insider research

Basing a project in your own workplace offers many potential bonuses. The key to this is often tailoring the project so that it is seen by managers as useful and likely to be of value to the working of the firm or business. If so (and it may call for negotiation on your part, perhaps modifying your original intentions and/or weaning the manager from their first thoughts about what is needed), you are more likely to be given time and the necessary resources to complete the project. Just as important are more intangible factors which open doors and facilitate progress. If managers are suspicious and only giving grudging approval to something which they view as only of value to you personally, it is all too easy for them to sabotage the project. Remember also that just because you have the active support of management in no way guarantees that the project will be viewed positively at all levels of the organization. Indeed, if labour relationships are poor, support from high levels can be unhelpful with other workers and union officials.

Practitioner researchers doing insider research in their own institutions while registered for an award as a student benefit particularly from carrying out a project perceived as valuable by managers in their institution. Not only is this likely to facilitate progress when carrying out the project but it also makes financial support for registration on the course more likely.

External funding

Getting funding for research is not easy. 'Track record' is an important factor in securing funding. If you can point to a number of successful projects, completed on time and within budget, and positively evaluated by reviewers, you are more likely to be successful. When research funding resources are inadequate, such that even proposals judged to be of high quality face rejection, it is understandable that proven success ranks highly. This is not good news for fledgling researchers (though one possibility is to collaborate initially with a colleague who has the requisite track record).

If you go solo, start small and spread your net wide when seeking funding. Charities, such as the Joseph Rowntree Foundation, Leverhulme Trust and Nuffield Foundation in the UK, are well worth considering if you can match your project to their priorities. There are large numbers of trusts and other bodies prepared to consider applications for small grants to carry out social research. The Directory of Social Change publishes a *Directory of Grant-making Trusts* (Smyth and Casson, 2007) available in many libraries (see also their 'Grants for Individuals' website available at http://www.grantsforindividuals.org.uk). See also http://www.charitychoice.co.uk, which includes a searchable directory of grant-giving charities. Note, however, that many trusts fund other activities rather than research and it can be very time-consuming finding those willing to fund research.

In the US, the Foundation Center publishes 'Foundation Directory Online', a massive searchable online database for funding research. The Association of Charitable Foundations website provides links to grant-making trusts and foundations in Europe and many other parts of the world (http://www.acf.org.uk/links/?id=384).

Tarling (2006, Chapter 4) provides a detailed review of funders of applied social research in the UK. The Economic and Social Research Council (ESRC) is the major funder by a large margin but other councils such as the Arts and Humanities Research Council and the Medical Research Council have some involvement. Much of the support is for large-scale programmes but several funders, including the ESRC, have 'small grants' schemes. Most UK government departments fund social research (see http://www.gsr.gov.uk for details). The European Union has also provided substantial social research funding for large projects, typically involving cooperation between institutions in two or more member states.

The ESRC and some major charities in the UK fund fellowships for individuals at various stages of a research career. The Social Science Research Council (SSRC) has an extensive fellowship programme in the US (see http://fellowships.ssrc.org/, which also provides links to other programmes). Fellowships, which are not necessarily linked to specific detailed projects, can be very helpful at the immediately post-doctoral stage when new researchers seek to get themselves established.

Further reading

The website gives annotated references to further reading for Chapter 16.

PART IV

Carrying out the project

Arranging the practicalities

Know what you are doing before starting the data collection

Persevering to this stage should have got you fully equipped with a focus for your project and some related research questions, which may be quite specific and concrete but are more likely to be relatively tentative. You will have given thought to the most appropriate research strategy and have sorted out the methods and techniques you need to implement this strategy.

Perhaps. This is the rational, sequential version of the research process. However, there is a 'reconstructed logic' to the process, mirroring that of the scientific paper (Silverman, 1985, p. 4). Buchanan, Boddy and McCalman (2013) emphasize the necessarily opportunistic flavour to much field research. For example,

> a friend made a casual enquiry about our research . . . he suggested that we study his own company . . . We then discussed what the company would be prepared to let us do, and the research design was settled over a mixed grill and two pints of beer . . . the following week, after a couple of telephone calls and an exchange of letters, we met the manager responsible . . . It became clear that we should interview the head of the new word-processing section . . . our first interview with him started there and then . . . the manager suggested that as the computer system was to be shut down on Wednesday . . . we could come back tomorrow . . . and interview our first batch of video typists. He also asked if we would like to see the minutes of the working party that had decided to install the system, and he produced from the drawer figures charting the performance of the company's typists since 1975 (pp. 54–5).

They stress that the published account (Buchanan & Boddy, 1982) implies that the research questions were based on a prior assessment of the literature, with the research strategy and methods being selected as most appropriate in this context. In fact there was no opportunity to carry out a formal literature review, explore other possible methods, or design and pilot interview schedules. In other words, real world research is very much the 'art of the possible'. *They were able to carry out the study successfully because of a prior familiarity with the literature and the field, which helped frame the research questions, and their experience in carrying out similar studies.*

There are several classic 'insider accounts' of research projects which make very valuable reading for anyone seeking to carry out a project. These include Bell and Encel (1978), and Bryman (1988). Deem (1996) provides an autobiographical account of her career as a researcher, emphasizing that, as in the progress of a research project: 'What has occurred has frequently been contingent, rarely linear, sometimes accidental and often serendipitous' (p. 6).

Such accounts reveal the fact that *experienced researchers can and do make a variety of mistakes*, including false starts and initial overambitiousness requiring substantial refocusing of the study. Novice researchers should take considerable heart from this. Such mistakes do not indicate that you are no good as a researcher; more that you are human. The accounts highlight the 'luck' or 'serendipity' factor (the 'happy knack of making fortunate discoveries'). It is also clear that the move from the traditional distant, uninvolved relationship between researcher and participant which is called for in most qualitative flexible design studies heightens the emotional dynamics of the research relationship, and is likely to generate considerable anxiety in the researcher. The emotional ante is raised for all concerned when sensitive topics are the focus of the study.

This injection of reality into the discussion does not indicate that consideration of the earlier sections of this text is a waste of time. The matters covered need to be internalized before you are in a position to follow this free-form approach. There are similarities to Martin's (1981) 'garbage can' model of research (Chapter 4, p. 73). Here the four elements of research – theory, methods, resources and solutions – swirl about in the garbage can or decision space of the research project. Each influences the others, and the assumption of a sequence of steps in the research process is discarded.

Negotiate access

Much real world research takes place in settings where you require *formal* agreement from someone to gain access. Issues about access vary to a considerable extent with the kind of task you are carrying out and the nature of the organization concerned. Hayes (2005) describes what he calls the 'long and winding road' gaining access to data sources in statutory social work agencies. Lindsay (2005) points out that negotiating access to a sample in a survey research project is an often unacknowledged process but it is crucial to the success of a project. To gain access to young workers in a study examining health risks of their social lives, she 'had to present the goals of the research to different audiences such as human resource managers, occupational health and safety managers, union officials, supervisors, heads of department, teachers, and the young workers themselves. Each of these audiences had to be convinced of the value of the research and the credibility of the researcher' (p. 121). Okumus, Altinay and Roper (2007), reflecting on their experience of case study research in large organizations, conclude that there is 'no single method or piece of advice related to gaining and maintaining access for a long period of time' (p. 22). They stress that while it is important to be organized, self-motivated, and persistent before and during the research, many external factors are beyond researchers' control. The implication is that you should remain flexible and learn to develop contingency strategies (Bondy, 2013; Feldman, Bell & Berger, 2003).

For more or less pure researchers, the task agenda is set by their perceptions of what is important in the academic discipline, say, in the development of a theoretical position, or in response to recent research. Thus it is the researcher's agenda that is important, and the access issue is essentially persuading people to let you in. If you are clear about your intentions, perhaps with a pretty tight, pre-structured, design, then the task is probably easier initially in that you can give them a good indication of what they are letting themselves in for. With a looser, more emergent design, there may be more difficulties as you are to some extent asking them to sign a 'blank cheque' as it is impossible to specify in advance exactly what you will do.

Studies with a more applied focus simplify some access problems and make others more complex, and more sensitive. If the study looks at 'practice' in some professional, industrial or business situation, there is the considerable advantage that you can legitimately present the study as relating to, and probably arising from, the concerns of practitioners. When you have been asked to do the study by persons from the institution or organization concerned, then at first sight this seems to solve problems of access. However, the investigator might, legitimately or not, be seen as a 'tool of management' supporting the squeezing of more blood out of the workers; or, conversely, as a dangerous agitator upsetting labour relations. In particular, studies with an overt 'change' approach are, almost by definition, disturbing. Even in a 'commissioned' study, you are very likely to want to observe and collect information from persons who were not party to the request for you to be involved.

Lofland, Snow, Anderson and Lofland (2006, pp. 41–7) suggest you are more likely to gain access if you have:

- *Connections*. Use friends, relatives and contacts wherever possible. If you don't have any existing links, identify key gatekeepers or others who might help you get in and try to develop ties.
- *Accounts*. Develop a careful explanation of your proposed research. Avoid jargon. Keep it brief. They want an answer to the question, 'Why should I let you in?' Don't identify yourself using off-putting labels. 'I'm a student (or on the staff) at Barsetshire College' is better than 'I'm a sociologist' (from wherever). 'Honest but vague' is sometimes suggested. Don't lie or misrepresent but something general about your interests is better than an attempt to detail the specifics of procedure, your theoretical rationale, etc. This is particularly important in flexible designs where you may end up doing something differently from your original plans. The form of your account should be tailored to the audience. If you need to persuade several different groups, the way in which you tell your story must be appropriate for each of the groups. Working in schools with young children, the account given to the children (see Chapter 10, p. 224 for the discussion on

seeking consent from the children themselves in school-based research) has to be differently expressed from that used with teachers and administrators.

- *Knowledge*. Lofland *et al.* advise that, to avoid being perceived as frivolous or stupid, you need to 'have enough knowledge about the setting or persons you wish to study to appear competent to do so' (p. 46). If you have a relevant professional or occupational background in a study (e.g. have worked as a midwife, or on a car assembly line, or whatever) it can help. Generally, knowing the 'lie of the land' (i.e. acquiring some prior knowledge about a setting and its ways) can help you avoid gaffes, not only in your initial presentations, but throughout your involvement.
- *Courtesy*. You are asking people to do you a favour. Behaving with courtesy and consideration in all your dealings is crucial – and it increases your chances of gaining access.

The checklist in the box below gives an indication of the things you might consider when negotiating access. Much of this is common sense and simply requires you to be sensitively alert to requirements of the situation. Given that you are inevitably going to trespass upon other people's time, and are probably giving them extra work to do, for you to be there in good faith you must believe, and do all you can to ensure, that they get something out of it. This can be at many levels. People often derive considerable satisfaction from talking about what they are doing to a disinterested but sympathetic ear.

Checklist on negotiating access

1. Establish points of contact and individuals from whom it is necessary to get permission.
2. Clear any necessary official channels by formally requesting permission to carry out the study. Permission may be needed at various 'levels'.
3. Prepare an outline of the study suitable for discussion with 'gatekeepers' (e.g. manager, head teacher).
4. Discuss the study with these gatekeepers. Go through study outline (purposes, conditions – including consent and participation). Attempt to anticipate potentially sensitive issues and areas.
5. Prepare an outline of the study suitable for discussion with likely participants.
6. Discuss the study with these likely participants. Go through outline, emphasizing aspects of likely interest or concern to them. May be with a group or with individuals, depending on circumstances.

Be prepared to modify the study in the light of these discussions (e.g. in respect of timing, treatment of sensitive issues).

Contract research involves a formal contract being drawn up between yourself (or the organization where you work) and whoever is providing the funding. Research organizations and funding bodies typically have contracts with pre-defined contents although some flexibility is usual. Grinyer (1999, p. 3) suggests that the contract should cover the following issues:

- What happens if the research focus changes?
- Are there limitations on the type of data to be collected and its subsequent use?
- Who approves any publications?
- Who controls dissemination of the findings?
- Does the client see material before publication?
- Who owns the intellectual property right?
- Can the client use the researcher's name and institution?
- What are the ethical implications and issues?
- How will the project be evaluated?
- Will the parties involved be continuously informed of the progress of the research?

Such questions arise in most real world research and are not exclusive to 'contract' research.

There is a distinction between what is *formally* necessary to gain access, and what may be necessary over and above this to gain support and acceptance. The 'system' may not require you to get formal approval from a deputy head in a school, but if she is hostile to the study, it is not difficult for her to subvert it by, say, changing the timetabling arrangements. Formalities are necessary, not only to get you in, but also to refer back to if something goes wrong. People forget what they have agreed to, particularly if they had not thought through some of its implications. It can help to remind them of their agreed conditions, although they should be able to withdraw from the study if they wish.

There is evidence from studies in school settings that the reduction in sample size which may result from this procedure has little or no biasing effect on the findings (Dent, Sussman & Stacy, 1997). The option of withdrawing from the study at a later time, without prejudice, is particularly necessary when relatively loose, emergent, designs are used. In these circumstances it may not be possible to foretell all that is involved when the respondent is first approached for consent (see the consent form and example Chapter 10, pp. 212 and 213).

A note on access and the 'insider'. It is increasingly common for researchers to carry out a study directly concerned with the setting in which they work. Teachers look at their own local authority, school or even classroom, social workers or 'health' personnel seek to evaluate or otherwise study some aspect of the service they are providing. The personnel department of a firm investigates its own interviewing procedures.

There are clear practical advantages to this kind of 'insider' research. You won't have to travel far. Generally you will have an intimate knowledge of the context of the study, both as it is at present and in a historical or developmental perspective. You should know the politics of the institution, not only of the formal hierarchy but also how it 'really works' (or, at least, an unexamined common-sense view of this). You will know how best to approach people. You should have 'street credibility' as someone who will understand what the job entails and what its stresses and strains are. In general, you will already have in your head a great deal of information which it takes an outsider a long time to acquire.

The disadvantages are, however, also pretty substantial. Adding the role of researcher to that of colleague is difficult both for yourself and for your colleagues. Interviewing colleagues can be an uncomfortable business, particularly so in hierarchical organizations if they are higher in status to you. Suppose that you obtain confidential information, appropriately enough within the conditions of confidentiality of the research. Is this going to affect your working relationship with colleagues? If you make mistakes during the study, you are going to have to live with them afterwards. More fundamentally, how are you going to maintain objectivity, given your previous and present close contact with the institution and your colleagues?

Grady and Wallston (1988, pp. 29–31) discuss these issues in the context of health care settings, but their principles are general:

- *Try to foresee likely conflicts.* For example, collecting data about drug and alcohol abuse by pregnant teenagers called for a non-reactive researcher; the same person as 'helping professional' appreciated the consequences of the abuse.
- *Make a plan to deal with them.* In the abuse example, non-reaction might be construed as acknowledgement that the behaviour was not harmful, or that no help was available, and so a procedure was developed to provide appropriate referrals at the end of the interview session when baseline data had been collected.
- *Record your responses.* It helps to have a full log with notes made after each session so that they can be subsequently scrutinized for possible contaminating effects on the research.
- *Where possible get the collaboration of researcher colleagues from outside the situation.* They will help you to maintain the researcher stance.

Leigh (2014) discusses some of the problems which arose when carrying out insider research in a social work setting. However, ' . . .by adopting a dual role and taking up the position of outsider in another similar setting, it was found that enough distance and space were created to encourage the author to employ reflexivity and overcome the difficulties experienced as a "native" at home' (p. 428).

Get yourself organized

As soon as is feasible, you need to work out schedules for the arrangement and timing of sessions for observation, interviewing, etc. The extent to which this is pre-plannable depends very much on the style of your enquiry but even with a flexible design, you are likely to be pressed for time and need (flexible) plans. Use calendars or wall charts to draw up timed and sequenced activity lists or flow charts. Sharp, Peters and Howard (2002, Chapter 3) suggest techniques useful for complex projects, including network analysis and control charts.

Pilot if at all possible

The first stage of any data gathering should, if at all possible, be a 'dummy run' – a pilot study. This helps you to throw up some of the inevitable problems of converting your design into reality. Some methods and techniques necessarily involve piloting in their use (e.g. in the development of a structured questionnaire or a direct observation instrument). An experiment or survey should be piloted on a small scale in virtually all circumstances. Most flexible designs can incorporate piloting within the study itself. The effort needed in gaining access and building up acceptance and trust is often such that one would be reluctant to regard a case study or ethnographic study simply as a pilot. Of course, if things go seriously wrong for whatever reason or it appears that the situation is not going to deliver in relation to your research questions, then it is better to cut it short and transfer your efforts elsewhere.

Work on your relationships

Formal approval from the boss may get you in but you then need informal agreement and acceptance from informants, respondents or participants in order to gather worthwhile data. This is largely a matter of relationships. You have to establish that you can be relied on to keep promises about confidentiality, etc. It is assumed that you are not proposing to deceive them and so you can share with them the general aims of your study and genuinely get over the message that you are there because you feel they can contribute. Maxwell (2013, pp. 90–6) discusses these issues in some detail. He emphasizes that they are not simply practical concerns but also raise design issues:

> You will need to reflect on the particular decisions (conscious or unconscious) that you make about your relationships, as well as on the relationship issues that you will face in doing the study, and the effects these can have on your research (p. 91).

Maxwell gives a good range of examples of accounts of relationship issues by qualitative researchers.

Don't just disappear at the end

It helps you, and everybody concerned, if your initial negotiations set a period for your involvement and a date for your departure. It can be difficult to leave, particularly when things have gone well and you are an accepted part of the scene. There will almost always be more data that it would be desirable to collect. However, in real world research, cutting your coat to fit a fixed length of cloth is often part of the reality, and it helps to concentrate your efforts.

Make sure that people know that you are going. Honour your commitments. Keep your bridges in good order so that you can return if necessary – and so that you haven't spoiled things for later researchers. Morse (1997) has useful advice if you have problems in bringing a project to an end.

Don't expect it to work out just as you planned

'Trouble awaits those unwary souls who believe that research flows smoothly and naturally from questions to answers via a well organized data collection system' (Hodgson & Rollnick, 1995, p. 3). It is as well to appreciate this from the start in real world research or you will be in for a dispiriting shock. Measles may play havoc with your carefully planned school sessions or unseasonal snow cut you off. Strikes shut down the plant or, even more frustrating, a 'work to rule' or 'withdrawal of goodwill' closes it to you. Communication channels do not function. The hospital you phoned yesterday to confirm an appointment denies your very existence. Hodgson and Rollnick provide a serious set of suggestions on 'how to survive in research' in a jocular manner. This includes a list of aphorisms well worth taking on board (*'Getting started will take at least as long as the data collection'; 'A research project will change twice in the middle'*; etc.) and a set of maxims for keeping going, based on the practices of Alcoholics Anonymous (e.g. 'one day at a time'; don't be overwhelmed by the size of the task; focus on smaller goals).

Having some flexibility built in and a 'forgiving' design (where it is possible to substitute one case or activity for another) helps. Experimental designs, sabotaged by breakdowns in sampling procedures or some other reason, can sometimes be patched up as quasi-experimental equivalents. Hakim (2000, pp. 150–2) provides a very useful section on 'trading down to a cheaper design' to cope with reductions in resources or time available.

PART V

Dealing with the data

A central, usually indispensable, part of a typical real world research project is the collection of data. No data – no project. In library, desk-based, projects someone else will have already collected the empirical data you discuss. Hence, much of the material in Part V is still relevant. How did they deal with this data? Do they give you sufficient information to evaluate the adequacy and appropriateness of what they did?

The specifics of data collection are bound up with the different methods of investigation. Whatever methods are used, there is a need for a systematic approach to the task – a need probably, paradoxically, at its greatest in so-called 'soft' methods such as participant observation and unstructured interviewing. Once you have data, the next steps are analysis and interpretation.

Collecting the data

Collecting the data is about using the selected method or methods of investigation. Doing it properly means using these methods in a systematic, professional fashion. The chapters in Part III covered the issues raised in the use of specific methods. At this stage you need to ask yourself the following questions:

Have you explored thoroughly the choice of methods?

There is no general 'best method'. The selection of methods should be driven by the kind of research questions you are seeking to answer. This has to be moderated by what is feasible in terms of time and other resources, by your skills and expertise and, in commissioned research, by the predilections of the sponsor.

What mix of methods do you propose to use?

The virtues of multi-strategy designs and the use of multiple methods have been emphasized in Chapters 8 *and* 15 respectively. All methods have strengths and weaknesses and you are seeking to match the strength of one to the weakness of another and vice versa. If it is impracticable to use more than one method, don't worry – many studies are still mono-method. Don't give up too easily though. It is often possible to devote a small fraction of your effort to a complementary method. This might be an unstructured interview session at the end of an experiment. Or, perhaps, two or three mini case studies based on observation, interview and document analysis – linked to a questionnaire survey.

Have you thought through potential problems in using the different methods?

You don't choose methods unless you have the skills and personality characteristics they call for (one of us would pay a fairly substantial amount not to have to do a telephone survey involving 'cold' calling). Nor if they would be unacceptable in the setting involved. Nor if they raise ethical concerns. Pilot work almost always brings out problems; better then than in the middle of a fixed design study.

Do the methods have the flexibility that you need?

You don't do fixed design research unless you have a clear idea about what you are doing before the main data collection starts. If not, you use some type of flexible design. The methods themselves in a flexible design study need to have a corresponding flexibility (e.g. relatively unstructured observation and interview). This does not preclude moving on to a confirmatory phase, using more structured instruments, at a later stage of the study in a multi-strategy design.

Whatever methods you use, data collection calls for commitment

You have to care – both about the substantive area and about your responsibilities as a researcher. This dual commitment is crucial. Caring solely about getting answers to the research questions, or about 'helping' the participants in some way, you are in danger of losing objectivity and the ability to appraise the evidence fairly. Caring only about doing a good piece of research may lead to the degree of detachment rightly castigated by feminist methodologists. And you need high commitment not only to do a quality job but also to get you through the inevitable bad times while you are doing it.

Analysing and interpreting data

After data have been collected in a project, they have at some stage to be analysed and interpreted. The traditional model in fixed design research is for this to take place after all the data are safely gathered in. It is, however, central to flexible design research that you start this analysis and interpretation at an earlier stage of the project. Analysis, at whatever stage, is necessary because, generally speaking, data in their raw form do not speak for themselves. The messages stay hidden and need careful teasing out. The process and products of analysis provide the bases for interpretation. It is often the case that, while in the middle of analysing data, ideas for interpretation arise (which is a major disadvantage of relying totally on the now virtually ubiquitous, and immensely useful, computer packages for analysis of quantitative data).

Analysis, then, is not an empty ritual, carried out for form's sake between doing the study and interpreting it. Nor is it a bolt-on feature which can be safely not thought about until all the data are collected. If you do this, you are likely to end up with an unanalysable mish-mash of quantitative data which no known test or procedure can redeem. Or a mountain of qualitative data which keeps you awake at night wondering what to do with it.

Hence, *as emphasized in Part II*, thinking about how the analysis *might* be carried out forms an integral part of the design process for any investigation. A particular disposition of your resources which, say, gets more data from a smaller number of respondents or fewer data from a greater number of respondents, might make all the difference between there being a straightforward path of analysis and a highly dubious one. If you have thought through such an analysis, that is available as a 'banker'. You can then, with confidence, explore the data when they are in and see if there are alternative or additional messages you can get from them.

The intention here is to sensitize you to analysis issues and to cover a range of ways of dealing with both quantitative and qualitative data. *Our aims are primarily to set out guidelines and principles to use in selecting appropriate procedure and to discuss how the results obtained from these procedures might be interpreted.*

Little attempt is made to cover computational aspects. The advent of powerful computers and wide-ranging program packages on statistical and other procedures obviate the need for factual knowledge about formulae or for craft skills in performing complex calculations. No doubt, inertia in the presentation of courses, and remnants of the puritan ethic, will force further generations of students through these satisfyingly labour-intensive hoops. However, there are more profitable ways of spending your time than doing something which a computer can do better, and more quickly. This does not gainsay, as mentioned above, the value to interpretation of really getting to know your data by playing about with them. And this is also something with which the computer can help.

Realist analysis and interpretation

The realist thread running through this text has, as its prime focus, the search for mechanisms. Taking a realist stance has many other implications covered in earlier chapters, but seeking an answer to the question behind almost all research of 'How can I understand what is going on here?' (in terms of 'What mechanisms are operating?') is central.

Once the task has been conceptualized in this way, it is not difficult to provide some kind of interpretation in mechanism terms for most if not all research projects. At issue, however, is the convincingness or plausibility of the operation of the proposed mechanisms, which depends partly on the design of the research and partly on the findings.

The work of Pawson and Tilley (1997) discussed in Chapter 2, p. 31, and at several points in the text has formed the basis for a wide range of projects and their analysis. Carter and New's

(2004) edited volume on *Making Realism Work* provides a varied range of exemplars. However, it has to be admitted that realist methodology is still in its infancy and the approaches to analysis in the following two chapters is largely traditional. This is, in part, because of deeply entrenched traditions of both quantitative and qualitative data analysis, and corresponding expectations of journal editors and reviewers. Also, particularly in the statistical analysis of quantitative data, traditional techniques can with minimal tweaking be adapted for realist purposes. This includes de-emphasizing the use of statistical significance and concentrating on other evidence for the importance (i.e. real significance) of findings using effect sizes and other measures as evidence for the operation of mechanisms – see Chapter 17, p. 441.

Why focus on mechanisms? While there may be resistance in some academic circles, other audiences including practitioners appear to find this helpful (see Chapter 2, p. 35). Also, as Pawson (2006) has argued with some passion, a focus solely on outcomes as in the process of 'systematic review' does little to develop a cumulative understanding of complex social interventions. Accounts of how they work can reach a better understanding of how theory may be improved.

Preparing for analysis

You have data, whether collected by yourself or some earlier researcher. You need to understand them. Data come in all sorts of shapes and sizes – audio- and video-tapes, sets of instrument readings or test results, responses to questionnaires, diary entries, reports of meetings, documents, etc., etc. Many of them fall effectively into two categories – words or numbers. Or they can, without too much difficulty, be turned into words or numbers. And some features of the words can be captured in numbers. So we have *qualitative analysis* (for words, and other data which come in a non-numerical form) and *quantitative analysis* (for numbers, and other data that can be transformed into numbers). Much real world research produces both and it is important that you are able to deal competently with the two kinds.

Keep quantitative analysis simple

Many researchers appear to think that the more complex the analysis you can do, the better. This is not true. You may be forced to get into, say, multivariate statistics by the conventions in your field or the expectations of supervisors or sponsors and/or journal editors, but fancy methods of analysis are no substitute for thought and reasoning when you are trying to understand and interpret your findings.

Simple descriptive statistics, tables and visual displays of the data are often all that you really need. If you need to persuade yourself, or others, on this point, classic papers by Rosnow and Rosenthal (1989) and, particularly, Cohen (1990) provide powerful ammunition. See also Gorard (2006) who argues convincingly that 'everyday numbers' can be used successfully for research purposes without the need for complex statistical techniques.

Seek advice about statistical analysis

If you need to carry out anything more than the simplest statistical analysis – beware. A vast technology on the carrying out of statistical analysis exists and it would be foolish to expect everyone carrying out real world research to have all of it at their finger-tips. There is a tendency to gain some familiarity with a narrow range of approaches and then be determined to use them. This means either inappropriate analyses or severe restrictions on the type of research questions you can tackle (the analytic equivalent of the one-track methods person who tackles everything with a questionnaire). The technique of 'analysis of variance', as used by some experimental psychologists, provides a case in point.

A more extreme, though not uncommon, response is to eschew all things quantitative and stick solely to qualitative analyses. Although this may be presented in terms of ideological objection to positivistic quantitative approaches, suspicion remains that there may be other blocks to the use of statistics.

One solution is to get advice from a consultant or other person familiar with a wide range of approaches to the quantitative analysis of social research data; and to get that advice at the design stage of your project, *before you have collected the data*. The advice should also, in many cases, home you in on a computer package which will do the analytical work for you. All this does not mean that you come naked to the consultant's table. It is important that you have at least an intuitive grasp of the kinds of approaches that might be taken, so that you know what is being talked about. Chapter 17 seeks to do that job. Even if you are on your own with no consultant available (or, as a student the rules say that you have to do it unaided in this way), it will sensitize you to a range of possibilities which, with further reading, you should be able to implement.

You are going to have to do much of the analysis of qualitative data for yourself

The analysis of qualitative data has now, like horticulture, moved out of the 'muck and magic' phase. It was commonly held that there was some ineffable mystique whereby the methods could only be used by experienced researchers admitted to the magic circle after a lengthy apprenticeship. Following Merton, Fiske and Kendall's insistence (1956, p. 17) that this is no 'private and incommunicable art', serious attempts have been made to show that qualitative analysis can be systematized and made widely accessible. *These approaches are* discussed in Chapter 18.

However, while there are helpful routines and procedures, they are less technical and differentiated than much statistical analysis – closer to codified common sense. It will undoubtedly be helpful to get external help and support to carry out qualitative analysis from someone with experience in this field. This, however, is more concerned with getting feedback on the processes you are using and checking the warrant for the interpretations you are making. There are computer packages to facilitate the process but they in no sense do the job of analysis for you in the way that a statistical package does.

Analysis or interpretation?

The traditional, and still widely used, terminology is to refer to the 'analysis' of data, whether quantitative or qualitative. Taken literally, analysis is a 'breaking up' of something complex into smaller parts and explaining the whole in terms of the properties of, and relations between, these parts. Not only is this, necessarily, a reductionist process but it is also seen by many as also necessarily reliant on the particular form of statistical reasoning where hypotheses are based on probability theory applied to sampling distributions. This approach, discussed in Chapter 17, has an important role when dealing with quantitative data from some experimental and other fixed designs. However, in real world research which generates quantitative data, it is rare to find that the rather restrictive design assumptions for the approach are met. The major research traditions in flexible design research are incompatible with the approach.

Interpretation carries very different conceptual baggage. Whereas the purpose of analysis is often seen as a search for causes (usually in the positivistic 'successionist' sense discussed in Chapter 2, p. 32), interpretation is considered to be about shedding light on meaning. This is a well-established view of the task when dealing with qualitative data, but Byrne (2002) makes a persuasive case for also focusing on the interpretation of quantitative data.

Quantitative and qualitative data – and their integration in multi-strategy designs

The following two chapters focus on the analysis and interpretation of quantitative and qualitative data respectively. Multi-strategy (mixed methods) designs will have substantial amounts of both types of data for which the techniques and approaches in the chapters can be used. They can make separate contributions to the findings of the study but there is also a possibility of their integration to take full advantage of the opportunity provided by this type of design. *The final section of* Chapter 18, p. 484 discusses some of the issues involved.

CHAPTER 17

The analysis and interpretation of quantitative data

This chapter:

- stresses the advantages of using a software package when analysing quantitative data and your likely need for help and advice when doing this;
- shows how to create a data set for entry into a computer;
- distinguishes between exploratory and confirmatory data analysis;
- explains statistical significance and discusses its controversial status;
- advocates greater reliance on measures of effect sizes;
- suggests how to explore, display, and summarize the data;
- discusses ways of analysing relationships between various types of data and a range of statistical tests that might be used;
- does the same thing for analysing differences between data; and
- considers issues specific to the analysis of quasi-experiments, single-case experiments, and non-experimental fixed designs.

Introduction

You would have to work quite hard in a research project not to have at least some data in the form of numbers, or which could be sensibly turned into numbers of some kind. Hence, techniques for dealing with such quantitative data are an essential feature of your professional toolkit. Their analysis covers a wide range of things, from simple organization of the data to complex statistical analysis. This chapter does not attempt a comprehensive treatment of all aspects of quantitative data analysis. Its main aim is to help you appreciate some of the issues involved so that you have a feeling for the questions you need to ask when deciding on an appropriate kind of analysis.

Some assumptions

1. *Everyone doing real world research needs to understand how to summarize and display quantitative data.* This applies not only to those using fixed and multi-strategy designs, but also to users of flexible designs where their data are essentially qualitative. Even die-hard qualitative researchers will often collect small amounts of numerical data or find advantage in turning some qualitative data into numbers for summary or display purposes. This does not necessarily call for the use of statistical tests. Simple techniques may be all you need to interpret your data.

2. *For relatively simple statistical tests specialist statistical software is not essential.* If you only have a very small amount of quantitative data, it may be appropriate for you to carry out analyses by 'hand' (or with the help of an electronic calculator). However, the drudgery and potential for error in such calculation, and the ease with which the computer can perform such mundane chores for you, suggest strongly that you make use of the new technology if at all possible. For such tasks, and for simple statistical tests, spreadsheet software such as Excel may be all that you need. 'Analyse-it' (http://www.analyse-it.com) is a straightforward package which can be used with Excel to produce most of the commonly used statistics and charts. Appendix A gives details. It has been used for several of the figures showing the results of different statistical analyses in this chapter.

3. *If you need to carry out complex statistical tests you will need to use a specialist statistical computer package. A range of commonly used statistical packages is discussed in Appendix A.* SPSS (the Statistical Package for the Social Sciences) is the market leader by some margin but other packages are well worth considering, particularly if you wish to follow the exploratory data analysis (EDA) approach highlighted in the chapter. Facility in the use of at least one specialist statistical package is a useful transferable skill for the real world researcher.

4. *You have some prior acquaintance with the basic concepts and language of statistical analysis.* If not, you are recommended to spend some time with one of the many texts covering this at an introductory level (e.g. Graham, 2013; Robson, 1994; Rowntree, 2000).

5. *You will seek help and advice in carrying out statistical analyses.* The field of statistical analysis is complex and specialized and it is unreasonable to expect everyone carrying out real world research to be a statistical specialist. It is, unfortunately, a field where it is not at all difficult to carry out an analysis which is simply wrong, or inappropriate, for your data or your purposes. And the negative side of readily available specialist statistical software is that it becomes that much easier to generate elegantly presented rubbish (remember GIGO – Garbage In, Garbage Out).

Preferably, such advice should come from an experienced statistician sympathetic to the particular difficulties involved in applied social research. Repeating the advice once more – it should be sought at the earliest possible stage in the *design* of your project. Inexperienced non-numerate researchers often have a touching faith that research is a linear process in which they first collect the data and then the statistician shows them the analysis to carry out. It is, however, all too easy to end up with unanalysable data, which, if they had been collected in a somewhat different way, would have been readily analysable. In the absence of personal statistical support, you should be able to use this chapter to get an introduction to the kind of approach you might take. The references provided should then help with more detailed coverage.

Organization of the chapter

The chapter first covers the creation of a 'data set' as a necessary precursor to data analysis. Suggestions are then made about how you might carry out various types of data analysis appropriate for different research designs and tasks.

Creating a data set

If you are to make use of a computer to help with analysis, then the data must be entered into the computer in the form required by the software you are using. This may be done in different ways:

1. *Direct automatic entry.* It may be feasible for the data to be generated in such a way that entry is automatic. For example, you may be using a structured observation schedule with some data collection device (either a specialized instrument or a laptop computer) so that the data as collected can be directly usable by the analysis software.
2. *Creation of a computer file which is then 'imported' to the analysis software.* It may be easier for your data to be entered into a computer after collection. For example, a survey might use questionnaires which are 'optically readable'. Respondents, or the person carrying out the survey, fill in boxes on the form corresponding to particular answers. The computer can directly transform this response into data which it can use. Such data form a computer 'file' which is then 'imported' into the particular analysis software being used. This is feasible with most statistical packages although you may need assistance to ensure that the transfer takes place satisfactorily.
3. *Direct 'keying' of data into analysis software.* For much small-scale research, automatic reading or conversion of the data into a computer file will either not be possible or not be economically justifiable. There is then the requirement for manual entry of data into the analysis software. The discussion below assumes that you will be entering the data in this way.

Whichever approach is used, the same principle applies. Try at the design stage to capture your data in a form which is going to simplify this entry process. Avoid intermediate systems where the original response has to be further categorized. The more times that data are transferred between coding systems, the greater the chance of error. *Single-transfer coding* (i.e. where the response is already in the form which has to be entered into the computer) is often possible with attitude and other scales, multiple-choice tests, inventories, checklists, and many questionnaires. In a postal or similar survey questionnaire, you will have to weigh up whether it is more important to simplify the task of the respondent or the task of the person transferring the code to the computer. Box 17.1 shows possible alternatives.

The conventions on coding are essentially common sense. Suggestions were made in Chapter 11 (p. 272) about how this might be dealt with in relation to questionnaires. Note that it is helpful to include the coding boxes on the questionnaire itself, conventionally in a column on the right-hand side of each page.

The data sets obtained from other types of project will be very various. However, it is almost always possible to have some sensible arrangement of the data into *rows* and *columns*. Typically each row corresponds to a *record* or *case*. This might be all of the data obtained from a particular

BOX 17.1

Question formats requiring (a) single-transfer coding and (b) double-transfer coding

(a) How many children are there in your school?

under	40	40–49	50–59	60–69	70–79	80–89	90–100	over 100
code	1	2	3	4	5	6	7	8

enter code ( )

(b) How many children are there in your school?
(please circle)

under   40   40–49   50–59   60–69   70–79   80–89   90–100   over 100

(response has then to be translated into appropriate code)

respondent. A record consists of *cells* which contain data. The cells in a column contain the data for a particular *variable*. Figure 17.1 presents a simple example derived from a survey-type study.

Student	Faculty	Sex	Entry points	Degree class	Income
1	A	F	14	2.1	14,120
2	EN	M	6	2.2	15,900
3	EN	M	5	Fail	11,200
4	ED	F	10	2.2	21,640
5	S	M	4	2.1	25,000
6	B	F	13	2.1	11,180
7	A	F	16	2.1	12,600
8	EN	M	6	3	9,300
9	ED	M	5	3	2,200
10	EN	M	*	2.2	17,880

Key: A = Arts; B = Business; Ed = Education; EN = Engineering; S = Sciences; M = Male; F = Female; * = missing data

Note: data are fictitious, but modelled on those in Linsell and Robson, 1987

Figure 17.1 Faculty, entry points, degree classification, and income two years after graduating of a sample of students.

A similar matrix would be obtained from a simple experiment where, say, the columns represent scores obtained under different experimental conditions.

Entering the data into the computer

The details of the procedure for entering this data set into the computer vary according to the particular software you are using. With early versions of software, this was quite complex but later versions are straightforward to use, particularly if you are familiar with the operation of spreadsheets.

Missing data

'The most acceptable solution to the problem of missing information is not to have any' (Youngman, 1979, p. 21). While this is obviously a counsel of perfection, it highlights the problem that there is no really satisfactory way of dealing with missing data. It may well be that the reason why data are missing is in some way related to the question being investigated. Those who avoid filling in the evaluation questionnaire, or who are not present at a session, may well have different views from those who responded. So it is well worth spending considerable time, effort and ingenuity in seeking to ensure a full response. Software normally has one or more ways of dealing with missing data when performing analyses and it may be necessary to investigate this further as different approaches can have substantially different effects on the results obtained.

Technically there is no particular problem in coding data as missing. There simply needs to be a signal code which is used for missing data, and only for missing data. Don't get in the habit of using 0 (zero) to code for missing data as this can cause confusion if the variable in question could have a zero value or if any analytic procedure treats it as a value of zero (99 or –1 are frequently used). Software packages should show the value that you have specified as missing data and deal with it intelligently (e.g. by computing averages based only on the data present).

It is worth noting that a distinction may need to be made between missing data where there is no response from someone, and a 'don't know' or 'not applicable' response, particularly if you have catered for possible responses of this type by including them as one of the alternatives.

Cleaning the data set after entry

Just as one needs to proof-read text for errors, so a computer data set needs to be checked for errors made while 'keying in' the data. One of the best ways of doing this is for the data to be entered twice, independently, by two people. Any discrepancies can then be resolved. This is time-consuming but may well be worthwhile, particularly if substantial data analysis is likely.

A valuable tip is to make use of 'categorical' variables whenever feasible. So, in the data set of Box 17.1 'degree class' has the categories 'first, 'upper second', etc. The advantage is that the software will clearly show where you have entered an invalid value.

While this eliminates several potential mistakes, it is, of course, still possible to enter the wrong class for an individual. The direct equivalent of proof-reading can be carried out by checking the computer data set carefully against the original set. Simple *frequency analyses* (see below) on each of the columns are helpful. This will throw up whether 'illegal', or highly unlikely, codes have been entered. For continuous variables *box plots* can be drawn, and potential 'outliers' highlighted (see p. 420).

Cross-tabulation

This involves counting the codes from one variable that occur for each code in a second variable. It can show up more subtle errors. Suppose that the two variables are 'withdrew before completing degree' and 'class of final degree'. *Cross-tabulation* might throw up one or two students who appeared to have withdrawn before completion but were nevertheless awarded a classified degree. These should then be checked, as while this might be legitimate (perhaps they returned), it could well be a miscoding. Cross-tabulation is easy when the variables have only a few values, as is the case with most categorical variables. However, it becomes very tedious when continuous variables such as age or income, which can take on many values, are involved. In this circumstance, *scattergrams/scatter plots* (see below) provide a useful tool. These are graphs in which corresponding codes from two variables give the horizontal and vertical scale values of points representing each record. 'Deviant' points which stand out from the general pattern can be followed up to see whether they are genuine or miscoded.

> *The 'cleaned' data set is an important resource for your subsequent analyses. It is prudent to keep a couple of copies, with one of the copies being at a separate physical location from the others. You will be likely to modify the set in various ways during analysis (e.g. by combining codes); however, you should always retain copies of the original data set.*

Starting data analysis

Now that you have a data set entered into the computer you are no doubt itching to do something with it. Data analysis is commonly divided into two broad types: exploratory and confirmatory. As the terms suggest, exploratory analysis explores the data trying to find out what they tell you. Confirmatory analysis seeks to establish whether you have actually got what you expected to find (for example on the basis of theory, such as predicting the operation of particular mechanisms).

With all data sets, and whatever type of research design, there is much to be said for having an initial exploration of the data. Try to get a feeling for what you have got and what it is trying to tell you. Play about with it. Draw up tables. Simple graphical displays help: charts, histograms, graphs, pie-charts, etc. Get summaries in the form of means and measures of the amount of variability, etc. (Details on what is meant by these terms, and how to do it, are presented later in the chapter.) Acquiring this working knowledge is particularly useful when you are going on to use various statistical tests with a software package. Packages will cheerfully and quickly produce complex nonsense if you ask them the wrong question or misunderstand how you enter the data. A good common-sense understanding of the data set will sensitize you against this.

Exploratory approaches of various kinds have been advocated at several points during this book. They are central to much flexible design research. While these designs mainly generate qualitative data, strategies such as case study commonly also result in quantitative data which we need to explore to see what has been found and to help direct later stages of data collection.

Much fixed design research is exclusively quantitative. The degree of pre-specification of design and of pre-thought about possible analyses called for in fixed design research means that the major task in data analysis is confirmatory; i.e. we are seeking to establish whether our predictions or hypotheses have been confirmed by the data. Such *confirmatory data analysis (CDA)* is the mainstream approach in statistical analysis.

However, there is an influential approach to quantitative analysis known as *exploratory data analysis (EDA)* advocated by Tukey (1977) – see also Myatt and Johnson (2014). Tukey's approach and influence come in at two levels. First, he has proposed several ingenious ways of displaying data diagrammatically. These devices, such as 'box plots', are non-controversial, deserve wider recognition, and are discussed below. The more revolutionary aspect of the EDA movement is the centrality it places on an informal, pictorial approach to data. EDA is criticized for implying that the pictures are all that you need; that the usual formal statistical procedures involving tests, *significance* levels, etc. are unnecessary. Tukey (1977) does acknowledge the need for CDA; in his view it complements EDA and provides a way of formally testing the relatively risky inductions made through EDA.

To a large extent, EDA simply regularizes the very common process whereby researchers make inferences about relationships between variables after data collection which their study was not designed to test formally – or which they had not expected prior to the research – and provides helpful tools for that task. It mirrors the suggestion made in Chapter 6 that while in fixed design research strong pre-specification is essential and you have clear expectations of what the results will show (i.e. the task of analysis is primarily confirmatory), this does not preclude additional exploration. Using EDA approaches, with a particular focus on graphical display, has been advocated by Connolly (2006) as a means of avoiding the ecological fallacy of making inferences about individuals from the group data provided from summary statistics.

In practice the EDA/CDA distinction isn't clear cut. As de Leeuw puts it (in Van de Geer, 1993), the view that:

> The scientist does all kinds of dirty things to his or her data . . . and at the end of this thoroughly unrespectable phase he or she comes up (miraculously) with a theory, model, or hypothesis. This hypothesis is then tested with the proper confirmatory statistical methods. [This] is a complete travesty of what *actually* goes on in all sciences some of the time and in some sciences all of the time. There are no two phases that can easily be distinguished (emphasis in original).

The treatment in this chapter is influenced by EDA and seeks to follow its spirit. However, there is no attempt to make a rigid demarcation between 'exploring' and 'confirming' aspects.

A note on 'levels' of measurement

A classic paper by Stevens (1946) suggested that there were four 'levels' of measurement ('nominal', 'ordinal', 'interval' and 'ratio'). Nominal refers to a set of categories used for classification purposes (e.g. marital status); ordinal also refers to a set of categories where they can be ordered in some meaningful way (e.g. social class); interval refers to a set of categories which are not only ordered but also have equal intervals on some *measurement scale* (e.g. calendar time); ratio is the same as interval level, but with a real or true zero (e.g. income).

Although very widely referred to in texts dealing with the analysis of quantitative data, the value of this typology has been queried by statisticians (e.g. Velleman and Wilkinson, 1993). Gorard (2006) considers it unnecessary and confusing. He claims that there is little practical difference between interval and ratio scales and points out that the same statistical procedures are traditionally suggested for both. Also that:

> So-called 'nominal' measures are, in fact, not numbers at all but categories of things that can be counted. The sex of an individual would, in traditional texts, be a nominal measure. But sex is clearly not a number . . . The only measure involved here is the frequency of individuals in each category of the variable 'sex' – i.e. how many females and how many males (p. 61).

Such frequencies are, of course, 'real numbers' and can be added, subtracted, multiplied and divided like other numbers. 'Ordinal' measures are also categories of things that can be counted and can be treated in exactly the same way. The only difference is in the possibility of ordering which can be used when describing and displaying frequencies.

He highlights the fact that a major problem arises when ordinal categories are treated as real numbers. For example examination grades, A, B, C, D and E may be given points scores, say that A is 10 points, B is 8 points, etc. As such points scores are essentially arbitrary; attempts to treat them as real numbers, for example by working out average points scores, lead to arbitrary results. Gorard's advice is to:

> . . . use your common sense but ignore the idea of 'levels' of measurement. If something is a real number then you can add it. If it is not a real number then it is not really any kind of number at all (p. 63).

Our advice is to take note of this advice but not to let it inhibit you from carrying out any of the statistical analyses (particularly the simple ones) covered in the chapter – providing you understand what you are doing, and it seems likely to shed light on what the data are trying to tell you. The notion that specific measurement scales are requirements for the use of particular statistical procedures, put forward by Stevens (1946), followed up in influential statistics textbooks (e.g. Siegel, 1959), and still commonly found, is rejected by many mathematical statisticians (see Gaito, 1980; Binder, 1984). There is nothing to stop you carrying out any analysis on quantitative data *on statistical grounds*. As Lord (1953) trenchantly put it in an early response to Stevens, 'the numbers do not know where they came from' (p. 751). The important thing is the *interpretation* of the results of the statistical analysis. It is here that the provenance of the numbers has to be considered, as well as other matters including the design of the study.

Exploring the data set

Frequency distributions and graphical displays

A simple means of exploring many data sets is to recast them in a way which counts the *frequency* (i.e. the number of times) that certain things happen and to find ways of displaying that information. For example, we could look at the number of students achieving different degree classifications. Some progress can be made by drawing up a *frequency distribution* as in Figure 17.2. This table can, alternatively, be presented as a *bar chart* (Figure 17.3).

Degree class	First	Upper second	Lower second	Third	Pass	Fail	Total
Frequency	9	64	37	30	7	3	150
Percentage	6	42.7	24.7	20	4.7	2	100

Note: 'Frequency' is the number of students with that degree class.

Figure 17.2 Frequency distribution of students across 'degree class'.

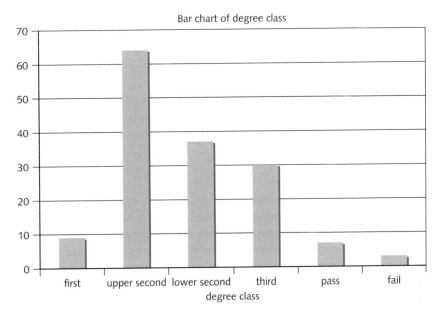

Figure 17.3 Bar chart showing distribution of students across 'degree class'.

The chart can be shown with either frequencies or percentages on the vertical axis; be sure to indicate which you have used. The classes of degree are ordered (here shown from first class 'downward' going from left to right). For some other variables (e.g. for faculties) the ordering is arbitrary. A distinction is sometimes made between histograms and bar charts. A bar chart is a histogram where the bars are separated from each other, rather than being joined together. The convention has been that histograms are only used for continuous variables (i.e. where the bar can take on any numerical value and is not, for example, limited to whole number values).

Pie charts provide an alternative way of displaying this kind of information (see Figure 17.4). Bar charts, *histograms* and pie charts are probably preferable ways of summarizing data to the corresponding tables of frequency distributions. It is claimed they are more quickly and easily understood by a variety of audiences – see Spence and Lewandowsky (1990) for a review of relevant empirical studies. Note, however, that with continuous variables (i.e. ones which can take on any numerical value, not simply whole numbers) both frequency tables and histograms may lose considerable detailed information. This is because of the need to group together a

Pie chart for faculty membership

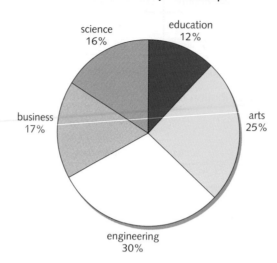

Figure 17.4 Pie chart showing relative numbers of students in different faculties.

range of values for a particular row of the frequency table or bar of the histogram. In all cases there will be a trade-off between decreasing the complexity of the display and losing information. An alternative EDA approach to displaying the data is the *box plot* (see p. 420).

Graphs (line charts) are well-known ways of displaying data. Excel, and statistical packages, provide ways of generating and displaying them although the quality of output many not be high enough for some needs. Specialized graphics packages (e.g. DeltaGraph, available from http://www.redrocksw.com) have a range of such displays available. Increasingly, professional standard displays are expected in presenting the results of projects, and apart from assisting communication, can help in getting over messages about the quality of the work. It is a matter of judgement whether or not any package to which you have access provides output of a quality adequate for presentation to a particular audience.

Marsh and Elliott (2008) give detailed, helpful and down-to-earth suggestions for producing numerical material clearly, in a section on 'Good Table Manners' (pp. 126–9). Tufte (2001) provides a fascinating compendium for anyone who needs to take graphical display seriously.

Summary or descriptive statistics

Summary statistics (also commonly known as *descriptive statistics*) are ways of representing some important aspect of a set of data by a single number. The two aspects most commonly dealt with in this way are the *level* of the distribution and its *spread* (otherwise known as *dispersion*). Statistics summarizing the level are known as *measures of central tendency*. Those summarizing the spread are called *measures of variability*. The *skewness* (asymmetricality), and other aspects of the shape of the distribution which are also sometimes summarized, are considered below in the context of the normal distribution (see p. 424).

Measures of central tendency

The notion here is to get a single figure which best represents the level of the distribution. The most common such measure to the layperson is the 'average', calculated by adding all of the scores together and then dividing by the number of scores. In statistical parlance, the figure obtained by carrying out this procedure is referred to as the *arithmetic mean*. This is because average, as a term in common use, suffers from being imprecise – some other more-or-less mid-value might also be referred to as average. There are, however, several other measures of central tendency in use, some appropriate for special purposes. Box 17.2 covers some of them.

Measures of variability

The extent to which the data values in a set of scores are tightly clustered or relatively widely spread out is a second important feature of a distribution for which several indices are in use. Box 17.3 gives details of the most commonly used measures. Several of them involve calculating *deviations* which are simply the difference between an individual score and the mean. Some individual scores are above the mean (positive deviations) and others below (negative deviations). It is an arithmetical feature of the mean that the sum of positive deviations is the same as the sum of negative deviations. Hence the *mean deviation* is calculated by ignoring the sign of the deviations, so that a non-zero total is obtained. The *standard deviation* and *variance* are probably the most widely used measures of variability, mainly because of their relationship to popular statistical tests such as the *t*-test and analysis of variance (discussed later in the chapter). However, Gorard (2006, pp. 17–19 and 63–73) makes a strong case for using the mean absolute deviation (i.e. ignoring the sign of the difference) rather than standard deviation, as it is simpler to compute, has a clear everyday meaning, and does not overemphasize extreme scores. This is part of his campaign in favour of 'using everyday numbers effectively in research'.

BOX 17.2

Measures of 'central tendency'

The most commonly used are:

- *Mean* (strictly speaking this should be referred to as the *arithmetic mean* as there are other, rarely used, kinds of mean) – this is the average, obtained by adding all the scores together and dividing by the number of scores.
- *Median* – this is the central value when all the scores are arranged in order of size (i.e. for 11 scores it is the sixth). It is also referred to as the '50th percentile' (i.e. it has 50 per cent of the scores below it, and 50 per cent above it).
- *Mode* – the most frequently occurring value.

   Note: Statistics texts give formulae and further explanation.

BOX 17.3

Measures of variability

Some commonly used measures are:

- *Range* – difference between the highest and the lowest score.
- *Midspread* or *inter-quartile range* – difference between the score which has one quarter of the scores below it (known as the 'first *quartile*', or '25th percentile') and that which has three-quarters of the scores below it (known as the 'third quartile', or '75th percentile').
- *Mean deviation* – the average of the deviations of individual scores from the mean (ignoring the sign or direction of the deviation).
- *Variance* – the average of the squared deviations of individual scores from the mean.
- *Standard deviation* – square root of the variance.
- *Standard error (SE)* – the standard deviation of the *mean* score.

   Note: Statistics texts give formulae and further explanation.

Statistics packages provide a very wide range of summary statistics, usually in the form of an optional menu of ways of summarizing any column within your data table.

Further graphical displays for single variables

It is possible to incorporate summary statistics into graphical displays in various ways.

Standard deviation error bars

A standard deviation error bar is a display showing the mean value as a dot, which has extending above and below it an 'error bar'. This represents one standard deviation unit above and below the mean. Typically, about two-thirds of the observed values will fall between these two limits (see the discussion of the normal distribution below).

   This is often a useful way of displaying the relative performance of sub-groups, and more generally of making comparisons. A similar-looking display is used to show the *confidence intervals* for the mean. These are limits within which we can be (probabilistically) sure that the *mean* value of the population from which our sample is drawn lies: 95 per cent limits (i.e. limits within which we can be 95 per cent sure) are commonly used, but others can be obtained. Figure 17.5 shows both error bar charts for one standard deviation and 95 per cent confidence intervals.

Box plots and whiskers

Figure 17.6 shows the general meaning of the box and its upper and lower 'whiskers'. Note that the plot is based on medians and other percentiles, rather than on means and standard deviations.

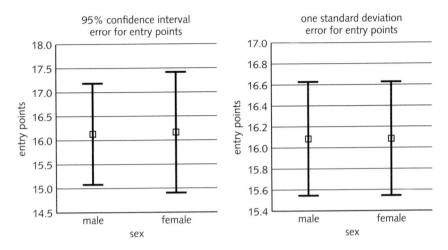

Figure 17.5 Display of error bar charts.

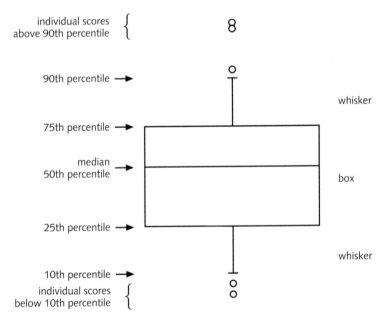

Figure 17.6 The 'box and whisker' plot.

Outliers

The term *outlier* is commonly used for a value which is a lot higher, or a lot lower, than the main body of the data. Marsh and Elliott (2008, pp. 168–71) suggest as a rule of thumb that values which are more than one and a half times the *inter-quartile range* ($Q_U - Q_L$) above the upper quartile, or more than one and a half times the inter-quartile range below the lower quartile, can be considered outliers. They term points as *far outliers* if they are more than three times the inter-quartile range above or below.

Outliers call for special attention. They can arise for a variety of reasons. For example, an error might be made in entering the data set where separate entries of '2' and '7' get entered together as '27'. If no objective reason of this kind can be unearthed, then its treatment is problematic. Many statistical procedures are very sensitive to the presence of outliers. For example, one advantage of the median over the mean as a measure of central tendency is its lack of such sensitivity. EDA has been much interested in outliers, both in their own right, and in the study of measures which are robust (i.e. relatively unaffected) in their presence.

Manipulating the data

Marsh and Elliott (2008, p. 57) point out that 'data are produced, not given'. This stance rejects our classical heritage in the sense that the derivation of the word 'data' is 'things given'.[1] The 'produced, not given' point is important. Many of the data that we collect are actually produced during the research itself. They tend not to be things lying around that we pick up. We often have a very active hand, not only in what is collected, but in how it is collected. The actual numbers that we subject to analysis are very much formed by a process of selection and choice – at a very simple level, for example, do we use grams, kilograms, ounces, pounds, tons . . .?

This basic choice will have been made at the time that the data are collected. In the example, this would probably now be metric in most countries, with the specific unit chosen to avoid very large, or very small, numbers (e.g. 5 grams rather than 0.005 kilograms; 2.3 kilograms rather than 2,300 grams). There is still the possibility of manipulating the data subsequently, so that it is easier to analyse, or so that attention can be focused on features of interest, or so that it is easier to compare two or more sets of data. As in so many aspects of research, this process is driven by your research questions. Are there things that you can do with your data that can help give clearer answers to these questions?

It perhaps needs saying that this is nothing to do with *How to Lie with Statistics* (Huff, 1991). 'Massaging' the data to give a biased or downright untruthful message should have no place in the kind of research covered in this book. The prime safeguard is your own honesty and integrity but this should be supported by detailed reporting of what you have done. Sufficient detail should be included to enable the sceptical reader to follow the trail from the collected data, through whatever you do to it, to the interpretation and conclusion.

Scaling data

The earlier section on descriptive statistics emphasized two aspects of a set of data: its *level* and its *spread*. The two simplest ways of scaling data involve these aspects directly.

---

[1] Also, in terms of its derivation the word is plural – one datum; two or more data. However, many people now use data as a singular noun. In a field where the term is used frequently, such as research reports, you may be perceived as ignorant of the 'correct' usage if you follow the popular trend. Not wanting to put you in that position, we shall stick to the plural use.

Adding or subtracting a constant

A straightforward way of focusing attention on a particular aspect of the data is to add or subtract a particular constant amount from each of the measurements. The most common tactic is to subtract the arithmetic mean from each score. As discussed above in connection with measures of variability, scores transformed in this way are referred to as *deviations*. A similar tactic can be used when the median, or some other measure of central tendency, has been employed.

Multiplying by a constant

This is sometimes referred to as scaling or rescaling the variable. It is what you do when changing from weight in imperial measure (pounds, ounces, etc.) to metric (kilograms, grams). This tactic is particularly useful in comparing different sets of data which have initially been measured on different scales. For example, the prices of goods or services in the UK and other European countries could be better compared by transforming them all into the standard 'euro'.

Other transformations

There are many other things that you can do. *Taking logarithms*, or *taking a power (e.g. square, square root, reciprocal)* are tactics commonly used when the distribution of the scores is asymmetrical or in some other way inappropriate for the type of statistical analysis proposed. Details are given in Marsh and Elliott (2008, Chapter 10).

Standardizing data

One way of manipulating data is very commonly used. It involves combining the two approaches covered above, i.e. subtracting a measure of level (central tendency) from an individual score, and then dividing by an appropriate measure of variability. The mean and standard deviation (or mean deviation) or median and mid-spread could be used. Distributions of scores that have been standardized in this way are much easier to compare, and in some circumstances combine, than unstandardized ones.

The normal distribution

The so-called *normal distribution* (or *Gaussian distribution*) is a theoretical distribution of scores for which the shape is completely determined once the mean and standard deviation (SD) are known. Its shape is shown as Figure 17.7. Many distributions of scores obtained in practice are reasonable approximations to the normal distribution. To find if this is the case for a particular set of scores, they are first standardized as shown above and then scrutinized to see whether the proportion of cases falling at different distances from the mean are as predicted from tables showing the theoretical distribution.

For example, the expectation is that:

- 68 per cent of cases are within one SD of the mean;
- 95 per cent of cases are within two SDs of the mean; and
- 99.7 per cent are within three SDs of the mean.

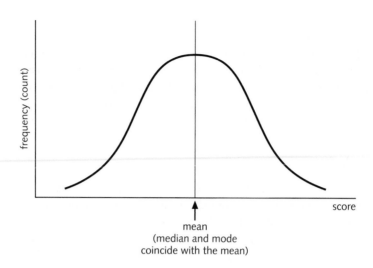

Figure 17.7 The theoretical 'normal' distribution.

Further details, and appropriate tables, are in many statistics texts (Robson, 1994, provides a simple account). It is possible to test the 'goodness of fit' of your data to the normal distribution by using a version of the chi-square test (see below).

Whether or not a distribution of scores can reasonably be represented as normal is then of value in describing, summarizing and comparing data. However, don't fall into the trap of thinking that 'only "normal" is normal'. Data won't necessarily fall into this pattern. This is no major disaster; your job is to seek to understand what you have got, playing about with the scale if this seems to help. Such transformations may bring the distribution closer to normal but in itself that may not further your understanding.

The normal distribution also has a part to play if one wants to go on to carry out formal statistical tests on the data. Many of the more commonly used tests are based on the assumption that a normal distribution is involved. Often these tests are *robust* in the sense that deviations from normality do not appear to have much effect on the outcome of the test. However there are 'distribution free' tests (commonly called 'non-parametric' tests) available (Pett, 1997; Higgins, 2003; Sprent & Smeeton, 2007) which do not make assumptions about the shape of the distributions involved.

Skewness

As can be seen from Figure 17.7, the normal distribution is symmetrical about its centre (which is where the mean, median and mode coincide). In practice, a distribution may be 'skewed' as shown in Figure 17.8. 'Negative' *skew* suggests that the majority of extreme observed values are less than the mean; 'positive' skew that the majority of extreme observed values are above the mean. A simple indication of this can be obtained by comparing the mean and median values. If the median is less than the mean, this suggests that over 50 per cent of the values are below the mean, and hence, to compensate, the right hand or upper tail of the distribution must extend further – indicating positive skew. Statistical packages usually provide a measure of the skewness of a distribution. A normal distribution (being symmetrical) has a value of 0; positive values indicate a distribution with a long right tail, negative values a distribution with a long left tail.

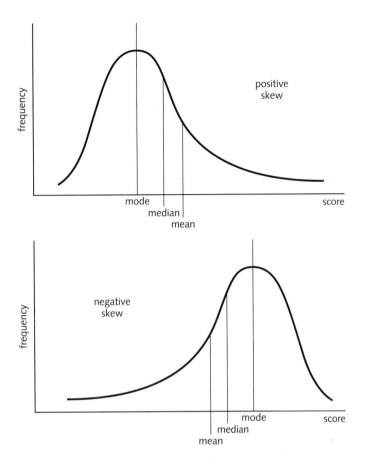

Figure 17.8 Positively and negatively skewed distributions.

Exploring relationships between two variables

Having considered how one might deal with individual variables, let us switch the focus to one of the main concerns in carrying out quantitative social research – looking for relationships between variables. Here we will limit ourselves to relations between two variables.

To say that there is a relationship between two variables means that the distribution of scores or values on one of the variables is in some way linked to the distribution of values on the second variable – that, say, higher scores on one variable for that case (person, perhaps) tend to occur when there are higher scores on the second variable for that case. An example would be the relationship between smoking and lung cancer; those who smoke are more likely to develop lung cancer.

Cross-tabulation

Cross-tabulation is a simple and frequently used way of displaying a relationship between two variables. It is an extension of the use of frequency tables as discussed in connection with the analysis of single variables. Take once more the data on student intake presented in Figure 17.1.

Let us say that we are interested in the relationship between faculty and the relative number of male and female students, i.e. between the variables 'faculty' and 'sex'. Figure 17.9 shows how these data could be presented in a *contingency table*. There are five faculties (five levels of the variable 'faculty') and two sexes (two values of the variable 'sex') and hence 10 (five times two) possible combinations of levels of the variables. The boxes in the table, corresponding to each of these combinations, are referred to as *cells*. The total for each row and each column is given at the end or margin of the row or column. These totals are called the *row marginals* and *column marginals* respectively.

The row total presentation shows the way in which females (and males) are distributed across the faculties labelled as 'counts'. The column total presentation shows the relative percentages (or proportions) of males and females in different faculties (e.g. the proportion of males in the science faculty). The contingency table, viewed in terms of percentages, helps to highlight any relationships between the two variables. Here the low percentage of females in the engineering faculty and high proportion in the arts is a striking, though unsurprising, feature.

Chi-square tests

Chi-square, in a contingency table, is a measure of the degree of association or linkage between the two variables. The more that there is a tendency for the relative number of males and females to vary from faculty to faculty, the greater is chi-square. It is based on the differences or discrepancies between the frequencies in the different cells (the 'counts') and those that you would expect if there was no association at all between the two variables (i.e. the ratio of males to females is the same in all faculties). These latter are known as the 'expected' counts and are shown in Figure 17.10.

You will often see assessments of the *statistical significance* of relationships in contingency tables. This concept, and some of the problems in its use, are discussed later in the chapter. It effectively tests the plausibility that a null hypothesis of no relationship is true. If the result you have obtained would be very unlikely if the null hypothesis were true, it becomes reasonable to rule out the possibility that purely random factors are involved. If its *probability* is sufficiently small (conventionally taken as 1 in 20, i.e. $p = 0.05$), the relationship is taken to be due to some non-chance factor. The chi-square (χ^2) test is commonly used to assess the statistical significance of such relationships in contingency tables. The probability in this example is less than 0.0005. This is clearly very much smaller than the conventional 0.05 and hence statistically *significant*. *Degrees of freedom (DF)* refers to a somewhat esoteric statistical concept linked to the number of cells in the contingency table, which is used when assessing the statistical significance of the value of chi-square.

	Arts	Engineering	Business	Science	Education	Total
Male	3	29	9	10	4	55
Female	22	1	8	6	8	45
Total	25	30	17	16	12	100

Figure 17.9 'Sex' by 'faculty' cross-tabulation.

		Faculty					
		Arts	Engineering	Business	Science	Education	Total
Male	Count	3	29	9	10	4	55
	Expected Count	13.8	16.5	9.4	8.8	6.6	55
Female	Count	22	1	8	6	8	45
	Expected Count	11.3	13.5	7.7	7.2	5.4	45
Total		25	30	17	16	12	100

Chi-square test result

Pearson chi-square   42.39
Degrees of freedom (DF)   4
$p < 0.05$ (exact p is 0.000 to three decimal places)

Note: No cells have an *expected* value of less than 5.

Figure 17.10 Results of a chi-square analysis of the 'sex' by 'faculty' cross-tabulation in Figure 17.9.

Statisticians warn against the use of chi-square when one or more *expected* frequencies fall below a particular value, usually taken as 5 in small tables. Fisher's Exact Test is a substitute which can be used in circumstances where the expected frequencies are too low for chi-square (see Pett, 1997).

A chi-square analysis, if statistically significant as in the present case, indicates that *overall* there is a relationship between the two variables (here 'faculty' and 'sex') which is unlikely to be explained by chance factors. In two-by-two contingency tables (where both variables only have two values) statisticians formerly had the practice of using a somewhat different formula incorporating a 'correction for continuity' (sometimes referred to as 'Yates' correction') for computing chi-square. This is now considered to be inappropriate (Richardson, 1990). Some statistical packages provide both chi-square and a 'corrected' value when analysing two-by-two tables producing an appropriately adjusted chi-square. You are recommended to ignore the corrected value.

Using chi-square to test for 'goodness of fit'

Chi-square can also be used to compare frequencies on a single variable to see how closely they 'fit' to those expected or predicted on some theoretical basis. A common theoretical expectation is for all frequencies to be the same; or perhaps it may be desired to test the goodness of fit to the frequencies expected if the data were normally distributed. The difference in terms of computation is that these expected frequencies have to be supplied, rather than being generated automatically from the observed frequencies.

Scattergrams

A *scattergram* (also known as a *scatter plot*) is a graphical representation of the relationship between two variables. It only makes sense when it is possible to order the values for each of the variables in some non-arbitrary manner. Hence in the data set of Figure 17.1 it would be reasonable to draw a scattergram for, say 'degree class' against 'entry points' but not for 'faculty' against 'entry points'. This is because any particular ordering of the faculties along an axis is arbitrary, and the apparent graphical relationship between the variables will vary with the ordering. Figure 17.11 presents a scattergram showing the relationship between 'entry points'

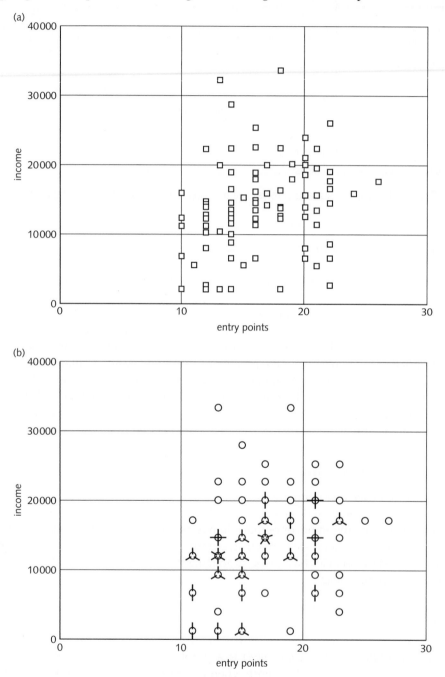

Figure 17.11 Scattergrams of 'entry points by income'.

and 'income' for a sample of graduates. It shows the position of each person on the two variables. For example, the far right point on the scattergram corresponds to someone who gained 26 entry points and has an income of about £18,000.

Scattergrams are a powerful pictorial device, giving a clear picture of the nature and strength of the relationship between the variables. They have their limitations, however. Many types of data are not readily amenable to display in this way, particularly when there are very few values on one or both of the variables. Nevertheless, unless you have data where the ordering of values is arbitrary, you should always consider the feasibility of drawing a scattergram for two-variable data. It is possible to produce contingency tables from the same data, summarizing by taking appropriate intervals along the variables when they take on many values.

Correlation coefficients

Measures of *correlation* (i.e. of the co-relationship between two variables) are referred to as *correlation coefficients*. They give an indication of both the strength and the direction of the relationship between the variables. The commonly used coefficients assume that there is a linear relationship between the two variables. Figure 17.12 demonstrates this in the idealized form of the 'perfect' linear correlation. However, perfection is not of this world. Certainly, you are very unlikely to get that degree of 'tightness' in the relationship, with data concerning humans and their doings. Figure 17.13 illustrates the kind of picture you are likely to see if there is a strong linear correlation. As you can see, the points fall within a cigar-shaped 'envelope'. The thinner the cigar, the stronger the relationship. With weaker correlations, the cigar is fatter; an essentially zero correlation shows no discernable pattern in the scattergram.

Commonly used correlation coefficients include Pearson's correlation coefficient (r), the Spearman rank correlation coefficient (known as Spearman's rho – ρ and Kendall's rank correlation coefficient (known as Kendall's Tau – τ). As their labels suggest, the latter two are used with data in the form of ranks, or orderings, of data (what is first, second, etc.). The data may have

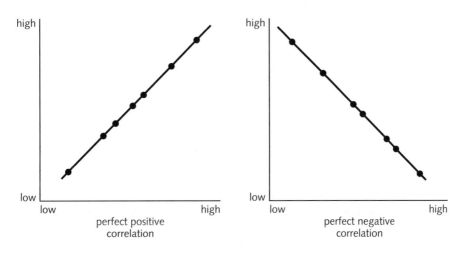

Figure 17.12 A 'perfect' linear correlation.

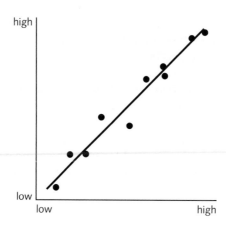

Figure 17.13 Example of a high positive correlation.

been collected in this form, perhaps through participants expressing their preferences for different objects or situations, or may have been collected in other forms and subsequently converted into ranks. They do not assume normal distribution of the data and hence may be used when that assumption, on which the Pearson's coefficient is based, is dubious. They are, however, measures of linear correlation (see below). The Spearman coefficient is effectively a Pearson coefficient performed on the ranks and is preferred by some on that ground, but most analysts appear to prefer Kendall's Tau, possibly because it deals with ties more consistently.

Proportion of variance explained (PVE)

While the correlation coefficient is a measure of the relationship between the variables, it is difficult to assess the strength of this relationship (real 'significance' or importance rather than statistical significance) from the correlation coefficient.

The square of the correlation coefficient (r^2) is a useful index, as it corresponds to the proportion of the variation in values of one of the variables which can be predicted from the variation in the other variable. Broadly speaking, if this is low (say less than 0.3 – but this will depend on circumstances) then it is unlikely to be profitable to exert much further time and effort in investigating the relationship. High values might suggest carrying out a subsequent *regression analysis* (see below).

Measuring the statistical significance of a correlation

The statistical significance of correlation coefficients is commonly computed. This concept, and some of the problems in its use, are discussed below.

It is important to appreciate that the size of correlation coefficient which reaches a particular statistical significance (conventionally $p = 0.05$ being taken as the largest acceptable probability for this type of significance) is very strongly affected by the size of the sample of data involved.

Thus for 20 pairs of scores the value of the Pearson correlation coefficient is 0.44 (two-tailed test – see below, p. 443); for 50 it is 0.28; for 100 less than 0.2; and for 500 less than 0.1. This illustrates the point that statistical significance has little to do with significance as commonly understood. Certainly, with a large sample such as 500, you can achieve statistical significance when less than 1 per cent of the variability in one variable is predictable from variation in the other variable; 99 per cent comes from other sources!

The message is that if the statistical significance of a correlation is to be quoted, make sure that both the size of the correlation (and/or of its square as a measure of the proportion of variance explained) and the size of the sample get quoted.

Non-linear relationships between variables

It is perfectly possible to have some form of non-linear relationship between two variables. One value of the scattergram is in highlighting such non-linearities, in part because they are likely to call for discussion and explanation. They should also give a warning against using statistical techniques which assume linearity. *Curvi-linear relationships* might be found. The envelope, instead of being cigar shaped, might be better represented by a banana or boomerang, as in Figure 17.14.

This is one situation where the data transformations discussed earlier in the chapter may be of value, as the appropriate transformation might convert the relationship in Figure 17.14 to something closely approaching linearity – and hence more amenable to statistical analysis. Even if this transformation does 'work' in that sense, there may be consequent problems of interpretation. To know that there is a strong linear correlation between one variable and, say, the square of another variable may be of descriptive and even predictive value, but defy your attempts at understanding. However, finding that a reciprocal transformation works, such that a non-linear relationship involving 'time elapsed' as one variable becomes linear when a 'rate' measure (i.e. reciprocal of time) is used, may well be readily interpretable.

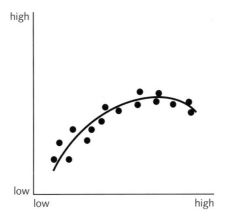

Figure 17.14 Example of a curvilinear relationship.

Lines of 'best fit'

It is possible to draw a line of best fit on a scattergram. This can be estimated by drawing a line having roughly equal numbers of points above and below it, and making each point as near to the line as possible (using the minimum, i.e. perpendicular, distance from the line in each case).

There are systematic means of drawing such a line, which should be employed if it is to be used in any formal way. One approach which is commonly used is *linear regression*. This involves finding the line for which the squared deviation of individual points from the line (in the vertical, i.e. the Y dimension) is a minimum. This can be routinely performed by many computer packages, including 'Analyse-it'. There are alternative ways of deriving these lines (see, for example, Marsh and Elliott, 2008, pp. 196–204, who advocate 'resistant lines'). When data are 'well behaved' (reasonably normal distributions with no problematic 'outliers'), linear regression is probably preferable, if only because of the ease with which the task can be completed.

The 'line of best fit', when obtained by one of the above means, is a powerful and useful way of summarizing the linear relationship between two variables. All straight lines can be expressed by a simple algebraic formula, one form of which is:

$$Y = bX + a,$$

where Y and X are the two variables (conventionally, when there are dependent and independent variables, Y is the dependent variable and X the independent variable); and a and b are constants which typify the particular line of best fit. The constant a is known as the *intercept* and is the point where the line cuts the vertical or Y axis; b is known as the *slope*. This is shown diagrammatically in Figure 17.15.

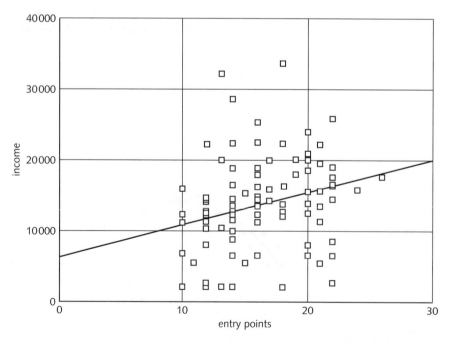

Figure 17.15 Fitting a 'regression line' for relationship between 'entry points' and 'income'.

In addition to providing an elegant way of summarizing the data, the line of best fit (or the coefficients a and b, which amount to the same thing) can be used for predictive purposes, for example, to give an estimate of the likely increase in income over a specified number of years.

There is a difficulty with the data in that the amount of variability of the points around the regression line is not constant. It appears to increase with higher values of entry points and income. This not uncommon feature goes by the somewhat fearsome name of *heteroscedasticity* and, strictly, violates one of the assumptions on which Pearson's correlation coefficient is based. Again, this is a situation where possible transformations of the data might be attempted.

Exploring relationships among three or more variables

Research designs often involve more than two variables, calling for different approaches to those covered already. Multivariate techniques which are concerned with the *joint* effects of multiple variables are covered later in the section. We will, however, first consider approaches which look at the effects of taking into account a third variable on the relationship between two variables.

Three-variable contingency tables: the 'elaboration' approach

With non-experimental strategies, it is often essential to explore the effects of other variables when seeking to understand the basis of a two-variable relationship. One set of techniques is known as *elaboration* analysis. It has been widely used in the analysis of data from surveys and other non-experimental designs. Marsh (1982, pp. 84–97) gives a very clear account of the underlying logic. It involves the following steps:

- establish a relationship between two variables;
- subdivide the data on the basis of the values of a third variable;
- review the original two-variable relationship for each of the sub-groups; and
- compare the relationship found in each sub-group with the original relationship.

The third variable is referred to as the *test variable* (or *control*) *variable*. The original relationship between the two variables, where the third variable is not being held constant at a particular value, is called the *zero-order relationship*. The relationship that is found for a particular value of the test variable is known as a *partial relationship*. See de Vaus (2014, pp. 293–315) for an account of the statistics involved.

The pattern of effects of the test variable on the zero-order relationship can help in interpreting and understanding what is going on.

The website gives details of the interpretation of various patterns obtained when exploring relationships among three variables.

This approach to data analysis is simply a somewhat more complex version of the use of contingency tables, which were covered earlier. It provides a way of testing out, and possibly modifying, the conceptual model you developed when designing the study (see Chapter 4, p. 72).

Or, in other words, identifying the causal links. In realist terms, this amounts to specifying which mechanisms are in operation. The real world is complex and analysis may well not generate clear-cut patterns. In practice it is likely that multiple causation is the norm for many of the phenomena which interest us and that models which allow for multiple independent variables are to be preferred (see below).

It is possible to extend this type of analysis to four or even more variables (i.e. to two or more test variables) but it rapidly becomes unwieldy, particularly when there are several categories on each variable. Unless large amounts of data have been collected, the database for each sub-group becomes very small. The choice of test variables for elaboration analysis is obviously of central importance as it is only possible to include very few of them. They have to be pre-specified at least to the extent that you have collected the necessary data (some of the variables on which data have been collected can, of course, be omitted at the analysis stage). The message for small-scale studies is to keep the conceptual model simple. As repeatedly emphasized in Chapter 6, if you are carrying out fixed design research with a view to understanding and explaining a phenomenon, you don't do this unless and until you have established a clear and simple conceptual framework.

Using partial correlations

Essentially the same type of logical analysis can be carried out using partial correlation coefficients, rather than proportions in contingency tables. This amounts to examining the correlation between two variables and then seeing how, if at all, it changes when one or more other variables are held constant.

In the three-variable case, the correlation matrix is first calculated, which gives each of the three possible correlations between the variables. A partial correlation matrix is then calculated. Interpretation of the relationship between the variables is based on the pattern of correlations and the logical potential link between the test variable and the two original variables (e.g. antecedent or intervening).

The partial correlation approach cannot be used when testing for a 'moderated' relationship (i.e. there is an interaction in the sense that the relationship between them is influenced by a third variable) because this depends on comparing the relationship for different categories of the test variable and the partial correlation effectively gives you a single averaged figure. There are also problems in computing the correlation coefficients if one of the variables has a small number of categories or values.

Multiple regression

Multiple regression is multiple in the sense that it involves a single dependent variable and two or more independent variables (or, in the terminology more commonly used in non-experimental research, a single response variable and more than one explanatory variable). It is a flexible, widely used approach which has been made readily accessible through computer packages.

Taking the simplest possible case for multiple regression of one dependent variable and two independent variables, the regression equation (refer back to p. 432) is:

$$y = a + b_1 x_1 + b_2 x_2$$

where y is the dependent variable, x_1 and x_2 are the two independent variables, a is the intercept, and b_1 and b_2 the regression coefficients for the two independent variables. The regression coefficient gives you the change in the dependent variable for each unit change in that independent variable, *with the effect of any of the independent variables controlled* (referred to as 'partialled out').

While multiple regression can be used in the same way as linear regression, to give a line of best fit and to provide predictions through substitutions of different values of x_1 and x_2, its main use is to provide an estimate of the relative importance of the different independent variables in producing changes in the dependent variable. To do this, it is necessary to convert the regression coefficients to allow for the different scales on which they have been measured. When this is done, they are referred to as *standardized regression coefficients* or *beta weights*. They then tell you how many standard deviation units the dependent variable will change for a unit change in that independent variable.

The output from a statistical package will provide various statistics, which may include:

- *R-squared.* This is the *multiple coefficient of determination*, a measure of the proportion of the variance in the dependent variable which is explained by the independent variables in the equation. If, for example, R^2 is 0.14, the proportion of variance explained is 14 per cent. An 'adjusted R^2' may also be produced. This will be smaller than R^2 and is adjusted in the sense that it takes into account the number of independent variables involved and would normally be preferred to the unadjusted value.
- *t-value of coefficients.* This presents a test of whether or not the associated beta coefficient is significantly different from zero. A probability value will usually be given in each case.
- *Standard error of coefficients.* This is a measure of the accuracy of the individual regression coefficients (see p. 435). This information is useful in assessing the likely accuracy of predictions based on the regression equation.
- *Analysis of variance (ANOVA) tables.* Discussed later in the chapter.

This discussion merely scratches the surface of multiple regression and its possibilities. If a major concern is in *developing* a model, effectively in deciding on an appropriate regression equation, then an option known as *stepwise regression* is worth considering. This starts with the simplest possible model and then step-by-step examines the implications of adding further independent variables to the equation.

If you already have an explicit model which you are testing, *hierarchical* (or *stepwise*) *multiple regression* is preferable. This involves entering the variables into the analysis in an order determined by your model.

You are strongly recommended to seek advice when considering using multiple regression, as not only is it complicated but it is particularly easy to do something silly and inappropriate with the packages available. It is worth noting, however, that multiple regression can be used with a wide variety of types of data. In particular, it can be used with categorical variables such as 'gender' and 'faculty' in the example we have been using. A difficulty here is that the ordering of categories is essentially arbitrary for such variables, and particularly when there are more than two categories for a variable, the ordering chosen would affect the result obtained. This can be handled by the use of so-called 'dummy variables'. It involves coding particular categories as 'present' (say coded '1') or absent (say coded '0'). Cramer (2003, Chapters 10–12) gives details. Alternatively, *logistic regression* may be used for both continuous and *categorical data*, as long as you have (or can produce) a categorical dependent variable (see Field, 2014, Chapter 19 for a thorough discussion).

Multivariate exploratory techniques

Strictly speaking, these involve more than one dependent or response variable and possibly additional explanatory variables (Ryan, 2008). This excludes multiple regression although it is commonly referred to as a multivariate technique. There is a wide variety of different exploratory techniques designed specifically to identify patterns in multivariate data sets of which *factor analysis* has been the most widely used.

Exploratory factor analysis

Factor analysis is an approach to making sense of a large number of correlations between variables. It has similarities with regression analysis but differs in that the variables all have equal status; no single variable is designated as the dependent or criterion variable. Factor analysis starts with a matrix of correlations.

Matrices of this type, particularly when they contain up to 100 or so variables, are very difficult to interpret. Factor analysis aids in this process by pointing to clusters of variables which are highly intercorrelated. The 'factors' referred to are hypothetical constructs developed to account for the intercorrelations between the variables. Factor analysis seeks to replace a large and unwieldy set of variables with a small and easily understood number of factors. Suppose that your correlation matrix arises from a 50-item questionnaire on aggression and aggressiveness. You find, say, that there are strong intercorrelations between 12 items concerning aggression towards family and friends, and similar intercorrelations between nine items concerning aggressiveness towards people in authority, but no other strong clusters. This then provides good evidence that two factors are important in understanding your results.

The technique is commonly used in the development of tests and scales (see, for example, Loewenthal, 2001). It allows you to assess the extent to which different test items are measuring the same concept (strong intercorrelations) or whether their answers to one set of questions are unrelated to their answers on a second set. Hence we get an assessment of whether the questions are measuring the same concepts or variables.

Factor analysis is typically used as an exploratory tool. There is an alternative version referred to as 'confirmatory factor analysis' – see below. Exploratory factor analysis starts with the correlation matrix. For it to be worthwhile to carry out the analysis, the matrix should show a substantial number of significant correlations (either positive or negative).

The number of respondents should exceed the number of variables. When the interest is not simply to describe the factors summarizing the relations between variables, but to try to get a reliable estimate of these underlying factors, then minima of five times the number of participants to the number of variables have been suggested. There are many versions of factor analysis including canonical, alpha, image and maximum likelihood factoring, but the most commonly used are *principal-components analysis* (strictly speaking a form of regression analysis) and *principal-axis factoring* (sometimes simply referred to as 'factor analysis'). Accounts of the process are found in specialized texts such as Loewenthal (2001), Child (2006) and Kline (1993).

SPSS provides most factor analysis options you may need. Bryman and Cramer (2008) provide details of the procedures to be followed and the kinds of output obtained when the SPSS is used to carry out principal-components and principal-axis analyses. Brief details of other multivariate techniques which can be used in an explanatory mode are given below. Further details, and examples which help in understanding the situations in which the techniques can be used, are given in the Electronic Statistics Textbook, available at http://www.statsoft.com/textbook. Hill and Lewicki (2006) is the corresponding paper version.

🖳 *The website includes a short discussion of additional multivariate exploratory techniques.*

Model-testing multivariate techniques

Although factor analysis is usually employed primarily as an exploratory tool, it can be used to assess the extent to which the solution obtained matches a hypothesized pattern and is therefore useful when we are testing a model or conceptual structure, when it is referred to as *confirmatory factor analysis* (Brown, 2015). Other multivariate approaches are specifically targeted at model testing. They include:

Path analysis

Sometimes referred to as *causal modelling*, the central idea in path analysis is that, if we can safely make assumptions about the chronological order of variables in our research, then we can use partialling of variance techniques from multiple regression to test models about the interrelationship of these variables. Causal models can only be built from what are effectively correlational techniques if other assumptions as well as the temporal assumptions about the effect of the variables apply. While this is a tool of considerable potential, the necessary assumptions are highly restrictive and there are many problems of interpretation (Olobatuyi, 2006).

Structural equation modelling (SEM)

This is a multivariate data analysis technique which combines elements of both multiple regression and factor analysis. Its goal is similar to that of factor analysis through providing a summary of the interrelationships among variables. It is similar to path analysis in that researchers can test models in the form of hypothesized relationships between constructs. A model can be tested statistically in a simultaneous analysis of the entire system of variables to assess its fit to the data. SEM has become increasingly popular in psychology and the social sciences for the analysis of non-experimental data and has also been quite intensively used in applied fields such as social work research (e.g. Guo, Perron & Gillespie, 2009).

Issues of interest in real world research are often complex and multidimensional in nature. However, until relatively recently researchers were dissuaded from working with complex research questions because the statistical techniques available did not easily allow for testing of multivariate models. Weston and Gore (2006), in an accessible brief guide to SEM, cite several applied examples where this approach has been valuable. For example, Tylka and Subich (2004) hypothesized that eating-disorder patterns in adult women were a function of personal, sociocultural, and relational factors. Using SEM they tested a multi-dimensional model about how these factors interact in complex ways to explain symptom severity and showed its close fit to the data. Using a similar approach, Long (1998) successfully tested a model of workplace stress and coping for employed women, which included constructs such as human agency, status, coping, work-environment demand, and distress, across levels of employment prestige.

It is important to stress that, just as with techniques discussed above, such as correlation, multiple regression, and path analysis, causality cannot be determined by the results of an SEM analysis – this is a judgement based on the adequacy of your underlying theory and research design. Also that, as Weston and Gore (2006) point out:

> researchers can easily misuse SEM. Just as researchers are free (although not encouraged) to conduct several different multiple regression models until they find a model to their liking, they can also analyze models in SEM, identify and remove weaknesses in the model, and then present the revised model as if it were the originally hypothesized model. Most users would likely agree that SEM's true power lies in the fact that researchers must specify complex relationships a priori and then test whether those relationships are reflected in the sample data. Optimally, researchers will draw these hypothesized relationships from previous research or theory and will present the results with integrity. Should the researcher detect weaknesses in the proposed model, he or she should further explore them using a modified model in a new sample (p. 733).

If you are considering using SEM, Blunch (2008) and Dattalo (2013, pp. 109–48) provide accessible introductions. Much of its popularity can be traced to the development of increasingly accessible and reliable software packages, which include LISREL, EQS and AMOS. Schumacker and Lomax (2004) provide a clear non-technical introduction covering each of these. However, SEM is complex statistically and calls for a great deal of judgement on the part of the researcher to avoid the misuse and misinterpretation of the results of analysis. It depends on an evaluation of multiple test statistics and indices to determine whether the model fits the data adequately and there is considerable controversy about what constitutes an acceptable fit. Weston and Gore (2006) provide a set of guidelines on how to avoid the pitfalls.

Analysing differences

So far, this chapter has focused on displaying, describing and summarizing quantitative data and on analysing relationships among data. We now turn to what has, traditionally, been viewed as the major task when analysing quantitative data. Are there *differences* between the scores, values or observations obtained under one condition and those obtained under another condition (or conditions)?

Looking for differences and looking for relationships are really two ways of viewing the same thing. Asking whether there are differences between the performance of three groups taught by different methods is essentially equivalent to asking whether there is a relationship between teaching method and performance.

It is to answer questions of difference that many of the *tests of statistical inference* have been developed. The basic logic behind such tests is not difficult, although its working out in specific tests can be complex. The test is commonly used to make decisions about the state of affairs in some 'population' as compared with the actual sample of scores or observations that we have obtained. For example, suppose we want to find out whether the ratio of men to women in a particular sample is such that we can consider it representative of a specific population where the ratio of men to women is known. If there is a 50-50 split in the population but there are no women in a randomly selected sample of 20 people from that population, then common sense might be unwilling to regard this as a representative sample and perhaps cast doubts upon the randomness of the procedure used to select the sample. However, even if we decide that the sample was not drawn from the 50-50 population, we could be wrong. A sample of 20 consisting of 20 women is in fact just as likely to occur as any other specific sample (the analogy often drawn is with tossing coins – it is possible to have a sequence of 20 heads in a row and that sequence is just as likely as any other specific sequence such as HTTHTTTHHTHHTHTTTTHH). There are, however, many possible ways in which one could end up with, say, 11 males and 9 females, but in fact only one sequence which gives all 20 females. It is then possible to come to the decision (based on probabilities) that the sample didn't come from the population when it in fact did, an error known as a *type one error*.

Statistical tests provide ways of assessing this type of error. This is where the term *statistical significance* rears its head. In situations like the one discussed, it refers to the probability of making a type one error (given the symbol alpha – α). The convention has also been mentioned of setting this at a probability of 0.05 (i.e. 5 per cent or 1 in 20). However, the fact that many computer programs typically generate exact probability figures for the chance of making a type one error, rather than saying that it is 'less than 0.05', means that there is an increasing tendency for such exact probabilities to be quoted.

There is also a *type two error*: that is, the probability of deciding that the sample came from the population when in fact it did not (given the symbol beta – β). There is an inverse relationship between the two types of error, in the sense that we can reduce our chances of making a type one error by setting the significance level at a very low probability (say 0.001, or 1 in 1,000). However, setting the decision line at this point produces a corresponding increase in the chances of making a type two error.

The *power* of a statistical test is the probability that the test will reject a false null hypothesis (that it will not make a type two error). As power increases, the chances of a type two error decrease. The probability of a type two error is referred to as the false negative rate (β). Therefore power is equal to $(1 - \beta)$. Cohen (1962) called attention to the poor *statistical power* of much published research – a situation which has not changed radically over 50 years later (see Cashen & Geiger, 2004).

Conventional statistical tests assume that we are dealing with randomly selected samples from known populations. This is rarely the case in experimental research. As discussed in Chapter 6, true experiments pay careful attention to the random *assignment* of a set of participants to different experimental treatments or conditions. However, it is relatively rare that serious attention is given to the random *selection* of these participants to ensure that, probabilistically, they are representative of known populations. Experimenters typically work with people they can persuade to take part, effectively a convenience sample.

This approach is justified by claiming that the interest is in testing for possible differences between the two conditions rather than in generalizing to the populations from which the samples are drawn. However, the theoretical basis to many of the statistics used does assume random selection. The general issue of statistical testing with non-random samples is discussed later in the chapter.

Statistical significance

For many statistically oriented social scientists, quantitative analysis is virtually synonymous with significance testing. The whole point and purpose of the exercise is taken to be: 'Have we got a significant result?' 'Is $p < 0.05$?' This refers to *statistical significance* (I [Robson] am grateful to a reviewer, Joe Maxwell, who pointed out the potentially misleading treatment of statistical significance in a draft version of an earlier edition of this text. The following discussion leans heavily on material which he kindly provided.)

The probability that a significance test gives you is *not* that a result is due to chance (as is commonly claimed). What a p value actually tells you is something that sounds very similar to this statement but is in fact quite different. It tells you how likely it *would be* that you would get the difference you did (or one more extreme), by chance alone, if there really is no difference between the categories represented by your groups, in the population from which you drew your sample. This assumption of 'no difference' is referred to as the *null hypothesis*. In other words, a statistical significance test 'tests' the plausibility that the null hypothesis – no difference between the population means – is true. If your result would be very unlikely *if* the null hypothesis were true, this makes it less plausible that the null hypothesis *is* true.

Thus, the result of a statistical significance test tells you nothing directly about the actual population to which you want to make inferences; it simply helps you rule out one possible validity threat to your result – namely, that the result could be due to random variation in your sample, rather than to real differences in the population. If your p value is small rather than large, this makes it less likely that your result is due to chance variation rather than to a true difference, other things being equal. However, the 'other things being equal' is very important, because the actual likelihood that your result is due to chance is not completely expressed by the p value. Statistical significance tests say *nothing* about all the other possible validity threats to the result, or how likely these are relative to the proposed explanation. For example, suppose you pull a coin out of your pocket or purse, flip it 10 times, and get 10 heads. This is an extremely unlikely occurrence (less than one chance in 1,000, or $p < 0.001$) if it is a fair coin (one that has an equal chance of coming up heads or tails – the null hypothesis). However, my judgement would be that it's still more likely that this particular result is due to chance than it is because the coin is biased. If it came up 50 times, the latter possibility becomes somewhat more plausible. Both explanations are unlikely, and if no other explanations can be put forward, then the more improbable it is that your result could have happened by chance if you have a fair coin. Hence, the more likely it is that the alternative explanation of bias, however implausible, is true.

Statistical significance testing is both deeply entrenched in practice and highly controversial. Meehl (1978) goes so far as to conclude that reliance on statistical significance was one of the ' . . . worst things that ever happened in the history of psychology' (p. 817). Haig (1996) considers that: 'It is a major professional embarrassment that researchers continue to employ such tests in the face of more than three decades of damning criticism.' Perhaps the most swingeing criticism comes from Ziliak and McCloskey (2008) in their text *The Cult of Statistical Significance*, who show convincingly, with evidence ranging from agronomy to zoology – taking in psychology, medicine and economics as major miscreants – how wide the disaster is and how bad it has been for the progress of science.

One problem, mentioned earlier in the chapter, is that statistical significance is not related to the size or importance of an effect or relationship, which is in many cases what we are really interested in. The chance of obtaining a statistically significant result increases as the sample size increases, because, for example, you then get a more sensitive test of any difference between the experimental and control groups in an RCT. But there is always likely to be some difference between the two conditions. Hence the common injunction to 'use a larger number of participants' may buy statistical significance at the expense of real life triviality. Paradoxically, if one is relying on statistical significance, there is much to be said for keeping the sample small so that only robust effects are going to be picked up.

Readers who wish to work out their own position on this controversy might review the interestingly titled *What If There Were No Significance Tests?* (Harlow, Mulaik and Steiger, 1997). See also Hagen (1997) and Gigerenzer, Krauss and Vitouch (2004) to get a flavour of the debate.

Measuring effect sizes

It would be helpful to use a statistic which is, unlike statistical significance, independent of sample size. When looking at the difference between the means of two sets of scores, this can be achieved by dividing the difference in means by the standard deviation in the population from which they come. So one obtains a difference expressed in standard deviation units; e.g. the difference in means is 0.6 standard deviations. The effect size is sometimes referred to as the *practical significance* of a result and it is not uncommon to find major discrepancies between this and statistical significance – a large effect size but lack of statistical significance; or the reverse (Alhija & Levy, 2009).

There are some underlying complexities. The population standard deviation is rarely known and a standard deviation estimated from the sample of scores available usually has to be substituted. Details of how this can be done are provided in texts concentrating on statistical analysis (e.g. Clark-Carter, 2009). There is also the issue of what constitutes a large enough difference to be taken note of. Cohen (1988) provides guidelines suggesting that a value of 0.2 is small; 0.5 is medium; and 0.8 is large. The use of *confidence intervals,* as discussed on p. 420, is another possibility. Confidence intervals are routinely computed by statistical packages. Effect sizes can be derived from the information about means and standard deviations. Details are given in Dancey and Reidy (2011). Gorard (2014) proposes using an effect size based on the mean difference between groups, divided by the mean absolute deviation of all scores (see p. 419). This is both easy to understand and to compute.

An alternative approach to measuring the size of an effect produced in a study involves evaluating the *proportion of variance explained* (PVE) by means of various statistics based on measures such as the square of the correlation between two variables. Rosnow and Rosenthal (1996) have suggested some convenient procedures for the compilation of both effect sizes and confidence intervals for several statistics.

A third, and more direct, approach to communicating the magnitude of the effect is to simply report the actual differences between the groups (as discussed below). This is often more meaningful to practitioners and other non-specialists than the two previous approaches.

Power analysis

The power of a statistical test is the probability that it will correctly lead to the rejection of a false null hypothesis – the probability that it will result in the conclusion that the phenomenon exists. A statistical power analysis can be used either retrospectively (i.e. after the study has been carried out) or prospectively (i.e. before it has been carried out). A prospective analysis is often used to determine a required sample size to achieve a target level of statistical power, while a retrospective analysis computes the statistical power of a test given the sample size and effect size. Cohen (1988) provides a very convenient source for formulas and tables to compute power in a range of common analyses. There are several websites which will calculate these statistics for you (e.g. http://www.danielsoper.com/statcalc/default.aspx#c17; see 'sample size' for prospective analyses, and 'statistical power' for retrospective analyses).

Although there are no formal standards for power, a value of 0.80 is commonly quoted as acceptable (i.e. at least an 80 per cent chance of rejecting a false null hypothesis). Setting the bar at this level can cause virtually insurmountable problems in some research contexts. For example McDonald and Fuller (1998) illustrate the difficulty in studying black bear cub survival in the wild. Although their data represented over 10 years of data collection, they could not generate a sufficiently large sample size to adequately test a simple hypothesis with the design and analytical methods they used.

A common misconception is that power is a property of a study or experiment. Any statistical result that has a p-value has an associated power. Hence if you are carrying out several tests there will be a different level of statistical power associated with each one. Statistical power provides vital additional information about the importance of non-significant test results that researchers should consider when drawing their conclusions. A non-significant result coupled with high statistical power to detect an effect of interest to the researcher increases confidence that the effect was not missed. On the other hand, a non-significant result coupled with low statistical power to detect the effect of interests suggests that another study, or more sampling, is required before strong conclusions can be drawn.

It is becoming common for funding agencies and boards reviewing research to request that prospective power analyses are carried out. The argument is that if a study is inadequately powered, there is no point in carrying it out.

Because significance testing is expected by many audiences, including sponsors and journal editors, it is advisable to give measures of statistical significance. However because of the various criticisms, you should not rely solely on them. Best practice, as recommended by the American Psychological Association, is to also include effect sizes and confidence intervals (Fritz, Scherndl & Kühberger, 2013).

Depending on the type of study this might be based on differences in means, correlation coefficients, and/or regression coefficients (each of these is discussed later in the chapter in connection with different analyses). These are simply ways of summarizing aspects of the data, i.e. summary or descriptive statistics (p. 418). Hence they do not carry with them the positivistic conceptual baggage associated with some uses of significance testing. With a realist approach, statistical analysis is used to confirm the existence of mechanisms whose operation we have predicted in the contexts set up in an experiment or other study. Large effect sizes provide confidence in their existence; hence they are what you are looking for. Significance levels play a subsidiary role, their inclusion perhaps lacking something in logic but sanctioned by convention.

Practical significance indices provide information about the size of observed difference or relationship (e.g. effect size). Clinical significance measures provide data regarding the extent to which the intervention makes a real difference to the quality of life of the participants or to those with whom they interact.

Single group tests

In most situations we are concerned with comparing the scores or values obtained under one condition with those obtained under another condition during the current project. However, you might want to compare what you have obtained with some expectation arising outside the study to see whether there is a difference.

Chi-square as a test of 'goodness of fit'

This test has already been mentioned (p. 427).

One-group *t*-test

The *t*-test is a very widely used to compare two means. In this version, the comparison is between a mean obtained from the particular sample of scores that you have obtained under some condition, and a hypothesized population mean. Figure 17.16 summarizes the output of a one-group *t*-test.

Probability values for the statistical significance of *t*-test results (and for many other statistical tests) can either be *one-tailed* or *two-tailed*. The 'two-tailed' description means that one is simply concerned with establishing the probability of a difference between the two means. With 'one-tailed' the hypothesis is that the difference will be in a particular direction (hence referred to as a 'directional' hypothesis'). So 'two-tailed' probabilities should be selected unless there is a strong *a priori* reason (e.g. from your model or other theory about what is happening) for expecting the difference to be in a particular direction. Details of the means themselves should always be reported.

		n	Mean	SE	SD
	Entry points	33	20.9	1.11	6.4
	Hypothesized		18.6		
	Mean	20.9			
	SE	1.11			
	t statistic	2.06			
	DF	32			
	2-tailed *p*	0.0477			

Key: SE = standard error; SD = standard deviation; DF = degrees of freedom
As $p < 0.05$ the difference in means is statistically significant

Note: The output from 'analyse-it' also gives 95% CI (confidence interval) values.

Figure 17.16 Results of a one-group *t*-test.

Two group tests

Many of the questions we are interested in when carrying out a study producing quantitative data boil down to whether there are differences between the scores obtained under two conditions or by two groups. Do mature students admitted without standard entry qualifications get poorer degrees than 18-year-old standard entrants? Do patients suffering from low back pain get better more quickly when treated by chiropractic methods than by drugs? And so on.

Two group t-tests

The *t*-test is very commonly used to compare the means of two groups. It comes in two versions. The *paired two-group t-test* (sometimes called the *dependent* samples *t*-test) should be used when there are pairs of scores. This would be, for example, if the same person provided a score in each of the conditions. The *unpaired two-group t-test* (otherwise known as the *independent samples t-test*) is where there is no such basis for putting together pairs of scores. Figure 17.17 gives an example of output from an independent samples *t*-test, and Figure 17.18 that from a dependent samples *t*-test.

Recall, once again, that it is good practice, when recording the results of such tests, to include not only the *t*-value and its statistical significance (the probability value, which must be lower than 0.05 for conventional statistical significance) but also the means and standard deviations of the two sets of scores. A minus sign for the value of *t* is not of importance and does not affect its significance; it simply indicates that the mean of whatever has been taken as the first set of scores is less than that for the second group of scores. The 'DF' which occurs in this and many

Gender	n	Mean	SE	SD
Female	12	119.3	6.20	21.5
Male	7	101.0	7.79	20.6
Mean difference	18.3			
SE	10.07			
t statistic	1.82			
DF	17.0			
2-tailed *p*	0.0864			

Key: SE = standard error; SD = standard deviation; DF = degrees of freedom
As *p* > 0.05 the difference in means is not statistically significant

Notes: (i) The output from 'analyse-it' also gives 95% CI (confidence interval) values. (ii) The example shows that it is possible to have unequal numbers in the two conditions. However, statistically, it is preferable to have equal sample sizes.

Figure 17.17 Results from an independent samples *t*-test.

Score	n	Mean	SE	SD
First measure	12	103	3.96	13.7
Second measure	12	107	4.09	14.2
Difference (first – second)	12	–4	2.58	8.9
Mean difference	–4			
SE	2.58			
t statistic	–1.55			
DF	11			
2-tailed p	0.1492			

Key: SE = standard error; SD = standard deviation; DF = degrees of freedom
As $p > 0.05$ the difference in means is not statistically significant

Note: The output from 'analyse-it' also gives 95% CI (confidence interval) values.

Figure 17.18 Results of a dependent samples t-test.

other printouts, refers to 'degrees of freedom'. It is a statistical concept of some importance but is in many cases, including this, simply related to the size of the sample. Packages also provide a test for equality of variances (the F-test, sometimes called a 'variance-ratio test'). As you might expect, this tells you if you have a statistically significant difference in the variances (concerned with the distribution of scores about the mean) of the two groups. If there is no significant difference, you can use the output for 'equal variances assumed' and if there is a *significant difference, use the output for 'equal variances not assumed'.*

Non-parametric equivalents to the t-test

Most statistical packages provide a range of *non-parametric tests*. Parametric tests (of which the t-test is an example) are ones that have been based in their derivation on certain assumptions as to the nature of the distributions from which the data come (usually that they are normal). Non-parametric tests are based on other principles and do not make this kind of assumption. Proponents of parametric tests argue that they are more *efficient* (in the sense that they will detect a significant difference with a smaller sample size than the corresponding non-parametric test – however, this is not always the case, see p. 440); that it is possible to carry out a greater range and variety of tests with them; and that they are *robust* (meaning that violations of the assumptions on which they are based, e.g. about the normality of the distribution from which the data samples are drawn, have little or no effect on the results they produce).

Advocates of non-parametric tests counter with the arguments that their tests tend to be easier to use and understand and hence less prone to mindless regurgitation, that because of their 'distribution-free' nature (i.e. no assumptions made about the type of distribution of the scores), they are usable in a wider variety of contexts. They have also been proposed as preferable when the assumption of *random sampling* from known populations, central to most conventional parametric statistics, cannot be assumed (see p. 451). The best of such tests are virtually identical efficiency-wise to parametric ones in situations where the latter can legitimately be used – and obviously preferable in other situations. There is now an adequate range of tests to deal with virtually any situation (Pett, 1997; Sprent & Smeeton, 2007; Corder & Foreman, 2014).

A pragmatic approach is suggested, driven mainly by the kind of data you have to deal with. If your data are obviously non-normal, or are in the form of ranks (i.e. first, second, etc.), then a non-parametric test is needed. Otherwise, the range of tests to which you have access through computer packages, and the expectations in the field in which you are working, are important considerations. Conventional parametric testing is the safe option as it is widely used, and with computer packages, you do not need to worry about the amount of computation required.

The *Mann-Whitney U test* is a non-parametric equivalent of the unpaired two-group *t*-test. The *Wilcoxon signed-rank test* is a non-parametric equivalent of the paired two-group *t*-test. Computation is straightforward and the output in both cases provides 'z'-scores (standardized scores expressed in standard deviation units) and associated probabilities. If there are ties in the scores, a corrected z-score is provided. Strictly, the tests should not be used if there is a substantial proportion of ties.

There are other non-parametric tests provided by some packages which are appropriate for use in the same type of situation as a Mann-Whitney U test. They are not widely used.

Three (or more) group tests

It is not uncommon, in experiments, to have three or more conditions. You may wish, for example, to compare the effects of 'high', 'medium' and 'low' stress levels on performance in some situation. It would be possible to take these conditions in pairs and carry out three separate *t*-tests. However, there are techniques which allow this to be done in a single, overall, test. It is necessary to separate out the 'independent samples' and 'paired samples' designs in the same kind of way as was done with the *t*-test.

Analysis of variance (single factor independent samples)

This situation requires the simplest version of a very widely used, and extremely versatile, technique known as *analysis of variance*. Figure 17.19 shows the format of data referred to. It is commonly referred to as a 'One-Way ANOVA'. Figure 17.20 illustrates the type of output generated for this design. The key finding here is that *there is an overall difference between the means under the different conditions*. This is shown by the F-test result and its associated probability, which is smaller than the 0.05 level. This is conventionally reported as: *the difference between groups is statistically significant ($F = 20.13$, $p < 0.0001$; with 3 and 14 DF)*.

When there is a significant overall difference between the groups, various additional statistics are available helping to pinpoint which of the differences between particular pairs of means are contributing to this overall difference. In Figure 17.20, the *Tukey test* has been used, but others are available. They are alternative ways of dealing with the problem of assessing significance level when a sequence of similar tests is carried out on a data set. Effectively what 'statistically

Experimental conditions (two or more)
i.e. 'levels' of the independent variable (X)

one	two	three	four

scores are the
values of the
dependent variable (Y)

Figure 17.19 Format of single-factor independent samples analysis of variance.

Conditions	n	Mean	SE	Pooled SE	SD
A	5	15.06	0.668	1.069	1.49
B	4	20.55	1.109	1.195	2.22
C	4	16.20	1.046	1.195	2.09
D	5	25.80	1.469	1.069	3.28
Source of variation	Sum squares	DF	Mean square	F statistic	p
Conditions	344.98	3	114.99	20.13	<0.0001
Residual	79.96	14	5.71		
Total	424.95	17			
Tukey					
Contrast	Difference	95% CI			
A v B	−5.49	−10.15	to −0.83	(significant)	
A v C	−1.14	−5.80	to 3.52		
A v D	−10.74	−15.13	to −6.35	(significant)	
B v C	4.35	−0.56	to 9.26		
B v D	−5.25	−9.91	to −0.59	(significant)	
C v D	−9.60	−14.26	to −4.94	(significant)	

Overall, the difference between conditions is statistically significant ($p < 0.0001$)

Note: The Tukey test is one of several available to test for the difference between pairs of conditions. The printout shows if a particular comparison between a pair ('contrast') is statistically significant ($p < 0.05$).

Figure 17.20 Results of a single factor independent samples analysis of variance.

significant at the 5 per cent level' means is that if you carry out, say, 20 tests, you would expect one of the 20 (5 per cent) to be significant even if there is no real effect and only random factors are at work. Any significant difference between two conditions should only be reported if the overall F-test is significant.

As with t-tests, it is helpful to report not only the results of the statistical test but also to give the summary statistics, such as the means, standard deviations, and confidence intervals under the different conditions. This applies when reporting any analysis of variance findings and helps you, and the reader, to appreciate what the analysis means.

Kruskal-Wallis test

This is a non-parametric equivalent to the above analysis of variance. It is simpler to compute manually but with computer assistance, there seems little reason to prefer it unless the data are in a form for which a parametric test is unsuitable.

Analysis of variance (single factor repeated measures)

The only difference between this design and the previous analysis of variance is that there is a basis for pairing individual scores across the conditions (usually because the same person produces a score under each condition, i.e. there are 'repeated measures'). The format of this design is given as Figure 17.21 and Figure 17.22 gives an example. In the example the same group of 'subjects' are each tested on a task at four yearly intervals. The use of the term 'subjects' rather than 'participants' is deeply engrained in the psyche of users of analysis of variance – sorry!

Friedman test

This is a non-parametric equivalent to the above paired samples analysis of variance. Again, it is relatively simple to compute manually but with computer assistance, there seems little reason to prefer it when the data are in a form for which a parametric test is suitable.

Experimental conditions (two or more)
i.e. 'levels' of the independent variable (X)

	one	two	three	four
participant 1				
participant 2		scores are the		
participant 3		values of the dependent variable (Y)		
participant 4				

Figure 17.21 Format of single-factor repeated measures analysis of variance.

Score	n	Mean	SE	SD	
1 year	12	103.0	3.96	13.7	
2 years	12	107.0	4.09	14.2	
3 years	12	110.0	3.85	13.3	
4 years	12	112.0	4.26	14.8	
Source of variation	Sum squares	DF	Mean square	F statistic	p
Score	552.0	3	184.0	3.03	0.0432
Subjects	6624.0	11	602.2	-	-
Residual	2006.0	33	60.8		
Total	9182.0	47			

Overall, the difference between the scores in different years is statistically significant ($p < 0.05$).

Figure 17.22 Results of single factor repeated measures analysis of variance.

Testing differences when two (or more) independent variables are involved

As discussed in Chapter 6, it is feasible to have two or more independent variables in an experiment, commonly in what are called factorial designs (p. 122). There is a plethora of different analyses for the many different designs. The following account simply tries to introduce some main issues.

Simple two-way independent samples analysis of variance

Figure 17.23 illustrates the form of the data with this design, and Figure 17.24 gives corresponding output. The analysis permits an assessment of the effect of each variable separately (the 'main effect' of variables A and B and also of any possible 'interaction' (or AB effect) between the two variables (refer back to Chapter 6, p. 124). In the case of the example shown in Figure 17.21 significant effects were found for both A and B variables. When the AB interaction is significant this means that the effect of one variable differs at different levels of the second variable. It is then not legitimate to talk about A or B having an overall effect. In this example the interaction is non-significant so the problem does not occur.

The pattern of results should be examined carefully. It helps to display any significant interaction graphically.

Two-variable (or factor) analysis of variance with repeated measures

A frequently used complication of the above design is to add repeated measures. Thus, participants are not simply tested once under a particular combination of levels of the two variables, but are given a series of trials.

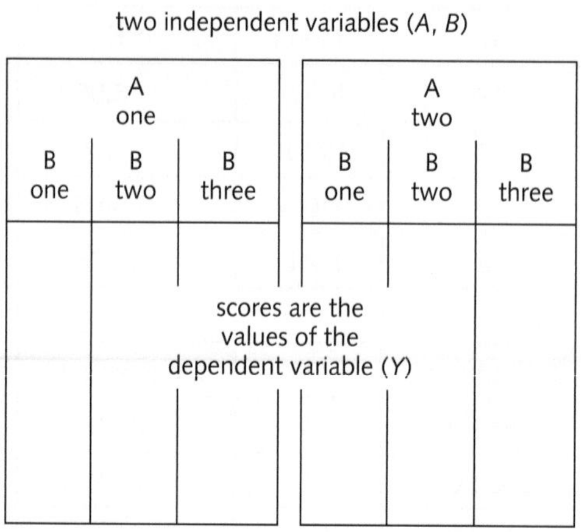

two independent variables (A, B)

Figure 17.23 Format for simple two-variable analysis of variance.

A	n	Mean	SE	Pooled SE	SD
A_1	10	175.8	3.90	4.92	12.3
A_2	10	203.7	4.75	4.92	15.0
A_3	10	197.0	7.07	4.92	22.4
B	n	Mean	SE	Pooled SE	SD
B_1	15	185.5	5.23	4.02	20.2
B_2	15	198.8	4.92	4.02	19.0
Source of variation	Sum squares	DF	Mean square	F statistic	p
A	4242.5	2	2121.2	8.75	0.0014
B	1320.0	1	1320.0	5.45	0.0283
AB	759.3	2	379.6	1.57	0.2294
Residual	5816.4	24	242.4		
Total	12138.2	29			

Figure 17.24 Results of a two-way independent samples analysis of variance.

Testing differences when two (or more) dependent variables are involved

The above analyses are all limited to dealing with a single dependent variable. In studies with more than one, it is possible simply to repeat the analysis for each dependent variable in turn. However, there are advantages in carrying out a single, global, analysis. One version of this is called *multivariate analysis of variance (MANOVA)*. The analysis and its interpretation are complex and should not be undertaken without advice.

Statistical testing and *non-random sampling*

The theoretical rationale of many of the statistical tests discussed in this chapter is based on an assumption of random sampling. However, in practice, much published research in fields covered in this text does not make use of random sampling techniques to select participants. How can this discrepancy be dealt with? Possibilities include:

Use random sampling whenever feasible

In some situations random sampling from known populations, if taken into account at the design stage, can be achieved without major problems. This is the preferred solution for those wishing to continue to use conventional parametric statistical tests.

Use randomization tests

While non-parametric tests, discussed earlier in the chapter, are presented as being 'distribution-free' (i.e. they are not dependent on assumptions about the type of distribution of scores, whereas conventional tests typically assume normal distributions) they can also be derived without assuming random sampling from known populations. However, random *assignment* to different conditions (as in true experiments) is assumed. The probability of particular patterns of results can be computed as an exercise in permutations and combinations (sometimes referred to as Monte Carlo techniques, where several thousand random repetitions are carried out to establish a very close approximation to the exact probability of different outcomes). Tests such as Mann-Whitney and Wilcoxon simplify the task by dealing with ranks rather than scores. They give tables of probabilities of different rankings, cutting out the need for complex computations.

The rapid increase in readily available computing power has extended the range and complexity of designs which can be analysed by randomization tests. Sprent and Smeeton (2007) give full coverage.

Joe Maxwell (personal communication, 21 July 2010) clarifies this point:

If an experimental study uses random assignment to conditions, but not random sampling from some population, then the result of a significance test tells you how likely it would be, if the random assignment were done repeatedly with the same sample, that you would get the difference you did (or a larger one) between the groups, by chance variation in assignment alone, if the intervention really had no overall causal effect on the outcome. However, it would not allow you make any statistical inferences to a larger population than the actual sample; any such inferences would have to be based on other arguments (such as the similarity of the sample to the population of interest – not always a reliable indicator). Box, Hunter, and Hunter (1978) are excellent on this issue, which is actually more complicated than suggested here.

Assume that the discrepancy is not important

This is the current default assumption. As analyses making this assumption continue to be widely published, you are unlikely to suffer if you do likewise. If you don't use random sampling but still want to assess the generalizability of your results to some population, you can (with some risk) assume that the distribution is not effectively different from random. In doing this, it seems prudent not to assume a normal distribution, and thus to use non-parametric tests.

In the context of survey research, Pruchno *et al.* (2008) show that respondents recruited using *convenience sampling* can differ on many variables from those recruited by random means. An unsurprising finding, but worth stressing.

Quantitative analysis and different fixed design research strategies

This chapter has not attempted to make one-to-one correspondences between the different fixed design research strategies and particular techniques of quantitative analysis. Ways of displaying, summarizing and manipulating data are essentially common to all strategies. Many of the ways of exploring relationships among the data are applicable to each of them. There are, admittedly, problems when tests of significance are used in the absence of *random allocation*, but they do not so much preclude their use in quasi-experiments or non-experimental fixed designs, as require the analyst to think very carefully about interpretation.

There are, of course, strong links between some analytical approaches and particular research strategies, which have been referred to at various points in the chapter. Analysis of variance was developed to deal with the analysis of the true experiment. Correlation matrices and associated techniques such as factor analysis are commonly used in surveys and similar non-experimental settings. However, labelling each test as appropriate only for a specific strategy would be as unnecessarily restrictive as insisting that a particular method of data collection, such as direct observation, should only be used in an experiment – when it could well play a part in a case study, or even in a survey.

It may be helpful, nevertheless, to highlight issues in the analysis of data from two types of experimental study likely to be of real world interest (quasi-experiments and single-case experiments) and the analysis of surveys and other non-experimental designs.

The analysis of quasi-experiments

Three possible quasi-experimental designs were recommended for serious consideration in Chapter 6: the pre-test post-test non-equivalent groups design, the interrupted time-series design, and the regression discontinuity design (p. 128). The three designs require differing approaches to their analysis.

Pre-test post-test non-equivalent groups design

This is a very common design and it is not unusual (though incorrect) for researchers to ignore the fact that it is not a true experiment and not to acknowledge this in either their description or analysis. The non-equivalence of the groups means that there are possible selection effects that may bias the results. Several techniques are available which attempt to separate out the treatment effect (i.e. the effect of the independent variable on the dependent variable) from the effect of selection differences. The most frequently used approaches are:

- simple analysis of variance;
- analysis of variance with blocking or matching of participants;
- analysis of variance based on 'gain' scores (e.g. difference between pre and post scores); and
- analysis of covariance (with either single or multiple covariates).

Reichardt (2005) provides details of each of these approaches and of the difficulties they raise. He concludes that 'any one of these statistical methods could be biased enough so that a useful treatment might look harmful and a harmful treatment could look benign or even beneficial'. His recommendation, in line with the general approach taken in this text, is not that we give up and regard the statistical procedures as worthless but that we give them a relatively minor role – by seeking to eliminate, or at least trying to reduce, the effect of selection and other threats through the *design* of the study rather than relying on the statistical analysis removing their effects. One interesting approach is to try to 'bracket' the effect of a treatment by using a variety of different but reasonable techniques of analysis (see the evaluation of the *Sesame Street* TV series by Cook *et al.*, 1975 for an example; Fisch and Truglio, 2001 include a wide range of related evaluations).

Interrupted time-series design

The approaches to the analysis of this design which are generally regarded as satisfactory (e.g. the use of autoregressive integrated moving average models – ARIMA models – as developed by Box and Jenkins, 1976) require a minimum sequence of about 50 data points, and preferably over 100 of them. Series of this length tend to be very rare in small-scale studies although, if anyone manages to generate this amount of data, the discussion by Glass, Willson and Gottman (2008) provides useful suggestions.

For smaller amounts of data, statistical analysis by standard methods is not advisable. Shadish, Cook, and Campbell (2002, pp. 198–203) suggest approaches which can be used to assist in making causal inferences. They point out that even short interrupted time series before and after an intervention can help in eliminating several threats to internal validity, depending on the pattern of results. They recommend adding design features such as control groups, multiple replications, etc. to enhance the interpretability of short time series. While several different statistical analyses have been used, there is little consensus about their worth. Their conclusion is that the best advice is to use several different statistical approaches. If the results from these converge, and are consistent with visual inspection, confidence in the findings is warranted. Gorman and Allison (1996) summarize the possible statistical tests that could be used.

Similar data patterns to those found in interrupted time-series designs occur with single-case designs, and hence the forms of analysis suggested for single-case designs may be appropriate in some cases (see the section below).

Regression discontinuity design

There are strong advocates, not only of the design itself as discussed in Chapter 6, p. 133, but also of its analysis using multiple regression techniques to provide unbiased estimates of treatment effects (e.g Vandenbroucke & le Cessie, 2014). Trochim is foremost as a proponent (see, for example, Trochim, 1984; 1990).[2] However, there is a continuing debate about appropriate statistical approaches (Stanley 1991; Reichardt, Trochim, & Cappelleri, 1995). As with interrupted time-series (and single-case experiments) visual inspection of the pattern of results may well be adequate to provide a convincing demonstration of an effect – or lack of it. If you feel that statistical analysis is called for, you are recommended to seek advice, and/or undertake further reading. The general introduction by Shadish *et al.* (2002, Chapter 7) is accessible and balanced, and includes an appendix on the various statistical approaches to the analysis of regression-discontinuity designs (pp. 243–5).

The analysis of single-case experiments

The simple form of a single-case experiment involves a single independent variable and a single dependent variable (traditionally the *rate* of some response, although this is not a necessary feature). It is, effectively, a time-series experiment carried out using a single 'case' (typically a single person; possibly replicated with a small number of other persons). Hence it might have been dealt with earlier together with other two-variable situations. However, there are major differences of ideology about purposes and procedures of analysis between single-case experimenters and others that warrant their separate consideration.

Researchers using single-case designs have traditionally avoided statistical analysis and relied upon 'eyeballing' the data – looking at a comparison, in graphical form, of the participant's performance (sometimes called 'charting') in the different phases of the study. They tend to claim that if statistical techniques were needed to tease out any effects, then the effects were not worth bothering about (see Sidman, 1960 for a clear exposition of the ideas underlying this methodology). This argument has undeniable force, though we will see that, as usual, things are more complicated. It arose in part because of the applied focus of many single-case studies (see the *Journal of Applied Behavior Analysis* for examples), where the distinction is commonly made between *clinical significance* and *statistical significance*. As discussed previously, the latter refers to the unlikeliness that a result is due to chance factors; clinical significance means that a treatment has produced a substantial effect such that, for example, a person with problems can now function adequately in society.

However, while Skinner and his fellow experimenters working with rats or pigeons in the laboratory were able to exert sufficient control so that stable base-lines could be obtained from

---

[2] See Trochim's website at http://www.socialresearchmethods.net/research/rd.htm, which gives free access to a full set of his publications on regression discontinuity.

which the performance in subsequent phases could be differentiated, this has not surprisingly proved more difficult in applied 'field' studies with humans. This once again illustrating the difference between 'open' and 'closed' systems discussed in Chapter 2. Some researchers with 'applied' interests have questioned the wisdom of ignoring non-dramatic changes, particularly in exploratory work (e.g. Barlow, Nock & Hersen, 2008). They argue that we should determine whether changes are reliable and then subsequently follow them up. It has also been demonstrated that the reliability of 'eyeballing' as a technique can leave a lot to be desired, with different individuals reaching different conclusions as to what the data were telling them. Hagopian, Fisher, Thompson and Owen-Deschryver (1997) have developed structured criteria which increase reliability. Gast and Spriggs (2014) give general coverage of the visual analysis of graphic data.

There is an increasing interest in, and use of, statistical tests of significance in single-case studies, although this is still a controversial area (Gorman & Allison, 1996; Kazdin, 2010). The techniques advocated are themselves the subject of controversy, largely for the same reason encountered in considering time-series quasi-experimental designs, namely, the lack of independence of successive data points obtained from the same individual. Again, the sequence of data points obtained in most real world single-case experiments is insufficient to use standard time-series approaches but they provide a good solution if extensive data are available.

Kazdin (2010, Appendix) gives details on various possible tests and their application. Dugard, File and Todman (2012) argue in favour of the use of randomization (exact) tests which can provide valid statistical analyses for all designs that incorporate a random procedure for assigning treatments to subjects or observation periods, including single-case designs. The tests have not been used widely until recently as they require substantial computational power. They give examples of the analysis of a wide range of single-case designs using Excel, with references to the use of SPSS and other statistical packages.

If it is important that you carry out a statistical analysis of the results of a single-case study (rather than simply performing a visual analysis), there is much to be said for introducing randomization at the design stage so that these tests can be used. Edgington (1996) provides a clear specification of what is required in design terms.

The analysis of surveys

Surveys, and many other non-experimental designs, in their simplest form produce a two dimensional rows and columns matrix coding data on a range of variables from a set of respondents. As ever, your research questions drive the form of analysis which you choose. If the study is purely descriptive, the techniques covered in the section on 'Exploring the data set' (p. 416) may be all that you need. Frequency distributions, graphical displays such as histograms and box plots, summary statistics such as means and standard deviations, will go a long way toward providing the answers required. You may need to go on to analyse relationships using contingency tables and correlation coefficients and/or analysing differences through t-tests and other statistics.

With studies seeking to explain or understand what is going on, you should still start with this exploratory, 'know your data', phase. However, when you have some conceptual model, possibly expressed in terms of mechanisms, which provides the basis for the research questions, you will need to take the analysis further following a more confirmatory style.

This may involve the testing of some specific two-variable relationships. The 'elaboration' approach (discussed on p. 433) can help to clarify the meaning of relationships between variables. More sophisticated analyses such as multiple linear regression perform a similar task in more complex situations. And modelling techniques such as SEM (p. 437) provide ways of quantifying and testing the conceptual model.

Causation in surveys and other non-experimental designs

Catherine Marsh (1982) accepts that '. . . the process of drawing causal inferences from surveys is problematic and indirect' (p. 69). Writing from a realist perspective she provides a very clear account of some ways of going about this difficult task (Chapter 3). Recall that the traditional positivist view of causation, known as 'constant conjunction', was found in Chapter 2 to be seriously wanting. Following realist precepts, we are concerned to establish a causal model which specifies the existence of a number of mechanisms or processes operating in particular contexts.

How can surveys help in doing this? Obviously correlations can be computed but the injunction that 'correlation does not imply causation' should be etched deeply on the cortex of anyone who has followed a course in statistics. The temptation to get a statistical package to cross-tabulate 'ALL' against 'ALL' (i.e. asking it to crunch out relationships between all the variables and then cherry-picking the significant ones) should be resisted. Working with a 5 per cent significance level means that we expect on average one in 20 of the results to be significant due to chance factors. While there are ways of dealing with the problem of chance correlations (e.g. by splitting the cases randomly into two equal subsets, exploring the correlations obtained with the first, then checking with the second), you still need to make *ad hoc* arguments to explain your pattern of findings.

One approach, simple in principle, involves the *elaboration* strategy discussed earlier in the chapter. If you have a thought-through proposed causal model involving a small number of possible mechanisms it can be tested in this way. Unfortunately, this process rapidly becomes unwieldy as more variables are included in the model. By going back and forth between model and data, gradually elaborating the model, it may be feasible to build up a more complex model. This process need not be totally 'pure'. While the unprincipled fishing trip is not a good way of developing a causal model, further development of the model based in part on hunches and insights that occur during analysis is well within the spirit of exploratory data analysis. Marsh and Elliott (2008) summarize the task as follows:

> In the absence of an experiment, a statistical effect of one variable on another cannot just be accepted as causal at face value. If we want to show that it is not *spurious*, we have to demonstrate that there are no plausible *prior variables* affecting both the variables of interest. If we want to argue that the *causal mechanism* is fairly direct, we have to control for similar intervening variables (p. 252, emphases added).

Marsh and Elliott (2008, especially Chapters 11 and 12) give an excellent account of the use of elaboration and related techniques to establish causation. It is stressed here as still being of value in small-scale real world study when data on a restricted set of variables have been collected, and the model to be tested is necessarily simple.

More generally, the more powerful multivariate techniques accessible via specialist statistical packages, in particular structural equation modelling (SEM), as discussed on p. 437, have tended to replace the type of sequential logic required when using elaboration.

A note on interactions

Formally, an interaction is when the effect of one variable on a second one depends on the value of a third variable. They were discussed earlier in the chapter in the context of two variable analyses of variance (p. 449). When such interactions exist – and they are extremely common in social research – they mean that any generalizations we seek to make about causal processes are limited. This is a serious obstacle to positivistic researchers who seek universal laws. However, it is entirely consistent with the realist view that mechanisms do not operate universally and that the research task is to specify the contexts in which they work.

A realist reminder on the analysis and interpretation of experiments

The realist view of experimentation, as discussed in Chapter 6 (p. 118), is fundamentally different from the traditional positivist one. The main remaining similarity is in the active role taken by the experimenter. It is her responsibility to so set up and manipulate the situation that predicted mechanisms are given the chance to operate. This calls for a considerable degree of prior knowledge and experience of the phenomenon or situation studied, so that a conceptual map or model can be developed with some confidence. This predicts likely mechanisms, the contexts in which they may work, and for whom they will work.

Viewing experiments in this light does not, in general, either preclude or privilege any of the experimental designs covered in Chapter 6, nor any of the analyses covered in this chapter. There may well be situations, as discussed by Pawson and Tilley (1997, pp. 34–54) where the nature of likely causal agents are such that, for example, randomized allocation to different conditions changes the nature of the phenomenon of interest. Hence control group methodology is inappropriate. Careful attention to such possible distortions is needed at the design stage.

Assuming the choice of an appropriate design, the question becomes one of deciding whether we have good evidence for the operation of the predicted mechanisms. In most cases, this boils down to deciding whether an obtained relationship or difference (typically of means) provides that evidence. While it will in many cases be feasible to generate statistical significance values, they need to be taken with even more than the usual pinch of salt (see p. 440). This is because their derivation has been within the positivistic conceptualization of experimental design. While it seems intuitively reasonable that, irrespective of this heritage, a lower probability value for the statistical significance of a difference gives greater confidence in the reality of that difference, it is difficult to go much further than that. Recall, however, that the advice has been throughout to place greater reliance on measures of effect sizes based on statistics such as confidence intervals and standardized differences in means (p. 441). Armed with these and graphical displays, you then have to judge the quality of the evidence.

Further reading

 The website gives annotated references to further reading for Chapter 17.

CHAPTER 18

The analysis and interpretation of qualitative data

This chapter:

- stresses the need for a systematic analysis of qualitative data;
- emphasizes the central role of the person doing the analysis, and warns about some deficiencies of the human as analyst;
- discusses the advantages and disadvantages of using specialist computer software;
- explains the Miles and Huberman approach to analysis which concentrates on reducing the bulk of qualitative data to manageable amounts and on displaying them to help draw conclusions;
- suggests thematic coding analysis as a generally useful technique when dealing with qualitative data;
- reviews the widely used grounded theory approach;
- summarizes a range of alternative approaches; and
- finally, considers issues involved in integrating qualitative and quantitative data in multi-strategy designs.

Introduction

Qualitative data have been described as an 'attractive nuisance' (Miles, 1979). Their attractiveness is undeniable. Words, which are by far the most common form of qualitative data, are a speciality of humans and their organizations. Narratives, accounts and other collections of words are variously described as 'rich', 'full' and 'real', and contrasted with the thin abstractions of number. Their collection is often straightforward. They lend verisimilitude to reports.

The 'nuisance' refers to the legal doctrine that if you leave an attractive object, such as an unlocked car, where children can play with it, you may be liable for any injuries they sustain.

Naive researchers may be injured by unforeseen problems with qualitative data. This can occur at the collection stage, where overload is a constant danger. But the main difficulty is in their analysis. There is no clear and universally accepted set of conventions for analysis corresponding to those observed with quantitative data. Indeed, many 'qualitative' workers would resist their development, viewing this enterprise as more of an art than a science. But for those who do wish to work within the kind of scientific framework advocated in this book, and who wish to persuade scientific or policy-making audiences, there are ways in which qualitative data can be dealt with systematically. This chapter seeks to provide an introduction to that task.

In the typology of research strategies that has been adopted in this text, the various types of flexible and multiple-strategy designs are the prime generators of large amounts of complex qualitative data.

Qualitative data are often useful in supplementing and illustrating the quantitative data obtained from an experiment or survey. Small amounts of qualitative data used as an adjunct within a largely quantitative fixed design study will not justify detailed and complex analysis. Often the need is simply to help the account 'live' and communicate to the reader through the telling quotation or apt example. However, when methods generating qualitative data form the only, or a substantial, aspect of the study, then serious and detailed attention needs to be given to the principles of their analysis.

Two assumptions

1. *If you have a substantial amount of qualitative data you will use some kind of software package to deal with it.* Standard software, even a simple word-processing package, can do much to reduce the sheer tedium of qualitative data analysis (see Hahn, 2008 on the use of standard Microsoft Office software for a small qualitative project). For anything other than a small amount of data, the amount of drudgery you can avoid, and the ease with which you can relate to the data, make the use of a computer near to essential. There are also specialist qualitative data analysis packages which aid the process even more. See Appendix B for further details.
2. *Unless you already have experience yourself, you will be helped or advised by someone who does have experience in this type of analysis.* The dominant model for carrying out qualitative analysis has in the past been that of apprenticeship. Without accepting all the implications of such a model (which tends, for example, to include a principled inarticulacy about process) there is undoubted value in expert advice. The help provided by software is very different from that in quantitative analysis. There the 'expert's' role is largely to point you towards an appropriate test and to ensure that you understand the outcome. In qualitative data analysis, both the experienced person and the computer help you through a not very well specified process.

Types of qualitative analysis

Box 18.1 provides a typology of possible approaches. Quasi-statistical approaches rely largely on the conversion of qualitative data into a quantitative format and have been covered under the heading of content analysis in Chapter 15. See also Abeyasekera (2005) who provides a range of suggestions.

BOX 18.1

Different approaches to qualitative analysis

1. *Quasi-statistical approaches*
   - Uses word or phrase frequencies and inter-correlations as key methods of determining the relative importance of terms and concepts.
   - Typified by content analysis.
2. *Thematic coding approach*
   - A generic approach not necessarily linked to a particular (or any) theoretical perspective.
   - All, or parts of, the data are coded (i.e. identified as representing something of potential interest) and labelled.
   - Codes with the same label are grouped together as a theme.
   - Codes and themes occurring in the data can be determined inductively from reviewing the data, and/or from relevance to your research questions, previous research, or theoretical considerations.
   - The themes then serve as a basis for further data analysis and interpretation.
   - Makes substantial use of summaries of the themes, supplemented by matrices, network maps, flow charts and diagrams.
   - Can be used on a purely descriptive or exploratory basis, or within a variety of theoretical frameworks.
3. *Grounded theory approach*
   - A version of thematic coding where, as a matter of principle, the codes arise from interaction with the data.
   - Codes are based on the researcher's interpretation of the meanings or patterns in the texts.
   - Used to develop a theory 'grounded' in the data.
   - Can be used very prescriptively following rules laid down by founders of the approach, or as a general style of analysis using a specialized terminology for different types of coding.

Note: There are other specialized approaches, including discourse and conversation analysis, and the analysis of narratives (i.e. stories in written, spoken or other forms). See Chapter 15, p. 361.

Thematic coding analysis is discussed in this chapter as a straightforward general approach which can be used in a wide variety of settings. The widespread popularity of grounded theory as a basis for qualitative data analysis demands its coverage in any treatment of the topic. There are a large number of other approaches, many of which call for an extensive understanding of their theoretical foundations. A brief introduction is provided in a later section of the chapter.

Whatever approach is taken, the researcher has the responsibility of describing it in detail. You have to be able to demonstrate the quality of your analysis, including how you got from the data to your interpretation.

The importance of the quality of the analyst

The central requirement in qualitative analysis is clear thinking on the part of the analyst. Fetterman (1998) considers that the analysis is as much a test of the researcher as it is a test of the data: 'First and foremost, analysis is a test of the ability to think – to process information in a meaningful and useful manner' (p. 93). As emphasized *at the beginning of Part V*, qualitative analysis remains much closer to codified common sense than the complexities of statistical analysis of quantitative data. However, humans as 'natural analysts' have deficiencies and biases corresponding to the problems that they have as observers (see Chapter 14, p. 320). Some of these are listed in Box 18.2. Systematic, documented approaches to analysis help minimize the effects of these human deficiencies. However, there is an inescapable emphasis on *interpretation* in dealing with much qualitative data which precludes reducing the task to a defined formula. Hence, the suggestions made in this chapter are more in the nature of guidelines rather than tight prescriptions.

BOX 18.2

Deficiencies of the human as analyst

1. *Data overload.* Limitations on the amount of data that can be dealt with (too much to receive, process and remember).
2. *First impressions.* Early input makes a large impression so that subsequent revision is resisted.
3. *Information availability.* Information which is difficult to get hold of gets less attention than that which is easier to obtain.
4. *Positive instances.* There is a tendency to ignore information conflicting with hypotheses already held and to emphasize information that confirms them.
5. *Internal consistency.* There is a tendency to discount the novel and unusual.
6. *Uneven reliability.* The fact that some sources are more reliable than others tends to be ignored.
7. *Missing information.* Something for which information is incomplete tends to be devalued.
8. *Revision of hypotheses.* There is a tendency either to over- or to under-react to new information.
9. *Fictional base.* The tendency to compare with a base or average when no base data is available.
10. *Confidence in judgement.* Excessive confidence is rested in one's judgement when once it is made.
11. *Co-occurrence.* Co-occurrence tends to be interpreted as strong evidence for correlation.
12. *Inconsistency.* Repeated evaluations of the same data tend to differ.

(adapted and abridged from Sadler, 1981, pp. 27–30)

Common features of qualitative data analysis

While the possible approaches to analysis are very diverse, there are recurring features. Miles, Huberman and Saldana (2014, p. 10) give a sequential list of what they describe as 'a fairly classic set of analytic moves':

- giving labels ('codes') to chunks (words, phrases, paragraphs, or whatever), labelling them as examples of a particular 'thing' which may be of interest in the initial set of materials obtained from observation, interviews, documentary analysis, etc.;
- adding comments, reflections, etc. (commonly referred to as 'memos');
- going through the materials trying to identify similar phrases, patterns, themes, relationships, sequences, differences between sub-groups, etc.;
- using these patterns, themes, etc. to help focus further data collection; gradually elaborating a small set of generalizations that cover the consistencies you discern in the data; and
- linking these generalizations to a formalized body of knowledge in the form of constructs or theories.

This general approach forms the basis of thematic coding analysis discussed below.

Similarity and contiguity relations

Maxwell and Miller (2008) are concerned that an emphasis on coding and categorizing is in danger of losing connections within accounts and other qualitative material. They make a distinction between *similarity relations* and *contiguity relations*. When using coding, similarities and differences are commonly used as the basis for categorization. Relationships based on contiguity involve seeing connections between things, rather than similarities or differences. We look for such relationships within a specific interview transcript or observational field notes, seeking connections between things which are close together in time or space. They can also be sought between categories and codes once they have been established as a next step in analysis.

Similar distinctions have been proposed previously, including Coffey and Atkinson's (1996) 'concepts and coding' as against 'narratives and stories' and Weiss's (1994) 'issue-focused' and 'case-focused' analysis.

Maxwell and Miller review several advantages of combining categorizing and connecting strategies for analysing qualitative data. They suggest that it may be useful to think in terms of:

> categorizing and connecting 'moves' in an analysis, rather than in terms of alternative or sequential overall strategies. At each point in the analysis, one can take either a categorising step looking for similarities and differences, or a connecting step, looking for actual (contiguity based) connections between things. In fact, it is often productive to alternate between categorizing and connecting moves (p. 470).

They provide an exemplar (pp. 471–2) illustrating one way in which the two strategies can be integrated.

In their view, the 'grounded theory' method discussed later in the chapter actually uses this strategy although with a different terminology. In particular, Corbin and Strauss's (2008) 'axial coding' is effectively the same as 'connecting analysis'. The other main approach *covered below*, 'thematic coding' analysis, while essentially based on categorizing, does not preclude following Maxwell and Miller's suggestions.

Using the computer for qualitative data analysis

The single constant factor reported by qualitative researchers is that such studies generate very large amounts of raw data. A small ethnographic style study will generate many pages of field notes including observations, records of informal interviews, conversations and discussions. This is likely to be supplemented by copies of various documents you have had access to, notes on your own thoughts and feelings, etc., etc. A multi-method case study will produce a similar range and amount of material. Even a strictly limited grounded theory study relying solely on interviews leaves you with 20 or more tapes to be transcribed and subsequently analysed.

Before getting on with any type of analysis, you need to ensure that you know what data you have available and that they are labelled, stored and, if necessary, edited and generally cleaned up so that they are both retrievable and understandable when you carry out the analysis. A typical first analytic task of labelling or coding the materials (e.g. deciding that a particular part or segment of an interview transcript falls into the category of 'requesting information' or 'expressing doubt' or whatever) involves not only assigning that code but also having a way of seeing it alongside other data you have coded in the same way.

In the pre-computer era, these tasks were accomplished by means of file folders containing the various sources of data, markers and highlighters, and copious photocopying. One strategy was to make as many photocopies of a page as there were different codes on that page, then to file all examples of a code together. It is clear that much of the drudgery of this task can be eliminated by using a word processor. Many data sources will either be directly in the form of computer files or can be converted into them without difficulty. It may be feasible to enter field notes directly into a laptop computer. An interview tape can be entered into the word processor as it is being transcribed. Incidentally, if you have to do this yourself there is much to be said for the use of speech recognition software for this task (listen to each sentence on the tape through headphones, then repeat it out loud to activate speech recognition). It will need to be checked but modern systems can reach high standards of accuracy. Similarly, if you have access to a scanner with optical character recognition software (OCR), it is now straightforward to convert many documents into word processor files. There are some types of data for which this may not be feasible (e.g. handwritten reports).

Word processors are a boon in storing, organizing and keeping track of your data. Obviously you need to observe good housekeeping practices and should take advice on how you can survive possible hard disk crashes, loss, theft, fire, etc. Essentially, this means having multiple copies of everything, regularly kept up to date in more than one location, and in both paper and computer file versions. Word processors can also help with the coding task through 'copy' and 'paste' functions. In this way it is easy to build up files containing all instances of a particular coding whilst retaining the original file with the original data to which codes have been added.

Word processors can also be used to assist in the 'connecting' (as against categorizing) analysis of qualitative data advocated by Maxwell and Miller (2008), discussed earlier in the chapter. Marking, extracting and putting together selected data from a longer text can greatly simplify the task of data reduction needed for producing case studies, narratives, etc.

Should you go beyond using standard word processors to one of the many specialist software packages designed to help with qualitative data analysis?

Using specialist qualitative data analysis (QDA) packages

There are many computer packages specifically designed for researchers to use when analysing qualitative data (commonly referred to as CAQDAS – computer-assisted qualitative data analysis). The most widely used has probably been NUD*IST (Non-numerical, Unstructured Data Indexing, Searching and Theorizing), a catchy acronym which encapsulates the central features of many of the packages – indexing, searching and theorizing. NUD*IST has now been superseded by NVivo, developed by the same organization, QSR International (http://www.qsrinternational.com). It can be used profitably in most situations where you have substantial amounts of qualitative data, and for many different types of study, including grounded theory, conversation and discourse analysis, ethnographic studies, phenomenological studies, action research, case studies, and mixed method research. If you have facility in its use it is also a valuable tool when carrying out literature reviews.

While NVivo is the preferred option for qualitative data analysis in many institutions and hence is likely to be readily available and to receive support, there are several other packages worth considering for particular situations or types of data – see Appendix B for details.

When deciding whether or not to use specialist software, the advantages of time-saving and efficiency when analysing large amounts of data (once you have gained familiarity with a package), should be weighed against the time and effort taken to gain that familiarity. Box 18.3 lists some general advantages and disadvantages in their use. García-Horta and Guerra-Ramos (2009) discuss the use of two different packages with interview data, concluding that 'CAQDAS is of great help and can enhance interview data analysis; however, careful and critical assessment of computer packages is encouraged. Their capabilities must not be overestimated, since computers are still unable to perform an independent rational process or substitute the analyst's capacities' (p. 151).

Richards (2002), the prime mover in the development of the NUD*IST and NVivo packages, expresses concerns that the full potential of computer-based analysis is not being realized. More seriously, the packages may actually be having negative effects. Because the coding and sorting tasks can be carried out more effectively and efficiently using a computer package, users tend to focus excessively on this aspect:

> The code-and-retrieve techniques most easily supported by computers and most demanded by users are techniques most researchers had used at some time, for sorting out the mess of complex data records. But they were not much discussed in the literature before computing, and not at all clearly associated with the goal of theorizing common to most qualitative methodologies. So computing became associated with techniques that are generic, easily learnt and that emphasize data management, and description. Significantly, these are aspects of practical research ignored or even spurned by theoretical writers (p. 266).

It could be argued that users are simply replicating their previous paper-based, cut and paste, highlighter employing, practices on the computer, but it is undoubtedly true that packages are capable of much more than this; for example, they can include tools for doing more

BOX 18.3

Advantages and disadvantages of specialist QDA packages

Advantages

- They provide an organized single location storage system for all stored material (also true of word processing programs).
- They give quick and easy access to coded material (e.g. examples of a particular theme) without using 'cut and paste' techniques.
- They can handle large amounts of data very quickly.
- They force detailed consideration of all text in the database on a line-by-line (or similar) basis.
- They help the development of consistent coding schemes.
- They can analyse differences, similarities and relationships between coded elements.
- Many have a range of ways of displaying results.

Disadvantages

- Proficiency in their use takes time and effort.
- There may be difficulties in changing, or reluctance to change, categories of information once they have been established.
- Particular programs tend to impose specific approaches to data analysis (depends on the program – see Appendix B).
- Tendency to think that simply because you have used specialist software you have carried out a worthwhile analysis. A focus on coding and other technical aspects can give less emphasis to interpretation.

interpretation once the coding is done. Encouragingly, theory-building software has in recent years been developed to such an extent that it is probably the most widely used type. While, as pointed out by Maxwell and Miller (2008), most of these uses have been based on a prior categorizing analysis, many of the current programs allow the user to create links among and between *any* segments, both within and between contexts, and to display the resulting networks.

Dealing with the quantity of qualitative data

Qualitative data can easily become overwhelming, even in small projects. Hence you need to find ways of keeping it manageable. This process starts before any data are collected when you focus the study and make sampling decisions about people to interview, places to visit, etc. During and after data collection you have to reduce the data mountain through the production of summaries and abstracts, writing memos, etc. Miles *et al.* (2014, p. 12) refer to this as *date condensation*. They emphasize that this is a part of analysis and not a separate activity. Decisions about what to select and to summarize, and how this is then to be organized, are analytic choices.

Good housekeeping

Even a small project producing qualitative data can easily leave you overwhelmed with lots of pieces of information of many different types. Possible ways of keeping track include the use of:

- *Session summary sheets.* Shortly after a data collection session (e.g. an interview or observation session) has taken place and the data have been processed, a single sheet should be prepared which summarizes what has been obtained. It is helpful if this sheet is in the form of answers to summarizing and focusing questions. These might include who was involved, what issues were covered, what is the relevance to your research questions (effectively what was the purpose of the session), new questions suggested and implications for subsequent data collection.
- *Document sheets.* A similar sheet prepared for each document collected. This clarifies its context and significance, as well as summarizing the content of lengthy documents. The session summary and document sheets assist in data reduction, an important part of the analysis process.
- *Memoing.* A memo can be anything that occurs to you during the project and its analysis. Memoing is a useful means of capturing ideas, views and intuitions at all stages of the data analysis process.
- *The interim summary.* This is an attempt to summarize what you have found out so far and highlight what still needs to be found out. It is recommended that this is done before you are halfway through the time you have available for data collection. The summary should cover not only what is known but also the confidence you have in that knowledge, so that gaps and deficiencies can be spotted and remedied. *Flexible designs enable you to do this in a way which would not be feasible in a fixed design study but to capitalize on this flexibility you must force yourself to find the time to do this interim summary while you can still take advantage of its findings to direct and focus the later phases of data collection.* The summary can also usefully incorporate a *data accounting sheet* which lists the different research questions and shows, for different informants, materials, settings, etc., whether adequate data concerning each of the questions have been collected.

Thematic coding analysis

Thematic coding analysis is presented here as a generic approach to the analysis of qualitative data. It can be used as a realist method, which reports experiences, meanings and the reality of participants or as a constructionist method, which examines the ways in which events, realities, meanings, and experiences are the effects of a range of discourses operating within society.

   Coding has a central role in qualitative analysis. Gibbs (2007), in a very clear and accessible discussion, introduces it as follows:

   Coding is how you define what the data you are analyzing are about. It involves identifying and recording one or more passages of text or other data items such as the parts of pictures that, in some sense, exemplify the same theoretical or descriptive idea. Usually, several passages are identified and they are then linked with a name for that idea – the code. Thus all the text and so on that is about the same thing or exemplifies the same thing is coded to the same name (p. 38).

Other terms are sometimes used instead of 'code', such as 'incidents', 'segments', 'units', 'data-bits' or 'chunks' (Ryan & Bernard, 2003, p. 87). Because the process involves comparing each new chunk of data with previous codes, so similar chunks will be labelled with the same code, it is sometimes referred to as *constant comparison analysis*.

Coding is followed by grouping the initial codes into a smaller number of *themes*. The term 'theme' is not tightly defined. It captures something of interest or importance in relation to your research question(s). Other terms including 'category', 'label' and 'code' itself are also used. For example, Miles and Huberman talk about first- and second-level coding. First-level coding is concerned with attaching labels to groups of words. Second-level coding groups the initial codes into a smaller number of themes. 'Theme' also tends to be associated with a phenomenological approach to analysis (e.g. Smith, Larkin & Flowers, 2009). However, it is here used more generally, without the implication of necessarily following a particular theoretical approach.

The development of possible themes should be an active concern when you are coding. You need to be continually asking yourself, 'What seems to go with what?' and elaborating on and checking these hunches. You will probably start with a very small number of potential themes, modify and add to them during the course of analysis (perhaps organizing them into major themes and sub-themes) and finally be left with a small number once more as various 'runners' are disconfirmed by the data. The work that you do in creating these codes is central to developing an understanding of your data. It lays the foundation for your subsequent analysis and interpretation.

Coding and the development of a thematic framework is central to many qualitative data analyses, although it is not without challenge (Coffey, Holbrook & Atkinson, 1996). In contrast to many 'named' approaches to qualitative data analysis (such as grounded theory, and discourse or conversation analysis), thematic coding analysis is not necessarily wedded to a particular theoretical framework. It has been used within different theoretical frameworks (*see the examples cited below*) and can also be used in purely descriptive or exploratory studies. Spencer, Ritchie, O'Connor, Morell and Ormston (2014) and Attride-Stirling (2001) provide introductions.

Guidelines for carrying out a thematic coding analysis

The steps listed below are not unique to thematic coding analysis; many approaches to the analysis of qualitative data have similar steps. Whenever feasible, analysis should be involved at an early stage of carrying out the project. From the start of data collection, you should be looking out for issues of interest in the data including possible patterns or themes. As the data collection proceeds, you move back and forward between the data itself, the extracts from the data which you have coded as possible themes and the analysis you are producing. The various techniques for data reduction, discussed earlier in the chapter, will help you to keep on top of this task. Use of memos to jot down ideas including thoughts about likely themes and sub-themes is particularly crucial. Ideas will always come but they can very easily go and be lost, unless you note them down.

Thematic coding analysis can be used inductively where the codes and themes emerge purely from your interaction with the data (as in the grounded theory approach discussed later in the chapter). However, there is nothing to stop you starting the analysis with predetermined codes or themes, perhaps arising from your reading of the research literature and/or the research questions you are interested in (as in *template analysis*, King, 2012). At a practical level it can be argued that such preconceptions can bias you toward some aspects of the data, perhaps leading to you ignoring other potentially important themes. An alternative view is that prior engagement with the literature can enhance your analysis by sensitizing you to features of the data that might otherwise be missed (Tuckett, 2005).

While the phases are, necessarily, presented sequentially, this should not be taken as implying that we are dealing with a linear process where one step is completed before moving to the next one. There is much movement to and fro, where the results of a later phase prompt you to return and rethink what you did at an earlier stage. Remember also that this is a process and it is counter-productive to try and rush it. Just as it is important to start the analysis at an early stage, it is important to give yourself time at the end to review the analysis. It is not unknown to have an epiphany at a late stage where you realize that the data are better interpreted in a radically different way!

Box 18.4 lists the steps involved, together with a brief description. In some circumstances, particularly in purely exploratory or descriptive studies, the analysis is terminated after the first three phases have been completed. A substantial proportion of published accounts are limited in this way. Providing that attention is given to demonstrating the quality of your analysis, and hence the trustworthiness of the findings, this may well be appropriate in a real world context. However, it is likely that it provides a very limited understanding of the meaning of your findings and how they might be interpreted, whether in terms of realist mechanisms or however. Box 18.5 reviews some of the advantages and disadvantages of thematic coding analysis.

Phase 1: Familiarizing yourself with your data

If you are collecting the data yourself, using a flexible design, this is an ongoing process. After initial data collection, give yourself time to immerse yourself in the data so you are really familiar with what you have collected. This usually involves repeated reading of the data, doing this

---

BOX 18.4

Phases of thematic coding analysis

1. *Familiarizing yourself with your data.* Transcribing data (if necessary), reading and re-reading the data, noting down initial ideas.
2. *Generating initial codes.* May be done by first devising a framework or template or inductively by interaction with the data. Extracts from the data are given codes in a systematic fashion across the entire data set, with similar extracts being given the same code.
3. *Identifying themes.* Collating codes into potential themes, gathering all data relevant to each potential theme. Checking if the themes work in relation to the coded extracts and the entire data set. Revising the initial codes and/or themes if necessary.
4. *Constructing thematic networks.* Developing a thematic 'map' of the analysis.
5. *Integration and interpretation.* Making comparisons between different aspects of the data using display techniques such as tables and networks. Exploring, describing, summarizing, and interpreting the patterns. Demonstrating the quality of the analysis.

BOX 18.5

Advantages and disadvantages of thematic coding analysis

Advantages

1. Very flexible, can be used with virtually all types of qualitative data.
2. By comparison with other approaches to qualitative data analysis which call for considerable time and effort to understand and require an appreciation of their philosophical and theoretical basis to use legitimately, it is a relatively easy and quick method to learn, and use.
3. It is accessible to researchers with little or no experience of qualitative research.
4. The results of the analysis can be communicated without major difficulties to practitioners, policy-makers and an educated general public.
5. It is a useful method to employ when working within a participatory research paradigm, where participants are acting as collaborators in the research and in the analysis of findings.
6. It provides a means of summarizing key features of large amounts of qualitative data, using a principled approach acceptable to fellow researchers and journal editors.
7. It is not tied to a particular level of interpretation and can be used in a wide variety of fields and disciplines.

Disadvantages

1. The flexibility of the method means that the potential range of things that can be said about your data is broad, which can be inhibiting to the researcher trying to decide what aspects of their data to focus on.
2. Thematic coding analysis is frequently limited to description or exploration with little attempt made at interpretation.
3. It is not uncommon to find reports where it is claimed that thematic coding analysis has been carried out, and themes are discussed, but there is little or no information about the details of the procedure.
4. Compared to 'branded' forms of analysis such as grounded theory, interpretative phenomenological analysis, discourse analysis or conversational analysis, it is a generic approach which currently has less kudos as an analytic method.

(based, in part, on Braun and Clarke, 2006, pp. 96–7)

in an active way where you are searching for meanings and patterns. If you are presented with data from some other source, or for some reason have the full data set before you start the analysis, it is absolutely crucial that you thoroughly immerse yourself in the data as the first step.

When collecting your own data, depending on the time-scale and organization of your project, you may have several bouts of data analysis before completing data collection. You then need to immerse yourself in the entire data set to confirm or modify your earlier views about meanings or patterns. While familiarizing yourself with the data you can, and should, be taking notes, writing yourself memos about ideas for formal coding and initial thoughts about themes. In practice, the first three phases shade into each other and are difficult to disentangle.

The familiarization process is time-consuming. Don't be tempted to skimp it or try to base it on a selection from the full data set.

Transcription issues

For many projects, much of the data may not be originally in the form of written text (e.g. audio recordings from interviews). It is not essential that you transcribe all (or even any) of such data into text format. It may be feasible to work directly from the original recording. However, having a detailed transcript of some, or all, of the data is often necessary to carry out the analysis. While this is a very time-consuming task (taking several times the period it took to make the recording), it is an excellent way of starting to familiarize yourself with the data. If you are in the fortunate position that someone else will do the transcription for you, it is important that you still have to spend time familiarizing yourself with the data and should also check the transcripts against the original recordings for accuracy. This should always be done with transcripts, of course.

Some forms of qualitative data analysis, such as conversation or discourse analysis, call for very detailed transcripts. Typically, thematic analysis does not require the same amount of detail. The necessity for a full 'verbatim' (i.e. word for word) account of all verbal utterances will depend on the nature of your project. It can help if the original recording is to hand when carrying out the analysis as intonation, pauses or other non-verbal features may clarify how a particular utterance should be coded.

Gibbs (2007, pp. 10–21) reviews the issues involved in detail.

Phase 2: Generating initial codes

To do this, you must be thoroughly familiar with the data available (whether this is the full, or an initial, data set), and have an initial set of ideas about what is in the data and what you feel is interesting, and may be important, about them.

Codes refer to 'the most basic segment, or element, of the raw data or information that can be assessed in a meaningful way regarding the phenomenon' (Boyatzis, 1998, p. 63). The process of coding is part of analysis as you are organizing your data into meaningful groups. Once you have coded the data you can start on deciding what themes you can see in the material. By working systematically through the entire data set and giving full attention to each data item, you will then try to identify interesting aspects in them which may form the basis of themes within the data set. Include rather than exclude when doing this. Code for as many potential themes as you can come up with. Include some of the context (i.e. surrounding text) if it looks as if it may be relevant when thinking about themes. You can code individual extracts of data in as many different themes as they fit into.

Your themes, which you start to develop in the next phase, are where the interpretative analysis of the data occurs. Coding will in part depend on whether the themes are 'data-driven' or 'theory-driven' (they can be both). In the former, the themes arise from consideration of the data. In the latter, you start by approaching the data with specific questions in mind. Extreme versions such as the 'framework approach' (Spencer *et al.* 2014) or 'template analysis' (King,

2012) depend on identifying examples of codes from a pre-existing list. Coding also depends on whether you aim to code the content of the entire data set or are simply coding to identify specific features of the data set. It can be performed totally manually (lots of printed copies of the data, a big table, highlighters, sticky notes, scissors, etc.) or using a word processor or other standard package, or specialist software (see Appendix B).

What do you code?

This depends on the kind of analysis you are planning to do, which is in turn dependent on your research question(s). As Gibbs (2007, p. 46) points out, fortunately, in much applied real world research, there is a lot of common ground in the kind of phenomena that researchers tend to look for when doing qualitative analysis. Typical things you might consider are listed in Box 18.6. Some codes are essentially descriptive, often in the participant's own words. At some stage in the process, you should be attempting to move from the descriptive (unless your research questions indicate purely descriptive concerns) to a more theoretically oriented search for categories and themes in the data. This is the central task in the next phase of thematic coding analysis but this should not inhibit you from using codes which themselves move beyond the descriptive.

BOX 18.6

What can you code?

1. *Specific acts, behaviours* – what people do or say (e.g. getting the opinions of friends).
2. *Events* – these are usually brief, one-off events or things someone has done. It is not uncommon for the respondent to tell them as a story (e.g. moving into a homeless hostel).
3. *Activities* – these are of longer duration than acts and often take place in a particular setting and may have several people involved (e.g. helping partner with dementia get washed and dressed).
4. *Strategies, practices or tactics* – activities aimed towards some goal (e.g. getting divorced for financial reasons).
5. *States* – general conditions experienced by people or found in organizations (e.g. working extra hours to get the job done).
6. *Meanings* – a wide range of phenomena at the core of much qualitative analysis. Meanings and interpretations are important parts of what directs participants' actions.
    (a) What concepts do participants use to understand their world? What norms, values, rules and mores guide their actions? (E.g. the idea of 'on-sight climbing' amongst rock climbers to describe doing a climb without artificial aids, etc. as a superior way of climbing.)
    (b) What meaning or significance does it have for participants, how do they construe events, what are their feelings? (E.g. 'His letter made me feel I was to blame.')
    (c) What symbols do people use to understand their situation? What names do they use for objects, events, persons, roles, settings and equipment? (E.g. teaching referred to as 'work at the chalkface').

7. *Participation* – people's involvement or adaptation to a setting (e.g. 'I find I have to be careful what I say now').

8. *Relationships or interaction* – between people, considered simultaneously (e.g. 'I'm enjoying the family now – the boys like to come home and have friends to stay').

9. *Conditions or constraints* – the precursor to or cause of events or actions, things that restrict behaviour or actions (e.g. firm's loss of markets before lay-offs).

10. *Consequences* – what happens if . . . ('People that haven't got no qualification, but have got a few months' experience are walking into jobs').

11. *Settings* – the entire context of the events under study (e.g. day-care centre).

12. *Reflexive* – the researcher's role in the process. How intervention generated the data (e.g. 'It must be hard for you in that situation').

(based on Gibbs, 2007, Table 4.1. pp. 47–8)

Marking the coding

Figure 18.1 shows how a short extract might look after coding. In a paper-based approach code names are written in the margin or marked in some way, perhaps using a highlighter pen. Words which stand out in some way (e.g. used for emphasis, unusual terms) could be circled. The figure illustrates several different types of codes, including *descriptive codes* (e.g. dancing, drive together); *categories* (e.g. joint activities ceased); and *analytic codes* (e.g. togetherness, core activity). The extract is unusually heavily coded to illustrate the process. Don't think that you have to code everything. You are just looking for extracts relevant to your analysis, either because they represent codes in the framework you are using or they seem potentially relevant as something likely to be of interest.

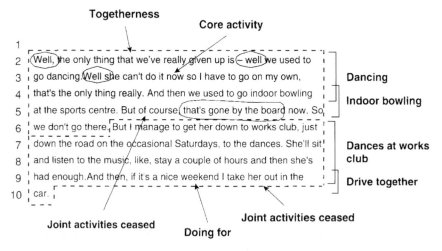

Figure 18.1 Response after coding.

While each code is only used once here, in practice, you would be looking for multiple examples from different parts of the text or from other participants. Don't be worried if you have inconsistencies and bits that don't seem to fit in. No data set is without contradictions.

An equivalent process takes place when coding using a software package such as NVivo. Whether paper- or computer-based, each coded extract should have a unique label to assist in retrieving it later. This indicates where it comes from (e.g. which document, person, or whatever), whereabouts in the document (e.g. line number) and other features you might use in the analysis (e.g. gender, age, job status).

Phase 3: Identifying themes

This aspect moves into centre stage when initial coding is completed and you have a long list of the different codes that you have identified. Your task is to sort the different codes into potential themes and to put together all the relevant coded data extracts within the themes you identify. This should have been at the back of your mind when doing the initial coding so it is likely that you will already have some candidates for themes.

Visual representations of various kinds, discussed in connection with the following phase, can also help here. Matrices (tables with rows and columns) and networks (sets of boxes with links between them) may assist in visualizing relationships between codes, between possible themes, and between different levels of themes (e.g. potential main themes and sub-themes within them). Having an initial attempt at the thematic 'map' *discussed below* may be useful. You may find that some initial codes may end up as themes in their own right, possibly even forming a main overarching theme. Others you will need to combine to form a theme or sub-theme. It is highly likely that several codes do not seem to belong anywhere. Put them, for the time being, in a residual category – perhaps a 'miscellaneous' theme. You may find a way of incorporating some of them as the analysis continues.

Box 18.7 suggests some of the things you can look out for when trying to identify themes. The techniques suggested tend to be at a more abstract level relating to the formal linguistic properties of the text than the suggestions for things to code in the previous box. However, there is no hard and fast distinction and it won't matter particularly if you find that you used one of these techniques when coding. Coding is only a tool to get at the themes in the data.

BOX 18.7

Techniques for identifying themes

1. *Repetitions.* One of the easiest ways to identify themes. Some of the most obvious themes are topics that occur and reoccur. The more the same concept occurs in a text, the more likely it is a theme. How many repetitions are enough to constitute an important theme, however, is an open question which only the investigator can decide.
2. *Indigenous categories.* Terms and concepts that participants themselves use. They may sound unfamiliar to the researcher or be used in unfamiliar ways, providing clues as to their existence. Contrasted with categories or typologies constructed by the analyst.

3. *Metaphors and analogies.* People often represent their thoughts, behaviours, and experiences with analogies and metaphors. For example Quinn (1996) found that people talk about their surprise at the breakup of a marriage using extensive metaphors (they thought the couple's marriage was 'like the Rock of Gibraltar' or 'nailed in cement').

4. *Transitions.* Naturally occurring shifts in content may be markers of themes. In written texts, new paragraphs may indicate shifts in topics. In speech, pauses, changes in voice tone, or the presence of particular phrases may indicate transitions.

5. *Similarities and differences.* Searching for similarities and differences by making systematic comparisons across units of data. How is a statement, text or whatever, similar to or different from those preceding or following? The abstract similarities and differences that this question generates are themes. If a particular theme is present in both expressions, then the next question to ask is, 'Is there any difference, in degree or kind, in which the theme is articulated in both of the expressions?' Degrees of strength in themes may lead to the naming of sub-themes.

6. *Linguistic connectors.* Look carefully for words and phrases such as 'because', 'since' and 'as a result', which often indicate causal relations. Words and phrases such as 'if' or 'then', 'rather than' and 'instead of' often signify conditional relations. Time-oriented relationships are expressed with words such as 'before', 'after', 'then' and 'next'. Ryan and Bernard list several other kinds of relationships that may be useful for identifying themes.

7. *Missing data.* Instead of asking about what is in the data, we can ask about what is missing. For example, in a study of birth planning in China, Greenhalgh (1994) reported that she could not ask direct questions about resistance to government policy but that respondents used silence to protest against aspects of the policy they did not like. Themes that are discovered like this will need to be carefully scrutinized to ensure that you are not just finding what you are looking for. A variant is to scrutinize any expressions that are not already associated with a theme by reading a text over and over.

8. *Theory-related material.* In addition to identifying indigenous themes that characterize the experience of informants, your research questions and issues of theoretical importance can be used to suggest possible themes.

(summarized from Ryan and Bernard, 2003, pp. 89–94)

With a collection of possible themes and sub-themes, and the extracts of data coded in relation to them, you start to refine them. The first step is to read all the collated extracts for each theme and consider whether they appear to form a coherent pattern. If they don't, is it because the theme itself is problematic? Or simply that some data extracts don't fit in the theme? Sort this out by reworking the theme, finding a new home for the extracts that don't fit or jettisoning them.

Once you are satisfied with this, re-read your entire data set. Do the themes seem to capture adequately what you have in the data? You should also look out for possible additional data extracts to code within your themes, which were missed in earlier coding stages. It is also likely that you now think you got some of the coding wrong, and need to re-code some extracts. Don't worry, this is an iterative process where you go from data to analysis, analysis to data, etc., until you feel reasonably satisfied. Again, don't expect perfection. You could go on for ever if you are not careful.

By the end of this phase, you should have at least an intuitive feeling about what the different themes are, how they fit together, and the overall story they tell about the data.

Phase 4: Constructing thematic networks and making comparisons

You now move to formalize the 'fitting together' of the themes into one or more maps or networks. Focus on ways in which themes can be put together, perhaps on the basis of content or on theoretical grounds. It may be that the themes are few enough and about similar enough issues to fit under one network. If they are too numerous, or they seem to be concerned with very different issues or aspects, then put them into two or more groupings. Each will represent a main theme with sub-themes. Attride-Stirling (2001) suggests using three levels of themes: 'global' (super-ordinate themes), 'organizing' (groups of basic themes), and 'basic'. While there are no hard and fast rules about how many themes should make a network, she recommends that from a practical stance, more than 15 may be too many to handle later on in the analysis and fewer than may not be enough to do justice to the data.

The main or global theme represents your view on what the sub-themes (organizing and basic) are about. It is the core, principal metaphor encapsulating the main point in the data set. If you see more than one such point, then split the themes into two or more networks with different main themes. Figure 18.2 shows an example of a thematic network. When you have produced the thematic network, it is good practice to go through the coded data extracts once more to satisfy yourself that the themes reflect the data and the data support the themes. Modify the themes or network if necessary.

Phase 5: Integration and interpretation

Thematic networks are a tool in analysis, not the analysis itself. Your next task is explore within and across the themes, to try to understand what the data are telling you. Miles *et al.* (2014, pp. 265–6) talk about this as 'generating meaning' and list a range of tactics you can use. These include:

- Noting patterns, themes and trends.
- Seeing plausibility. Do the trends, patterns and conclusions make sense?

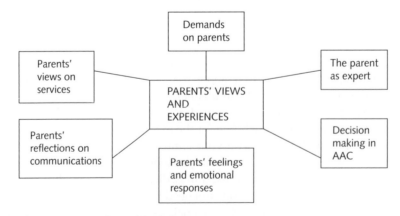

AAC = American College of Cardiology

Figure 18.2 Example of a thematic network.

- Clustering. Grouping events, places, people, processes, etc. together if they appear to have similar patterns or characteristics.
- Making metaphors. Metaphors are rich, data-reducing and pattern-making devices which help to connect data with theory.
- Counting. Helps to see what's there by counting frequency of occurrence of recurrent events.
- Making contrasts and comparisons. Establishing similarities and differences between and within data sets.
- Partitioning variables. Splitting variables may help in finding more coherent descriptions and explanations.
- Subsuming particulars into the general. Linking specific data to general concepts and categories.
- Factoring. Attempting to discover the factors underlying the process under investigation.
- Noting relations between variables. Using matrix displays and other methods to study interrelationships between different parts of the data.
- Finding intervening variables. Trying to establish the presence and effects of variables intervening between observed variables.
- Building a logical chain of evidence. Trying to understand trends and patterns through developing logical relationships.
- Making conceptual/theoretical coherence. Moving from data to constructs to theories through analysis and categorization.

Some of the tactics have already been used when coding, identifying themes and the relations between them in the thematic network. Many of them are unexceptionable in that they simply represent a labelling of common practices but several, such as 'factoring' and the use of 'variable-speak', reveal Miles *et al.*'s direct translation of concepts from quantitative analysis into qualitative analysis. Researchers used to working with qualitative data may well view this as inappropriate. They may also resist the 'counting' tactic, turning qualitative data into numbers, while happily using pseudo-numbers such as 'few', 'many', 'almost all', etc.

However, there is no requirement to take these tactics *en bloc* – or to use their terminology.

Using tables for comparative analysis

Several of the tactics call for making comparisons between different aspects of the data. Displaying the data, in the form of tables with rows and columns, provides a simple and useful technique. As discussed in Chapter 17, tables are widely used in quantitative analyses where they are referred to as cross-tabulations (p. 425). Qualitative tables provide a convenient way of displaying text from different parts of the data to make systematic comparisons. There are many different possible types, including:

- Time-ordered tables where the columns are arranged in time sequence. A specific version of this is known as an event listing, where concrete events, sorted into categories, are arranged into time sequence.
- Role-ordered tables where the rows represent data from sets of individuals occupying different roles (e.g. doctor/nurse/administrator/patient).

- Conceptually clustered tables where the columns are arranged to being together items 'belonging together' (e.g. relating to same theme).
- Effects tables which display data on outcomes.
- Issues tables where the columns concern issues and what happens in connection with them (e.g. who does what).

Using networks

Networks (i.e. a set of boxes or 'nodes' with links between them) are also useful display techniques when you seek to understand patterns and relationships in your data. The thematic network developed in the previous phase is one example. The various types include:

- Context charts showing interrelationships between roles, groups, organizations, etc., which provide the context for the situation studied.
- Event flow networks which show how events (e.g. experiences, incidents) are ordered by time and sequence.
- Activity records displaying a specific recurring activity (e.g. a classroom lesson) as a sequential pattern with specific actions each assigned to a link.
- Flow charts giving sequential decisions made. Conceptually ordered tree diagrams showing how phenomena are classified and sub-categorized.
- Cognitive maps displaying a person's representation of concepts about a particular domain or area of interest, showing the relationships between them.
- Causal networks consisting of boxes showing the most important variables or factors in a study, with arrows showing the relationships between them.

Your task is to tell the story of your data in a way which convinces the reader of the merit and trustworthiness of your analysis (discussed below in terms of assessing the quality of your analysis). As Braun and Clarke (2006) put it, you have to provide:

> a concise, coherent, logical, non-repetitive and interesting account of the story the data tell – within and across themes. Your write-up must provide sufficient evidence of the themes within the data – i.e. enough data extracts to demonstrate the prevalence of the theme. Choose particularly vivid examples, or extracts which capture the essence of the point you are demonstrating, without unnecessary complexity. The extract should be easily identifiable as an example of the issue. However, your write-up needs to do more than just provide data. Extracts need to be embedded within an analytic narrative that compellingly illustrates the story you are telling about your data, and your analytic narrative needs to go *beyond* description of the data, and make an *argument* in relation to your research question (p. 93, emphasis in original).

Demonstrating the quality of the analysis

Box 18.8 lists tactics you might use when assessing the trustworthiness of your analysis.

BOX 18.8

Assessing the quality of qualitative data analysis

Assessing data quality

1. *Checking for representativeness.* There are many pitfalls to the gathering of representative data. The informants, and the events or activities sampled, may be non-representative. Safeguards include the use of random sampling where feasible; triangulation through multiple methods of data collection; constructing data display matrices; and seeking data for empty or weakly sampled cells. Your analysis may be biased, not only because you are drawing inferences from non-representative processes, but also because of your own biases as an information processor (p. 462). Auditing processes by colleagues help guard against this.

2. *Checking for researcher effects.* These come in two versions; the effects you have on the case, and the effects your involvement with the case has on you. They have been discussed previously (p. 462).

3. *Triangulation.* Again discussed earlier (Chapters 8 and 15). Not a panacea and it has its own problems (what, for example, do you do when two data sources are inconsistent or conflicting? Answer, you investigate further, possibly ending up with a more complex set of understandings.) However, it is very important: '. . . triangulation is not so much a tactic as a way of life. If you self-consciously set out to collect and double-check findings, using multiple sources and modes of evidence, the verification process will largely be built into data collection as you go' (Miles & Huberman, 1994, p. 267).

4. *Weighting the evidence.* Some data are stronger than others and you naturally place greater reliance on conclusions based on them. Stronger data are typically those you collect first-hand; which you have observed directly; which come from trusted informants; which are collected when the respondent is alone rather than in a group setting; and which arise from repeated contact.

Testing patterns

5. *Checking the meaning of outliers.* These are the exceptions, the ones that don't fit into the overall pattern of findings or lie at the extremes of a distribution. Outliers can be people, cases, settings, treatments or events. Don't be tempted to hide or forget them. Evaluating an in-service training package, we found very high levels of teacher satisfaction with its effectiveness, with a very small number of dissidents. Further interviews with the latter established that in all cases an element of the package involving role-playing sessions had been omitted or problematic. This both strengthened the explanation and helped isolate the mechanisms involved.

6. *Using extreme cases.* These are outliers of a particular type, defined in terms of being atypical situations or persons rather than by the data they provide, which may or may not be atypical. An innovation which failed in a school where the circumstances

(continued)

appeared close to ideal appeared linked to the unexpressed resistance of the deputy head teacher responsible for timetabling, hence suggesting a key factor.

7. *Following up surprises*. Surprises can be salutary. You may well be surprised because something is at variance with your (possibly implicit and not thought-through) theory of what is going on. This then provides the opportunity to surface that theory, to possibly revise it and to search for evidence relevant to the revision.

8. *Looking for negative evidence*. This is the tactic of actively seeking disconfirmation of what you think is true. While this is in principle straightforward, you are likely to have some reluctance to spending a large amount of effort on this activity. Miles and Huberman (1994, p. 271) make the helpful suggestion of giving a colleague your conclusions and free access to your original data with a brief to try to find evidence which would disconfirm your conclusion. If they manage to do this, then your task is to come up with an alternative or elaborated explanation.

Testing explanations

9. *Making if–then tests*. Testing possible relationships; i.e. if one condition obtains or is the case, look to see if a second one is. If it is, we are on the way to understanding what is going on and can make further similar tests. If it isn't true, we have to make other conjectures.

10. *Ruling out spurious relationships*. If you appear to have established a relationship consider whether there may be a third factor or variable which underlies, influences or causes the apparent relationship. In the relationship between guardsmen fainting on parade and the softness of the tar in the asphalt of the parade ground, it appears highly likely that the temperature is providing an intervening causal link rather than noxious fumes from the tar having a direct effect. Note that this is essentially the same tactic discussed above under the heading of 'Finding intervening variables' but used for a different purpose. It can also be thought of as finding rival explanations for a relationship.

11. *Replicating a finding*. If a finding can be repeated in a different context or data set, then it is more dependable. Given that once you find a relationship or develop a theory, there is a strong tendency for you to find confirming evidence (and to ignore disconfirming evidence), it is even better if someone else, not privy to your findings, confirms it. Note that this is a particular type of triangulation.

12. *Checking out rival explanations*. It is good practice to try to come up with one or more rival explanations which could account for all or part of the phenomena you are studying. Keeping these 'in play' while you are analysing and gathering further data helps to prevent the premature closure effect discussed above.

13. *Getting feedback from informants*. This process of 'member checking' performs several useful functions. It honours the implicit (or preferably explicit) contract between researcher and informant to provide feedback about the findings. It also provides an invaluable means of corroborating them. While problems of jargon and terminology may need to be attended to, you should be able to present findings in a way that communicates with informants and allows them to evaluate the findings in the light of their superior experience of the setting.

(summarized from Miles and Huberman, 1994, p. 262–77)

The website gives further examples of research using thematic coding analysis.

Data analysis in grounded theory studies

Many analyses of qualitative data are influenced by grounded theory. They typically reference the work of either or both of the originators of the approach, Barney Glaser and Anselm Strauss, which was explored in Chapter 7, p. 161. However, while some of these analyses follow the detailed prescriptions and terminology discussed in the following sections, others are much more 'in the general style of' and virtually indistinguishable from the thematic coding approach detailed in the previous section.

The aim of grounded theory analysis

The aim is to *generate* a theory to explain what is central in the data. Your task is to find a central core category which is both at a high level of abstraction and grounded in (i.e. derived from) the data you have collected and analysed. This is done in three stages:

1. Find conceptual categories in the data;
2. Find relationships between these categories;
3. Conceptualize and account for these relationships though finding core categories.

   It is achieved by carrying out three kinds of coding:

- *Open coding* to find the categories;
- *Axial coding* to interconnect them; and
- *Selective coding* to establish the core category or categories (Corbin & Strauss, 2008).

   Throughout, the analysis theory is built through interaction with the data, making comparisons and asking questions of the data. It is sometimes referred to as the *method of constant comparison* (Pidgeon & Henwood, 1996; pp. 92–4).

Open coding

Here data (interview transcripts, field notes, documents, etc.) are split into discrete parts. The size of the part chosen is whatever seems to be a unit in the data, perhaps a sentence, or an utterance, or a paragraph. The question asked is, 'What is this piece of data an example of?' The code applied is a label. It is provisional and may be changed. A piece of data may have several codes (labels), i.e. it may be considered to fall within more than one conceptual category. Labels can be of whatever kind that seems appropriate, including descriptive (e.g. 'accepting advice'), *in vivo* (i.e. a direct quotation from the data) or more inferential.

   These conceptual categories arise from the data. Using predetermined coding categories and seeking to fit data into such categories is against the spirit of grounded theory. However, this distinction is somewhat metaphysical as the 'conceptual baggage' you bring to your data (whether derived from a pre-existing theory or from analysis of data collected earlier) will inevitably have some influence on what you are likely to 'see' in the data.

Open coding is essentially interpreting rather than summarizing. It is about teasing out the theoretical possibilities in the data. There is much to be said for doing it in a small group. This will enhance the ideas pool about what the data are examples of and it will assist in keeping individuals 'on task'. Is a particular code really grounded in the data? Is the central purpose of open coding being kept in mind?

While carrying out open coding, you should bear in mind any ideas that occur from working with the data about relationships between the categories, and even first thoughts about the core category. This can be encouraged by stepping back from the data from time to time and getting an overall feel for what is going on. As with other approaches to flexible design this initial analysis will be taking place before data collection is complete. There is no requirement to code all the data fully at this stage but you do need to have done a substantial amount of coding and to have a good appreciation of what you have captured overall in the various data sets arising from the interviews, field notes, etc. In an ideal world, you will have reached the stage where the various categories are 'saturated'. That is, you have squeezed as much conceptual juice as you can out of the data so that continuing analysis is giving severely diminished returns in the new categories and insights that it is yielding.

Axial coding

Axial, or *theoretical*, coding is about linking together the categories developed through the process of open coding. Glaser and Strauss, the begetters of grounded theory, now have diverging views about the approach to be taken when trying to establish these relationships. Strauss works within an interactionist paradigm where axial coding is viewed as leading to an understanding of the central phenomenon in the data in terms of its context, the conditions which gave rise to it, the action and interaction strategies by which it is dealt with, and their consequences (see Corbin & Strauss, 2008). Glaser (1992) takes a more purist grounded line. He argues that the axial codes, and the form that they take, should emerge from the data rather than being forced into any particular predetermined format.

Whichever line is taken, axial coding is about in some way putting together again the data which have been effectively split apart into categories by open coding. As Mertens (2014) puts it:

> During this phase, you build a model of the phenomena that includes the conditions under which it occurs (or does not occur), the context in which it occurs, the action and interactional strategies that describe the phenomena, and the consequences of these actions. You continue to ask questions of the data; however, now the questions focus on relationships between the categories.

If you are simply concerned with exploring or describing the phenomena being studied, this completes the analysis. However, grounded theory, as the term suggests, seeks to go further. For this, you need to go on to selective coding.

Selective coding

In this third stage, selective coding, you select one aspect as the *core category* and focus on it. The basis for doing this arises from axial coding which provides you with a picture of the relationships between various categories. In doing this, you should begin to get a feeling for what the study is about. In what way can you understand and explain the overall picture? This may well involve limiting the study to the major relationships which fit with this conceptualization.

In grounded theory, there must be a central integrating focus to those aspects which remain in the study. If more than one remain, the notion is that they have to be integrated into a single focus at a higher degree of abstraction. This must remain grounded in the data but is abstract and integrated as well as being highly condensed. The core category is the centrepiece of your analysis. It is the central phenomenon around which the categories arising from axial coding are integrated.

Corbin and Strauss (2008) approach this task via the *story line*. This starts as a description of what axial coding has produced. You have to move from this descriptive account to a conceptualization of the story line. In other words, you are seeking a core conceptual category which enables you to understand the story line.

Doing a grounded theory style analysis

The preceding section is intended to give the 'flavour' of a grounded theory analysis. Studied in conjunction with one or more of the examples provided on the website, it should be of assistance to anyone wanting to carry out an analysis following a general grounded theory style. Madill, Jordan and Shirley (2000) discuss two simple studies which use grounded theory to analyse interviews with relatives of individuals diagnosed as schizophrenic. They compare analyses carried out using realist, contextualist and radical constructionist epistemologies.

Much published research gives little or no attention to the theoretical background to grounded theory. It is simply regarded as a set of procedures, and as such can be regarded as a particular version of thematic coding analysis covered earlier in the chapter. Substantial further reading is called for if you wish to get on top of its theoretical background preparatory to doing a genuine grounded theory analysis. Punch (2013, Chapter 9) provides a helpful introduction. Denzin, cited by Punch (2005), warns that, just as grounded theory is being widely adopted in many areas of social research:

> it is being challenged by a new body of work coming from the neighboring fields of anthropology and cultural studies . . . [They] are proposing that postmodern ethnography can no longer follow the guidelines of positivist social science. Gone are words like theory, hypothesis, concept, indicator, coding scheme, sampling, validity, and reliability. In their place comes a new language; readerly texts, modes of discourse, cultural poetics, deconstruction, interpretation, domination, the authority of the text, the author's voice, feminism, genre, grammatology, hermeneutics, inscription, master narrative, narrative structures, otherness, postmodernism, redemptive ethnography, semiotics, subversion, textuality, tropes (Denzin, 1988a, p. 432).

This is a reprise of an earlier theme in this book: the demise of positivism and the challenge of interpretive, constructivist and relativist voices (see Chapter 2, pp. 21–4). The argument put forward there was not to deny the value of this new body of approaches but to insist that there were continuing virtues in maintaining a broad scientific approach for real world research. And that realism provides a viable means of doing this in a post-positivist scientific era. Admittedly some of the language and terminology traditional in grounded theory harks back to an earlier era but there appears to be no basic incompatibility between grounded theory and realism. The approach is one way of finding out underlying structures and mechanisms, and realism has no quarrel with theory being generated from analysis of the data gathered in a study.

The website gives examples of research using a grounded theory analysis.

Alternative approaches to qualitative analysis

As discussed in Chapter 7, there is a wide range of other traditions of flexible research design additional to the three types selected as particularly appropriate for real world research. Of those covered in that chapter, the *phenomenological* tradition has a detailed and fully developed approach to analysis. Creswell (2013) provides an introduction; Moustakas (1994) a detailed account. Smith *et al.* (2009) discuss in detail a version known as 'interpretative phenomenological analysis' which has been recently recommended for use in a range of different fields including music education (Joseph, 2014) and the study of pain (Smith & Osborn, 2014). There are also specific strategies for analysing text central to *hermeneutic* research. Bentz and Shapiro (1998, pp. 105–20) provide references. *Narrative methods* also have distinctive approaches to analysis. Creswell (2013) provides an introduction, Riessman (2008) a detailed account.

There are many other possibilities. The reader still unsure about which route to take may well find inspiration in Coffey and Atkinson (1996) where a single data set is analysed using a range of different strategies, including different versions of narrative analysis, linguistic or *semiotic analyses*, types of *textual analysis* and interpretive or *hermeneutic* goals.

Integrating qualitative and quantitative data in multi-strategy designs

Multi-strategy (mixed methods) designs, discussed in Chapter 8, are characterized by the collection of substantial amounts of both qualitative and quantitative data. Depending on the particular design selected, qualitative data collection may precede that of quantitative data, or vice versa, or the collection may be in tandem. The techniques and approaches discussed in this chapter and the preceding one can be used for separate analysis of the two types of data. Again depending on the type of design, and in particular on your research questions, such separate analyses and their interpretation may be all that is envisaged. Bryman (2007) makes the point that, even when the initial intentions are not to integrate the findings, there can be value in exploring the connections between the qualitative and quantitative findings. Seeking the opportunity to integrate them in some way takes fuller advantage of the potential benefits of multi-strategy designs, as rehearsed in Chapter 8, Box 8.2 (p. 179).

Onwuegbuzie and Teddlie (2003, p. 375) suggest the following steps in the process of data analysis (not necessarily followed in a linear sequence):

1. *Data reduction.* Involves summarizing quantitative data (e.g. using descriptive statistics) and qualitative data (e.g. using thematic analysis).
2. *Data display.* Using tables, graphs, etc., with quantitative data and matrices, charts, networks, etc. with qualitative data.
3. *Data transformation.* 'Qualitizing' quantitative data and/or 'quantizing' qualitative data.[1]
4. *Data correlation.* Correlating quantitative data with qualitized data.
5. *Data consolidation.* Combining both data types to create new variables or data sets.
6. *Data comparison.* Comparing data from different data sources.
7. *Data integration.* Integrating all data into a coherent whole, or separate quantitative and qualitative coherent wholes.

Slate, LaPrairie, Schulte and Onwuegbuzie (2009) provide a clear example of the process involved. Caracelli and Greeene (1993) discuss several of these strategies in detail and consider their appropriateness for different research designs.

Bryman (2007), in a paper on the barriers to integration, focused on the degree to which researchers link the quantitative and qualitative in the course of analysing and writing up their findings. He cites evidence that reviewers have found this a problem area in published research. His own research (Bryman, 2006a) which carried out a content analysis of over 200 mixed methods research articles, found fewer than one in five 'genuinely integrated' their qualitative and quantitative findings (i.e. analysed, interpreted, and wrote up the research in such a way that the two components were mutually illuminating).

Integrated analyses

Rather than viewing the qualitative and quantitative data analyses as initially separate, with or without subsequent attempts to integrate the two sets of findings, an alternative approach is to bring the two aspects together at an early stage. This strategy is commonly used in case study research, as discussed in Chapter 7, p. 150, although for largely historical reasons it is usually discussed under a separate heading to multi-strategy designs.

Bazeley (2009), in a review of current developments in the integration of data analysis, lists a range of possible strategies summarized in Box 18.9. She also points out the value of computer software in the task of integrating analyses. The use of the widely available spreadsheet software package Excel was discussed in connection with quantitative analysis in Chapter 17, p. 410 – see also Appendix A. It is also a useful tool for tasks involving synthesis of varied forms of data from

---

[1] As the term suggests, 'qualitising' refers to turning quantitative data into a qualitative form (e.g. by converting them into narrative codes that can be analysed qualitatively). 'Quantising' refers to turning qualitative data into a quantitative form (e.g. by determining the frequency of occurrence of themes in a thematic analysis). While quantising involves data reduction, qualitising is an interpretive step which adds information (Maxwell, 2010).

> ## BOX 18.9
>
> ## Strategies for integrating quantitative and qualitative data through analysis
>
> - Employment of the results from analysis of one form of data in approaching the analysis of another form of data;
> - Synthesis of data generated from a variety of sources, for further joint interpretation;
> - Comparison of coded or thematic qualitative data across groups defined by categorical or scaled variables (matched, where possible, on an individual basis);
> - Pattern analysis using matrices;
> - Conversion of qualitative to quantitative coding to allow for descriptive, inferential, or exploratory statistical analysis;
> - Conversion of quantitative data into narrative form (e.g. for profiling);
> - Inherently mixed data analysis, where a single source gives rise to both qualitative and quantitative information (e.g. some forms of social network analysis); and
> - Iterative analyses involving multiple, sequenced phases where the conduct of each phase arises out of or draws on the analysis of the preceding phase.
>
> (based on Bazeley, 2009, p. 205)

a range of sources (Niglas, 2007). Several of the Computer Assisted Qualitative Data Analysis (CAQDAS) packages discussed in Appendix B (e.g. NVivo, MAXQDA and QDA Miner), although designed primarily for qualitative analysis, support the combination of quantitative variable data within the qualitative database for matrix-based analyses of coded text and the conversion of qualitative coding to variable data (Bazeley, 2006).

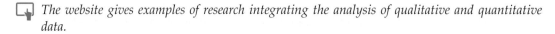 *The website gives examples of research integrating the analysis of qualitative and quantitative data.*

Further reading

The website gives annotated references to further reading for Chapter 18.

CHAPTER 19

Reporting, disseminating and moving forward

This chapter:

- emphasizes the importance of considering your intended audience when writing a report;
- stresses the difference between writing for academic and other audiences;
- covers conventions of the traditional scientific journal format;
- considers approaches to the reporting of flexible design studies;
- emphasizes the special nature of evaluation reports;
- discusses issues in writing for clients;
- reviews a range of alternative ways of disseminating findings;
- provides advice on writing; and
- concludes by discussing where to go next in terms of research, career development and training.

Introduction

Reports get written for many reasons, not least because you have to. For students, no report – no award. For contract researchers it is part of the contract, and if you don't deliver you won't secure further contracts. Reports are often thought of as the end of the research process, but are often only the starting point of a wider *dissemination strategy*:

> The object of dissemination is to maximize the impact of the project by getting the messages across to those who could benefit from the research or to those who simply need to be informed (Tarling, 2006, p. 125).

This has become an important factor for researchers, especially those in universities in the UK, as research is now measured on the basis of the impact that it has at an institutional, research council and governmental level.

Additional or alternative approaches to dissemination are discussed below.

Consideration of the form that a report of your research might take highlights the notion of *audience*. Who is the report for? What are you seeking to achieve by reporting to them?

Reporting what you have found

Reporting is an essential part of the research process

For a study to count in research terms, it must be made public. Reporting is one way that you do this.

The appropriate format for a report depends on the nature and purpose of the research

If you are seeking publication in an academic or professional journal you use whatever format they ask for. Similarly, as a student, you will be told what format to use, which may well be a journal format. For other purposes, other formats may well communicate better.

You need not be limited to a single type of report

Real world research often seeks to inform and influence several different audiences. It is unlikely that the same style of report will be best suited to all of them. There is nothing (apart from the effort involved) to stop you producing several different reports. They don't (all) have to be written reports and often can also be presentations, summaries, etc.

Real world research calls for professional standards of reporting and presentation

This applies if you are simply seeking to inform. It is probably even more important if you want the report and findings to be acted on in some way.

Writing for academic audiences almost always has to follow strict rules. The conventions and expectations in report writing for academic audiences for fixed designs and flexible designs differ considerably. They are therefore considered separately. When reporting to other audiences, the central issue is the format and approach which best delivers your message to them.

Ethics and reporting

Several parties or stakeholders are likely to be concerned with what is reported and with how it is reported. You have both an interest in, and a responsibility for, ensuring that the results of your study get into the 'public domain' (to publish is, literally, to make public). 'Publish or perish' may be overdramatic but it is inescapable that if your role permits you to carry out research, then a likely index of your work and worth will be the quantity and quality of the reports that you produce.

Participants in the research may well be concerned with how they appear in the report and whether their interests, individually or collectively, are affected by publication. Can you keep to the assurances of anonymity and confidentiality that you gave them? Surveys and experiments are usually straightforward in this respect. But flexible and multi-strategy design projects such as case studies, where the context is important, pose problems. Obviously it is possible to use pseudonyms for persons and settings, but this may not guarantee anonymity (particularly internally) and further changes that you make to seek disguise may distance your report from the reality it is trying to describe or understand. The basic stance usually adopted is to take reasonable precautions to ensure anonymity and then publish.

When the study has been carried out in an organization, or for sponsors, they also have concerns. How are they, and/or whoever they represent, being portrayed? Will the report be used by others to criticize, compete with or undermine them? Can they stop you (discussed below)? 'Gatekeepers' will be interested in the outcomes of any approval they gave for the study to take place. Are they going to be hassled by others as a result (see Box 10.13, for an example of the tensions in this situation)?

Misrepresentation, plagiarism and assistance from others

A more straightforward set of issues concerns your own ethical standards when reporting. You should, of course, try to produce an honest and truthful account of what you have done. Claiming to do work which you have not done, or exaggerating its amount, or fabricating results or findings is unforgivable as it strikes at the heart of trust in research. If suspected, it should be investigated thoroughly (with protection for the 'whistle-blower') and if substantiated, should be severely punished. Instances of such cheating are, unfortunately, not unknown (see Chapter 10, p. 230) and pressures to publish may well increase their incidence.

A basic rule is that you should not try to pass off someone else's work or ideas as your own. It is highly unlikely, and in most cases highly undesirable, that you will have carried out a research project without in some sense having assistance from others. In any report, this assistance should be acknowledged. Typically, this is done by formal referencing of previously published material or by explicit acknowledgement of ideas or advice from colleagues or others. Above all, you do not copy material from others without making this clear. Similarly, if you are doing a replication study (which may well be very valuable), this has to be made clear.

In some situations, such as presenting material for an academic award, there will be an expectation that the research itself is 'all your own work', which you may be called on to certify. In many real world settings this is unrealistic, as parts of the data collection may have been carried out on a group basis; or some stakeholders may have contributed in various ways; or you may have received support from a statistician for statistical analysis; or you may be reporting on part of a larger study where it is necessary for you to also include the work of colleagues to make what you have done understandable. In an individual assessment situation, the need is to make clear to the reader exactly what contribution you have made, so that a judgement can be made about its value.

A convention of academic reporting is that quoting a reference implies that you have read it yourself rather than seen it quoted by someone else (where you use 'cited by' and give the full reference to the work doing the citing). Observing this convention would help stop the transmission of mistakes and misattributions through generations of such references.

Sexist language

Sexist language is offensive to many as, in the language of the legal definition, the male term is simply assumed to 'embrace the female'. It can also be ambiguous, as in the use of 'businessman' (as a generic term in the sense of covering females as well as males), when it is then not clear whether or not only male managers are being referred to. Empirical studies have shown that the use of sexist language does make a difference in the inferences that readers draw (e.g. Miller & Swift, 1995).

Several sets of guidelines exist aiming to sensitize people to the forms that sexist language takes and suggesting non-sexist alternatives. For example, suggestions in 'Language and the BSA: Sex and Gender' (British Sociological Association, 2004a) include:

Sexist	Non-sexist
man in the street	people in general, people
man-made	synthetic, artificial, manufactured
manpower	workforce staff, labour force
manhours	workhours
forefathers	ancestors
master copy	top copy, original

There is a corresponding set of issues concerning racist language (see e.g. British Sociological Association, 2005) and on language and disability (e.g. British Sociological Association, 2004b).

Report quality

The quality of a research report raises ethical issues. Spending time and resources on carrying out a project can be justified if there is an outcome of some type. The outcome will not necessarily be a publishable report. It can be an 'apprentice piece' where the experience and learning which has taken place (by the researcher at least, but hopefully participants and others) has been worthwhile. For students on courses or doing research degrees, the gaining of an award is a personal outcome. For funded real world researchers, the outcome will be a report which may not be formally published, in part depending on the view that the person, or organization, providing the funding takes of it and its findings – and of the political climate. If not, your effort is justified when, and if, some change or improvement takes place.

However, formal publication of an article based on the findings, preferably in a prestigious refereed journal, is the lifeblood of career researchers, whether real world or academic. Note that, although a journal article may be based on a report it does not simply replicate it. Some reports can be the basis for several journal articles, whereas other reports may struggle to produce a single one. In producing a journal article you are writing for a different audience from the original one. This audience looks for different qualities in research which you need to consider before submitting it. Always research the requirements of a journal prior to submission so that you can maximize your chances of publication.

The quality of submitted articles is a matter of debate, as is what 'quality' means (see Becker, Bryman & Sempik, 2007; Sempik, Becker & Bryman, 2007). Analyses of published research papers reveal worrying deficiencies. Webb (2004) found fewer than half of 256 empirical papers published in the high-ranking *Journal of Advanced Nursing* throughout 2002 explicitly identified the research methodology used, while more than a third did not include the sample size). An editorial by Rushby (2006) identified a catalogue of weaknesses in the 'great bulk' of papers submitted to the *British Journal of Educational Technology*, including the following:

- They are verbose – the writers do not follow the obvious discipline of restricting themselves to what their readers will want to read. Some appear to be trying to impress, but to impress whom?
- They lack knowledge of the relevant literature;
- They do not understand the concept of assembling and analysing data drawn, and of tabling well-founded conclusions – and reservations; and
- Even if their research and reporting is sound, they may lead to conclusions and findings that are probably of little use to readers of the journal.

Reporting fixed design research

There is a traditional model for the format of written reports on fixed design research in academic journals. If you do not follow the model, you are very unlikely to be published in such journals. Broadly speaking, the same conventions apply to reporting of fixed design research in professional journals, although some which are specifically aimed at practitioners may adopt a more relaxed stance. There are other ways of disseminating findings to fellow researchers and professionals, most notably through conference papers (and other conference activities such as 'poster sessions' where you display a summary of your research and stand by the posters to answer questions and discuss the work with interested conference members) and seminar papers. There is sometimes an unexamined assumption that these latter types of activities should mimic the journal paper in style. As with many unexamined assumptions, this is highly questionable, and you may well communicate more effectively face-to-face by adopting one of the more informal formats covered later in the chapter.

The student on a degree or postgraduate course is also commonly required to follow the scientific paper format for all quantitative fixed design reports. Similar expectations exist for dissertations produced by doctoral and other research students. There is a strong case for students being required to gain skills in other kinds of presentation. Report writing for academic audiences is likely to be a high-frequency activity for only a small minority of students in their subsequent careers. Many more will have to produce reports for other audiences.

The scientific journal format

Almost all journals require contributors to follow a specific format and to keep within certain areas of subject content and limits of length. Instructions are given on the journal's website and may include reference to a 'style manual' of which probably the most common in the psychological field is that published by the American Psychological Association (APA) – see American Psychological Association (2009). Educational, clinical, and other professional psychological journals typically follow similar formats. Other social science disciplines differ somewhat; legal journals vary even more. In any of these cases, a good strategy is to search the websites of appropriate journals and check recent issues to find a suitable model. Reading past issues of the journals will inform you whether the topic of your article is appropriate for the journal in question. Even though a journal may cover the same general field or discipline, it may have a theoretical slant, and not be interested in applied or empirical work.

The traditional writing style expected has been impersonal, past tense, and in the passive voice (as in 'subjects were asked to complete all questions'). This is understandable as an attempt to demonstrate the scientific credentials of the activity but can lead to a dryness and lack of impact in the writing. Several journals do not now require the passive impersonal style (e.g. 'We found that . . .' is accepted instead of the traditional 'It was found that . . .'). Conversely, too much authorial intrusion, with 'I did this and then I . . .' can sound naive and possibly suggest author bias.

Continued use of the past tense for things that have already happened (for previous studies referred to, and also what *was* done in the one you are reporting on) does, however, seem justified. Calling those who have taken part in the study 'subjects' has also been criticized, in part as suggesting an inappropriate role – that they are 'subjected' to various things. The term 'participant' is now recommended by the British Psychological Society (BPS), British Sociology Association (BSA) and British Society of Criminology (BSC) as well as medical and social work bodies. In some contexts 'respondent', 'informant', or just 'person' may be appropriate. Sexist, racist and other discriminatory language should be avoided, as discussed above and in Chapter 10 (p. 239).

See the website for a checklist of areas typically covered in a scientific journal report.

Reminders about pitfalls in the use of the term 'significant' in quantitative research (discussed in Chapter 17, p. 440) are perhaps worth repeating here. Significance in the '$p < 0.05$' sense should always be reported as 'statistical significance' rather than just 'significance'. The practical importance, or 'clinical significance', of a finding is another thing entirely. The common conclusion following a non-'statistically significant' finding in a small-scale experiment that 'the study should be replicated on a larger scale' with the implicit or explicit inference that a statistically significant result would thereby be obtained, is a truism. Achievement of statistical significance is a direct function of sample size; if you wish to obtain statistical significance, simply run a large enough study.

It is always important to consider sample size when claiming the significance (i.e. importance) of findings in research, whether qualitative or quantitative. Researchers are prone to overstating the importance of studies with relatively small samples. In that situation it is advisable to use cautious terms such as 'suggest' or 'recommend'. Similar caution is advised when claiming generalizability for findings.

To make progress as a professional researcher, writing accounts in a scientific journal format is a 'real world' activity for you. Reputation, progress and research money are strongly related to the number and quality of articles accepted for publication in reputable, refereed journals.

And rightly so. The conventions of this style of publication, with detailed and explicit concern for descriptions of procedure and analysis, together with the system of anonymous review by peers, provide important safeguards for the quality of the collective scientific endeavour. Scandals where the system breaks down, due to fraud, delusion or collusion, are not unknown (see Chapter 10, p. 230). The system within science, in principle though not always in practice, should be self-correcting because of the replicability of findings (maverick findings are highly likely to be checked by others and faked results will not replicate).

There are potential difficulties and tensions in reporting applied studies to both academic and other audiences. Many concentrate on specific settings, persons or organizations, selected because of practical concerns rather than through some representative sampling procedure. Such studies may be difficult to fit into the traditional format. In particular, you must ensure that problems in the interpretation of statistical findings produced by such sampling are made explicit in your report. Further details on the 'scientific journal' format for reporting case studies are presented in a following section.

Some journals catering for specialized fields can have different reporting guidelines and conventions. If you are writing in a practitioner journal they may encourage reflection, personalization and a focus on skills development. In a law journal you might write a comment (a brief note around a case or an issue) which would be tightly focused on the topic and would be expected to quote the literature heavily, provide context and include the personal experience of the author. Writing in an 'industry' journal, you would be expected to talk to the aims and main issues of that industry.

Reporting flexible design studies

There is little consensus on the format for reporting qualitative research in academic or professional journals. Again the best advice is to study carefully any guidelines included in the websites of journals (or paper copies of the journals themselves) which interest you and the actual reports printed in recent volumes. Some 'qualitative' journals expect the use of the first person and the active voice. Several have an explicit policy of encouraging alternative formats. For example, *Qualitative Social Work* welcomes:

> Articles by oppressed voices that often have been silenced, and from authors working in contexts that are new to publishing on qualitative research and practice and are exploring new possibilities for the use of qualitative research and practice. We welcome articles from practitioners, new researchers and others who are finding creative ways to work with and write about qualitative research and practice (from Manuscript submission guidelines; available at http://www.sagepub.com/journalsProdManSub.nav?prodId=Journal201566).

General features

Commentators such as Stainback and Stainback (1988) suggest the need for 'deep and valid description', and 'well-grounded theories emerging from a wide variety of data'. Mertens (2005) adds to this 'contextual meaning'; i.e. an ' . . . attempt to understand the social and cultural context in which the statements are made and the behaviors exhibited', including ' . . . a description of relevant contextual variables, such as home, community, history, educational background, physical arrangements, emotional climate, and rules'(p. 433). Padgett (2008) encapsulates the task concisely: 'Our basic goal is to produce a report that is scholarly, trustworthy, and readable' (p. 104).

Miles and Huberman (1994) have produced a set of guidelines which are sufficiently general to cover many types of qualitative research, given as Box 19.1. Silverman (2013, Part 5454) gives detailed and very helpful consideration of how to write up this type of report.

See the website for a checklist of areas typically covered in a report of a qualitative study.

Working in this way produces a conventionally structured, mainstream report of a qualitative study. There are additional features of the research which might be included in the report, and alternative possible structures. If, for example, you are working in a field or area where quantitative research is the norm, it may be politic to provide a detailed defence of the legitimacy of a qualitative approach. However, in most areas there is now sufficient experience of qualitative research for this to be unnecessary (there is still, as with quantitative designs, a need to justify why specific methods or approaches have been taken in relation to their appropriateness for the research questions).

Punch (1986) considers that the reader ought to know more about the 'muddy boots and grubby hands' aspect of doing fieldwork, by including in the report such things as the:

- problems encountered getting into and out of the field;
- micro-politics of the site and the role played by your study; and
- conflicts, ambiguities, and more sordid understandings (!) gained during fieldwork.

BOX 19.1

Guidelines for qualitative reports

1. The report should tell us what the study was about or came to be about.
2. It should communicate a clear sense of the social and historical context of the setting(s) where data were collected.
3. It should provide us with what Erickson (1986) calls the 'natural history of the inquiry', so we see clearly what was done, by whom, and how. More deeply than in a sheer 'methods' account, we should see how key concepts emerged over time, which variables appeared and disappeared, which codes led into important insights.
4. A good report should provide basic data, preferably in focused form (vignettes, organized narrative, photographs, or data displays) so that the reader can, in parallel with the researcher, draw warranted conclusions.
5. Finally, researchers should articulate their conclusions and describe their broader meaning in the worlds of ideas and action they affect.

(after Miles, Huberman & Saldana, 2014, pp. 333–4)

Wolcott (2009, pp. 67–70) discusses the issue of the 'lit review' in a report of a qualitative study and the appropriateness of a free-standing literature review chapter early in the report. An alternative is to draw upon the literature selectively and appropriately as needed when telling your story. Particularly if a grounded theory approach has been adopted, there is a good case for introducing and discussing theories arising from the literature toward the end of a study.

The most common means of organizing the data chapters is probably through a discussion of the research questions one by one and the evidence you have from the data about how they might be answered. Again this does not sit easily with an inductive, grounded theory approach. It is also to a greater or lesser extent a reconstructed account of what you eventually made of the data, and likely to lose any feeling for the process of the analysis. An alternative but similar version is advocated by Corbin and Strauss (2008).

Reporting on multi-strategy design studies

In multi-strategy designs with both fixed and flexible design elements or phases resulting in substantial amounts of quantitative and qualitative data, the safe reporting strategy is to follow the fixed design reporting conventions for the fixed design aspect and the flexible design conventions for the flexible design aspect. The detailed presentation depends very much on the specific multi-strategy design chosen. With separate fixed and flexible design phases, it is simplest to mimic this when reporting. With other designs where there are simultaneous fixed and flexible elements, there are no general answers. Go for whatever approach best tells the story that you are presenting.

When a serious attempt to integrate the findings from the qualitative and quantitative data is being made this aspect effectively requires that you present the two together. This should not preclude separate discussion of the steps taken to assure the reader of the trustworthiness of the different sets of data in appropriate terms.

Reporting on case studies

Case studies can be written up in many different ways. Before suggesting some alternatives it is worth emphasizing that, as with the design and analysis of any flexible design study (and multi-strategy design studies with a substantial use of qualitative data collection), reporting is not a once-only event tagged on to the end of the process. Yin (2009, Chapter 6) discusses different possible structures and also the situation where the case study is a part of a larger mixed-strategy design study. The general advice to start writing early, and not to regard it as something you only think about when all the data are in, applies strongly here. Start composing parts of the report (e.g. the bibliography) at an early stage, and keep drafting and re-drafting other parts of the report (e.g. the methodological section) rather than waiting for the end of the data analysis process.

The 'scientific journal' case study format

Use of this standard approach for structuring research reports is feasible with many case studies and has the advantage that it is familiar to the person steeped in the traditions of laboratory-based enquiry. It is similarly the style of presentation least likely to raise hackles in academic circles. Conversely, it is unlikely to be the most appropriate format in communicating to other audiences.

The 'issue/methods/findings/conclusions' structure provides the broad framework. Lincoln and Guba (1985, Chapter 13) suggest a two-part structure, with a main report consisting of:

1. an explanation of the focus of the case study (e.g. problem, issue, policy option, topic of evaluation);
2. a description of the context or setting in which the enquiry took place, and with which it was concerned;
3. a description and analysis of the data obtained; and
4. a discussion of the outcomes of the enquiry; followed by a methodological appendix containing a description of:
5. the credentials of the investigator(s), to include training and experience, together with a statement about the methodological predispositions and any biases towards the problem or setting;
6. the methods employed and the nature of the design as finally implemented; and
7. the methods used to enhance and assess trustworthiness.

Lincoln and Guba also stress the need for assessing each of these considerations at several different times in the study so that the report incorporates what was *intended* in respect of each of them and what was actually *implemented*.

The website gives details of other formats for case study reports.

Many real world studies can legitimately seek to reach multiple audiences through multiple publications. The sponsor, the wider practitioner and lay audiences can receive appropriate treatment(s), while the scientific audience can be reached through thesis and journal article.

Reporting on literature reviews

In recent years more journals are starting to accept extended literature reviews. These are, in the main, reviews of existing bodies of literature that either update, condense or rationalize a body of knowledge, or reinterpret existing bodies of literature in a new way. Literature review articles can be generated from a larger research project such as a PhD or funded project, or they can be a project within themselves (see Chapter 5).

There is an expectation that a journal article focused around a literature review would follow the basic approach of a systematic review (see Chapter 5, p. 84). This means that it would have a well-developed methodology explaining the search terms used, the search engines, the criteria for selection of literature, and a discussion of how the literature, once selected, was analysed.

This is not a traditional narrative literature review. As ever, check possible journals and home in on those which accept reviews of this kind and look at recent examples. Check the journal website for their criteria for acceptance.

Writing for non-academic audiences – the technical report

Many real world projects involve carrying out research for someone, whom we will refer to here as the client. Evaluations, for example, often come into this category. The client may be an outside agency of some kind which has given you financial and other assistance to do a project, probably on a contractual basis. Or the research might be a normal part of your job where you have been asked to do it by your boss, section head or manager, where she is the client. Or, you have set yourself up as a research consultant (see Barrington (2012), who provides useful suggestions on how to do this). Or, again within your job, it might be a part of your professional responsibility to carry out projects, largely on your own initiative. In this latter case, and to some extent in the previous ones, the clients may be thought of as the persons forming the focus of the study, for example, staff and children in schools, or nurses, doctors and patients in hospitals.

The nature of report for a sponsor or superior, which we will refer to as a *technical report*, is very much conditioned by their requirements and expectations. For some, the required report is very much along the lines of the 'scientific journal article' model. For other clients, this may be totally inappropriate.

The Rowntree Trust (n.d.), a major British funder of applied social research, requires projects to be of value to policy-makers, decision-takers and practitioners and is hence concerned to ensure that research findings:

> are presented in a form which can be grasped quickly by influential people who are normally too busy to read long reports or books. The Trust attaches importance to reports which are short, to the point and written in plain English. Compact summaries of research findings are likely to provide the basis of the Trust's Dissemination activities . . . it seriously doubts whether scholarly publications ever represent an effective means of communication with policy makers and practitioners, certainly in the short term (p. 10).

Burningham and Thrush (2001) is a good example of the kind of report this leads to. The Canadian Health Services Research Foundation takes a similar stance. They fund practically-oriented work research done in collaboration with the people who run the healthcare system, to answer their very concrete questions about how to make the system work better, and require 'a different style of writing for your final report. Writing a research summary for decision makers is not the same as writing an article for an academic journal. It has a different objective, and it takes a different approach' (CHSRF, 2001). Every report prepared for the Foundation has the same guidelines: start with one page of main messages; follow that with a three-page executive summary; present your findings in no more than 25 pages of writing, in language a bright, educated, but not research-trained person would understand.

In contract research, the type, length and date of presentation of the final report is usually specified in the terms of the contract itself. The issue here is whether you can live with these terms. They may be negotiable but are frequently standard. The degree of control that the sponsors have over content and publication should be clarified in the initial contract. Some may expect a power of veto and modification or exclusion of things they object to (e.g. Jenkins, 1984). Others simply expect consultation at a draft stage. The issue may be not so much about your report to them, but whether they seek restrictions on further reports to other audiences. This is a particularly contested area with evaluation studies, largely because of the likely sensitivity of the findings for both sponsors and other parties. There are no general answers here apart from making sure that you know where you stand before you get into the project and feeling that you can live with the constraints, both practically and ethically. Having a frank conversation with the client or sponsor early on in the research process is essential, so that there is no confusion. This is particularly so in the current academic climate whereby reports, or academic publications from reports, can be used as evidence of your, or your institution's, research contribution. For example, in the UK as part of their REF ('Research Excellence Framework') submissions or impact case studies.

The sponsors should appreciate, however, that they are paying for your expertise and that your concern is to 'tell it as it is'. If they seek to muffle or distort that message, then to an extent they are wasting their money.

Practicalities of technical report writing

Find out what is expected

Ask. Some clients will want everything included, perhaps an adaptation of the 'scientific journal' format but with minimal use of jargon, particularly of statistical terminology. Others may simply want major findings. Implications and suggested courses of action may either be specifically required, or excluded. It often helps to check the form, style and length of any similar reports for the same sponsor – ask to see any they thought to be particularly helpful, good models, etc. Be ruthless on length; do not exceed what they have asked for.

Provide an 'executive summary'

This is a short (usually one page), punchy summary, usually covering the problem, methods used, results and conclusion.

Put as much material as possible into appendices

Any supplementary materials which you feel should be included, but which are not crucial to understanding what has been done, should be put in appendices. Put them in a separate volume if they are likely to make the report appear off-puttingly large; alternatively, you may want them in the same volume to emphasize how much work you have done with the client's money. Their main function is to provide additional detail for readers with specialized interests. Typical appendix items would be:

- detailed tables, charts and statistical analyses (summary charts would usually be in the main report);
- copies of instruments and documents used (e.g. questionnaires, coding and other instructions, observation schedules, form letters); and
- a glossary of terms, including acronyms used (also explained on first use in the main body of the report).

Onwuegbuzie, Leech and Whitcome (2008) suggest that the lack of impact of educational research on practice in schools can, in part, be attributed to the complex statistical language used in research reports and demonstrate how the presentation of a published report can be greatly simplified and reduced in length by placing technical information in appendices.

Make sure that the presentation of the report is to a professional standard

The sponsor has the right to expect professionalism in presentation of the report, just as much as in your carrying out and analysing the study. Anyhow, good presentation aids communication. *See the general comments on writing and presentation below.*

 See the website for details of the format required by the Canadian Health Services Research Foundation.

Special features of evaluation reports

A distinctive feature of many evaluation reports is the emphasis on *recommendations*. Box 19.2 provides suggestions on the writing of effective recommendations (i.e. ones likely to be acted on).

BOX 19.2

Recommendations in evaluation reports

1. *The most important aspects are that recommendations should*:
   (a) be *clearly derived from the data*; and
   (b) be *practical* (i.e. *capable of implementation*).
2. It is helpful to distinguish:
   (a) *findings* – information about the situation;
   (b) *interpretations* – explanations offered about the findings;
   (c) *judgements* – values brought to bear on the data; and
   (d) *recommendations* – suggested courses of action.

   Patton (1982) describes exercises designed to develop skills in making these distinctions. He suggests taking a set of data and writing a final section of the report in which

   (continued)

the findings, interpretations, judgements and subsequent recommendations are summarized *in one place*. The reasonableness of a recommendation depends on its being logically backed up by a set of findings, a reasonable interpretation of the findings and a judgement applied to them. Criteria for the making of judgements should be made explicit. Interpretations are necessarily speculative and may be the subject of dispute. Resolution should be sought through discussion, and returning to the findings, to ensure that interpretations are grounded in these findings.

3. The process of generating recommendations takes time. A carefully carried out evaluation can be ruined by seeking to produce recommendations under severe time pressure. There should be the opportunity to discuss provisional recommendations with those holding a stake in the evaluation.

4. Consider presenting recommendations as a *set of options*. Given a list of findings, there may be several reasonable interpretations and different value positions which will generate a whole range of options. Each should be fully documented, showing fairly how the findings, interpretations and judgements support the option.

5. The nature of recommendations should be negotiated with decision-makers, or whoever forms the audience for the report, at an early stage. This will have implications for the kind of evaluation carried out and the questions addressed. Note that it is possible that decision-makers may not want the evaluator to present recommendations but simply deliver findings, with or without analysis and interpretation.

6. The people who will make use of the evaluation information should be closely involved in generating the recommendations. They are more likely to act on things that they have thought out for themselves than on ideas foisted on them by an outside evaluator. From your point of view as an evaluator, they are a valuable resource enabling you to escape being over-influenced by your own prejudices. This does mean that they will have to be prepared to invest time and effort in making the progression from facts to recommendations. Getting them in the way of doing this may have spin-offs way beyond the particular evaluation.

Alternative forms of presentation

Real world research may be most effectively communicated to some audiences through forms different from a written report – whether in scientific paper, case study or technical report format. Alternatives include oral presentations, audio-visual ones of various kinds and literary forms other than the report. They are thought of here mainly as supplementary ways of communicating what you have done and form part of disseminating your findings. They are adding to some kind of report in which you can demonstrate, both to your own and to others' satisfaction, the rigour and quality of your study – although there may be circumstances in which, say, a video-tape by itself provides the best means of communication to your main audience.

It is increasingly common for the culmination of a piece of funded research with an applied focus to involve not simply a technical report and journal publication but also oral presentations both to the funding body and other audiences. For some studies, there may be the need for workshop sessions with practitioner groups where the implications of the study for action form the bases of practical sessions.

Practical constraints will often have a major influence on these alternative forms of presentation. You may have 15 minutes with the board of directors or the team of community workers in a particular area. Or a one-day in-service training course for teachers. Or a four-page A5 supplement to a newsletter sent out to proprietors of private residential homes for the elderly. Each of those would present a substantial, and different, presentational challenge.

Comments are made below on a few possibilities. The suggestions are all obvious and owe more to common sense than systematic analysis but the abysmal quality of many presentations indicates they may be helpful.

Oral presentations

Professional standards here are just as important as with the report, and are easy to achieve using presentational packages such as PowerPoint (see however the trenchant criticisms of the strait-jacketing influence of the near ubiquitous use of this package made by Tufte, 2006). Particular attention should be given to the quality and legibility of lettering, its size being such that it is easily read by all those present – check by viewing your material from the back of the room before the audience arrives. A handout which complements the oral presentation is helpful. Mere repetition in the handout of what is said is a waste of time and opportunity, as is the habitual reading out of the contents of PowerPoint slides.

Alternative literary presentations

A greater degree of creativity in this respect seems to have been shown by evaluators in conducting and disseminating their research than those doing other types of study, although there seems to be no reason against them being used more widely. Approaches include the following:

Pamphlet production

The task of compressing an account of a project into a short pamphlet for a general audience is daunting. Emphasis should be on the findings and on implications for action. Jargon should be ruthlessly excised. An attractive, uncluttered layout with strong headings and use of photographs, drawings and simple tables is needed. Resist the temptation to get in as many words as you can. Give an indication of what the interested reader can do to follow up, by providing references to other publications and an address.

This kind of short document is one way in which you can fulfil promises made to participants to let them know about the outcome of the project. The full report is not usually suitable for this purpose, although it should normally be available on request. 'Member checking' and the production of 'negotiated accounts' represent a very different kind of activity and responsibility to participants and must be completed prior to publication of any final reports (see Chapter 18, p. 480).

News releases

One way of reaching a wider audience is through newspapers, and radio and television stations. For a small-scale study, the local and possibly regional media are the likely targets. A short news release, usually on one side of A4, written in a lively style with an eye-catching heading, is required. Regard it as a further boiling down of the pamphlet described in the previous section. Give a telephone contact number and try to prepare for questions, so that you can avoid injudicious quotations.

A problem is that you do not have control over what they will write. Busy journalists are likely to use at least parts of the release verbatim – a likelihood enhanced by your lively writing – but they will be prone to inserting their own distortions and (mis)interpretations. While it may be wisest not to seek publicity for studies carried out in some sensitive areas, there is a general responsibility to help promote a better informed general public that all who carry out real world research should recognize.

Blogs and online forums

Increasingly, more and more researchers of all kinds are using social media to communicate to a variety of audiences. These are forums with a wide reach and, potentially, an impact which can be used for dissemination of research. Researchers can use traditional social media such as Facebook, Twitter and Linkedin to provide interested parties with a signpost to their research. There is a skill to writing short, snappy segments about your research and practice is advised. There is also a growing body of reputable blogs run by academic institutions, research councils, publishers and professional organization (e.g. charities, government agencies, etc.). Authors produce a 500–800 word summary of their research – a streamlined version of their findings. More generally, online blogs can be a useful way of disseminating findings to interested peers or other parties who can then be directed towards the full report. If you are interested in blogs, or other social media, contact the blog owner or administrator to gauge their interest in your piece prior to writing it. Often there will be style guidelines to consider and contributions may be peer reviewed.

Writing skills

The actual activity of writing receives scant attention in most books on the doing of research (Lofland, Snow, Anderson & Lofland, 2006, Chapter 10 is an honourable exception). It is similarly rarely dealt with explicitly on research methods courses – apart from that form of summative evaluation of reports of investigations, otherwise known as marking or assessment. Hartley (1994) provides a practical guide, which, although oriented toward instructional text such as textbooks, contains much of relevance to anyone seeking to communicate through writing. It includes selection of paper size and page layout, through composition of clear text, to the use of diagrams and illustrations. Persuasive psychological reasons are given for making one choice rather than another on vocabulary, line length, or paragraph spacing. There is a useful section dealing with electronic text and tips for producing screen layouts which people will actually read. And a comprehensive analysis of the visual presentation of information, with subtle distinctions noted between pie charts and bar charts. It is, incidentally, very readable!

As with other skills, writing benefits from practice, particularly if detailed and early feedback can be provided by a constructive colleague.

The first draft

The importance of having a clear sense of audience has already been stressed in relation to style, length and general approach. If you have followed the suggestions for a structured approach to design, data collection and analysis made in earlier chapters, this should have provided you with a substantial base of material for the report. The advice, stressed in connection with flexible design studies, of starting to write parts of the report while still involved with data collection, could usefully be generalized to all research projects. Even so, there has to be a period toward the end of a study where the major task is writing – putting it all together, and getting the 'first draft'.

There are major individual differences in preferred approach to this task. The word processor has much to commend it, particularly in the ease with which amendments to drafts can be made, both in content and in sequence. Many users report a liberating effect with proficiency in word processing, where a more 'playful' writing style emerges, with lower barriers both to starting (the 'blank page' phenomenon) and continuation. However, it is important that you possess a good working knowledge of the system and its features; and absolutely crucial that you stick to 'good housekeeping' principles including regular saving of what you have typed, backing up of copies of computer files and the equally regular printing out of drafts of what you have produced.

Notwithstanding its advantages, there is no rule which says that you must use a word processor if you are to produce a good report. If you can best deliver when writing longhand or speaking into a dictating machine, then go ahead. *What is essential is that you allow yourself sufficient uninterrupted time for the activity*. And go for 'prime time'. Writing is difficult and you should devote the time of the day when you are most effective to it. For many people, this is the first two or three working hours in the day, but it could well be in the evening or some other time. A regular schedule helps.

Interruptions reduce efficiency. Try to organize a period when you are incommunicado. Persuade a partner to look after the children – out of earshot somewhere. Switch off that mobile/cell phone. Set up your system so that incoming e-mails are only attended to when you have finished writing for the day. An answering machine or colleague (possibly on a reciprocal basis) can deal with the phone. Make it known and respected that you are not available for discussion, or whatever, at that time. Obviously, details depend on your individual circumstances but the principle is that this is an important activity which has to take precedence if you are to do your job properly.

Starting is often difficult, both right at the beginning and at each writing session. This argues for putting your available time into substantial-sized blocks. One tactic is to finish a session in mid-paragraph so that you know exactly where to pick things up next time. Outlines and structures, as discussed earlier in the chapter, are helpful, but don't feel that you must go through them in a linear manner. In particular, with the scientific journal format, early parts such as the title, abstract, and the final version of the introduction are best left until you see what the rest of the report is going to look like.

Revising the draft

There are, again, individual differences in preferred approach. It is often recommended that in producing the first draft, you should concern yourself primarily with content and leave style of writing as a task that you concentrate on when revising the draft.

The aim is to communicate. Go for clear, simple and lively English. There are several useful general guides to writing style (e.g. Strunk and White, 2014[1]). Trask (1997) is helpful on the often vexed topic of punctuation. For specific usages and controversial topics such as split infinitives, the best known is probably Fowler's *Modern English Usage* (Burchfield, 2004) – which covers both 'English' English and 'American' English. More specific texts include Day and Gastel (2011) on writing scientific papers. See also Daryl Bem's classic paper on 'Writing the empirical journal article' available at http://dbem.ws/WritingArticle.pdf (Bem, 2003). Barzun and Graff (2003), although oriented towards research in the humanities, has much that is generally valuable on writing. Box 19.3 suggests some guidelines for revising text.

BOX 19.3

Guidelines for revising the first draft

Whether you can work on the paper as a whole, or sections of it at a time, obviously depends on its length.

1. Read the text through.
2. Read the text again and ask yourself:
   • What am I trying to say?
   • Who is the text for?
3. Read the text again and ask yourself:
   • What changes will make the text clearer and easier to follow?
4. To make these changes, you may need:
   • to make *global* or big changes (e.g. rewriting sections); or
   • to make *minor* text changes.

   You need to decide whether you are going to focus first on global changes or first on text changes.

5. *Global* changes you might like to consider in turn are:
   • reordering parts of the text;
   • rewriting sections;
   • adding examples;
   • changing the examples for better ones;
   • deleting parts that seem confusing.

---

[1] This classic text exists in many, relatively unchanged, editions.

6. *Text* changes you might like to consider in turn are:
   - using simpler wording;
   - using shorter sentences;
   - using shorter paragraphs;
   - using active rather than passive tenses;
   - substituting positive constructions for negatives;
   - writing sequences in order;
   - spacing numbered sequences or lists down the page (as here).
7. Read the revised text through to see if you want to make any further global changes.
8. Finally, repeat this whole procedure some time (at least 24 hours) after making your original revisions and do it without looking back at the original text.

(adapted from Hartley, 1994)

Computers can assist in revising drafts. Word-processors usually incorporate a spelling checker, and there is also 'thesaurus' software useful for suggesting alternatives to words that you may tend to over-use. Various 'writer's aids' programs are available which provide facilities such as checking on punctuation as well as on spelling errors, repeated words, split infinitives, long sentences, sexist language, readability indices, etc. However, don't let the 'style police' iron out all individuality in your writing; stylistic conventions should work in the service of communication rather than of total conformity.

The final typescript

This should be a polished jewel. Spelling, punctuation and typing should be perfect. There should be a simple and consistent system of headings and subheadings and of spacing between sections. If the report is intended for publication in some form, the publishers will have requirements or preferences about format as well as style. Double spacing and wide margins are required. References often cause problems. These include inconsistency in format, parts missing, references mentioned in the text but not present in the reference list (and vice versa) and inconsistencies between the name(s) or dates in the text and those in the list. Check the reference system they require. Although there are many referencing systems around, only two are commonly used. The Harvard system is the most widely used system in the social sciences. The Vancouver system (sometimes referred to as the 'numeric' system) is used in some fields, particularly in medicine and some health-related areas. Many academic libraries provide helpful guides (e.g. Harvard, http://libweb.anglia.ac.uk/referencing/harvard.htm; Vancouver, http://www.le.ac.uk/li/research/vancouver.html). Some journals insist on the APA (American Psychological Association) reference style, included within American Psychological Association (2009).

Assuming that you are using a word processor, it is at this stage that your expertise in its use and attention to detail will be tested. If you can't reach a high standard, give the job to someone who can. Tables and figures for work sent for publication go at the end of the text with their position indicated in the text. Computer packages are available for graphics (see, for example the 'DeltaGraph' software http://www.redrocksw.com). Even relatively cheap systems can produce very high-quality work but again require facility in their use and you may have to use the services of a professional graphic illustrator.

There is no substitute for painstaking proof-reading, preferably by someone else. This is not simply because this is a very boring job, but mainly because your familiarity with the text is likely to impede your effectiveness at the task. Parry (1996) provides a more detailed account of preparing the final typescript, angled towards the scientific journal paper, taking the process beyond this stage to the independent review system and possible outcomes.

Where next?

When you have finished your research project and delivered your final report, or published your findings via a more academic route, what do you do next? This chapter has sought to involve you in disseminating the results of your activities in a variety of ways. But after that? In some situations the answer can present itself.

Undergraduate

A next step can be a postgraduate taught course. Consider your discipline choice well because, more so than with your undergraduate course, it often defines your area of future employment. If you are interested in research generally, the possibilities include a 'research methods' master's programme. If you have a firm idea of going into a particular field there are many specialized programmes in different areas. Depending on your background it may be advisable to first obtain experience, and possibly a qualification, in applied fields (e.g. in teaching if you hope to become an educational psychologist). Then a generic research methods master's degree might be best. If you are considering going into a specific field, such as criminological or health research, a specialized master's would be better.

Shop around for possible postgraduate courses in the same way that you would for first degrees. In addition, look at the research profile and interests of the department and staff in question as you could be doing an extended project with them. For very specific interests, check that there are staff with interests and experience in that area.

Postgraduate

Following a taught postgraduate course, or with a successful research master's programme behind you, the next obvious step for an intending researcher is to seek a doctoral qualification. There are a couple of options open to you including applying for a PhD in your area of interest. This is essential if you are to have a chance of a traditional academic post, as most universities will not employ a lecturer unless they have completed or are close to completing a PhD/DPhil. When applying for a PhD there are sites that can help with this, as well as university sites. In deciding to do a PhD you are committing at least three, possibly more, years of your life, so it's not a decision to be taken lightly. Think it through; consider the programme; funding opportunities; the university department and university; the town or city that you will move to; and the topic area. The key to getting a PhD and completing it is often endurance, so don't enter into it half-heartedly.

An alternative is to follow a doctoral programme on a part-time basis. One way of doing this is to find a job where you can do the research linked to your employment. This is more feasible when you have been working in the post for a few years or following professional training in, say, an area of health or teaching.

Another potential route open to you is working for a research organization (private, public, state or university orientated) as an entry level researcher.

Post-doctoral

Generally at this stage you will find yourself working for a research organization or for a university. As a post-doctoral researcher you will generally need to apply for research funding to sustain your position, especially if you work at a university. This means being on the lookout for funding opportunities, either from research councils, government/policy groups or universities themselves. The majority of post-doc researchers work in this way for a few years until, hopefully, they gain a permanent position either as an academic or a full-time researcher.

Career researcher

In this instance you will have a full-time post as a researcher, either as an academic or in a research organization. Part of your role will be to apply for research funding and then disseminate the findings. This means that when you have one grant completed, usually while you are disseminating the findings, you will be applying for the next research grant. The cyclical process of writing grant applications, research and dissemination is an integral part of any full-time research post.

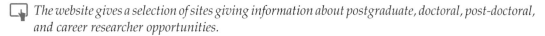 *The website gives a selection of sites giving information about postgraduate, doctoral, post-doctoral, and career researcher opportunities.*

Whatever research career, if any, that you decide to pursue, the main thing to keep in mind is – does doing research on this topic, or in this field of activity, really interest me? If the answer is 'Yes, definitely' then great; if 'No' or 'I'm not sure' then it's probably best to think about some other career!

Further reading

The website gives annotated references to further reading for Chapter 19.

APPENDIX A

Using specialist software for quantitative analysis

This appendix contains information about specialist computer programs which can be used for the analysis of quantitative data. The message in this text has been to keep statistical analysis simple whenever feasible. Not only are you less likely to make mistakes – not so much computational ones now that computers can deal with the drudgery involved, but more by misapplication, which is easy to do with complex statistical techniques.

Using Excel with 'Analyse-it'

The analyses and many of the figures in Chapter 17 were prepared using the spreadsheet program Excel together with 'Analyse-it' (http://www.analyse-it.com/), a very accessible package which covers a good range of the most widely used statistics, as listed in Box A.1. It does not call for training in its use. If you can handle a spreadsheet and have a basic statistical background, you should be up and running quickly.

SOFA statistics

'SOFA statistics' – statistics open for all – (http://www.sofastatistics.com/home.php) is a free and very user-friendly, open-source statistics, analysis, and reporting package. The SOFA statistics website includes several easy-to-follow videos and sequences of screen-shots which effectively form a short workbook.

BOX A.1

Statistical tests available in 'Analyse-it'

The categories used here follow those in the program for ease of reference. The tests listed here are those covered in Chapter 17; several others are also included in the package.

Comparing groups

F-test; independent samples *t*-test; one-way analysis of variance; two-way analysis of variance; Mann-Whitney test; Kruskal-Wallis test

Comparing groups (categorical data)

Chi-square test; Fisher exact test

Comparing pairs

Dependent samples *t*-test; one-way repeated measures analysis of variance; Wilcoxon test; Friedman test

Correlation

Pearson test; Spearman test; Kendall's tau

Describe

One-group *t*-test

Regression

Linear regression; multiple linear regression.

Notes: A wide range of descriptive/summary statistics including means, medians, variance, standard deviation and standard error, confidence intervals, etc. are also provided, as are various displays including error bars, outliers, box and whisker plots, scatter plots, etc. They are linked to the various data types and analysis techniques listed above.

Examples of each of the tests and the output produced are included, together with a video run-through of the steps involved and a short instruction booklet.

Using SPSS

There is something approaching consensus that researchers using quantitative methods are expected to have facility in the use of SPSS (the Statistical Package for the Social Sciences, http://www-01.ibm.com/software/analytics/spss/). It has been the market leader for some time. It is now relatively straightforward and intuitive to use and covers a very wide range of statistical tests and procedures. SPSS is likely to be available, and supported in various ways, at virtually all universities and higher education institutions. Nevertheless, it does take a non-negligible time and effort to acquire proficiency. And it includes many tests, often routinely provided as output, which are rarely used. SPSS is expensive and licensed on a time-limited basis.

The following section discusses strategies for developing the necessary skills.

Acquiring skills in using SPSS

- *The most effective way to acquire the necessary skills is to book into a practical hands-on workshop.* Many institutions run such workshops as do the developers of the package. Their website (http://www-01.ibm.com/software/analytics/spss/resources.html) gives details of workshops in a wide range of countries.
- *Use workbooks (user guides) linked to the workshop and for subsequent reference.* They give step-by-step instructions and show screen-shots for the different procedures.
- (If you do not have access to a practical workshop) *use a workbook independently.* SPSS restricts access to persons registered on their courses. Workbooks have also been developed by a wide range of universities. Some of these are only available to registered students but several are open access. Good examples include the Research Analytics Group at Indiana University (rt.uits.iu.edu/visualization/analytics) which, amongst other material, has detailed workbooks covering SPSS. Workbooks are typically updated when new versions of packages are released.
- *Use specialist texts which cover statistics using SPSS.* They suffer from the disadvantage that specific details of the actions to be taken, including screen-shots, are keyed to the version of the software current at the time that the text was written. While there are frequent changes of version, which can make it confusing if you have a different version to that covered in the book, such changes are now usually pretty minimal.

SPSS based statistics texts include Cramer (2014) and Field (2014). It will be worth checking if more recent editions are available if, and when, you propose to use one.

Other statistical packages

Minitab (http://www.minitab.com), although marketed as primarily for 'quality improvement', covers a good range of statistics, is very easy to use and is particularly valuable for exploratory data analysis. Individual licences are perpetual though not cheap. The advice given above for developing skills in SPSS applies equally for Minitab. Many institutions run practical hands-on workshops as do the developers of the package (see their website for details of workshops in a wide range of countries). Minitab makes pdf versions of workbooks in several languages available without charge. The texts by Bryman and Cramer (1996), Carver (2003) and Weatherup (2007) are based on Minitab.

Other packages, which tend to assume a greater background in statistics, include:

- *SAS* (http://www.sas.com). This is a 'heavyweight' package used by many businesses and large organizations. Such organizations should have support units to provide help in using the software
- *R* (https://www.r-project.org/). R is a widely used, free, programming language package which also provides a wide variety of statistical tests. It can be used for various types of modelling, time-series analysis, classification and clustering. A notable feature is the ability to produce high-quality graphs which can include mathematical symbols. Crawley (2014) provides an accessible introduction, while Crawley (2012) has comprehensive coverage.
- *Stata* (http://www.stata.com). This is a general-purpose statistical software package marketed commercially. It is used widely by statisticians and researchers in business and academic institutions. It is particularly popular in the fields of economics, political science, and sociology. Acock (2014) provides a 'gentle' introduction; Mitchell (2010) a detailed handbook.

Note: There are several packages which provide assistance in the production of web-based surveys, some of which include assistance in dealing with the data produced. See Chapter 11, p. 256).

APPENDIX B

Using specialist software for qualitative analysis

This appendix contains information about specialist computer programs which can be used for the analysis of qualitative data, known as Computer Assisted Qualitative Data Analysis (CAQDAS) packages. Chapter 18 discussed the use of general word processors for this task and made the point that while there are substantial advantages from using specialist computer programs, there are disadvantages.

Box B.1 gives an overview of the kinds of things that the packages can do. Typically a package will cover several of these different functions. Popular packages as of 2015 include:

- *Atlas.ti*
- *HyperRESEARCH*
- *MAXqda*
- *QDA Miner and*
- *QSR NVivo.*

NUD.IST, one of the first CAQDAS programs to be developed in the late 1980s, has now been largely superseded by NVivo. Features continue to be added to the programs, for example, several can now capture feeds from Twitter, Facebook and LinkedIn. Others, such as QDA Miner, are designed to be used with a wide variety of different types of material, and have links with tools for statistical data analysis and content analysis. *Dedoose* was created to deal with integrating qualitative and quantitative methods.

The Online QDA project provides valuable information about these packages and others; what they are capable of; their strengths; and comparative reviews. This is a field where new versions of the packages appear frequently and it is advisable to check the current situation at the time you are considering using one.

BOX B.1

Types of specialist CAQDAS packages

Text retrievers/content analysis. These include programs, many of them aimed at businesses, to help researchers find text and terms in very large databases and collections of documents. As these programs have developed, they have moved more into supporting businesses in organizing and giving staff intelligent access to large amounts of corporate data. They are very strong on finding data but do not support the ability to code data.

Code-and-retrieve packages. This is the kind of program that started computer-aided qualitative data analysis back in the 1980s. The simple aim was to allow researchers to code text (i.e. mark it and link it to a name that indicated the marked text's thematic content). Most support simple retrieval, that is, the collecting together of all text coded in the same way. Many of these programs have developed into the next type, theory-building software.

Theory-building software. These programs build on the code-and-retrieve functions and add facilities such as sophisticated searches (both text/lexical and code based), diagrams and networks, memos, and ways of developing the code list or codebook.

Concordance. This software was developed to assist language and text researchers undertake quantitative analysis of language use. They are usually designed to work on a large collection of text, called a corpus (plural, corpora) that is, representative of some use of language or its use in a certain context. A concordance is a listing of some or all the words used in that corpus, showing each in its context (e.g. 10 words either side). Some of the facilities of these programs are now being built into the most recent versions of theory-building software.

Audio and video analysis. Most of these programs share functions with the code-and-retrieve and theory-building programs but add to them the ability to deal with audio and video recordings and not just text. Early versions of these programs worked with audio- and video-tape recorders to use their analogue recordings. Now, most work with digital video and audio files. Some theory-building software has the ability to work with digital video and audio files.

Concept maps and diagrams. Some theory-building software now includes diagram and chart features, but this software allows much more sophisticated production of diagrams and charts, particularly focusing on concept maps.

Data conversion/collection. Although it is possible to work with digital audio and video data (see the software listed above) most researchers still work with text. Converting video and audio into text is still laborious but there is some software that can help. This includes optical character recognition software, that can convert printed documents into digital text files, and voice recognition software, that can convert the spoken voice into digital text files.

Note: Based on material from the 'Online QDA' project (see onlineqda.hud.ac.uk). Details are provided of the packages which can help with each of these tasks.

Acquiring skills in using specialist software for qualitative analysis

- *The most effective way to acquire the necessary skills is to book into a practical hands-on workshop or to find an experienced colleague willing to help you.* Many institutions run workshops, as do the developers of the packages.
- *Use workbooks (user guides) linked to the workshop and for subsequent reference.* They give step-by-step instructions and show screen-shots for the different procedures.
- (If you do not have access to a practical workshop) *use a workbook independently.* Workbooks are typically updated when new versions of packages are released.
- *Use specialist texts which cover Computer Assisted Qualitative Data Analysis (CAQDAS) packages.* They suffer from the disadvantage that specific details of the actions to be taken, including screen-shots, are keyed to the version of the software current at the time that the text was written. While there are frequent changes of version, which can make it confusing if you have a different version from that covered in the book, such changes are now usually pretty minimal. See Gibbs (2002; 2007); Gregorio and Davidson (2008); and Lewins and Silver (2014).

SUBJECT INDEX

Note: Page numbers in *italics* refer to illustrations